PARADISE LOST

AND

SELECTED POETRY AND PROSE

JOHN MILTON

EDITED WITH AN INTRODUCTION BY NORTHROP FRYE

Holt, Rinehart and Winston, Inc.

NEW YORK • CHICAGO • SAN FRANCISCO • ATLANTA • DALLAS
MONTREAL • TORONTO • LONDON • SYDNEY

Typography and Cover Design by Stefan Salter
ISBN 0-03-008480-6
Printed in the United States of America
8910 095 3837363534

INTRODUCTION

I. *Early Poetry,* 1629–1640

The first poem of Milton's to show major genius, the poem generally called the *Nativity Ode,* was written during the Christmas season of 1629. Not many of us can have much idea of what it would feel like to have such a poem as that tearing itself loose from one's brain at the age of twenty-one. The shock of its emergence is recorded in a Latin poem, later known as the *Sixth Elegy,* which Milton sent to his friend Charles Diodati at that time. In this poem Milton says that the major poet must think of himself as a priest of poetry, "making augury before the wrathful gods." For "the bard (*vates*) is sacred to the gods; he is their priest; from both his hidden heart and his lips he breathes Jove."

The poet's images are derived from human life, but the major poet must also use those human symbols to convey to man some inkling of the eternal worlds beyond human knowledge, "singing now the holy counsels of the gods above, and now the deep regions where the fierce dog (Cerberus) barks," to quote again from the *Sixth Elegy*. He must use all the resources of human wisdom and sensibility, but in doing so he will show how limited and finite the human perspective is. If the poet is an "augur," he must bend every effort of imagination and will to formulate the questions in which human experience ends. And when he has done all he can, he may, in those moments of involuntary inspiration that the poet can do nothing but wait for, get some of the answers.

The *Sixth Elegy* uses Classical imagery, and therefore speaks of priests and oracles. But Milton was a Christian, and for him the Christian poet follows the track of the Hebrew prophets and the Christian apostles, whose work was based on the belief in a "Word of God," a verbal revelation from God to man. Milton pictures God as surrounded by tense and waiting angels, listening constantly for messages. It is this sense of the dedication of his genius that gives Milton's poetry its deep impersonality and reserve. For his rare love poems, even for his more intimate touches of personal feeling, he seeks the shelter of Latin or Italian. His poetry is rarely inspired by his personal moods; it is usually a response to a definite occasion. A friend dies, and Milton writes an elegy; Christmas comes and he writes a *Nativity Ode;* he is asked for a masque, and he produces *Comus;* the sonnets are nearly all comments on events, personal or political.

The commonest type of occasion, up to 1640, is a death. Almost any death will do: "a fair infant dying of a cough," the university beadle, the Vice-Chancellor, are all metrically commemorated. Two great funeral poems, the English *Lycidas* and the Latin *Epitaphium Damonis,* mark the end of the early poetry. It is not hard to understand Milton's preference for elegiac subjects. Death marks the limit of knowledge as well as life: the first question that man asks at the oracle of the gods is about death. The answer that comes from the Christian oracle, the vision of resurrection and immortality, is implied or expressed at the end of all Milton's elegies. The funeral elegy, then, is for Milton one of the most concentrated forms of poetry, as it brings the human and the divine worlds into direct alignment. The relation between them must still be expressed in human imagery, however, and the traditional symbol of the mystery of death and resurrection is the cycle of nature, the daily victory of dawn over night, the annual victory of spring over winter.

Thus the hero of *Lycidas* is not so much Milton's friend

Edward King as a larger being, what in paganism would be called a god, who personifies both the sun that falls into the western ocean at night and the vegetable life that dies in the autumn. In this latter aspect Lycidas is the Adonis or Tammuz whose "annual wound," as Milton calls it elsewhere, was the subject of a ritual lament in Mediterranean religion. Out of the lament for Adonis there developed the convention of the pastoral elegy, the lament for the death of a friend symbolized by the passing of summer. Milton's approach to his subject commits him to the use of this convention. As a poet, Lycidas is similarly linked with Orpheus, who also died young and was flung into the water, and as priest, with Peter, who would have drowned on the "Galilean lake" without the help of Christ. Each aspect of Lycidas poses the question of premature death as it relates to the life of man, of poetry, and of the Church. The central theme and its two episodes (often absurdly called "digressions") are all contained in the figure of Christ, the young dying god who is eternally alive, the Word that contains all poetry, the head and body of the Church, the good Shepherd whose pastoral world sees no winter, the Sun of righteousness that never sets, and whose power can raise Lycidas, like Peter, out of the waves. Christ does not enter the poem as a character, but he pervades every line of it, supplying the continuous answer of revelation to the repeated questions of ignorance. And so, although Lycidas becomes the "Genius of the shore," a deified nature spirit like those in pagan mythology, that, for Milton, is only a minor function of what Lycidas has really become, a Christian angel, a member of those "solemn troops and sweet societies" who are in a world lifted clear of the wheel of time.

It is not only in the elegiac poems that the contrasts of night and day, and of winter and summer, represent the contrast between the human world that ends in death and the world of eternal life beyond it. The crucial importance of this symbolism meets us everywhere in Milton's poetry. His nephew even tells us, whatever significance it may have, that "his vein never happily flowed but from the autumnal equinoctial to the vernal." In the *Nativity Ode,* for instance, the barren frozen world of the winter solstice, with the steady advance of the long nights haunted by the sinister and gloomy gods that man has made in his own image, is our own world, the darkness that does not comprehend the new light. The world of Moloch and Osiris is also the world of Comus, the master of illusion, whose habitat is in the night and the forest, and whose power over the Lady is broken by the nymph of the Severn River, as spring rains release life from the paralysis of winter.

But *Comus* presents a moral problem as well: it is the first of Milton's four great temptation poems. The whole of nature, the whole "fallen" world that man lives in, is the real domain of Comus, and of the false gods of the *Nativity Ode* as well; spring as well as winter, day as well as night. The natural images of dawn and spring in Milton's poetry represent something much larger than themselves: they represent the passing from the world of the temporal alternation of seasons to a world of perpetual spring. This latter is the Paradisal world or "Gardens of Adonis" to which the Attendant Spirit who watches over the Lady belongs. Comus tempts the Lady's chastity with "natural" arguments: he seems to represent the free abandon of nature in contrast to the Lady's starched and sterile prurience. But the apparent situation is the opposite of the real one. The Lady's chastity is the condition of life on the upper or spiritual level: it enables one to possess the joy and freedom that will satisfy a conscious being. Comus is preaching passion, and at the core of passion lies passivity, the helpless servitude to desire that we see at the end of all lust. All passions are ruling passions, and their rule is tyranny. The conflict of the dancing Comus and the frozen Lady is the same paradoxical conflict that we get later in *Paradise Regained.* The tempter attracts all our attention and most of our sympathy because he is constantly in action, but the goal of his activity is death, and to find the principle of real energy we must turn to the motionless figure in the center.

We have moralized on *Comus* because it shows that the ignorance and confusion of human life is, in terms of action, slavery and bondage. It is not only enlightenment that man wants from the gods, but emancipation. For Milton the capacity to emancipate man is what distinguishes Christianity. The pagans had seen clearly that man is, in Christian terms, "fallen," bound by his human nature to the state of nature, which is a state of tyranny. But they had seen only the contrast, along with the irony and tragedy which that contrast suggests. "The gods alone are free," Homer says. The New Testament on the contrary insists that God wills this freedom for man as well as for himself. Thus the Christian poet, who breathes Christ rather than Jove, will, if society is relatively secure and at peace, devote himself to making poems out of the Christian vision of life; but, if society is in crisis, he will turn to prose and fight for liberty.

II. *Prose and Controversy,* 1640–1660

After 1640, then, Milton turned to controversial prose, and to working out the conception of liberty which was the central theme of his prose. In a later pamphlet he divides liberty into three categories: religious, involving the question of church government; domestic, relating to private life; and civil, relating to public life. But liberty for him, in contrast with the Romantic poets, does not begin with man; it begins with God. God wills liberty for man, and if man submits himself to God he gains liberty, which means that "none can love liberty heartily but good men; the rest love not liberty but license." The instrument of God's revelation to man is a book, the Bible or Word of God, and the messengers or prophets of God will normally be people with special capacities for handling words. But in the attaining of human liberty, God is the only free agent. Man can do nothing directly to achieve his own freedom: what he can do is to indicate his willingness to be set free by knocking down his idols, and so allow the Word of God to circulate freely in human society. The prophet is not a Utopian or a social planner, but an iconoclast, a breaker of the false images that man worships.

One obvious place to look for these images is in the Christian Church itself, and Milton's first issue is an ecclesiastical one. For Milton, the Church is a community in which all the members are made free and equal by their faith. In such a community the only authority is spiritual, and spiritual authority, the reverence aroused by sanctity, has, in contrast to temporal authority, no power to coerce, and cannot take the form of an institutional hierarchy, as sanctity cannot be delegated. When the principle of temporal authority enters the Church, the Church is being made a worldly institution. Such a corruption set in when the purely spiritual authority of the apostles was replaced by a hierarchy of bishops, Christians with temporal authority over other Christians. With such arguments as these Milton defends the Puritan system of church government against the Anglican one. The logical end of the episcopal system, Milton says, is the Papacy, and Milton thinks of the Papacy as the chief obstacle to Christian liberty within Christianity, the autonomous church which has, so to speak, swallowed the Word of God by claiming the monopoly of interpreting it. On the other hand, Milton was not a Bibliolater: the revelation of God to man does not remain in the Bible, but passes through it. The Holy Spirit builds up from it a structure of wisdom and energy in the human mind which does not override the intelligence and will already there, but emancipates and fulfills them.

For Milton the Church's whole duty is to study the Bible and recognize its spiritual authority. And the Bible must be interpreted by what Milton terms the "rule of charity." The Bible is designed to free man from a state of slavery, and therefore any passage in it which seems to confirm or approve the bondage of man has not been rightly understood. Churches pervaded by temporal authority could, from Milton's point of view, hardly avoid uncharitable conceptions of Scripture, and Milton found a crucial example of such an uncharitable conception in the ecclesiastical view of marriage and divorce. Milton's unfortunate first marriage may have awakened, as it certainly embittered, his interest in this subject; but it is hard to see how he could have avoided writing about the one conspicuous case in which a passage from the Gospels has been made the basis of common law.

The argument of the divorce pamphlets is, briefly: Moses allowed for divorce in the marriage law; Jesus declared marriage to be indissoluble. But Jesus' words form part of the gospel, and thus relate, not to the law of marriage, which remains unchanged, but to marriage as God sees it in relation to the free life of man: a lifetime companionship which can be "consummated," which means finished, only by the death of one of the partners. Marriage as Jesus sees it is like the innocent love of Adam and Eve before the Fall, for each of whom there was, very literally, no one else. The *law* of marriage relates only to a sexual union in the fallen world, and divorce must always be a part of marriage law. For if a divorce is necessary, the gospel marriage, the lifetime companionship, is simply not there, and man can always put asunder what God has never joined together in the first place. Milton is thus not preferring the law to the gospel; he is attacking the Christian Pharisaism that makes a new law out of the gospel.

The effect of this argument is to separate still more widely the spheres of spiritual and temporal authority. The church which, by a legalistic interpretation of the gospel, perverts a reasonable law into a superstitious taboo is revealed as a force making for tyranny within the state. The next step is to redefine the two spheres so as to show that, as there is a temporal church, so there may be spiritual authority outside the Church. In *Areopagitica* the conception of spiritual authority bursts out of the Church and overflows into fields that the Church itself usually calls "worldly." Prophets and apostles spoke in the marketplace and the court, and their descendants today may be writers of books as well as preachers. *Areopagitica* is an attack on censorship of books before publication in which Milton explains that the censor of the creative process, like the bishop and the indissoluble marriage contract, stands for the perversion of the spiritual power that frees into the temporal power that compels. The censor is the agent of the bondage of the moral law; his function is to ensure that man will hear only what he already knows. This means that he will never hear the revelation of God, which is always foreign to man's nature in every age, and always sounds disturbingly new and dangerous.

So far Milton had not committed himself on the subject of temporal authority. In fact, he never developed a positive theory of temporal government, and his political views were shaped largely by the course of events. After the execution of King Charles and the "purging" of the Long Parliament, Milton stepped forward in defense of "civil liberty," as a spokesman for the Cromwellian party; but what he defended was the regicide itself rather than the form of government established after it took place.

Nevertheless, Milton did claim to speak for the republic and the English people against the tyranny of Charles, and so he was forced to include a rudimentary theory of contract resembling the one later developed by Locke. The king, he says, is responsible to the people for his authority, and may be removed if he is irresponsible. But Milton is uneasy with this argument: "people," for him, are mostly unregenerate men who prefer tyranny to freedom anyway. It is the people of God, the free and equal society of believers, with whom temporal authority must come to terms. From a Christian point of view, tyranny is essentially a violation of Christian conscience, an attempt on the part of Caesar to seize the tribute that belongs to God. A monarchy is particularly vulnerable to this form of tyranny, because the reverence paid to the king is apt to turn him into another human idol. The more his power is withdrawn from the Christian community, the more likely this is to happen. There is thus a kind of revolutionary dynamic within the Church itself that first neutralizes the anti-Christian tendencies in temporal power, and then forces temporal power to fall in line with its own pattern of a free society. For a brief moment Milton felt that the reformed Church of England was beginning to assimilate the English nation to this pattern.

Milton's objections to monarchy apply with even greater force to dictatorship; but the "judges" of the Bible indicate that a strong man may be useful in guiding an ignorant and confused populace past the initial crises of a bid for freedom. Milton accepted the Cromwellian regime as a temporary measure, with many qualifications and warnings. After Cromwell's death, he proposed that the power of holding the new republic together should be entrusted to a permanent senate, a sort of reconstituted Long Parliament. He thus never arrived at what we should now consider a liberal or democratic position, partly because, being in a revolutionary situation, he was trying to see what would fit that situation, not what would be on paper the best form of government.

From one point of view, Milton's political theories seem to be a series of helpless rationalizations of every major change that occurred, until he was finally checkmated by the Restoration. He certainly illustrates the plight of the liberal intellectual who sees in every revolution an apocalyptic struggle of tyranny and freedom and finds it so hard to understand that revolution is a technique of transferring power from one class to another. The Restoration was a perfectly logical way of showing that the wealthy and powerful class which had risen in revolt against Charles I had achieved its ends. Charles II, though he did not have as great a mind as Milton, understood that very well. But to Milton the Restoration was the deliberate refusal of the freedom which God had offered "first to his Englishmen." The people who had had the chance of becoming a second Israel, a people chosen for the gospel instead of the law, had preferred "a captain back for Egypt," and had turned again to rolling up the same old Sisyphus stone of human history.

There is clearly a certain unreality in Milton's application of his vision to England, and it is the long-range values in his political writing that are important to us: those moments in which he looks over the head of the immediate situation to a greater vision beyond it. He saw that the only permanent support on which man can rely for preserving his freedom is education. As there can be no freedom without social responsibility and discipline, the students in Milton's treatise *Of Education* are conceived as a potential ruling class. Their education is based on the pattern which the Renaissance humanists, whom Milton is following, had derived from the great Classical writers. For the humanist, if a man wished to understand literary style, he read Cicero and Quintilian; if medicine, Hippocrates and Galen; if architecture, Vitruvius; if agriculture, Columella and Varro, and so on. There had been an end to the making of Classical books, and it was possible for a single diligent student to attain a considerable grasp of what had survived from that era. Thus the humanist ideal was encyclopaedic, designed to give one a comprehensive grasp of human knowledge. The keystone of all this learning was for Milton the Bible, the end of education being "to repair the ruin of our first parents by regaining to know God aright."

The assumption in *Of Education* is that the freedom which education brings makes the individual responsible to society. The end of human learning is not a selfish or parasitic "culture," but a knowledge of social and moral questions; the end of religious learning is not contemplation but prophecy, teaching others how it is God's will that they should be free. *Areopagitica* makes the complementary assumption: that the individuals who have been made free by liberal education and Christian liberty, and are trying to free others, constitute the only freedom that society has. In the foreground of Milton's social thought, therefore, is an intellectual élite of Christian humanists, including himself, the agents of spiritual authority. But in the background is his great vision of the free nation which is the fulfillment of their work, absorbed in the serene excitement of civilized life even with an enemy at its gates, disputing of the highest and deepest secrets of religion, culture, and politics. As he says more plainly in a later pamphlet, all such words as "heretic" or "blasphemer," which mean very little except that some human mind is determined to impose its own limitations on the infinite mind of God, will soon become obsolete if people will only use the talents and the birthright that have been given them.

III. *The Final Period,* 1660–1674

In an enlightened age like ours, a politically active poet could not possibly survive four revolutions. And there are many today who would admire Milton more if he had been executed in 1660. We should then have seen him as a man who, after showing that he could write poetry better than anyone else, walked contemptuously off into prose and died a martyr to the cause of real life. However, he was allowed to finish his work and die in his bed. As a result, though he still remains our greatest revolutionary genius, both in the content and in the form of his work, we can also see a more traditional strain in him, as we watch his life moving toward a final statement of everything he had to say.

It was an axiom of Renaissance criticism that, as there were major poets, so there were major poetic forms, in which alone a major poet's genius could find adequate expression. There was also general agreement that there were two such major forms, epic and tragedy. Milton had stated this doctrine as early as 1642, except that he divides the epic into two species:

the "diffuse," the full-dress epic in twelve books, or some multiple of twelve, of which Homer and Virgil are the models, and the "brief," the model of which Milton cites as the Book of Job. The models of tragedy for Milton are also Biblical as well as Classical. The close correspondence of this threefold scheme with the forms of *Paradise Lost, Paradise Regained,* and *Samson Agonistes,* respectively, produced so many years later, is a good illustration of the consistency of Milton's thinking. Around 1640, apparently, Milton thought that his "diffuse" epic would be, like Spenser's *Faerie Queene,* a patriotic epic with the legendary Arthur as its hero. He seems to have considered the theme of *Paradise Lost* at first as a possible subject for tragedy, and presumably it was his political disillusionment that pushed into the more conspicuous place of the diffuse epic the story of how man lost his liberty, and how he still resists all God's efforts to give it back to him. Similarly his tragedy of Samson is a grimly ironic comment on the great passage in *Areopagitica* which speaks of England as a "nation rousing herself like a strong man after sleep, and shaking her invincible locks."

Most Renaissance critics regarded the epic as a greater form than tragedy: this fact is to be connected with the humanist sense already referred to of the encyclopaedic range of knowledge to be derived from the study of the classics. For the difference between an epic and an ordinary narrative poem lies chiefly in the encyclopaedic quality of the epic. The epics of Homer, Virgil, Dante, and Milton are vast syntheses of religious, philosophical, political and even scientific ideas: they integrate not only the poet's own thinking, but the whole culture of their times. An epic of this sort can only be written in an age which possesses some kind of encyclopaedic vision. For Milton, the humanist synthesis of knowledge was in its turn contained within Christianity. The Bible, as Milton saw it, transcends all secular knowledge, but comprehends it too, and is also encyclopaedic, though on a far bigger scale. It begins where time begins, at the Creation; it ends where time ends, in the Apocalypse; and it surveys the entire life of man between these two points. Yet these two points are at the same point in the eternity of God, and thus time goes in a circle, proceeding from God and returning to him.

This last point indicates that the Bible is in form not only encyclopaedic but cyclic, and the same cyclic movement is to be found in the great epics as well. The total action of the *Iliad* moves from Greece to Troy and back again; the total movement of the *Odyssey* is from Ithaca back to Ithaca; the *Aeneid* moves from the old Troy to the new one at Rome. In each case the final goal is the starting point renewed and transformed by the heroic quest which is the epic theme. Similarly the total action in *Paradise Lost* is a cyclic movement from the begetting of the Son by the Father to the reabsorption of all things in the Father, transformed by the heroic quest of Christ to release man from his bondage.

Traditionally, the epic begins at a low point in the middle of the action: the *Iliad,* at a moment of despair in the Greek camp; the *Odyssey,* at the widest point of separation of Ulysses from his home; the *Aeneid,* with the hero shipwrecked at the enemy city of Carthage. The foreground action of *Paradise Lost* is similarly at the furthest point from God, the fall of Satan and Adam. The epic picks up the thread of action in the middle, from which we can see the beginning and the end hanging down in separate strands. In *Paradise Lost* these two strands are traced out by the speeches of Raphael and Michael, which work back to the beginning and forward to the end of the total action respectively. The cyclic action of *Paradise Lost* is thus also that of the Bible itself, the whole of the Christian revelation from creation to apocalypse focused on, and implicit in, the story of one of its most important episodes, the fall of man.

Traditionally, too, the theme of the epic is heroic action, and all the conventional features that Milton takes over from the Classical epic—the similes, the battles, the set speeches, the invocations to Muses, the councils of gods and leaders—are concerned essentially with this theme. But Milton was sick of what the world calls heroism, and he no longer believed that there could be such a thing as a "Christian hero," the role that he makes Jesus reject with such contempt in *Paradise Regained.* There are three orders of existence in *Paradise Lost:* those of heaven, earth, and hell; and there are correspondingly three types of action. The essentially human act of Adam and Eve is the act of disobedience, which is not really an act at all, any more than jumping over a precipice is a real act. Adam is faced with the choice of preserving his freedom and of throwing it away, and when he throws it away his freedom to act comes to an end. With his fall human history begins, and human history is pervaded by that fundamental inertia and incapacity known as "original sin," which makes history a record of spasmodic but always unsuccessful efforts to reach peace, freedom, and justice.

The essentially divine act is the act of creation, which in *Paradise Lost* shows itself not only in the Creation proper, the separation of cosmos from chaos, but in redemption, the re-creation of order and reason in man out of the chaos he fell into. All the divine acts are performed by the Son of God, to whom the Father transfers all his power, retiring from the action, though not nearly far enough. The reasons for Milton's grotesque failure to portray the Father as anything better than a smug and wily old hypocrite are too complicated to examine here: we are concerned only with the fact that Christ is the real hero of *Paradise Lost.* He gets this title by default, as he is the only character in the poem who does perform a positive act; nevertheless, the only men who deserve to be called heroic are his prophets, who carry on his work even when it means ostracism or persecution. Their prototype in *Paradise Lost* is Abdiel, the faithful angel. Milton's epic thus closes up the gap between the hero and the poet who celebrates him, as for him the true hero and the true poet are engaged in the same work.

The question of Satan's heroism is quite different. The essential demonic act is rebellion, and rebellion, as distinct from mere disobedience, involves an attempt at rivalry with God. Satan could not have fallen at all without convincing himself that God was not God but *a* god, and he himself therefore another god. Hence he sets up a kingdom in hell which is a close parody of the kingdom of heaven. To the heroism of Christ, which is to show itself in *Paradise Regained* as persistence in obedience, there is opposed the heroism of Satan, who is usually the model for man when man tries to be heroic. Satan is thus the hero of a kind of mock-heroic epic within *Paradise Lost,* which incorporates the heroic mood of the non-Christian epic. Satan is the haughty Achilles, the crafty Ulysses, the knight-errant who achieves the perilous quest of chaos, and all through the first four books he is surrounded with the rumors and the panoply of war. The trouble is that such heroism is founded on pride, and pride is evil. We like to distinguish moral levels in evil: we feel that hurling defiance in the teeth of God is more admirable than, say, stealing pennies out of a blind beggar's cup. But for Milton all evil is in one piece, and Satan, merely by the compulsion of obeying his own nature, is forced to become more and more debased. By the time he has got himself disguised as a talking snake and is congratulating himself on catching Eve alone with the man of the house away, the sombre Promethean rebel of the opening books seems remote. Yet even so Milton never suggests the comic or ridiculous devil who was such a favorite of the Middle Ages. Satan may be ridiculous to God, but man cannot take God's attitude, and even as a snake or a toad he is still a gigantic and terrifying angel.

The sinister figure of Nimrod, who appears at the beginning of the last book, marks the change in human life from disobedience to rebellion. From now on man is capable of worshiping devils, of mistaking the demonic for the divine, and the sign of it is the appearance in human life of hell's parody of the kingdom of heaven, the substitution of a society of slavery and compulsion for a society of love and freedom. In heaven God is an absolute monarch whose angels wait on his will; but, for Milton, human attempts to imitate this government produce only something more like the dictatorial hierarchy of hell. Michael explains to Adam that Satan is reborn in every tyrant, every seeker of earthly power and glory, every human leader that man turns to when he turns away from God. Spiritual authority, the element in human life that tries to redeem and emancipate it, remains apart from this demonic social order, outcast and ridiculed, forced, like Christ in *Paradise Regained,* to wander starving in the wilderness, and hunted down and persecuted even there. Yet the vision of a lost paradise can never be itself quite lost, and when Adam and Eve join hands as they walk slowly out of their garden, we know that another kind of human society has already been formed, and one that no tyranny can ever penetrate.

Milton said that *Samson Agonistes* was not intended for the stage: he meant the Restoration stage, and we should not conclude that it is not a real play. The greatest contemporary dramatist, Racine, also turned at the end of his life to the same combination of Old Testament subject and classical treatment. No one can forget, in reading *Samson Agonistes,* that its author was also a blind giant in the power of Philistines, but it sums up Milton's life far more profoundly than that. The great champion of Israel is now enslaved; he cannot free himself, but he can destroy the idols of his servitude. His father appears, offering ransom; his wife, the Philistine Delilah, comes seeking reconciliation, and a giant comes to bully him. Samson beats them all off, like the poet who fought religious, domestic, and civil tyranny all in turn. He is summoned to the Philistine temple and refuses to go: it is right that he should refuse, but he has come to the end of his own will. At that point a mysterious change in his will takes place (the "peripety" or turning point in the tragic action); he goes to the temple and brings it crashing into the dust. The cowering Israelites, though free for the moment, have still to wait a long time for their redemption, and meanwhile their champion is dead. But the temple of ignorance and superstition no longer has any pillars.

According to Milton's view of the Bible, the ultimate author of the story of Samson was Christ himself, and the tragedy of Samson is thus one of Christ's parables. To the Greeks, tragedy was primarily a vision of law, of the nemesis that follows pride, of the social contract that replaces the fury of revenge in Aeschylus' *Oresteia*. For a religion concerned with deliverance from the law, the source of tragedy comes to be thought of as increasingly cruel and malignant. In the Book of Job, for instance, it is Satan; but while Satan is the ultimate source in *Samson Agonistes* too, he operates mainly through the Nimrods of human tyranny, who in this case are the Philistine lords. Samson is thus, somewhat as Christ was to be later himself, a tragic hero to his oppressed followers and simultaneously the buffoon of a Philistine carnival. As soon as God has taken charge of his will, the two aspects of the drama are reversed: the tragedy ends in triumph and the carnival in confusion. But the Israel who triumphs is not the Israel that reluctantly followed and then deserted Samson: they have little part in his victory, and will be enslaved many times again. It is the Christian Israel, the city of God, whose power to destroy tyranny Samson has vindicated, and the serene quiet in which the poem ends vibrates with the presence of the same "solemn troops and sweet societies" that welcome Lycidas, though nothing can actually be seen but bewildered slaves with no masters, a city wailing to its helpless gods, and a dead giant in a pile of broken stones.

IV. *The Poetry of Milton*

Some poets—Spenser is a good example—start with experiment and end with conventional forms. Milton, like Shakespeare, begins in convention and becomes increasingly radical as he develops. The *Nativity Ode* is written in a tight, intricate stanza: the rhythm is not thereby prevented from bringing out every ripple and curve of the meaning—

> She, crowned with olive green, came softly sliding
> Down through the turning air

—but it is still exactly confined to the pattern of the stanza. It is a miraculous feat of technical skill, but even Milton could not always be performing miracles. He began a complementary poem on the Passion, but abandoned it after eight stanzas, and the stanzaic poem along with it. In the lovely tripping octosyllabics of *L'Allegro* and *Il Penseroso* he escaped into a more freely moving and continuous rhythm, and one that he uses for a good part of *Comus*. From that time on he sought mainly for long-range rhythmical units, and consequently moved away from rhyme, with its emphatic recurrence of sound, to the more austere but freer patterns of blank verse. He had a keen appreciation of music, and perhaps the continuity of rhythm in music influenced his poetry: it is noteworthy that in the Preface to *Paradise Lost* he speaks of "musical delight" as consisting among other things in "the sense variously drawn out from one verse [that is, line] into another."

The epic in any case makes heavy demands on the more sustained and cumulative rhythms, and Milton may have found his twenty years of practice in writing prose also of some help. Prose gives the fullest scope for long-range rhythmical construction, and Milton, though he complains about having only the use of his "left hand" in prose, took every advantage of what prose had to give him. His vast periodic sentences that almost never end, his dizzy flights of prayer and peroration, and his labyrinths of subordinate clauses, qualifying epithets, and parenthetical allusions do not always make for what we should now consider ideal prose. But they may well have played some part in developing the motor power that makes

Paradise Lost, apart from all its other qualities, the most readable epic in English. Milton's long postponement of his epic had its reward in the almost effortless mastery of the final performance. His reference to "Easy my unpremeditated verse" is no idle boast, and from beginning to end it is clear that *Paradise Lost* was not so much written as written out.

As Milton moves from the stanza into the more linear and continuous pentameter forms, a much bigger type of stanza develops, containing a number of pentameter lines in a rhythmic unit for which the most convenient name is "verse paragraph." The opening lines of *Lycidas,* down to "without the meed of some melodious tear," constitute an intricately organized verse paragraph, held together by the rhymes to "sere" in the second line and by a varied but consistent pattern of alliteration. The real secret of the unity behind its irregularity, however (the first line, for instance, is unrhymed and the fourth line is not a pentameter), defies all critical analysis. Many of the sonnets, too, are much more verse paragraphs than they are conventional sonnets. This paragraph forms a larger rhythmical unit in *Paradise Lost* too, and its presence enables Milton to handle the pentameter line with such a large number of run-on lines and medial pauses. In *Samson Agonistes* the paragraph achieves a much greater independence from the line and forms the basis for those amazing passages of recitativo which are perhaps the "freest" and most radically experimental verse that English poetry has yet reached.

The elements of versification are sound, vocabulary, rhythm, and imagery, and all four demand the closest attention from the reader of major poetry. Let us take a passage from *L'Allegro* and compare it with one from *Il Penseroso:*

> While the cock with lively din,
> Scatters the rear of darkness thin,
> And to the stack, or the barn-door,
> Stoutly struts his dames before.

To behold the wandering moon,
Riding near her highest noon,
Like one that had been led astray
Through the heaven's wide pathless way.

We can see how each of these four elements helps to make the contrast between the two poems. The *L'Allegro* passage has sharp, light vowels and abrupt, explosive consonants; the *Il Penseroso* one has resonant vowels and soft liquids. *L'Allegro* has vigorous words like "scatters," "struts," and "din"; *Il Penseroso,* quiet and pensive words like "wandering" and "behold." The *L'Allegro* rhythm flutters away in the almost unscannable third line and swaggers in the fourth; the *Il Penseroso* rhythm, especially in the fourth line, is full of slow and sonorous heavy accents. The first passage describes the clucks and crows of a poultry yard at dawn; the second dwells on the silence of a moonlit night. These points are simple enough, though it takes the highest kind of genius to produce the simplicity, and the principles involved are applicable everywhere in Milton.

Every language has its own body of descriptive sounds, and every poet accepts what his language affords him as a matter of course. *S* is always a hissing letter, suitable for serpents:

And Dipsas (not so thick swarmed once the soil . . .)

R (which Milton is said to have pronounced very hard) is a martial one:

Innumerable force of spirits armed;

W is for loneliness and terror:

Through the world's wilderness long wandered man

and the long *a* and *o* sounds (even more resonant in seventeenth-century pronunciation) herald the approach of the prince of darkness:

> Meanwhile upon the firm opacous globe
> Of this round world, whose first convex divides
> The luminous inferior orbs, enclosed
> From Chaos and th' inroad of darkness old,
> Satan alighted walks.

Milton's poetry is proverbial for its resonance: the sonnet on the massacre in Piedmont, for instance, is a deeply felt and powerfully indignant poem, but this does not prevent it from being also a kind of étude, a technical exercise in sombre vowels. It is natural that we should find what makes most noise easiest to hear. This is one reason why Satan makes the strongest initial impact on the reader of *Paradise Lost,* for in the great variety of Milton's orchestration Satan gets most of the heavy brass. It is true also that the gloom and terror of hell is not less impressive for being obviously impressive. But it would be a pity to neglect the woodwinds and strings, and fail to hear how the brothers in *Comus* murmur to each other what they have read in praise of chastity; how the flowers are dropped one by one on Lycidas' grave; how the Christ child lies asleep with his legions of angels sitting quietly around him; how the fragrance of Eden is diffused over the earth by lazy breezes. The great hymn of creation in the seventh book of *Paradise Lost,* in which everything seems to dance in the joy of its deliverance from chaos and the release of its form, is a particularly wonderful example of Milton's skill in the subtler and softer harmonies:

> Forth flourished thick the clustering vine, forth crept
> The smelling gourd, up stood the corny reed
> Embattled in her field; and th' humble shrub

And bush with frizzled hair implicit: last
Rose, as in dance, the stately trees.

Passing from the sounds to the words, we notice that Milton uses an unusually large proportion of long words of Latin origin. Also that he often uses such words in an original Latin sense different from ours: "frequent" means crowded, "horrid" means bristling, "explode" means to hiss off or drive away, and so on. Many of these Latin words have become dead robot words in our speech, with nothing left in them of the vivid concrete metaphors they once were. But Milton uses them with the whole weight of their etymology behind them, and in reading him we have to wake up this part of our vocabulary. It comes as something of a shock to read in *Paradise Regained* of "elephants endorsed with towers," because we no longer think of *dorsum,* back, in connection with the word. But in Milton "astonished" means not mildly surprised but struck with thunder; "aspect" and "influence" are still partly technical terms in astrology, and "insinuating" has its visual meaning of wriggling as well as its abstract meaning. This principle of traditional weight applies not only to words, but to phrases as well, and the reader should be warned that it is precisely in such lines as "He for God only, she for God in him," where Milton seems to be most typically Miltonic, that he is most likely to be quoting verbatim from the Bible.

Another feature of Milton's vocabulary, the catalogues of proper names, also needs a word of warning. There are two reasons for which these catalogues are never used. They are never used to show off Milton's learning, and they are never used as an easy way of increasing the resonance. When they are lists of strange gods, they suggest the incantation or muttered spell of the magician who commands them, as in the summoning of Sabrina in *Comus,* and, less obviously, in the roll call of baffled demons in the *Nativity Ode*. In *Paradise Lost* the rumble and crash of Satan's armies is echoed in the place names of epic and romance; the garden of Eden calls up the luxuriant and fruitful spots of earth, and the storms of advancing chaos sweep from point to point over the wastes of Asia and America. In each case the reader who has to look up several dozen references at once may miss the fact that the vagueness and strangeness of the names is exactly the poet's reason for using them. There are exceptions to this, of course: one should not miss the irony of "Vallombrosa," with its echo of "valley of shadows" in reference to hell, nor of the fateful epithet of Eden, "this Assyrian garden," which links it prophetically with the ferocious children of Nimrod who annihilated the Ten Tribes.

Some of the peculiar features of Milton's rhythm have been mentioned. The prosody of *Paradise Lost* has been exhaustively studied, but the general principle is that Milton can do anything he likes with the pentameter line. One may notice particularly the use of trochaic rhythms to describe falling movement:

> Hurled headlong flaming from th' ethereal sky,
>
> Exhausted, spiritless, afflicted, fallen;

the placing of two strong accents together in the middle of a line to describe something ominous or foreboding:

> Which tasted works knowledge of good and evil,
>
> Deep malice to conceal, couched with revenge;

the use of extra syllables to suggest relaxation or lateral movement:

> Luxuriant; meanwhile murmuring waters fall;

and the use of a weak or enjambed ending that pushes the

rhythm into the next line to describe the completing of a movement:

Intelligent of seasons, and set forth
Their airy caravan high over seas
Flying.

The long Latin words in Milton's vocabulary also have the rhythmical function of relaxing or increasing the speed. A monosyllable always means a separate accent, however slight, and a series of them produces a slow, emphatic sonority that would soon become intolerable unless relieved:

Scarce half I seem to live, dead more than half.
O dark, dark, dark, amid the blaze of noon,
Irrecoverably dark!

The same principles of variation apply to the other verse forms as well as to the pentameter, and usually the sense will warn us when a change of pace is coming:

I can fly, or I can run
Quickly to the green earth's end,
Where the bowed welkin slow doth bend.

Milton's imagery is more difficult to appreciate than any other aspect of his work. Except perhaps in *L'Allegro* and *Il Penseroso,* he is not one of the intensely visualizing poets: we are more conscious of degrees of light and shade than of sharply outlined objects. In this Milton is more characteristic of his age than elsewhere: in such painters as Rembrandt and Claude Lorrain, who were Milton's contemporaries, we find the same mysterious shadows and diffused brilliance that we find in Milton's hell and heaven. The relative vagueness of vision in *Paradise Lost* can hardly be due primarily to Milton's blindness, for we find it also in the early poems: in the formless shadows of the old gods retreating from the tiny point of light at the center of the *Nativity Ode;* in the dark wood of *Comus* and in the stylized pastoral world of *Lycidas.* In *Samson Agonistes,* where the hero is blind, the vision is outside the poem: it is focused with unbearable intensity on the hero himself, whose inability to stare back is his greatest torment, an agony of humiliation that makes him, in one of the most dreadful passages in all drama, scream at Delilah that he will tear her to pieces if she touches him. The precision of Milton's poetry is aural rather than visual, musical rather than pictorial. When we read, for instance:

> Immediately the mountains huge appear
> Emergent, and their broad bare backs upheave

the mountains cannot be *seen:* it is the ear that must hear in "emergent" the splash of the water falling from them, and in the long and level monosyllables the clear blue line of the horizon. In every major poem of Milton's there is some reason why the ear predominates over the eye. In the *Nativity Ode,* it is because of the pattern of light and shade already mentioned; in *Comus,* it is because of the dark "leafy labyrinth" where one listens intently for rustles and whispers; in *Lycidas,* it is because the ritual lament generalizes the imagery; in *Paradise Lost* it is because the three states of existence, heaven, hell, and Paradise, all transcend visualization; in *Samson Agonistes* it is because the Classical form of the tragedy makes it a discussion or reporting of offstage events. The prominence of temptation among Milton's themes is significant too, as temptation is an attempt to persuade one through aural suggestion to seize something that is illusory.

In *Paradise Lost* Milton uses the same Ptolemaic onion-shaped universe that Dante does, with the earth at the center and the *primum mobile* at the circumference. But Dante puts heaven and hell inside this universe; Milton puts them outside, and the impersonal remoteness of the Copernican universe, with its unthinkable stretches of empty space, thus forms part of his poetic vision. Dante relies on symmetry; Milton on disproportion. Satan is a colossal angel and a toad; Christ is to become a despised son of the Adam he creates; Raphael is a hero of a war that rocks heaven, yet he drops in on Adam and Eve for a cold lunch; all the armies of heaven and hell and the fate of the created universe hang on one apple, and on whether or not a hungry girl will reach for it. What holds this farrago together is nothing that the eye or mind can accept, but the steady flow of the powerful working words that, exactly like the temptations in the poems, persuade us to seize the illusion. Milton, the agent of the Word of God, is trying to awaken with his words a vision in us which is, in his own language, the Word of God in the heart, and in the possession of which we may say with Job, "I have heard thee with the hearing of the ear, but now mine eye seeth thee." If we surrender to his charming and magical spell, and seize his fables of hell and Paradise, they will become realities of earth, and the stories of Adam and Samson our own story. And then, perhaps, we may consider a further question:

> what if Earth
> Be but the shadow of Heaven, and things therein
> Each to other like, more than on Earth is thought?

NORTHROP FRYE

Victoria College in the
University of Toronto
June, 1950

CHRONOLOGICAL TABLE OF EVENTS IN MILTON'S LIFE

1608. Born in Bread Street, Cheapside, London, Dec. 9.

1611. Authorized version of the Bible published, the last great effort of cooperation between Anglicans and Puritans.

1615. Possible date of Milton's entrance into St. Paul's School, where he studied under Alexander Gill.

1618. Thomas Young, a Scottish Puritan, Milton's tutor.

1625. Milton enters Christ's College, Cambridge. James I dies and is succeeded by Charles I.

1626. Earliest Latin elegies written.

1628. *At a Vacation Exercise*. Parliament passes Petition of Right.

1629. Milton takes B.A. at Cambridge. *Nativity Ode*. Charles tries to reign without a Parliament.

1630. *On Shakespeare, The Passion,* and other minor poems.

1631. Several minor poems written: possible date of *L'Allegro* and *Il Penseroso*.

1632. Milton takes M.A. and retires to Horton, where he engages in a period of study and preparation for an as yet undetermined career, rejecting the Church because of its episcopal organization. Possible date of his first masque, *Arcades*.

1634. *Comus* performed at Ludlow Castle.

1637. *Lycidas* written for the death of Edward King. Death of Milton's mother.

1638. Milton leaves Horton for Italy, visiting Florence, Rome, and Naples.

1639. Milton visits Florence and Geneva and returns to England. *To Mansus.* First Bishops' War (attempt of Charles I to force the episcopal system on the Church of Scotland).

1640. Milton engaged in teaching. First sketches for *Paradise Lost. Epitaphium Damonis* (on the death of his friend Charles Diodati). Second Bishops' War. Charles's attempt to reign alone breaks down and he summons the Short and Long Parliaments.

1641. Milton enters the religious controversy on the Puritan side and publishes three anti-episcopal pamphlets, *Of Reformation, Of Prelatical Episcopacy,* and *Animadversions.* Grand Remonstrance passed by Parliament and Strafford, Charles's chief minister, impeached and executed.

1642. Two more anti-episcopal pamphlets, *Reason of Church Government* and *Apology for "Smectymnuus"* (a group of Puritan pamphleteers associated with Milton: the "ty" was Thomas Young, mentioned above). First marriage, to Mary Powell (d. 1652). Civil War begins, Aug. 22.

1643. Year of Royalist successes. *Doctrine and Discipline of Divorce.*

1644. *The Judgment of Martin Bucer Concerning Divorce. Of Education. Areopagitica.* Battle of Marston Moor and emergence of Cromwell as revolutionary leader.

1645. Milton's early poems published. *Tetrachordon* and *Colasterion* (last divorce pamphlets). First Civil War ends with defeat of Charles at Naseby. Archbishop Laud executed.

1647. Death of Milton's father.

1648. Second Civil War begins (Cromwellians against a coalition of Royalists, Scotch, and Irish).

1649. Charles I beheaded, Jan. 30, and the Long Parliament reduced to a "Rump." Milton appointed Latin Secretary and publishes two pamphlets defending the regicide, *Tenure of Kings and Magistrates* and *Eikonoklastes* (attack on *Eikon Basilike,* a devotional work attributed to Charles I).

1651. *Defensio Prima pro Populo Anglicano* (against Salmasius). Second Civil War ends with the Battle of Worcester.

1652. Milton totally blind. Sonnets to Cromwell and Vane.

1653. Cromwell dissolves Rump and becomes Lord Protector. Metrical versions of Psalms.

1654. *Defensio Secunda* (against Salmasius and Alexander More).

1655. Sonnets on his blindness, on the massacre in Piedmont, etc.

1656. Second marriage, to Katharine Woodcock (d. 1658).

1658. Death of Oliver Cromwell, Sept. 3.

1659. *Treatise of Civil Power; Likeliest Means to Remove Hirelings.* Richard Cromwell abdicates and Rump returns.

1660. *Ready and Easy Way.* Rump dissolves; General Monk reconstitutes the Long Parliament. Restoration of Charles II, May 29. Milton arrested and released, and deprived of public office.

1663. Third marriage, to Elizabeth Minshull (d. 1727).

1665. *Paradise Lost* completed.

1667. First edition of *Paradise Lost* published, in ten books.

1671. *Paradise Regained* and *Samson Agonistes* published.

1673. *Of True Religion* (pamphlet designed to unite Protestants). Second edition of early poems.

1674. Second edition of *Paradise Lost,* in twelve books. Milton dies at Bunhill Fields, London, Nov. 8.

BIBLIOGRAPHICAL NOTE

The definitive modern edition of Milton's works is that of the Columbia University Press, edited by F. A. Patterson and others, in 18 vols., 1931–1938, a complete critical edition (with a two-volume index) with revised translations of the Latin works. The best-known annotated single texts are those of A. W. Verity, Pitt Press Series, Cambridge (England), 1891–1912, and include most of the works reprinted here. See also *Of Education,* edited by Ainsworth (New Haven, 1928); *Areopagitica,* edited by Hales (Oxford, 1898); *Paradise Lost,* edited by M. Y. Hughes (New York, 1935); *The Sonnets of Milton,* edited by J. S. Smart (Glasgow, 1921).

For the primary sources of Milton criticism and biography see: Helen Darbishire, *Early Lives of Milton* (London, 1932); J. S. Diekhoff, *Milton on Himself* (New York, 1939); W. R. Parker, *Milton's Contemporary Reputation* (Columbus, 1940); James Thorpe, *Milton Criticism, Selections from Four Centuries* (New York, 1950). The best contemporary biography is J. H. Hanford, *John Milton Englishman* (New York, 1949).

The basis of modern Milton scholarship is *The Life of John Milton . . .* by David Masson, 7 Vols. with index (London, 1859–1894) (rev. 1881–1896). Of general introductions to Milton, many of the older ones are still good, including: John C. Bailey, *Milton* (Home University Library) (London, 1915); Mark Pattison, *Milton* (English Men of Letters Series) (London, 1879); Sir Walter Raleigh, *Milton* (London, 1914). More recent ones, which the modern reader will probably want to look at first, include: J. H. Hanford, *A Milton Handbook,* 3rd ed. (New York, 1939); Denis Saurat, *Milton, Man and Thinker* (New York, 1925) (rev. 1944); E. M. W. Tillyard, *Milton* (New York, 1930).

The best study of the period 1640–60 is Arthur Barker, *Milton and the Puritan Dilemma* (Toronto, 1942). For *Paradise Lost* see: Douglas Bush, *Paradise Lost in Our Time* (Ithaca, 1945); J. S. Diekhoff, *Milton's Paradise Lost* (New York, 1946); C. S. Lewis, *A Preface to Paradise Lost* (London, 1942); Grant McColley, *Paradise Lost* (Chicago, 1940). For *Samson Agonistes* see especially W. R. Parker, *Milton's Debt to Greek Tragedy in Samson Agonistes* (Baltimore, 1937).

A few of the vast number of special studies are the following, their general reference being indicated in their titles: Herbert Agar, *Milton and Plato* (Princeton, 1928); Robert Bridges, *Milton's Prosody* (rev. ed., Oxford, 1921); R. D. Havens, *The Influence of Milton on English Poetry* (Cambridge (Mass.), 1922); B. Rajan, *Paradise Lost and the Seventeenth Century Reader* (London, 1947); M. M. Ross, *Milton's Royalism* (Ithaca, 1943); Sigmund Spaeth, *Milton's Knowledge of Music* (Princeton, 1913); G. W. Whiting, *Milton's Literary Milieu* (Chapel Hill, 1939); Don M. Wolfe, *Milton in the Puritan Revolution* (New York, 1941).

For the literary, philosophical and religious background, see: C. M. Bowra, *From Virgil to Milton* (London, 1945); Douglas Bush, *Mythology and the Renaissance Tradition in English Poetry* (Minneapolis, 1932), and *English Literature in the Earlier Seventeenth Century* (Oxford, 1945); Sir Herbert Grierson, *Cross Currents in English Literature of the Seventeenth Century* (London, 1929), and *Milton and Wordsworth* (Cambridge (England), 1937); E. M. W. Tillyard, *The Miltonic Setting Past and Present* (Cambridge (England), 1938); Basil Willey, *The Seventeenth Century Background* (London, 1934). Two standard histories of the period are Godfrey Davies, *The Early Stuarts* (Oxford, 1937), and G. M. Trevelyan, *England Under the Stuarts* (19th ed., London, 1946). Of special value as background for Milton are: E. Dowden, *Puritan and Anglican* (London, 1900); W. H. Haller, *The Rise of Puritanism* (New York, 1938); A. S. P. Woodhouse, *Puritanism and Liberty* . . . (London, 1938).

A few briefer essays and periodical articles of general interest are: Arthur Barker, "The Pattern of Milton's Nativity Ode," *University of Toronto Quarterly,* X (1941); T. S. Eliot, "A Note on the Verse of John Milton," *Essays and Studies of the English Association,* Oxford, 1936, and *Milton* (British Academy Lecture), London, 1947; Charles Williams's introduction to the World's Classics edition of the *English Poems,* Oxford, 1940; A. S. P. Woodhouse, "The Argument of Milton's Comus," *University of Toronto Quarterly,* XI (1941); Mario Praz, "Milton and Poussin," and E. M. W. Tillyard, "Milton and the English Epic Tradition," both in *Seventeenth Century Studies Presented to Sir Herbert Grierson* (Oxford, 1938).

Of the present text about all that need be said is that it has been completely modernized in spelling, punctuation, and capitalization, and attempts to be as accurate as possible within the limits of such modernization.

TABLE OF CONTENTS

SELECTED PROSE

PARADISE LOST

THE VERSE

The measure is English heroic verse without rhyme, as that of Homer in Greek, and of Virgil in Latin—rhyme being no necessary adjunct or true ornament of poem or good verse, in longer works especially, but the invention of a barbarous age, to set off wretched matter and lame metre; graced indeed since by the use of some famous modern poets, carried away by custom, but much to their own vexation, hindrance, and constraint to express many things otherwise, and for the most part worse, than else they would have expressed them. Not without cause therefore some both Italian and Spanish poets of prime note have rejected rhyme both in longer and shorter works, as have also long since our best English tragedies, as a thing of itself, to all judicious ears, trivial and of no true musical delight; which consists only in apt numbers, fit quantity of syllables and the sense variously drawn out from one verse into another, not in the jingling sound of like endings—a fault avoided by the learned ancients both in poetry and all good oratory. This neglect then of rhyme so little is to be taken for a defect, though it may seem so perhaps to vulgar readers, that it rather is to be esteemed an example set, the first in English, of ancient liberty recovered to heroic poem from the troublesome and modern bondage of rhyming.

BOOK I

THE ARGUMENT

This First Book proposes, first in brief, the whole subject—Man's disobedience, and the loss thereupon of Paradise, wherein he was placed: then touches the prime cause of his fall—the Serpent, or rather Satan in the Serpent; who, revolting from God, and drawing to his side many legions of Angels, was, by the command of God, driven out of Heaven, with all his crew, into the great Deep. Which action passed over, the Poem hastes into the midst of things; presenting Satan, with his Angels, now fallen into Hell—described here not in the centre (for heaven and earth may be supposed as yet not made, certainly not yet accursed), but in a place of utter darkness, fitliest called Chaos. Here Satan, with his Angels lying on the burning lake, thunderstruck and astonished, after a certain space recovers, as from confusion; calls up him who, next in order and dignity, lay by him: they confer of their miserable fall. Satan awakens all his legions, who lay till then in the same manner confounded. They rise: their numbers; array of battle; their chief leaders named, according to the idols known afterwards in Canaan and the countries adjoining. To these Satan directs his speech; comforts them with hope yet of regaining Heaven; but tells them, lastly, of a new world and new kind of creature to be created, according to an ancient prophecy, or report, in Heaven—for that Angels were long before this visible creation was the opinion of many ancient Fathers. To find out the truth of this prophecy, and what to determine thereon, he refers to a full council. What his associates thence attempt. Pandemonium, the palace of Satan, rises, suddenly built out of the Deep: the infernal Peers there sit in council.

Of Man's first disobedience, and the fruit
Of that forbidden tree whose mortal taste
Brought death into the World, and all our woe,
With loss of Eden, till one greater Man
Restore us, and regain the blissful seat,
Sing, Heavenly Muse, that, on the secret top

Of Oreb, or of Sinai, didst inspire
That shepherd who first taught the chosen seed
In the beginning how the heavens and earth
Rose out of Chaos: or, if Sion hill
Delight thee more, and Siloa's brook that flowed
Fast by the oracle of God, I thence
Invoke thy aid to my adventurous song,
That with no middle flight intends to soar
Above th' Aonian mount, while it pursues
Things unattempted yet in prose or rhyme.
And chiefly thou, O Spirit, that dost prefer
Before all temples th' upright heart and pure,
Instruct me, for thou know'st; thou from the first
Wast present, and, with mighty wings outspread,
Dove-like sat'st brooding on the vast Abyss,
And mad'st it pregnant: what in me is dark
Illumine, what is low raise and support;
That, to the height of this great argument,
I may assert Eternal Providence,
And justify the ways of God to men.
  Say first—for Heaven hides nothing from thy view,
Nor the deep tract of Hell—say first what cause
Moved our grand parents, in that happy state,
Favoured of Heaven so highly, to fall off
From their Creator, and transgress his will
For one restraint, lords of the World besides.
Who first seduced them to that foul revolt?
  Th' infernal Serpent; he it was whose guile,
Stirred up with envy and revenge, deceived
The mother of mankind, what time his pride
Had cast him out from Heaven, with all his host
Of rebel Angels, by whose aid, aspiring
To set himself in glory above his peers,
He trusted to have equalled the Most High,
If he opposed, and with ambitious aim
Against the throne and monarchy of God,
Raised impious war in Heaven and battle proud,

With vain attempt. Him the Almighty Power
Hurled headlong flaming from th' ethereal sky,
With hideous ruin and combustion, down
To bottomless perdition, there to dwell
In adamantine chains and penal fire,
Who durst defy th' Omnipotent to arms.
  Nine times the space that measures day and night
To mortal men, he, with his horrid crew,
Lay vanquished, rolling in the fiery gulf,
Confounded, though immortal. But his doom
Reserved him to more wrath; for now the thought
Both of lost happiness and lasting pain
Torments him: round he throws his baleful eyes,
That witnessed huge affliction and dismay,
Mixed with obdúrate pride and steadfast hate.
At once, as far as Angels ken, he views
The dismal situation waste and wild.
A dungeon horrible, on all sides round,
As one great furnace flamed; yet from those flames
No light; but rather darkness visible
Served only to discover sights of woe,
Regions of sorrow, doleful shades, where peace
And rest can never dwell, hope never comes
That comes to all, but torture without end
Still urges, and a fiery deluge, fed
With ever-burning sulphur unconsumed.
Such place Eternal Justice had prepared
For those rebellious; here their prison ordained
In utter darkness, and their portion set,
As far removed from God and light of Heaven
As from the centre thrice to th' utmost pole.
Oh how unlike the place from whence they fell!
There the companions of his fall, o'erwhelmed
With floods and whirlwinds of tempestuous fire,
He soon discerns; and, weltering by his side,
One next himself in power, and next in crime,
Long after known in Palestine, and named

Beëlzebub. To whom th' Arch-Enemy,
And thence in Heaven called Satan, with bold words
Breaking the horrid silence, thus began:—
"If thou beest he—but O how fallen! how changed
From him who, in the happy realms of light
Clothed with transcendent brightness, didst outshine
Myriads, though bright!—if he whom mutual league,
United thoughts and counsels, equal hope
And hazard in the glorious enterprise,
Joined with me once, now misery hath joined
In equal ruin; into what pit thou seest
From what height fallen: so much the stronger proved
He with his thunder: and till then who knew
The force of those dire arms? Yet not for those,
Nor what the potent Victor in his rage
Can else inflict, do I repent, or change,
Though changed in outward lustre, that fixed mind,
And high disdain from sense of injured merit,
That with the Mightiest raised me to contend,
And to the fierce contentions brought along
Innumerable force of Spirits armed,
That durst dislike his reign, and, me preferring,
His utmost power with adverse power opposed
In dubious battle on the plains of Heaven,
And shook his throne. What though the field be lost?
All is not lost—the unconquerable will,
And study of revenge, immortal hate,
And courage never to submit or yield:
And what is else not to be overcome?
That glory never shall his wrath or might
Extort from me. To bow and sue for grace
With suppliant knee, and deify his power
Who, from the terror of this arm, so late
Doubted his empire—that were low indeed;
That were an ignominy and shame beneath
This downfall; since, by fate, the strength of Gods,
And this empyreal substance, cannot fail;

Since, through experience of this great event,
In arms not worse, in foresight much advanced,
We may with more successful hope resolve
To wage by force or guile eternal war,
Irreconcilable to our grand Foe,
Who now triúmphs, and in th' excess of joy
Sole reigning holds the tyranny of Heaven."
  So spake th' apostate Angel, though in pain,
Vaunting aloud, but racked with deep despair;
And him thus answered soon his bold compeer:—
  "O Prince, O Chief of many thronèd Powers
That led th' embattled Seraphim to war
Under thy conduct, and, in dreadful deeds
Fearless, endangered Heaven's perpetual King,
And put to proof his high supremacy,
Whether upheld by strength, or chance, or fate,
Too well I see and rue the dire event
That, with sad overthrow and foul defeat,
Hath lost us Heaven, and all this mighty host
In horrible destruction laid thus low,
As far as Gods and heavenly Essences
Can perish: for the mind and spirit remains
Invincible, and vigour soon returns,
Though all our glory extinct, and happy state
Here swallowed up in endless misery.
But what if he our Conqueror (whom I now
Of force believe almighty, since no less
Than such could have o'erpowered such force as ours)
Have left us this our spirit and strength entire,
Strongly to suffer and support our pains,
That we may so suffice his vengeful ire,
Or do him mightier service as his thralls
By right of war, whate'er his business be,
Here in the heart of Hell to work in fire,
Or do his errands in the gloomy Deep?
What can it then avail though yet we feel
Strength undiminished, or eternal being

To undergo eternal punishment?"
  Whereto with speedy words th' Arch-Fiend replied:—
"Fallen Cherub, to be weak is miserable,
Doing or suffering: but of this be sure—
To do aught good never will be our task,
But ever to do ill our sole delight,
As being the contrary to his high will
Whom we resist. If then his providence
Out of our evil seek to bring forth good,
Our labour must be to pervert that end,
And out of good still to find means of evil;
Which ofttimes may succeed so as perhaps
Shall grieve him, if I fail not, and disturb
His inmost counsels from their destined aim.
But see! the angry Victor hath recalled
His ministers of vengeance and pursuit
Back to the gates of Heaven: the sulphurous hail,
Shot after us in storm, o'erblown hath laid
The fiery surge that from the precipice
Of Heaven received us falling; and the thunder,
Winged with red lightning and impetuous rage,
Perhaps hath spent his shafts, and ceases now
To bellow through the vast and boundless Deep.
Let us not slip th' occasion, whether scorn
Or satiate fury yield it from our Foe.
Seest thou yon dreary plain, forlorn and wild,
The seat of desolation, void of light,
Save what the glimmering of these livid flames
Casts pale and dreadful? Thither let us tend
From off the tossing of these fiery waves;
There rest, if any rest can harbour there;
And, re-assembling our afflicted powers,
Consult how we may henceforth most offend
Our enemy, our own loss how repair,
How overcome this dire calamity,
What reinforcement we may gain from hope,
If not, what resolution from despair."

Thus Satan, talking to his nearest mate,
With head uplift above the wave, and eyes
That sparkling blazed; his other parts besides
Prone on the flood, extended long and large,
Lay floating many a rood, in bulk as huge
As whom the fables name of monstrous size,
Titanian or Earth-born, that warred on Jove,
Briareos or Typhon, whom the den
By ancient Tarsus held, or that sea-beast
Leviathan, which God of all his works
Created hugest that swim th' ocean-stream.
Him, haply slumbering on the Norway foam,
The pilot of some small night-foundered skiff,
Deeming some island, oft, as seamen tell,
With fixèd anchor in his scaly rind,
Moors by his side under the lee, while night
Invests the sea, and wishèd morn delays.
So stretched out huge in length the Arch-fiend lay,
Chained on the burning lake; nor ever thence
Had risen, or heaved his head, but that the will
And high permission of all-ruling Heaven
Left him at large to his own dark designs,
That with reiterated crimes he might
Heap on himself damnation, while he sought
Evil to others, and enraged might see
How all his malice served but to bring forth
Infinite goodness, grace, and mercy, shewn
On Man by him seduced, but on himself
Treble confusion, wrath, and vengeance poured.
Forthwith upright he rears from off the pool
His mighty stature; on each hand the flames
Driven backward slope their pointing spires, and, rolled
In billows, leave i' th' midst a horrid vale.
Then with expanded wings he steers his flight
Aloft, incumbent on the dusky air,
That felt unusual weight; till on dry land
He lights—if it were land that ever burned

With solid, as the lake with liquid fire,
And such appeared in hue as when the force
Of subterranean wind transports a hill
Torn from Pelorus, or the shattered side
Of thundering Etna, whose combustible
And fuelled entrails, thence conceiving fire,
Sublimed with mineral fury, aid the winds,
And leave a singèd bottom all involved
With stench and smoke. Such resting found the sole
Of unblest feet. Him followed his next mate;
Both glorying to have scaped the Stygian flood
As gods, and by their own recovered strength,
Not by the sufferance of supernal Power.
"Is this the region, this the soil, the clime,"
Said then the lost Archangel, "this the seat
That we must change for Heaven?—this mournful gloom
For that celestial light? Be it so, since he
Who now is sovereign can dispose and bid
What shall be right: farthest from him is best,
Whom reason hath equalled, force hath made supreme
Above his equals. Farewell, happy fields,
Where joy for ever dwells! Hail, horrors! hail,
Infernal world! and thou, profoundest Hell,
Receive thy new possessor—one who brings
A mind not to be changed by place or time.
The mind is its own place, and in itself
Can make a Heaven of Hell, a Hell of Heaven.
What matter where, if I be still the same,
And what I should be, all but less than he
Whom thunder hath made greater? Here at least
We shall be free; th' Almighty hath not built
Here for his envy, will not drive us hence:
Here we may reign secure; and, in my choice,
To reign is worth ambition, though in Hell:
Better to reign in Hell than serve in Heaven.
But wherefore let we then our faithful friends,
Th' associates and co-partners of our loss,

Lie thus astonished on th' oblivious pool,
And call them not to share with us their part
In this unhappy mansion, or once more
With rallied arms to try what may be yet
Regained in Heaven, or what more lost in Hell?"
  So Satan spake; and him Beëlzebub
Thus answered:—"Leader of those armies bright
Which, but th' Omnipotent, none could have foiled!
If once they hear that voice, their liveliest pledge
Of hope in fears and dangers—heard so oft
In worst extremes, and on the perilous edge
Of battle, when it raged, in all assaults
Their surest signal—they will soon resume
New courage and revive, though now they lie
Grovelling and prostrate on yon lake of fire,
As we erewhile, astounded and amazed;
No wonder, fallen such a pernicious height!"
  He scarce had ceased when the superior Fiend
Was moving toward the shore; his ponderous shield,
Ethereal temper, massy, large, and round,
Behind him cast. The broad circumference
Hung on his shoulders like the moon, whose orb
Through optic glass the Tuscan artist views
At evening, from the top of Fesolè,
Or in Valdarno, to descry new lands,
Rivers, or mountains, in her spotty globe.
His spear—to equal which the tallest pine
Hewn on Norwegian hills, to be the mast
Of some great ammiral, were but a wand—
He walked with, to support uneasy steps
Over the burning marl, not like those steps
On Heaven's azure; and the torrid clime
Smote on him sore besides, vaulted with fire.
Nathless he so endured, till on the beach
Of that inflamèd sea he stood, and called
His legions—Angel Forms, who lay entranced
Thick as autumnal leaves that strow the brooks

In Vallombrosa, where th' Etrurian shades
High over-arched embower; or scattered sedge
Afloat, when with fierce winds Orion armed
Hath vexed the Red-Sea coast, whose waves o'erthrew
Busiris and his Memphian chivalry,
While with perfidious hatred they pursued
The sojourners of Goshen, who beheld
From the safe shore their floating carcases
And broken chariot-wheels. So thick bestrown,
Abject and lost, lay these, covering the flood,
Under amazement of their hideous change.
He called so loud that all the hollow deep
Of Hell resounded:—"Princes, Potentates,
Warriors, the Flower of Heaven—once yours; now lost,
If such astonishment as this can seize
Eternal Spirits! Or have ye chosen this place
After the toil of battle to repose
Your wearied virtue, for the ease you find
To slumber here, as in the vales of Heaven?
Or in this abject posture have ye sworn
To adore the Conqueror, who now beholds
Cherub and Seraph rolling in the flood
With scattered arms and ensigns, till anon
His swift pursuers from Heaven-gates discern
Th' advantage, and, descending, tread us down
Thus drooping, or with linkèd thunderbolts
Transfix us to the bottom of this gulf?
Awake, arise, or be for ever fallen!"
  They heard, and were abashed, and up they sprung
Upon the wing, as when men wont to watch
On duty, sleeping found by whom they dread,
Rouse and bestir themselves ere well awake.
Nor did they not perceive the evil plight
In which they were, or the fierce pains not feel;
Yet to their General's voice they soon obeyed
Innumerable. As when the potent rod
Of Amram's son, in Egypt's evil day,

Waved round the coast, up-called a pitchy cloud
Of locusts, warping on the eastern wind,
That o'er the realm of impious Pharaoh hung
Like Night, and darkened all the land of Nile;
So numberless were those bad Angels seen
Hovering on wing under the cope of Hell,
'Twixt upper, nether, and surrounding fires;
Till, as a signal given, th' uplifted spear
Of their great Sultan waving to direct
Their course, in even balance down they light
On the firm brimstone, and fill all the plain:
A multitude like which the populous North
Poured never from her frozen loins to pass
Rhene or the Danaw, when her barbarous sons
Came like a deluge on the South, and spread
Beneath Gibraltar to the Libyan sands.
Forthwith, from every squadron and each band,
The heads and leaders thither haste where stood
Their great Commander—godlike Shapes, and Forms
Excelling human; princely Dignities;
And Powers that erst in Heaven sat on thrones,
Though on their names in Heavenly records now
Be no memorial, blotted out and rased
By their rebellion from the Books of Life.
Nor had they yet among the sons of Eve
Got them new names, till, wandering o'er the earth,
Through God's high sufferance for the trial of man,
By falsities and lies the greatest part
Of mankind they corrupted to forsake
God their Creator, and th' invisible
Glory of him that made them to transform
Oft to the image of a brute, adorned
With gay religions full of pomp and gold,
And devils to adore for deities:
Then were they known to men by various names,
And various idols through the heathen world.
Say, Muse, their names then known, who first, who last,

Roused from the slumber on that fiery couch,
At their great Emperor's call, as next in worth
Came singly where he stood on the bare strand,
While the promiscuous crowd stood yet aloof?
  The chief were those who, from the pit of Hell
Roaming to seek their prey on Earth, durst fix
Their seats, long after, next the seat of God,
Their altars by his altar, gods adored
Among the nations round, and durst abide
Jehovah thundering out of Sion, throned
Between the Cherubim; yea, often placed
Within his sanctuary itself their shrines,
Abominations; and with cursèd things
His holy rites and solemn feasts profaned,
And with their darkness durst affront his light.
First, Moloch, horrid king, besmeared with blood
Of human sacrifice, and parents' tears;
Though, for the noise of drums and timbrels loud,
Their children's cries unheard that passed through fire
To his grim idol. Him the Ammonite
Worshiped in Rabba and her watery plain,
In Argob and in Basan, to the stream
Of utmost Arnon. Nor content with such
Audacious neighbourhood, the wisest heart
Of Solomon he led by fraud to build
His temple right against the temple of God
On that opprobrious hill, and made his grove
The pleasant valley of Hinnom, Tophet thence
And black Gehenna called, the type of Hell.
Next Chemos, th' obscene dread of Moab's sons,
From Aroar to Nebo and the wild
Of southmost Abarim; in Hesebon
And Horonaim, Seon's realm, beyond
The flowery dale of Sibma clad with vines,
And Elealè to th' Asphaltic Pool:
Peor his other name, when he enticed
Israel in Sittim, on their march from Nile,

To do him wanton rites, which cost them woe.
Yet thence his lustful orgies he enlarged
Even to that hill of scandal, by the grove
Of Moloch homicide, lust hard by hate,
Till good Josiah drove them thence to Hell.
With these came they who, from the bordering flood
Of old Euphrates to the brook that parts
Egypt from Syrian ground, had general names
Of Baalim and Ashtaroth—those male,
These feminine. For Spirits, when they please,
Can either sex assume, or both; so soft
And uncompounded is their essence pure,
Not tied or manacled with joint or limb,
Nor founded on the brittle strength of bones,
Like cumbrous flesh; but, in what shape they choose,
Dilated or condensed, bright or obscure,
Can execute their airy purposes,
And works of love or enmity fulfil.
For those the race of Israel oft forsook
Their Living Strength, and unfrequented left
His righteous altar, bowing lowly down
To bestial gods; for which their heads as low
Bowed down in battle, sunk before the spear
Of despicable foes. With these in troop
Came Astoreth, whom the Phoenicians called
Astartè, queen of heaven, with crescent horns;
To whose bright image nightly by the moon
Sidonian virgins paid their vows and songs;
In Sion also not unsung, where stood
Her temple on th' offensive mountain, built
By that uxorious king whose heart, though large,
Beguiled by fair idolatresses, fell
To idols foul. Thammuz came next behind,
Whose annual wound in Lebanon allured
The Syrian damsels to lament his fate
In amorous ditties all a summer's day,
While smooth Adonis from his native rock

Ran purple to the sea, supposed with blood
Of Thammuz yearly wounded: the love-tale
Infected Sion's daughters with like heat,
Whose wanton passions in the sacred porch
Ezekiel saw, when, by the vision led,
His eye surveyed the dark idolatries
Of alienated Judah. Next came one
Who mourned in earnest, when the captive ark
Maimed his brute image, head and hands lopt off,
In his own temple, on the grunsel-edge,
Where he fell flat and shamed his worshippers:
Dagon his name, sea-monster, upward man
And downward fish; yet had his temple high
Reared in Azotus, dreaded through the coast
Of Palestine, in Gath and Ascalon,
And Accaron and Gaza's frontier bounds.
Him followed Rimmon, whose delightful seat
Was fair Damascus, on the fertile banks
Of Abbana and Pharphar, lucid streams.
He also against the house of God was bold:
A leper once he lost, and gained a king—
Ahaz, his sottish conqueror, whom he drew
God's altar to disparage and displace
For one of Syrian mode, whereon to burn
His odious offerings, and adore the gods
Whom he had vanquished. After these appeared
A crew who, under names of old renown—
Osiris, Isis, Orus, and their train—
With monstrous shapes and sorceries abused
Fanatic Egypt and her priests to seek
Their wandering gods disguised in brutish forms
Rather than human. Nor did Israel scape
Th' infection, when their borrowed gold composed
The calf in Oreb; and the rebel king
Doubled that sin in Bethel and in Dan,
Likening his Maker to the grazèd ox—
Jehovah, who, in one night, when he passed

From Egypt marching, equalled with one stroke
Both her first-born and all her bleating gods.
Belial came last; than whom a Spirit more lewd
Fell not from Heaven, or more gross to love
Vice for itself. To him no temple stood
Or altar smoked; yet who more oft than he
In temples and at altars, when the priest
Turns atheist, as did Eli's sons, who filled
With lust and violence the house of God?
In courts and palaces he also reigns,
And in luxurious cities, where the noise
Of riot ascends above their loftiest towers,
And injury and outrage; and, when night
Darkens the streets, then wander forth the sons
Of Belial, flown with insolence and wine.
Witness the streets of Sodom, and that night
In Gibeah, when the hospitable door
Exposed a matron, to avoid worse rape.
These were the prime in order and in might:
The rest were long to tell; though far renowned
Th' Ionian gods—of Javan's issue held
Gods, yet confessed later than Heaven and Earth,
Their boasted parents;—Titan, Heaven's first-born,
With his enormous brood, and birthright seized
By younger Saturn: he from mightier Jove,
His own and Rhea's son, like measure found;
So Jove usurping reigned. These, first in Crete
And Ida known, thence on the snowy top
Of cold Olympus ruled the middle air,
Their highest heaven; or on the Delphian cliff,
Or in Dodona, and through all the bounds
Of Doric land; or who with Saturn old
Fled over Adria to th' Hesperian fields,
And o'er the Celtic roamed the utmost Isles.
All these and more came flocking; but with looks
Downcast and damp; yet such wherein appeared
Obscure some glimpse of joy to have found their Chief

Not in despair, to have found themselves not lost
In loss itself; which on his countenance cast
Like doubtful hue. But he, his wonted pride
Soon recollecting, with high words, that bore
Semblance of worth, not substance, gently raised
Their fainting courage, and dispelled their fears:
Then straight commands that, at the warlike sound
Of trumpets loud and clarions, be upreared
His mighty standard. That proud honour claimed
Azazel as his right, a Cherub tall:
Who forthwith from the glittering staff unfurled
Th' imperial ensign; which, full high advanced,
Shone like a meteor streaming to the wind,
With gems and golden lustre rich emblazed,
Seraphic arms and trophies; all the while
Sonorous metal blowing martial sounds:
At which the universal host up-sent
A shout that tore Hell's concave, and beyond
Frighted the reign of Chaos and old Night.
All in a moment through the gloom were seen
Ten thousand banners rise into the air,
With orient colours waving: with them rose
A forest huge of spears; and thronging helms
Appeared, and serried shields in thick array
Of depth immeasurable. Anon they move
In perfect phalanx to the Dorian mood
Of flutes and soft recorders—such as raised
To height of noblest temper heroes old
Arming to battle, and instead of rage
Deliberate valour breathed, firm, and unmoved
With dread of death to flight or foul retreat;
Nor wanting power to mitigate and swage
With solemn touches troubled thoughts, and chase
Anguish and doubt and fear and sorrow and pain
From mortal or immortal minds. Thus they,
Breathing united force with fixèd thought,
Moved on in silence to soft pipes that charmed

Their painful steps o'er the burnt soil. And now
Advanced in view they stand—a horrid front
Of dreadful length and dazzling arms, in guise
Of warriors old, with ordered spear and shield,
Awaiting what command their mighty Chief
Had to impose. He through the armèd files
Darts his experienced eye, and soon traverse
The whole battalion views—their order due,
Their visages and stature as of gods;
Their number last he sums. And now his heart
Distends with pride, and, hardening in his strength,
Glories: for never, since created Man,
Met such embodied force as, named with these,
Could merit more than that small infantry
Warred on by cranes—though all the giant brood
Of Phlegra with th' heroic race were joined
That fought at Thebes and Ilium, on each side
Mixed with auxiliar gods; and what resounds
In fable or romance of Uther's son,
Begirt with British and Armoric knights;
And all who since, baptized or infidel,
Jousted in Aspramont, or Montalban,
Damasco, or Marocco, or Trebisond,
Or whom Biserta sent from Afric shore
When Charlemain with all his peerage fell
By Fontarabbia. Thus far these beyond
Compare of mortal prowess, yet observed
Their dread Commander. He, above the rest
In shape and gesture proudly eminent,
Stood like a tower. His form had yet not lost
All her original brightness, nor appeared
Less than Archangel ruined, and th' excess
Of glory obscured: as when the sun new-risen
Looks through the horizontal misty air
Shorn of his beams, or, from behind the moon,
In dim eclipse, disastrous twilight sheds
On half the nations, and with fear of change

Perplexes monarchs. Darkened so, yet shone
Above them all th' Archangel: but his face
Deep scars of thunder had intrenched, and care
Sat on his faded cheek, but under brows
Of dauntless courage, and considerate pride
Waiting revenge. Cruel his eye, but cast
Signs of remorse and passion, to behold
The fellows of his crime, the followers rather
(Far other once beheld in bliss), condemned
For ever now to have their lot in pain—
Millions of Spirits for his fault amerced
Of Heaven, and from eternal splendours flung
For his revolt—yet faithful how they stood,
Their glory withered; as, when heaven's fire
Hath scathed the forest oaks or mountain pines,
With singèd top their stately growth, though bare,
Stands on the blasted heath. He now prepared
To speak; whereat their doubled ranks they bend
From wing to wing, and half enclose him round
With all his peers: attention held them mute.
Thrice he assayed, and thrice, in spite of scorn,
Tears, such as Angels weep, burst forth: at last
Words interwove with sighs found out their way:—
"O myriads of immortal Spirits! O Powers
Matchless, but with th' Almighty!—and that strife
Was not inglorious, though th' event was dire,
As this place testifies, and this dire change,
Hateful to utter. But what power of mind,
Foreseeing or presaging, from the depth
Of knowledge past or present, could have feared
How such united force of gods, how such
As stood like these, could ever know repulse?
For who can yet believe, though after loss,
That all these puissant legions, whose exile
Hath emptied Heaven, shall fail to re-ascend,
Self-raised, and repossess their native seat?
For me, be witness all the host of Heaven,

If counsels different, or danger shunned
By me, have lost our hopes. But he who reigns
Monarch in Heaven till then as one secure
Sat on his throne, upheld by old repute,
Consent or custom, and his regal state
Put forth at full, but still his strength concealed—
Which tempted our attempt, and wrought our fall.
Henceforth his might we know, and know our own,
So as not either to provoke, or dread
New war provoked: our better part remains
To work in close design, by fraud or guile,
What force effected not; that he no less
At length from us may find, who overcomes
By force hath overcome but half his foe.
Space may produce new Worlds; whereof so rife
There went a fame in Heaven that he ere long
Intended to create, and therein plant
A generation whom his choice regard
Should favour equal to the Sons of Heaven.
Thither, if but to pry, shall be perhaps
Our first eruption—thither, or elsewhere;
For this infernal pit shall never hold
Celestial Spirits in bondage, nor th' Abyss
Long under darkness cover. But these thoughts
Full counsel must mature. Peace is despaired;
For who can think submission? War, then, war
Open or understood, must be resolved."
He spake; and, to confirm his words, outflew
Millions of flaming swords, drawn from the thighs
Of mighty Cherubim; the sudden blaze
Far round illumined Hell. Highly they raged
Against the Highest, and fierce with graspèd arms
Clashed on their sounding shields the din of war,
Hurling defiance toward the vault of Heaven.
There stood a hill not far, whose grisly top
Belched fire and rolling smoke; the rest entire
Shone with a glossy scurf—undoubted sign

That in his womb was hid metallic ore,
The work of sulphur. Thither, winged with speed,
A numerous brígade hastened: as when bands
Of pioneers, with spade and pickaxe armed,
Forerun the royal camp, to trench a field,
Or cast a rampart. Mammon led them on—
Mammon, the least erected Spirit that fell
From Heaven; for even in Heaven his looks and thoughts
Were always downward bent, admiring more
The riches of Heaven's pavement, trodden gold,
Than aught divine or holy else enjoyed
In vision beatific. By him first
Men also, and by his suggestion taught,
Ransacked the centre, and with impious hands
Rifled the bowels of their mother Earth
For treasures better hid. Soon had his crew
Opened into the hill a spacious wound,
And digged out ribs of gold. Let none admire
That riches grow in Hell; that soil may best
Deserve the precious bane. And here let those
Who boast in mortal things, and wondering tell
Of Babel, and the works of Memphian kings,
Learn how their greatest monuments of fame
And strength, and art, are easily outdone
By Spirits reprobate, and in an hour
What in an age they, with incessant toil
And hands innumerable, scarce perform.
Nigh on the plain, in many cells prepared,
That underneath had veins of liquid fire
Sluiced from the lake, a second multitude
With wondrous art founded the massy ore,
Severing each kind, and scummed the bullion-dross.
A third as soon had formed within the ground
A various mould, and from the boiling cells
By strange conveyance filled each hollow nook;
As in an organ, from one blast of wind,
To many a row of pipes the sound-board breathes.

Anon out of the earth a fabric huge
Rose like an exhalation, with the sound
Of dulcet symphonies and voices sweet—
Built like a temple, where pilasters round
Were set, and Doric pillars overlaid
With golden architrave; nor did there want
Cornice or frieze, with bossy sculptures graven;
The roof was fretted gold. Not Babylon
Nor great Alcairo such magnificence
Equalled in all their glories, to enshrine
Belus or Serapis their gods, or seat
Their kings, when Egypt with Assyria strove
In wealth and luxury. Th' ascending pile
Stood fixed her stately height; and straight the doors,
Opening their brazen folds, discover, wide
Within, her ample spaces o'er the smooth
And level pavement: from the archèd roof,
Pendent by subtle magic, many a row
Of starry lamps and blazing cressets, fed
With naphtha and asphaltus, yielded light
As from a sky. The hasty multitude
Admiring entered; and the work some praise,
And some the architect. His hand was known
In Heaven by many a towered structure high,
Where sceptred Angels held their residence,
And sat as Princes, whom the supreme King
Exalted to such power, and gave to rule,
Each in his Hierarchy, the Orders bright.
Nor was his name unheard or unadored
In ancient Greece; and in Ausonian land
Men called him Mulciber; and how he fell
From Heaven they fabled, thrown by angry Jove
Sheer o'er the crystal battlements: from morn
To noon he fell, from noon to dewy eve,
A summer's day, and with the setting sun
Dropt from the zenith, like a falling star,
On Lemnos, th' Aegaean isle. Thus they relate,

Erring; for he with this rebellious rout
Fell long before; nor aught availed him now
To have built in Heaven high towers; nor did he scape
By all his engines, but was headlong sent,
With his industrious crew, to build in Hell.
  Meanwhile the wingèd Heralds, by command
Of sovereign power, with awful ceremony
And trumpet's sound, throughout the host proclaim
A solemn council forthwith to be held
At Pandemonium, the high capital
Of Satan and his peers. Their summons called
From every band and squarèd regiment
By place or choice the worthiest: they anon
With hundreds and with thousands trooping came
Attended. All access was thronged; the gates
And porches wide, but chief the spacious hall
(Though like a covered field, where champions bold
Wont ride in armed, and at the Soldan's chair
Defied the best of Paynim chivalry
To mortal combat, or career with lance),
Thick swarmed, both on the ground and in the air,
Brushed with the hiss of rustling wings. As bees
In spring-time, when the Sun with Taurus rides,
Pour forth their populous youth about the hive
In clusters; they among fresh dews and flowers
Fly to and fro, or on the smoothèd plank,
The suburb of their straw-built citadel,
New rubbed with balm, expatiate, and confer
Their state-affairs: so thick the airy crowd
Swarmed and were straitened; till, the signal given,
Behold a wonder! They but now who seemed
In bigness to surpass Earth's giant sons,
Now less than smallest dwarfs, in narrow room
Throng numberless—like that pygmean race
Beyond the Indian mount; or faery elves,
Whose midnight revels, by a forest-side
Or fountain, some belated peasant sees,

Or dreams he sees, while overhead the Moon
Sits arbitress, and nearer to the Earth
Wheels her pale course: they, on their mirth and dance
Intent, with jocund music charm his ear;
At once with joy and fear his heart rebounds.
Thus incorporeal Spirits to smallest forms
Reduced their shapes immense, and were at large,
Though without number still, amidst the hall
Of that infernal court. But far within,
And in their own dimensions like themselves,
The great Seraphic Lords and Cherubim
In close recess and secret conclave sat,
A thousand demi-gods on golden seats,
Frequent and full. After short silence then,
And summons read, the great consult began.

THE END OF THE FIRST BOOK

BOOK II

THE ARGUMENT

The consultation begun, Satan debates whether another battle be to be hazarded for the recovery of Heaven: some advise it, others dissuade. A third proposal is preferred, mentioned before by Satan—to search the truth of that prophecy or tradition in Heaven concerning another world, and another kind of Creature, equal, or not much inferior, to themselves, about this time to be created. Their doubt who shall be sent on this difficult search: Satan, their chief, undertakes alone the voyage; is honoured and applauded. The council thus ended, the rest betake them several ways and to several employments, as their inclinations lead them, to entertain the time till Satan return. He passes on his journey to Hell-gates; finds them shut, and who sat there to guard them; by whom at length they are opened, and discover to him the great gulf between Hell and Heaven. With what difficulty he passes through, directed by Chaos, the Power of that place, to the sight of this new World which he sought.

High on a throne of royal state, which far
Outshone the wealth of Ormus and of Ind,
Or where the gorgeous East with richest hand
Showers on her kings barbaric pearl and gold,
Satan exalted sat, by merit raised
To that bad eminence; and, from despair
Thus high uplifted beyond hope, aspires
Beyond thus high, insatiate to pursue
Vain war with Heaven; and, by success untaught,
His proud imaginations thus displayed:—
"Powers and Dominions, Deities of Heaven!—
For, since no deep within her gulf can hold
Immortal vigour, though oppressed and fallen,
I give not Heaven for lost: from this descent
Celestial Virtues rising will appear
More glorious and more dread than from no fall,

And trust themselves to fear no second fate!—
Me though just right, and the fixed laws of Heaven,
Did first create your leader—next, free choice,
With what besides in council or in fight
Hath been achieved of merit—yet this loss,
Thus far at least recovered, hath much more
Established in a safe, unenvied throne,
Yielded with full consent. The happier state
In Heaven, which follows dignity, might draw
Envy from each inferior; but who here
Will envy whom the highest place exposes
Foremost to stand against the Thunderer's aim
Your bulwark, and condemns to greatest share
Of endless pain? Where there is, then, no good
For which to strive, no strife can grow up there
From faction: for none sure will claim in Hell
Precedence; none whose portion is so small
Of present pain that with ambitious mind
Will covet more! With this advantage, then,
To union, and firm faith, and firm accord,
More than can be in Heaven, we now return
To claim our just inheritance of old,
Surer to prosper than prosperity
Could have assured us; and by what best way,
Whether of open war or covert guile,
We now debate. Who can advise may speak."
He ceased; and next him Moloch, sceptred king,
Stood up—the strongest and the fiercest Spirit
That fought in Heaven, now fiercer by despair.
His trust was with th' Eternal to be deemed
Equal in strength, and rather than be less
Cared not to be at all; with that care lost
Went all his fear: of God, or Hell, or worse,
He recked not, and these words thereafter spake:—
"My sentence is for open war. Of wiles,
More unexpert, I boast not: them let those
Contrive who need, or when they need; not now.

For, while they sit contriving, shall the rest—
Millions that stand in arms, and longing wait
The signal to ascend—sit lingering here,
Heaven's fugitives, and for their dwelling-place
Accept this dark opprobrious den of shame,
The prison of his tyranny who reigns
By our delay? No! let us rather choose,
Armed with Hell-flames and fury, all at once
O'er Heaven's high towers to force resistless way,
Turning our tortures into horrid arms
Against the Torturer; when, to meet the noise
Of his almighty engine, he shall hear
Infernal thunder, and, for lightning, see
Black fire and horror shot with equal rage
Among his Angels, and his throne itself
Mixed with Tartarean sulphur and strange fire,
His own invented torments. But perhaps
The way seems difficult, and steep to scale
With upright wing against a higher foe!
Let such bethink them, if the sleepy drench
Of that forgetful lake benumb not still,
That in our proper motion we ascend
Up to our native seat; descent and fall
To us is adverse. Who but felt of late,
When the fierce foe hung on our broken rear
Insulting, and pursued us through the Deep,
With what compulsion and laborious flight
We sunk thus low? Th' ascent is easy, then;
Th' event is feared! Should we again provoke
Our stronger, some worse way his wrath may find
To our destruction, if there be in Hell
Fear to be worse destroyed! What can be worse
Than to dwell here, driven out from bliss, condemned
In this abhorrèd deep to utter woe!
Where pain of unextinguishable fire
Must exercise us without hope of end
The vassals of his anger, when the scourge

Inexorably, and the torturing hour,
Calls us to penance? More destroyed than thus,
We should be quite abolished, and expire.
What fear we then? what doubt we to incense
His utmost ire? which, to the height enraged,
Will either quite consume us, and reduce
To nothing this essential—happier far
Than miserable to have eternal being!—
Or, if our substance be indeed divine,
And cannot cease to be, we are at worst
On this side nothing; and by proof we feel
Our power sufficient to disturb his Heaven,
And with perpetual inroads to alarm,
Though inaccessible, his fatal throne:
Which, if not victory, is yet revenge."
  He ended frowning, and his look denounced
Desperate revenge, and battle dangerous
To less than gods. On th' other side up rose
Belial, in act more graceful and humane.
A fairer person lost not Heaven; he seemed
For dignity composed, and high exploit.
But all was false and hollow; though his tongue
Dropped manna, and could make the worse appear
The better reason, to perplex and dash
Maturest counsels: for his thoughts were low—
To vice industrious, but to nobler deeds
Timorous and slothful. Yet he pleased the ear,
And with persuasive accent thus began:—
  "I should be much for open war, O Peers,
As not behind in hate, if what was urged
Main reason to persuade immediate war
Did not dissuade me most, and seem to cast
Ominous conjecture on the whole success;
When he who most excels in fact of arms,
In what he counsels and in what excels
Mistrustful, grounds his courage on despair
And utter dissolution, as the scope

Of all his aim, after some dire revenge.
First, what revenge? The towers of Heaven are filled
With armèd watch, that render all access
Impregnable: oft on the bordering Deep
Encamp their legions, or with obscure wing
Scout far and wide into the realm of Night,
Scorning surprise. Or, could we break our way
By force, and at our heels all Hell should rise
With blackest insurrection to confound
Heaven's purest light, yet our great Enemy,
All incorruptible, would on his throne
Sit unpolluted, and th' ethereal mould,
Incapable of stain, would soon expel
Her mischief, and purge off the baser fire,
Victorious. Thus repulsed, our final hope
Is flat despair: we must exasperate
Th' Almighty Victor to spend all his rage;
And that must end us; that must be our cure—
To be no more. Sad cure! for who would lose,
Though full of pain, this intellectual being,
Those thoughts that wander through eternity,
To perish rather, swallowed up and lost
In the wide womb of uncreated Night,
Devoid of sense and motion? And who knows,
Let this be good, whether our angry Foe
Can give it, or will ever? How he can
Is doubtful; that he never will is sure.
Will he, so wise, let loose at once his ire,
Belike through impotence or unaware,
To give his enemies their wish, and end
Them in his anger whom his anger saves
To punish endless? 'Wherefore cease we, then?'
Say they who counsel war; 'we are decreed,
Reserved, and destined to eternal woe;
Whatever doing, what can we suffer more,
What can we suffer worse?' Is this, then, worst—
Thus sitting, thus consulting, thus in arms?

What when we fled amain, pursued and struck
With Heaven's afflicting thunder, and besought
The Deep to shelter us? This Hell then seemed
A refuge from those wounds. Or when we lay
Chained on the burning lake? That sure was worse.
What if the breath that kindled those grim fires,
Awaked, should blow them into sevenfold rage,
And plunge us in the flames; or from above
Should intermitted vengeance arm again
His red right hand to plague us? What if all
Her stores were opened, and this firmament
Of Hell should spout her cataracts of fire,
Impendent horrors, threatening hideous fall
One day upon our heads; while we perhaps,
Designing or exhorting glorious war,
Caught in a fiery tempest, shall be hurled,
Each on his rock transfixed, the sport and prey
Of racking whirlwinds, or for ever sunk
Under yon boiling ocean, wrapt in chains,
There to converse with everlasting groans,
Unrespited, unpitied, unreprieved,
Ages of hopeless end? This would be worse.
War, therefore, open or concealed, alike
My voice dissuades; for what can force or guile
With him, or who deceive his mind, whose eye
Views all things at one view? He from Heaven's height
All these our motions vain sees and derides,
Not more almighty to resist our might
Than wise to frustrate all our plots and wiles.
Shall we, then, live thus vile—the race of Heaven
Thus trampled, thus expelled, to suffer here
Chains and these torments? Better these than worse,
By my advice; since fate inevitable
Subdues us, and omnipotent decree,
The Victor's will. To suffer, as to do,
Our strength is equal; nor the law unjust
That so ordains. This was at first resolved,

If we were wise, against so great a foe
Contending, and so doubtful what might fall.
I laugh when those who at the spear are bold
And venturous, if that fail them, shrink, and fear
What yet they know must follow—to endure
Exile, or ignominy, or bonds, or pain,
The sentence of their Conqueror. This is now
Our doom; which if we can sustain and bear,
Our Supreme Foe in time may much remit
His anger, and perhaps, thus far removed,
Not mind us not offending, satisfied
With what is punished; whence these raging fires
Will slacken, if his breath stir not their flames.
Our purer essence then will overcome
Their noxious vapour; or, inured, not feel;
Or, changed at length, and to the place conformed
In temper and in nature, will receive
Familiar the fierce heat; and, void of pain,
This horror will grow mild, this darkness light;
Besides what hope the never-ending flight
Of future days may bring, what chance, what change
Worth waiting—since our present lot appears
For happy though but ill, for ill not worst,
If we procure not to ourselves more woe."
  Thus Belial, with words clothed in reason's garb,
Counselled ignoble ease and peaceful sloth,
Not peace; and after him thus Mammon spake:—
  "Either to disenthrone the King of Heaven
We war, if war be best, or to regain
Our own right lost. Him to unthrone we then
May hope, when everlasting Fate shall yield
To fickle Chance, and Chaos judge the strife.
The former, vain to hope, argues as vain
The latter; for what place can be for us
Within Heaven's bound, unless Heaven's Lord supreme
We overpower? Suppose he should relent,
And publish grace to all, on promise made

Of new subjection; with what eyes could we
Stand in his presence humble, and receive
Strict laws imposed, to celebrate his throne
With warbled hymns, and to his Godhead sing
Forced hallelujahs, while he lordly sits
Our envied sovereign, and his altar breathes
Ambrosial odours and ambrosial flowers,
Our servile offerings? This must be our task
In Heaven, this our delight. How wearisome
Eternity so spent in worship paid
To whom we hate! Let us not then pursue,
By force impossible, by leave obtained
Unácceptable, though in Heaven, our state
Of splendid vassalage; but rather seek
Our own good from ourselves, and from our own
Live to ourselves, though in this vast recess,
Free and to none accountable, preferring
Hard liberty before the easy yoke
Of servile pomp. Our greatness will appear
Then most conspicuous when great things of small,
Useful of hurtful, prosperous of adverse,
We can create, and in what place soe'er
Thrive under evil, and work ease out of pain
Through labour and endurance. This deep world
Of darkness do we dread? How oft amidst
Thick clouds and dark doth Heaven's all-ruling Sire
Choose to reside, his glory unobscured,
And with the majesty of darkness round
Covers his throne, from whence deep thunders roar,
Mustering their rage, and Heaven resembles Hell!
As he our darkness, cannot we his light
Imitate when we please? This desert soil
Wants not her hidden lustre, gems and gold;
Nor want we skill or art from whence to raise
Magnificence; and what can Heaven show more?
Our torments also may, in length of time,
Become our elements, these piercing fires

As soft as now severe, our temper changed
Into their temper; which must needs remove
The sensible of pain. All things invite
To peaceful counsels, and the settled state
Of order, how in safety best we may
Compose our present evils, with regard
Of what we are and where, dismissing quite
All thoughts of war. Ye have what I advise."
He scarce had finished, when such murmur filled
Th' assembly as when hollow rocks retain
The sound of blustering winds, which all night long
Had roused the sea, now with hoarse cadence lull
Seafaring men o'erwatched, whose bark by chance,
Or pinnace, anchors in a craggy bay
After the tempest. Such applause was heard
As Mammon ended, and his sentence pleased,
Advising peace: for such another field
They dreaded worse than Hell; so much the fear
Of thunder and the sword of Michaël
Wrought still within them; and no less desire
To found this nether empire, which might rise,
By policy and long process of time,
In emulation opposite to Heaven.
Which when Beëlzebub perceived—than whom,
Satan except, none higher sat—with grave
Aspect he rose, and in his rising seemed
A pillar of state. Deep on his front engraven
Deliberation sat, and public care;
And princely counsel in his face yet shone,
Majestic, though in ruin. Sage he stood,
With Atlantean shoulders, fit to bear
The weight of mightiest monarchies; his look
Drew audience and attention still as night
Or summer's noontide air, while thus he spake:—
"Thrones and Imperial Powers, Offspring of Heaven,
Ethereal Virtues! or these titles now
Must we renounce, and, changing style, be called

Princes of Hell? for so the popular vote
Inclines—here to continue, and build up here
A growing empire; doubtless! while we dream,
And know not that the King of Heaven hath doomed
This place our dungeon, not our safe retreat
Beyond his potent arm, to live exempt
From Heaven's high jurisdiction, in new league
Banded against his throne, but to remain
In strictest bondage, though thus far removed,
Under th' inevitable curb, reserved
His captive multitude. For he, be sure,
In height or depth, still first and last will reign
Sole king, and of his kingdom lose no part
By our revolt, but over Hell extend
His empire, and with iron sceptre rule
Us here, as with his golden those in Heaven.
What sit we then projecting peace and war?
War hath determined us and foiled with loss
Irreparable; terms of peace yet none
Vouchsafed or sought; for what peace will be given
To us enslaved, but custody severe,
And stripes and arbitrary punishment
Inflicted? and what peace can we return,
But, to our power, hostility and hate,
Untamed reluctance, and revenge, though slow,
Yet ever plotting how the Conqueror least
May reap his conquest, and may least rejoice
In doing what we most in suffering feel?
Nor will occasion want, nor shall we need
With dangerous expedition to invade
Heaven, whose high walls fear no assault or siege,
Or ambush from the Deep. What if we find
Some easier enterprise? There is a place
(If ancient and prophetic fame in Heaven
Err not)—another World, the happy seat
Of some new race, called Man, about this time
To be created like to us, though less

In power and excellence, but favoured more
Of him who rules above; so was his will
Pronounced among the Gods, and by an oath
That shook Heaven's whole circumference confirmed.
Thither let us bend all our thoughts, to learn
What creatures there inhabit, of what mould
Or substance, how endued, and what their power
And where their weakness: how attempted best,
By force or subtlety. Though Heaven be shut,
And Heaven's high Arbitrator sit secure
In his own strength, this place may lie exposed,
The utmost border of his kingdom, left
To their defence who hold it: here, perhaps,
Some advantageous act may be achieved
By sudden onset—either with Hell-fire
To waste his whole creation, or possess
All as our own, and drive, as we were driven,
The puny habitants; or, if not drive,
Seduce them to our party, that their God
May prove their foe, and with repenting hand
Abolish his own works. This would surpass
Common revenge, and interrupt his joy
In our confusion, and our joy upraise
In his disturbance; when his darling sons,
Hurled headlong to partake with us, shall curse
Their frail original, and faded bliss—
Faded so soon! Advise if this be worth
Attempting, or to sit in darkness here
Hatching vain empires." Thus Beëlzebub
Pleaded his devilish counsel—first devised
By Satan, and in part proposed: for whence,
But from the author of all ill, could spring
So deep a malice, to confound the race
Of mankind in one root, and Earth with Hell
To mingle and involve, done all to spite
The great Creator? But their spite still serves
His glory to augment. The bold design

Pleased highly those infernal States, and joy
Sparkled in all their eyes: with full assent
They vote: whereat his speech he thus renews:—
"Well have ye judged, well ended long debate,
Synod of Gods, and, like to what ye are,
Great things resolved, which from the lowest deep
Will once more lift us up, in spite of fate,
Nearer our ancient seat—perhaps in view
Of those bright confines, whence, with neighbouring arms,
And opportune excursion, we may chance
Re-enter Heaven; or else in some mild zone
Dwell, not unvisited of Heaven's fair light,
Secure, and at the brightening orient beam
Purge off this gloom: the soft delicious air,
To heal the scar of these corrosive fires,
Shall breathe her balm. But, first, whom shall we send
In search of this new World? whom shall we find
Sufficient? who shall tempt with wandering feet
The dark, unbottomed, infinite Abyss,
And through the palpable obscure find out
His uncouth way, or spread his airy flight,
Upborne with indefatigable wings
Over the vast abrupt, ere he arrive
The happy Isle? What strength, what art, can then
Suffice, or what evasion bear him safe,
Through the strict senteries and stations thick
Of Angels watching round? Here he had need
All circumspection: and we now no less
Choice in our suffrage; for on whom we send
The weight of all, and our last hope, relies."
  This said, he sat; and expectation held
His look suspense, awaiting who appeared
To second, or oppose, or undertake
The perilous attempt. But all sat mute,
Pondering the danger with deep thoughts; and each
In other's countenance read his own dismay,
Astonished. None among the choice and prime

Of those Heaven-warring champions could be found
So hardy as to proffer or accept,
Alone, the dreadful voyage; till, at last,
Satan, whom now transcendent glory raised
Above his fellows, with monarchal pride
Conscious of highest worth, unmoved thus spake:—
"O Progeny of Heaven! Empyreal Thrones!
With reason hath deep silence and demur
Seized us, though undismayed. Long is the way
And hard, that out of Hell leads up to light.
Our prison strong, this huge convex of fire,
Outrageous to devour, immures us round
Ninefold; and gates of burning adamant,
Barred over us, prohibit all egress.
These passed, if any pass, the void profound
Of unessential Night receives him next,
Wide-gaping, and with utter loss of being
Threatens him, plunged in that abortive gulf.
If thence he scape, into whatever world,
Or unknown region, what remains him less
Than unknown dangers, and as hard escape?
But I should ill become this throne, O Peers,
And this imperial sovereignty, adorned
With splendour, armed with power, if aught proposed
And judged of public moment in the shape
Of difficulty or danger, could deter
Me from attempting. Wherefore do I assume
These royalties, and not refuse to reign,
Refusing to accept as great a share
Of hazard as of honour, due alike
To him who reigns, and so much to him due
Of hazard more as he above the rest
High honoured sits? Go, therefore, mighty Powers,
Terror of Heaven, though fallen; intend at home,
While here shall be our home, what best may ease
The present misery, and render Hell
More tolerable; if there be cure or charm

To respite, or deceive, or slack the pain
Of this ill mansion: intermit no watch
Against a wakeful foe, while I abroad
Through all the coasts of dark destruction seek
Deliverance for us all. This enterprise
None shall partake with me." Thus saying, rose
The Monarch, and prevented all reply;
Prudent lest, from his resolution raised,
Others among the chief might offer now,
Certain to be refused, what erst they feared,
And, so refused, might in opinion stand
His rivals, winning cheap the high repute
Which he through hazard huge must earn. But they
Dreaded not more th' adventure than his voice
Forbidding; and at once with him they rose.
Their rising all at once was as the sound
Of thunder heard remote. Towards him they bend
With awful reverence prone, and as a God
Extol him equal to the Highest in Heaven.
Nor failed they to express how much they praised
That for the general safety he despised
His own: for neither do the Spirits damned
Lose all their virtue; lest bad men should boast
Their specious deeds on earth, which glory excites,
Or close ambition varnished o'er with zeal.
  Thus they their doubtful consultations dark
Ended, rejoicing in their matchless Chief:
As, when from mountain-tops the dusky clouds
Ascending, while the north wind sleeps, o'erspread
Heaven's cheerful face, the louring element
Scowls o'er the darkened landscape snow or shower,
If chance the radiant sun, with farewell sweet,
Extend his evening beam, the fields revive,
The birds their notes renew, and bleating herds
Attest their joy, that hill and valley rings.
O shame to men! Devil with devil damned
Firm concord holds; men only disagree

Of creatures rational, though under hope
Of heavenly grace, and, God proclaiming peace,
Yet live in hatred, enmity, and strife
Among themselves, and levy cruel wars
Wasting the earth, each other to destroy:
As if (which might induce us to accord)
Man had not hellish foes enow besides,
That day and night for his destruction wait!
  The Stygian council thus dissolved; and forth
In order came the grand infernal Peers:
Midst came their mighty Paramount, and seemed
Alone th' antagonist of Heaven, nor less
Than Hell's dread Emperor, with pomp supreme,
And god-like imitated state: him round
A globe of fiery Seraphim enclosed
With bright emblazonry, and horrent arms.
Then of their session ended they bid cry
With trumpet's regal sound the great result:
Toward the four winds four speedy Cherubim
Put to their mouths the sounding alchemy,
By herald's voice explained; the hollow Abyss
Heard far and wide, and all the host of Hell
With deafening shout returned them loud acclaim.
Thence more at ease their minds, and somewhat raised
By false presumptuous hope, the rangèd Powers
Disband; and, wandering, each his several way
Pursues, as inclination or sad choice
Leads him perplexed, where he may likeliest find
Truce to his restless thoughts, and entertain
The irksome hours, till his great Chief return.
Part on the plain, or in the air sublime,
Upon the wing or in swift race contend,
As at th' Olympian games or Pythian fields;
Part curb their fiery steeds, or shun the goal
With rapid wheels, or fronted brígades form:
As when, to warn proud cities, war appears
Waged in the troubled sky, and armies rush

To battle in the clouds; before each van
Prick forth the airy knights, and couch their spears,
Till thickest legions close; with feats of arms
From either end of heaven the welkin burns.
Others, with vast Typhoean rage, more fell,
Rend up both rocks and hills, and ride the air
In whirlwind; Hell scarce holds the wild uproar:—
As when Alcides, from Oechalia crowned
With conquest, felt th' envenomed robe, and tore
Through pain up by the roots Thessalian pines,
And Lichas from the top of Oeta threw
Into th' Euboic sea. Others, more mild,
Retreated in a silent valley, sing
With notes angelical to many a harp
Their own heroic deeds, and hapless fall
By doom of battle, and complain that Fate
Free Virtue should enthrall to Force or Chance.
Their song was partial; but the harmony
(What could it less when Spirits immortal sing?)
Suspended Hell, and took with ravishment
The thronging audience. In discourse more sweet
(For Eloquence the Soul, Song charms the Sense)
Others apart sat on a hill retired,
In thoughts more elevate, and reasoned high
Of Providence, Foreknowledge, Will, and Fate—
Fixed fate, free will, foreknowledge absolute,
And found no end, in wandering mazes lost.
Of good and evil much they argued then,
Of happiness and final misery,
Passion and apathy, and glory and shame:
Vain wisdom all, and false philosophy!—
Yet, with a pleasing sorcery, could charm
Pain for a while or anguish, and excite
Fallacious hope, or arm th' obdurèd breast
With stubborn patience as with triple steel.
Another part, in squadrons and gross bands,
On bold adventure to discover wide

That dismal world, if any clime perhaps
Might yield them easier habitation, bend
Four ways their flying march, along the banks
Of four infernal rivers, that disgorge
Into the burning lake their baleful streams—
Abhorrèd Styx, the flood of deadly hate;
Sad Acheron of sorrow, black and deep;
Cocytus, named of lamentation loud
Heard on the rueful stream; fierce Phlegeton,
Whose waves of torrent fire inflame with rage.
Far off from these, a slow and silent stream,
Lethe, the river of oblivion, rolls
Her watery labyrinth, whereof who drinks
Forthwith his former state and being forgets—
Forgets both joy and grief, pleasure and pain.
Beyond this flood a frozen continent
Lies dark and wild, beat with perpetual storms
Of whirlwind and dire hail, which on firm land
Thaws not, but gathers heap, and ruin seems
Of ancient pile; all else deep snow and ice,
A gulf profound as that Serbonian bog
Betwixt Damiata and Mount Casius old,
Where armies whole have sunk: the parching air
Burns frore, and cold performs th' effect of fire.
Thither, by harpy-footed Furies haled,
At certain revolutions all the damned
Are brought; and feel by turns the bitter change
Of fierce extremes, extremes by change more fierce,
From beds of raging fire to starve in ice
Their soft ethereal warmth, and there to pine
Immovable, infixed, and frozen round
Periods of time,—thence hurried back to fire.
They ferry over this Lethean sound
Both to and fro, their sorrow to augment,
And wish and struggle, as they pass, to reach
The tempting stream, with one small drop to lose
In sweet forgetfulness all pain and woe,

All in one moment, and so near the brink;
But Fate withstands, and, to oppose th' attempt,
Medusa with Gorgonian terror guards
The ford, and of itself the water flies
All taste of living wight, as once it fled
The lip of Tantalus. Thus roving on
In confused march forlorn, th' adventurous bands,
With shuddering horror pale, and eyes aghast,
Viewed first their lamentable lot, and found
No rest. Through many a dark and dreary vale
They passed, and many a region dolorous,
O'er many a frozen, many a fiery alp,
Rocks, caves, lakes, fens, bogs, dens, and shades of death—
A universe of death, which God by curse
Created evil, for evil only good;
Where all life dies, death lives, and Nature breeds,
Perverse, all monstrous, all prodigious things,
Abominable, inutterable, and worse
Than fables yet have feigned or fear conceived,
Gorgons, and Hydras, and Chimeras dire.
  Meanwhile the Adversary of God and Man,
Satan, with thoughts inflamed of highest design,
Puts on swift wings, and toward the gates of Hell
Explores his solitary flight: sometimes
He scours the right hand coast, sometimes the left;
Now shaves with level wing the deep, then soars
Up to the fiery concave towering high.
As when far off at sea a fleet descried
Hangs in the clouds, by equinoctial winds
Close sailing from Bengala, or the isles
Of Ternate and Tidore, whence merchants bring
Their spicy drugs; they on the trading flood,
Through the wide Ethiopian to the Cape,
Ply stemming nightly toward the pole: so seemed
Far off the flying Fiend. At last appear
Hell-bounds, high reaching to the horrid roof,
And thrice threefold the gates; three folds were brass,

Three iron, three of adamantine rock,
Impenetrable, impaled with circling fire,
Yet unconsumed. Before the gates there sat
On either side a formidable Shape.
The one seemed woman to the waist, and fair,
But ended foul in many a scaly fold,
Voluminous and vast—a serpent armed
With mortal sting. About her middle round
A cry of Hell-hounds never-ceasing barked
With wide Cerberean mouths full loud, and rung
A hideous peal; yet, when they list, would creep,
If aught disturbed their noise, into her womb,
And kennel there; yet there still barked and howled
Within unseen. Far less abhorred than these
Vexed Scylla, bathing in the sea that parts
Calabria from the hoarse Trinacrian shore;
Nor uglier follow the night-hag, when, called
In secret, riding through the air she comes,
Lured with the smell of infant blood, to dance
With Lapland witches, while the labouring moon
Eclipses at their charms. The other Shape—
If shape it might be called that shape had none
Distinguishable in member, joint, or limb;
Or substance might be called that shadow seemed,
For each seemed either—black it stood as Night,
Fierce as ten Furies, terrible as Hell,
And shook a dreadful dart: what seemed his head
The likeness of a kingly crown had on.
Satan was now at hand, and from his seat
The monster moving onward came as fast
With horrid strides; Hell trembled as he strode.
Th' undaunted Fiend what this might be admired—
Admired, not feared (God and his Son except,
Created thing naught valued he nor shunned),
And with disdainful look thus first began:—
"Whence and what art thou, execrable Shape,
That dar'st, though grim and terrible, advance

Thy miscreated front athwart my way
To yonder gates? Through them I mean to pass,
That be assured, without leave asked of thee.
Retire; or taste thy folly, and learn by proof,
Hell-born, not to contend with Spirits of Heaven."
  To whom the Goblin, full of wrath, replied:—
"Art thou that traitor Angel? art thou he,
Who first broke peace in Heaven and faith, till then
Unbroken, and in proud rebellious arms
Drew after him the third part of Heaven's sons,
Conjured against the Highest—for which both thou
And they, outcast from God, are here condemned
To waste eternal days in woe and pain?
And reckon'st thou thyself with Spirits of Heaven,
Hell-doomed, and breath'st defiance here and scorn,
Where I reign king, and, to enrage thee more,
Thy king and lord? Back to thy punishment,
False fugitive; and to thy speed add wings,
Lest with a whip of scorpions I pursue
Thy lingering, or with one stroke of this dart
Strange horror seize thee, and pangs unfelt before."
  So spake the grisly Terror, and in shape,
So speaking and so threatening, grew tenfold,
More dreadful and deform. On th' other side,
Incensed with indignation, Satan stood
Unterrified, and like a comet burned,
That fires the length of Ophiuchus huge
In th' arctic sky, and from his horrid hair
Shakes pestilence and war. Each at the head
Levelled his deadly aim; their fatal hands
No second stroke intend; and such a frown
Each cast at th' other as when two black clouds,
With heaven's artillery fraught, come rattling on
Over the Caspian,—then stand front to front
Hovering a space, till winds the signal blow
To join their dark encounter in mid-air.
So frowned the mighty combatants that Hell

Grew darker at their frown; so matched they stood;
For never but once more was either like
To meet so great a foe. And now great deeds
Had been achieved, whereof all Hell had rung,
Had not the snaky Sorceress, that sat
Fast by Hell-gate and kept the fatal key,
Risen, and with hideous outcry rushed between.
"O father, what intends thy hand," she cried,
"Against thy only son? What fury, O son,
Possesses thee to bend that mortal dart
Against thy father's head? And know'st for whom?
For him who sits above, and laughs the while
At thee, ordained his drudge to execute
Whate'er his wrath, which he calls justice, bids—
His wrath, which one day will destroy ye both!"
She spake, and at her words the hellish Pest
Forbore: then these to her Satan returned:—
"So strange thy outcry, and thy words so strange
Thou interposest, that my sudden hand,
Prevented, spares to tell thee yet by deeds
What it intends, till first I know of thee
What thing thou art, thus double-formed, and why,
In this infernal vale first met, thou call'st
Me father, and that phantasm call'st my son.
I know thee not, nor ever saw till now
Sight more detestable than him and thee."
T' whom thus the Portress of Hell-gate replied:—
"Hast thou forgot me, then; and do I seem
Now in thine eye so foul?—once deemed so fair
In Heaven, when at th' assembly, and in sight
Of all the Seraphim with thee combined
In bold conspiracy against Heaven's King,
All on a sudden miserable pain
Surprised thee, dim thine eyes and dizzy swum
In darkness, while thy head flames thick and fast
Threw forth, till on the left side opening wide,
Likest to thee in shape and countenance bright,

Then shining heavenly fair, a goddess armed,
Out of thy head I sprung. Amazement seized
All th' host of Heaven; back they recoiled afraid
At first, and called me *Sin*, and for a sign
Portentous held me; but, familiar grown,
I pleased, and with attractive graces won
The most averse—thee chiefly, who, full oft
Thyself in me thy perfect image viewing,
Becam'st enamoured; and such joy thou took'st
With me in secret that my womb conceived
A growing burden. Meanwhile war arose,
And fields were fought in Heaven: wherein remained
(For what could else?) to our Almighty Foe
Clear victory; to our part loss and rout
Through all the Empyrean. Down they fell,
Driven headlong from the pitch of Heaven, down
Into this Deep; and in the general fall
I also: at which time this powerful key
Into my hands was given, with charge to keep
These gates for ever shut, which none can pass
Without my opening. Pensive here I sat
Alone; but long I sat not, till my womb,
Pregnant by thee, and now excessive grown,
Prodigious motion felt and rueful throes.
At last this odious offspring whom thou seest,
Thine own begotten, breaking violent way,
Tore through my entrails, that, with fear and pain
Distorted, all my nether shape thus grew
Transformed: but he my inbred enemy
Forth issued, brandishing his fatal dart,
Made to destroy. I fled, and cried out *Death!*
Hell trembled at the hideous name, and sighed
From all her caves, and back resounded *Death!*
I fled; but he pursued (though more, it seems,
Inflamed with lust than rage), and, swifter far,
Me overtook, his mother, all dismayed,
And, in embraces forcible and foul

Engendering with me, of that rape begot
These yelling monsters, that with ceaseless cry
Surround me, as thou saw'st—hourly conceived
And hourly born, with sorrow infinite
To me; for, when they list, into the womb
That bred them they return, and howl, and gnaw
My bowels, their repast; then, bursting forth
Afresh, with conscious terrors vex me round,
That rest or intermission none I find.
Before mine eyes in opposition sits
Grim Death, my son and foe, who sets them on,
And me, his parent, would full soon devour
For want of other prey, but that he knows
His end with mine involved, and knows that I
Should prove a bitter morsel, and his bane,
Whenever that shall be: so Fate pronounced.
But thou, O father, I forewarn thee, shun
His deadly arrow; neither vainly hope
To be invulnerable in those bright arms,
Though tempered heavenly; for that mortal dint,
Save he who reigns above, none can resist."
  She finished; and the subtle Fiend his lore
Soon learned, now milder, and thus answered smooth:—
  "Dear daughter—since thou claim'st me for thy sire,
And my fair son here show'st me, the dear pledge
Of dalliance had with thee in Heaven, and joys
Then sweet, now sad to mention, through dire change
Befallen us unforeseen, unthought-of—know,
I come no enemy, but to set free
From out this dark and dismal house of pain
Both him and thee, and all the heavenly host
Of Spirits that, in our just pretences armed,
Fell with us from on high. From them I go
This uncouth errand sole, and one for all
Myself expose, with lonely steps to tread
Th' unfounded Deep, and through the void immense
To search, with wandering quest, a place foretold

Should be—and, by concurring signs, ere now
Created vast and round—a place of bliss
In the purlieus of Heaven; and therein placed
A race of upstart creatures, to supply
Perhaps our vacant room, though more removed,
Lest Heaven, surcharged with potent multitude,
Might hap to move new broils. Be this, or aught
Than this more secret, now designed, I haste
To know; and, this once known, shall soon return,
And bring ye to the place where thou and Death
Shall dwell at ease, and up and down unseen
Wing silently the buxom air, embalmed
With odours. There ye shall be fed and filled
Immeasurably; all things shall be your prey."
He ceased; for both seemed highly pleased, and Death
Grinned horrible a ghastly smile, to hear
His famine should be filled, and blessed his maw
Destined to that good hour. No less rejoiced
His mother bad, and thus bespake her sire:—
"The key of this infernal Pit, by due
And by command of Heaven's all-powerful King,
I keep, by him forbidden to unlock
These adamantine gates; against all force
Death ready stands to interpose his dart,
Fearless to be o'ermatched by living might.
But what owe I to his commands above,
Who hates me, and hath hither thrust me down
Into this gloom of Tartarus profound,
To sit in hateful office here confined,
Inhabitant of Heaven and heavenly born—
Here in perpetual agony and pain,
With terrors and with clamours compassed round
Of mine own brood, that on my bowels feed?
Thou art my father, thou my author, thou
My being gav'st me; whom should I obey
But thee? whom follow? Thou wilt bring me soon
To that new world of light and bliss, among

The gods who live at ease, where I shall reign
At thy right hand voluptuous, as beseems
Thy daughter and thy darling, without end."
  Thus saying, from her side the fatal key,
Sad instrument of all our woe, she took;
And, towards the gate rolling her bestial train,
Forthwith the huge portcullis high up-drew,
Which, but herself, not all the Stygian Powers
Could once have moved; then in the key-hole turns
Th' intricate wards, and every bolt and bar
Of massy iron or solid rock with ease
Unfastens. On a sudden open fly,
With impetuous recoil and jarring sound,
Th' infernal doors, and on their hinges grate
Harsh thunder, that the lowest bottom shook
Of Erebus. She opened; but to shut
Excelled her power: the gates wide open stood,
That with extended wings a bannered host,
Under spread ensigns marching, might pass through
With horse and chariots ranked in loose array;
So wide they stood, and like a furnace-mouth
Cast forth redounding smoke and ruddy flame.
Before their eyes in sudden view appear
The secrets of the hoary Deep—a dark
Illimitable ocean, without bound,
Without dimension; where length, breadth, and height,
And time, and place, are lost; where eldest Night
And Chaos, ancestors of Nature, hold
Eternal anarchy, amidst the noise
Of endless wars, and by confusion stand.
For Hot, Cold, Moist, and Dry, four champions fierce,
Strive here for mastery, and to battle bring
Their embryon atoms: they around the flag
Of each his faction, in their several clans,
Light-armed or heavy, sharp, smooth, swift, or slow,
Swarm populous, unnumbered as the sands
Of Barca or Cyrenè's torrid soil,

Levied to side with warring winds, and poise
Their lighter wings. To whom these most adhere
He rules a moment: Chaos umpire sits,
And by decision more embroils the fray
By which he reigns: next him, high arbiter,
Chance governs all. Into this wild Abyss,
The womb of Nature, and perhaps her grave,
Of neither sea, nor shore, nor air, nor fire,
But all these in their pregnant causes mixed
Confusedly, and which thus must ever fight,
Unless th' Almighty Maker them ordain
His dark materials to create more worlds—
Into this wild Abyss the wary Fiend
Stood on the brink of Hell and looked a while,
Pondering his voyage; for no narrow frith
He had to cross. Nor was his ear less pealed
With noises loud and ruinous (to compare
Great things with small) than when Bellona storms
With all her battering engines, bent to rase
Some capital city; or less than if this frame
Of Heaven were falling, and these elements
In mutiny had from her axle torn
The steadfast Earth. At last his sail-broad vans
He spread for flight, and, in the surging smoke
Uplifted, spurns the ground; thence many a league,
As in a cloudy chair, ascending rides
Audacious; but, that seat soon failing, meets
A vast vacuity. All unawares,
Fluttering his pennons vain, plumb-down he drops
Ten thousand fathom deep, and to this hour
Down had been falling, had not, by ill chance,
The strong rebuff of some tumultuous cloud,
Instinct with fire and nitre, hurried him
As many miles aloft. That fury stayed—
Quenched in a boggy Syrtis, neither sea,
Nor good dry land—nigh foundered, on he fares,
Treading the crude consistence, half on foot,

Half flying; behoves him now both oar and sail.
As when a gryphon through the wilderness
With wingèd course, o'er hill or moory dale,
Pursues the Arimaspian, who by stealth
Had from his wakeful custody purloined
The guarded gold; so eagerly the Fiend
O'er bog or steep, through strait, rough, dense, or rare,
With head, hands, wings, or feet, pursues his way,
And swims, or sinks, or wades, or creeps, or flies.
At length a universal hubbub wild
Of stunning sounds, and voices all confused,
Borne through the hollow dark, assaults his ear
With loudest vehemence. Thither he plies
Undaunted, to meet there whatever Power
Or Spirit of the nethermost Abyss
Might in that noise reside, of whom to ask
Which way the nearest coast of darkness lies
Bordering on light; when straight behold the throne
Of Chaos, and his dark pavilion spread
Wide on the wasteful Deep! With him enthroned
Sat sable-vested Night, eldest of things,
The consort of his reign; and by them stood
Orcus and Ades, and the dreaded name
Of Demogorgon; Rumour next, and Chance,
And Tumult, and Confusion, all embroiled,
And Discord with a thousand various mouths.
T' whom Satan, turning boldly, thus:—"Ye Powers
And Spirits of this nethermost Abyss,
Chaos and ancient Night, I come no spy
With purpose to explore or to disturb
The secrets of your realm; but, by constraint
Wandering this darksome desert, as my way
Lies through your spacious empire up to light,
Alone and without guide, half lost, I seek,
What readiest path leads where your gloomy bounds
Confine with Heaven; or, if some other place,
From your dominion won, th' Ethereal King

Possesses lately, thither to arrive
I travel this profound. Direct my course:
Directed, no mean recompense it brings
To your behoof, if I that region lost,
All usurpation thence expelled, reduce
To her original darkness and your sway
(Which is my present journey), and once more
Erect the standard there of ancient Night.
Yours be th' advantage all, mine the revenge!"
  Thus Satan; and him thus the Anarch old,
With faltering speech and visage incomposed,
Answered:—"I know thee, stranger, who thou art—
That mighty leading Angel, who of late
Made head against Heaven's King, though overthrown.
I saw and heard; for such a numerous host
Fled not in silence through the frighted Deep,
With ruin upon ruin, rout on rout,
Confusion worse confounded; and Heaven-gates
Poured out by millions her victorious bands,
Pursuing. I upon my frontiers here
Keep residence; if all I can will serve
That little which is left so to defend,
Encroached on still through our intestine broils
Weakening the sceptre of old Night: first, Hell,
Your dungeon, stretching far and wide beneath;
Now lately Heaven and Earth, another world
Hung o'er my realm, linked in a golden chain
To that side Heaven from whence your legions fell!
If that way be your walk, you have not far;
So much the nearer danger. Go, and speed;
Havoc, and spoil, and ruin, are my gain."
  He ceased; and Satan stayed not to reply,
But, glad that now his sea should find a shore,
With fresh alacrity and force renewed
Springs upward, like a pyramid of fire,
Into the wild expanse, and through the shock
Of fighting elements, on all sides round

Environed, wins his way; harder beset
And more endangered than when Argo passed
Through Bosporus betwixt the justling rocks,
Or when Ulysses on the larboard shunned
Charybdis, and by th' other whirlpool steered.
So he with difficulty and labour hard
Moved on, with difficulty and labour he;
But, he once passed, soon after, when Man fell,
Strange alteration! Sin and Death amain,
Following his track (such was the will of Heaven)
Paved after him a broad and beaten way
Over the dark Abyss, whose boiling gulf
Tamely endured a bridge of wondrous length,
From Hell continued, reaching th' utmost orb
Of this frail World; by which the Spirits perverse
With easy intercourse pass to and fro
To tempt or punish mortals, except whom
God and good Angels guard by special grace.
  But now at last the sacred influence
Of light appears, and from the walls of Heaven
Shoots far into the bosom of dim Night
A glimmering dawn. Here Nature first begins
Her farthest verge, and Chaos to retire,
As from her outmost works, a broken foe,
With tumult less and with less hostile din;
That Satan with less toil, and now with ease,
Wafts on the calmer wave by dubious light,
And, like a weather-beaten vessel, holds
Gladly the port, though shrouds and tackle torn;
Or in the emptier waste, resembling air,
Weighs his spread wings, at leisure to behold
Far off th' empyreal Heaven, extended wide
In circuit, undetermined square or round,
With opal towers and battlements adorned
Of living sapphire, once his native seat;
And, fast by, hanging in a golden chain,
This pendent World, in bigness as a star

Of smallest magnitude close by the moon.
Thither, full fraught with mischievous revenge,
Accursed, and in a cursèd hour, he hies.

THE END OF THE SECOND BOOK

BOOK III

THE ARGUMENT

God, sitting on his throne, sees Satan flying towards this World, then newly created; shows him to the Son, who sat at his right hand; foretells the success of Satan in perverting mankind; clears his own justice and wisdom from all imputation, having created Man free, and able enough to have withstood his Tempter; yet declares his purpose of grace towards him, in regard he fell not of his own malice, as did Satan, but by him seduced. The Son of God renders praises to his Father for the manifestation of his gracious purpose towards Man: but God again declares that grace cannot be extended towards Man without the satisfaction of Divine Justice; Man hath offended the majesty of God by aspiring to Godhead, and therefore, with all his progeny, devoted to death, must die, unless some one can be found sufficient to answer for his offence, and undergo his punishment. The Son of God freely offers himself a ransom for Man: the Father accepts him, ordains his incarnation, pronounces his exaltation above all names in Heaven and Earth; commands all the Angels to adore him. They obey, and, hymning to their harps in full choir, celebrate the Father and the Son. Meanwhile Satan alights upon the bare convex of this World's outermost orb; where wandering he first finds a place since called the Limbo of Vanity; what persons and things fly up thither: thence comes to the gate of Heaven, described ascending by stairs, and the waters above the firmament that flow about it. His passage thence to the orb of the Sun: he finds there Uriel, the regent of that orb, but first changes himself into the shape of a meaner Angel, and, pretending a zealous desire to behold the new Creation, and Man whom God placed here, inquires of him the place of his habitation, and is directed: alights first on Mount Niphates.

Hail, holy Light, offspring of Heaven first-born!
Or of th' Eternal coeternal beam
May I express thee unblamed? since God is light,
And never but in unapproachèd light

Dwelt from eternity—dwelt then in thee,
Bright effluence of bright essence increate!
Or hear'st thou rather pure ethereal stream,
Whose fountain who shall tell? Before the Sun,
Before the heavens, thou wert, and at the voice
Of God, as with a mantle, didst invest
The rising world of waters dark and deep,
Won from the void and formless Infinite!
Thee I revisit now with bolder wing,
Escaped the Stygian Pool, though long detained
In that obscure sojourn, while in my flight,
Through utter and through middle Darkness borne,
With other notes than to th' Orphean lyre
I sung of Chaos and eternal Night,
Taught by the Heavenly Muse to venture down
The dark descent, and up to re-ascend,
Though hard and rare. Thee I revisit safe,
And feel thy sovereign vital lamp; but thou
Revisit'st not these eyes, that roll in vain
To find thy piercing ray, and find no dawn;
So thick a drop serene hath quenched their orbs,
Or dim suffusion veiled. Yet not the more
Cease I to wander where the Muses haunt
Clear spring, or shady grove, or sunny hill,
Smit with the love of sacred song; but chief
Thee, Sion, and the flowery brooks beneath,
That wash thy hallowed feet, and warbling flow,
Nightly I visit: nor sometimes forget
Those other two equalled with me in fate,
So were I equalled with them in renown,
Blind Thamyris and blind Maeonides,
And Tiresias and Phineus, prophets old:
Then feed on thoughts that voluntary move
Harmonious numbers; as the wakeful bird
Sings darkling, and, in shadiest covert hid,
Tunes her nocturnal note. Thus with the year
Seasons return; but not to me returns

Day, or the sweet approach of even or morn,
Or sight of vernal bloom, or summer's rose,
Or flocks, or herds, or human face divine;
But cloud instead and ever-during dark
Surrounds me, from the cheerful ways of men
Cut off, and, for the book of knowledge fair,
Presented with a universal blank
Of Nature's works, to me expunged and rased,
And wisdom at one entrance quite shut out.
So much the rather thou, Celestial Light,
Shine inward, and the mind through all her powers
Irradiate; there plant eyes; all mist from thence
Purge and disperse, that I may see and tell
Of things invisible to mortal sight.
  Now had the Almighty Father from above,
From the pure Empyrean where he sits
High throned above all height, bent down his eye,
His own works and their works at once to view:
About him all the Sanctities of Heaven
Stood thick as stars, and from his sight received
Beatitude past utterance; on his right
The radiant image of his glory sat,
His only Son. On Earth he first beheld
Our two first parents, yet the only two
Of mankind, in the Happy Garden placed,
Reaping immortal fruits of joy and love,
Uninterrupted joy, unrivalled love,
In blissful solitude. He then surveyed
Hell and the gulf between, and Satan there
Coasting the wall of Heaven on this side Night,
In the dun air sublime, and ready now
To stoop, with wearied wings and willing feet,
On the bare outside of this World, that seemed
Firm land imbosomed without firmament,
Uncertain which, in ocean or in air.
Him God beholding from his prospect high,
Wherein past, present, future, he beholds,

Thus to his only Son foreseeing spake:—
"Only-begotten Son, seest thou what rage
Transports our Adversary? whom no bounds
Prescribed, no bars of Hell, nor all the chains
Heaped on him there, nor yet the main Abyss
Wide interrupt, can hold; so bent he seems
On desperate revenge, that shall redound
Upon his own rebellious head. And now,
Through all restraint broke loose, he wings his way
Not far off Heaven, in the precincts of light,
Directly towards the new-created World,
And Man there placed, with purpose to assay
If him by force he can destroy, or, worse,
By some false guile pervert: and shall pervert;
For Man will hearken to his glozing lies,
And easily transgress the sole command,
Sole pledge of his obedience so will fall
He and his faithless progeny. Whose fault?
Whose but his own? Ingrate, he had of me
All he could have; I made him just and right,
Sufficient to have stood, though free to fall.
Such I created all th' ethereal Powers
And Spirits, both them who stood and them who failed;
Freely they stood who stood, and fell who fell.
Not free, what proof could they have given sincere
Of true allegiance, constant faith, or love,
Where only what they needs must do appeared,
Not what they would? What praise could they receive,
What pleasure I, from such obedience paid,
When Will and Reason (Reason also is Choice),
Useless and vain, of freedom both despoiled,
Made passive both, had served Necessity,
Not me? They, therefore, as to right belonged,
So were created, nor can justly accuse
Their Maker, or their making, or their fate,
As if predestination overruled
Their will, disposed by absolute decree

Or high foreknowledge. They themselves decreed
Their own revolt, not I. If I foreknew,
Foreknowledge had no influence on their fault,
Which had no less proved certain unforeknown.
So without least impulse or shadow of fate,
Or aught by me immutably foreseen,
They trespass, authors to themselves in all,
Both what they judge and what they choose; for so
I formed them free, and free they must remain
Till they enthrall themselves: I else must change
Their nature, and revoke the high decree
Unchangeable, eternal, which ordained
Their freedom; they themselves ordained their fall.
The first sort by their own suggestion fell,
Self-tempted, self-depraved; Man falls, deceived
By the other first: Man, therefore, shall find grace;
The other, none. In mercy and justice both,
Through Heaven and Earth, so shall my glory excel;
But mercy, first and last, shall brightest shine."
Thus while God spake ambrosial fragrance filled
All Heaven, and in the blessèd Spirits elect
Sense of new joy ineffable diffused.
Beyond compare the Son of God was seen
Most glorious; in him all his Father shone
Substantially expressed; and in his face
Divine compassion visibly appeared,
Love without end, and without measure grace;
Which uttering, thus he to his Father spake:—
"O Father, gracious was that word which closed
Thy sovereign sentence, that Man should find grace;
For which both Heaven and Earth shall high extol
Thy praises, with th' innumerable sound
Of hymns and sacred songs, wherewith thy throne
Encompassed shall resound thee ever blest.
For, should Man finally be lost—should Man,
Thy creature late so loved, thy youngest son,
Fall circumvented thus by fraud, though joined

With his own folly? That be from thee far,
That far be from thee, Father, who art judge
Of all things made, and judgest only right!
Or shall the Adversary thus obtain
His end, and frustrate thine? shall he fulfil
His malice, and thy goodness bring to naught
Or proud return, though to his heavier doom
Yet with revenge accomplished, and to Hell
Draw after him the whole race of mankind,
By him corrupted? Or wilt thou thyself
Abolish thy creation, and unmake,
For him, what for thy glory thou hast made?
So should thy goodness and thy greatness both
Be questioned and blasphemed without defence."
  To whom the great Creator thus replied:—
"O Son, in whom my soul hath chief delight,
Son of my bosom, Son who art alone
My word, my wisdom, and effectual might,
All hast thou spoken as my thoughts are, all
As my eternal purpose hath decreed.
Man shall not quite be lost, but saved who will;
Yet not of will in him, but grace in me
Freely vouchsafed. Once more I will renew
His lapsèd powers, though forfeit, and enthralled
By sin to foul exorbitant desires:
Upheld by me, yet once more he shall stand
On even ground against his mortal foe,
By me upheld, that he may know how frail
His fallen condition is, and to me owe
All his deliverance, and to none but me.
Some I have chosen of peculiar grace,
Elect above the rest; so is my will:
The rest shall hear me call, and oft be warned
Their sinful state, and to appease betimes
Th' incensèd Deity, while offered grace
Invites; for I will clear their senses dark
What may suffice, and soften stony hearts

To pray, repent, and bring obedience due.
To prayer, repentance, and obedience due,
Though but endeavoured with sincere intent,
Mine ear shall not be slow, mine eye not shut.
And I will place within them as a guide
My umpire Conscience; whom if they will hear,
Light after light well used they shall attain,
And to the end persisting safe arrive.
This my long sufferance, and my day of grace,
They who neglect and scorn shall never taste;
But hard be hardened, blind be blinded more,
That they may stumble on, and deeper fall;
And none but such from mercy I exclude.
But yet all is not done. Man disobeying,
Disloyal, breaks his fealty, and sins
Against the high supremacy of Heaven,
Affecting Godhead, and, so losing all,
To expiate his treason hath naught left,
But, to destruction sacred and devote,
He with his whole posterity must die;—
Die he or Justice must; unless for him
Some other, able, and as willing, pay
The rigid satisfaction, death for death.
Say, Heavenly Powers, where shall we find such love?
Which of ye will be mortal, to redeem
Man's mortal crime, and just, th' unjust to save?
Dwells in all Heaven charity so dear?"
He asked, but all the heavenly choir stood mute,
And silence was in Heaven: on Man's behalf
Patron or intercessor none appeared—
Much less that durst upon his own head draw
The deadly forfeiture, and ransom set.
And now without redemption all mankind
Must have been lost, adjudged to Death and Hell
By doom severe, had not the Son of God,
In whom the fulness dwells of love divine,
His dearest mediation thus renewed:—

"Father, thy word is passed, Man shall find grace;
And shall Grace not find means, that finds her way,
The speediest of thy wingèd messengers,
To visit all thy creatures, and to all
Comes unprevented, unimplored, unsought?
Happy for Man, so coming! He her aid
Can never seek, once dead in sins and lost—
Atonement for himself, or offering meet,
Indebted and undone, hath none to bring.
Behold me, then: me for him, life for life,
I offer; on me let thine anger fall;
Account me Man: I for his sake will leave
Thy bosom, and this glory next to thee
Freely put off, and for him lastly die
Well pleased; on me let Death wreak all his rage.
Under his gloomy power I shall not long
Lie vanquished. Thou hast given me to possess
Life in myself for ever; by thee I live;
Though now to Death I yield, and am his due,
All that of me can die, yet, that debt paid,
Thou wilt not leave me in the loathsome grave
His prey, nor suffer my unspotted soul
For ever with corruption there to dwell;
But I shall rise victorious, and subdue
My vanquisher, spoiled of his vaunted spoil.
Death his death's wound shall then receive, and stoop
Inglorious, of his mortal sting disarmed;
I through the ample air in triumph high
Shall lead Hell captive maugre Hell, and show
The powers of Darkness bound. Thou, at the sight
Pleased, out of Heaven shalt look down and smile,
While, by thee raised, I ruin all my foes—
Death last, and with his carcase glut the grave;
Then, with the multitude of my redeemed,
Shall enter Heaven, long absent, and return,
Father, to see thy face, wherein no cloud
Of anger shall remain, but peace assured

And reconcilement: wrath shall be no more
Thenceforth, but in thy presence joy entire."
His words here ended; but his meek aspéct
Silent yet spake, and breathed immortal love
To mortal men, above which only shone
Filial obedience: as a sacrifice
Glad to be offered, he attends the will
Of his great Father. Admiration seized
All Heaven, what this might mean, and whither tend,
Wondering; but soon th' Almighty thus replied:—
"O thou in Heaven and Earth the only peace
Found out for mankind under wrath, O thou
My sole complacence! well thou know'st how dear
To me are all my works; nor Man the least,
Though last created, that for him I spare
Thee from my bosom and right hand, to save,
By losing thee a while, the whole race lost!
Thou, therefore, whom thou only canst redeem,
Their nature also to thy nature join;
And be thyself Man among men on Earth,
Made flesh, when time shall be, of virgin seed,
By wondrous birth; be thou in Adam's room
The head of all mankind, though Adam's son.
As in him perish all men, so in thee,
As from a second root, shall be restored
As many as are restored; without thee, none.
His crime makes guilty all his sons; thy merit,
Imputed, shall absolve them who renounce
Their own both righteous and unrighteous deeds,
And live in thee transplanted, and from thee
Receive new life. So Man, as is most just,
Shall satisfy for Man, be judged and die,
And dying rise, and, rising, with him raise
His brethren, ransomed with his own dear life.
So heavenly love shall outdo hellish hate,
Giving to death, and dying to redeem,
So dearly to redeem what hellish hate

So easily destroyed, and still destroys
In those who, when they may, accept not grace.
Nor shalt thou, by descending to assume
Man's nature, lessen or degrade thine own.
Because thou hast, though throned in highest bliss
Equal to God, and equally enjoying
God-like fruition, quitted all to save
A world from utter loss, and hast been found
By merit more than birthright Son of God,
Found worthiest to be so by being good,
Far more than great or high; because in thee
Love hath abounded more than glory abounds;
Therefore thy humiliation shall exalt
With thee thy manhood also to this throne:
Here shalt thou sit incarnate, here shalt reign
Both God and Man, Son both of God and Man,
Anointed universal King. All power
I give thee; reign for ever, and assume
Thy merits; under thee, as Head Supreme,
Thrones, Princedoms, Powers, Dominions, I reduce:
All knees to thee shall bow of them that bide
In Heaven, or Earth, or under Earth in Hell.
When thou, attended gloriously from Heaven,
Shalt in the sky appear, and from thee send
The summoning Archangels to proclaim
Thy dread tribunal, forthwith from all winds
The living, and forthwith the cited dead
Of all past ages, to the general doom
Shall hasten; such a peal shall rouse their sleep.
Then, all thy Saints assembled, thou shalt judge
Bad men and Angels; they arraigned shall sink
Beneath thy sentence; Hell, her numbers full,
Thenceforth shall be for ever shut. Meanwhile
The World shall burn, and from her ashes spring
New Heaven and Earth, wherein the just shall dwell,
And, after all their tribulations long,
See golden days, fruitful of golden deeds,

With Joy and Love triúmphing, and fair Truth.
Then thou thy regal sceptre shalt lay by;
For regal sceptre then no more shall need;
God shall be all in all. But all ye Gods,
Adore him who, to compass all this, dies;
Adore the Son, and honour him as me."
No sooner had th' Almighty ceased but all
The multitude of Angels, with a shout
Loud as from numbers without number, sweet
As from blest voices, uttering joy, Heaven rung
With jubilee, and loud hosannas filled
Th' eternal regions. Lowly reverent
Towards either throne they bow, and to the ground
With solemn adoration down they cast
Their crowns, inwove with amarant and gold,—
Immortal amarant, a flower which once
In Paradise, fast by the Tree of Life,
Began to bloom, but soon for Man's offence
To Heaven removed where first it grew, there grows
And flowers aloft, shading the Fount of Life,
And where the River of Bliss through midst of Heaven
Rolls o'er Elysian flowers her amber stream.
With these, that never fade, the Spirits elect
Bind their resplendent locks, inwreathed with beams.
Now in loose garlands thick thrown off, the bright
Pavement, that like a sea of jasper shone,
Impurpled with celestial roses smiled.
Then, crowned again, their golden harps they took—
Harps ever tuned, that glittering by their side
Like quivers hung; and with preamble sweet
Of charming symphony they introduce
Their sacred song, and waken raptures high:
No voice exempt, no voice but well could join
Melodious part; such concord is in Heaven.
Thee, Father, first they sung, Omnipotent,
Immutable, Immortal, Infinite,
Eternal King; thee, Author of all being,

Fountain of light, thyself invisible
Amidst the glorious brightness where thou sitt'st
Throned inaccessible, but when thou shad'st
The full blaze of thy beams, and through a cloud
Drawn round about thee like a radiant shrine
Dark with excessive bright thy skirts appear,
Yet dazzle Heaven, that brightest Seraphim
Approach not, but with both wings veil their eyes.
Thee next they sang, of all creation first,
Begotten Son, Divine Similitude,
In whose conspicuous countenance, without cloud
Made visible, th' Almighty Father shines,
Whom else no creature can behold: on thee
Impressed the effulgence of his glory abides;
Transfused on thee his ample Spirit rests.
He Heaven of Heavens, and all the Powers therein,
By thee created; and by thee threw down
Th' aspiring Dominations. Thou that day
Thy Father's dreadful thunder didst not spare,
Nor stop thy flaming chariot-wheels, that shook
Heaven's everlasting frame, while o'er the necks
Thou drov'st of warring Angels disarrayed.
Back from pursuit, thy Powers with loud acclaim
Thee only extolled, Son of thy Father's might,
To execute fierce vengeance on his foes.
Not so on Man: him, through their malice fallen,
Father of mercy and grace, thou didst not doom
So strictly, but much more to pity incline.
No sooner did thy dear and only Son
Perceive thee purposed not to doom frail Man
So strictly, but much more to pity inclined,
He, to appease thy wrath, and end the strife
Of mercy and justice in thy face discerned,
Regardless of the bliss wherein he sat
Second to thee, offered himself to die
For Man's offence. O unexampled love!
Love nowhere to be found less than Divine!

Hail, Son of God, Saviour of men! Thy name
Shall be the copious matter of my song
Henceforth, and never shall my harp thy praise
Forget, nor from thy Father's praise disjoin!
  Thus they in Heaven, above the starry sphere,
Their happy hours in joy and hymning spent.
Meanwhile, upon the firm opacous globe
Of this round World, whose first convex divides
The luminous inferior orbs, enclosed
From Chaos and th' inroad of Darkness old,
Satan alighted walks. A globe far off
It seemed; now seems a boundless continent,
Dark, waste, and wild, under the frown of Night
Starless exposed, and ever-threatening storms
Of Chaos blustering round, inclement sky,
Save on that side which from the wall of Heaven,
Though distant far, some small reflection gains
Of glimmering air less vexed with tempest loud.
Here walked the Fiend at large in spacious field.
As when a vulture, on Imaus bred,
Whose snowy ridge the roving Tartar bounds,
Dislodging from a region scarce of prey,
To gorge the flesh of lambs or yeanling kids
On hills where flocks are fed, flies toward the springs
Of Ganges or Hydaspes, Indian streams,
But in his way lights on the barren plains
Of Sericana, where Chineses drive
With sails and wind their cany waggons light;
So, on this windy sea of land, the Fiend
Walked up and down alone, bent on his prey:
Alone, for other creature in this place,
Living or lifeless, to be found was none;—
None yet; but store hereafter from the Earth
Up hither like aerial vapours flew
Of all things transitory and vain, when sin
With vanity had filled the works of men—
Both all things vain, and all who in vain things

Built their fond hopes of glory or lasting fame,
Or happiness in this or th' other life.
All who have their reward on earth, the fruits
Of painful superstition and blind zeal,
Naught seeking but the praise of men, here find
Fit retribution, empty as their deeds;
All th' unaccomplished works of Nature's hand,
Abortive, monstrous, or unkindly mixed,
Dissolved on Earth, fleet hither, and in vain,
Till final dissolution, wander here—
Not in the neighbouring moon, as some have dreamed:
Those argent fields more likely habitants,
Translated Saints, or middle Spirits hold,
Betwixt th' angelical and human kind.
Hither, of ill-joined sons and daughters born,
First from the ancient world those giants came,
With many a vain exploit, though then renowned:
The builders next of Babel on the plain
Of Sennaar, and still with vain design
New Babels, had they wherewithal, would build:
Others came single; he who, to be deemed
A god, leaped fondly into Etna flames,
Empedocles, and he who, to enjoy
Plato's Elysium, leaped into the sea,
Cleombrotus; and many more, too long,
Embryos and idiots, eremites and friars,
White, black, and grey, with all their trumpery.
Here pilgrims roam, that strayed so far to seek
In Golgotha him dead who lives in Heaven;
And they who, to be sure of Paradise,
Dying put on the weeds of Dominic,
Or in Franciscan think to pass disguised.
They pass the planets seven, and pass the fixed,
And that crystalline sphere whose balance weighs
The trepidation talked, and that first moved;
And now Saint Peter at Heaven's wicket seems
To wait them with his keys, and now at foot

Of Heaven's ascent they lift their feet, when, lo!
A violent cross wind from either coast
Blows them transverse ten thousand leagues awry,
Into the devious air. Then might ye see
Cowls, hoods, and habits, with their wearers, tost
And fluttered into rags; then relics, beads,
Indulgences, dispenses, pardons, bulls,
The sport of winds: all these, upwhirled aloft,
Fly o'er the backside of the World far off
Into a Limbo large and broad, since called
The Paradise of Fools; to few unknown
Long after, now unpeopled and untrod.
All this dark globe the Fiend found as he passed;
And long he wandered, till at last a gleam
Of dawning light turned thitherward in haste
His travelled steps. Far distant he descries,
Ascending by degrees magnificent
Up to the wall of Heaven, a structure high;
At top whereof, but far more rich, appeared
The work as of a kingly palace-gate,
With frontispiece of diamond and gold
Embellished; thick with sparkling orient gems
The portal shone, inimitable on Earth
By model, or by shading pencil drawn.
The stairs were such as whereon Jacob saw
Angels ascending and descending, bands
Of guardians bright, when he from Esau fled
To Padan-Aram, in the field of Luz
Dreaming by night under the open sky,
And waking cried, *This is the gate of Heaven.*
Each stair mysteriously was meant, nor stood
There always, but drawn up to Heaven sometimes
Viewless; and underneath a bright sea flowed
Of jasper, or of liquid pearl, whereon
Who after came from Earth sailing arrived
Wafted by Angels, or flew o'er the lake
Rapt in a chariot drawn by fiery steeds.

The stairs were then let down, whether to dare
The Fiend by easy ascent, or aggravate
His sad exclusion from the doors of bliss:
Direct against which opened from beneath,
Just o'er the blissful seat of Paradise,
A passage down to th' Earth—a passage wide;
Wider by far than that of after-times
Over Mount Sion, and, though that were large,
Over the Promised Land to God so dear,
By which, to visit oft those happy tribes,
On high behests his Angels to and fro
Passed frequent, and his eye with choice regard
From Paneas, the fount of Jordan's flood,
To Beërsaba, where the Holy Land
Borders on Egypt and the Arabian shore.
So wide the opening seemed, where bounds were set
To darkness, such as bound the ocean wave.
Satan from hence, now on the lower stair,
That scaled by steps of gold to Heaven-gate,
Looks down with wonder at the sudden view
Of all this World at once. As when a scout,
Through dark and desert ways with peril gone
All night, at last by break of cheerful dawn
Obtains the brow of some high-climbing hill,
Which to his eye discovers unaware
The goodly prospect of some foreign land
First seen, or some renowned metropolis
With glistering spires and pinnacles adorned,
Which now the rising sun gilds with his beams;
Such wonder seized, though after Heaven seen,
The Spirit malign, but much more envy seized,
At sight of all this World beheld so fair.
Round he surveys (and well might, where he stood
So high above the circling canopy
Of Night's extended shade) from eastern point
Of Libra to the fleecy star that bears
Andromeda far off Atlantic seas

Beyond th' horizon; then from pole to pole
He views in breadth,—and, without longer pause,
Down right into the World's first region throws
His flight precipitant, and winds with ease
Through the pure marble air his oblique way
Amongst innumerable stars, that shone
Stars distant, but nigh-hand seemed other worlds.
Or other worlds they seemed, or happy isles,
Like those Hesperian Gardens famed of old,
Fortunate fields, and groves, and flowery vales;
Thrice happy isles! But who dwelt happy there
He stayed not to inquire: above them all
The golden Sun, in splendour likest Heaven,
Allured his eye. Thither his course he bends,
Through the calm firmament (but up or down,
By centre or eccentric, hard to tell,
Or longitude) where the great luminary,
Aloof the vulgar constellations thick,
That from his lordly eye keep distance due,
Dispenses light from far. They, as they move
Their starry dance in numbers that compute
Days, months, and years, towards his all-cheering lamp
Turn swift their various motions, or are turned
By his magnetic beam, that gently warms
The Universe, and to each inward part
With gentle penetration, though unseen,
Shoots invisible virtue even to the Deep;
So wondrously was set his station bright.
There lands the Fiend, a spot like which perhaps
Astronomer in the Sun's lucent orb
Through his glazed optic tube yet never saw.
The place he found beyond expression bright,
Compared with aught on Earth, metal or stone—
Not all parts like, but all alike informed
With radiant light, as glowing iron with fire.
If metal, part seemed gold, part silver clear;
If stone, carbuncle most or chrysolite,

Ruby or topaz, to the twelve that shone
In Aaron's breast-plate, and a stone besides,
Imagined rather oft than elsewhere seen—
That stone, or like to that, which here below
Philosophers in vain so long have sought;
In vain, though by their powerful art they bind
Volatile Hermes, and call up unbound
In various shapes old Proteus from the sea,
Drained through a limbec to his native form.
What wonder then if fields and regions here
Breathe forth elixir pure, and rivers run
Potable gold, when, with one virtuous touch,
Th' arch-chemic Sun, so far from us remote,
Produces, with terrestrial humour mixed,
Here in the dark so many precious things
Of colour glorious and effect so rare?
Here matter new to gaze the Devil met
Undazzled. Far and wide his eye commands;
For sight no obstacle found here, nor shade,
But all sunshine, as when his beams at noon
Culminate from th' equator, as they now
Shot upward still direct, whence no way round
Shadow from body opaque can fall; and the air,
Nowhere so clear, sharpened his visual ray
To objects distant far, whereby he soon
Saw within ken a glorious Angel stand,
The same whom John saw also in the Sun.
His back was turned, but not his brightness hid;
Of beaming sunny rays a golden tiar
Circled his head, nor less his locks behind
Illustrious on his shoulders fledge with wings
Lay waving round: on some great charge employed
He seemed, or fixed in cogitation deep.
Glad was the Spirit impure, as now in hope
To find who might direct his wandering flight
To Paradise, the happy seat of Man,
His journey's end, and our beginning woe.

But first he casts to change his proper shape,
Which else might work him danger or delay:
And now a stripling Cherub he appears,
Not of the prime, yet such as in his face
Youth smiled celestial, and to every limb
Suitable grace diffused; so well he feigned.
Under a coronet his flowing hair
In curls on either cheek played; wings he wore
Of many a coloured plume sprinkled with gold,
His habit fit for speed succinct, and held
Before his decent steps a silver wand.
He drew not nigh unheard; the Angel bright,
Ere he drew nigh, his radiant visage turned,
Admonished by his ear, and straight was known
Th' Archangel Uriel—one of the seven
Who in God's presence, nearest to his throne,
Stand ready at command, and are his eyes
That run through all the Heavens, or down to th' Earth
Bear his swift errands over moist and dry,
O'er sea and land. Him Satan thus accosts:—
"Uriel! for thou of those seven Spirits that stand
In sight of God's high throne, gloriously bright,
The first art wont his great authentic will
Interpreter through highest heaven to bring,
Where all his Sons thy embassy attend,
And here art likeliest by supreme decree
Like honour to obtain, and as his eye
To visit oft this new Creation round—
Unspeakable desire to see and know
All these his wondrous works, but chiefly Man,
His chief delight and favour, him for whom
All these his works so wondrous he ordained,
Hath brought me from the choirs of Cherubim
Alone thus wandering. Brightest Seraph, tell
In which of all these shining orbs hath Man
His fixèd seat—or fixèd seat hath none,
But all these shining orbs his choice to dwell—

That I may find him, and with secret gaze
Or open admiration him behold
On whom the great Creator hath bestowed
Worlds, and on whom hath all these graces poured;
That both in him and all things, as is meet,
The Universal Maker we may praise;
Who justly hath driven out his rebel foes
To deepest Hell, and, to repair that loss,
Created this new happy race of Men
To serve him better: wise are all his ways!"
So spake the false dissembler unperceived;
For neither man nor angel can discern
Hypocrisy—the only evil that walks
Invisible, except to God alone,
By his permissive will, through Heaven and Earth;
And oft, though Wisdom wake, Suspicion sleeps
At Wisdom's gate, and to Simplicity
Resigns her charge, while Goodness thinks no ill
Where no ill seems: which now for once beguiled
Uriel, though Regent of the Sun, and held
The sharpest-sighted Spirit of all in Heaven;
Who to the fraudulent impostor foul,
In his uprightness, answer thus returned:—
"Fair Angel, thy desire, which tends to know
The works of God, thereby to glorify
The great Work-master, leads to no excess
That reaches blame, but rather merits praise
The more it seems excess, that led thee hither
From thy empyreal mansion thus alone,
To witness with thine eyes what some perhaps,
Contented with report, hear only in Heaven:
For wonderful indeed are all his works,
Pleasant to know, and worthiest to be all
Had in remembrance always with delight!
But what created mind can comprehend
Their number, or the wisdom infinite
That brought them forth, but hid their causes deep?

I saw when, at his word, the formless mass,
This World's material mould, came to a heap:
Confusion heard his voice, and wild Uproar
Stood ruled, stood vast Infinitude confined;
Till, at his second bidding, Darkness fled,
Light shone, and order from disorder sprung.
Swift to their several quarters hasted then
The cumbrous elements—Earth, Flood, Air, Fire;
And this ethereal quintessence of Heaven
Flew upward, spirited with various forms,
That rolled orbicular, and turned to stars
Numberless, as thou seest, and how they move:
Each had his place appointed, each his course;
The rest in circuit walls this Universe.
Look downward on that globe, whose hither side
With light from hence, though but reflected, shines:
That place is Earth, the seat of Man; that light
His day, which else, as th' other hemisphere,
Night would invade, but there the neighbouring Moon
(So call that opposite fair star) her aid
Timely interposes, and, her monthly round
Still ending, still renewing, through mid-heaven,
With borrowed light her countenance triform
Hence fills and empties, to enlighten th' Earth,
And in her pale dominion checks the night.
That spot to which I point is Paradise,
Adam's abode; those lofty shades his bower.
Thy way thou canst not miss; me mine requires."
  Thus said, he turned; and Satan, bowing low,
As to superior Spirits is wont in Heaven,
Where honour due and reverence none neglects,
Took leave, and toward the coast of Earth beneath,
Down from th' ecliptic, sped with hoped success,
Throws his steep flight in many an airy wheel,
Nor stayed, till on Niphates' top he lights.

THE END OF THE THIRD BOOK

BOOK IV

THE ARGUMENT

Satan, now in prospect of Eden, and nigh the place where he must now attempt the bold enterprise which he undertook alone against God and Man, falls into many doubts with himself, and many passions—fear, envy, and despair; but at length confirms himself in evil; journeys on to Paradise, whose outward prospect and situation is described; overleaps the bounds; sits, in the shape of a cormorant, on the Tree of Life, as highest in the Garden, to look about him. The Garden described; Satan's first sight of Adam and Eve; his wonder at their excellent form and happy state, but with resolution to work their fall; overhears their discourse; thence gathers that the Tree of Knowledge was forbidden them to eat of under penalty of death, and thereon intends to found his temptation by seducing them to transgress; then leaves them a while, to know further of their state by some other means. Meanwhile Uriel, descending on a sunbeam, warns Gabriel, who had in charge the gate of Paradise, that some evil Spirit had escaped the Deep, and passed at noon by his Sphere, in the shape of a good Angel, down to Paradise, discovered after by his furious gestures in the mount. Gabriel promises to find him ere morning. Night coming on, Adam and Eve discourse of going to their rest: their bower described; their evening worship. Gabriel, drawing forth his bands of night-watch to walk the rounds of Paradise, appoints two strong Angels to Adam's bower, lest the evil Spirit should be there doing some harm to Adam or Eve sleeping: there they find him at the ear of Eve, tempting her in a dream, and bring him, though unwilling, to Gabriel: by whom questioned, he scornfully answers; prepares resistance; but, hindered by a sign from Heaven, flies out of Paradise.

O for that warning voice, which he who saw
Th' Apocalypse heard cry in Heaven aloud,
Then when the Dragon, put to second rout,
Came furious down to be revenged on men,
Woe to the inhabitants on Earth! that now,

While time was, our first parents had been warned
The coming of their secret foe, and scaped,
Haply so scaped, his mortal snare! For now
Satan, now first inflamed with rage, came down,
The tempter, ere th' accuser, of mankind,
To wreak on innocent frail Man his loss
Of that first battle, and his flight to Hell.
Yet not rejoicing in his speed, though bold
Far off and fearless, nor with cause to boast,
Begins his dire attempt; which, nigh the birth
Now rolling, boils in his tumultuous breast,
And like a devilish engine back recoils
Upon himself. Horror and doubt distract
His troubled thoughts, and from the bottom stir
The hell within him; for within him Hell
He brings, and round about him, nor from Hell
One step, no more than from himself, can fly
By change of place. Now Conscience wakes Despair
That slumbered; wakes the bitter memory
Of what he was, what is, and what must be
Worse; of worse deeds worse sufferings must ensue.
Sometimes towards Eden, which now in his view
Lay pleasant, his grieved look he fixes sad;
Sometimes towards Heaven and the full-blazing Sun,
Which now sat high in his meridian tower:
Then, much revolving, thus in sighs began:—
"O thou that, with surpassing glory crowned,
Look'st from thy sole dominion like the god
Of this new World—at whose sight all the stars
Hide their diminished heads—to thee I call,
But with no friendly voice, and add thy name,
O Sun, to tell thee how I hate thy beams,
That bring to my remembrance from what state
I fell, how glorious once above thy sphere,
Till pride and worse ambition threw me down,
Warring in Heaven against Heaven's matchless King!
Ah, wherefore? He deserved no such return

From me, whom he created what I was
In that bright eminence, and with his good
Upbraided none; nor was his service hard.
What could be less than to afford him praise,
The easiest recompense, and pay him thanks,
How due! Yet all his good proved ill in me,
And wrought but malice. Lifted up so high,
I 'sdained subjection, and thought one step higher
Would set me highest, and in a moment quit
The debt immense of endless gratitude,
So burdensome, still paying, still to owe;
Forgetful what from him I still received;
And understood not that a grateful mind
By owing owes not, but still pays, at once
Indebted and discharged—what burden then?
Oh, had his powerful destiny ordained
Me some inferior Angel, I had stood
Then happy; no unbounded hope had raised
Ambition. Yet why not? Some other Power
As great might have aspired, and me, though mean,
Drawn to his part. But other Powers as great
Fell not, but stand unshaken, from within
Or from without to all temptations armed!
Hadst thou the same free will and power to stand?
Thou hadst. Whom hast thou then, or what, to accuse,
But Heaven's free love dealt equally to all?
Be then his love accursed, since, love or hate,
To me alike it deals eternal woe.
Nay, cursed be thou; since against his thy will
Chose freely what it now so justly rues.
Me miserable! which way shall I fly
Infinite wrath and infinite despair?
Which way I fly is Hell; myself am Hell;
And, in the lowest deep, a lower deep
Still threatening to devour me opens wide,
To which the Hell I suffer seems a Heaven.
O, then, at last relent! Is there no place

Left for repentance, none for pardon left?
None left but by submission; and that word
Disdain forbids me, and my dread of shame
Among the Spirits beneath, whom I seduced
With other promises and other vaunts
Than to submit, boasting I could subdue
Th' Omnipotent. Ay me! they little know
How dearly I abide that boast so vain,
Under what torments inwardly I groan.
While they adore me on the throne of Hell,
With diadem and sceptre high advanced,
The lower still I fall, only supreme
In misery: such joy ambition finds!
But say I could repent, and could obtain,
By act of grace, my former state, how soon
Would height recall high thoughts, how soon unsay
What feigned submission swore! Ease would recant
Vows made in pain, as violent and void
(For never can true reconcilement grow
Where wounds of deadly hate have pierced so deep);
Which would but lead me to a worse relapse
And heavier fall: so should I purchase dear
Short intermission, bought with double smart.
This knows my Punisher; therefore as far
From granting he, as I from begging, peace.
All hope excluded thus, behold, instead
Of us, outcast, exiled, his new delight,
Mankind, created, and for him this World!
So farewell hope, and, with hope, farewell fear,
Farewell remorse! All good to me is lost;
Evil, be thou my good: by thee at least
Divided empire with Heaven's King I hold,
By thee, and more than half perhaps will reign;
As Man ere long, and this new World, shall know."
  Thus while he spake, each passion dimmed his face,
Thrice changed with pale—ire, envy, and despair;
Which marred his borrowed visage, and betrayed

Him counterfeit, if any eye beheld:
For heavenly minds from such distempers foul
Are ever clear. Whereof he soon aware
Each perturbation smoothed with outward calm,
Artificer of fraud; and was the first
That practised falsehood under saintly show,
Deep malice to conceal, couched with revenge:
Yet not enough had practised to deceive
Uriel, once warned; whose eye pursued him down
The way he went, and on th' Assyrian mount
Saw him disfigured, more than could befall
Spirit of happy sort: his gestures fierce
He marked and mad demeanour, then alone,
As he supposed, all unobserved, unseen.
  So on he fares, and to the border comes
Of Eden, where delicious Paradise,
Now nearer, crowns with her enclosure green,
As with a rural mound, the champaign head
Of a steep wilderness, whose hairy sides
With thicket overgrown, grotesque and wild,
Access denied, and overhead up-grew
Insuperable height of loftiest shade,
Cedar, and pine, and fir, and branching palm,
A sylvan scene, and, as the ranks ascend
Shade above shade, a woody theatre
Of stateliest view. Yet higher than their tops
The verdurous wall of Paradise up-sprung;
Which to our general sire gave prospect large
Into his nether empire neighbouring round.
And higher than that wall a circling row
Of goodliest trees, loaden with fairest fruit,
Blossoms and fruits at once of golden hue,
Appeared, with gay enamelled colours mixed;
On which the sun more glad impressed his beams
Than in fair evening cloud, or humid bow,
When God hath showered the earth: so lovely seemed
That landscape. And of pure now purer air

Meets his approach, and to the heart inspires
Vernal delight and joy, able to drive
All sadness but despair. Now gentle gales,
Fanning their odoriferous wings, dispense
Native perfumes, and whisper whence they stole
Those balmy spoils. As, when to them who sail
Beyond the Cape of Hope, and now are past
Mozambic, off at sea north-east winds blow
Sabean odours from the spicy shore
Of Araby the Blest, with such delay
Well pleased they slack their course, and many a league
Cheered with the grateful smell old Ocean smiles;
So entertained those odorous sweets the Fiend
Who came their bane, though with them better pleased
Than Asmodeus with the fishy fume
That drove him, though enamoured, from the spouse
Of Tobit's son, and with a vengeance sent
From Media post to Egypt, there fast bound.
Now to th' ascent of that steep savage hill
Satan had journeyed on, pensive and slow;
But further way found none; so thick entwined,
As one continued brake, the undergrowth
Of shrubs and tangling bushes had perplexed
All path of man or beast that passed that way.
One gate there only was, and that looked east
On th' other side. Which when th' Arch-Felon saw,
Due entrance he disdained, and, in contempt,
At one slight bound high overleaped all bound
Of hill or highest wall, and sheer within
Lights on his feet. As when a prowling wolf,
Whom hunger drives to seek new haunt for prey,
Watching where shepherds pen their flocks at eve,
In hurdled cotes amid the field secure,
Leaps o'er the fence with ease into the fold;
Or as a thief, bent to unhoard the cash
Of some rich burgher, whose substantial doors,
Cross-barred and bolted fast, fear no assault,

In at the window climbs, or o'er the tiles;
So clomb this first grand Thief into God's fold:
So since into his Church lewd hirelings climb.
Thence up he flew, and on the Tree of Life,
The middle tree and highest there that grew,
Sat like a cormorant; yet not true life
Thereby regained, but sat devising death
To them who lived; nor on the virtue thought
Of that life-giving plant, but only used
For prospect, what well used had been the pledge
Of immortality. So little knows
Any, but God alone, to value right
The good before him, but perverts best things
To worst abuse, or to their meanest use.
Beneath him, with new wonder, now he views,
To all delight of human sense exposed,
In narrow room Nature's whole wealth; yea, more,
A Heaven on Earth: for blissful Paradise
Of God the garden was, by him in the east
Of Eden planted. Eden stretched her line
From Auran eastward to the royal towers
Of great Seleucia, built by Grecian kings,
Or where the sons of Eden long before
Dwelt in Telassar. In this pleasant soil
His far more pleasant garden God ordained.
Out of the fertile ground he caused to grow
All trees of noblest kind for sight, smell, taste.
And all amid them stood the Tree of Life,
High eminent, blooming ambrosial fruit
Of vegetable gold, and next to life,
Our death, the Tree of Knowledge, grew fast by—
Knowledge of good, bought dear by knowing ill.
Southward through Eden went a river large,
Nor changed his course, but through the shaggy hill
Passed underneath ingulfed; for God had thrown
That mountain, as his garden-mould, high raised
Upon the rapid current, which, through veins

Of porous earth with kindly thirst up-drawn,
Rose a fresh fountain, and with many a rill
Watered the garden; thence united fell
Down the steep glade, and met the nether flood,
Which from his darksome passage now appears,
And now, divided into four main streams,
Runs diverse, wandering many a famous realm
And country whereof here needs no account;
But rather to tell how, if Art could tell
How, from that sapphire fount the crispèd brooks,
Rolling on orient pearl and sands of gold,
With mazy error under pendent shades
Ran nectar, visiting each plant, and fed
Flowers worthy of Paradise, which not nice Art
In beds and curious knots, but Nature boon
Poured forth profuse on hill, and dale, and plain,
Both where the morning sun first warmly smote
The open field, and where the unpierced shade
Imbrowned the noontide bowers. Thus was this place,
A happy rural seat of various view:
Groves whose rich trees wept odorous gums and balm;
Others whose fruit, burnished with golden rind,
Hung amiable—Hesperian fables true,
If true, here only—and of delicious taste.
Betwixt them lawns, or level downs, and flocks
Grazing the tender herb, were interposed,
Or palmy hillock; or the flowery lap
Of some irriguous valley spread her store,
Flowers of all hue, and without thorn the rose.
Another side, umbrageous grots and caves
Of cool recess, o'er which the mantling vine
Lays forth her purple grape, and gently creeps
Luxuriant; meanwhile murmuring waters fall
Down the slope hills dispersed, or in a lake,
That to the fringèd bank with myrtle crowned
Her crystal mirror holds, unite their streams.
The birds their choir apply; airs, vernal airs,

Breathing the smell of field and grove, attune
The trembling leaves, while universal Pan,
Knit with the Graces and the Hours in dance,
Led on th' eternal Spring. Not that fair field
Of Enna, where Proserpin gathering flowers,
Herself a fairer flower, by gloomy Dis
Was gathered—which cost Ceres all that pain
To seek her through the world—nor that sweet grove
Of Daphne, by Orontes and th' inspired
Castalian spring, might with this Paradise
Of Eden strive; nor that Nyseian isle,
Girt with the river Triton, where old Cham,
Whom Gentiles Ammon call and Libyan Jove,
Hid Amalthea, and her florid son,
Young Bacchus, from his stepdame Rhea's eye;
Nor, where Abassin kings their issue guard,
Mount Amara (though this by some supposed
True Paradise) under the Ethiop line
By Nilus' head, enclosed with shining rock,
A whole day's journey high, but wide remote
From this Assyrian garden, where the Fiend
Saw undelighted all delight, all kind
Of living creatures, new to sight and strange.
Two of far nobler shape, erect and tall,
God-like erect, with native honour clad
In naked majesty, seemed lords of all,
And worthy seemed; for in their looks divine
The image of their glorious Maker shone,
Truth, wisdom, sanctitude severe and pure—
Severe, but in true filial freedom placed,
Whence true authority in men: though both
Not equal, as their sex not equal seemed;
For contemplation he and valour formed,
For softness she and sweet attractive grace;
He for God only, she for God in him.
His fair large front and eye sublime declared
Absolute rule; and hyacinthine locks

Round from his parted forelock manly hung
Clustering, but not beneath his shoulders broad:
She, as a veil down to the slender waist,
Her unadornèd golden tresses wore
Dishevelled, but in wanton ringlets waved
As the vine curls her tendrils, which implied
Subjection, but required with gentle sway,
And by her yielded, by him best received
Yielded, with coy submission, modest pride,
And sweet, reluctant, amorous delay.
Nor those mysterious parts were then concealed;
Then was not guilty shame. Dishonest shame
Of Nature's works, honour dishonourable,
Sin-bred, how have ye troubled all mankind
With shows instead, mere shows of seeming pure,
And banished from man's life his happiest life,
Simplicity and spotless innocence!
So passed they naked on, nor shunned the sight
Of God or Angel; for they thought no ill:
So hand in hand they passed, the loveliest pair
That ever since in love's embraces met—
Adam the goodliest man of men since born
His sons; the fairest of her daughters Eve.
Under a tuft of shade that on a green
Stood whispering soft, by a fresh fountain-side,
They sat them down; and, after no more toil
Of their sweet gardening labour than sufficed
To recommend cool Zephyr, and make ease
More easy, wholesome thirst and appetite
More grateful, to their supper-fruits they fell—
Nectarine fruits, which the compliant boughs
Yielded them, sidelong as they sat recline
On the soft downy bank damasked with flowers.
The savoury pulp they chew, and in the rind,
Still as they thirsted, scoop the brimming stream;
Nor gentle purpose, nor endearing smiles
Wanted, nor youthful dalliance, as beseems

Fair couple linked in happy nuptial league,
Alone as they. About them frisking played
All beasts of th' earth, since wild, and of all chase
In wood or wilderness, forest or den.
Sporting the lion ramped, and in his paw
Dandled the kid; bears, tigers, ounces, pards,
Gambolled before them; th' unwieldy elephant,
To make them mirth, used all his might, and wreathed
His lithe proboscis; close the serpent sly,
Insinuating, wove with Gordian twine
His braided train, and of his fatal guile
Gave proof unheeded. Others on the grass
Couched, and, now filled with pasture, gazing sat,
Or bedward ruminating; for the sun,
Declined, was hasting now with prone career
To th' ocean isles, and in th' ascending scale
Of Heaven the stars that usher evening rose:
When Satan, still in gaze as first he stood,
Scarce thus at length failed speech recovered sad:—
"O Hell! what do mine eyes with grief behold?
Into our room of bliss thus high advanced
Creatures of other mould—Earth-born perhaps,
Not Spirits, yet to heavenly Spirits bright
Little inferior—whom my thoughts pursue
With wonder, and could love; so lively shines
In them divine resemblance, and such grace
The hand that formed them on their shape hath poured.
Ah! gentle pair, ye little think how nigh
Your change approaches, when all these delights
Will vanish, and deliver ye to woe—
More woe, the more your taste is now of joy:
Happy, but for so happy ill secured
Long to continue, and this high seat, your Heaven,
Ill fenced for Heaven to keep out such a foe
As now is entered; yet no purposed foe
To you, whom I could pity thus forlorn,
Though I unpitied. League with you I seek,

And mutual amity, so strait, so close,
That I with you must dwell, or you with me,
Henceforth. My dwelling, haply, may not please,
Like this fair Paradise, your sense; yet such
Accept your Maker's work; he gave it me,
Which I as freely give. Hell shall unfold,
To entertain you two, her widest gates,
And send forth all her kings; there will be room,
Not like these narrow limits, to receive
Your numerous offspring; if no better place,
Thank him who puts me, loath, to this revenge
On you, who wrong me not, for him who wronged.
And, should I at your harmless innocence
Melt, as I do, yet public reason just—
Honour and empire with revenge enlarged
By conquering this new World—compels me now
To do what else, though damned, I should abhor."
  So spake the Fiend, and with necessity,
The tyrant's plea, excused his devilish deeds.
Then from his lofty stand on that high tree
Down he alights among the sportful herd
Of those four-footed kinds, himself now one,
Now other, as their shape served best his end
Nearer to view his prey, and, unespied,
To mark what of their state he more might learn
By word or action marked. About them round
A lion now he stalks with fiery glare;
Then as a tiger, who by chance hath spied
In some purlieu two gentle fawns at play,
Straight crouches close; then, rising, changes oft
His couchant watch, as one who chose his ground,
Whence rushing he might surest seize them both
Gripped in each paw: when Adam, first of men,
To first of women, Eve, thus moving speech,
Turned him all ear to hear new utterance flow:—
  "Sole partner and sole part of all these joys,
Dearer thyself than all, needs must the Power

That made us, and for us this ample World,
Be infinitely good, and of his good
As liberal and free as infinite;
That raised us from the dust, and placed us here
In all this happiness, who at his hand
Have nothing merited, nor can perform
Aught whereof he hath need; he who requires
From us no other service than to keep
This one, this easy charge—of all the trees
In Paradise that bear delicious fruit
So various, not to taste that only Tree
Of Knowledge, planted by the Tree of Life;
So near grows death to life, whate'er death is—
Some dreadful thing no doubt; for well thou know'st
God hath pronounced it death to taste that Tree:
The only sign of our obedience left
Among so many signs of power and rule
Conferred upon us, and dominion given
Over all other creatures that possess
Earth, Air, and Sea. Then let us not think hard
One easy prohibition, who enjoy
Free leave so large to all things else, and choice
Unlimited of manifold delights;
But let us ever praise him, and extol
His bounty, following our delightful task,
To prune these growing plants, and tend these flowers;
Which, were it toilsome, yet with thee were sweet."
To whom thus Eve replied:—"O thou for whom
And from whom I was formed flesh of thy flesh,
And without whom am to no end, my guide
And head! what thou hast said is just and right.
For we to him, indeed, all praises owe,
And daily thanks—I chiefly, who enjoy
So far the happier lot, enjoying thee
Pre-eminent by so much odds, while thou
Like consort to thyself canst nowhere find.
That day I oft remember, when from sleep

I first awaked, and found myself reposed,
Under a shade, on flowers, much wondering where
And what I was, whence thither brought, and how.
Not distant far from thence a murmuring sound
Of waters issued from a cave, and spread
Into a liquid plain; then stood unmoved,
Pure as th' expanse of Heaven. I thither went
With unexperienced thought, and laid me down
On the green bank, to look into the clear
Smooth lake, that to me seemed another sky.
As I bent down to look, just opposite
A shape within the watery gleam appeared,
Bending to look on me. I started back,
It started back; but pleased I soon returned,
Pleased it returned as soon with answering looks
Of sympathy and love. There I had fixed
Mine eyes till now, and pined with vain desire,
Had not a voice thus warned me: 'What thou seest,
What there thou seest, fair creature, is thyself;
With thee it came and goes: but follow me,
And I will bring thee where no shadow stays
Thy coming, and thy soft embraces—he
Whose image thou art; him thou shalt enjoy
Inseparably thine; to him shalt bear
Multitudes like thyself, and thence be called
Mother of human race.' What could I do,
But follow straight, invisibly thus led?
Till I espied thee, fair, indeed, and tall,
Under a platan; yet methought less fair,
Less winning soft, less amiably mild,
Than that smooth watery image. Back I turned;
Thou, following, cried'st aloud, 'Return, fair Eve;
Whom fliest thou? Whom thou fliest, of him thou art,
His flesh, his bone; to give thee being I lent
Out of my side to thee, nearest my heart,
Substantial life, to have thee by my side
Henceforth an individual solace dear:

Part of my soul I seek thee, and thee claim
My other half.' With that thy gentle hand
Seized mine: I yielded, and from that time see
How beauty is excelled by manly grace
And wisdom, which alone is truly fair."
  So spake our general mother, and, with eyes
Of conjugal attraction unreproved,
And meek surrender, half-embracing leaned
On our first father; half her swelling breast
Naked met his, under the flowing gold
Of her loose tresses hid. He, in delight
Both of her beauty and submissive charms,
Smiled with superior love, as Jupiter
On Juno smiles when he impregns the clouds
That shed May flowers, and pressed her matron lip
With kisses pure. Aside the Devil turned
For envy; yet with jealous leer malign
Eyed them askance, and to himself thus plained:—
  "Sight hateful, sight tormenting! Thus these two,
Imparadised in one another's arms,
The happier Eden, shall enjoy their fill
Of bliss on bliss; while I to Hell am thrust,
Where neither joy nor love, but fierce desire,
Among our other torments not the least,
Still unfulfilled, with pain of longing pines!
Yet let me not forget what I have gained
From their own mouths. All is not theirs, it seems;
One fatal tree there stands, of Knowledge called,
Forbidden them to taste. Knowledge forbidden?
Suspicious, reasonless! Why should their Lord
Envy them that? Can it be sin to know?
Can it be death? And do they only stand
By ignorance? Is that their happy state,
The proof of their obedience and their faith?
O fair foundation laid whereon to build
Their ruin! Hence I will excite their minds
With more desire to know, and to reject

Envious commands, invented with design
To keep them low, whom knowledge might exalt
Equal with gods. Aspiring to be such,
They taste and die: what likelier can ensue?
But first with narrow search I must walk round
This garden, and no corner leave unspied;
A chance but chance may lead where I may meet
Some wandering Spirit of Heaven, by fountain-side,
Or in thick shade retired, from him to draw
What further would be learned. Live while ye may,
Yet happy pair; enjoy, till I return,
Short pleasures; for long woes are to succeed!"
  So saying, his proud step he scornful turned,
But with sly circumspection, and began
Through wood, through waste, o'er hill, o'er dale, his roam.
Meanwhile in utmost longitude, where Heaven
With Earth and Ocean meets, the setting Sun
Slowly descended, and with right aspect
Against the eastern gate of Paradise
Levelled his evening rays. It was a rock
Of alabaster, piled up to the clouds,
Conspicuous far, winding with one ascent
Accessible from Earth, one entrance high;
The rest was craggy cliff, that overhung
Still as it rose, impossible to climb.
Betwixt these rocky pillars Gabriel sat,
Chief of th' angelic guards, awaiting night;
About him exercised heroic games
Th' unarmèd youth of Heaven; but nigh at hand
Celestial armoury, shields, helms, and spears,
Hung high, with diamond flaming and with gold.
Thither came Uriel, gliding through the even
On a sunbeam, swift as a shooting star
In autumn thwarts the night, when vapours fired
Impress the air, and shows the mariner
From what point of his compass to beware
Impetuous winds. He thus began in haste:—

"Gabriel, to thee thy course by lot hath given
Charge and strict watch that to this happy place
No evil thing approach or enter in.
This day at height of noon came to my sphere
A Spirit, zealous, as he seemed, to know
More of th' Almighty's works, and chiefly Man,
God's latest image. I described his way
Bent all on speed, and marked his airy gait,
But in the mount that lies from Eden north,
Where he first lighted, soon discerned his looks
Alien from Heaven, with passions foul obscured.
Mine eye pursued him still, but under shade
Lost sight of him. One of the banished crew,
I fear, hath ventured from the Deep, to raise
New troubles; him thy care must be to find."
To whom the wingèd Warrior thus returned:—
"Uriel, no wonder if thy perfect sight,
Amid the Sun's bright circle where thou sitt'st,
See far and wide. In at this gate none pass
The vigilance here placed, but such as come
Well known from Heaven; and since meridian hour
No creature thence. If Spirit of other sort,
So minded, have o'erleaped these earthy bounds
On purpose, hard thou know'st it to exclude
Spiritual substance with corporeal bar.
But, if within the circuit of these walks,
In whatsoever shape, he lurk of whom
Thou tell'st, by morrow dawning I shall know."
So promised he; and Uriel to his charge
Returned on that bright beam, whose point now raised
Bore him slope downward to the Sun, now fallen
Beneath th' Azores; whether the Prime Orb,
Incredible how swift, had thither rolled
Diurnal, or this less volúbile Earth,
By shorter flight to th' east, had left him there
Arraying with reflected purple and gold
The clouds that on his western throne attend.

Now came still Evening on, and Twilight grey
Had in her sober livery all things clad;
Silence accompanied; for beast and bird,
They to their grassy couch, these to their nests
Were slunk, all but the wakeful nightingale.
She all night long her amorous descant sung:
Silence was pleased. Now glowed the firmament
With living sapphires; Hesperus, that led
The starry host, rode brightest, till the Moon,
Rising in clouded majesty, at length
Apparent queen, unveiled her peerless light,
And o'er the dark her silver mantle threw;
When Adam thus to Eve:—"Fair consort, th' hour
Of night, and all things now retired to rest,
Mind us of like repose; since God hath set
Labour and rest, as day and night, to men
Successive, and the timely dew of sleep,
Now falling with soft slumberous weight, inclines
Our eyelids. Other creatures all day long
Rove idle, unemployed, and less need rest;
Man hath his daily work of body or mind
Appointed, which declares his dignity,
And the regard of Heaven on all his ways;
While other animals unactive range,
And of their doings God takes no account.
To-morrow, ere fresh morning streak the east
With first approach of light, we must be risen,
And at our pleasant labour, to reform
Yon flowery arbours, yonder alleys green,
Our walk at noon, with branches overgrown,
That mock our scant manuring, and require
More hands than ours to lop their wanton growth.
Those blossoms also, and those dropping gums,
That lie bestrewn, unsightly and unsmooth,
Ask riddance, if we mean to tread with ease.
Meanwhile, as Nature wills, Night bids us rest."
To whom thus Eve, with perfect beauty adorned:—

"My author and disposer, what thou bidd'st
Unargued I obey. So God ordains:
God is thy law, thou mine: to know no more
Is woman's happiest knowledge, and her praise.
With thee conversing, I forget all time,
All seasons, and their change; all please alike.
Sweet is the breath of Morn, her rising sweet,
With charm of earliest birds; pleasant the Sun,
When first on this delightful land he spreads
His orient beams, on herb, tree, fruit, and flower,
Glistering with dew; fragrant the fertile Earth
After soft showers; and sweet the coming on
Of grateful Evening mild, then silent Night,
With this her solemn bird, and this fair Moon,
And these the gems of Heaven, her starry train:
But neither breath of Morn, when she ascends
With charm of earliest birds; nor rising Sun
On this delightful land; nor herb, fruit, flower,
Glistering with dew; nor fragrance after showers;
Nor grateful Evening mild, nor silent Night,
With this her solemn bird, nor walk by Moon,
Or glittering starlight, without thee is sweet.
But wherefore all night long shine these? for whom
This glorious sight, when sleep hath shut all eyes?"
  To whom our general ancestor replied.—
"Daughter of God and Man, accomplished Eve,
Those have their course to finish round the Earth
By morrow evening, and from land to land
In order, though to nations yet unborn,
Ministering light prepared, they set and rise;
Lest total Darkness should by night regain
Her old possession, and extinguish life
In nature and all things; which these soft fires
Not only enlighten, but with kindly heat
Of various influence foment and warm,
Temper or nourish, or in part shed down
Their stellar virtue on all kinds that grow

On Earth, made hereby apter to receive
Perfection from the Sun's more potent ray.
These, then, though unbeheld in deep of night,
Shine not in vain. Nor think, though men were none,
That Heaven would want spectators, God want praise.
Millions of spiritual creatures walk the Earth
Unseen, both when we wake, and when we sleep:
All these with ceaseless praise his works behold
Both day and night. How often, from the steep
Of echoing hill or thicket, have we heard
Celestial voices to the midnight air,
Sole, or responsive each to other's note,
Singing their great Creator! Oft in bands
While they keep watch, or nightly rounding walk,
With heavenly touch of instrumental sounds
In full harmonic number joined, their songs
Divide the night, and lift our thoughts to Heaven."
  Thus talking, hand in hand alone they passed
On to their blissful bower. It was a place
Chosen by the sovereign Planter, when he framed
All things to Man's delightful use. The roof
Of thickest covert was inwoven shade,
Laurel and myrtle, and what higher grew
Of firm and fragrant leaf; on either side
Acanthus, and each odorous bushy shrub,
Fenced up the verdant wall; each beauteous flower,
Iris all hues, roses, and jessamine,
Reared high their flourished heads between, and wrought
Mosaic; under foot the violet,
Crocus, and hyacinth, with rich inlay
Broidered the ground, more coloured than with stone
Of costliest emblem. Other creature here,
Beast, bird, insect, or worm, durst enter none;
Such was their awe of Man. In shadier bower
More sacred and sequestered, though but feigned,
Pan or Sylvanus never slept, nor Nymph
Nor Faunus haunted. Here, in close recess,

With flowers, garlands, and sweet-smelling herbs,
Espousèd Eve decked her first nuptial bed,
And heavenly choirs the hymenaean sung,
What day the genial Angel to our sire
Brought her, in naked beauty more adorned,
More lovely, than Pandora, whom the gods
Endowed with all their gifts; and, O! too like
In sad event, when, to the unwiser son
Of Japhet brought by Hermes, she ensnared
Mankind with her fair looks, to be avenged
On him who had stole Jove's authentic fire.
  Thus at their shady lodge arrived, both stood,
Both turned, and under open sky adored
The God that made both Sky, Air, Earth, and Heaven,
Which they beheld, the Moon's resplendent globe,
And starry Pole:—" Thou also mad'st the Night,
Maker Omnipotent; and thou the Day,
Which we, in our appointed work employed,
Have finished, happy in our mutual help
And mutual love, the crown of all our bliss
Ordained by thee; and this delicious place,
For us too large, where thy abundance wants
Partakers, and uncropt falls to the ground.
But thou hast promised from us two a race
To fill the Earth, who shall with us extol
Thy goodness infinite, both when we wake,
And when we seek, as now, thy gift of sleep."
  This said unanimous, and other rites
Observing none, but adoration pure,
Which God likes best, into their inmost bower
Handed they went; and, eased the putting-off
These troublesome disguises which we wear,
Straight side by side were laid; nor turned, I ween,
Adam from his fair spouse, nor Eve the rites
Mysterious of connubial love refused:
Whatever hypocrites austerely talk
Of purity, and place, and innocence,

Defaming as impure what God declares
Pure, and commands to some, leaves free to all.
Our Maker bids increase; who bids abstain
But our destroyer, foe to God and Man?
Hail, wedded Love, mysterious law, true source
Of human offspring, sole propriety
In Paradise of all things common else!
By thee adulterous lust was driven from men
Among the bestial herds to range; by thee,
Founded in reason, loyal, just, and pure,
Relations dear, and all the charities
Of father, son, and brother, first were known.
Far be it that I should write thee sin or blame,
Or think thee unbefitting holiest place,
Perpetual fountain of domestic sweets,
Whose bed is undefiled and chaste pronounced,
Present, or past, as saints and patriarchs used.
Here Love his golden shafts employs, here lights
His constant lamp, and waves his purple wings,
Reigns here and revels; not in the bought smile
Of harlots—loveless, joyless, unendeared,
Casual fruition; nor in court amours,
Mixed dance, or wanton mask, or midnight ball,
Or serenade, which the starved lover sings
To his proud fair, best quitted with disdain.
These, lulled by nightingales, embracing slept,
And on their naked limbs the flowery roof
Showered roses, which the morn repaired. Sleep on,
Blest pair! and, O! yet happiest, if ye seek
No happier state, and know to know no more!
  Now had Night measured with her shadowy cone
Halfway uphill this vast sublunar vault,
And from their ivory port the Cherubim
Forth issuing, at th' accustomed hour, stood armed
To their night-watches in warlike parade;
When Gabriel to his next in power thus spake:—
  "Uzziel, half these draw off, and coast the south

With strictest watch; these other wheel the north:
Our circuit meets full west." As flame they part,
Half wheeling to the shield, half to the spear.
From these, two strong and subtle Spirits he called
That near him stood, and gave them thus in charge:—
"Ithuriel and Zephon, with winged speed
Search through this Garden; leave unsearched no nook;
But chiefly where those two fair creatures lodge,
Now laid perhaps asleep, secure of harm.
This evening from the Sun's decline arrived
Who tells of some infernal Spirit seen
Hitherward bent (who could have thought?), escaped
The bars of Hell, on errand bad, no doubt:
Such, where ye find, seize fast, and hither bring."
So saying, on he led his radiant files,
Dazzling the Moon; these to the bower direct
In search of whom they sought. Him there they found
Squat like a toad, close at the ear of Eve,
Assaying by his devilish art to reach
The organs of her fancy, and with them forge
Illusions as he list, phantasms and dreams;
Or if, inspiring venom, he might taint
Th' animal spirits, that from pure blood arise
Like gentle breaths from rivers pure, thence raise,
At least distempered, discontented thoughts,
Vain hopes, vain aims, inordinate desires,
Blown up with high conceits engendering pride.
Him thus intent Ithuriel with his spear
Touched lightly; for no falsehood can endure
Touch of celestial temper, but returns
Of force to its own likeness. Up he starts,
Discovered and surprised. As, when a spark
Lights on a heap of nitrous powder, laid
Fit for the tun, some magazine to store
Against a rumoured war, the smutty grain,
With sudden blaze diffused, inflames the air;
So started up, in his own shape, the Fiend.

Back stept those two fair Angels, half amazed
So sudden to behold the grisly King;
Yet thus, unmoved with fear, accost him soon:—
  " Which of those rebel Spirits adjudged to Hell
Com'st thou, escaped thy prison? and, transformed,
Why satt'st thou like an enemy in wait,
Here watching at the head of these that sleep? "
  " Know ye not, then," said Satan, filled with scorn,
" Know ye not me? Ye knew me once no mate
For you, there sitting where ye durst not soar!
Not to know me argues yourselves unknown,
The lowest of your throng; or, if ye know,
Why ask ye, and superfluous begin
Your message, like to end as much in vain? "
  To whom thus Zephon, answering scorn with scorn:—
" Think not, revolted Spirit, thy shape the same,
Or undiminished brightness, to be known
As when thou stood'st in Heaven upright and pure.
That glory then, when thou no more wast good,
Departed from thee; and thou resemblest now
Thy sin and place of doom obscure and foul.
But come; for thou, be sure, shalt give account
To him who sent us, whose charge is to keep
This place inviolable, and these from harm."
  So spake the Cherub; and his grave rebuke,
Severe in youthful beauty, added grace
Invincible. Abashed the Devil stood,
And felt how awful goodness is, and saw
Virtue in her shape how lovely—saw, and pined
His loss; but chiefly to find here observed
His lustre visibly impaired; yet seemed
Undaunted. " If I must contend," said he,
" Best with the best—the sender, not the sent:
Or all at once: more glory will be won,
Or less be lost." " Thy fear," said Zephon bold,
" Will save us trial what the least can do
Single against thee wicked, and thence weak."

The Fiend replied not, overcome with rage;
But, like a proud steed reined, went haughty on,
Champing his iron curb. To strive or fly
He held it vain; awe from above had quelled
His heart, not else dismayed. Now drew they nigh
The western point, where those half-rounding guards
Just met, and, closing, stood in squadron joined,
Awaiting next command. To whom their chief,
Gabriel, from the front thus called aloud:—
"O friends, I hear the tread of nimble feet
Hasting this way, and now by glimpse discern
Ithuriel and Zephon through the shade;
And with them comes a third, of regal port,
But faded splendour wan, who by his gait
And fierce demeanour seems the Prince of Hell—
Not likely to part hence without contést.
Stand firm, for in his look defiance lours."
He scarce had ended, when those two approached,
And brief related whom they brought, where found,
How busied, in what form and posture couched.
To whom, with stern regard, thus Gabriel spake:—
"Why hast thou, Satan, broke the bounds prescribed
To thy transgressions, and disturbed the charge
Of others, who approve not to transgress
By thy example, but have power and right
To question thy bold entrance on this place;
Employed, it seems, to violate sleep, and those
Whose dwelling God hath planted here in bliss?"
To whom thus Satan, with contemptuous brow:—
"Gabriel, thou hadst in Heaven th' esteem of wise;
And such I held thee; but this question asked
Puts me in doubt. Lives there who loves his pain?
Who would not, finding way, break loose from Hell,
Though thither doomed? Thou wouldst thyself, no doubt,
And boldly venture to whatever place
Farthest from pain, where thou mightst hope to change
Torment with ease, and soonest recompense

Dole with delight; which in this place I sought:
To thee no reason, who know'st only good,
But evil hast not tried. And wilt object
His will who bound us? Let him surer bar
His iron gates, if he intends our stay
In that dark durance. Thus much what was asked:
The rest is true; they found me where they say;
But that implies not violence or harm."
  Thus he in scorn. The warlike Angel moved,
Disdainfully half smiling, thus replied:—
"O loss of one in Heaven to judge of wise,
Since Satan fell, whom folly overthrew,
And now returns him from his prison scaped,
Gravely in doubt whether to hold them wise
Or not who ask what boldness brought him hither
Unlicensed from his bounds in Hell prescribed!
So wise he judges it to fly from pain
However, and to scape his punishment!
So judge thou still, presumptuous, till the wrath,
Which thou incurr'st by flying, meet thy flight
Sevenfold, and scourge that wisdom back to Hell,
Which taught thee yet no better that no pain
Can equal anger infinite provoked.
But wherefore thou alone? Wherefore with thee
Came not all Hell broke loose? Is pain to them
Less pain, less to be fled? or thou than they
Less hardy to endure? Courageous chief,
The first in flight from pain, hadst thou alleged
To thy deserted host this cause of flight,
Thou surely hadst not come sole fugitive."
  To which the Fiend thus answered, frowning stern:—
"Not that I less endure, or shrink from pain,
Insulting Angel! well thou know'st I stood
Thy fiercest, when in battle to thy aid
The blasting volleyed thunder made all speed
And seconded thy else not dreaded spear.
But still thy words at random, as before,

Argue thy inexperience what behoves,
From hard assays and ill successes past,
A faithful leader—not to hazard all
Through ways of danger by himself untried.
I, therefore, I alone, first undertook
To wing the desolate Abyss, and spy
This new-created World, whereof in Hell
Fame is not silent, here in hope to find
Better abode, and my afflicted Powers
To settle here on Earth, or in mid Air;
Though for possession put to try once more
What thou and thy gay legions dare against;
Whose easier business were to serve their Lord
High up in Heaven, with songs to hymn his throne,
And practised distances to cringe, not fight."
To whom the warrior Angel soon replied:—
"To say and straight unsay, pretending first
Wise to fly pain, professing next the spy,
Argues no leader, but a liar traced,
Satan; and couldst thou 'faithful' add? O name,
O sacred name of faithfulness profaned!
Faithful to whom? to thy rebellious crew?
Army of fiends, fit body to fit head!
Was this your discipline and faith engaged,
Your military obedience, to dissolve
Allegiance to th' acknowledged Power supreme?
And thou, sly hypocrite, who now wouldst seem
Patron of liberty, who more than thou
Once fawned, and cringed, and servilely adored
Heaven's awful Monarch? wherefore, but in hope
To dispossess him, and thyself to reign?
But mark what I areed thee now: Avaunt!
Fly thither whence thou fledd'st. If from this hour
Within these hallowed limits thou appear,
Back to th' infernal Pit I drag thee chained,
And seal thee so as henceforth not to scorn,
The facile gates of Hell too slightly barred."

So threatened he; but Satan to no threats
Gave heed, but waxing more in rage, replied:—
"Then, when I am thy captive, talk of chains,
Proud limitary Cherub! but ere then
Far heavier load thyself expect to feel
From my prevailing arm, though Heaven's King
Ride on thy wings, and thou with thy compeers,
Used to the yoke, draw'st his triumphant wheels
In progress through the road of Heaven star-paved."
While thus he spake, th' angelic squadron bright
Turned fiery red, sharpening in mooned horns
Their phalanx, and began to hem him round
With ported spears, as thick as when a field
Of Ceres ripe for harvest waving bends
Her bearded grove of ears which way the wind
Sways them; the careful plowman doubting stands,
Lest on the threshing-floor his hopeful sheaves
Prove chaff. On th' other side, Satan, alarmed,
Collecting all his might, dilated stood,
Like Teneriff or Atlas, unremoved:
His stature reached the sky, and on his crest
Sat Horror plumed; nor wanted in his grasp
What seemed both spear and shield. Now dreadful deeds
Might have ensued; nor only Paradise,
In this commotion, but the starry cope
Of Heaven perhaps, or all the elements
At least, had gone to wrack, disturbed and torn
With violence of this conflict, had not soon
Th' Eternal, to prevent such horrid fray,
Hung forth in Heaven his golden scales, yet seen
Betwixt Astraea and the Scorpion sign,
Wherein all things created first he weighed,
The pendulous round Earth with balanced air
In counterpoise, now ponders all events,
Battles and realms. In these he put two weights,
The sequel each of parting and of fight:
The latter quick up flew, and kicked the beam;

Which Gabriel spying thus bespake the Fiend:—
"Satan, I know thy strength, and thou know'st mine,
Neither our own, but given; what folly then
To boast what arms can do! since thine no more
Than Heaven permits, nor mine, though doubled now
To trample thee as mire. For proof look up,
And read thy lot in yon celestial sign,
Where thou art weighed, and shown how light, how weak
If thou resist." The Fiend looked up, and knew
His mounted scale aloft: nor more, but fled
Murmuring; and with him fled the shades of Night.

THE END OF THE FOURTH BOOK

BOOK V

THE ARGUMENT

Morning approached, Eve relates to Adam her troublesome dream; he likes it not, yet comforts her: they come forth to their day labours: their morning hymn at the door of their bower. God, to render Man inexcusable, sends Raphael to admonish him of his obedience, of his free estate, of his enemy near at hand, who he is, and why his enemy, and whatever else may avail Adam to know. Raphael comes down to Paradise; his appearance described; his coming discerned by Adam afar off, sitting at the door of his bower; he goes out to meet him, brings him to his lodge, entertains him with the choicest fruits of Paradise, got together by Eve; their discourse at table. Raphael performs his message, minds Adam of his state and of his enemy; relates, at Adam's request, who that enemy is, and how he came to be so, beginning from his first revolt in Heaven, and the occasion thereof; how he drew his legions after him to the parts of the North, and there incited them to rebel with him, persuading all but only Abdiel, a Seraph, who in argument dissuades and opposes him, then forsakes him.

Now Morn, her rosy steps in th' eastern clime
Advancing, sowed the earth with orient pearl,
When Adam waked, so customed; for his sleep
Was airy light, from pure digestion bred,
And temperate vapours bland, which th' only sound
Of leaves and fuming rills, Aurora's fan,
Lightly dispersed, and the shrill matin song
Of birds on every bough. So much the more
His wonder was to find unwakened Eve,
With tresses discomposed, and glowing cheek,
As through unquiet rest. He, on his side
Leaning half raised, with looks of cordial love
Hung over her enamoured, and beheld
Beauty which, whether waking or asleep,

Shot forth peculiar graces; then, with voice
Mild as when Zephyrus on Flora breathes,
Her hand soft touching, whispered thus:—" Awake,
My fairest, my espoused, my latest found,
Heaven's last, best gift, my ever-new delight!
Awake! the morning shines, and the fresh field
Calls us; we lose the prime to mark how spring
Our tended plants, how blows the citron grove,
What drops the myrrh, and what the balmy reed,
How Nature paints her colours, how the bee
Sits on the bloom extracting liquid sweet."
  Such whispering waked her, but with startled eye
On Adam; whom embracing, thus she spake:—
  " O sole in whom my thoughts find all repose,
My glory, my perfection! glad I see
Thy face, and morn returned; for I this night
(Such night till this I never passed) have dreamed,
If dreamed, not, as I oft am wont, of thee,
Works of day past, or morrow's next design;
But of offence and trouble, which my mind
Knew never till this irksome night. Methought
Close at mine ear one called me forth to walk
With gentle voice; I thought it thine. It said,
'Why sleep'st thou, Eve? now is the pleasant time,
The cool, the silent, save where silence yields
To the night-warbling bird, that now awake
Tunes sweetest his love-laboured song; now reigns
Full-orbed the Moon, and, with more pleasing light,
Shadowy sets off the face of things—in vain,
If none regard. Heaven wakes with all his eyes;
Whom to behold but thee, Nature's desire,
In whose sight all things joy, with ravishment
Attracted by thy beauty still to gaze?'
I rose as at thy call, but found thee not:
To find thee I directed then my walk;
And on, methought, alone I passed through ways
That brought me on a sudden to the Tree

Of interdicted Knowledge. Fair it seemed,
Much fairer to my fancy than by day;
And, as I wondering looked, beside it stood
One shaped and winged like one of those from Heaven
By us oft seen; his dewy locks distilled
Ambrosia. On that tree he also gazed;
And, 'O fair plant,' said he, 'with fruit surcharged,
Deigns none to ease thy load, and taste thy sweet,
Nor God nor Man? Is knowledge so despised?
Or envy, or what reserve forbids to taste?
Forbid who will, none shall from me withhold
Longer thy offered good, why else set here?'
This said, he paused not, but with venturous arm
He plucked, he tasted. Me damp horror chilled
At such bold words vouched with a deed so bold;
But he thus, overjoyed: 'O fruit divine,
Sweet of thyself, but much more sweet thus cropt,
Forbidden here, it seems, as only fit
For gods, yet able to make gods of men!
And why not gods of men, since good, the more
Communicated, more abundant grows,
The author not impaired, but honoured more?
Here, happy creature, fair angelic Eve!
Partake thou also: happy though thou art,
Happier thou may'st be, worthier canst not be.
Taste this, and be henceforth among the gods
Thyself a goddess; not to Earth confined,
But sometimes in the Air, as we; sometimes
Ascend to Heaven, by merit thine, and see
What life the gods live there, and such live thou.'
So saying, he drew nigh, and to me held,
Even to my mouth, of that same fruit held part
Which he had plucked: the pleasant savoury smell
So quickened appetite that I, methought,
Could not but taste. Forthwith up to the clouds
With him I flew, and underneath beheld
The Earth outstretched immense, a prospect wide

And various. Wondering at my flight and change
To this high exaltation, suddenly
My guide was gone, and I, methought, sunk down,
And fell asleep; but O how glad I waked
To find this but a dream!" Thus Eve her night
Related, and thus Adam answered sad:—
"Best image of myself, and dearer half,
The trouble of thy thoughts this night in sleep
Affects me equally; nor can I like
This uncouth dream—of evil sprung, I fear;
Yet evil whence? In thee can harbour none,
Created pure. But know that in the soul
Are many lesser faculties, that serve
Reason as chief. Among these Fancy next
Her office holds; of all external things,
Which the five watchful senses represent,
She forms imaginations, airy shapes,
Which Reason, joining or disjoining, frames
All what we affirm or what deny, and call
Our knowledge or opinion; then retires
Into her private cell when Nature rests.
Oft, in her absence, mimic Fancy wakes
To imitate her; but, misjoining shapes,
Wild work produces oft, and most in dreams,
Ill matching words and deeds long past or late.
Some such resemblances, methinks, I find
Of our last evening's talk in this thy dream,
But with addition strange. Yet be not sad:
Evil into the mind of God or Man
May come and go, so unapproved, and leave
No spot or blame behind; which gives me hope
That what in sleep thou didst abhor to dream
Waking thou never wilt consent to do.
Be not disheartened, then, nor cloud those looks,
That wont to be more cheerful and serene
Than when fair Morning first smiles on the world;
And let us to our fresh employments rise

Among the groves, the fountains, and the flowers,
That open now their choicest bosomed smells,
Reserved from night, and kept for thee in store."
  So cheered he his fair spouse; and she was cheered,
But silently a gentle tear let fall
From either eye, and wiped them with her hair:
Two other precious drops that ready stood,
Each in their crystal sluice, he, ere they fell,
Kissed as the gracious signs of sweet remorse
And pious awe, that feared to have offended.
  So all was cleared, and to the field they haste.
But first, from under shady arborous roof
Soon as they forth were come to open sight
Of day-spring, and the Sun—who, scarce uprisen,
With wheels yet hovering o'er the ocean-brim,
Shot parallel to the Earth his dewy ray,
Discovering in wide landscape all the east
Of Paradise and Eden's happy plains—
Lowly they bowed, adoring, and began
Their orisons, each morning duly paid
In various style; for neither various style
Nor holy rapture wanted they to praise
Their Maker, in fit strains pronounced, or sung
Unmeditated; such prompt eloquence
Flowed from their lips, in prose or numerous verse,
More tuneable than needed lute or harp
To add more sweetness: and they thus began:—
  "These are thy glorious works, Parent of good,
Almighty! thine this universal frame,
Thus wondrous fair: thyself how wondrous then!
Unspeakable! who sitt'st above these heavens
To us invisible, or dimly seen
In these thy lowest works; yet these declare
Thy goodness beyond thought, and power divine
Speak, ye who best can tell, ye Sons of light,
Angels—for ye behold him, and with songs
And choral symphonies, day without night,

Circle his throne, rejoicing—ye in Heaven;
On Earth join, all ye creatures, to extol
Him first, him last, him midst, and without end.
Fairest of Stars, last in the train of night,
If better thou belong not to the dawn,
Sure pledge of day, that crown'st the smiling morn
With thy bright circlet, praise him in thy sphere
While day arises, that sweet hour of prime.
Thou Sun, of this great World both eye and soul,
Acknowledge him thy greater; sound his praise
In thy eternal course, both when thou climb'st,
And when high noon hast gained, and when thou fall'st.
Moon, that now meet'st the orient Sun, now fliest,
With the fixed Stars, fixed in their orb that flies;
And ye five other wandering Fires, that move
In mystic dance, not without song, resound
His praise who out of Darkness called up Light.
Air, and ye Elements, the eldest birth
Of Nature's womb, that in quaternion run
Perpetual circle, multiform, and mix
And nourish all things, let your ceaseless change
Vary to our great Maker still new praise.
Ye Mists and Exhalations, that now rise
From hill or steaming lake, dusky or grey,
Till the sun paint your fleecy skirts with gold,
In honour to the World's great Author rise;
Whether to deck with clouds the uncoloured sky,
Or wet the thirsty earth with falling showers,
Rising or falling, still advance his praise.
His praise, ye Winds, that from four quarters blow,
Breathe soft or loud; and wave your tops, ye Pines,
With every Plant, in sign of worship wave.
Fountains, and ye that warble, as ye flow,
Melodious murmurs, warbling tune his praise.
Join voices, all ye living Souls. Ye Birds,
That, singing, up to Heaven-gate ascend,
Bear on your wings and in your notes his praise.

Ye that in waters glide, and ye that walk
The earth, and stately tread, or lowly creep,
Witness if I be silent, morn or even,
To hill or valley, fountain, or fresh shade,
Made vocal by my song, and taught his praise.
Hail, universal Lord! Be bounteous still
To give us only good; and, if the night
Have gathered aught of evil, or concealed,
Disperse it, as now light dispels the dark."
  So prayed they innocent, and to their thoughts
Firm peace recovered soon, and wonted calm.
On to their morning's rural work they haste,
Among sweet dews and flowers, where any row
Of fruit-trees, over-woody, reached too far
Their pampered boughs, and needed hands to check
Fruitless embraces: or they led the vine
To wed her elm; she, spoused, about him twines
Her marriageable arms, and with her brings
Her dower, th' adopted clusters, to adorn
His barren leaves. Them thus employed beheld
With pity Heaven's high King, and to him called
Raphael, the sociable Spirit, that deigned
To travel with Tobias, and secured
His marriage with the seven-times-wedded maid.
  "Raphael," said he, "thou hear'st what stir on Earth
Satan, from Hell scaped through the darksome gulf,
Hath raised in Paradise, and how disturbed
This night the human pair; how he designs
In them at once to ruin all mankind.
Go, therefore; half this day, as friend with friend,
Converse with Adam, in what bower or shade
Thou find'st him from the heat of noon retired
To réspite his day-labour with repast
Or with repose; and such discourse bring on
As may advise him of his happy state—
Happiness in his power left free to will,
Left to his own free will, his will though free

Yet mutable. Whence warn him to beware
He swerve not, too secure: tell him withal
His danger, and from whom; what enemy,
Late fallen himself from Heaven, is plotting now
The fall of others from like state of bliss.
By violence? no, for that shall be withstood;
But by deceit and lies. This let him know,
Lest, wilfully transgressing, he pretend
Surprisal, unadmonished, unforewarned."
  So spake th' Eternal Father, and fulfilled
All justice. Nor delayed the wingèd Saint
After his charge received; but from among
Thousand celestial Ardours, where he stood
Veiled with his gorgeous wings, upspringing light,
Flew through the midst of Heaven. Th' angelic choirs,
On each hand parting, to his speed gave way
Through all th' empyreal road, till, at the gate,
Of Heaven arrived, the gate self-opened wide,
On golden hinges turning, as by work
Divine the sovereign Architect had framed.
From hence—no cloud or, to obstruct his sight,
Star interposed, however small—he sees,
Not unconform to other shining globes,
Earth, and the Garden of God, with cedars crowned
Above all hills; as when by night the glass
Of Galileo, less assured, observes
Imagined lands and regions in the Moon;
Or pilot from amidst the Cyclades
Delos or Samos first appearing kens,
A cloudy spot. Down thither prone in flight
He speeds, and through the vast ethereal sky
Sails between worlds and worlds, with steady wing
Now on the polar winds; then with quick fan
Winnows the buxom air, till, within soar
Of towering eagles, to all the fowls he seems
A phoenix, gazed by all, as that sole bird,
When, to enshrine his relics in the Sun's

Bright temple, to Egyptian Thebes he flies.
At once on th' eastern cliff of Paradise
He lights, and to his proper shape returns,
A Seraph winged. Six wings he wore, to shade
His lineaments divine: the pair that clad
Each shoulder broad came mantling o'er his breast
With regal ornament; the middle pair
Girt like a starry zone his waist, and round
Skirted his loins and thighs with downy gold
And colours dipped in heaven; the third his feet
Shadowed from either heel with feathered mail,
Sky-tinctured grain. Like Maia's son he stood,
And shook his plumes, that heavenly fragrance filled
The circuit wide. Straight knew him all the bands
Of Angels under watch, and to his state
And to his message high in honour rise;
For on some message high they guessed him bound.
Their glittering tents he passed, and now is come
Into the blissful field, through groves of myrrh,
And flowering odours, cassia, nard, and balm,
A wilderness of sweets; for Nature here
Wantoned as in her prime, and played at will
Her virgin fancies, pouring forth more sweet,
Wild above rule or art, enormous bliss.
Him, through the spicy forest onward come,
Adam discerned, as in the door he sat
Of his cool bower, while now the mounted Sun
Shot down direct his fervid rays, to warm
Earth's inmost womb, more warmth than Adam needs;
And Eve, within, due at her hour, prepared
For dinner savoury fruits, of taste to please
True appetite, and not disrelish thirst
Of nectarous draughts between, from milky stream,
Berry or grape: to whom thus Adam called:—
"Haste hither, Eve, and, worth thy sight, behold
Eastward among those trees what glorious Shape
Comes this way moving; seems another morn

Risen on mid-noon. Some great behest from Heaven
To us perhaps he brings, and will vouchsafe
This day to be our guest. But go with speed,
And what thy stores contain bring forth, and pour
Abundance fit to honour and receive
Our heavenly stranger; well we may afford
Our givers their own gifts, and large bestow
From large bestowed, where Nature multiplies
Her fertile growth, and by disburdening grows
More fruitful; which instructs us not to spare."
 To whom thus Eve—"Adam, Earth's hallowed mould,
Of God inspired, small store will serve where store,
All seasons, ripe for use hangs on the stalk;
Save what, by frugal storing, firmness gains
To nourish, and superfluous moist consumes.
But I will haste, and from each bough and brake,
Each plant and juiciest gourd, will pluck such choice
To entertain our Angel guest, as he
Beholding, shall confess that here on Earth
God hath dispensed his bounties as in Heaven."
 So saying, with dispatchful looks in haste
She turns, on hospitable thoughts intent
What choice to choose for delicacy best,
What order so contrived as not to mix
Tastes, not well joined, inelegant, but bring
Taste after taste upheld with kindliest change:
Bestirs her then, and from each tender stalk
Whatever Earth, all-bearing mother, yields
In India East or West, or middle shore
In Pontus or the Punic coast, or where
Alcinous reigned, fruit of all kinds, in coat
Rough or smooth rined, or bearded husk, or shell
She gathers, tribute large, and on the board
Heaps with unsparing hand. For drink the grape
She crushes, inoffensive must, and meaths
From many a berry, and from sweet kernels pressed
She tempers dulcet creams—nor these to hold

Wants her fit vessels pure; then strews the ground
With rose and odours from the shrub unfumed.
  Meanwhile our primitive great sire, to meet
His godlike guest, walks forth, without more train
Accompanied than with his own complete
Perfections; in himself was all his state,
More solemn than the tedious pomp that waits
On princes, when their rich retínue long
Of horses led and grooms besmeared with gold
Dazzles the crowd and sets them all agape.
Nearer his presence, Adam, though not awed,
Yet with submiss approach and reverence meek,
As to a superior nature, bowing low,
Thus said:—"Native of Heaven (for other place
None can than Heaven such glorious Shape contain),
Since, by descending from the Thrones above,
Those happy places thou hast deigned a while
To want, and honour these, vouchsafe with us,
Two only, who yet by sovereign gift possess
This spacious ground, in yonder shady bower
To rest, and what the Garden choicest bears
To sit and taste, till this meridian heat
Be over, and the sun more cool decline."
  Whom thus the angelic Virtue answered mild:—
"Adam, I therefore came; nor art thou such
Created, or such place hast here to dwell,
As may not oft invite, though Spirits of Heaven,
To visit thee. Lead on then, where thy bower
O'ershades; for these mid-hours, till evening rise,
I have at will." So to the sylvan lodge
They came, that like Pomona's arbour smiled,
With flowerets decked and fragrant smells. But Eve,
Undecked, save with herself, more lovely fair
Than wood-nymph, or the fairest goddess feigned
Of three that in Mount Ida naked strove,
Stood to entertain her guest from Heaven; no veil
She needed, virtue proof; no thought infirm

Altered her cheek. On whom the Angel "Hail!"
Bestowed—the holy salutation used
Long after to blest Mary, second Eve:—
"Hail! Mother of mankind, whose fruitful womb
Shall fill the world more numerous with thy sons
Than with these various fruits the trees of God
Have heaped this table!" Raised of grassy turf
Their table was, and mossy seats had round,
And on her ample square, from side to side,
All Autumn piled, though Spring and Autumn here
Danced hand-in-hand. A while discourse they hold—
No fear lest dinner cool—when thus began
Our author:—"Heavenly Stranger, please to taste
These bounties, which our Nourisher, from whom
All perfect good, unmeasured-out, descends,
To us for food and for delight hath caused
The Earth to yield: unsavoury food, perhaps,
To spiritual natures; only this I know,
That one Celestial Father gives to all."
To whom the Angel:—"Therefore, what he gives
(Whose praise be ever sung) to Man, in part
Spiritual, may of purest Spirits be found
No ingrateful food: and food alike those pure
Intelligential substances require
As doth your rational; and both contain
Within them every lower faculty
Of sense, whereby they hear, see, smell, touch, taste,
Tasting concoct, digest, assimilate,
And corporeal to incorporeal turn.
For know, whatever was created needs
To be sustained and fed. Of elements
The grosser feeds the purer: Earth the Sea;
Earth and the Sea feed Air; the Air those Fires
Ethereal, and, as lowest, first the Moon;
Whence in her visage round those spots, unpurged
Vapours not yet into her substance turned.
Nor doth the Moon no nourishment exhale

From her moist continent to higher orbs.
The Sun, that light imparts to all, receives
From all his alimental recompense
In humid exhalations, and at even
Sups with the Ocean. Though in Heaven the trees
Of life ambrosial fruitage bear, and vines
Yield nectar—though from off the boughs each morn
We brush mellifluous dews and find the ground
Covered with pearly grain—yet God hath here
Varied his bounty so with new delights
As may compare with Heaven; and to taste
Think not I shall be nice." So down they sat,
And to their viands fell; nor seemingly
The Angel, nor in mist—the common gloss
Of theologians—but with keen dispatch
Of real hunger, and concoctive heat
To transubstantiate: what redounds transpires
Through Spirits with ease; nor wonder, if by fire
Of sooty coal the empiric alchemist
Can turn, or holds it possible to turn,
Metals of drossiest ore to perfect gold,
As from the mine. Meanwhile at table Eve
Ministered naked, and their flowing cups
With pleasant liquors crowned. O innocence
Deserving Paradise! If ever, then,
Then had the Sons of God excuse to have been
Enamoured at that sight. But in those hearts
Love unlibidinous reigned, nor jealousy
Was understood, the injured lover's hell.
  Thus when with meats and drinks they had sufficed,
Not burdened nature, sudden mind arose
In Adam not to let th' occasion pass,
Given him by this great conference, to know
Of things above his World, and of their being
Who dwell in Heaven, whose excellence he saw
Transcend his own so far, whose radiant forms,
Divine effulgence, whose high power so far

Exceeded human; and this wary speech
Thus to th' empyreal minister he framed:—
"Inhabitant with God, now know I well
Thy favour, in his honour done to Man;
Under whose lowly roof thou hast vouchsafed
To enter, and these earthly fruits to taste,
Food not of Angels, yet accepted so
As that more willingly thou could'st not seem
At Heaven's high feasts to have fed: yet what compare!"
To whom the winged Hierarch replied:—
"O Adam, one Almighty is, from whom
All things proceed, and up to him return,
If not depraved from good, created all
Such to perfection; one first matter all,
Endued with various forms, various degrees
Of substance, and, in things that live, of life;
But more refined, more spirituous and pure,
As nearer to him placed or nearer tending
Each in their several active spheres assigned,
Till body up to spirit work, in bounds
Proportioned to each kind. So from the root
Springs lighter the green stalk, from thence the leaves
More airy, last the bright consummate flower
Spirits odorous breathes: flowers and their fruit,
Man's nourishment, by gradual scale sublimed,
To vital spirits aspire, to animal,
To intellectual; give both life and sense,
Fancy and understanding; whence the Soul
Reason receives, and Reason is her being,
Discursive, or intuitive: discourse
Is oftest yours, the latter most is ours,
Differing but in degree, of kind the same.
Wonder not, then, what God for you saw good
If I refuse not, but convert, as you,
To proper substance. Time may come when Men
With Angels may participate, and find
No inconvenient diet, nor too light fare;

And from these corporal nutriments, perhaps,
Your bodies may at last turn all to spirit,
Improved by tract of time, and winged ascend
Ethereal, as we, or may at choice
Here or in heavenly paradises dwell,
If ye be found obedient, and retain
Unalterably firm his love entire
Whose progeny you are. Meanwhile enjoy
Your fill, what happiness this happy state
Can comprehend, incapable of more."
  To whom the Patriarch of Mankind replied:—
"O favourable Spirit, propitious guest,
Well hast thou taught the way that might direct
Our knowledge, and the scale of Nature set
From centre to circumference, whereon,
In contemplation of created things,
By steps we may ascend to God. But say,
What meant that caution joined, *If ye be found*
Obedient? Can we want obedience, then,
To him, or possibly his love desert,
Who formed us from the dust, and placed us here
Full to the utmost measure of what bliss
Human desires can seek or apprehend?"
  To whom the Angel:—"Son of Heaven and Earth,
Attend! That thou art happy, owe to God;
That thou continuest such, owe to thyself,
That is, to thy obedience; therein stand.
This was that caution given thee; be advised.
God made thee perfect, not immutable;
And good he made thee; but to persevere
He left it in thy power—ordained thy will
By nature free, not over-ruled by fate
Inextricable, or strict necessity.
Our voluntary service he requires,
Not our necessitated. Such with him
Finds no acceptance, nor can find; for how
Can hearts not free be tried whether they serve

Willing or no, who will but what they must
By destiny, and can no other choose?
Myself, and all th' angelic host, that stand
In sight of God enthroned, our happy state
Hold, as you yours, while our obedience holds.
On other surety none: freely we serve,
Because we freely love, as in our will
To love or not; in this we stand or fall.
And some are fallen, to disobedience fallen,
And so from Heaven to deepest Hell. O fall
From what high state of bliss into what woe!"
  To whom our great progenitor:—"Thy words
Attentive, and with more delighted ear,
Divine instructor, I have heard, than when
Cherubic songs by night from neighbouring hills
Aërial music send. Nor knew I not
To be, both will and deed, created free.
Yet that we never shall forget to love
Our Maker, and obey him whose command
Single is yet so just, my constant thoughts
Assured me, and still assure; though what thou tell'st
Hath passed in Heaven some doubt within me move,
But more desire to hear, if thou consent,
The full relation, which must needs be strange,
Worthy of sacred silence to be heard.
And we have yet large day, for scarce the Sun
Hath finished half his journey, and scarce begins
His other half in the great zone of heaven."
  Thus Adam made request; and Raphael,
After short pause assenting, thus began:—
  "High matter thou enjoin'st me, O prime of Men—
Sad task and hard; for how shall I relate
To human sense th' invisible exploits
Of warring Spirits? how, without remorse,
The ruin of so many, glorious once
And perfect while they stood? how, last, unfold
The secrets of another world, perhaps

Not lawful to reveal? Yet for thy good
This is dispensed; and what surmounts the reach
Of human sense I shall delineate so,
By likening spiritual to corporal forms,
As may express them best—though what if Earth
Be but the shadow of Heaven, and things therein
Each to other like, more than on Earth is thought?
"As yet this World was not, and Chaos wild
Reigned where these heavens now roll, where Earth now rests
Upon her centre poised, when on a day
(For Time, though in Eternity, applied
To motion, measures all things durable
By present, past, and future), on such day
As Heaven's great year brings forth, th' empyreal host
Of Angels, by imperial summons called,
Innumerable before th' Almighty's throne
Forthwith from all the ends of Heaven appeared
Under their Hierarchs in Orders bright.
Ten thousand thousand ensigns high advanced,
Standards and gonfalons, 'twixt van and rear
Stream in the air, and for distinction serve
Of hierarchies, of orders, and degrees;
Or in their glittering tissues bear emblazed
Holy memorials, acts of zeal and love
Recorded eminent. Thus when in orbs
Or circuit inexpressible they stood,
Orb within orb, the Father Infinite,
By whom in bliss embosomed sat the Son,
Amidst, as from a flaming mount, whose top
Brightness had made invisible, thus spake:—
" 'Hear, all ye Angels, Progeny of Light,
Thrones, Dominations, Princedoms, Virtues, Powers,
Hear my decree, which unrevoked shall stand!
This day I have begot whom I declare
My only Son, and on this holy hill
Him have anointed, whom ye now behold
At my right hand. Your head I him appoint,

And by myself have sworn to him shall bow
All knees in Heaven, and shall confess him Lord.
Under his great vicegerent reign abide,
United as one individual soul,
For ever happy. Him who disobeys
Me disobeys, breaks union, and, that day,
Cast out from God and blessèd vision, falls
Into utter darkness, deep ingulfed, his place
Ordained without redemption, without end.'
"So spake th' Omnipotent, and with his words
All seemed well pleased; all seemed, but were not all.
That day, as other solemn days, they spent
In song and dance about the sacred hill—
Mystical dance, which yonder starry sphere
Of planets, and of fixed, in all her wheels
Resembles nearest; mazes intricate,
Eccentric, intervolved, yet regular
Then most when most irregular they seem;
And in their motions harmony divine
So smooths her charming tones that God's own ear
Listens delighted. Evening now approached
(For we have also our evening and our morn—
We ours for change delectable, not need),
Forthwith from dance to sweet repast they turn
Desirous: all in circles as they stood,
Tables are set, and on a sudden piled
With Angels' food; and rubied nectar flows
In pearl, in diamond, and massy gold,
Fruit of delicious vines, the growth of Heaven.
On flowers reposed, and with fresh flowerets crowned,
They eat, they drink, and in communion sweet
Quaff immortality and joy, secure
Of surfeit where full measure only bounds
Excess, before th' all-bounteous King, who showered
With copious hand, rejoicing in their joy.
Now when ambrosial Night, with clouds exhaled
From that high mount of God, whence light and shade

Spring both, the face of brightest Heaven had changed
To grateful twilight (for Night comes not there
In darker veil), and roseate dews disposed
All but the unsleeping eyes of God to rest,
Wide over all the plain, and wider far
Than all this globous Earth in plain outspread
(Such are the courts of God), th' angelic throng,
Dispersed in bands and files, their camp extend
By living streams among the trees of life—
Pavilions numberless and sudden reared,
Celestial tabernacles, where they slept,
Fanned with cool winds; save those who, in their course,
Melodious hymns about the sovereign throne
Alternate all night long. But not so waked
Satan—so call him now; his former name
Is heard no more in Heaven. He, of the first,
If not the first Archangel, great in power,
In favour, and pre-eminence, yet fraught
With envy against the Son of God, that day
Honoured by his great Father, and proclaimed
Messiah, King Anointed, could not bear,
Through pride, that sight, and thought himself impaired.
Deep malice thence conceiving and disdain,
Soon as midnight brought on the dusky hour
Friendliest to sleep and silence, he resolved
With all his legions to dislodge, and leave
Unworshipped, unobeyed, the Throne supreme,
Contemptuous, and, his next subordinate
Awakening, thus to him in secret spake:—
"'Sleep'st thou, companion dear? what sleep can close
Thy eyelids? and rememb'rest what decree,
Of yesterday, so late hath passed the lips
Of Heaven's Almighty? Thou to me thy thoughts
Wast wont, I mine to thee was wont to impart;
Both waking we were one; how then can now
Thy sleep dissent? New laws thou seest imposed;
New laws from him who reigns new minds may raise

In us who serve—new counsels, to debate
What doubtful may ensue. More in this place
To utter is not safe. Assemble thou
Of all those myriads which we lead the chief;
Tell them that, by command, ere yet dim Night
Her shadowy cloud withdraws, I am to haste,
And all who under me their banners wave,
Homeward with flying march where we possess
The quarters of the North, there to prepare
Fit entertainment to receive our King,
The great Messiah, and his new commands,
Who speedily through all the Hierarchies
Intends to pass triumphant, and give laws.'
"So spake the false Archangel, and infused
Bad influence into th' unwary breast
Of his associate. He together calls,
Or several one by one, the regent Powers,
Under him regent; tells, as he was taught,
That, the Most High commanding, now ere Night,
Now ere dim Night had disencumbered Heaven,
The great hierarchal standard was to move;
Tells the suggested cause, and casts between
Ambiguous words and jealousies, to sound
Or taint integrity. But all obeyed
The wonted signal, and superior voice
Of their great Potentate; for great indeed
His name, and high was his degree in Heaven:
His countenance, as the morning-star that guides
The starry flock, allured them, and with lies
Drew after him the third part of Heaven's host.
Meanwhile, th' Eternal Eye, whose sight discerns
Abstrusest thoughts, from forth his holy Mount,
And from within the golden lamps that burn
Nightly before him, saw without their light
Rebellion rising—saw in whom, how spread
Among the Sons of Morn, what multitudes
Were banded to oppose his high decree;

And, smiling, to his only Son thus said:—
" 'Son, thou in whom my glory I behold
In full resplendence, Heir of all my might,
Nearly it now concerns us to be sure
Of our omnipotence, and with what arms
We mean to hold what anciently we claim
Of deity or empire: such a foe
Is rising, who intends to erect his throne
Equal to ours, throughout the spacious North;
Nor so content, hath in his thought to try
In battle what our power is or our right.
Let us advise, and to this hazard draw
With speed what force is left, and all employ
In our defence, lest unawares we lose
This our high place, our sanctuary, our hill.'
"To whom the Son, with calm aspect and clear
Lightening divine, ineffable, serene,
Made answer:— 'Mighty Father, thou thy foes
Justly hast in derision, and secure
Laugh'st at their vain designs and tumults vain—
Matter to me of glory, whom their hate
Illustrates, when they see all regal power
Given me to quell their pride, and in event
Know whether I be dextrous to subdue
Thy rebels, or be found the worst in Heaven.'
"So spake the Son; but Satan with his Powers
Far was advanced on wingèd speed, an host
Innumerable as the stars of night,
Or stars of morning, dew-drops which the sun
Impearls on every leaf and every flower.
Regions they passed, the mighty regencies
Of Seraphim and Potentates and Thrones
In their triple degrees—regions to which
All thy dominion, Adam, is no more
Than what this garden is to all the earth
And all the sea, from one entire globose
Stretched into longitude; which having passed,

At length into the limits of the North
They came, and Satan to his royal seat
High on a hill, far blazing, as a mount
Raised on a mount, with pyramids and towers
From diamond quarries hewn and rocks of gold—
The palace of great Lucifer (so call
That structure, in the dialect of men
Interpreted) which, not long after, he,
Affecting all equality with God,
In imitation of that mount whereon
Messiah was declared in sight of Heaven,
The Mountain of the Congregation called;
For thither he assembled all his train,
Pretending so commanded to consult
About the great reception of their King
Thither to come, and with calumnious art
Of counterfeited truth thus held their ears:—
" 'Thrones, Dominations, Princedoms, Virtues, Powers—
If these magnific titles yet remain
Not merely titular, since by decree
Another now hath to himself engrossed
All power, and us eclipsed under the name
Of King Anointed; for whom all this haste
Of midnight march, and hurried meeting here,
This only to consult, how we may best,
With what may be devised of honours new,
Receive him coming to receive from us
Knee-tribute yet unpaid, prostration vile!
Too much to one! but double, how endured—
To one and to his image now proclaimed?
But what if better counsels might erect
Our minds, and teach us to cast off this yoke?
Will ye submit your necks, and choose to bend
The supple knee? Ye will not, if I trust
To know ye right, or if ye know yourselves
Natives and Sons of Heaven possessed before
By none, and, if not equal all, yet free,

Equally free; for orders and degrees
Jar not with liberty, but well consist.
Who can in reason, then, or right, assume
Monarchy over such as live by right
His equals—if in power and splendour less,
In freedom equal? or can introduce
Law and edict on us, who without law
Err not? much less for this to be our Lord,
And look for adoration, to th' abuse
Of those imperial titles which assert
Our being ordained to govern, not to serve!'
"Thus far his bold discourse without control
Had audience, when, among the Seraphim,
Abdiel, than whom none with more zeal adored
The Deity, and divine commands obeyed,
Stood up, and in a flame of zeal severe
The current of his fury thus opposed:—
"'O argument blasphémous, false, and proud—
Words which no ear ever to hear in Heaven
Expected; least of all from thee, ingrate,
In place thyself so high above thy peers!
Canst thou with impious obloquy condemn
The just decree of God, pronounced and sworn,
That to his only Son, by right endued
With regal sceptre, every soul in Heaven
Shall bend the knee, and in that honour due
Confess him rightful King? Unjust, thou say'st,
Flatly unjust, to bind with laws the free,
And equal over equals to let reign,
One over all with unsucceeded power!
Shalt thou give law to God? shalt thou dispute
With him the points of liberty, who made
Thee what thou art, and formed the Powers of Heaven
Such as he pleased, and circumscribed their being?
Yet, by experience taught, we know how good,
And of our good and of our dignity
How provident, he is—how far from thought

To make us less; bent rather to exalt
Our happy state, under one head more near
United. But—to grant it thee unjust
That equal over equals monarch reign—
Thyself, though great and glorious, dost thou count,
Or all angelic nature joined in one,
Equal to him, begotten Son, by whom,
As by his Word, the mighty Father made
All things, even thee, and all the Spirits of Heaven
By him created in their bright degrees,
Crowned them with glory and to their glory named
Thrones, Dominations, Princedoms, Virtues, Powers?—
Essential Powers; nor by his reign obscured,
But more illustrious made since he, the head,
One of our number thus reduced becomes;
His laws our laws; all honour to him done
Returns our own. Cease, then, this impious rage,
And tempt not these; but hasten to appease
Th' incensèd Father and th' incensèd Son
While pardon may be found, in time besought.'
"So spake the fervent Angel; but his zeal
None seconded, as out of season judged,
Or singular and rash. Whereat rejoiced
Th' Apostate, and, more haughty, thus replied:—
" 'That we were formed, then, say'st thou? and the work
Of secondary hands, by task transferred
From Father to his Son? Strange point and new!
Doctrine which we would know whence learned! Who saw
When this creation was? Remember'st thou
Thy making, while the Maker gave thee being?
We know no time when we were not as now;
Know none before us, self-begot, self-raised
By our own quickening power when fatal course
Had circled his full orb, the birth mature
Of this our native Heaven, ethereal Sons.
Our puissance is our own; our own right hand
Shall teach us highest deeds, by proof to try

Who is our equal. Then thou shalt behold
Whether by supplication we intend
Address, and to begirt th' Almighty Throne
Beseeching or besieging. This report,
These tidings, carry to th' Anointed King;
And fly, ere evil intercept thy flight.'
"He said; and, as the sound of waters deep,
Hoarse murmur echoed to his words applause
Through the infinite host. Nor less for that
The flaming Seraph, fearless, though alone,
Encompassed round with foes, thus answered bold:–
" 'O alienate from God, O Spirit accursed,
Forsaken of all good! I see thy fall
Determined, and thy hapless crew involved
In this perfidious fraud, contagion spread
Both of thy crime and punishment. Henceforth
No more be troubled how to quit the yoke
Of God's Messiah. Those indulgent laws
Will not be now vouchsafed; other decrees
Against thee are gone forth without recall;
That golden sceptre which thou didst reject
Is now an iron rod to bruise and break
Thy disobedience. Well thou didst advise;
Yet not for thy advice or threats I fly
These wicked tents devoted, lest the wrath
Impendent, raging into sudden flame,
Distinguish not: for soon expect to feel
His thunder on thy head, devouring fire.
Then who created thee lamenting learn,
When who can uncreate thee thou shalt know.'
"So spake the Seraph Abdiel, faithful found;
Among the faithless faithful only he;
Among innumerable false unmoved,
Unshaken, unseduced, unterrified,
His loyalty he kept, his love, his zeal;
Nor number nor example with him wrought
To swerve from truth, or change his constant mind,

Though single. From amidst them forth he passed,
Long way through hostile scorn, which he sustained
Superior, nor of violence feared aught;
And with retorted scorn his back he turned
On those proud towers, to swift destruction doomed."

THE END OF THE FIFTH BOOK

BOOK VI

THE ARGUMENT

Raphael continues to relate how Michael and Gabriel were sent forth to battle against Satan and his Angels. The first fight described: Satan and his Powers retire under night. He calls a council; invents devilish engines, which, in the second day's fight, put Michael and his Angels to some disorder; but they at length, pulling up mountains, overwhelmed both the force and machines of Satan. Yet, the tumult not so ending, God, on the third day, sends Messiah his Son, for whom he had reserved the glory of that victory. He, in the power of his Father, coming to the place, and causing all his legions to stand still on either side, with his chariot and thunder driving into the midst of his enemies, pursues them, unable to resist, towards the wall of Heaven; which opening, they leap down with horror and confusion into the place of punishment prepared for them in the Deep. Messiah returns with triumph to his Father.

"All night the dreadless Angel, unpursued,
Through Heaven's wide champaign held his way, till Morn,
Waked by the circling Hours, with rosy hand
Unbarred the gates of Light. There is a cave
Within the Mount of God, fast by his throne,
Where Light and Darkness in perpetual round
Lodge and dislodge by turns—which makes through Heaven
Grateful vicissitude, like day and night;
Light issues forth, and at the other door
Obsequious Darkness enters, till her hour
To veil the heaven, though darkness there might well
Seem twilight here. And now went forth the Morn
Such as in highest heaven, arrayed in gold
Empyreal; from before her vanished Night,
Shot through with orient beams; when all the plain
Covered with thick embattled squadrons bright,
Chariots, and flaming arms, and fiery steeds,

Reflecting blaze on blaze, first met his view.
War he perceived, war in procinct, and found
Already known what he for news had thought
To have reported. Gladly then he mixed
Among those friendly Powers, who him received
With joy and acclamations loud, that one,
That of so many myriads fallen yet one,
Returned not lost. On to the sacred hill
They led him, high applauded, and present
Before the seat supreme; from whence a voice,
From midst a golden cloud, thus mild was heard:—
"'Servant of God, well done! Well hast thou fought
The better fight, who single hast maintained
Against revolted multitudes the cause
Of truth, in word mightier than they in arms,
And for the testimony of truth hast borne
Universal reproach, far worse to bear
Than violence; for this was all thy care—
To stand approved in sight of God, though worlds
Judged thee perverse. The easier conquest now
Remains thee—aided by this host of friends,
Back on thy foes more glorious to return
Than scorned thou didst depart; and to subdue
By force who reason for their law refuse—
Right reason for their law, and for their King
Messiah, who by right of merit reigns.
Go, Michael, of celestial armies prince,
And thou, in military prowess next,
Gabriel; lead forth to battle these my sons
Invincible; lead forth my armèd Saints,
By thousands and by millions ranged for fight,
Equal in number to that godless crew
Rebellious. Them with fire and hostile arms
Fearless assault; and, to the brow of Heaven
Pursuing, drive them out from God and bliss
Into their place of punishment, the gulf
Of Tartarus, which ready opens wide

His fiery chaos to receive their fall.'
"So spake the sovereign voice; and clouds began
To darken all the hill, and smoke to roll
In dusky wreaths reluctant flames, the sign
Of wrath awaked; nor with less dread the loud
Ethereal trumpet from on high gan blow.
At which command the Powers militant
That stood for Heaven, in mighty quadrate joined
Of union irresistible, moved on
In silence their bright legions to the sound
Of instrumental harmony, that breathed
Heroic ardour to adventurous deeds
Under their godlike leaders, in the cause
Of God and his Messiah. On they move,
Indissolubly firm; nor obvious hill,
Nor straitening vale, nor wood, nor stream, divides
Their perfect ranks; for high above the ground
Their march was, and the passive air upbore
Their nimble tread. As when the total kind
Of birds, in orderly array on wing,
Came summoned over Eden to receive
Their names of thee; so over many a tract
Of Heaven they marched, and many a province wide,
Tenfold the length of this terrene. At last,
Far in th' horizon, to the north, appeared
From skirt to skirt a fiery region, stretched
In battailous aspéct; and, nearer view,
Bristled with upright beams innumerable
Of rigid spears, and helmets thronged, and shields
Various, with boastful argument portrayed,
The banded Powers of Satan hasting on
With furious expedition; for they weened
That self-same day, by fight or by surprise,
To win the Mount of God, and on his throne
To set the envier of his state, the proud
Aspirer. But their thoughts proved fond and vain
In the mid-way; though strange to us it seemed

At first that Angel should with Angel war,
And in fierce hosting meet, who wont to meet
So oft in festivals of joy and love
Unanimous, as sons of one great Sire,
Hymning th' Eternal Father. But the shout
Of battle now began, and rushing sound
Of onset ended soon each milder thought.
High in the midst, exalted as a God,
Th' Apostate in his sun-bright chariot sat,
Idol of majesty divine, enclosed
With flaming Cherubim and golden shields;
Then lighted from his gorgeous throne—for now
'Twixt host and host but narrow space was left,
A dreadful interval, and front to front
Presented stood, in terrible array
Of hideous length. Before the cloudy van,
On the rough edge of battle ere it joined,
Satan, with vast and haughty strides advanced,
Came towering, armed in adamant and gold.
Abdiel that sight endured not, where he stood
Among the mightiest, bent on highest deeds,
And thus his own undaunted heart explores:—
" 'O Heaven! that such resemblance of the Highest
Should yet remain, where faith and realty
Remain not! Wherefore should not strength and might
There fail where virtue fails, or weakest prove
Where boldest, though to sight unconquerable?
His puissance, trusting in th' Almighty's aid,
I mean to try, whose reason I have tried
Unsound and false; nor is it aught but just
That he who in debate of truth hath won
Should win in arms, in both disputes alike
Victor. Though brutish that contést and foul,
When reason hath to deal with force, yet so
Most reason is that reason overcome.'
" So pondering, and from his armèd peers
Forth-stepping opposite, half-way he met

His daring foe, at this prevention more
Incensed, and thus securely him defied:—
"'Proud, art thou met? Thy hope was to have reached
The height of thy aspiring unopposed—
The throne of God unguarded, and his side
Abandoned at the terror of thy power
Or potent tongue. Fool! not to think how vain
Against th' Omnipotent to rise in arms;
Who, out of smallest things, could without end
Have raised incessant armies to defeat
Thy folly; or with solitary hand,
Reaching beyond all limit, at one blow,
Unaided could have finished thee, and whelmed
Thy legions under darkness! But thou seest
All are not of thy train; there be who faith
Prefer, and piety to God, though then
To thee not visible when I alone
Seemed in thy world erroneous to dissent
From all: my sect thou seest; now learn too late
How few sometimes may know when thousands err.'
"Whom the grand Foe, with scornful eye askance,
Thus answered:—'Ill for thee, but in wished hour
Of my revenge, first sought for, thou return'st
From flight, seditious Angel, to receive
Thy merited reward, the first assay
Of this right hand provoked, since first that tongue,
Inspired with contradiction, durst oppose
A third part of the gods, in synod met
Their deities to assert: who, while they feel
Vigour divine within them, can allow
Omnipotence to none. But well thou com'st
Before thy fellows, ambitious to win
From me some plume, that thy success may show
Destruction to the rest. This pause between
(Unanswered lest thou boast) to let thee know.—
At first I thought that liberty and Heaven
To heavenly souls had been all one; but now

I see that most through sloth had rather serve,
Ministering Spirits, trained up in feast and song:
Such hast thou armed, the ministrelsy of heaven—
Servility with freedom to contend,
As both their deeds compared this day shall prove.'
"To whom, in brief, thus Abdiel stern replied:—
'Apostate! still thou err'st, nor end wilt find
Of erring, from the path of truth remote.
Unjustly thou deprav'st it with the name
Of servitude, to serve whom God ordains,
Or Nature: God and Nature bid the same,
When he who rules is worthiest, and excels
Them whom he governs. This is servitude—
To serve th' unwise, or him who hath rebelled
Against his worthier, as thine now serve thee,
Thyself not free, but to thyself enthralled;
Yet lewdly dar'st our ministering upbraid.
Reign thou in Hell, thy kingdom; let me serve
In Heaven God ever blest, and his divine
Behests obey, worthiest to be obeyed.
Yet chains in Hell, not realms, expect: meanwhile,
From me returned, as erst thou saidst, from flight,
This greeting on thy impious crest receive.'
"So saying, a noble stroke he lifted high,
Which hung not, but so swift with tempest fell
On the proud crest of Satan that no sight,
Nor motion of swift thought, less could his shield,
Such ruin intercept. Ten paces huge
He back recoiled; the tenth on bended knee
His massy spear upstayed: as if, on earth,
Winds under ground, or waters forcing way,
Sidelong had pushed a mountain from his seat,
Half-sunk with all his pines. Amazement seized
The rebel Thrones, but greater rage, to see
Thus foiled their mightiest; ours joy filled, and shout,
Presage of victory, and fierce desire
Of battle: whereat Michaël bid sound

Th' Archangel trumpet. Through the vast of Heaven
It sounded, and the faithful armies rung
Hosanna to the Highest; nor stood at gaze
The adverse legions, nor less hideous joined
The horrid shock. Now storming fury rose,
And clamour such as heard in Heaven till now
Was never; arms on armour clashing brayed
Horrible discord, and the madding wheels
Of brazen chariots raged; dire was the noise
Of conflict; overhead the dismal hiss
Of fiery darts in flaming volleys flew,
And, flying, vaulted either host with fire.
So under fiery cope together rushed
Both battles main with ruinous assault
And inextinguishable rage. All Heaven
Resounded; and, had Earth been then, all Earth
Had to her centre shook. What wonder, when
Millions of fierce encountering Angels fought
On either side, the least of whom could wield
These elements, and arm him with the force
Of all their regions? How much more of power
Army against army numberless to raise
Dreadful combustion warring, and disturb,
Though not destroy, their happy native seat;
Had not th' Eternal King Omnipotent
From his strong hold of Heaven high overruled
And limited their might, though numbered such
As each divided legion might have seemed
A numerous host, in strength each armed hand
A legion; led in fight, yet leader seemed
Each warrior single as in chief; expert
When to advance, or stand, or turn the sway
Of battle, open when, and when to close
The ridges of grim war. No thought of flight,
None of retreat, no unbecoming deed
That argued fear; each on himself relied
As only in his arm the moment lay

Of victory. Deeds of eternal fame
Were done, but infinite; for wide was spread
That war, and various: sometimes on firm ground
A standing fight; then, soaring on main wing,
Tormented all the air; all air seemed then
Conflicting fire. Long time in even scale
The battle hung; till Satan, who that day
Prodigious power had shown, and met in arms
No equal, ranging through the dire attack
Of fighting Seraphim confused, at length
Saw where the sword of Michael smote, and felled
Squadrons at once: with huge two-handed sway
Brandished aloft, the horrid edge came down
Wide-wasting. Such destruction to withstand
He hasted, and opposed the rocky orb
Of tenfold adamant, his ample shield,
A vast circumference. At his approach
The great Archangel from his warlike toil
Surceased, and, glad, as hoping here to end
Intestine war in Heaven, the Arch-foe subdued,
Or captive dragged in chains, with hostile frown
And visage all inflamed, first thus began:—
"'Author of evil, unknown till thy revolt,
Unnamed in Heaven, now plenteous as thou seest
These acts of hateful strife—hateful to all,
Though heaviest, by just measure, on thyself
And thy adherents—how hast thou disturbed
Heaven's blessed peace, and into Nature brought
Misery, uncreated till the crime
Of thy rebellion! how hast thou instilled
Thy malice into thousands, once upright
And faithful, now proved false! But think not here
To trouble holy rest; Heaven casts thee out
From all her confines; Heaven, the seat of bliss,
Brooks not the works of violence and war.
Hence, then, and Evil go with thee along,
Thy offspring, to the place of evil, Hell—

Thou and thy wicked crew! there mingle broils!
Ere this avenging sword begin thy doom,
Or some more sudden vengeance, winged from God,
Precipitate thee with augmented pain.'
"So spake the Prince of Angels; to whom thus
The Adversary:— 'Nor think thou with wind
Of airy threats to awe whom yet with deeds
Thou canst not. Hast thou turned the least of these
To flight—or, if to fall, but that they rise
Unvanquished—easier to transact with me
That thou shouldst hope, imperious, and with threats
To chase me hence? Err not that so shall end
The strife which thou call'st evil, but we style
The strife of glory; which we mean to win,
Or turn this Heaven itself into the Hell
Thou fablest; here, however, to dwell free,
If not to reign. Meanwhile, thy utmost force—
And join him named Almighty to thy aid—
I fly not, but have sought thee far and nigh.'
"They ended parle, and both addressed for fight
Unspeakable; for who, though with the tongue
Of Angels, can relate, or to what things
Liken on Earth conspicuous, that may lift
Human imagination to such height
Of godlike power? for likest gods they seemed,
Stood they or moved, in stature, motion, arms,
Fit to decide the empire of great Heaven.
Now waved their fiery swords, and in the air
Made horrid circles; two broad suns their shields
Blazed opposite, while Expectation stood
In horror; from each hand with speed retired,
Where erst was thickest fight, th' angelic throng,
And left large field, unsafe within the wind
Of such commotion: such as (to set forth
Great things by small) if, Nature's concord broke,
Among the constellations war were sprung,
Two planets, rushing from aspéct malign

Of fiercest opposition in mid sky,
Should combat, and their jarring spheres confound.
Together both, with next to almighty arm
Uplifted imminent, one stroke they aimed
That might determine, and not need repeat
As not of power, at once; nor odds appeared
In might or swift prevention. But the sword
Of Michael from the armoury of God
Was given him tempered so, that neither keen
Nor solid might resist that edge: it met
The sword of Satan, with steep force to smite
Descending, and in half cut sheer; nor stayed,
But, with swift wheel reverse, deep entering, shared
All his right side. Then Satan first knew pain,
And writhed him to and fro convolved; so sore
The griding sword with discontinuous wound
Passed through him. But th' ethereal substance closed,
Not long divisible; and from the gash
A stream of nectarous humour issuing flowed
Sanguine, such as celestial Spirits may bleed,
And all his armour stained, erewhile so bright.
Forthwith, on all sides, to his aid was run
By Angels many and strong, who interposed
Defence, while others bore him on their shields
Back to his chariot where it stood retired
From off the files of war: there they him laid
Gnashing for anguish, and despite, and shame
To find himself not matchless, and his pride
Humbled by such rebuke, so far beneath
His confidence to equal God in power.
Yet soon he healed; for Spirits, that live throughout
Vital in every part—not, as frail Man,
In entrails, heart or head, liver or reins—
Cannot but by annihilating die;
Nor in their liquid texture mortal wound
Receive, no more than can the fluid air:
All heart they live, all head, all eye, all ear,

All intellect, all sense; and as they please
They limb themselves, and colour, shape, or size
Assume, as likes them best, condense or rare.
"Meanwhile, in other parts, like deeds deserved
Memorial, where the might of Gabriel fought,
And with fierce ensigns pierced the deep array
Of Moloch, furious king, who him defied,
And at his chariot-wheels to drag him bound
Threatened, nor from the Holy One of Heaven
Refrained his tongue blasphémous, but anon,
Down cloven to the waist, with shattered arms
And uncouth pain fled bellowing. On each wing
Uriel and Raphaël his vaunting foe,
Though huge and in a rock of diamond armed,
Vanquished Adramelech and Asmadai,
Two potent Thrones, that to be less than Gods
Disdained, but meaner thoughts learned in their flight,
Mangled with ghastly wounds through plate and mail.
Nor stood unmindful Abdiel to annoy
The atheist crew, but with redoubled blow
Ariel, and Arioch, and the violence
Of Ramiel, scorched and blasted, overthrew.
I might relate of thousands, and their names
Eternize here on Earth; but those elect
Angels, contented with their fame in Heaven,
Seek not the praise of men: the other sort,
In might though wondrous and in acts of war,
Nor of renown less eager, yet by doom
Cancelled from Heaven and sacred memory,
Nameless in dark oblivion let them dwell.
For strength from truth divided, and from just,
Illaudable, nought merits but dispraise
And ignominy, yet to glory aspires,
Vain-glorious, and through infamy seeks fame:
Therefore eternal silence be their doom.
"And now, their mightiest quelled, the battle swerved,
With many an inroad gored; deformèd rout

Entered, and foul disorder; all the ground
With shivered armour strewn, and on a heap
Chariot and charioteer lay overturned,
And fiery foaming steeds; what stood recoiled,
O'er-wearied, through the faint Satanic host,
Defensive scarce, or with pale fear surprised—
Then first with fear surprised and sense of pain—
Fled ignominious, to such evil brought
By sin of disobedience, till that hour
Not liable to fear, or flight, or pain.
Far otherwise th' inviolable Saints
In cubic phalanx firm advanced entire,
Invulnerable, impenetrably armed;
Such high advantages their innocence
Gave them above their foes—not to have sinned,
Not to have disobeyed; in fight they stood
Unwearied, unobnoxious to be pained
By wound, though from their place by violence moved.
"Now Night her course began, and, over Heaven
Inducing darkness, grateful truce imposed,
And silence on the odious din of war.
Under her cloudy covert both retired,
Victor and vanquished. On the foughten field
Michaël and his Angels, prevalent
Encamping, placed in guard their watches round,
Cherubic waving fires: on th' other part,
Satan with his rebellious disappeared,
Far in the dark dislodged, and, void of rest,
His potentates to council called by night,
And in the midst thus undismayed began:—
"'O now in danger tried, now known in arms
Not to be overpowered, companions dear,
Found worthy not of liberty alone—
Too mean pretence—but, what we more affect,
Honour, dominion, glory, and renown;
Who have sustained one day in doubtful fight
(And, if one day, why not eternal days?)

What Heaven's Lord had powerfullest to send
Against us from about his throne, and judged
Sufficient to subdue us to his will,
But proves not so: then fallible, it seems,
Of future we may deem him, though till now
Omniscient thought! True is, less firmly armed,
Some disadvantage we endured, and pain—
Till now not known, but, known, as soon contemned;
Since now we find this our empyreal form
Incapable of mortal injury,
Imperishable, and, though pierced with wound,
Soon closing, and by native vigour healed.
Of evil, then, so small, as easy think
The remedy: perhaps more valid arms,
Weapons more violent, when next we meet
May serve to better us and worse our foes,
Or equal what between us made the odds,
In nature none. If other hidden cause
Left them superior, while we can preserve
Unhurt our minds, and understanding sound,
Due search and consultation will disclose.'
"He sat; and in th' assembly next upstood
Nisroch, of Principalities the prime.
As one he stood escaped from cruel fight
Sore toiled, his riven arms to havoc hewn,
And, cloudy in aspéct, thus answering spake:—
"'Deliverer from new Lords, leader to free
Enjoyment of our rights as Gods! yet hard
For Gods, and too unequal work, we find
Against unequal arms to fight in pain,
Against unpained, impassive; from which evil
Ruin must needs ensue. For what avails
Valour or strength, though matchless, quelled with pain,
Which all subdues, and makes remiss the hands
Of mightiest? Sense of pleasure we may well
Spare out of life perhaps, and not repine,
But live content—which is the calmest life;

But pain is perfect misery, the worst
Of evils, and, excessive, overturns
All patience. He who, therefore, can invent
With what more forcible we may offend
Our yet unwounded enemies, or arm
Ourselves with like defence, to me deserves
No less than for deliverance what we owe.'
"Whereto, with look composed, Satan replied:—
'Not uninvented that, which thou aright
Believ'st so main to our success, I bring.
Which of us who beholds the bright surfáce
Of this ethereous mould whereon we stand—
This continent of spacious Heaven, adorned
With plant, fruit, flower ambrosial, gems and gold—
Whose eye so superficially surveys
These things as not to mind from whence they grow
Deep under ground: materials dark and crude,
Of spirituous and fiery spume, till, touched
With Heaven's ray, and tempered, they shoot forth
So beauteous, opening to the ambient light?
These in their dark nativity the Deep
Shall yield us, pregnant with infernal flame;
Which, into hollow engines long and round
Thick-rammed, at th' other bore with touch of fire
Dilated and infuriate, shall send forth
From far, with thundering noise, among our foes
Such implements of mischief as shall dash
To pieces and o'erwhelm whatever stands
Adverse, that they shall fear we have disarmed
The Thunderer of his only dreaded bolt.
Nor long shall be our labour; yet ere dawn
Effect shall end our wish. Meanwhile revive;
Abandon fear; to strength and counsel joined
Think nothing hard, much less to be despaired.'
"He ended; and his words their drooping cheer
Enlightened, and their languished hope revived.
Th' invention all admired, and each how he

To be th' inventor missed; so easy it seemed
Once found, which yet unfound most would have thought
Impossible! Yet, haply, of thy race,
In future days, if malice should abound,
Some one, intent on mischief, or inspired
With devilish machination, might devise
Like instrument to plague the sons of men
For sin, on war and mutual slaughter bent.
Forthwith from council to the work they flew;
None arguing stood; innumerable hands
Were ready; in a moment up they turned
Wide the celestial soil, and saw beneath
Th' originals of Nature in their crude
Conception; sulphurous and nitrous foam
They found, they mingled, and, with subtle art
Concocted and adusted, they reduced
To blackest grain, and into store conveyed.
Part hidden veins digged up (nor hath this Earth
Entrails unlike) of mineral and stone,
Whereof to found their engines and their balls
Of missive ruin; part incentive reed
Provide, pernicious with one touch to fire.
So all ere day-spring, under conscious Night,
Secret they finished, and in order set,
With silent circumspection, unespied.
"Now, when fair Morn orient in Heaven appeared,
Up rose the victor Angels, and to arms
The matin trumpet sung. In arms they stood
Of golden panoply, refulgent host,
Soon banded; others from the dawning hills
Looked round, and scouts each coast light-armèd scour,
Each quarter, to descry the distant foe,
Where lodged, or whither fled, or if for fight,
In motion or in halt. Him soon they met
Under spread ensigns moving nigh, in slow
But firm battalion: back with speediest sail
Zophiel, of Cherubim the swiftest wing,

Came flying, and in mid air aloud thus cried:—
" 'Arm, Warriors, arm for fight! The foe at hand,
Whom fled we thought, will save us long pursuit
This day; fear not his flight; so thick a cloud
He comes, and settled in his face I see
Sad resolution and secure. Let each
His adamantine coat gird well, and each
Fit well his helm, grip fast his orbèd shield,
Borne even or high; for this day will pour down,
If I conjecture aught, no drizzling shower,
But rattling storm of arrows barbed with fire.'
" So warned he them, aware themselves, and soon
In order, quit of all impediment.
Instant, without disturb, they took alarm,
And onward move embattled: when, behold,
Not distant far, with heavy pace the foe
Approaching gross and huge, in hollow cube
Training his devilish enginry, impaled
On every side with shadowing squadrons deep,
To hide the fraud. At interview both stood
A while; but suddenly at head appeared
Satan, and thus was heard commanding loud:—
" 'Vanguard, to right and left the front unfold,
That all may see who hate us how we seek
Peace and composure, and with open breast
Stand ready to receive them, if they like
Our overture, and turn not back perverse:
But that I doubt. However, witness Heaven!
Heaven, witness thou anon! while we discharge
Freely our part. Ye, who appointed stand,
Do as you have in charge, and briefly touch
What we propound, and loud that all may hear.'
" So scoffing in ambiguous words, he scarce
Had ended, when to right and left the front
Divided, and to either flank retired;
Which to our eyes discovered, new and strange,
A triple mounted row of pillars laid

On wheels (for like to pillars most they seemed,
Or hollowed bodies made of oak or fir,
With branches lopt, in wood or mountain felled),
Brass, iron, stony mould, had not their mouths
With hideous orifice gaped on us wide,
Portending hollow truce. At each, behind,
A Seraph stood, and in his hand a reed
Stood waving, tipt with fire; while we, suspense,
Collected stood within our thoughts amused.
Not long! for sudden all at once their reeds
Put forth, and to a narrow vent applied
With nicest touch. Immediate in a flame,
But soon obscured with smoke, all Heaven appeared,
From those deep-throated engines belched, whose roar
Embowelled with outrageous noise the air,
And all her entrails tore, disgorging foul
Their devilish glut, chained thunderbolts and hail
Of iron globes; which, on the victor host
Levelled, with such impetuous fury smote,
That whom they hit none on their feet might stand
Though standing else as rocks, but down they fell
By thousands, Angel on Archangel rolled,
The sooner for their arms. Unarmed, they might
Have easily, as Spirits, evaded swift
By quick contraction or remove; but now
Foul dissipation followed, and forced rout;
Nor served it to relax their serried files.
What should they do? If on they rushed, repulse
Repeated, and indecent overthrow
Doubled, would render them yet more despised,
And to their foes a laughter—for in view
Stood ranked of Seraphim another row,
In posture to displode their second tire
Of thunder; back defeated to return
They worse abhorred. Satan beheld their plight,
And to his mates thus in derision called:—
" 'O friends, why come not on these victors proud?

Erewhile they fierce were coming; and, when we,
To entertain them fair with open front
And breast (what could we more?), propounded terms
Of composition, straight they changed their minds,
Flew off, and into strange vagaries fell,
As they would dance. Yet for a dance they seemed
Somewhat extravagant and wild; perhaps
For joy of offered peace. But I suppose,
If our proposals once again were heard,
We should compel them to a quick result.'
"To whom thus Belial, in like gamesome mood: —
'Leader, the terms we sent were terms of weight,
Of hard contents, and full of force urged home,
Such as we might perceive amused them all,
And stumbled many. Who receives them right
Had need from head to foot well understand;
Not understood, this gift they have besides—
They show us when our foes walk not upright.'
"So they among themselves in pleasant vein
Stood scoffing, heightened in their thoughts beyond
All doubt of victory; Eternal Might
To match with their inventions they presumed
So easy, and of his thunder made a scorn,
And all his host derided, while they stood
A while in trouble. But they stood not long;
Rage prompted them at length, and found them arms
Against such hellish mischief fit to oppose.
Forthwith (behold the excellence, the power,
Which God hath in his mighty Angels placed!)
Their arms away they threw, and to the hills
(For Earth hath this variety from Heaven
Of pleasure situate in hill and dale)
Light as the lightning-glimpse they ran, they flew;
From their foundations, loosening to and fro,
They plucked the seated hills, with all their load,
Rocks, waters, woods, and, by the shaggy tops
Uplifting, bore them in their hands. Amaze,

Be sure, and terror, seized the rebel host,
When coming towards them so dread they saw
The bottom of the mountains upward turned,
Till on those cursèd engines' triple row
They saw them whelmed, and all their confidence
Under the weight of mountains buried deep;
Themselves invaded next, and on their heads
Main promontories flung, which in the air
Came shadowing, and oppressed whole legions armed.
Their armour helped their harm, crushed in and bruised,
Into their substance pent—which wrought them pain
Implacable, and many a dolorous groan,
Long struggling underneath, ere they could wind
Out of such prison, though Spirits of purest light,
Purest at first, now gross by sinning grown.
The rest, in imitation, to like arms
Betook them, and the neighbouring hills uptore;
So hills amid the air encountered hills,
Hurled to and fro with jaculation dire,
That underground they fought in dismal shade:
Infernal noise! war seemed a civil game
To this uproar; horrid confusion heaped
Upon confusion rose. And now all Heaven
Had gone to wrack, with ruin overspread,
Had not th' Almighty Father, where he sits
Shrined in his sanctuary of Heaven secure,
Consulting on the sum of things, foreseen
This tumult, and permitted all, advised,
That his great purpose he might so fulfil,
To honour his anointed Son, avenged
Upon his enemies, and to declare
All power on him transferred. Whence to his Son,
Th' assessor of his throne, he thus began:—
" 'Effulgence of my glory, Son beloved,
Son in whose face invisible is beheld
Visibly, what by Deity I am,
And in whose hand what by decree I do,

Second Omnipotence! two days are passed,
Two days, as we compute the days of Heaven,
Since Michael and his Powers went forth to tame
These disobedient. Sore hath been their fight,
As likeliest was when two such foes met armed:
For to themselves I left them; and thou know'st
Equal in their creation they were formed,
Save what sin hath impaired—which yet hath wrought
Insensibly, for I suspend their doom:
Whence in perpetual fight they needs must last
Endless, and no solution will be found.
War wearied hath performed what war can do,
And to disordered rage let loose the reins,
With mountains, as with weapons, armed; which makes
Wild work in Heaven, and dangerous to the main.
Two days are therefore passed; the third is thine:
For thee I have ordained it, and thus far
Have suffered, that the glory may be thine
Of ending this great war, since none but thou
Can end it. Into thee such virtue and grace
Immense I have transfused, that all may know
In Heaven and Hell thy power above compare,
And this perverse commotion governed thus,
To manifest thee worthiest to be Heir
Of all things—to be Heir, and to be King
By sacred unction, thy deservèd right.
Go, then, thou Mightiest, in thy Father's might;
Ascend my chariot; guide the rapid wheels
That shake Heaven's basis; bring forth all my war:
My bow and thunder, my almighty arms,
Gird on, and sword upon thy puissant thigh;
Pursue these Sons of Darkness, drive them out
From all Heaven's bounds into the utter Deep;
There let them learn, as likes them, to despise
God, and Messiah his anointed King.'

"He said, and on his Son with rays direct
Shone full. He all his Father full expressed

Ineffably into his face received:
And thus the Filial Godhead answering spake:—
"'O Father, O Supreme of Heavenly Thrones,
First, Highest, Holiest, Best, thou always seek'st
To glorify thy Son; I always thee,
As is most just. This I my glory account,
My exaltation, and my whole delight,
That thou in me, well pleased, declar'st thy will
Fulfilled, which to fulfil is all my bliss.
Sceptre and power, thy giving, I assume,
And gladlier shall resign when in the end
Thou shalt be all in all, and I in thee
For ever, and in me all whom thou lov'st.
But whom thou hat'st I hate, and can put on
Thy terrors, as I put thy mildness on,
Image of thee in all things: and shall soon,
Armed with thy might, rid Heaven of these rebelled,
To their prepared ill mansion driven down,
To chains of darkness and th' undying worm,
That from thy just obedience could revolt,
Whom to obey, is happiness entire.
Then shall thy Saints, unmixed, and from th' impure
Far separate, circling thy holy Mount,
Unfeignèd hallelujahs to thee sing,
Hymns of high praise, and I among them chief.'
"So said, he, o'er his sceptre bowing, rose
From the right hand of Glory where he sat;
And the third sacred morn began to shine,
Dawning through Heaven. Forth rushed with whirlwind sound
The chariot of Paternal Deity,
Flashing thick flames, wheel within wheel; undrawn,
Itself instinct with spirit, but convoyed
By four cherubic Shapes. Four faces each
Had wondrous; as with stars, their bodies all
And wings were set with eyes; with eyes the wheels
Of beryl, and careering fires between;
Over their heads a crystal firmament,

Whereon a sapphire throne, inlaid with pure
Amber and colours of the showery arch.
He, in celestial panoply all armed
Of radiant Urim, work divinely wrought,
Ascended; at his right hand Victory
Sat eagle-winged; beside him hung his bow,
And quiver, with three-bolted thunder stored;
And from about him fierce effusion rolled
Of smoke and bickering flame and sparkles dire.
Attended with ten thousand thousand Saints,
He onward came; far off his coming shone;
And twenty thousand (I their number heard)
Chariots of God, half on each hand, were seen.
He on the wings of Cherub rode sublime
On the crystalline sky, in sapphire throned—
Illustrious far and wide, but by his own
First seen. Them unexpected joy surprised
When the great ensign of Messiah blazed
Aloft, by Angels borne, his sign in Heaven;
Under whose conduct Michael soon reduced
His army, circumfused on either wing,
Under their Head embodied all in one.
Before him Power Divine his way prepared;
At his command the uprooted hills retired
Each to his place; they heard his voice, and went
Obsequious; Heaven his wonted face renewed,
And with fresh flowerets hill and valley smiled.
"This saw his hapless foes, but stood obdured,
And to rebellious fight rallied their Powers,
Insensate, hope conceiving from despair.
In heavenly Spirits could such perverseness dwell?
But to convince the proud what signs avail,
Or wonders move th' obdúrate to relent?
They, hardened more by what might most reclaim,
Grieving to see his glory, at the sight
Took envy, and, aspiring to his height,
Stood re-embattled fierce, by force or fraud

Weening to prosper, and at length prevail
Against God and Messiah, or to fall
In universal ruin last; and now
To final battle drew, disdaining flight,
Or faint retreat: when the great Son of God
To all his host on either hand thus spake:—
"'Stand still in bright array, ye Saints; here stand,
Ye Angels armed; this day from battle rest.
Faithful hath been your warfare, and of God
Accepted, fearless in his righteous cause;
And, as ye have received, so have ye done,
Invincibly. But of this cursèd crew
The punishment to other hand belongs;
Vengeance is his, or whose he sole appoints.
Number to this day's work is not ordained,
Nor multitude; stand only and behold
God's indignation on these godless poured
By me. Not you, but me, they have despised,
Yet envied; against me is all their rage,
Because the Father, t' whom in Heaven supreme
Kingdom and power and glory appertains,
Hath honoured me, according to his will.
Therefore to me their doom he hath assigned,
That they may have their wish, to try with me
In battle which the stronger proves—they all,
Or I alone against them; since by strength
They measure all, of other excellence
Not emulous, nor care who them excels;
Nor other strife with them do I vouchsafe.'
"So spake the Son, and into terror changed
His countenance, too severe to be beheld,
And full of wrath bent on his enemies.
At once the Four spread out their starry wings
With dreadful shade contiguous, and the orbs
Of his fierce chariot rolled, as with the sound
Of torrent floods, or of a numerous host.
He on his impious foes right onward drove,

Gloomy as Night. Under his burning wheels
The steadfast Empyrean shook throughout,
All but the throne itself of God. Full soon
Among them he arrived, in his right hand
Grasping ten thousand thunders, which he sent
Before him, such as in their souls infixed
Plagues. They, astonished, all resistance lost,
All courage; down their idle weapons dropped;
O'er shields, and helms, and helmèd heads he rode
Of Thrones and mighty Seraphim prostráte,
That wished the mountains now might be again
Thrown on them, as a shelter from his ire.
Nor less on either side tempestuous fell
His arrows, from the fourfold-visaged Four,
Distinct with eyes, and from the living wheels,
Distinct alike with multitude of eyes;
One spirit in them ruled, and every eye
Glared lightning, and shot forth pernicious fire
Among th' accursed, that withered all their strength,
And of their wonted vigour left them drained,
Exhausted, spiritless, afflicted, fallen.
Yet half his strength he put not forth, but checked
His thunder in mid-volley; for he meant
Not to destroy, but root them out of Heaven.
The overthrown he raised, and, as a herd
Of goats or timorous flock together thronged,
Drove them before him thunderstruck, pursued
With terrors and with furies to the bounds
And crystal wall of Heaven; which, opening wide,
Rolled inward, and a spacious gap disclosed
Into the wasteful Deep. The monstrous sight
Struck them with horror backward; but far worse
Urged them behind: headlong themselves they threw
Down from the verge of Heaven: eternal wrath
Burnt after them to the bottomless pit.
"Hell heard th' unsufferable noise; Hell saw
Heaven ruining from Heaven, and would have fled

Affrighted; but strict Fate had cast too deep
Her dark foundations, and too fast had bound.
Nine days they fell; confounded Chaos roared,
And felt tenfold confusion in their fall
Through his wild anarchy; so huge a rout
Encumbered him with ruin. Hell at last,
Yawning, received them whole, and on them closed—
Hell, their fit habitation, fraught with fire
Unquenchable, the house of woe and pain.
Disburdened Heaven rejoiced, and soon repaired
Her mural breach, returning whence it rolled.
Sole victor, from th' expulsion of his foes
Messiah his triumphal chariot turned.
To meet him all his Saints, who silent stood
Eye-witnesses of his almighty acts,
With jubilee advanced; and, as they went,
Shaded with branching palm, each order bright
Sung triumph, and him sung victorious King,
Son, Heir, and Lord, to him dominion given,
Worthiest to reign. He celebrated rode,
Triumphant through mid Heaven, into the courts
And temple of his mighty Father throned
On high; who into glory him received,
Where now he sits at the right hand of bliss.
"Thus, measuring things in Heaven by things on Earth,
At thy request, and that thou may'st beware
By what is past, to thee I have revealed
What might have else to human race been hid—
The discord which befell, and war in Heaven
Among th' angelic Powers, and the deep fall
Of those too high aspiring who rebelled
With Satan: he who envies now thy state,
Who now is plotting how he may seduce
Thee also from obedience, that, with him
Bereaved of happiness, thou may'st partake
His punishment, eternal misery;
Which would be all his solace and revenge,

As a despite done against the Most High,
Thee once to gain companion of his woe.
But listen not to his temptations; warn
Thy weaker; let it profit thee to have heard,
By terrible example, the reward
Of disobedience. Firm they might have stood,
Yet fell. Remember, and fear to transgress."

THE END OF THE SIXTH BOOK

BOOK VII

THE ARGUMENT

Raphael, at the request of Adam, relates how and wherefore this World was first created:—that God, after the expelling of Satan and his Angels out of Heaven, declared his pleasure to create another World, and other creatures to dwell therein; sends his Son with glory, and attendance of Angels, to perform the work of creation in six days: the Angels celebrate with hymns the performance thereof, and his reascension into Heaven.

Descend from Heaven, Urania, by that name
If rightly thou art called, whose voice divine
Following, above th' Olympian hill I soar,
Above the flight of Pegasean wing!
The meaning, not the name, I call; for thou
Nor of the Muses nine, nor on the top
Of old Olympus dwell'st; but, heavenly-born,
Before the hills appeared or fountain flowed,
Thou with Eternal Wisdom didst converse,
Wisdom thy sister, and with her didst play
In presence of th' Almighty Father, pleased
With thy celestial song. Up led by thee,
Into the Heaven of Heavens I have presumed,
An earthly guest, and drawn empyreal air,
Thy tempering. With like safety guided down,
Return me to my native element;
Lest, from this flying steed unreined (as once
Bellerophon, though from a lower clime)
Dismounted, on th' Aleian field I fall,
Erroneous there to wander and forlorn.
Half yet remains unsung, but narrower bound
Within the visible diurnal sphere.
Standing on Earth, not rapt above the pole,
More safe I sing with mortal voice, unchanged

To hoarse or mute, though fallen on evil days,
On evil days though fallen, and evil tongues,
In darkness, and with dangers compassed round,
And solitude; yet not alone, while thou
Visit'st my slumbers nightly, or when Morn
Purples the East. Still govern thou my song,
Urania, and fit audience find, though few.
But drive far off the barbarous dissonance
Of Bacchus and his revellers, the race
Of that wild rout that tore the Thracian bard
In Rhodope, where woods and rocks had ears
To rapture, till the savage clamour drowned
Both harp and voice; nor could the Muse defend
Her son. So fail not thou who thee implores;
For thou art heavenly, she an empty dream.
  Say, Goddess, what ensued when Raphael,
The affable Archangel, had forewarned
Adam, by dire example, to beware
Apostasy, by what befell in Heaven
To those apostates, lest the like befall
In Paradise to Adam or his race,
Charged not to touch the interdicted Tree,
If they transgress, and slight that sole command,
So easily obeyed amid the choice
Of all tastes else to please their appetite,
Though wandering. He, with his consorted Eve,
The story heard attentive, and was filled
With admiration and deep muse, to hear
Of things so high and strange—things to their thought
So unimaginable as hate in Heaven,
And war so near the peace of God in bliss,
With such confusion; but the evil, soon
Driven back, redounded as a flood on those
From whom it sprung, impossible to mix
With blessedness. Whence Adam soon repealed
The doubts that in his heart arose; and, now
Led on, yet sinless, with desire to know

What nearer might concern him—how this World
Of heaven and earth conspicuous first began;
When, and whereof, created; for what cause;
What within Eden, or without, was done
Before his memory—as one whose drouth,
Yet scarce allayed, still eyes the current stream,
Whose liquid murmur heard new thirst excites,
Proceeded thus to ask his Heavenly Guest:—
"Great things, and full of wonder in our ears,
Far differing from this World, thou hast revealed,
Divine Interpreter! by favour sent
Down from the Empyrean to forewarn
Us timely of what might else have been our loss,
Unknown, which human knowledge could not reach;
For which to the infinitely Good we owe
Immortal thanks, and his admonishment
Receive with solemn purpose to observe
Immutably his sovereign will, the end
Of what we are. But, since thou hast vouchsafed
Gently, for our instruction, to impart
Things above earthly thought, which yet concerned
Our knowing, as to highest Wisdom seemed,
Deign to descend now lower, and relate—
What may no less perhaps avail us known—
How first began this Heaven which we behold
Distant so high, with moving fires adorned
Innumerable; and this which yields or fills
All space, the ambient Air, wide interfused,
Embracing round this florid Earth; what cause
Moved the Creator, in his holy rest
Through all eternity, so late to build
In Chaos; and, the work begun, how soon
Absolved: if unforbid thou may'st unfold
What we not to explore the secrets ask
Of his eternal empire, but the more
To magnify his works the more we know.
And the great Light of Day yet wants to run

Much of his race, though steep. Suspense in heaven,
Held by thy voice, thy potent voice he hears,
And longer will delay, to hear thee tell
His generation, and the rising birth
Of Nature from the unapparent deep:
Or, if the Star of Evening and the Moon
Haste to thy audience, Night with her will bring
Silence, and Sleep listening to thee will watch;
Or we can bid his absence till thy song
End, and dismiss thee ere the morning shine."
  Thus Adam his illustrious guest besought;
And thus the godlike Angel answered mild:—
  "This also thy request, with caution asked,
Obtain; though to recount almighty works
What words or tongue of Seraph can suffice,
Or heart of man suffice to comprehend?
Yet what thou canst attain, which best may serve
To glorify the Maker, and infer
Thee also happier, shall not be withheld
Thy hearing. Such commission from above
I have received, to answer thy desire
Of knowledge within bounds; beyond abstain
To ask, nor let thine own inventions hope
Things not revealed, which th' invisible King,
Only omniscient, hath suppressed in night,
To none communicable in Earth or Heaven.
Enough is left beside to search and know;
But Knowledge is as food, and needs no less
Her temperance over appetite, to know
In measure what the mind may well contain;
Oppresses else with surfeit, and soon turns
Wisdom to folly, as nourishment to wind.
  "Know then that, after Lucifer from Heaven
(So call him, brighter once amidst the host
Of Angels than that star the stars among)
Fell with his flaming legions through the Deep
Into his place, and the great Son returned

Victorious with his Saints, th' Omnipotent
Eternal Father from his throne beheld
Their multitude, and to his Son thus spake:—
" 'At least our envious foe hath failed, who thought
All like himself rebellious; by whose aid
This inaccessible high strength, the seat
Of Deity supreme, us dispossessed,
He trusted to have seized, and into fraud
Drew many whom their place knows here no more.
Yet far the greater part have kept, I see,
Their station; Heaven, yet populous, retains
Number sufficient to possess her realms,
Though wide, and this high temple to frequent
With ministeries due and solemn rites.
But, lest his heart exalt him in the harm
Already done, to have dispeopled Heaven—
My damage fondly deemed—I can repair
That detriment, if such it be to lose
Self-lost, and in a moment will create
Another world; out of one man a race
Of men innumerable, there to dwell,
Not here, till by degrees of merit raised,
They open to themselves at length the way
Up hither, under long obedience tried,
And Earth be changed to Heaven, and Heaven to Earth,
One kingdom, joy and union without end.
Meanwhile inhabit lax, ye Powers of Heaven;
And thou, my Word, begotten Son, by thee
This I perform; speak thou, and be it done!
My overshadowing Spirit and might with thee
I send along; ride forth, and bid the Deep
Within appointed bounds be heaven and earth.
Boundless the Deep, because I am who fill
Infinitude; nor vacuous the space,
Though I, uncircumscribed, myself retire,
And put not forth my goodness, which is free
To act or not. Necessity and Chance

Approach not me, and what I will is Fate.'
"So spake th' Almighty; and to what he spake
His Word, the Filial Godhead, gave effect.
Immediate are the acts of God, more swift
Than time or motion, but to human ears
Cannot without procéss of speech be told,
So told as earthly notion can receive.
Great triumph and rejoicing was in Heaven
When such was heard declared the Almighty's will.
Glory they sung to the Most High, good-will
To future men, and in their dwellings peace—
Glory to him whose just avenging ire
Had driven out th' ungodly from his sight
And th' habitations of the just; to him
Glory and praise whose wisdom had ordained
Good out of evil to create—instead
Of Spirits malign, a better race to bring
Into their vacant room, and thence diffuse
His good to worlds and ages infinite.
"So sang the Hierarchies. Meanwhile the Son
On his great expedition now appeared,
Girt with omnipotence, with radiance crowned
Of majesty divine, sapience and love
Immense; and all his Father in him shone.
About his chariot numberless were poured
Cherub and Seraph, Potentates and Thrones,
And Virtues, wingèd Spirits, and chariots winged
From the armoury of God, where stand of old
Myriads, between two brazen mountains lodged
Against a solemn day, harnessed at hand,
Celestial equipage; and now came forth
Spontaneous, for within them Spirit lived,
Attendant on their Lord. Heaven opened wide
Her ever-during gates, harmonious sound
On golden hinges moving, to let forth
The King of Glory, in his powerful Word
And Spirit coming to create new worlds.

On Heavenly ground they stood, and from the shore
They viewed the vast immeasurable Abyss,
Outrageous as a sea, dark, wasteful, wild,
Up from the bottom turned by furious winds
And surging waves, as mountains to assault
Heaven's height, and with the centre mix the pole.
"'Silence, ye troubled waves, and, thou Deep, peace!'
Said then th' omnific Word: 'your discord end!'
Nor stayed; but, on the wings of Cherubim
Uplifted, in paternal glory rode
Far into Chaos and the World unborn;
For Chaos heard his voice. Him all his train
Followed in bright procession, to behold
Creation, and the wonders of his might.
Then stayed the fervid wheels, and in his hand
He took the golden compasses, prepared
In God's eternal store, to circumscribe
This Universe, and all created things.
One foot he centred, and the other turned
Round through the vast profundity obscure,
And said, 'Thus far extend, thus far thy bounds:
This be thy just circumference, O World!'
Thus God the Heaven created, thus the Earth,
Matter unformed and void. Darkness profound
Covered th' Abyss; but on the watery calm
His brooding wings the Spirit of God outspread,
And vital virtue infused, and vital warmth,
Throughout the fluid mass, but downward purged
The black, tartareous, cold, infernal dregs,
Adverse to life; then founded, then conglobed,
Like things to like, the rest to several place
Disparted, and between spun out the Air,
And Earth, self-balanced, on her centre hung.
"'Let there be Light!' said God; and forthwith Light
Ethereal, first of things, quintessence pure,
Sprung from the Deep, and from her native East
To journey through the airy gloom began,

Sphered in a radiant cloud—for yet the Sun
Was not; she in a cloudy tabernacle
Sojourned the while. God saw the Light was good;
And light from darkness by the hemisphere
Divided: Light the Day, and Darkness Night,
He named. Thus was the first Day even and morn;
Nor passed uncelebrated, nor unsung
By the celestial choirs, when orient light
Exhaling first from darkness they beheld,
Birth-day of Heaven and Earth. With joy and shout
The hollow universal orb they filled,
And touched their golden harps, and hymning praised
God and his works; Creator him they sung,
Both when first evening was, and when first morn.
"Again God said, 'Let there be firmament
Amid the waters, and let it divide
The waters from the waters!' And God made
The firmament, expanse of liquid, pure,
Transparent, elemental air diffused
In circuit to the uttermost convex
Of this great round—partition firm and sure,
The waters underneath from those above
Dividing; for as Earth, so he the World
Built on circumfluous waters calm, in wide
Crystálline ocean, and the loud misrule
Of Chaos far removed, lest fierce extremes
Contiguous might distemper the whole frame:
And heaven he named the Firmament. So even
And morning chorus sung the second Day.
"The Earth was formed, but, in the womb as yet
Of waters, embryon immature, involved,
Appeared not; over all the face of Earth
Main Ocean flowed, not idle, but, with warm
Prolific humour softening all her globe,
Fermented the great mother to conceive,
Satiate with genial moisture; when God said,
'Be gathered now, ye waters under heaven,

Into one place, and let dry land appear!'
Immediately the mountains huge appear
Emergent, and their broad bare backs upheave
Into the clouds; their tops ascend the sky.
So high as heaved the tumid hills, so low
Down sunk a hollow bottom broad and deep,
Capacious bed of waters. Thither they
Hasted with glad precipitance, uprolled,
As drops on dust conglobing, from the dry:
Part rise in crystal wall, or ridge direct,
For haste; such flight the great command impressed
On the swift floods. As armies at the call
Of trumpet (for of armies thou hast heard)
Troop to the standard, so the watery throng
Wave rolling after wave, where way they found—
If steep, with torrent rapture, if through plain,
Soft-ebbing; nor withstood them rock or hill;
But they, or underground, or circuit wide
With serpent error wandering, found their way,
And on the washy ooze deep channels wore:
Easy, ere God had bid the ground be dry,
All but within those banks where rivers now
Stream, and perpetual draw their humid train.
The dry land Earth, and the great receptacle
Of congregated waters he called Seas;
And saw that it was good, and said, 'Let th' Earth
Put forth the verdant grass, herb yielding seed,
And fruit-tree yielding fruit after her kind,
Whose seed is in herself upon the Earth!'
He scarce had said when the bare Earth, till then
Desert and bare, unsightly, unadorned,
Brought forth the tender grass, whose verdure clad
Her universal face with pleasant green;
Then herbs of every leaf, that sudden flowered,
Opening their various colours, and made gay
Her bosom, smelling sweet; and, these scarce blown,
Forth flourished thick the clustering vine, forth crept

The smelling gourd, up stood the corny reed
Embattled in her field: and the humble shrub,
And bush with frizzled hair implicit: last
Rose, as in dance, the stately trees, and spread
Their branches hung with copious fruit, or gemmed
Their blossoms. With high woods the hills were crowned,
With tufts the valleys and each fountain-side,
With borders long the rivers, that Earth now
Seemed like to Heaven, a seat where Gods might dwell,
Or wander with delight, and love to haunt
Her sacred shades; though God had yet not rained
Upon the Earth, and man to till the ground
None was, but from the Earth a dewy mist
Went up and watered all the ground, and each
Plant of the field, which ere it was in the Earth
God made, and every herb before it grew
On the green stem. God saw that it was good;
So even and morn recorded the third Day.
"Again th' Almighty spake, 'Let there be Lights
High in th' expanse of Heaven, to divide
The Day from Night; and let them be for signs,
For seasons, and for days, and circling years;
And let them be for lights, as I ordain
Their office in the firmament of heaven,
To give light on the Earth!' and it was so.
And God made two great Lights, great for their use
To Man, the greater to have rule by day,
The less by night, altern; and made the Stars,
And set them in the firmament of heaven
To illuminate the Earth, and rule the day
In their vicissitude, and rule the night,
And light from darkness to divide. God saw,
Surveying his great work, that it was good:
For, of celestial bodies, first the Sun
A mighty sphere he framed, unlightsome first,
Though of ethereal mould; then formed the Moon
Globose, and every magnitude of Stars,

And sowed with stars the heaven thick as a field.
Of light by far the greater part he took,
Transplanted from her cloudy shrine, and placed
In the Sun's orb, made porous to receive
And drink the liquid light, firm to retain
Her gathered beams, great palace now of light.
Hither, as to their fountain, other stars
Repairing in their golden urns draw light,
And hence the morning planet gilds her horns;
By tincture or reflection they augment
Their small peculiar, though, from human sight
So far remote, with diminution seen.
First in his east the glorious lamp was seen,
Regent of day, and all th' horizon round
Invested with bright rays, jocund to run
His longitude through heaven's high road; the grey
Dawn, and the Pleiades, before him danced,
Shedding sweet influence. Less bright the Moon,
But opposite in levelled west, was set,
His mirror, with full face borrowing her light
From him; for other light she needed none
In that aspect, and still that distance keeps
Till night; then in the east her turn she shines,
Revolved on heaven's great axle, and her reign
With thousand lesser lights dividual holds,
With thousand thousand stars, that then appeared
Spangling the hemisphere. Then first adorned
With her bright luminaries, that set and rose,
Glad evening and glad morn crowned the fourth Day.
"And God said, 'Let the waters generate
Reptile with spawn abundant, living soul;
And let fowl fly above the earth, with wings
Displayed on the open firmament of heaven!'
And God created the great whales, and each
Soul living, each that crept, which plenteously
The waters generated by their kinds,
And every bird of wing after his kind,

And saw that it was good, and blessed them, saying,
'Be fruitful, multiply, and, in the seas,
And lakes, and running streams, the waters fill;
And let the fowl be multiplied on the earth!'
Forthwith the sounds and seas, each creek and bay,
With fry innumerable swarm, and shoals
Of fish that, with their fins and shining scales,
Glide under the green wave in sculls that oft
Bank the mid-sea. Part, single or with mate,
Graze the sea-weed, their pasture, and through groves
Of coral stray, or, sporting with quick glance,
Show to the sun their waved coats dropped with gold,
Or, in their pearly shells at ease, attend
Moist nutriment, or under rocks their food
In jointed armour watch; on smooth the seal
And bended dolphins play: part, huge of bulk,
Wallowing unwieldy, enormous in their gait,
Tempest the ocean. There leviathan,
Hugest of living creatures, on the deep
Stretched like a promontory, sleeps or swims,
And seems a moving land, and at his gills
Draws in, and at his trunk spouts out, a sea.
Meanwhile the tepid caves, and fens, and shores,
Their brood as numerous hatch from the egg, that soon,
Bursting with kindly rupture, forth disclosed
Their callow young; but feathered soon and fledge
They summed their pens, and, soaring th' air sublime,
With clang despised the ground, under a cloud
In prospect. There the eagle and the stork
On cliffs and cedar-tops their eyries build.
Part loosely wing the region; part, more wise,
In common, ranged in figure, wedge their way,
Intelligent of seasons, and set forth
Their airy caravan, high over seas
Flying, and over lands, with mutual wing
Easing their flight: so steers the prudent crane
Her annual voyage, borne on winds: the air

Floats as they pass, fanned with unnumbered plumes.
From branch to branch the smaller birds with song
Solaced the woods, and spread their painted wings,
Till even; nor then the solemn nightingale
Ceased warbling, but all night tuned her soft lays.
Others, on silver lakes and rivers, bathed
Their downy breast; the swan, with archèd neck
Between her white wings mantling proudly, rows
Her state with oary feet; yet oft they quit
The dank, and, rising on stiff pennons, tower
The mid aerial sky. Others on ground
Walked firm—the crested cock, whose clarion sounds
The silent hours, and th' other, whose gay train
Adorns him, coloured with the florid hue
Of rainbows and starry eyes. The waters thus
With fish replenished, and the air with fowl,
Evening and morn solemnized the fifth Day.
"The sixth, and of Creation last, arose
With evening harps and matin; when God said,
'Let th' Earth bring forth soul living in her kind,
Cattle, and creeping things, and beast of the earth,
Each in their kind!' The Earth obeyed, and, straight
Opening her fertile womb, teemed at a birth
Innumerous living creatures, perfect forms,
Limbed and full-grown. Out of the ground up rose,
As from his lair, the wild beast, where he wons
In forest wild, in thicket, brake, or den—
Among the trees in pairs they rose, they walked;
The cattle in the fields and meadows green:
Those rare and solitary, these in flocks
Pasturing at once and in broad herds, upsprung.
The grassy clods now calved; now half appeared
The tawny lion, pawing to get free
His hinder parts—then springs, as broke from bonds,
And rampant shakes his brinded mane; the ounce,
The libbard, and the tiger, as the mole
Rising, the crumbled earth above them threw

In hillocks; the swift stag from underground
Bore up his branching head; scarce from his mould
Behemoth, biggest born of earth, upheaved
His vastness; fleeced the flocks and bleating rose,
As plants; ambiguous between sea and land,
The river-horse and scaly crocodile.
At once came forth whatever creeps the ground,
Insect or worm. Those waved their limber fans
For wings, and smallest lineaments exact
In all the liveries decked of summer's pride,
With spots of gold and purple, azure and green;
These as a line their long dimension drew,
Streaking the ground with sinuous trace; not all
Minims of nature; some of serpent kind,
Wondrous in length and corpulence, involved
Their snaky folds, and added wings. First crept
The parsimonious emmet, provident
Of future, in small room large heart enclosed—
Pattern of just equality perhaps
Hereafter—joined in her popular tribes
Of commonalty. Swarming next appeared
The female bee, that feeds her husband drone
Deliciously, and builds her waxen cells
With honey stored. The rest are numberless,
And thou their natures know'st, and gav'st them names,
Needless to thee repeated; nor unknown
The serpent, subtlest beast of all the field,
Of huge extent sometimes, with brazen eyes
And hairy mane terrific, though to thee
Not noxious, but obedient at thy call.
"Now Heaven in all her glory shone, and rolled
Her motions, as the great First Mover's hand
First wheeled their course; Earth, in her rich attire
Consummate, lovely smiled; air, water, earth,
By fowl, fish, beast, was flown, was swum, was walked,
Frequent; and of the sixth Day yet remained.
There wanted yet the master-work, the end

Of all yet done—a creature who, not prone
And brute as other creatures, but endued
With sanctity of reason, might erect
His stature, and upright with front serene
Govern the rest, self-knowing, and from thence
Magnanimous to correspond with Heaven,
But grateful to acknowledge whence his good
Descends; thither with heart, and voice, and eyes
Directed in devotion, to adore
And worship God Supreme, who made him chief
Of all his works. Therefore the Omnipotent
Eternal Father (for where is not he
Present?) thus to his Son audibly spake:—
'Let us make now Man in our image, Man
In our similitude, and let them rule
Over the fish and fowl of sea and air,
Beast of the field, and over all the earth,
And every creeping thing that creeps the ground!'
This said, he formed thee, Adam, thee, O Man,
Dust of the ground, and in thy nostrils breathed
The breath of life; in his own image he
Created thee, in the image of God
Express, and thou becam'st a living soul.
Male he created thee, but thy consort
Female, for race; then blessed mankind, and said,
'Be fruitful, multiply, and fill the Earth;
Subdue it, and throughout dominion hold
Over fish of the sea, and fowl of the air,
And every living thing that moves on the Earth!'
Wherever thus created—for no place
Is yet distinct by name—thence, as thou know'st,
He brought thee into this delicious grove,
This Garden, planted with the trees of God,
Delectable both to behold and taste,
And freely all their pleasant fruit for food
Gave thee. All sorts are here that all th' earth yields,
Variety without end; but of the tree

Which tasted works knowledge of good and evil
Thou may'st not; in the day thou eat'st, thou diest.
Death is the penalty imposed; beware,
And govern well thy appetite, lest Sin
Surprise thee, and her black attendant Death.
"Here finished he, and all that he had made
Viewed, and, behold! all was entirely good.
So even and morn accomplished the sixth Day;
Yet not till the Creator, from his work
Desisting, though unwearied, up returned,
Up to the Heaven of Heavens, his high abode,
Thence to behold this new-created World,
Th' addition of his empire, how it showed
In prospect from his throne, how good, how fair,
Answering his great idea. Up he rode,
Followed with acclamation, and the sound
Symphonious of ten thousand harps, that tuned
Angelic harmonies. The Earth, the Air
Resounded (thou remember'st, for thou heard'st),
The heavens and all the constellations rung,
The planets in their stations listening stood,
While the bright pomp ascended jubilant.
'Open, ye everlasting gates!' they sung;
'Open, ye Heavens, your living doors! let in
The great Creator, from his work returned
Magnificent, his six days' work, a World!
Open, and henceforth oft; for God will deign
To visit oft the dwellings of just men
Delighted, and with frequent intercourse
Thither will send his wingèd messengers
On errands of supernal grace.' So sung
The glorious train ascending. He through Heaven,
That opened wide her blazing portals, led
To God's eternal house direct the way—
A broad and ample road, whose dust is gold,
And pavement, stars, as stars to thee appear
Seer in the Galaxy, that milky way

Which nightly as a circling zone thou seest
Powdered with stars. And now on Earth the seventh
Evening arose in Eden—for the sun
Was set, and twilight from the east came on,
Forerunning night, when at the holy Mount
Of Heaven's high-seated top, th' imperial throne
Of Godhead, fixed for ever firm and sure,
The Filial Power arrived, and sat him down
With his great Father; for he also went
Invisible, yet stayed (such privilege
Hath Omnipresence) and the work ordained,
Author and end of all things, and, from work
Now resting, blessed and hallowed the seventh Day,
As resting on that day from all his work;
But not in silence holy kept: the harp
Had work, and rested not; the solemn pipe
And dulcimer, all organs of sweet stop,
All sounds on fret by string or golden wire,
Tempered soft tunings, intermixed with voice
Choral or unison; of incense clouds,
Fuming from golden censers, hid the Mount.
Creation and the Six Days' acts they sung:—
'Great are thy works, Jehovah! infinite
Thy power! what thought can measure thee, or tongue
Relate thee—greater now in thy return
Than from the Giant-angels! Thee that day
Thy thunders magnified; but to create
Is greater than created to destroy.
Who can impair thee, mighty King, or bound
Thy empire? Easily the proud attempt
Of Spirits apostate, and their counsels vain,
Thou hast repelled, while impiously they thought
Thee to diminish, and from thee withdraw
The number of thy worshippers. Who seeks
To lessen thee, against his purpose, serves
To manifest the more thy might; his evil
Thou usest, and from thence creat'st more good.

Witness this new-made World, another Heaven
From Heaven-gate not far, founded in view
On the clear hyaline, the glassy sea;
Of amplitude almost immense, with stars
Numerous, and every star perhaps a world
Of destined habitation—but thou know'st
Their seasons; among these the seat of men,
Earth, with her nether ocean circumfused,
Their pleasant dwelling-place. Thrice happy men,
And sons of men, whom God hath thus advanced,
Created in his image, there to dwell
And worship him, and in reward to rule
Over his works, on earth, in sea, or air,
And multiply a race of worshippers
Holy and just! thrice happy, if they know
Their happiness, and persevere upright!'
"So sung they, and the Empyrean rung
With hallelujahs. Thus was Sabbath kept.
And thy request think now fulfilled, that asked
How first this World and face of things began,
And what before thy memory was done
From the beginning, that posterity,
Informed by thee, might know. If else thou seek'st
Aught, not surpassing human measure, say."

THE END OF THE SEVENTH BOOK

BOOK VIII

THE ARGUMENT

Adam inquires concerning celestial motions; is doubtfully answered, and exhorted to search rather things more worthy of knowledge. Adam assents, and, still desirous to detain Raphael, relates to him what he remembered since his own creation—his placing in Paradise; his talk with God concerning solitude and fit society; his first meeting and nuptials with Eve. His discourse with the Angel thereupon; who, after admonitions repeated, departs.

The Angel ended, and in Adam's ear
So charming left his voice that he a while
Thought him still speaking, still stood fixed to hear;
Then, as new-waked, thus gratefully replied:—
"What thanks sufficient, or what recompense
Equal, have I to render thee, divine
Historian, who thus largely hast allayed
The thirst I had of knowledge, and vouchsafed
This friendly condescension, to relate
Things else by me unsearchable—now heard
With wonder, but delight, and, as is due,
With glory attributed to the high
Creator? Something yet of doubt remains,
Which only thy solution can resolve.
When I behold this goodly frame, this World,
Of Heaven and Earth consisting, and compute
Their magnitudes—this Earth, a spot, a grain,
An atom, with the firmament compared
And all her numbered stars, that seem to roll
Spaces incomprehensible (for such
Their distance argues, and their swift return
Diurnal) merely to officiate light
Round this opacous Earth, this punctual spot,

One day and night, in all their vast survey
Useless besides—reasoning, I oft admire
How Nature, wise and frugal, could commit
Such disproportions, with superfluous hand
So many nobler bodies to create,
Greater so manifold, to this one use,
For aught appears, and on their orbs impose
Such restless revolution day by day
Repeated, while the sedentary Earth,
That better might with far less compass move,
Served by more noble than herself, attains
Her end without least motion, and receives,
As tribute, such a sumless journey brought
Of incorporeal speed, her warmth and light:
Speed, to describe whose swiftness number fails."
So spake our sire, and by his countenance seemed
Entering on studious thoughts abstruse; which Eve
Perceiving, where she sat retired in sight,
With lowliness majestic from her seat,
And grace that won who saw to wish her stay,
Rose, and went forth among her fruits and flowers,
To visit how they prospered, bud and bloom,
Her nursery; they at her coming sprung,
And, touched by her fair tendance, gladlier grew.
Yet went she not as not with such discourse
Delighted, or not capable her ear
Of what was high. Such pleasure she reserved,
Adam relating, she sole auditress;
Her husband the relater she preferred
Before the Angel, and of him to ask
Chose rather; he, she knew, would intermix
Grateful digressions, and solve high dispute
With conjugal caresses: from his lip
Not words alone pleased her. Oh, when meet now
Such pairs, in love and mutual honour joined?
With goddess-like demeanour forth she went,
Not unattended; for on her as queen

A pomp of winning Graces waited still,
And from about her shot darts of desire
Into all eyes, to wish her still in sight.
And Raphael now to Adam's doubt proposed
Benevolent and facile thus replied:—
"To ask or search I blame thee not; for Heaven
Is as the Book of God before thee set,
Wherein to read his wondrous works, and learn
His seasons, hours, or days, or months, or years.
This to attain, whether Heaven move or Earth
Imports not, if thou reckon right; the rest
From Man or Angel the great Architect
Did wisely to conceal, and not divulge
His secrets, to be scanned by them who ought
Rather admire. Or, if they list to try
Conjecture, he his fabric of the Heavens
Hath left to their disputes—perhaps to move
His laughter at their quaint opinions wide
Hereafter, when they come to model heaven,
And calculate the stars; how they will wield
The mighty frame; how build, unbuild, contrive
To save appearances; how gird the sphere
With centric and eccentric scribbled o'er,
Cycle and epicycle, orb in orb.
Already by thy reasoning this I guess,
Who art to lead thy offspring, and supposest
That bodies bright and greater should not serve
The less not bright, nor Heaven such journeys run,
Earth sitting still, when she alone receives
The benefit. Consider, first, that great
Or bright infers not excellence. The Earth,
Though, in comparison of Heaven, so small,
Nor glistering, may of solid good contain
More plenty than the Sun that barren shines,
Whose virtue on itself works no effect,
But in the fruitful Earth; there first received,
His beams, unactive else, their vigour find.

Yet not to Earth are those bright luminaries
Officious, but to thee, Earth's habitant.
And, for the Heaven's wide circuit, let it speak
The Maker's high magnificence, who built
So spacious, and his line stretched out so far,
That Man may know he dwells not in his own—
An edifice too large for him to fill,
Lodged in a small partition, and the rest
Ordained for uses to his Lord best known.
The swiftness of those circles attribute,
Though numberless, to his omnipotence,
That to corporeal substances could add
Speed almost spiritual. Me thou think'st not slow,
Who since the morning-hour set out from Heaven
Where God resides, and ere mid-day arrived
In Eden—distance inexpressible
By numbers that have name. But this I urge,
Admitting motion in the Heavens, to show
Invalid that which thee to doubt it moved;
Not that I so affirm, though so it seem
To thee who hast thy dwelling here on Earth.
God, to remove his ways from human sense,
Placed Heaven from Earth so far, that earthly sight,
If it presume, might err in things too high,
And no advantage gain. What if the Sun
Be centre to the World, and other stars,
By his attractive virtue and their own
Incited, dance about him various rounds?
Their wandering course, now high, now low, then hid.
Progressive, retrograde, or standing still,
In six thou seest; and what if, seventh to these,
The planet Earth, so steadfast though she seem,
Insensibly three different motions move?
Which else to several spheres thou must ascribe,
Moved contrary with thwart obliquities,
Or save the Sun his labour, and that swift
Nocturnal and diurnal rhomb supposed,

Invisible else above all stars, the wheel
Of Day and Night; which needs not thy belief,
If Earth, industrious of herself, fetch Day,
Travelling east, and with her part averse
From the Sun's beam meet Night, her other part
Still luminous by his ray. What if that light,
Sent from her through the wide transpicuous air,
To the terrestrial Moon be as a star,
Enlightening her by day, as she by night
This Earth—reciprocal, if land be there,
Fields and inhabitants? Her spots thou seest
As clouds, and clouds may rain, and rain produce
Fruits in her softened soil, for some to eat
Allotted there; and other Suns, perhaps,
With their attendant Moons, thou wilt descry,
Communicating male and female light—
Which two great sexes animate the World,
Stored in each orb perhaps with some that live.
For such vast room in Nature unpossessed
By living soul, desert and desolate,
Only to shine, yet scarce to contribute
Each orb a glimpse of light, conveyed so far
Down to this habitable, which returns
Light back to them, is obvious to dispute.
But whether thus these things, or whether not—
Whether the Sun, predominant in heaven,
Rise on the Earth, or Earth rise on the Sun;
He from the east his flaming road begin,
Or she from west her silent course advance
With inoffensive pace that spinning sleeps
On her soft axle, while she paces even,
And bears thee soft with the smooth air along—
Solicit not thy thoughts with matters hid;
Leave them to God above; him serve and fear.
Of other creatures as him pleases best,
Wherever placed, let him dispose; joy thou
In what he gives to thee, this Paradise

And thy fair Eve; Heaven is for thee too high
To know what passes there. Be lowly wise;
Think only what concerns thee and thy being;
Dream not of other worlds, what creatures there
Live, in what state, condition, or degree—
Contented that thus far hath been revealed
Not of Earth only, but of highest Heaven."
 To whom thus Adam, cleared of doubt, replied:—
"How fully hast thou satisfied me, pure
Intelligence of Heaven, Angel serene,
And, freed from intricacies, taught to live
The easiest way, nor with perplexing thoughts
To interrupt the sweet of life, from which
God hath bid dwell far off all anxious cares,
And not molest us, unless we ourselves
Seek them with wandering thoughts, and notions vain!
But apt the mind or fancy is to rove
Unchecked; and of her roving is no end,
Till warned, or by experience taught, she learn
That not to know at large of things remote
From use, obscure and subtle, but to know
That which before us lies in daily life,
Is the prime wisdom: what is more is fume,
Or emptiness, or fond impertinence,
And renders us in things that most concern
Unpractised, unprepared, and still to seek.
Therefore from this high pitch let us descend
A lower flight, and speak of things at hand
Useful; whence, haply, mention may arise
Of something not unseasonable to ask,
By sufferance, and thy wonted favour, deigned.
Thee I have heard relating what was done
Ere my remembrance; now hear me relate
My story, which, perhaps, thou hast not heard.
And day is yet not spent; till then thou seest
How subtly to detain thee I devise,
Inviting thee to hear while I relate—

Fond, were it not in hope of thy reply.
For, while I sit with thee, I seem in Heaven;
And sweeter thy discourse is to my ear
Than fruits of palm-tree, pleasantest to thirst
And hunger both, from labour, at the hour
Of sweet repast. They satiate, and soon fill,
Though pleasant; but thy words, with grace divine
Imbued, bring to their sweetness no satiety."
  To whom thus Raphael answered, heavenly meek:—
"Nor are thy lips ungraceful, Sire of Men,
Nor tongue ineloquent; for God on thee
Abundantly his gifts hath also poured,
Inward and outward both, his image fair:
Speaking, or mute, all comeliness and grace
Attends thee, and each word, each motion, forms.
Nor less think we in Heaven of thee on Earth
Than of our fellow-servant, and inquire
Gladly into the ways of God with Man;
For God, we see, hath honoured thee, and set
On Man his equal love. Say therefore on;
For I that day was absent, as befell,
Bound on a voyage uncouth and obscure,
Far on excursion toward the gates of Hell,
Squared in full legion (such command we had),
To see that none thence issued forth a spy
Or enemy, while God was in his work,
Lest he, incensed at such eruption bold,
Destruction with Creation might have mixed.
Not that they durst without his leave attempt;
But us he sends upon his high behests
For state, as sovereign King, and to inure
Our prompt obedience. Fast we found, fast shut,
The dismal gates, and barricadoed strong,
But, long ere our approaching, heard within
Noise, other than the sound of dance or song—
Torment, and loud lament, and furious rage.
Glad we returned up to the coasts of light

Ere Sabbath-evening; so we had in charge.
But thy relation now; for I attend,
Pleased with thy words no less than thou with mine."
  So spake the godlike Power, and thus our sire:—
"For Man to tell how human life began
Is hard; for who himself beginning knew?
Desire with thee still longer to converse
Induced me. As new-waked from soundest sleep,
Soft on the flowery herb I found me laid,
In balmy sweat, which with his beams the Sun
Soon dried, and on the reeking moisture fed.
Straight toward Heaven my wondering eyes I turned,
And gazed a while the ample sky, till, raised
By quick instinctive motion, up I sprung,
As thitherward endeavouring, and upright
Stood on my feet. About me round I saw
Hill, dale, and shady woods, and sunny plains,
And liquid lapse of murmuring streams; by these,
Creatures that lived and moved, and walked or flew,
Birds on the branches warbling: all things smiled;
With fragrance and with joy my heart o'erflowed.
Myself I then perused, and limb by limb
Surveyed, and sometimes went, and sometimes ran
With supple joints, as lively vigour led;
But who I was, or where, or from what cause,
Knew not. To speak I tried, and forthwith spake;
My tongue obeyed, and readily could name
Whate'er I saw. 'Thou Sun,' said I, 'fair light,
And thou enlightened Earth, so fresh and gay,
Ye hills and dales, ye rivers, woods, and plains,
And ye that live and move, fair creatures, tell,
Tell, if ye saw, how came I thus, how here!
Not of myself; by some great Maker then,
In goodness and in power pre-eminent.
Tell me, how may I know him, how adore,
From whom have I that thus I move and live,
And feel that I am happier than I know!'

While thus I called, and strayed I knew not whither,
From where I first drew air, and first beheld
This happy light, when answer none returned,
On a green shady bank, profuse of flowers,
Pensive I sat me down. There gentle sleep
First found me, and with soft oppression seized
My drowsèd sense, untroubled, though I thought
I then was passing to my former state
Insensible, and forthwith to dissolve:
When suddenly stood at my head a dream,
Whose inward apparition gently moved
My fancy to believe I yet had being,
And lived. One came, methought, of shape divine,
And said, 'Thy mansion wants thee, Adam; rise,
First Man, of men innumerable ordained
First father! called by thee, I come thy guide
To the garden of bliss, thy seat prepared.'
So saying, by the hand he took me, raised,
And over fields and waters, as in air
Smooth sliding without step, last led me up
A woody mountain, whose high top was plain,
A circuit wide, enclosed, with goodliest trees
Planted, with walks and bowers, that what I saw
Of Earth before scarce pleasant seemed. Each tree
Loaden with fairest fruit, that hung to the eye
Tempting, stirred in me sudden appetite
To pluck and eat; whereat I waked, and found
Before mine eyes all real, as the dream
Had lively shadowed. Here had new begun
My wandering, had not he who was my guide
Up hither from among the trees appeared,
Presence Divine. Rejoicing, but with awe,
In adoration at his feet I fell
Submiss. He reared me, and, 'Whom thou sought'st I am,'
Said mildly, 'Author of all this thou seest
Above, or round about thee, or beneath.
This Paradise I give thee; count it thine

To till and keep, and of the fruit to eat.
Of every tree that in the garden grows
Eat freely with glad heart; fear here no dearth.
But of the tree whose operation brings
Knowledge of good and ill, which I have set,
The pledge of thy obedience and thy faith,
Amid the garden by the Tree of Life—
Remember what I warn thee—shun to taste,
And shun the bitter consequence: for know,
The day thou eat'st thereof, my sole command
Transgressed, inevitably thou shalt die,
From that day mortal, and this happy state
Shalt lose, expelled from hence into a world
Of woe and sorrow.' Sternly he pronounced
The rigid interdiction, which resounds
Yet dreadful in mine ear, though in my choice
Not to incur; but soon his clear aspéct
Returned, and gracious purpose thus renewed:—
'Not only these fair bounds, but all the Earth
To thee and to thy race I give; as lords
Possess it, and all things that therein live,
Or live in sea or air, beast, fish, and fowl.
In sign whereof, each bird and beast behold
After their kind; I bring them to receive
From thee their names, and pay thee fealty
With low subjection. Understand the same
Of fish within their watery residence,
Not hither summoned, since they cannot change
Their element to draw the thinner air.'
As thus he spake, each bird and beast behold
Approaching two and two—these cowering low
With blandishment; each bird stooped on his wing.
I named them as they passed, and understood
Their nature; with such knowledge God endued
My sudden apprehension. But in these
I found not what methought I wanted still,
And to the Heavenly Vision thus presumed:—

"'O, by what name—for thou above all these,
Above mankind, or aught than mankind higher,
Surpassest far my naming—how may I
Adore thee, Author of this Universe,
And all this good to Man, for whose well-being
So amply, and with hands so liberal,
Thou hast provided all things? But with me
I see not who partakes. In solitude
What happiness? who can enjoy alone,
Or, all enjoying, what contentment find?'
Thus I, presumptuous; and the Vision bright,
As with a smile more brightened, thus replied:—
"'What call'st thou solitude? Is not the Earth
With various living creatures, and the Air,
Replenished, and all these at thy command
To come and play before thee? Know'st thou not
Their language and their ways? They also know,
And reason not contemptibly; with these
Find pastime, and bear rule; thy realm is large.'
So spake the Universal Lord, and seemed
So ordering. I, with leave of speech implored,
And humble deprecation, thus replied:—
"'Let not my words offend thee, Heavenly Power;
My Maker, be propitious while I speak.
Hast thou not made me here thy substitute,
And these inferior far beneath me set?
Among unequals what society
Can sort, what harmony or true delight?
Which must be mutual, in proportion due
Given and received; but, in disparity,
The one intense, the other still remiss,
Cannot well suit with either, but soon prove
Tedious alike. Of fellowship I speak
Such as I seek, fit to participate
All rational delight, wherein the brute
Cannot be human consort. They rejoice
Each with their kind, lion with lioness;

So fitly them in pairs thou hast combined:
Much less can bird with beast, or fish with fowl,
So well converse, nor with the ox the ape;
Worse, then, can man with beast, and least of all.'
"Whereto th' Almighty answered, not displeased:—
'A nice and subtle happiness, I see,
Thou to thyself proposest, in the choice
Of thy associates, Adam, and wilt taste
No pleasure, though in pleasure, solitary.
What think'st thou then of me, and this my state?
Seem I to thee sufficiently possessed
Of happiness, or not, who am alone
From all eternity? for none I know
Second to me or like, equal much less.
How have I, then, with whom to hold converse,
Save with the creatures which I made, and those
To me inferior infinite descents
Beneath what other creatures are to thee?'
"He ceased. I lowly answered:—'To attain
The height and depth of thy eternal ways
All human thoughts come short, Supreme of things!
Thou in thyself art perfect, and in thee
Is no deficience found. Not so is Man,
But in degree—the cause of his desire
By conversation with his like to help
Or solace his defects. No need that thou
Should'st propagate, already infinite,
And through all numbers absolute, though one;
But Man by number is to manifest
His single imperfection, and beget
Like of his like, his image multiplied,
In unity defective; which requires
Collateral love and dearest amity.
Thou, in thy secrecy although alone,
Best with thyself accompanied, seek'st not
Social communication—yet, so pleased,
Canst raise thy creature to what height thou wilt

Of union or communion, deified;
I, by conversing, cannot these erect
From prone, nor in their ways complacence find.'
Thus I emboldened spake, and freedom used
Permissive, and acceptance found; which gained
This answer from the gracious Voice Divine:—
"'Thus far to try thee, Adam, I was pleased,
And find thee knowing not of beasts alone,
Which thou hast rightly named, but of thyself—
Expressing well the spirit within thee free,
My image, not imparted to the brute;
Whose fellowship, therefore, unmeet for thee,
Good reason was thou freely shouldst dislike.
And be so minded still. I, ere thou spak'st,
Knew it not good for Man to be alone,
And no such company as then thou saw'st
Intended thee—for trial only brought,
To see how thou couldst judge of fit and meet.
What next I bring shall please thee, be assured,
Thy likeness, thy fit help, thy other self,
Thy wish exactly to thy heart's desire.'
"He ended, or I heard no more; for now
My earthly, by his heavenly overpowered,
Which it had long stood under, strained to the height
In that celestial colloquy sublime,
As with an object that excels the sense,
Dazzled and spent, sunk down, and sought repair
Of sleep, which instantly fell on me, called
By Nature as in aid, and closed mine eyes.
Mine eyes he closed, but open left the cell
Of fancy, my internal sight; by which,
Abstract as in a trance, methought I saw,
Though sleeping, where I lay, and saw the Shape
Still glorious before whom awake I stood;
Who, stooping, opened my left side, and took
From thence a rib, with cordial spirits warm,
And life-blood streaming fresh; wide was the wound,

But suddenly with flesh filled up and healed.
The rib he formed and fashioned with his hands;
Under his forming hands a creature grew,
Man-like, but different sex, so lovely fair
That what seemed fair in all the world seemed now
Mean, or in her summed up, in her contained
And in her looks, which from that time infused
Sweetness into my heart unfelt before,
And into all things from her air inspired
The spirit of love and amorous delight.
She disappeared, and left me dark; I waked
To find her, or for ever to deplore
Her loss, and other pleasures all abjure:
When, out of hope, behold her not far off,
Such as I saw her in my dream, adorned
With what all Earth or Heaven could bestow
To make her amiable. On she came,
Led by her Heavenly Maker, though unseen
And guided by his voice, nor uninformed
Of nuptial sanctity and marriage rites.
Grace was in all her steps, Heaven in her eye.
In every gesture dignity and love.
I, overjoyed, could not forbear aloud:—
"'This turn hath made amends; thou hast fulfilled
Thy words, Creator bounteous and benign,
Giver of all things fair—but fairest this
Of all thy gifts!—nor enviest. I now see
Bone of my bone, flesh of my flesh, my self
Before me. Woman is her name, of Man
Extracted; for this cause he shall forgo
Father and mother, and to his wife adhere,
And they shall be one flesh, one heart, one soul.'
"She heard me thus; and, though divinely brought,
Yet innocence and virgin modesty,
Her virtue, and the conscience of her worth,
That would be wooed, and not unsought be won,

Not obvious, not obtrusive, but retired,
The more desirable—or, to say all,
Nature herself, though pure of sinful thought—
Wrought in her so, that, seeing me, she turned.
I followed her; she what was honour knew,
And with obsequious majesty approved
My pleaded reason. To the nuptial bower
I led her blushing like the Morn; all Heaven,
And happy constellations, on that hour
Shed their selectest influence; the Earth
Gave sign of gratulation, and each hill;
Joyous the birds; fresh gales and gentle airs
Whispered it to the woods, and from their wings
Flung rose, flung odours from the spicy shrub,
Disporting, till the amorous bird of night
Sung spousal, and bid haste the Evening-star
On his hill-top to light the bridal lamp.
"Thus have I told thee all my state, and brought
My story to the sum of earthly bliss
Which I enjoy, and must confess to find
In all things else delight indeed, but such
As, used or not, works in the mind no change,
Nor vehement desire—these delicacies
I mean of taste, sight, smell, herbs, fruits, and flowers,
Walks, and the melody of birds: but here,
Far otherwise, transported I behold,
Transported touch; here passion first I felt,
Commotion strange, in all enjoyments else
Superior and unmoved, here only weak
Against the charm of beauty's powerful glance.
Or Nature failed in me, and left some part
Not proof enough such object to sustain,
Or, from my side subducting, took perhaps
More than enough—at least on her bestowed
Too much of ornament, in outward show
Elaborate, of inward less exact.

For well I understand in the prime end
Of Nature her th' inferior, in the mind
And inward faculties, which most excel;
In outward also her resembling less
His image who made both, and less expressing
The character of that dominion given
O'er other creatures. Yet when I approach
Her loveliness, so absolute she seems
And in herself complete, so well to know
Her own, that what she wills to do or say
Seems wisest, virtuousest, discreetest, best.
All higher Knowledge in her presence falls
Degraded; Wisdom in discourse with her
Loses, discountenanced, and like Folly shows;
Authority and Reason on her wait,
As one intended first, not after made
Occasionally; and, to consummate all,
Greatness of mind and nobleness their seat
Build in her loveliest, and create an awe
About her, as a guard angelic placed."
  To whom the Angel, with contracted brow:—
"Accuse not Nature! she hath done her part;
Do thou but thine! and be not diffident
Of Wisdom; she deserts thee not, if thou
Dismiss not her, when most thou need'st her nigh,
By attribúting overmuch to things
Less excellent, as thou thyself perceiv'st.
For, what admir'st thou, what transports thee so?
An outside—faïr, no doubt, and worthy well
Thy cherishing, thy honouring, and thy love;
Not thy subjection. Weigh with her thyself;
Then value. Oft-times nothing profits more
Than self-esteem, grounded on just and right
Well managed. Of that skill the more thou know'st,
The more she will acknowledge thee her head,
And to realities yield all her shows—

Made so adorn for thy delight the more,
So awful, that with honour thou may'st love
Thy mate, who sees when thou art seen least wise.
But, if the sense of touch, whereby mankind
Is propagated, seem such dear delight
Beyond all other, think the same vouchsafed
To cattle and each beast; which would not be
To them made common and divulged, if aught
Therein enjoyed were worthy to subdue
The soul of Man, or passion in him move.
What higher in her society thou find'st
Attractive, human, rational, love still:
In loving thou dost well; in passion not,
Wherein true Love consists not. Love refines
The thoughts, and heart enlarges—hath his seat
In Reason, and is judicious, is the scale
By which to heavenly Love thou may'st ascend,
Not sunk in carnal pleasure; for which cause
Among the beasts no mate for thee was found."
  To whom thus, half-abashed, Adam replied:—
" Neither her outside formed so fair, nor aught
In procreation, common to all kinds
(Though higher of the genial bed by far,
And with mysterious reverence, I deem),
So much delights me as those graceful acts,
Those thousand decencies, that daily flow
From all her words and actions, mixed with love
And sweet compliance, which declare unfeigned
Union of mind, or in us both one soul—
Harmony to behold in wedded pair
More grateful than harmonious sound to the ear.
Yet these subject not; I to thee disclose
What inward thence I feel, not therefore foiled,
Who meet with various objects, from the sense
Variously representing, yet, still free,
Approve the best, and follow what I approve.

To love thou blam'st me not—for Love, thou say'st,
Leads up to Heaven, is both the way and guide;
Bear with me, then, if lawful what I ask.
Love not the heavenly Spirits, and how their love
Express they—by looks only, or do they mix
Irradiance, virtual or immediate touch?"
 To whom the Angel, with a smile that glowed
Celestial rosy-red, Love's proper hue,
Answered:—" Let it suffice thee that thou know'st
Us happy, and without Love no happiness.
Whatever pure thou in the body enjoy'st
(And pure thou wert created) We enjoy
In eminence, and obstacle find none
Of membrane, joint, or limb, exclusive bars.
Easier than air with air, if Spirits embrace,
Total they mix, union of pure with pure
Desiring, nor restrained conveyance need
As flesh to mix with flesh, or soul with soul.
But I can now no more: the parting Sun
Beyond the Earth's green Cape and verdant Isles
Hesperean sets, my signal to depart.
Be strong, live happy, and love! but first of all
Him whom to love is to obey, and keep
His great command; take heed lest passion sway
Thy judgment to do aught which else free-will
Would not admit; thine and of all thy sons
The weal or woe in thee is placed; beware!
I in thy persevering shall rejoice,
And all the Blest. Stand fast; to stand or fall
Free in thine own arbitrement it lies.
Perfect within, no outward aid require;
And all temptation to transgress repel."
 So saying, he arose; whom Adam thus
Followed with benediction:—" Since to part,
Go, Heavenly Guest, Ethereal Messenger,
Sent from whose sovereign goodness I adore!

Gentle to me and affable hath been
Thy condescension, and shall be honoured ever
With graceful memory. Thou to mankind
Be good and friendly still, and oft return!"
  So parted they, the Angel up to Heaven
From the thick shade, and Adam to his bower.

THE END OF THE EIGHTH BOOK

BOOK IX

THE ARGUMENT

***Satan,** having compassed the Earth, with meditated guile returns as a mist by night into Paradise; enters into the Serpent sleeping. Adam and Eve in the morning go forth to their labours, which Eve proposes to divide in several places, each labouring apart: Adam consents not, alleging the danger lest that enemy of whom they were forewarned should attempt her found alone. Eve, loath to be thought not circumspect or firm enough, urges her going apart, the rather desirous to make trial of her strength; Adam at last yields. The Serpent finds her alone: his subtle approach, first gazing, then speaking, with much flattery extolling Eve above all other creatures. Eve, wondering to hear the Serpent speak, asks how he attained to human speech and such understanding not till now; the Serpent answers that by tasting of a certain tree in the garden he attained both to speech and reason, till then void of both. Eve requires him to bring her to that tree, and finds it to be the Tree of Knowledge forbidden: the Serpent, now grown bolder, with many wiles and arguments induces her at length to eat. She, pleased with the taste, deliberates a while whether to impart thereof to Adam or not; at last brings him of the fruit; relates what persuaded her to eat thereof. Adam, at first amazed, but perceiving her lost, resolves, through vehemence of love, to perish with her, and, extenuating the trespass, eats also of the fruit. The effects thereof in them both; they seek to cover their nakedness; then fall to variance and accusation of one another.*

No more of talk where God or Angel Guest
With Man, as with his friend, familiar used
To sit indulgent, and with him partake
Rural repast, permitting him the while
Venial discourse unblamed. I now must change
Those notes to tragic—foul distrust, and breach
Disloyal, on the part of man, revolt
And disobedience; on the part of Heaven,

Now alienated, distance and distaste,
Anger and just rebuke, and judgment given,
That brought into this World a world of woe,
Sin and her shadow Death, and Misery,
Death's harbinger. Sad task! yet argument
Not less but more heroic than the wrath
Of stern Achilles on his foe pursued
Thrice fugitive about Troy wall; or rage
Of Turnus for Lavinia disespoused;
Or Neptune's ire, or Juno's, that so long
Perplexed the Greek, and Cytherea's son:
If answerable style I can obtain
Of my celestial Patroness, who deigns
Her nightly visitation unimplored,
And dictates to me slumbering, or inspires
Easy my unpremeditated verse,
Since first this subject for heroic song
Pleased me, long choosing and beginning late,
Not sedulous by nature to indite
Wars, hitherto the only argument
Heroic deemed, chief mastery to dissect
With long and tedious havoc fabled knights
In battles feigned (the better fortitude
Of patience and heroic martyrdom
Unsung), or to describe races and games,
Or tilting furniture, emblazoned shields,
Impreses quaint, caparisons and steeds,
Bases and tinsel trappings, gorgeous knights
At joust and tournament; then marshalled feast
Served up in hall with sewers and seneschals:
The skill of artifice or office mean;
Not that which justly gives heroic name
To person or to poem. Me, of these
Nor skilled nor studious, higher argument
Remains, sufficient of itself to raise
That name, unless an age too late, or cold
Climate, or years, damp my intended wing

Depressed; and much they may if all be mine,
Not hers who brings it nightly to my ear.
  The Sun was sunk, and after him the Star
Of Hesperus, whose office is to bring
Twilight upon the Earth, short arbiter
'Twixt day and night, and now from end to end
Night's hemisphere had veiled the horizon round,
When Satan, who late fled before the threats
Of Gabriel out of Eden, now improved
In meditated fraud and malice, bent
On Man's destruction, maugre what might hap
Of heavier on himself, fearless returned.
By night he fled, and at midnight returned
From compassing the Earth—cautious of day
Since Uriel, Regent of the Sun, descried
His entrance, and forewarned the Cherubim
That kept their watch. Thence, full of anguish, driven,
The space of seven continued nights he rode
With darkness—thrice the equinoctial line
He circled, four times crossed the car of Night
From pole to pole, traversing each colure—
On the eighth returned, and on the coast averse
From entrance or cherubic watch by stealth
Found unsuspected way. There was a place
(Now not, though Sin, not Time, first wrought the change)
Where Tigris, at the foot of Paradise,
Into a gulf shot under ground, till part
Rose up a fountain by the Tree of Life.
In with the river sunk, and with it rose,
Satan, involved in rising mist; then sought
Where to lie hid. Sea he had searched and land
From Eden over Pontus, and the Pool
Maeotis, up beyond the river Ob;
Downward as far antarctic; and, in length,
West from Orontes to the ocean barred
At Darien, thence to the land where flows
Ganges and Indus. Thus the orb he roamed

With narrow search, and with inspection deep
Considered every creature, which of all
Most opportune might serve his wiles, and found
The Serpent subtlest beast of all the field.
Him, after long debate, irresolute
Of thoughts revolved, his final sentence chose
Fit vessel, fittest imp of fraud, in whom
To enter, and his dark suggestions hide
From sharpest sight; for in the wily snake
Whatever sleights none would suspicious mark,
As from his wit and native subtlety
Proceeding, which, in other beasts observed,
Doubt might beget of diabolic power
Active within beyond the sense of brute.
Thus he resolved, but first from inward grief
His bursting passion into plaints thus poured:—
"O Earth, how like to Heaven, if not preferred
More justly, seat worthier of Gods, as built
With second thought, reforming what was old!
For what God, after better, worse would build?
Terrestrial Heaven, danced round by other Heavens,
That shine, yet bear their bright officious lamps,
Light above light, for thee alone, as seems,
In thee concentring all their precious beams
Of sacred influence! As God in Heaven
Is centre, yet extends to all, so thou
Centring receiv'st from all those orbs; in thee,
Not in themselves, all their known virtue appears,
Productive in herb, plant, and nobler birth
Of creatures animate with gradual life
Of growth, sense, reason, all summed up in Man.
With what delight could I have walked thee round,
If I could joy in aught—sweet interchange
Of hill and valley, rivers, woods, and plains,
Now land, now sea, and shores with forest crowned,
Rocks, dens, and caves! But I in none of these
Find place or refuge; and the more I see

Pleasures about me, so much more I feel
Torment within me, as from the hateful siege
Of contraries; all good to me becomes
Bane, and in Heaven much worse would be my state.
But neither here seek I, no, nor in Heaven,
To dwell, unless by mastering Heaven's Supreme;
Nor hope to be myself less miserable
By what I seek, but others to make such
As I, though thereby worse to me redound.
For only in destroying I find ease
To my relentless thoughts; and him destroyed,
Or won to what may work his utter loss,
For whom all this was made, all this will soon
Follow, as to him linked in weal or woe:
In woe then, that destruction wide may range!
To me shall be the glory sole among
The infernal Powers, in one day to have marred
What he, Almighty styled, six nights and days
Continued making, and who knows how long
Before had been contriving? though perhaps
Not longer than since I in one night freed
From servitude inglorious well-nigh half
Th' angelic name, and thinner left the throng
Of his adorers. He, to be avenged,
And to repair his numbers thus impaired—
Whether such virtue, spent of old, now failed
More Angels to create (if they at least
Are his created), or to spite us more—
Determined to advance into our room
A creature formed of earth, and him endow,
Exalted from so base original,
With heavenly spoils, our spoils. What he decreed
He effected; Man he made, and for him built
Magnificent this World, and Earth his seat,
Him Lord pronounced, and, O indignity!
Subjected to his service Angel-wings
And flaming ministers, to watch and tend

Their earthy charge. Of these the vigilance
I dread, and to elude, thus wrapt in mist
Of midnight vapour, glide obscure, and pry
In every bush and brake, where hap may find
The Serpent sleeping, in whose mazy folds
To hide me, and the dark intent I bring.
O foul descent! that I, who erst contended
With Gods to sit the highest, am now constrained
Into a beast, and, mixed with bestial slime,
This essence to incarnate and imbrute,
That to the height of deity aspired!
But what will not ambition and revenge
Descend to? Who aspires must down as low
As high he soared, obnoxious, first or last,
To basest things. Revenge, at first though sweet,
Bitter ere long back on itself recoils.
Let it; I reck not, so it light well aimed,
Since higher I fall short, on him who next
Provokes my envy, this new favourite
Of Heaven, this Man of clay, son of despite,
Whom, us the more to spite, his Maker raised
From dust: spite then with spite is best repaid."
  So saying, through each thicket, dank or dry,
Like a black mist low-creeping, he held on
His midnight search, where soonest he might find
The Serpent. Him fast sleeping soon he found,
In labyrinth of many a round self-rolled,
His head the midst, well stored with subtle wiles:
Not yet in horrid shade or dismal den,
Nor nocent yet, but on the grassy herb,
Fearless, unfeared, he slept. In at his mouth
The Devil entered, and his brutal sense,
In heart or head, possessing soon inspired
With act intelligential; but his sleep
Disturbed not, waiting close th' approach of morn.
  Now, whenas sacred light began to dawn
In Eden on the humid flowers, that breathed

Their morning incense, when all things that breathe
From th' Earth's great altar send up silent praise
To the Creator, and his nostrils fill
With grateful smell, forth came the human pair,
And joined their vocal worship to the choir
Of creatures wanting voice; that done, partake
The season, prime for sweetest scents and airs;
Then cómmune how that day they best may ply
Their growing work—for much their work outgrew
The hands' dispatch of two gardening so wide:
And Eve first to her husband thus began:—
"Adam, well may we labour still to dress
This garden, still to tend plant, herb, and flower,
Our pleasant task enjoined; but, till more hands
Aid us, the work under our labour grows,
Luxurious by restraint: what we by day
Lop overgrown, or prune, or prop, or bind,
One night or two with wanton growth derides,
Tending to wild. Thou, therefore, now advise,
Or hear what to my mind first thoughts present.
Let us divide our labours—thou where choice
Leads thee, or where most needs, whether to wind
The woodbine round this arbour, or direct
The clasping ivy where to climb; while I
In yonder spring of roses intermixed
With myrtle find what to redress till noon.
For, while so near each other thus all day
Our task we choose, what wonder if so near
Looks intervene and smiles, or objects new
Casual discourse draw on, which intermits
Our day's work, brought to little, though begun
Early, and th' hour of supper comes unearned!"
To whom mild answer Adam thus returned:—
"Sole Eve, associate sole, to me beyond
Compare above all living creatures dear!
Well hast thou motioned, well thy thoughts employed
How we might best fulfil the work which here

God hath assigned us, nor of me shalt pass
Unpraised; for nothing lovelier can be found
In woman than to study household good,
And good works in her husband to promote.
Yet not so strictly hath our Lord imposed
Labour as to debar us when we need
Refreshment, whether food or talk between,
Food of the mind, or this sweet intercourse
Of looks and smiles; for smiles from reason flow,
To brute denied, and are of love the food—
Love, not the lowest end of human life.
For not to irksome toil, but to delight,
He made us, and delight to reason joined.
These paths and bowers doubt not but our joint hands
Will keep from wilderness with ease, as wide
As we need walk, till younger hands ere long
Assist us. But, if much converse perhaps
Thee satiate, to short absence I could yield;
For solitude sometimes is best society,
And short retirement urges sweet return.
But other doubt possesses me, lest harm
Befall thee, severed from me; for thou know'st
What hath been warned us—what malicious foe,
Envying our happiness, and of his own
Despairing, seeks to work us woe and shame
By sly assault, and somewhere nigh at hand
Watches, no doubt, with greedy hope to find
His wish and best advantage, us asunder,
Hopeless to circumvent us joined, where each
To other speedy aid might lend at need.
Whether his first design be to withdraw
Our fealty from God, or to disturb
Conjugal love—than which perhaps no bliss
Enjoyed by us excites his envy more—
Or this, or worse, leave not the faithful side
That gave thee being, still shades thee and protects.
The wife, where danger or dishonour lurks,

Safest and seemliest by her husband stays,
Who guards her, or with her the worst endures."
To whom the virgin majesty of Eve,
As one who loves, and some unkindness meets,
With sweet austere composure thus replied:—
"Offspring of Heaven and Earth, and all Earth's lord!
That such an enemy we have, who seeks
Our ruin, both by thee informed I learn,
And from the parting Angel overheard,
As in a shady nook I stood behind,
Just then returned at shut of evening flowers.
But that thou shouldst my firmness therefore doubt
To God or thee, because we have a foe
May tempt it, I expected not to hear.
His violence thou fear'st not, being such
As we, not capable of death or pain,
Can either not receive, or can repel.
His fraud is, then, thy fear; which plain infers
Thy equal fear that my firm faith and love
Can by his fraud be shaken or seduced:
Thoughts, which how found they harbour in thy breast,
Adam! misthought of her to thee so dear?"
To whom, with healing words, Adam replied:—
"Daughter of God and Man, immortal Eve!—
For such thou art, from sin and blame entire—
Not diffident of thee do I dissuade
Thy absence from my sight, but to avoid
Th' attempt itself, intended by our foe.
For he who tempts, though in vain, at least asperses
The tempted with dishonour foul, supposed
Not incorruptible of faith, not proof
Against temptation. Thou thyself with scorn
And anger wouldst resent the offered wrong,
Though ineffectual found; misdeem not, then,
If such affront I labour to avert
From thee alone, which on us both at once
The enemy, though bold, will hardly dare;

Or, daring, first on me th' assault shall light.
Nor thou his malice and false guile contemn—
Subtle he needs must be who could seduce
Angels—nor think superfluous others' aid.
I from the influence of thy looks receive
Access in every virtue—in thy sight
More wise, more watchful, stronger, if need were
Of outward strength; while shame, thou looking on,
Shame to be overcome or overreached,
Would utmost vigour raise, and raised unite.
Why shouldst not thou like sense within thee feel
When I am present, and thy trial choose
With me, best witness of thy virtue tried?"
  So spake domestic Adam in his care
And matrimonial love; but Eve, who thought
Less áttributed to her faith sincere,
Thus her reply with accent sweet renewed—
  "If this be our condition, thus to dwell
In narrow circuit straitened by a foe,
Subtle or violent, we not endued
Single with like defence wherever met,
How are we happy, still in fear of harm?
But harm precedes not sin: only our foe
Tempting affronts us with his foul esteem
Of our integrity: his foul esteem
Sticks no dishonour on our front, but turns
Foul on himself; then wherefore shunned or feared
By us, who rather double honour gain
From his surmise proved false, find peace within,
Favour from Heaven, our witness, from th' event?
And what is faith, love, virtue, unassayed
Alone, without exterior help sustained?
Let us not then suspect our happy state
Left so imperfect by the Maker wise
As not secure to single or combined.
Frail is our happiness, if this be so;
And Eden were no Eden, thus exposed."

To whom thus Adam fervently replied:—
"O Woman, best are all things as the will
Of God ordained them; his creating hand
Nothing imperfect or deficient left
Of all that he created—much less Man,
Or aught that might his happy state secure,
Secure from outward force. Within himself
The danger lies, yet lies within his power;
Against his will he can receive no harm.
But God left free the Will; for what obeys
Reason is free; and Reason he made right,
But bid her well beware, and still erect,
Lest, by some fair appearing good surprised,
She dictate false, and misinform the Will
To do what God expressly hath forbid.
Not then mistrust, but tender love, enjoins
That I should mind thee oft; and mind thou me.
Firm we subsist, yet possible to swerve,
Since Reason not impossibly may meet
Some specious object by the foe suborned,
And fall into deception unaware,
Not keeping strictest watch, as she was warned.
Seek not temptation, then, which to avoid
Were better, and most likely if from me
Thou sever not: trial will come unsought.
Wouldst thou approve thy constancy, approve
First thy obedience; th' other who can know,
Not seeing thee attempted, who attest?
But if thou think trial unsought may find
Us both securer than thus warned thou seem'st,
Go; for thy stay, not free, absents thee more.
Go in thy native innocence; rely
On what thou hast of virtue; summon all;
For God towards thee hath done his part: do thine."
So spake the Patriarch of Mankind; but Eve
Persisted; yet submiss, though last, replied:—
"With thy permission, then, and thus forewarned,

Chiefly by what thy own last reasoning words
Touched only, that our trial, when least sought,
May find us both perhaps far less prepared,
The willinger I go, nor much expect
A foe so proud will first the weaker seek;
So bent, the more shall shame him his repulse."
  Thus saying, from her husband's hand her hand
Soft she withdrew, and, like a wood-nymph light,
Oread or Dryad, or of Delia's train,
Betook her to the groves, but Delia's self
In gait surpassed and goddess-like deport,
Though not as she with bow and quiver armed,
But with such gardening tools as Art, yet rude,
Guiltless of fire had formed, or Angels brought.
To Pales, or Pomona, thus adorned,
Likest she seemed—Pomona when she fled
Vertumnus—or to Ceres in her prime,
Yet virgin of Proserpina from Jove.
Her long with ardent look his eye pursued
Delighted, but desiring more her stay.
Oft he to her his charge of quick return
Repeated; she to him as oft engaged
To be returned by noon amid the bower,
And all things in best order to invite
Noontide repast, or afternoon's repose.
O much deceived, much failing, hapless Eve,
Of thy presumed return! event perverse!
Thou never from that hour in Paradise
Found'st either sweet repast or sound repose:
Such ambush, hid among sweet flowers and shades,
Waited, with hellish rancour imminent,
To intercept thy way, or send thee back
Despoiled of innocence, of faith, of bliss.
For now, and since first break of dawn, the Fiend,
Mere serpent in appearance, forth was come,
And on his quest where likeliest he might find
The only two of mankind, but in them

The whole included race, his purposed prey.
In bower and field he sought, where any tuft
Of grove or garden-plot more pleasant lay,
Their tendance or plantation for delight;
By fountain or by shady rivulet
He sought them both, but wished his hap might find
Eve separate; he wished, but not with hope
Of what so seldom chanced, when to his wish,
Beyond his hope, Eve separate he spies,
Veiled in a cloud of fragrance, where she stood,
Half-spied, so thick the roses bushing round
About her glowed, oft stooping to support
Each flower of tender stalk, whose head, though gay
Carnation, purple, azure, or specked with gold,
Hung drooping unsustained. Them she upstays
Gently with myrtle band, mindless the while
Herself, though fairest unsupported flower,
From her best prop so far, and storm so nigh.
Nearer he drew, and many a walk traversed
Of stateliest covert, cedar, pine, or palm;
Then voluble and bold, now hid, now seen
Among thick-woven arborets, and flowers
Imbordered on each bank, the hand of Eve:
Spot more delicious than those gardens feigned
Or of revived Adonis, or renowned
Alcinoüs, host of old Laertes' son,
Or that, not mystic, where the sapient king
Held dalliance with his fair Egyptian spouse.
Much he the place admired, the person more.
As one who, long in populous city pent,
Where houses thick and sewers annoy the air,
Forth issuing on a summer's morn, to breathe
Among the pleasant villages and farms
Adjoined, from each thing met conceives delight—
The smell of grain, or tedded grass, or kine,
Or dairy, each rural sight, each rural sound—
If chance with nymph-like step fair virgin pass,

What pleasing seemed, for her now pleases more,
She most, and in her look sums all delight:
Such pleasure took the Serpent to behold
This flowery plat, the sweet recess of Eve
Thus early, thus alone. Her heavenly form
Angelic, but more soft and feminine,
Her graceful innocence, her every air
Of gesture or least action, overawed
His malice, and with rapine sweet bereaved
His fierceness of the fierce intent it brought.
That space the Evil One abstracted stood
From his own evil, and for the time remained
Stupidly good, of enmity disarmed,
Of guile, of hate, of envy, of revenge.
But the hot hell that always in him burns,
Though in mid Heaven, soon ended his delight
And tortures him now more, the more he sees
Of pleasure not for him ordained. Then soon
Fierce hate he recollects, and all his thoughts
Of mischief, gratulating, thus excites:—
  "Thoughts, whither have ye led me? with what sweet
Compulsion thus transported to forget
What hither brought us? hate, not love, nor hope
Of Paradise for Hell, hope her to taste
Of pleasure, but all pleasure to destroy,
Save what is in destroying; other joy
To me is lost. Then let me not let pass
Occasion which now smiles. Behold alone
The Woman, opportune to all attempts;
Her husband, for I view far round, not nigh,
Whose higher intellectual more I shun,
And strength, of courage haughty, and of limb
Heroic built, though of terrestrial mould;
Foe not informidable, exempt from wound—
I not; so much hath Hell debased, and pain
Enfeebled me, to what I was in Heaven.
She fair, divinely fair, fit love for Gods,

Not terrible, though terror be in love,
And beauty, not approached by stronger hate,
Hate stronger under show of love well feigned,
The way which to her ruin now I tend."
  So spake the Enemy of Mankind, enclosed
In serpent, inmate bad, and toward Eve
Addressed his way—not with indented wave,
Prone on the ground, as since, but on his rear,
Circular base of rising folds, that towered
Fold above fold, a surging maze; his head
Crested aloft, and carbuncle his eyes;
With burnished neck of verdant gold, erect
Amidst his circling spires, that on the grass
Floated redundant. Pleasing was his shape
And lovely; never since of serpent kind
Lovelier—not those that in Illyria changed
Hermione and Cadmus, or the god
In Epidaurus: nor to which transformed
Ammonian Jove, or Capitoline, was seen,
He with Olympias, this with her who bore
Scipio, the height of Rome. With tract oblique
At first, as one, who sought access but feared
To interrupt, sidelong he works his way.
As when a ship, by skilful steersman wrought
Nigh river's mouth, or foreland, where the wind
Veers oft, as oft so steers, and shifts her sail,
So varied he, and of his tortuous train
Curled many a wanton wreath in sight of Eve,
To lure her eye. She, busied, heard the sound
Of rustling leaves, but minded not, as used
To such disport before her through the field
From every beast, more duteous at her call
Than at Circean call the herd disguised.
He, bolder now, uncalled before her stood,
But as in gaze admiring. Oft he bowed
His turret crest and sleek enamelled neck,
Fawning, and licked the ground whereon she trod.

His gentle dumb expression turned at length
The eye of Eve to mark his play; he, glad
Of her attention gained, with serpent-tongue
Organic, or impulse of vocal air,
His fraudulent temptation thus began:—
"Wonder not, sovereign mistress (if perhaps
Thou canst who art sole wonder), much less arm
Thy looks, the heaven of mildness, with disdain,
Displeased that I approach thee thus, and gaze
Insatiate, I thus single, nor have feared
Thy awful brow, more awful thus retired.
Fairest resemblance of thy Maker fair,
Thee all things living gaze on, all things thine
By gift, and thy celestial beauty adore,
With ravishment beheld—there best beheld
Where universally admired. But here,
In this enclosure wild, these beasts among,
Beholders rude, and shallow to discern
Half what in thee is fair, one man except,
Who sees thee (and what is one?) who shouldst be seen
A Goddess among Gods, adored and served
By Angels numberless, thy daily train?"
So glozed the Tempter, and his proem tuned.
Into the heart of Eve his words made way,
Though at the voice much marvelling; at length,
Not unamazed, she thus in answer spake:—
"What may this mean? Language of Man pronounced
By tongue of brute, and human sense expressed!
The first at least of these I thought denied
To beasts, whom God on their creation-day
Created mute to all articulate sound;
The latter I demur, for in their looks
Much reason, and in their actions, oft appears.
Thee, Serpent, subtlest beast of all the field
I knew, but not with human voice endued;
Redouble then this miracle, and say,
How cam'st thou speakable of mute, and how

To me so friendly grown above the rest
Of brutal kind that daily are in sight:
Say, for such wonder claims attention due."
  To whom the guileful Tempter thus replied:—
"Empress of this fair World, resplendent Eve!
Easy to me it is to tell thee all
What thou command'st, and right thou shouldst be obeyed.
I was at first as other beasts that graze
The trodden herb, of abject thoughts and low,
As was my food, nor aught but food discerned
Or sex, and apprehended nothing high:
Till on a day, roving the field, I chanced
A goodly tree far distant to behold,
Loaden with fruit of fairest colours mixed,
Ruddy and gold. I nearer drew to gaze;
When from the boughs a savoury odour blown,
Grateful to appetite, more pleased my sense
Than smell of sweetest fennel, or the teats
Of ewe or goat dropping with milk at even,
Unsucked of lamb or kid, that tend their play.
To satisfy the sharp desire I had
Of tasting those fair apples, I resolved
Not to defer; hunger and thirst at once,
Powerful persuaders, quickened at the scent
Of that alluring fruit, urged me so keen.
About the mossy trunk I wound me soon;
For, high from ground, the branches would require
Thy utmost reach, or Adam's: round the tree
All other beasts that saw, with like desire
Longing and envying stood, but could not reach.
Amid the tree now got, where plenty hung
Tempting so nigh, to pluck and eat my fill
I spared not; for such pleasure till that hour
At feed or fountain never had I found.
Sated at length, ere long I might perceive
Strange alteration in me, to degree
Of reason in my inward powers, and speech

Wanted not long, though to this shape retained.
Thenceforth to speculations high or deep
I turned my thoughts, and with capacious mind
Considered all things visible in Heaven,
Or Earth, or Middle, all things fair and good.
But all that fair and good in thy divine
Semblance and in thy beauty's heavenly ray,
United I beheld—no fair to thine
Equivalent or second; which compelled
Me thus, though importune perhaps, to come
And gaze, and worship thee of right declared
Sovereign of creatures, universal Dame!"
  So talked the spirited sly Snake; and Eve,
Yet more amazed, unwary thus replied:—
  "Serpent, thy overpraising leaves in doubt
The virtue of that fruit, in thee first proved.
But say, where grows the tree? from hence how far?
For many are the trees of God that grow
In Paradise, and various, yet unknown
To us; in such abundance lies our choice
As leaves a greater store of fruit untouched,
Still hanging incorruptible, till men
Grow up to their provision, and more hands
Help to disburden Nature of her bearth."
  To whom the wily Adder, blithe and glad:—
"Empress, the way is ready, and not long—
Beyond a row of myrtles, on a flat,
Fast by a fountain, one small thicket past
Of blowing myrrh and balm. If thou accept
My conduct, I can bring thee thither soon."
  "Lead, then," said Eve. He, leading, swiftly rolled
In tangles, and made intricate seem straight,
To mischief swift. Hope elevates, and joy
Brightens his crest. As when a wandering fire,
Compact of unctuous vapour, which the night
Condenses, and the cold environs round,
Kindled through agitation to a flame

(Which oft, they say, some evil spirit attends),
Hovering and blazing with delusive light,
Misleads th' amazed night-wanderer from his way
To bogs and mires, and oft through pond or pool,
There swallowed up and lost, from succour far:
So glistered the dire Snake, and into fraud
Led Eve, our credulous mother, to the Tree
Of Prohibition, root of all our woe;
Which when she saw, thus to her guide she spake:—
"Serpent, we might have spared our coming hither,
Fruitless to me, though fruit be here to excess,
The credit of whose virtue rest with thee—
Wondrous indeed, if cause of such effects!
But of this tree we may not taste or touch;
God so commanded, and left that command
Sole daughter of his voice: the rest, we live
Law to ourselves; our reason is our law."
To whom the Tempter guilefully replied:—
"Indeed! Hath God then said that of the fruit
Of all these garden-trees ye shall not eat,
Yet lords declared of all in earth or air?"
To whom thus Eve, yet sinless:— "Of the fruit
Of each tree in the garden we may eat;
But of the fruit of this fair tree, amidst
The garden, God hath said, 'Ye shall not eat
Thereof, nor shall ye touch it, lest ye die.'"
She scarce had said, though brief, when now more bold
The Tempter, but with show of zeal and love
To Man, and indignation at his wrong,
New part puts on, and, as to passion moved,
Fluctuates disturbed, yet comely, and in act
Raised, as of some great matter to begin.
As when of old some orator renowned
In Athens or free Rome, where eloquence
Flourished, since mute, to some great cause addressed,
Stood in himself collected, while each part,
Motion, each act, won audience ere the tongue

Sometimes in height began, as no delay
Of preface brooking through his zeal of right:
So standing, moving, or to height upgrown,
The Tempter, all impassioned, thus began:—
"O sacred, wise, and wisdom-giving Plant,
Mother of science! now I feel thy power
Within me clear, not only to discern
Things in their causes, but to trace the ways
Of highest agents, deemed however wise.
Queen of this Universe! do not believe
Those rigid threats of death. Ye shall not die.
How should ye? By the fruit? it gives you life
To knowledge. By the Threatener? look on me,
Me who have touched and tasted, yet both live,
And life more perfect have attained than Fate
Meant me, by venturing higher than my lot.
Shall that be shut to Man which to the beast
Is open? or will God incense his ire
For such a petty trespass, and not praise
Rather your dauntless virtue, whom the pain
Of death denounced, whatever thing Death be,
Deterred not from achieving what might lead
To happier life, knowledge of good and evil?
Of good, how just? of evil—if what is evil
Be real, why not known, since easier shunned?
God therefore cannot hurt ye, and be just;
Not just, not God; not feared then, nor obeyed;
Your fear itself of death removes the fear.
Why, then, was this forbid? Why but to awe,
Why but to keep ye low and ignorant,
His worshippers? He knows that in the day
Ye eat thereof your eyes, that seem so clear,
Yet are but dim, shall perfectly be then
Opened and cleared, and ye shall be as Gods,
Knowing both good and evil, as they know.
That ye should be as Gods, since I as Man,
Internal Man, is but proportion meet—

I, of brute, human; ye, of human, Gods.
So ye shall die perhaps, by putting off
Human, to put on Gods—death to be wished,
Though threatened, which no worse than this can bring!
And what are Gods, that Man may not become
As they, participating godlike food?
The Gods are first, and that advantage use
On our belief, that all from them proceeds.
I question it; for this fair Earth I see,
Warmed by the Sun, producing every kind;
Them nothing. If they all things, who enclosed
Knowledge of good and evil in this tree,
That whoso eats thereof forthwith attains
Wisdom without their leave? and wherein lies
Th' offence, that Man should thus attain to know?
What can your knowledge hurt him, or this tree
Impart against his will, if all be his?
Or is it envy? and can envy dwell
In heavenly breasts? These, these and many more
Causes import your need of this fair fruit.
Goddess humane, reach, then, and freely taste!"
  He ended; and his words, replete with guile,
Into her heart too easy entrance won.
Fixed on the fruit she gazed, which to behold
Might tempt alone; and in her ears the sound
Yet rung of his persuasive words, impregned
With reason, to her seeming, and with truth.
Meanwhile the hour of noon drew on, and waked
An eager appetite, raised by the smell
So savoury of that fruit, which with desire,
Inclinable now grown to touch or taste,
Solicited her longing eye; yet first,
Pausing a while, thus to herself she mused:—
  "Great are thy virtues, doubtless, best of fruits,
Though kept from Man, and worthy to be admired,
Whose taste, too long forborne, at first assay
Gave elocution to the mute, and taught

The tongue not made for speech to speak thy praise.
Thy praise he also who forbids thy use
Conceals not from us, naming thee the Tree
Of Knowledge, knowledge both of good and evil;
Forbids us then to taste. But his forbidding
Commends thee more, while it infers the good
By thee communicated, and our want;
For good unknown sure is not had, or, had
And yet unknown, is as not had at all.
In plain, then, what forbids he but to know?
Forbids us good, forbids us to be wise!
Such prohibitions bind not. But, if Death
Bind us with after-bands, what profits then
Our inward freedom? In the day we eat
Of this fair fruit, our doom is we shall die!
How dies the Serpent? He hath eaten, and lives,
And knows, and speaks, and reasons, and discerns,
Irrational till then. For us alone
Was death invented? or to us denied
This intellectual food, for beasts reserved?
For beasts it seems; yet that one beast which first
Hath tasted envies not, but brings with joy
The good befallen him, author unsuspect,
Friendly to Man, far from deceit or guile.
What fear I, then? rather, what know to fear
Under this ignorance of good and evil,
Of God or Death, of law or penalty?
Here grows the cure of all, this fruit divine,
Fair to the eye, inviting to the taste,
Of virtue to make wise. What hinders, then,
To reach, and feed at once both body and mind?"
So saying, her rash hand in evil hour
Forth-reaching to the fruit, she plucked, she eat.
Earth felt the wound, and Nature from her seat,
Sighing through all her works, gave signs of woe
That all was lost. Back to the thicket slunk
The guilty Serpent, and well might, for Eve,

Intent now wholly on her taste, naught else
Regarded; such delight till then, as seemed,
In fruit she never tasted, whether true,
Or fancied so through expectation high
Of knowledge; nor was Godhead from her thought.
Greedily she ingorged without restraint,
And knew not eating death. Satiate at length,
And heightened as with wine, jocund and boon,
Thus to herself she pleasingly began:—
"O sovereign, virtuous, precious of all trees
In Paradise! of operation blest
To sapience, hitherto obscured, infamed,
And thy fair fruit let hang, as to no end
Created! but henceforth my early care,
Not without song, each morning, and due praise,
Shall tend thee, and the fertile burden ease
Of thy full branches, offered free to all;
Till, dieted by thee, I grow mature
In knowledge, as the Gods who all things know.
Though others envy what they cannot give—
For, had the gift been theirs, it had not here
Thus grown! Experience, next to thee I owe,
Best guide: not following thee, I had remained
In ignorance; thou open'st Wisdom's way,
And giv'st access, though secret she retire.
And I perhaps am secret: Heaven is high—
High, and remote to see from thence distinct
Each thing on Earth; and other care perhaps
May have diverted from continual watch
Our great Forbidder, safe with all his spies
About him. But to Adam in what sort
Shall I appear? Shall I to him make known
As yet my change, and give him to partake
Full happiness with me, or rather not,
But keep the odds of knowledge in my power
Without copartner? so to add what wants
In female sex, the more to draw his love,

And render me more equal, and perhaps—
A thing not undesirable—sometime
Superior; for, inferior, who is free?
This may be well; but what if God have seen,
And death ensue? Then I shall be no more;
And Adam, wedded to another Eve,
Shall live with her enjoying, I extinct!
A death to think! Confirmed, then, I resolve
Adam shall share with me in bliss or woe.
So dear I love him that with him all deaths
I could endure, without him live no life."
So saying, from the tree her step she turned,
But first low reverence done, as to the Power
That dwelt within, whose presence had infused
Into the plant sciential sap, derived
From nectar, drink of Gods. Adam the while,
Waiting desirous her return, had wove
Of choicest flowers a garland, to adorn
Her tresses, and her rural labours crown,
As reapers oft are wont their harvest-queen.
Great joy he promised to his thoughts, and new
Solace in her return, so long delayed;
Yet oft his heart, divine of something ill,
Misgave him. He the faltering measure felt,
And forth to meet her went, the way she took
That morn when first they parted. By the Tree
Of Knowledge he must pass; there he her met,
Scarce from the tree returning; in her hand
A bough of fairest fruit, that downy smiled,
New gathered, and ambrosial smell diffused.
To him she hasted; in her face excuse
Came prologue, and apology to prompt,
Which, with bland words at will, she thus addressed:—
"Hast thou not wondered, Adam, at my stay?
Thee I have missed, and thought it long, deprived
Thy presence—agony of love till now
Not felt, nor shall be twice; for never more

Mean I to try, what rash untried I sought,
The pain of absence from thy sight. But strange
Hath been the cause, and wonderful to hear.
This tree is not, as we are told, a tree
Of danger tasted, nor to evil unknown
Opening the way, but of divine effect
To open eyes, and make them Gods who taste;
And hath been tasted such. The Serpent wise,
Or not restrained as we, or not obeying,
Hath eaten of the fruit, and is become
Not dead, as we are threatened, but thenceforth
Endued with human voice and human sense,
Reasoning to admiration, and with me
Persuasively hath so prevailed that I
Have also tasted, and have also found
Th' effects to correspond—opener mine eyes,
Dim erst, dilated spirits, ampler heart,
And growing up to Godhead; which for thee
Chiefly I sought, without thee can despise.
For bliss, as thou hast part, to me is bliss;
Tedious, unshared with thee, and odious soon.
Thou, therefore, also taste, that equal lot
May join us, equal joy, as equal love;
Lest, thou not tasting, different degree
Disjoin us, and I then too late renounce
Deity for thee, when Fate will not permit."
  Thus Eve with countenance blithe her story told;
But in her cheek distemper flushing glowed.
On th' other side, Adam, soon as he heard
The fatal trespass done by Eve, amazed,
Astonied stood and blank, while horror chill
Ran through his veins, and all his joints relaxed.
From his slack hand the garland wreathed for Eve
Down dropt, and all the faded roses shed.
Speechless he stood and pale, till thus at length
First to himself he inward silence broke:—
  "O fairest of creation, last and best

Of all God's works, creature in whom excelled
Whatever can to sight or thought be formed,
Holy, divine, good, amiable, or sweet!
How art thou lost! how on a sudden lost,
Defaced, deflowered, and now to death devote!
Rather, how hast thou yielded to transgress
The strict forbiddance, how to violate
The sacred fruit forbidden? Some cursèd fraud
Of enemy hath beguiled thee, yet unknown,
And me with thee hath ruined; for with thee
Certain my resolution is to die.
How can I live without thee; how forgo
Thy sweet converse, and love so dearly joined,
To live again in these wild woods forlorn?
Should God create another Eve, and I
Another rib afford, yet loss of thee
Would never from my heart. No, no! I feel
The link of nature draw me: flesh of flesh,
Bone of my bone thou art, and from thy state
Mine never shall be parted, bliss or woe."
  So having said, as one from sad dismay
Recomforted, and, after thoughts disturbed,
Submitting to what seemed remediless,
Thus in calm mood his words to Eve he turned:—
  "Bold deed thou hast presumed, adventurous Eve,
And peril great provoked, who thus hast dared
Had it been only coveting to eye
That sacred food, sacred to abstinence;
Much more to taste it, under ban to touch.
But past who can recall, or done undo?
Not God Omnipotent, nor Fate! Yet so
Perhaps thou shalt not die; perhaps the fact
Is no so heinous now—foretasted fruit,
Profaned first by the Serpent, by him first
Made common and unhallowed ere your taste,
Nor yet on him found deadly. He yet lives—
Lives, as thou saidst, and gains to live, as Man,

Higher degree of life: inducement strong
To us, as likely, tasting, to attain
Proportional ascent; which cannot be
But to be Gods, or Angels, demi-gods.
Nor can I think that God, Creator wise,
Though threatening, will in earnest so destroy
Us, his prime creatures, dignified so high,
Set over all his works; which, in our fall,
For us created, needs with us must fail,
Dependent made. So God shall uncreate,
Be frustrate, do, undo, and labour lose—
Not well conceived of God; who, though his power
Creation could repeat, yet would be loath
Us to abolish, lest the Adversary
Triumph and say: 'Fickle their state whom God
Most favours; who can please him long? Me first
He ruined, now Mankind; whom will he next?'—
Matter of scorn not to be given the Foe.
However, I with thee have fixed my lot,
Certain to undergo like doom. If death
Consort with thee, death is to me as life;
So forcible within my heart I feel
The bond of Nature draw me to my own—
My own in thee; for what thou art is mine.
Our state cannot be severed; we are one,
One flesh; to lose thee were to lose myself."
  So Adam; and thus Eve to him replied:—
"O glorious trial of exceeding love,
Illustrious evidence, example high!
Engaging me to emulate; but, short
Of thy perfection, how shall I attain,
Adam? from whose dear side I boast me sprung,
And gladly of our union hear thee speak,
One heart, one soul in both; whereof good proof
This day affords, declaring thee resolved,
Rather than death, or aught than death more dread,
Shall separate us, linked in love so dear,

To undergo with me one guilt, one crime,
If any be, of tasting this fair fruit;
Whose virtue (for of good still good proceeds,
Direct, or by occasion) hath presented
This happy trial of thy love, which else
So eminently never had been known
Were it I thought death menaced would ensue
This my attempt, I would sustain alone
The worst, and not persuade thee—rather die
Deserted than oblige thee with a fact
Pernicious to thy peace, chiefly assured
Remarkably so late of thy so true,
So faithful, love unequalled. But I feel
Far otherwise th' event—not death, but life
Augmented, opened eyes, new hopes, new joys,
Taste so divine that what of sweet before
Hath touched my sense flat seems to this and harsh.
On my experience, Adam, freely taste,
And fear of death deliver to the winds."
  So saying, she embraced him, and for joy
Tenderly wept, much won that he his love
Had so ennobled, as of choice to incur
Divine displeasure for her sake, or death.
In recompense (for such compliance bad
Such recompense best merits), from the bough
She gave him of that fair enticing fruit
With liberal hand. He scrupled not to eat,
Against his better knowledge, not deceived,
But fondly overcome with female charm.
Earth trembled from her entrails, as again
In pangs, and Nature gave a second groan;
Sky loured, and, muttering thunder, some sad drops
Wept at completing of the mortal sin
Original; while Adam took no thought,
Eating his fill, nor Eve to iterate
Her former trespass feared, the more to soothe
Him with her loved society; that now.

As with new wine intoxicated both,
They swim in mirth, and fancy that they feel
Divinity within them breeding wings
Wherewith to scorn the Earth. But that false fruit
Far other operation first displayed,
Carnal desire inflaming. He on Eve
Began to cast lascivious eyes; she him
As wantonly repaid; in lust they burn,
Till Adam thus 'gan Eve to dalliance move:—
"Eve, now I see thou art exact of taste
And elegant—of sapience no small part;
Since to each meaning savour we apply,
And palate call judicious. I the praise
Yield thee; so well this day thou hast purveyed.
Much pleasure we have lost, while we abstained
From this delightful fruit, nor known till now
True relish, tasting. If such pleasure be
In things to us forbidden, it might be wished
For this one tree had been forbidden ten.
But come; so well refreshed, now let us play,
As meet is, after such delicious fare;
For never did thy beauty, since the day
I saw thee first and wedded thee, adorned
With all perfections, so inflame my sense
With ardour to enjoy thee, fairer now
Than ever—bounty of this virtuous tree!"
So said he, and forbore not glance or toy
Of amorous intent, well understood
Of Eve, whose eye darted contagious fire.
Her hand he seized, and to a shady bank,
Thick overhead with verdant roof embowered,
He led her, nothing loath; flowers were the couch,
Pansies, and violets, and asphodel,
And hyacinth—Earth's freshest, softest lap.
There they their fill of love and love's disport
Took largely, of their mutual guilt the seal,
The solace of their sin, till dewy sleep

Oppressed them, wearied with their amorous play.
  Soon as the force of that fallacious fruit,
That with exhilarating vapour bland
About their spirits had played, and inmost powers
Made err, was now exhaled, and grosser sleep,
Bred of unkindly fumes, with conscious dreams
Encumbered, now had left them, up they rose
As from unrest, and each the other viewing,
Soon found their eyes how opened, and their minds
How darkened. Innocence, that as a veil
Had shadowed them from knowing ill, was gone;
Just confidence, and native righteousness,
And honour, from about them, naked left
To guilty Shame: he covered, but his robe
Uncovered more. So rose the Danite strong,
Herculean Samson, from the harlot-lap
Of Philistean Dalilah, and waked
Shorn of his strength; they destitute and bare
Of all their virtue. Silent, and in face
Confounded, long they sat, as stricken mute;
Till Adam, though not less than Eve abashed,
At length gave utterance to these words constrained:—
  "O Eve, in evil hour thou didst give ear
To that false Worm, of whomsoever taught
To counterfeit Man's voice—true in our fall,
False in our promised rising; since our eyes
Opened we find indeed, and find we know
Both good and evil, good lost and evil got:
Bad fruit of knowledge, if this be to know,
Which leaves us naked thus, of honour void,
Of innocence, of faith, of purity,
Our wonted ornaments now soiled and stained,
And in our faces evident the signs
Of foul concupiscence; whence evil store,
Even shame, the last of evils; of the first
Be sure then. How shall I behold the face
Henceforth of God or Angel, erst with joy

And rapture so oft beheld? Those heavenly Shapes
Will dazzle now this earthly with their blaze
Insufferably bright. Oh, might I here
In solitude live savage, in some glade
Obscured, where highest woods, impenetrable
To star or sunlight, spread their umbrage broad,
And brown as evening! Cover me, ye pines!
Ye cedars, with innumerable boughs
Hide me, where I may never see them more!
But let us now, as in bad plight, devise
What best may, for the present, serve to hide
The parts of each from other that seem most
To shame obnoxious, and unseemliest seen—
Some tree, whose broad smooth leaves, together sewed,
And girded on our loins, may cover round
Those middle parts, that this new comer, Shame,
There sit not, and reproach us as unclean."
So counselled he, and both together went
Into the thickest wood. There soon they chose
The fig-tree—not that kind for fruit renowned,
But such as, at this day, to Indians known,
In Malabar or Decan spreads her arms
Branching so broad and long that in the ground
The bended twigs take root, and daughters grow
About the mother tree, a pillared shade
High overarched, and echoing walks between:
There oft the Indian herdsman, shunning heat,
Shelters in cool, and tends his pasturing herds
At loop-holes cut through thickest shade. Those leaves
They gathered, broad as Amazonian targe,
And with what skill they had together sewed,
To gird their waist—vain covering, if to hide
Their guilt and dreaded shame! O how unlike
To that first naked glory! Such of late
Columbus found th' American, so girt
With feathered cincture, naked else and wild,
Among the trees on isles and woody shores.

Thus fenced, and, as they thought, their shame in part
Covered, but not at rest or ease of mind,
They sat them down to weep. Nor only tears
Rained at their eyes, but high winds worse within
Began to rise, high passions—anger, hate,
Mistrust, suspicion, discord—and shook sore
Their inward state of mind, calm region once
And full of peace, now tost and turbulent:
For Understanding ruled not, and the Will
Heard not her lore, both in subjection now
To sensual Appetite, who, from beneath
Usurping over sovereign Reason, claimed
Superior sway. From thus distempered breast
Adam, estranged in look and altered style,
Speech intermitted thus to Eve renewed:—
"Would thou hadst hearkened to my words, and stayed
With me, as I besought thee, when that strange
Desire of wandering, this unhappy morn,
I know not whence possessed thee! We had then
Remained still happy—not, as now, despoiled
Of all our good, shamed, naked, miserable!
Let none henceforth seek needless cause to approve
The faith they owe; when earnestly they seek
Such proof, conclude they then begin to fail."
To whom, soon moved with touch of blame, thus Eve:—
"What words have passed thy lips, Adam severe?
Imput'st thou that to my default, or will
Of wandering, as thou call'st it, which who knows
But might as ill have happened thou being by,
Or to thyself perhaps? Hadst thou been there,
Or here th' attempt, thou couldst not have discerned
Fraud in the Serpent, speaking as he spake;
No ground of enmity between us known.
Why he should mean me ill or seek to harm,
Was I to have never parted from thy side?
As good have grown there still, a lifeless rib.
Being as I am, why didst not thou, the head,

Command me absolutely not to go,
Going into such danger, as thou saidst?
Too facile then, thou didst not much gainsay,
Nay, didst permit, approve, and fair dismiss.
Hadst thou been firm and fixed in thy dissent,
Neither had I transgressed, nor thou with me."
To whom, then first incensed, Adam replied:—
"Is this the love, is this the recompense
Of mine to thee, ingrateful Eve, expressed
Immutable when thou wert lost, not I—
Who might have lived, and joyed immortal bliss,
Yet willingly chose rather death with thee?
And am I now upbraided as the cause
Of thy transgressing? not enough severe,
It seems, in thy restraint! What could I more?
I warned thee, I admonished thee, foretold
The danger, and the lurking enemy
That lay in wait; beyond this had been force,
And force upon free will hath here no place.
But confidence then bore thee on, secure
Either to meet no danger, or to find
Matter of glorious trial; and perhaps
I also erred in overmuch admiring
What seemed in thee so perfect that I thought
No evil durst attempt thee. But I rue
That error now, which is become my crime,
And thou th' accuser. Thus it shall befall
Him who, to worth in women overtrusting,
Lets her will rule: restraint she will not brook;
And, left to herself, if evil thence ensue,
She first his weak indulgence will accuse."
Thus they in mutual accusation spent
The fruitless hours, but neither self-condemning;
And of their vain contést appeared no end.

THE END OF THE NINTH BOOK

BOOK X

THE ARGUMENT

Man's transgression known, the guardian Angels forsake Paradise, and return up to Heaven to approve their vigilance, and are approved; God declaring that the entrance of Satan could not be by them prevented. He sends his Son to judge the transgressors; who descends, and gives sentence accordingly; then, in pity, clothes them both, and reascends. Sin and Death sitting till then at the gates of Hell, by wondrous sympathy feeling the success of Satan in this new World, and the sin by Man there committed, resolve to sit no longer confined in Hell, but to follow Satan, their sire, up to the place of Man: to make the way easier from Hell to this World to and fro, they pave a broad highway or bridge over Chaos, according to the track that Satan first made; then, preparing for Earth, they meet him, proud of his success, returning to Hell; their mutual gratulation. Satan arrives at Pandemonium; in full assembly relates, with boasting, his success against Man; instead of applause is entertained with a general hiss by all his audience, transformed, with himself also, suddenly into Serpents, according to his doom given in Paradise; then, deluded with a show of the Forbidden Tree springing up before them, they, greedily reaching to take of the fruit, chew dust and bitter ashes. The proceedings of Sin and Death: God foretells the final victory of his Son over them, and the renewing of all things; but, for the present, commands his Angels to make several alterations in the Heavens and Elements. Adam, more and more perceiving his fallen condition, heavily bewails, rejects the condolement of Eve; she persists, and at length appeases him: then, to evade the curse likely to fall on their offspring, proposes to Adam violent ways; which he approves not, but, conceiving better hope, puts her in mind of the late promise made them, that her seed should be revenged on the Serpent, and exhorts her, with him, to seek peace of the offended Deity by repentance and supplication.

Meanwhile the heinous and despiteful act
Of Satan done in Paradise, and how
He, in the Serpent, had perverted Eve,

Her husband she, to taste the fatal fruit,
Was known in Heaven; for what can scape the eye
Of God all-seeing, or deceive his heart
Omniscient? who, in all things wise and just,
Hindered not Satan to attempt the mind
Of Man, with strength entire and free will armed
Complete to have discovered and repulsed
Whatever wiles of foe or seeming friend.
For still they knew, and ought to have still remembered,
The high injunction not to taste that fruit,
Whoever tempted; which they not obeying
Incurred (what could they less?) the penalty,
And, manifold in sin, deserved to fall.
Up into Heaven from Paradise in haste
Th' angelic guards ascended, mute and sad
For Man; for of his state by this they knew,
Much wondering how the subtle Fiend had stolen
Entrance unseen. Soon as th' unwelcome news
From Earth arrived at Heaven-gate, displeased
All were who heard; dim sadness did not spare
That time celestial visages, yet, mixed
With pity, violated not their bliss.
About the new-arrived, in multitudes,
Th' ethereal people ran, to hear and know
How all befell. They towards the throne supreme,
Accountable, made haste, to make appear,
With righteous plea, their utmost vigilance,
And easily approved; when the Most High,
Eternal Father, from his secret cloud
Amidst, in thunder uttered thus his voice:—
"Assembled Angels, and ye Powers returned
From unsuccessful charge, be not dismayed
Nor troubled at these tidings from the Earth,
Which your sincerest care could not prevent,
Foretold so lately what would come to pass,
When first this Tempter crossed the gulf from Hell.
I told ye then he should prevail, and speed

On his bad errand—Man should be seduced,
And flattered out of all, believing lies
Against his Maker; no decree of mine,
Concurring to necessitate his fall,
Or touch with lightest moment of impulse
His free will, to her own inclining left
In even scale. But fallen he is; and now
What rests, but that the mortal sentence pass
On his transgression, Death denounced that day?
Which he presumes already vain and void,
Because not yet inflicted, as he feared,
By some immediate stroke, but soon shall find
Forbearance no acquittance ere day end.
Justice shall not return, as bounty, scorned.
But whom send I to judge them? whom but thee,
Vicegerent Son? To thee I have transferred
All judgment, whether in Heaven, or Earth, or Hell.
Easy it may be seen that I intend
Mercy colleague with justice, sending thee,
Man's friend, his Mediator, his designed
Both ransom and Redeemer voluntary,
And destined Man himself to judge Man fallen."
  So spake the Father; and, unfolding bright
Toward the right hand his glory, on the Son
Blazed forth unclouded deity. He full
Resplendent all his Father manifest
Expressed, and thus divinely answered mild:—
  "Father Eternal, thine is to decree;
Mine both in Heaven and Earth to do thy will
Supreme, that thou in me, thy Son beloved,
May'st ever rest well pleased. I go to judge
On Earth these thy transgressors; but thou know'st,
Whoever judged, the worst on me must light,
When time shall be; for so I undertook
Before thee, and, not repenting, this obtain
Of right, that I may mitigate their doom
On me derived. Yet I shall temper so

Justice with mercy as may illustrate most
Them fully satisfied, and thee appease.
Attendance none shall need, nor train, where none
Are to behold the judgment but the judged,
Those two; the third best absent is condemned,
Convict by flight, and rebel to all law;
Conviction to the Serpent none belongs."
  Thus saying, from his radiant seat he rose
Of high collateral glory. Him Thrones and Powers,
Princedoms, and Dominations ministrant,
Accompanied to Heaven-gate, from whence
Eden and all the coast in prospect lay.
Down he descended straight; the speed of Gods
Time counts not, though with swiftest minutes winged.
  Now was the Sun in western cadence low
From noon, and gentle airs due at their hour
To fan the Earth now waked, and usher in
The evening cool, when he, from wrath more cool,
Came, the mild judge and intercessor both,
To sentence Man. The voice of God they heard
Now walking in the garden, by soft winds
Brought to their ears, while day declined; they heard,
And from his presence hid themselves among
The thickest trees, both man and wife, till God,
Approaching, thus to Adam called aloud:—
  "Where art thou, Adam, wont with joy to meet
My coming, seen far off? I miss thee here,
Not pleased, thus entertained with solitude,
Where obvious duty erewhile appeared unsought.
Or come I less conspicuous, or what change
Absents thee, or what chance detains? Come forth!"
  He came, and with him Eve, more loath, though first
To offend, discountenanced both, and discomposed.
Love was not in their looks, either to God
Or to each other, but apparent guilt,
And shame, and perturbation, and despair,
Anger, and obstinacy, and hate, and guile.

Whence Adam, faltering long, thus answered brief:—
"I heard thee in the garden, and, of thy voice
Afraid, being naked, hid myself." To whom
The gracious Judge, without revile, replied:—
"My voice thou oft hast heard, and hast not feared,
But still rejoiced; how is it now become
So dreadful to thee? That thou art naked, who
Hath told thee? Hast thou eaten of the tree
Whereof I gave thee charge thou shouldst not eat?"
To whom thus Adam, sore beset, replied:—
"O Heaven! in evil strait this day I stand
Before my Judge—either to undergo
Myself the total crime, or to accuse
My other self, the partner of my life,
Whose failing, while her faith to me remains,
I should conceal, and not expose to blame
By my complaint. But strict necessity
Subdues me, and calamitous constraint,
Lest on my head both sin and punishment,
However insupportable, be all
Devolved; though, should I hold my peace, yet thou
Wouldst easily detect what I conceal.
This Woman, whom thou mad'st to be my help,
And gav'st me as thy perfect gift, so good,
So fit, so acceptable, so divine,
That from her hand I could suspect no ill,
And what she did, whatever in itself,
Her doing seemed to justify the deed—
She gave me of the tree, and I did eat."
To whom the Sovereign Presence thus replied:—
"Was she thy God, that her thou didst obey
Before his voice? or was she made thy guide,
Superior, or but equal, that to her
Thou didst resign thy manhood, and the place
Wherein God set thee above her, made of thee
And for thee, whose perfection far excelled
Hers in all real dignity? Adorned

She was indeed, and lovely, to attract
Thy love, not thy subjection; and her gifts
Were such as under government well seemed—
Unseemly to bear rule; which was thy part
And person, hadst thou known thyself aright."
So having said, he thus to Eve in few:—
"Say, Woman, what is this which thou hast done?"
To whom said Eve, with shame nigh overwhelmed,
Confessing soon, yet not before her Judge
Bold or loquacious, thus abashed replied—
"The Serpent me beguiled, and I did eat."
Which when the Lord God heard, without delay
To judgment he proceeded on th' accused
Serpent, though brute, unable to transfer
The guilt on him who made him instrument
Of mischief, and polluted from the end
Of his creation—justly then accursed,
As vitiated in nature. More to know
Concerned not Man (since he no further knew),
Nor altered his offence; yet God at last
To Satan, first in sin, his doom applied,
Though in mysterious terms, judged as then best;
And on the Serpent thus his curse let fall:—
"Because thou hast done this, thou art accursed
Above all cattle, each beast of the field;
Upon thy belly grovelling thou shalt go,
And dust shalt eat all the days of thy life.
Between thee and the Woman I will put
Enmity, and between thine and her seed;
Her seed shall bruise thy head, thou bruise his heel."
So spake this oracle—then verified
When Jesus, son of Mary, second Eve,
Saw Satan fall like lightning down from Heaven,
Prince of the Air; then, rising from his grave,
Spoiled Principalities and Powers, triumphed
In open show, and, with ascension bright,
Captivity led captive through the Air,

The realm itself of Satan, long usurped,
Whom he shall tread at last under our feet,
Even he who now foretold his fatal bruise,
And to the Woman thus his sentence turned:—
"Thy sorrow I will greatly multiply
By thy conception; children thou shalt bring
In sorrow forth, and to thy husband's will
Thine shall submit; he over thee shall rule."
On Adam last thus Judgment he pronounced:—
"Because thou hast hearkened to the voice of thy wife,
And eaten of the tree concerning which
I charged thee, saying, *Thou shalt not eat thereof*,
Cursed is the ground for thy sake; thou in sorrow
Shalt eat thereof all the days of thy life;
Thorns also and thistles it shall bring thee forth
Unbid; and thou shalt eat th' herb of th' field;
In the sweat of thy face shalt thou eat bread,
Till thou return unto the ground; for thou
Out of the ground wast taken: know thy birth,
For dust thou art, and shalt to dust return."
So judged he Man, both Judge and Saviour sent,
And th' instant stroke of death, denounced that day,
Removed far off; then, pitying how they stood
Before him naked to the air, that now
Must suffer change, disdained not to begin
Thenceforth the form of servant to assume.
As when he washed his servants' feet, so now,
As father of his family, he clad
Their nakedness with skins of beasts, or slain,
Or, as the snake, with youthful coat repaid;
And thought not much to clothe his enemies.
Nor he their outward only with the skins
Of beasts, but inward nakedness, much more
Opprobrious, with his robe of righteousness
Arraying, covered from his Father's sight.
To him with swift ascent he up returned,
Into his blissful bosom reassumed

In glory as of old; to him, appeased,
All, though all-knowing, what had passed with Man
Recounted, mixing intercession sweet.
Meanwhile, ere thus was sinned and judged on Earth,
Within the gates of Hell sat Sin and Death,
In counterview within the gates, that now
Stood open wide, belching outrageous flame
Far into Chaos, since the Fiend passed through,
Sin opening; who thus now to Death began:—
"O son, why sit we here, each other viewing
Idly, while Satan, our great author, thrives
In other worlds, and happier seat provides
For us, his offspring dear? It cannot be
But that success attends him; if mishap,
Ere this he had returned, with fury driven
By his avengers, since no place like this
Can fit his punishment, or their revenge.
Methinks I feel new strength within me rise,
Wings growing, and dominion given me large
Beyond this Deep—whatever draws me on,
Or sympathy, or some connatural force,
Powerful at greatest distance to unite
With secret amity things of like kind
By secretest conveyance. Thou, my shade
Inseparable, must with me along;
For Death from Sin no power can separate.
But, lest the difficulty of passing back
Stay his return perhaps over this gulf
Impassable, impervious, let us try
(Adventurous work, yet to thy power and mine
Not unagreeable!) to found a path
Over this main from Hell to that new World
Where Satan now prevails—a monument
Of merit high to all th' infernal host,
Easing their passage hence, for intercourse
Or transmigration, as their lot shall lead.
Nor can I miss the way, so strongly drawn

By this new-felt attraction and instinct."
  Whom thus the meagre Shadow answered soon:—
"Go whither fate and inclination strong
Leads thee; I shall not lag behind, nor err
The way, thou leading: such a scent I draw
Of carnage, prey innumerable, and taste
The savour of death from all things there that live.
Nor shall I to the work thou enterprisest
Be wanting, but afford thee equal aid."
  So saying, with delight he snuffed the smell
Of mortal change on Earth. As when a flock
Of ravenous fowl, though many a league remote,
Against the day of battle, to a field
Where armies lie encamped come flying, lured
With scent of living carcases designed
For death the following day in bloody fight;
So scented the grim Feature, and upturned
His nostril wide into the murky air,
Sagacious of his quarry from so far.
Then both, from out Hell-gates, into the waste
Wide anarchy of Chaos, damp and dark,
Flew diverse, and, with power (their power was great)
Hovering upon the waters, what they met
Solid or slimy, as in raging sea
Tossed up and down, together crowded drove,
From each side shoaling, towards the mouth of Hell;
As when two polar winds, blowing adverse
Upon the Cronian sea, together drive
Mountains of ice, that stop th' imagined way
Beyond Petsora eastward to the rich
Cathaian coast. The aggregated soil
Death with his mace petrific, cold and dry,
As with a trident smote, and fixed as firm
As Delos, floating once; the rest his look
Bound with Gorgonian rigour not to move,
And with asphaltic slime; broad as the gate,
Deep to the roots of Hell the gathered beach

They fastened, and the mole immense wrought on
Over the foaming Deep high-arched, a bridge
Of length prodigious, joining to the wall
Immovable of this now fenceless World,
Forfeit to Death—from hence a passage broad,
Smooth, easy, inoffensive, down to Hell.
So, if great things to small may be compared,
Xerxes, the liberty of Greece to yoke,
From Susa, his Memnonian palace high,
Came to the sea, and over Hellespont
Bridging his way, Europe with Asia joined,
And scourged with many a stroke th' indignant waves.
Now had they brought the work by wondrous art
Pontifical—a ridge of pendent rock
Over the vexed Abyss, following the track
Of Satan, to the self-same place where he
First lighted from his wing and landed safe
From out of Chaos—to the outside bare
Of this round World. With pins of adamant
And chains they made all fast, too fast they made
And durable; and now in little space
The confines met of empyrean Heaven
And of this World, and on the left hand Hell,
With long reach interposed; three several ways
In sight to each of these three places led.
And now their way to Earth they had descried,
To Paradise first tending, when, behold
Satan, in likeness of an Angel bright,
Betwixt the Centaur and the Scorpion steering
His zenith, while the Sun in Aries rose:
Disguised he came; but those his children dear
Their parent soon discerned, though in disguise.
He, after Eve seduced, unminded slunk
Into the wood fast by, and, changing shape
To observe the sequel, saw his guileful act
By Eve, though all unweeting, seconded
Upon her husband—saw their shame that sought

Vain covertures; but, when he saw descend
The Son of God to judge them, terrified
He fled, not hoping to escape, but shun
The present—fearing, guilty, what his wrath
Might suddenly inflict; that past, returned
By night, and, listening where the hapless pair
Sat in their sad discourse and various plaint,
Thence gathered his own doom; which understood
Not instant, but of future time, with joy
And tidings fraught, to Hell he now returned,
And at the brink of Chaos, near the foot
Of this new wondrous pontifice, unhoped
Met who to meet him came, his offspring dear.
Great joy was at their meeting, and at sight
Of that stupendous bridge his joy increased.
Long he admiring stood, till Sin, his fair
Enchanting daughter, thus the silence broke:—
"O parent, these are thy magnific deeds,
Thy trophies! which thou view'st as not thine own;
Thou art their author and prime architect.
For I no sooner in my heart divined
(My heart, which by a secret harmony
Still moves with thine, joined in connexion sweet)
That thou on Earth hadst prospered, which thy looks
Now also evidence, but straight I felt—
Though distant from thee worlds between, yet felt—
That I must after thee with this thy son;
Such fatal consequence unites us three.
Hell could no longer hold us in her bounds,
Nor this unvoyageable gulf obscure
Detain from following thy illustrious track.
Thou hast achieved our liberty, confined
Within Hell-gates till now; thou us empowered
To fortify thus far, and overlay
With this portentous bridge the dark Abyss.
Thine now is all this World; thy virtue hath won
What thy hands builded not; thy wisdom gained,

With odds, what war hath lost, and fully avenged
Our foil in Heaven. Here thou shalt monarch reign,
There didst not; there let him still victor sway,
As battle hath adjudged, from this new World
Retiring, by his own doom alienated,
And henceforth monarchy with thee divide
Of all things, parted by th' empyreal bounds,
His quadrature, from thy orbicular World,
Or try thee now more dangerous to his throne."
  Whom thus the Prince of Darkness answered glad:—
"Fair daughter, and thou, son and grandchild both,
High proof ye now have given to be the race
Of Satan (for I glory in the name,
Antagonist of Heaven's Almighty King),
Amply have merited of me, of all
Th' infernal empire, that so near Heaven's door
Triumphal with triumphal act have met,
Mine with this glorious work, and made one realm
Hell and this World—one realm, one continent
Of easy thoroughfare. Therefore, while I
Descend through Darkness, on your road with ease,
To my associate Powers, them to acquaint
With these successes, and with them rejoice,
You two this way, among these numerous orbs,
All yours, right down to Paradise descend;
There dwell, and reign in bliss; thence on the Earth
Dominion exercise and in the air,
Chiefly on Man, sole lord of all declared;
Him first make sure your thrall, and lastly kill.
My substitutes I send ye, and create
Plenipotent on Earth, of matchless might
Issuing from me. On your joint vigour now
My hold of this new kingdom all depends,
Through Sin to Death exposed by my exploit.
If your joint power prevail, th' affairs of Hell
No detriment need fear; go, and be strong."
  So saying, he dismissed them; they with speed

Their course through thickest constellations held,
Spreading their bane; the blasted stars looked wan,
And planets, planet-struck, real eclipse
Then suffered. Th' other way Satan went down
The causey to Hell-gate; on either side
Disparted Chaos overbuilt exclaimed,
And with rebounding surge the bars assailed,
That scorned his indignation. Through the gate,
Wide open and unguarded, Satan passed,
And all about found desolate; for those
Appointed to sit there had left their charge,
Flown to the upper World; the rest were all
Far to the inland retired, about the walls
Of Pandemonium, city and proud seat
Of Lucifer, so by allusion called
Of that bright star to Satan paragoned.
There kept their watch the legions, while the Grand
In council sat, solicitous what chance
Might intercept their Emperor sent; so he
Departing gave command, and they observed.
As when the Tartar from his Russian foe,
By Astracan, over the snowy plains,
Retires, or Bactrian Sophi, from the horns
Of Turkish crescent, leaves all waste beyond
The realm of Aladule, in his retreat
To Tauris or Casbeen; so these, the late
Heaven-banished host, left desert utmost Hell
Many a dark league, reduced in careful watch
Round their metropolis, and now expecting
Each hour their great Adventurer from the search
Of foreign worlds. He through the midst unmarked,
In show plebeian Angel militant
Of lowest order, passed, and, from the door
Of that Plutonian hall, invisible
Ascended his high throne, which, under state
Of richest texture spread, at th' upper end
Was placed in regal lustre. Down a while

He sat, and round about him saw, unseen.
At last, as from a cloud, his fulgent head
And shape star-bright appeared, or brighter, clad
With what permissive glory since his fall
Was left him, or false glitter. All amazed
At that so sudden blaze, the Stygian throng
Bent their aspéct, and whom they wished beheld,
Their mighty Chief returned: loud was th' acclaim.
Forth rushed in haste the great consulting Peers,
Raised from their dark Divan, and with like joy
Congratulant approached him, who with hand
Silence, and with these words attention, won:—
"Thrones, Dominations, Princedoms, Virtues, Powers!
For in possession such, not only of right,
I call ye, and declare ye now, returned,
Successful beyond hope, to lead ye forth
Triumphant out of this infernal pit
Abominable, accursed, the house of woe,
And dungeon of our tyrant! Now possess,
As lords, a spacious World, to our native Heaven
Little inferior, by my adventure hard
With peril great achieved. Long were to tell
What I have done, what suffered, with what pain
Voyaged th' unreal, vast, unbounded Deep
Of horrible confusion—over which
By Sin and Death a broad way now is paved,
To expedite your glorious march; but I
Toiled out my uncouth passage, forced to ride
Th' untractable Abyss, plunged in the womb
Of unoriginal Night and Chaos wild,
That, jealous of their secrets, fiercely opposed
My journey strange, with clamorous uproar
Protesting Fate supreme; thence how I found
The new-created World, which fame in Heaven
Long had foretold, a fabric wonderful,
Of absolute perfection; therein Man
Placed in a paradise, by our exile

Made happy. Him by fraud I have seduced
From his Creator, and, the more to increase
Your wonder, with an apple! He, thereat
Offended—worth your laughter!—hath given up
Both his belovèd Man and all his World
To Sin and Death a prey, and so to us,
Without our hazard, labour, or alarm,
To range in, and to dwell, and over Man
To rule, as over all he should have ruled.
True is, me also he hath judged; or rather
Me not, but the brute Serpent, in whose shape
Man I deceived. That which to me belongs
Is enmity, which he will put between
Me and Mankind: I am to bruise his heel;
His seed—when, is not set—shall bruise my head!
A world who would not purchase with a bruise,
Or much more grievous pain? Ye have th' account
Of my performance; what remains, ye Gods,
But up and enter now into full bliss?"
  So having said, a while he stood, expecting
Their universal shout and high applause
To fill his ear; when, contrary, he hears,
On all sides, from innumerable tongues
A dismal universal hiss, the sound
Of public scorn. He wondered, but not long
Had leisure, wondering at himself now more.
His visage drawn he felt to sharp and spare,
His arms clung to his ribs, his legs entwining
Each other, till, supplanted, down he fell,
A monstrous serpent on his belly prone,
Reluctant, but in vain; a greater power
Now ruled him, punished in the shape he sinned,
According to his doom. He would have spoke,
But hiss for hiss returned with forkèd tongue
To forkèd tongue; for now were all transformed
Alike, to serpents all, as accessories
To his bold riot. Dreadful was the din

Of hissing through the hall, thick-swarming now
With complicated monsters, head and tail—
Scorpion, and Asp, and Amphisbaena dire,
Cerastes horned, Hydrus, and Ellops drear,
And Dipsas (not so thick swarmed once the soil
Bedropped with blood of Gorgon, or the isle
Ophiusa); but still greatest he the midst,
Now Dragon grown, larger than whom the Sun
Engendered in the Pythian vale on slime,
Huge Python; and his power no less he seemed
Above the rest still to retain. They all
Him followed, issuing forth to th' open field,
Where all yet left of that revolted rout,
Heaven-fallen, in station stood or just array.
Sublime with expectation when to see
In triumph issuing forth their glorious Chief.
They saw, but other sight instead—a crowd
Of ugly serpents. Horror on them fell,
And horrid sympathy; for what they saw
They felt themselves now changing. Down their arms,
Down fell both spear and shield; down they as fast,
And the dire hiss renewed, and the dire form
Catched by contagion, like in punishment
As in their crime. Thus was th' applause they meant
Turned to exploding hiss, triumph to shame
Cast on themselves from their own mouths. There stood
A grove hard by, sprung up with this their change,
His will who reigns above, to aggravate
Their penance, laden with fair fruit, like that
Which grew in Paradise, the bait of Eve
Used by the Tempter. On that prospect strange
Their earnest eyes they fixed, imagining
For one forbidden tree a multitude
Now risen, to work them further woe or shame;
Yet, parched with scalding thirst and hunger fierce,
Though to delude them sent, could not abstain,
But on they rolled in heaps, and, up the trees

Climbing, sat thicker than the snaky locks
That curled Megaera. Greedily they plucked
The fruitage fair to sight, like that which grew
Near that bituminous lake where Sodom flamed;
This, more delusive, not the touch, but taste
Deceived; they, fondly thinking to allay
Their appetite with gust, instead of fruit
Chewed bitter ashes, which th' offended taste
With spattering noise rejected. Oft they assayed,
Hunger and thirst constraining; drugged as oft,
With hatefulest disrelish writhed their jaws
With soot and cinders filled; so oft they fell
Into the same illusion, not as Man
Whom they triumphed once lapsed. Thus were they plagued,
And worn with famine long, and ceaseless hiss,
Till their lost shape, permitted, they resumed—
Yearly enjoined, some say, to undergo
This annual humbling certain numbered days,
To dash their pride, and joy for Man seduced.
However, some tradition they dispersed
Among the heathen of their purchase got,
And fabled how the Serpent, whom they called
Ophion, with Eurynome (the wide-
Encroaching Eve perhaps), had first the rule
Of high Olympus, thence by Saturn driven
And Ops, ere yet Dictaean Jove was born.
  Meanwhile in Paradise the hellish pair
Too soon arrived—Sin, there in power before
Once actual, now in body, and to dwell
Habitual habitant; behind her Death,
Close following pace for pace, not mounted yet
On his pale horse; to whom Sin thus began:—
  "Second of Satan sprung, all-conquering Death!
What think'st thou of our empire now? though earned
With travail difficult, not better far
Than still at Hell's dark threshold to have sat watch,
Unnamed, undreaded, and thyself half-starved?"

Whom thus the Sin-born Monster answered soon:—
"To me, who with eternal famine pine,
Alike is Hell, or Paradise, or Heaven—
There best where most with ravin I may meet:
Which here, though plenteous, all too little seems
To stuff this maw, this vast unhide-bound corpse."
To whom th' incestuous Mother thus replied:—
"Thou, therefore, on these herbs, and fruits, and flowers,
Feed first, on each beast next, and fish, and fowl—
No homely morsels; and whatever thing
The scythe of Time mows down devour unspared
Till I, in Man residing through the race,
His thoughts, his looks, words, actions, all infect,
And season him thy last and sweetest prey."
This said, they both betook them several ways,
Both to destroy, or unimmortal make
All kinds, and for destruction to mature
Sooner or later; which th' Almighty seeing,
From his transcendent seat the Saints among,
To those bright Orders uttered thus his voice:—
"See with what heat these dogs of Hell advance
To waste and havoc yonder World, which I
So fair and good created, and had still
Kept in that state, had not the folly of Man
Let in these wasteful furies, who impute
Folly to me (so doth the Prince of Hell
And his adherents), that with so much ease
I suffer them to enter and possess
A place so heavenly, and, conniving, seem
To gratify my scornful enemies,
That laugh, as if, transported with some fit
Of passion, I to them had quitted all,
At random yielded up to their misrule;
And know not that I called and drew them thither,
My Hell-hounds, to lick up the draff and filth
Which Man's polluting sin with taint hath shed
On what was pure; till, crammed and gorged, nigh burst

With sucked and glutted offal, at one sling
Of thy victorious arm, well-pleasing Son,
Both Sin and Death, and yawning Grave, at last
Through Chaos hurled, obstruct the mouth of Hell
For ever, and seal up his ravenous jaws.
Then Heaven and Earth, renewed, shall be made pure
To sanctity that shall receive no stain:
Till then the curse pronounced on both precedes."
He ended, and the Heavenly audience loud
Sung hallelujah, as the sound of seas,
Through multitude that sung:—"Just are thy ways,
Righteous are thy decrees on all thy works;
Who can extenuate thee? Next, to the Son,
Destined restorer of Mankind, by whom
New Heaven and Earth shall to the ages rise,
Or down from Heaven descend." Such was their song,
While the Creator, calling forth by name
His mighty Angels, gave them several charge,
As sorted best with present things. The Sun
Had first his precept so to move, so shine,
As might affect the Earth with cold and heat
Scarce tolerable, and from the north to call
Decrepit winter, from the south to bring
Solstitial summer's heat. To the blanc Moon
Her office they prescribed; to th' other five
Their planetary motions and aspécts,
In sextile, square, and trine, and opposite,
Of noxious efficacy, and when to join
In synod unbenign; and taught the fixed
Their influence malignant when to shower—
Which of them, rising with the Sun or falling,
Should prove tempestuous. To the winds they set
Their corners, when with bluster to confound
Sea, air, and shore; the thunder when to roll
With terror through the dark aerial hall.
Some say he bid his Angels turn askance
The poles of Earth twice ten degrees and more

From the Sun's axle; they with labour pushed
Oblique the centric Globe: some say the Sun
Was bid turn reins from th' equinoctial road
Like distant breadth to Taurus with the seven
Atlantic Sisters, and the Spartan Twins,
Up to the Tropic Crab; thence down amain
By Leo, and the Virgin, and the Scales,
As deep as Capricorn; to bring in change
Of seasons to each clime. Else had the spring
Perpetual smiled on Earth with verdant flowers,
Equal in days and nights, except to those
Beyond the polar circles; to them day
Had unbenighted shone, while the low Sun,
To recompense his distance, in their sight
Had rounded still th' horizon, and not known
Or east or west—which had forbid the snow
From cold Estotiland, and south as far
Beneath Magellan. At that tasted fruit,
The Sun, as from Thyestean banquet, turned
His course intended; else how had the world
Inhabited, though sinless, more than now
Avoided pinching cold and scorching heat?
These changes in the heavens, though slow, produced
Like change on sea and land—sideral blast,
Vapour, and mist, and exhalation hot,
Corrupt and pestilent. Now from the north
Of Norumbega, and the Samoed shore,
Bursting their brazen dungeon, armed with ice,
And snow, and hail, and stormy gust and flaw,
Boreas and Caecias and Argestes loud
And Thrascias rend the woods, and seas upturn;
With adverse blasts upturns them from the south
Notus and Afer, black with thunderous clouds
From Serraliona; thwart of these, as fierce
Forth rush the Levant and the Ponent winds,
Eurus and Zephyr, with their lateral noise,
Sirocco and Libecchio. Thus began

Outrage from lifeless things; but Discord first,
Daughter of Sin, among th' irrational
Death introduced through fierce antipathy.
Beast now with beast 'gan war, and fowl with fowl,
And fish with fish. To graze the herb all leaving
Devoured each other; nor stood much in awe
Of Man, but fled him, or with countenance grim
Glared on him passing. These were from without
The growing miseries; which Adam saw
Already in part, though hid in gloomiest shade,
To sorrow abandoned, but worse felt within,
And, in a troubled sea of passion tost,
Thus to disburden sought with sad complaint:—
"O miserable of happy! Is this the end
Of this new glorious World, and me so late
The glory of that glory? who now, become
Accursed of blessèd, hide me from the face
Of God, whom to behold was then my height
Of happiness! Yet well, if here would end
The misery! I deserved it, and would bear
My own deservings. But this will not serve:
All that I eat or drink, or shall beget,
Is propagated curse. O voice, once heard
Delightfully, '*Increase and multiply*';
Now death to hear! for what can I increase
Or multiply, but curses on my head?
Who, of all ages to succeed, but, feeling
The evil on him brought by me, will curse
My head? 'Ill fare our ancestor impure!
For this we may thank Adam!' but his thanks
Shall be the execration. So, besides
Mine own that bide upon me, all from me
Shall with a fierce reflux on me redound—
On me, as on their natural centre, light;
Heavy, though in their place. O fleeting joys
Of Paradise, dear bought with lasting woes!
Did I request thee, Maker, from my clay

To mould me Man? Did I solicit thee
From darkness to promote me, or here place
In this delicious garden? As my will
Concurred not to my being, it were but right
And equal to reduce me to my dust,
Desirous to resign and render back
All I received, unable to perform
Thy terms too hard, by which I was to hold
The good I sought not. To the loss of that,
Sufficient penalty, why hast thou added
The sense of endless woes? Inexplicable
Thy justice seems. Yet, to say truth, too late
I thus contest; then should have been refused
Those terms, whatever, when they were proposed.
Thou didst accept them: wilt thou enjoy the good,
Then cavil the conditions? And, though God
Made thee without thy leave, what if thy son
Prove disobedient, and, reproved, retort,
'Wherefore didst thou beget me? I sought it not!'
Wouldst thou admit for his contempt of thee
That proud excuse? yet him not thy election,
But natural necessity, begot.
God made thee of choice his own, and of his own
To serve him; thy reward was of his grace;
Thy punishment, then, justly is at his will.
Be it so, for I submit; his doom is fair,
That dust I am, and shall to dust return.
O welcome hour, whenever! Why delays
His hand to execute what his decree
Fixed on this day? Why do I overlive?
Why am I mocked with death, and lengthened out
To deathless pain? How gladly would I meet
Mortality, my sentence, and be earth
Insensible! how glad would lay me down
As in my mother's lap! There I should rest,
And sleep secure; his dreadful voice no more
Would thunder in my ears; no fear of worse

To me and to my offspring would torment me
With cruel expectation. Yet one doubt
Pursues me still—lest all I cannot die;
Lest that pure breath of life, the Spirit of Man
Which God inspired, cannot together perish
With this corporeal clod. Then, in the grave,
Or in some other dismal place, who knows
But I shall die a living death? O thought
Horrid, if true! Yet why? It was but breath
Of life that sinned: what dies but what had life
And sin? The body properly hath neither.
All of me, then, shall die: let this appease
The doubt, since human reach no further knows.
For, though the Lord of all be infinite,
Is his wrath also? Be it, Man is not so,
But mortal doomed. How can he exercise
Wrath without end on Man, whom death must end?
Can he make deathless death? That were to make
Strange contradiction; which to God himself
Impossible is held, as argument
Of weakness, not of power. Will he draw out,
For anger's sake, finite to infinite
In punished Man, to satisfy his rigour
Satisfied never? That were to extend
His sentence beyond dust and Nature's law;
By which all causes else, according still
To the reception of their matter, act,
Not to th' extent of their own sphere. But say
That death be not one stroke, as I supposed,
Bereaving sense, but endless misery
From this day onward, which I feel begun
Both in me and without me, and so last
To perpetuity—Ay me! that fear
Comes thundering back with dreadful revolution
On my defenceless head! Both Death and I
Am found eternal, and incorporate both:
Nor I on my part single; in me all

Posterity stands cursed. Fair patrimony
That I must leave ye, sons! Oh, were I able
To waste it all myself, and leave ye none!
So disinherited, how would ye bless
Me, now your curse! Ah, why should all mankind,
For one man's fault, thus guiltless be condemned?
If guiltless! But from me what can proceed
But all corrupt—both mind and will depraved
Not to do only, but to will the same
With me? How can they, then, acquitted stand
In sight of God? Him, after all disputes,
Forced I absolve. All my evasions vain
And reasonings, though through mazes, lead me still
But to my own conviction: first and last
On me, me only, as the source and spring
Of all corruption, all the blame lights due.
So might the wrath! Fond wish! couldst thou support
That burden, heavier than the Earth to bear—
Than all the world much heavier, though divided
With that bad Woman? Thus, what thou desir'st,
And what thou fear'st, alike destroys all hope
Of refuge, and concludes thee miserable
Beyond all past example and futúre—
To Satan only like, both crime and doom.
O Conscience! into what abyss of fears
And horrors hast thou driven me; out of which
I find no way, from deep to deeper plunged!"
  Thus Adam to himself lamented loud
Through the still night—not now, as ere Man fell,
Wholesome and cool and mild, but with black air
Accompanied, with damps and dreadful gloom;
Which to his evil conscience represented
All things with double terror. On the ground
Outstretched he lay, on the cold ground, and oft
Cursed his creation; Death as oft accused
Of tardy execution, since denounced
The day of his offence. "Why comes not Death,"

Said he, "with one thrice-ácceptable stroke
To end me? Shall Truth fail to keep her word,
Justice divine not hasten to be just?
But Death comes not at call; Justice divine
Mends not her slowest pace for prayers or cries.
O woods, O fountains, hillocks, dales, and bowers!
With other echo late I taught your shades
To answer, and resound far other song."
Whom thus afflicted when sad Eve beheld,
Desolate where she sat, approaching nigh,
Soft words to his fierce passion she assayed;
But her, with stern regard, he thus repelled:—
"Out of my sight, thou serpent! That name best
Befits thee, with him leagued, thyself as false
And hateful: nothing wants, but that thy shape
Like his, and colour serpentine, may show
Thy inward fraud, to warn all creatures from thee
Henceforth, lest that too heavenly form, pretended
To hellish falsehood, snare them. But for thee
I had persisted happy, had not thy pride
And wandering vanity when least was safe,
Rejected my forewarning, and disdained
Not to be trusted—longing to be seen,
Though by the Devil himself; him overweening
To overreach; but, with the Serpent meeting,
Fooled and beguiled; by him thou, I by thee,
To trust thee from my side, imagined wise,
Constant, mature, proof against all assaults,
And understood not all was but a show,
Rather than solid virtue, all but a rib
Crooked by nature—bent, as now appears,
More to the part sinister—from me drawn;
Well if thrown out, as supernumerary
To my just number found! Oh, why did God,
Creator wise, that peopled highest Heaven
With Spirits masculine, create at last
This novelty on Earth, this fair defect

Of Nature, and not fill the World at once
With men as Angels, without feminine;
Or find some other way to generate
Mankind? This mischief had not then befallen,
And more that shall befall—innumerable
Disturbances on Earth through female snares,
And strait conjunction with this sex. For either
He never shall find out fit mate, but such
As some misfortune brings him, or mistake;
Or whom he wishes most shall seldom gain,
Through her perverseness, but shall see her gained
By a far worse, or, if she love, withheld
By parents; or his happiest choice too late
Shall meet, already linked and wedlock-bound
To a fell adversary, his hate or shame:
Which infinite calamity shall cause
To human life, and household peace confound."
He added not, and from her turned; but Eve,
Not so repulsed, with tears that ceased not flowing,
And tresses all disordered, at his feet
Fell humble, and, embracing them, besought
His peace, and thus proceeded in her plaint:—
"Forsake me not thus, Adam! witness Heaven
What love sincere and reverence in my heart
I bear thee, and unweeting have offended,
Unhappily deceived! Thy suppliant
I beg, and clasp thy knees; bereave me not
Whereon I live, thy gentle looks, thy aid,
Thy counsel in this uttermost distress,
My only strength and stay. Forlorn of thee,
Whither shall I betake me, where subsist?
While yet we live, scarce one short hour perhaps,
Between us two let there be peace; both joining,
As joined in injuries, one enmity
Against a foe by doom express assigned us,
That cruel Serpent. On me exercise not
Thy hatred for this misery befallen—

On me already lost, me than thyself
More miserable. Both have sinned; but thou
Against God only; I against God and thee,
And to the place of judgment will return,
There with my cries importune Heaven, that all
The sentence, from thy head removed, may light
On me, sole cause to thee of all this woe,
Me, me only, just object of his ire."
She ended, weeping; and her lowly plight,
Immovable till peace obtained from fault
Acknowledged and deplored, in Adam wrought
Commiseration. Soon his heart relented
Towards her, his life so late, and sole delight,
Now at his feet submissive in distress—
Creature so fair his reconcilement seeking,
His counsel whom she had displeased, his aid.
As one disarmed, his anger all he lost,
And thus with peaceful words upraised her soon:—
" Unwary, and too desirous, as before
So now, of what thou know'st not, who desir'st
The punishment all on thyself! Alas!
Bear thine own first, ill able to sustain
His full wrath whose thou feel'st as yet least part,
And my displeasure bear'st so ill. If prayers
Could alter high decrees, I to that place
Would speed before thee, and be louder heard,
That on my head all might be visited,
Thy frailty and infirmer sex forgiven,
To me committed, and by me exposed.
But rise; let us no more contend, nor blame
Each other, blamed enough elsewhere, but strive
In offices of love how we may lighten
Each other's burden in our share of woe;
Since this day's death denounced, if aught I see,
Will prove no sudden, but a slow-paced evil,
A long day's dying, to augment our pain,
And to our seed (O hapless seed!) derived."

To whom thus Eve, recovering heart, replied:—
"Adam, by sad experiment I know
How little weight my words with thee can find,
Found so erroneous, thence by just event
Found so unfortunate. Nevertheless,
Restored by thee, vile as I am, to place
Of new acceptance, hopeful to regain
Thy love, the sole contentment of my heart,
Living or dying from thee I will not hide
What thoughts in my unquiet breast are risen,
Tending to some relief of our extremes,
Or end, though sharp and sad, yet tolerable,
As in our evils, and of easier choice.
If care of our descent perplex us most,
Which must be born to certain woe, devoured
By Death at last (and miserable it is
To be to others cause of misery,
Our own begotten, and of our loins to bring
Into this cursèd world a woeful race,
That, after wretched life, must be at last
Food for so foul a monster), in thy power
It lies, yet ere conception, to prevent
The race unblest, to being yet unbegot.
Childless thou art; childless remain. So Death
Shall be deceived his glut, and with us two
Be forced to satisfy his ravenous maw.
But, if thou judge it hard and difficult,
Conversing, looking, loving, to abstain
From love's due rites, nuptial embraces sweet,
And with desire to languish without hope
Before the present object languishing
With like desire—which would be misery
And torment less than none of what we dread—
Then, both ourselves and seed at once to free
From what we fear for both, let us make short;
Let us seek Death, or, he not found, supply
With our own hands his office on ourselves.

Why stand we longer shivering under fears
That show no end but death, and have the power,
Of many ways to die the shortest choosing,
Destruction with destruction to destroy?"
  She ended here; or vehement despair
Broke off the rest; so much of death her thoughts
Had entertained as dyed her cheeks with pale.
But Adam, with such counsel nothing swayed,
To better hopes his more attentive mind
Labouring had raised, and thus to Eve replied:—
  "Eve, thy contempt of life and pleasure seems
To argue in thee something more sublime
And excellent than what thy mind contemns:
But self-destruction therefore sought refutes
That excellence thought in thee, and implies
Not thy contempt, but anguish and regret
For loss of life and pleasure overloved.
Or, if thou covet death, as utmost end
Of misery, so thinking to evade
The penalty pronounced, doubt not but God
Hath wiselier armed his vengeful ire than so
To be forestalled. Much more I fear lest death
So snatched will not exempt us from the pain
We are by doom to pay; rather such acts
Of contumacy will provoke the Highest
To make death in us live. Then let us seek
Some safer resolution—which methinks
I have in view, calling to mind with heed
Part of our sentence, that thy seed shall bruise
The Serpent's head. Piteous amends! unless
Be meant whom I conjecture, our grand foe,
Satan, who in the Serpent hath contrived
Against us this deceit. To crush his head
Would be revenge indeed—which will be lost
By death brought on ourselves, or childless days
Resolved as thou proposest; so our foe
Shall scape his punishment ordained, and we

Instead shall double ours upon our heads.
No more be mentioned, then, of violence
Against ourselves, and wilful barrenness
That cuts us off from hope, and savours only
Rancour and pride, impatience and despite,
Reluctance against God and his just yoke
Laid on our necks. Remember with what mild
And gracious temper he both heard and judged,
Without wrath or reviling. We expected
Immediate dissolution, which we thought
Was meant by death that day; when, lo! to thee
Pains only in child-bearing were foretold,
And bringing forth, soon recompensed with joy,
Fruit of thy womb. On me the curse aslope
Glanced on the ground. With labour I must earn
My bread; what harm? Idleness had been worse;
My labour will sustain me; and, lest cold
Or heat should injure us, his timely care
Hath, unbesought, provided, and his hands
Clothed us unworthy, pitying while he judged.
How much more, if we pray him, will his ear
Be open, and his heart to pity incline,
And teach us further by what means to shun
Th' inclement seasons, rain, ice, hail, and snow!
Which now the sky, with various face, begins
To show us in this mountain, while the winds
Blow moist and keen, shattering the graceful locks
Of these fair spreading trees; which bids us seek
Some better shroud, some better warmth to cherish
Our limbs benumbed—ere this diurnal star
Leave cold the night, how we his gathered beams
Reflected may with matter sere foment,
Or by collision of two bodies grind
The air attrite to fire; as late the clouds,
Justling, or pushed with winds, rude in their shock,
Tine the slant lightning, whose thwart flame, driven down,
Kindles the gummy bark of fir or pine,

And sends a comfortable heat from far,
Which might supply the sun. Such fire to use,
And what may else be remedy or cure
To evils which our own misdeeds have wrought,
He will instruct us praying, and of grace
Beseeching him; so as we need not fear
To pass commodiously this life, sustained
By him with many comforts, till we end
In dust, our final rest and native home.
What better can we do than, to the place
Repairing where he judged us, prostrate fall
Before him reverent, and there confess
Humbly our faults, and pardon beg, with tears
Watering the ground, and with our sighs the air
Frequenting, sent from hearts contrite, in sign
Of sorrow unfeigned and humiliation meek?
Undoubtedly he will relent, and turn
From his displeasure, in whose look serene,
When angry most he seemed and most severe,
What else but favour, grace, and mercy shone?"
  So spake our Father penitent; nor Eve
Felt less remorse. They, forthwith to the place
Repairing where he judged them, prostrate fell
Before him reverent, and both confessed
Humbly their faults, and pardon begged, with tears
Watering the ground, and with their sighs the air
Frequenting, sent from hearts contrite, in sign
Of sorrow unfeigned and humiliation meek.

THE END OF THE TENTH BOOK

BOOK XI

THE ARGUMENT

The Son of God presents to his Father the prayers of our first parents now repenting, and intercedes for them. God accepts them, but declares that they must no longer abide in Paradise; sends Michael with a band of Cherubim to dispossess them, but first to reveal to Adam future things: Michael's coming down. Adam shows to Eve certain ominous signs: he discerns Michael's approach; goes out to meet him: the Angel denounces their departure. Eve's lamentation. Adam pleads, but submits; the Angel leads him up to a high hill; sets before him in vision what shall happen till the Flood.

Thus they, in lowliest plight, repentant stood
Praying; for from the mercy-seat above
Prevenient grace descending had removed
The stony from their hearts, and made new flesh
Regenerate grow instead, that sighs now breathed
Unutterable, which the Spirit of prayer
Inspired, and winged for Heaven with speedier flight
Than loudest oratory. Yet their port
Not of mean suitors; nor important less
Seemed their petition, than when th' ancient pair
In fables old, less ancient yet than these,
Deucalion and chaste Pyrrha, to restore
The race of mankind drowned, before the shrine
Of Themis stood devout. To Heaven their prayers
Flew up, nor missed the way, by envious winds
Blown vagabond or frustrate: in they passed
Dimensionless through heavenly doors; then, clad
With incense, where the golden altar fumed,
By their great Intercessor, came in sight
Before the Father's throne. Them the glad Son
Presenting thus to intercede began:—

"See, Father, what first-fruits on Earth are sprung
From thy implanted grace in Man—these sighs
And prayers, which in this golden censer, mixed
With incense, I, thy priest, before thee bring;
Fruits of more pleasing savour, from thy seed
Sown with contrition in his heart, than those
Which, his own hand manuring, all the trees
Of Paradise could have produced, ere fallen
From innocence. Now, therefore, bend thine ear
To supplication; hear his sighs, though mute;
Unskilful with what words to pray, let me
Interpret for him, me his advocate
And propitiation; all his works on me,
Good or not good, ingraft; my merit those
Shall perfect, and for these my death shall pay.
Accept me, and in me from these receive
The smell of peace toward Mankind; let him live,
Before thee reconciled, at least his days
Numbered, though sad, till death, his doom (which I
To mitigate thus plead, not to reverse),
To better life shall yield him, where with me
All my redeemed may dwell in joy and bliss,
Made one with me, as I with thee am one."
To whom the Father, without cloud, serene:—
"All thy request for Man, accepted Son,
Obtain; all thy request was my decree.
But longer in that Paradise to dwell
The law I gave to Nature him forbids;
Those pure immortal elements, that know
No gross, no unharmonious mixture foul,
Eject him, tainted now, and purge him off,
As a distemper, gross, to air as gross,
And mortal food, as may dispose him best
For dissolution wrought by sin, that first
Distempered all things, and of incorrupt
Corrupted. I at first with two fair gifts
Created him endowed—with Happiness

And Immortality; that fondly lost,
This other served but to eternize woe,
Till I provided Death: so Death becomes
His final remedy, and, after life
Tried in sharp tribulation, and refined
By faith and faithful works, to second life,
Waked in the renovation of the just,
Resigns him up with Heaven and Earth renewed.
But let us call to synod all the Blest
Through Heaven's wide bounds; from them I will not hide
My judgments—how with Mankind I proceed,
As how with peccant Angels late they saw,
And in their state, though firm, stood more confirmed."
He ended, and the Son gave signal high
To the bright Minister that watched. He blew
His trumpet, heard in Oreb since perhaps
When God descended, and perhaps once more
To sound at general doom. Th' angelic blast
Filled all the regions: from their blissful bowers
Of amarantine shade, fountain or spring,
By the waters of life, where'er they sat
In fellowships of joy, the Sons of Light
Hasted, resorting to the summons high,
And took their seats, till from his throne supreme
Th' Almighty thus pronounced his sovereign will:—
"O Sons, like one of us Man is become
To know both good and evil, since his taste
Of that defended fruit; but let him boast
His knowledge of good lost and evil got,
Happier had it sufficed him to have known
Good by itself and evil not at all.
He sorrows now, repents, and prays contrite—
My motions in him; longer than they move,
His heart I know how variable and vain,
Self-left. Lest, therefore, his now bolder hand
Reach also of the Tree of Life, and eat,
And live for ever, dream at least to live

For ever, to remove him I decree,
And send him from the garden forth, to till
The ground whence he was taken, fitter soil.
Michael, this my behest have thou in charge:
Take to thee from among the Cherubim
Thy choice of flaming warriors, lest the Fiend,
Or in behalf of Man, or to invade
Vacant possession, some new trouble raise;
Haste thee, and from the Paradise of God
Without remorse drive out the sinful pair,
From hallowed ground th' unholy, and denounce
To them, and to their progeny, from thence
Perpetual banishment. Yet lest they faint
At the sad sentence rigorously urged
(For I behold them softened, and with tears
Bewailing their excess), all terror hide.
If patiently thy bidding they obey,
Dismiss them not disconsolate; reveal
To Adam what shall come in future days,
As I shall thee enlighten; intermix
My covenant in the Woman's seed renewed.
So send them forth, though sorrowing, yet in peace;
And on the east side of the garden place,
Where entrance up from Eden easiest climbs,
Cherubic watch, and of a sword the flame
Wide-waving, all approach far off to fright,
And guard all passage to the Tree of Life;
Lest Paradise a receptácle prove
To Spirits foul, and all my trees their prey,
With whose stolen fruit Man once more to delude."
  He ceased, and th' archangelic Power prepared
For swift descent; with him the cohort bright
Of watchful Cherubim. Four faces each
Had, like a double Janus; all their shape
Spangled with eyes more numerous than those
Of Argus, and more wakeful than to drowse,
Charmed with Arcadian pipe, the pastoral reed

Of Hermes, or his opiate rod. Meanwhile,
To resalute the World with sacred light,
Leucóthea waked, and with fresh dews embalmed
The Earth, when Adam and first matron Eve
Had ended now their orisons, and found
Strength added from above, new hope to spring
Out of despair, joy, but with fear yet linked;
Which thus to Eve his welcome words renewed:—
  "Eve, easily may faith admit that all
The good which we enjoy from Heaven descends;
But that from us aught should ascend to Heaven
So prevalent as to concern the mind
Of God high-blest, or to incline his will,
Hard to belief may seem. Yet this will prayer,
Or one short sigh of human breath, upborne
Even to the seat of God. For, since I sought
By prayer th' offended Deity to appease,
Kneeled and before him humbled all my heart,
Methought I saw him placable and mild,
Bending his ear; persuasion in me grew
That I was heard with favour; peace returned
Home to my breast, and to my memory
His promise that thy seed shall bruise our Foe;
Which, then not minded in dismay, yet now
Assures me that the bitterness of death
Is past, and we shall live. Whence hail to thee!
Eve rightly called, Mother of all Mankind,
Mother of all things living, since by thee
Man is to live, and all things live for Man."
  To whom thus Eve with sad demeanour meek:—
"Ill-worthy I such title should belong
To me transgressor, who, for thee ordained
A help, became thy snare; to me reproach
Rather belongs, distrust, and all dispraise.
But infinite in pardon was my Judge,
That I, who first brought death on all, am graced
The source of life; next favourable thou,

Who highly thus to entitle me vouchsaf'st,
Far other name deserving. But the field
To labour calls us, now with sweat imposed,
Though after sleepless night; for see! the Morn,
All unconcerned with our unrest, begins
Her rosy progress smiling. Let us forth,
I never from thy side henceforth to stray,
Where'er our day's work lies, though now enjoined
Laborious, till day droop. While here we dwell,
What can be toilsome in these pleasant walks?
Here let us live, though in fallen state, content."
  So spake, so wished, much-humbled Eve; but Fate
Subscribed not. Nature first gave signs, impressed
On bird, beast, air—air suddenly eclipsed,
After short blush of morn. Nigh in her sight
The bird of Jove, stooped from his airy tower,
Two birds of gayest plume before him drove;
Down from a hill the beast that reigns in woods,
First hunter then, pursued a gentle brace,
Goodliest of all the forest, hart and hind;
Direct to th' eastern gate was bent their flight.
Adam observed, and, with his eye the chase
Pursuing, not unmoved to Eve thus spake:—
  "O Eve, some further change awaits us nigh,
Which Heaven by these mute signs in Nature shows,
Forerunners of his purpose, or to warn
Us, haply too secure of our discharge
From penalty because from death released
Some days: how long, and what till then our life,
Who knows, or more than this, that we are dust,
And thither must return, and be no more?
Why else this double object in our sight,
Of flight pursued in th' air and o'er the ground
One way the self-same hour? Why in the east
Darkness ere day's mid-course, and morning light
More orient in yon western cloud, that draws
O'er the blue firmament a radiant white,

And slow descends, with something heavenly fraught?"
He erred not; for, by this, the heavenly bands
Down from a sky of jasper lighted now
In Paradise, and on a hill made halt—
A glorious apparition, had not doubt
And carnal fear that day dimmed Adam's eye.
Not that more glorious, when the Angels met
Jacob in Mahanaim, where he saw
The field pavilioned with his guardians bright;
Nor that which on the flaming mount appeared
In Dothan, covered with a camp of fire,
Against the Syrian king, who, to surprise
One man, assassin-like, had levied war,
War unproclaimed. The princely Hierarch
In their bright stand there left his Powers to seize
Possession of the garden; he alone,
To find where Adam sheltered, took his way,
Not unperceived of Adam; who to Eve,
While the great visitant approached, thus spake:—
"Eve, now expect great tidings, which, perhaps,
Of us will soon determine, or impose
New laws to be observed; for I descry,
From yonder blazing cloud that veils the hill,
One of the heavenly host, and, by his gait,
None of the meanest—some great Potentate
Or of the Thrones above, such majesty
Invests him coming; yet not terrible,
That I should fear, nor sociably mild,
As Raphael, that I should much confide,
But solemn and sublime; whom, not to offend,
With reverence I must meet, and thou retire."
He ended; and th' Archangel soon drew nigh,
Not in his shape celestial, but as man
Clad to meet man. Over his lucid arms
A military vest of purple flowed,
Livelier than Meliboean, or the grain
Of Sarra, worn by kings and heroes old

In time of truce; Iris had dipped the woof.
His starry helm unbuckled showed him prime
In manhood where youth ended; by his side,
As in a glistering zodiac, hung the sword,
Satan's dire dread, and in his hand the spear.
Adam bowed low; he, kingly, from his state
Inclined not, but his coming thus declared:—
"Adam, Heaven's high behest no preface needs.
Sufficient that thy prayers are heard, and Death,
Then due by sentence when thou didst transgress,
Defeated of his seizure many days,
Given thee of grace, wherein thou may'st repent,
And one bad act with many deeds well done
May'st cover. Well may then thy Lord, appeased,
Redeem thee quite from Death's rapacious claim;
But longer in this Paradise to dwell
Permits not. To remove thee I am come,
And send thee from the garden forth, to till
The ground whence thou wast taken, fitter soil."
He added not; for Adam, at the news
Heart-struck, with chilling gripe of sorrow stood,
That all his senses bound; Eve, who unseen
Yet all had heard, with audible lament
Discovered soon the place of her retire:—
"O unexpected stroke, worse than of Death!
Must I thus leave thee, Paradise? thus leave
Thee, native soil? these happy walks and shades,
Fit haunt of Gods, where I had hope to spend,
Quiet, though sad, the respite of that day
That must be mortal to us both? O flowers,
That never will in other climate grow,
My early visitation, and my last
At even, which I bred up with tender hand
From the first opening bud, and gave ye names,
Who now shall rear ye to the Sun, or rank
Your tribes, and water from th' ambrosial fount?
Thee, lastly, nuptial bower, by me adorned

With what to sight or smell was sweet, from thee
How shall I part, and whither wander down
Into a lower world, to this obscure
And wild? How shall we breathe in other air
Less pure, accustomed to immortal fruits?"
Whom thus the Angel interrupted mild:—
"Lament not, Eve, but patiently resign
What justly thou hast lost; nor set thy heart,
Thus over-fond, on that which is not thine.
Thy going is not lonely; with thee goes
Thy husband; him to follow thou art bound;
Where he abides, think there thy native soil."
Adam, by this from the cold sudden damp
Recovering, and his scattered spirits returned,
To Michael thus his humble words addressed:—
"Celestial, whether among the Thrones, or named
Of them the highest—for such of shape may seem
Prince above princes—gently hast thou told
Thy message, which might else in telling wound,
And in performing end us. What besides
Of sorrow, and dejection, and despair,
Our frailty can sustain, thy tidings bring—
Departure from this happy place, our sweet
Recess, and only consolation left
Familiar to our eyes; all places else
Inhospitable appear, and desolate,
Nor knowing us, nor known. And, if by prayer
Incessant I could hope to change the will
Of him who all things can, I would not cease
To weary him with my assiduous cries;
But prayer against his absolute decree
No more avails than breath against the wind,
Blown stifling back on him that breathes it forth:
Therefore to his great bidding I submit.
This most afflicts me—that, departing hence,
As from his face I shall be hid, deprived
His blessèd countenance. Here I could frequent,

With worship, place by place where he vouchsafed
Presence Divine, and to my sons relate,
'On this mount he appeared; under this tree
Stood visible; among these pines his voice
I heard; here with him at this fountain talked.'
So many grateful altars I would rear
Of grassy turf, and pile up every stone
Of lustre from the brook, in memory
Or monument to ages, and thereon
Offer sweet-smelling gums, and fruits, and flowers.
In yonder nether world where shall I seek
His bright appearances, or footstep trace?
For, though I fled him angry, yet, recalled
To life prolonged and promised race, I now
Gladly behold though but his utmost skirts
Of glory, and far off his steps adore."
  To whom thus Michael, with regard benign:—
"Adam, thou know'st Heaven his, and all the Earth,
Not this rock only; his omnipresence fills
Land, sea, and air, and every kind that lives,
Fomented by his virtual power and warmed.
All th' Earth he gave thee to possess and rule,
No despicable gift; surmise not, then,
His presence to these narrow bounds confined
Of Paradise or Eden. This had been
Perhaps thy capital seat, from whence had spread
All generations, and had hither come,
From all the ends of th' Earth, to celebrate
And reverence thee their great progenitor.
But this pre-eminence thou hast lost, brought down
To dwell on even ground now with thy sons:
Yet doubt not but in valley and in plain
God is, as here, and will be found alike
Present, and of his presence many a sign
Still following thee, still compassing thee round
With goodness and paternal love, his face
Express, and of his steps the track divine.

Which that thou may'st believe, and be confirmed
Ere thou from hence depart, know I am sent
To show thee what shall come in future days
To thee and to thy offspring. Good with bad
Expect to hear, supernal grace contending
With sinfulness of men—thereby to learn
True patience, and to temper joy with fear
And pious sorrow, equally inured
By moderation either state to bear,
Prosperous or adverse: so shalt thou lead
Safest thy life, and best prepared endure
Thy mortal passage when it comes. Ascend
This hill; let Eve (for I have drenched her eyes)
Here sleep below while thou to foresight wak'st,
As once thou slept'st while she to life was formed."
  To whom thus Adam gratefully replied:—
"Ascend, I follow thee, safe Guide, the path
Thou lead'st me, and to the hand of Heaven submit,
However chastening—to the evil turn
My obvious breast, arming to overcome
By suffering, and earn rest from labour won,
If so I may attain." So both ascend
In the visions of God. It was a hill,
Of Paradise the highest, from whose top
The hemisphere of Earth in clearest ken
Stretched out to the amplest reach of prospect lay.
Not higher that hill, nor wider looking round,
Whereon for different cause the Tempter set
Our second Adam, in the wilderness,
To show him all Earth's kingdoms and their glory.
His eye might there command wherever stood
City of old or modern fame, the seat
Of mightiest empire, from the destined walls
Of Cambalu, seat of Cathaian Khan,
And Samarchand by Oxus, Temir's throne,
To Paquin, of Sinaean kings, and thence
To Agra and Lahor of Great Mogul,

Down to the golden Chersonese, or where
The Persian in Ecbatan sat, or since
In Hispahan, or where the Russian Ksar
In Mosco, or the Sultan in Bizance,
Turchestan-born; nor could his eye not ken
Th' empire of Negus to his utmost port
Ercoco, and the less marítime kings,
Mombaza, and Quiloa, and Melind,
And Sofala (thought Ophir), to the realm
Of Congo, and Angola farthest south,
Or thence from Niger flood to Atlas mount,
The kingdoms of Almansor, Fez and Sus,
Marocco, and Algiers, and Tremisen;
On Europe thence, and where Rome was to sway
The world: in spirit perhaps he also saw
Rich Mexico, the seat of Montezume,
And Cusco in Peru, the richer seat
Of Atabalipa, and yet unspoiled
Guiana, whose great city Geryon's sons
Call El Dorado. But to nobler sights
Michael from Adam's eyes the film removed,
Which that false fruit that promised clearer sight
Had bred; then purged with euphrasy and rue
The visual nerve, for he had much to see,
And from the Well of Life three drops instilled.
So deep the power of these ingredients pierced,
Even to the inmost seat of mental sight,
That Adam, now enforced to close his eyes,
Sunk down, and all his spirits became entranced.
But him the gentle Angel by the hand
Soon raised, and his attention thus recalled:—
"Adam, now ope thine eyes, and first behold
Th' effects which thy original crime hath wrought
In some to spring from thee, who never touched
Th' excepted tree, nor with the Snake conspired,
Nor sinned thy sin, yet from that sin derive
Corruption to bring forth more violent deeds."

His eyes he opened, and beheld a field,
Part arable and tilth, whereon were sheaves
New-reaped, the other part sheep-walks and folds;
I' th' midst an altar as the landmark stood,
Rustic, of grassy sward. Thither anon
A sweaty reaper from his tillage brought
First-fruits, the green ear and the yellow sheaf,
Unculled, as came to hand. A shepherd next,
More meek, came with the firstlings of his flock,
Choicest and best; then, sacrificing, laid
The inwards and their fat, with incense strewed,
On the cleft wood, and all due rites performed.
His offering soon propitious fire from Heaven
Consumed, with nimble glance and grateful steam;
The other's not, for his was not sincere:
Whereat he inly raged, and, as they talked,
Smote him into the midriff with a stone
That beat out life; he fell, and, deadly pale,
Groaned out his soul, with gushing blood effused.
Much at that sight was Adam in his heart
Dismayed, and thus in haste to th' Angel cried:—
"O Teacher, some great mischief hath befallen
To that meek man, who well had sacrificed.
Is piety thus and pure devotion paid?"
T' whom Michael thus, he also moved, replied:—
"These two are brethren, Adam, and to come
Out of thy loins. Th' unjust the just hath slain,
For envy that his brother's offering found
From Heaven acceptance; but the bloody fact
Will be avenged, and th' other's faith approved
Lose no reward, though here thou see him die,
Rolling in dust and gore." To which our sire:—
"Alas, both for the deed and for the cause!
But have I now seen Death? Is this the way
I must return to native dust? O sight
Of terror, foul and ugly to behold!
Horrid to think, how horrible to feel!"

To whom thus Michael:—" Death thou hast seen
In his first shape on Man; but many shapes
Of Death, and many are the ways that lead
To his grim cave—all dismal, yet to sense
More terrible at th' entrance than within.
Some, as thou saw'st, by violent stroke shall die,
By fire, flood, famine; by intemperance more
In meats and drinks, which on the Earth shall bring
Diseases dire, of which a monstrous crew
Before thee shall appear, that thou may'st know
What misery th' inabstinence of Eve
Shall bring on men." Immediately a place
Before his eyes appeared, sad, noisome, dark;
A lazar-house it seemed, wherein were laid
Numbers of all diseased—all maladies
Of ghastly spasm, or racking torture, qualms
Of heart-sick agony, all feverous kinds,
Convulsions, epilepsies, fierce catarrhs,
Intestine stone and ulcer, colic pangs,
Demoniac frenzy, moping melancholy,
And moon-struck madness, pining atrophy,
Marasmus, and wide-wasting pestilence,
Dropsies and asthmas, and joint-racking rheums.
Dire was the tossing, deep the groans; Despair
Tended the sick, busiest from couch to couch;
And over them triumphant Death his dart
Shook, but delayed to strike, though oft invoked
With vows, as their chief good and final hope.
Sight so deform what heart of rock could long
Dry-eyed behold? Adam could not, but wept,
Though not of woman born: compassion quelled
His best of man, and gave him up to tears
A space, till firmer thoughts restrained excess,
And, scarce recovering words, his plaint renewed:—
" O miserable mankind, to what fall
Degraded, to what wretched state reserved!
Better end here unborn. Why is life given

To be thus wrested from us? rather why
Obtruded on us thus? who, if we knew
What we receive, would either not accept
Life offered, or soon beg to lay it down,
Glad to be so dismissed in peace. Can thus
Th' image of God in Man, created once
So goodly and erect, though faulty since,
To such unsightly sufferings be debased
Under inhuman pains? Why should not Man,
Retaining still divine similitude
In part, from such deformities be free,
And for his Maker's image' sake exempt?"
"Their Maker's image," answered Michael, "then
Forsook them, when themselves they vilified
To serve ungoverned Appetite, and took
His image whom they served—a brutish vice,
Inductive mainly to the sin of Eve.
Therefore so abject is their punishment,
Disfiguring not God's likeness, but their own;
Or, if his likeness, by themselves defaced
While they pervert pure Nature's healthful rules
To loathsome sickness—worthily, since they
God's image did not reverence in themselves."
"I yield it just," said Adam, "and submit.
But is there yet no other way, besides
These painful passages, how we may come
To death, and mix with our connatural dust?"
"There is," said Michael, "if thou well observe
The rule of *Not too much*, by temperance taught
In what thou eat'st and drink'st, seeking from thence
Due nourishment, not gluttonous delight,
Till many years over thy head return.
So may'st thou live, till, like ripe fruit, thou drop
Into thy mother's lap, or be with ease
Gathered, not harshly plucked, for death mature.
This is old age; but then thou must outlive
Thy youth, thy strength, thy beauty, which will change

To withered, weak, and grey; thy senses then,
Obtuse, all taste of pleasure must forgo
To what thou hast; and, for the air of youth,
Hopeful and cheerful, in thy blood will reign
A melancholy damp of cold and dry,
To weigh thy spirits down, and last consume
The balm of life." To whom our ancestor:—
"Henceforth I fly not death, nor would prolong
Life much—bent rather how I may be quit,
Fairest and easiest, of this cumbrous charge,
Which I must keep till my appointed day
Of rendering up, and patiently attend
My dissolution." Michaël replied:—
"Nor love thy life, nor hate; but what thou liv'st
Live well; how long or short permit to Heaven.
And now prepare thee for another sight."
He looked, and saw a spacious plain, whereon
Were tents of various hue: by some were herds
Of cattle grazing: others whence the sound
Of instruments that made melodious chime
Was heard, of harp and organ, and who moved
Their stops and chords was seen: his volant touch
Instinct through all proportions low and high
Fled and pursued transverse the resonant fugue.
In other part stood one who, at the forge
Labouring, two massy clods of iron and brass
Had melted (whether found where casual fire
Had wasted woods, on mountain or in vale,
Down to the veins of earth, thence gliding hot
To some cave's mouth, or whether washed by stream
From underground); the liquid ore he drained
Into fit moulds prepared; from which he formed
First his own tools, then what might else be wrought
Fusil or graven in metal. After these,
But on the hither side, a different sort
From the high neighbouring hills, which was their seat,
Down to the plain descended: by their guise

Just men they seemed, and all their study bent
To worship God aright, and know his works
Not hid; nor those things last which might preserve
Freedom and peace to men. They on the plain
Long had not walked, when from the tents behold
A bevy of fair women, richly gay
In gems and wanton dress: to the harp they sung
Soft amorous ditties, and in dance came on.
The men, though grave, eyed them, and let their eyes
Rove without rein, till, in the amorous net
Fast caught, they liked, and each his liking chose.
And now of love they treat, till th' evening-star,
Love's harbinger, appeared; then, all in heat,
They light the nuptial torch, and bid invoke
Hymen, then first to marriage rites invoked:
With feast and music all the tents resound.
Such happy interview, and fair event
Of love and youth not lost, songs, garlands, flowers,
And charming symphonies, attached the heart
Of Adam, soon inclined to admit delight,
The bent of Nature; which he thus expressed:—
  "True opener of mine eyes, prime Angel blest,
Much better seems this vision, and more hope
Of peaceful days portends, than those two past:
Those were of hate and death, or pain much worse;
Here Nature seems fulfilled in all her ends."
  To whom thus Michael:—"Judge not what is best
By pleasure, though to Nature seeming meet,
Created, as thou art, to nobler end,
Holy and pure, conformity divine.
Those tents thou saw'st so pleasant were the tents
Of wickedness, wherein shall dwell his race
Who slew his brother: studious they appear
Of arts that polish life, inventors rare;
Unmindful of their Maker, though his Spirit
Taught them; but they his gifts acknowledged none.
Yet they a beauteous offspring shall beget;

For that fair female troop thou saw'st, that seemed
Of goddesses, so blithe, so smooth, so gay,
Yet empty of all good wherein consists
Woman's domestic honour and chief praise;
Bred only and completed to the taste
Of lustful appetence, to sing, to dance,
To dress, and troll the tongue, and roll the eye;—
To these that sober race of men, whose lives
Religious titled them the Sons of God,
Shall yield up all their virtue, all their fame,
Ignobly, to the trains and to the smiles
Of these fair atheists, and now swim in joy
(Erelong to swim at large) and laugh; for which
The world erelong a world of tears must weep."
  To whom thus Adam, of short joy bereft:—
"O pity and shame, that they who to live well
Entered so fair, should turn aside to tread
Paths indirect, or in the midway faint!
But still I see the tenor of Man's woe
Holds on the same, from Woman to begin."
  "From Man's effeminate slackness it begins,"
Said th' Angel, "who should better hold his place
By wisdom, and superior gifts received.
But now prepare thee for another scene."
  He looked, and saw wide territory spread
Before him—towns, and rural works between,
Cities of men with lofty gates and towers,
Concourse in arms, fierce faces threatening war,
Giants of mighty bone and bold emprise.
Part wield their arms, part curb the foaming steed,
Single or in array of battle ranged
Both horse and foot, nor idly mustering stood.
One way a band select from forage drives
A herd of beeves, fair oxen and fair kine,
From a fat meadow-ground, or fleecy flock,
Ewes and their bleating lambs, over the plain,
Their booty; scarce with life the shepherds fly,

But call in aid, which makes a bloody fray:
With cruel tournament the squadrons join;
Where cattle pastured late, now scattered lies
With carcases and arms th' ensanguined field
Deserted. Others to a city strong
Lay siege, encamped, by battery, scale, and mine,
Assaulting; others from the wall defend
With dart and javelin, stones and sulphurous fire;
On each hand slaughter and gigantic deeds.
In other part the sceptred heralds call
To council in the city-gates: anon
Grey-headed men and grave, with warriors mixed,
Assemble, and harangues are heard; but soon
In factious opposition, till at last
Of middle age one rising, eminent
In wise deport, spake much of right and wrong,
Of justice, of religion, truth, and peace,
And judgment from above: him old and young
Exploded, and had seized with violent hands,
Had not a cloud descending snatched him thence,
Unseen amid the throng. So violence
Proceeded, and oppression, and sword-law,
Through all the plain, and refuge none was found.
Adam was all in tears, and to his guide
Lamenting turned full sad:—" Oh, what are these?
Death's ministers, not men! who thus deal death
Inhumanly to men, and multiply
Ten thousandfold the sin of him who slew
His brother; for of whom such massacre
Make they but of their brethren, men of men?
But who was that just man, whom had not Heaven
Rescued, had in his righteousness been lost? "
To whom thus Michael:—" These are the product
Of those ill-mated marriages thou saw'st,
Where good with bad were matched; who of themselves
Abhor to join, and, by imprudence mixed,
Produce prodigious births of body or mind.

Such were these Giants, men of high renown;
For in those days might only shall be admired,
And valour and heroic virtue called.
To overcome in battle, and subdue
Nations, and bring home spoils with infinite
Manslaughter, shall be held the highest pitch
Of human glory, and, for glory done,
Of triumph, to be styled great conquerors,
Patrons of mankind, gods, and sons of gods—
Destroyers rightlier called, and plagues of men.
Thus fame shall be achieved, renown on earth,
And what most merits fame in silence hid.
But he, the seventh from thee, whom thou beheld'st
The only righteous in a world perverse,
And therefore hated, therefore so beset
With foes, for daring single to be just,
And utter odious truth, that God would come
To judge them with his Saints—him the Most High,
Rapt in a balmy cloud, with wingèd steeds,
Did, as thou saw'st, receive, to walk with God
High in salvation and the climes of bliss,
Exempt from death, to show thee what reward
Awaits the good, the rest what punishment;
Which now direct thine eyes and soon behold."
  He looked, and saw the face of things quite changed.
The brazen throat of war had ceased to roar;
All now was turned to jollity and game,
To luxury and riot, feast and dance,
Marrying or prostituting, as befell,
Rape or adultery, where passing fair
Allured them; thence from cups to civil broils.
At length a reverend sire among them came,
And of their doings great dislike declared,
And testified against their ways. He oft
Frequented their assemblies, whereso met,
Triumphs or festivals, and to them preached
Conversion and repentance, as to souls

In a prison, under judgments imminent;
But all in vain. Which when he saw, he ceased
Contending, and removed his tents far off;
Then, from the mountain hewing timber tall,
Began to build a vessel of huge bulk,
Measured by cubit, length, and breadth, and height,
Smeared round with pitch, and in the side a door
Contrived, and of provisions laid in large
For man and beast: when lo! a wonder strange!
Of every beast, and bird, and insect small,
Came sevens and pairs, and entered in, as taught
Their order; last, the sire and his three sons,
With their four wives; and God made fast the door.
Meanwhile the south wind rose, and, with black wings
Wide-hovering, all the clouds together drove
From under heaven; the hills to their supply
Vapour, and exhalation dusk and moist,
Sent up amain; and now the thickened sky
Like a dark ceiling stood: down rushed the rain
Impetuous, and continued till the earth
No more was seen. The floating vessel swum
Uplifted, and secure with beakèd prow
Rode tilting o'er the waves; all dwellings else
Flood overwhelmed, and them with all their pomp
Deep under water rolled; sea covered sea,
Sea without shore: and in their palaces,
Where luxury late reigned, sea-monsters whelped
And stabled: of mankind, so numerous late,
All left in one small bottom swum embarked.
How didst thou grieve then, Adam, to behold
The end of all thy offspring, end so sad,
Depopulation! Thee another flood,
Of tears and sorrow a flood thee also drowned,
And sunk thee as thy sons; till, gently reared
By th' Angel, on thy feet thou stood'st at last,
Though comfortless, as when a father mourns
His children, all in view destroyed at once,

And scarce to th' Angel utter'dst thus thy plaint:—
"O visions ill foreseen! Better had I
Lived ignorant of future—so had borne
My part of evil only, each day's lot
Enough to bear. Those now that were dispensed
The burden of many ages on me light
At once, by my foreknowledge gaining birth
Abortive, to torment me, ere their being,
With thought that they must be. Let no man seek
Henceforth to be foretold what shall befall
Him or his children—evil, he may be sure,
Which neither his foreknowing can prevent,
And he the future evil shall no less
In apprehension than in substance feel
Grievous to bear. But that care now is past;
Man is not whom to warn; those few escaped,
Famine and anguish will at last consume,
Wandering that watery desert. I had hope,
When violence was ceased and war on Earth,
All would have then gone well, peace would have crowned
With length ot happy days the race of Man;
But I was far deceived, for now I see
Peace to corrupt no less than war to waste.
How comes it thus? Unfold, Celestial Guide,
And whether here the race of Man will end."
To whom thus Michael:—"Those whom last thou saw'st
In triumph and luxurious wealth, are they
First seen in acts of prowess eminent
And great exploits, but of true virtue void;
Who, having spilt much blood, and done much waste,
Subduing nations, and achieved thereby
Fame in the world, high titles, and rich prey,
Shall change their course to pleasure, ease, and sloth,
Surfeit, and lust, till wantonness and pride
Raise out of friendship hostile deeds in peace.
The conquered, also, and enslaved by war,
Shall, with their freedom lost, all virtue lose,

And fear of God—from whom their piety feigned
In sharp contést of battle found no aid
Against invaders; therefore, cooled in zeal,
Thenceforth shall practise how to live secure,
Worldly or dissolute, on what their lords
Shall leave them to enjoy; for th' Earth shall bear
More than enough, that temperance may be tried.
So all shall turn degenerate, all depraved,
Justice and temperance, truth and faith, forgot;
One man except, the only son of light
In a dark age, against example good,
Against allurement, custom, and a world
Offended. Fearless of reproach and scorn,
Or violence, he of their wicked ways
Shall them admonish, and before them set
The paths of righteousness, how much more safe
And full of peace, denouncing wrath to come
On their impenitence, and shall return
Of them derided, but of God observed
The one just man alive: by his command
Shall build a wondrous ark, as thou beheld'st,
To save himself and household from amidst
A world devote to universal wrack.
No sooner he, with them of man and beast
Select for life, shall in the ark be lodged
And sheltered round, but all the cataracts
Of Heaven set open on the Earth shall pour
Rain day and night; all fountains of the deep,
Broke up, shall heave the ocean to usurp
Beyond all bounds, till inundation rise
Above the highest hills. Then shall this Mount
Of Paradise by might of waves be moved
Out of his place, pushed by the hornèd flood,
With all his verdure spoiled, and trees adrift,
Down the great river to the opening gulf,
And there take root, an island salt and bare,
The haunt of seals, and orcs, and sea-mews' clang—

To teach thee that God áttributes to place
No sanctity, if none be thither brought
By men who there frequent or therein dwell.
And now what further shall ensue behold."
He looked, and saw the ark hull on the flood,
Which now abated; for the clouds were fled,
Driven by a keen north wind, that, blowing dry,
Wrinkled the face of deluge, as decayed;
And the clear sun on his wide watery glass
Gazed hot, and of the fresh wave largely drew,
As after thirst; which made their flowing shrink
From standing lake to tripping ebb, that stole
With soft foot towards the deep, who now had stopped
His sluices, as the heaven his windows shut.
The ark no more now floats, but seems on ground,
Fast on the top of some high mountain fixed.
And now the tops of hills as rocks appear;
With clamour thence the rapid currents drive
Towards the retreating sea their furious tide.
Forthwith from out the ark a raven flies,
And, after him, the surer messenger,
A dove, sent forth once and again to spy
Green tree or ground whereon his foot may light;
The second time returning, in his bill
An olive-leaf he brings, pacific sign.
Anon dry ground appears, and from his ark
The ancient sire descends, with all his train;
Then, with uplifted hands, and eyes devout,
Grateful to Heaven, over his head beholds
A dewy cloud, and in the cloud a bow
Conspicuous with three listed colours gay,
Betokening peace from God, and covenant new.
Whereat the heart of Adam, erst so sad,
Greatly rejoiced; and thus his joy broke forth:—
"O thou, who future things canst represent
As present, Heavenly Instructor, I revive
At this last sight, assured that Man shall live,

With all the creatures, and their seed preserve.
Far less I now lament for one whole world
Of wicked sons destroyed, than I rejoice
For one man found so perfect, and so just,
That God vouchsafes to raise another world
From him, and all his anger to forget.
But say, what mean those coloured streaks in Heaven,
Distended as the brow of God appeased?
Or serve they as a flowery verge to bind
The fluid skirts of that same watery cloud,
Lest it again dissolve and shower the Earth?"
  To whom th' Archangel:—" Dextrously thou aim'st.
So willingly doth God remit his ire:
Though late repenting him of Man depraved,
Grieved at his heart, when, looking down, he saw
The whole Earth filled with violence, and all flesh
Corrupting each their way; yet, those removed,
Such grace shall one just man find in his sight
That he relents, not to blot out mankind,
And makes a covenant never to destroy
The Earth again by flood, nor let the sea
Surpass his bounds, nor rain to drown the world
With man therein or beast; but, when he brings
Over the Earth a cloud, will therein set
His triple-coloured bow, whereon to look
And call to mind his covenant. Day and night,
Seed-time and harvest, heat and hoary frost,
Shall hold their course, till fire purge all things new,
Both Heaven and Earth, wherein the just shall dwell."

THE END OF THE ELEVENTH BOOK

BOOK XII

THE ARGUMENT

The Angel Michael continues, from the Flood, to relate what shall succeed; then, in the mention of Abraham, comes by degrees to explain who that Seed of the Woman shall be which was promised Adam and Eve in the Fall: his incarnation, death, resurrection, and ascension: the state of the Church till his second coming. Adam, greatly satisfied and recomforted by these relations and promises, descends the hill with Michael; wakens Eve, who all this while had slept, but with gentle dreams composed to quietness of mind and submission. Michael in either hand leads them out of Paradise, the fiery sword waving behind them, and the Cherubim taking their stations to guard the place.

As one who in his journey bates at noon,
Though bent on speed, so here the Archangel paused
Betwixt the world destroyed and world restored,
If Adam aught perhaps might interpose;
Then, with transition sweet, new speech resumes:—
"Thus thou hast seen one world begin and end,
And Man as from a second stock proceed.
Much thou hast yet to see; but I perceive
Thy mortal sight to fail; objects divine
Must needs impair and weary human sense.
Henceforth what is to come I will relate;
Thou, therefore, give due audience, and attend.
"This second source of men, while yet but few,
And while the dread of judgment past remains
Fresh in their minds, fearing the Deity,
With some regard to what is just and right
Shall lead their lives, and multiply apace,
Labouring the soil, and reaping plenteous crop,
Corn, wine, and oil; and, from the herd or flock
Oft sacrificing bullock, lamb, or kid,

With large wine-offerings poured, and sacred feast,
Shall spend their days in joy unblamed, and dwell
Long time in peace, by families and tribes,
Under paternal rule: till one shall rise,
Of proud, ambitious heart, who, not content,
With fair equality, fraternal state,
Will arrogate dominion undeserved
Over his brethren, and quite dispossess
Concord and law of Nature from the Earth—
Hunting (and men, not beasts, shall be his game)
With war and hostile snare such as refuse
Subjection to his empire tyrannous.
A mighty hunter thence he shall be styled
Before the Lord, as in despite of Heaven,
Or from Heaven claiming second sovereignty,
And from rebellion shall derive his name,
Though of rebellion others he accuse.
He, with a crew, whom like ambition joins
With him or under him to tyrannize,
Marching from Eden towards the west, shall find
The plain, wherein a black bituminous gurge
Boils out from under ground, the mouth of Hell.
Of brick, and of that stuff, they cast to build
A city and tower, whose top may reach to Heaven;
And get themselves a name, lest, far dispersed
In foreign lands, their memory be lost—
Regardless whether good or evil fame.
But God, who oft descends to visit men
Unseen, and through their habitations walks,
To mark their doings, them beholding soon,
Comes down to see their city, ere the tower
Obstruct Heaven-towers, and in derision sets
Upon their tongues a various spirit, to rase
Quite out their native language, and, instead,
To sow a jangling noise of words unknown.
Forthwith a hideous gabble rises loud
Among the builders; each to other calls,

Not understood—till, hoarse and all in rage,
As mocked they storm. Great laughter was in Heaven,
And looking down to see the hubbub strange
And hear the din. Thus was the building left
Ridiculous, and the work *Confusion* named."
  Whereto thus Adam, fatherly displeased:—
"O execrable son, so to aspire
Above his brethren, to himself assuming
Authority usurped, from God not given!
He gave us only over beast, fish, fowl,
Dominion absolute; that right we hold
By his donation: but man over men
He made not lord—such title to himself
Reserving, human left from human free.
But this usurper his encroachment proud
Stays not on Man; to God his tower intends
Siege and defiance. Wretched man! what food
Will he convey up thither, to sustain
Himself and his rash army, where thin air
Above the clouds will pine his entrails gross,
And famish him of breath, if not of bread?"
  To whom thus Michael:—"Justly thou abhorr'st
That son, who on the quiet state of men
Such trouble brought, affecting to subdue
Rational liberty; yet know withal,
Since thy original lapse, true liberty
Is lost, which always with right reason dwells
Twinned, and from her hath no dividual being.
Reason in Man obscured, or not obeyed,
Immediately inordinate desires
And upstart passions catch the government
From Reason, and to servitude reduce
Man, till then free. Therefore, since he permits
Within himself unworthy powers to reign
Over free reason, God, in judgment just,
Subjects him from without to violent lords,
Who oft as undeservedly enthrall

His outward freedom. Tyranny must be,
Though to the tyrant thereby no excuse.
Yet sometimes nations will decline so low
From virtue, which is reason, that no wrong,
But justice and some fatal curse annexed,
Deprives them of their outward liberty,
Their inward lost: witness th' irreverent son
Of him who built the ark, who, for the shame
Done to his father, heard this heavy curse,
Servant of servants, on his vicious race.
Thus will this latter, as the former world,
Still tend from bad to worse, till God at last,
Wearied with their iniquities, withdraw
His presence from among them, and avert
His holy eyes, resolving from thenceforth
To leave them to their own polluted ways,
And one peculiar nation to select
From all the rest, of whom to be invoked—
A nation from one faithful man to spring.
Him on this side Euphrates yet residing,
Bred up in idol-worship—Oh, that men
(Canst thou believe?) should be so stupid grown,
While yet the patriarch lived who scaped the Flood,
As to forsake the living God, and fall
To worship their own work in wood and stone
For gods!—yet him God the Most High vouchsafes
To call by wisdom from his father's house,
His kindred, and false gods, into a land
Which he will show him, and from him will raise
A mighty nation, and upon him shower
His benediction so that in his seed
All nations shall be blest. He straight obeys;
Not knowing to what land, yet firm believes.
I see him, but thou canst not, with what faith
He leaves his gods, his friends, and native soil,
Ur of Chaldaea, passing now the ford
To Haran—after him a cumbrous train

Of herds and flocks, and numerous servitude—
Not wandering poor, but trusting all his wealth
With God, who called him, in a land unknown.
Canaan he now attains; I see his tents
Pitched about Sechem, and the neighbouring plain
Of Moreh. There, by promise, he receives
Gift to his progeny of all that land,
From Hamath northward to the Desert south
(Things by their names I call, though yet unnamed),
From Hermon east to the great western sea;
Mount Hermon, yonder sea, each place behold
In prospect, as I point them: on the shore,
Mount Carmel; here, the double-founted stream,
Jordan, true limit eastward; but his sons
Shall dwell to Senir, that long ridge of hills.
This ponder, that all nations of the Earth
Shall in his seed be blessèd. By that seed
Is meant thy great Deliverer, who shall bruise
The Serpent's head; whereof to thee anon
Plainlier shall be revealed. This patriarch blest,
Whom *faithful Abraham* due time shall call,
A son, and of his son a grandchild, leaves,
Like him in faith, in wisdom, and renown.
The grandchild, with twelve sons increased, departs
From Canaan to a land hereafter called
Egypt, divided by the river Nile;
See where it flows, disgorging at seven mouths
Into the sea. To sojourn in that land
He comes, invited by a younger son
In time of dearth—a son whose worthy deeds
Raise him to be the second in that realm
Of Pharaoh. There he dies, and leaves his race
Growing into a nation, and now grown
Suspected to a sequent king, who seeks
To stop their overgrowth, as inmate guests
Too numerous; whence of guests he makes them slaves
Inhospitably, and kills their infant males:

Till, by two brethren (those two brethren call
Moses and Aaron) sent from God to claim
His people from enthrallment, they return,
With glory and spoil, back to their promised land.
But first the lawless tyrant, who denies
To know their God, or message to regard,
Must be compelled by signs and judgments dire:
To blood unshed the rivers must be turned;
Frogs, lice, and flies must all his palace fill
With loathed intrusion, and fill all the land;
His cattle must of rot and murrain die;
Botches and blains must all his flesh emboss,
And all his people; thunder mixed with hail,
Hail mixed with fire, must rend th' Egyptian sky,
And wheel on th' earth, devouring where it rolls;
What it devours not, herb, or fruit, or grain,
A darksome cloud of locusts swarming down
Must eat, and on the ground leave nothing green;
Darkness must overshadow all his bounds,
Palpable darkness, and blot out three days;
Last, with one midnight-stroke, all the first-born
Of Egypt must lie dead. Thus with ten wounds
The river-dragon tamed at length submits
To let his sojourners depart, and oft
Humbles his stubborn heart, but still as ice
More hardened after thaw; till in his rage,
Pursuing whom he late dismissed, the sea
Swallows him with his host, but them lets pass,
As on dry land, between two crystal walls,
Awed by the rod of Moses so to stand
Divided till his rescued gain their shore:
Such wondrous power God to his Saint will lend,
Though present in his Angel, who shall go
Before them in a cloud, and pillar of fire—
By day a cloud, by night a pillar of fire—
To guide them in their journey, and remove
Behind them, while th' obdúrate king pursues.

All night he will pursue, but his approach
Darkness defends between till morning-watch;
Then through the fiery pillar and the cloud
God looking forth will trouble all his host,
And craze their chariot-wheels: when, by command,
Moses once more his potent rod extends
Over the sea; the sea his rod obeys;
On their embattled ranks the waves return,
And overwhelm their war. The race elect
Safe towards Canaan, from the shore, advance
Through the wild Desert—not the readiest way,
Lest, entering on the Canaanite alarmed,
War terrify them inexpert, and fear
Return them back to Egypt, choosing rather
Inglorious life with servitude; for life
To noble and ignoble is more sweet
Untrained in arms, where rashness leads not on.
This also shall they gain by their delay
In the wide wilderness: there they shall found
Their government, and their great Senate choose
Through the twelve tribes, to rule by laws ordained.
God, from the Mount of Sinai, whose grey top
Shall tremble, he descending, will himself,
In thunder, lightning, and loud trumpet's sound,
Ordain them laws—part, such as appertain
To civil justice; part, religious rites
Of sacrifice, informing them, by types
And shadows, of that destined Seed to bruise
The Serpent, by what means he shall achieve
Mankind's deliverance. But the voice of God
To mortal ear is dreadful: they beseech
That Moses might report to them his will,
And terror cease; he grants what they besought,
Instructed that to God is no access
Without Mediator, whose high office now
Moses in figure bears, to introduce
One greater, of whose day he shall foretell,

And all the Prophets, in their age, the times
Of great Messiah shall sing. Thus laws and rites
Established, such delight hath God in men
Obedient to his will that he vouchsafes
Among them to set up his tabernacle—
The Holy One with mortal men to dwell.
By his prescript a sanctuary is framed
Of cedar overlaid with gold; therein
An ark, and in the ark his testimony,
The records of his covenant; over these
A mercy-seat of gold, between the wings
Of two bright Cherubim; before him burn
Seven lamps, as in a zodiac representing
The heavenly fires. Over the tent a cloud
Shall rest by day, a fiery gleam by night,
Save when they journey; and at length they come,
Conducted by his Angel, to the land
Promised to Abraham and his seed. The rest
Were long to tell—how many battles fought;
How many kings destroyed, and kingdoms won;
Or how the sun shall in mid-heaven stand still
A day entire, and night's due course adjourn,
Man's voice commanding, 'Sun, in Gibeon stand,
And thou, Moon, in the vale of Aialon,
Till Israel overcome!'—so call the third
From Abraham, son of Isaac, and from him
His whole descent, who thus shall Canaan win."
  Here Adam interposed:—"O sent from Heaven,
Enlightener of my darkness, gracious things
Thou hast revealed, those chiefly which concern
Just Abraham and his seed. Now first I find
Mine eyes true opening, and my heart much eased,
Erewhile perplexed with thoughts what would become
Of me and all mankind; but now I see
His day, in whom all nations shall be blest—
Favour unmerited by me, who sought
Forbidden knowledge by forbidden means.

This yet I apprehend not—why to those
Among whom God will deign to dwell on Earth
So many and so various laws are given.
So many laws argue so many sins
Among them; how can God with such reside?"
  To whom thus Michael:—"Doubt not but that sin
Will reign among them, as of thee begot;
And therefore was law given them, to evince
Their natural pravity, by stirring up
Sin against Law to fight, that, when they see
Law can discover sin, but not remove,
Save by those shadowy expiations weak,
The blood of bulls and goats, they may conclude
Some blood more precious must be paid for Man,
Just for unjust, that in such righteousness,
To them by faith imputed, they may find
Justification towards God, and peace
Of conscience, which the law by ceremonies
Cannot appease, nor man the moral part
Perform, and not performing cannot live.
So Law appears imperfect, and but given
With purpose to resign them, in full time,
Up to a better covenant, disciplined
From shadowy types to truth, from flesh to spirit,
From imposition of strict laws to free
Acceptance of large grace, from servile fear
To filial, works of law to works of faith.
And therefore shall not Moses, though of God
Highly beloved, being but the minister
Of Law, his people into Canaan lead;
But Joshua, whom the Gentiles Jesus call,
His name and office bearing who shall quell
The adversary Serpent, and bring back
Through the world's wilderness long-wandered Man
Safe to eternal Paradise of rest.
Meanwhile they, in their earthly Canaan placed,
Long time shall dwell and prosper, but when sins

National interrupt their public peace,
Provoking God to raise them enemies—
From whom as oft he saves them penitent,
By judges first, then under kings; of whom
The second, both for piety renowned
And puissant deeds, a promise shall receive
Irrevocable, that his regal throne
For ever shall endure. The like shall sing
All Prophecy—that of the royal stock
Of David (so I name this king) shall rise
A son, the Woman's Seed to thee foretold,
Foretold to Abraham as in whom shall trust
All nations, and to kings foretold of kings
The last, for of his reign shall be no end.
But first a long succession must ensue;
And his next son, for wealth and wisdom famed,
The clouded ark of God, till then in tents
Wandering, shall in a glorious temple enshrine.
Such follow him as shall be registered
Part good, part bad; of bad the longer scroll:
Whose foul idolatries and other faults,
Heaped to the popular sum, will so incense
God, as to leave them, and expose their land,
Their city, his temple, and his holy ark,
With all his sacred things, a scorn and prey
To that proud city whose high walls thou saw'st
Left in confusion, Babylon thence called.
There in captivity he lets them dwell
The space of seventy years; then brings them back,
Remembering mercy, and his covenant sworn
To David, stablished as the days of Heaven.
Returned from Babylon by leave of kings,
Their lords, whom God disposed, the house of God
They first re-edify, and for a while
In mean estate live moderate, till, grown
In wealth and multitude, factious they grow.
But first among the priests dissension springs—

Men who attend the altar, and should most
Endeavour peace: their strife pollution brings
Upon the temple itself; at last they seize
The sceptre, and regard not David's sons;
Then lose it to a stranger, that the true
Anointed King Messiah might be born
Barred of his right. Yet at his birth a star,
Unseen before in heaven, proclaims him come,
And guides the eastern sages, who inquire
His place, to offer incense, myrrh, and gold:
His place of birth a solemn Angel tells
To simple shepherds, keeping watch by night;
They gladly thither haste, and by a choir
Of squadroned Angels hear his carol sung.
A Virgin is his mother, but his Sire
The Power of the Most High. He shall ascend
The throne hereditary, and bound his reign
With Earth's wide bounds, his glory with the Heavens."
  He ceased, discerning Adam with such joy
Surcharged as had, like grief, been dewed in tears,
Without the vent of words; which these he breathed:—
  "O prophet of glad tidings, finisher
Of utmost hope! now clear I understand
What oft my steadiest thoughts have searched in vain—
Why our great Expectation should be called
The Seed of Woman. Virgin Mother, hail!
High in the love of Heaven, yet from my loins
Thou shalt proceed, and from thy womb the Son
Of God Most High; so God with Man unites.
Needs must the Serpent now his capital bruise
Expect with mortal pain. Say where and when
Their fight, what stroke shall bruise the Victor's heel."
  To whom thus Michael:—"Dream not of their fight
As of a duel, or the local wounds
Of head or heel. Not therefore joins the Son
Manhood to Godhead, with more strength to foil
Thy enemy; nor so is overcome

Satan, whose fall from Heaven, a deadlier bruise,
Disabled not to give thee thy death's wound;
Which he who comes thy Saviour shall recure,
Not by destroying Satan, but his works
In thee and in thy seed. Nor can this be,
But by fulfilling that which thou didst want,
Obedience to the law of God, imposed
On penalty of death, and suffering death,
The penalty to thy transgression due,
And due to theirs which out of thine will grow:
So only can high justice rest appaid.
The law of God exact he shall fulfil
Both by obedience and by love, though love
Alone fulfil the Law; thy punishment
He shall endure, by coming in the flesh
To a reproachful life and cursèd death,
Proclaiming life to all who shall believe
In his redemption, and that his obedience
Imputed becomes theirs by faith—his merits
To save them, not their own, though legal, works.
For this he shall live hated, be blasphemed,
Seized on by force, judged, and to death condemned
A shameful and accursed, nailed to the cross
By his own nation, slain for bringing life;
But to the cross he nails thy enemies—
The Law that is against thee, and the sins
Of all mankind, with him there crucified,
Never to hurt them more who rightly trust
In this his satisfaction. So he dies,
But soon revives; Death over him no power
Shall long usurp. Ere the third dawning light
Return, the stars of morn shall see him rise
Out of his grave, fresh as the dawning light,
Thy ransom paid, which Man from Death redeems—
His death for Man, as many as offered life
Neglect not, and the benefit embrace
By faith not void of works. This godlike act

Annuls thy doom, the death thou shouldst have died,
In sin for ever lost from life; this act
Shall bruise the head of Satan, crush his strength,
Defeating Sin and Death, his two main arms,
And fix far deeper in his head their stings
Than temporal death shall bruise the Victor's heel,
Or theirs whom he redeems—a death like sleep,
A gentle wafting to immortal life.
Nor after resurrection shall he stay
Longer on Earth than certain times to appear
To his disciples—men who in his life
Still followed him; to them shall leave in charge
To teach all nations what of him they learned
And his salvation, them who shall believe
Baptizing in the profluent stream—the sign
Of washing them from guilt of sin to life
Pure, and in mind prepared, if so befall,
For death like that which the Redeemer died.
All nations they shall teach; for from that day
Not only to the sons of Abraham's loins
Salvation shall be preached, but to the sons
Of Abraham's faith wherever through the world;
So in his seed all nations shall be blest.
Then to the Heaven of Heavens he shall ascend
With victory, triúmphing through the air
Over his foes and thine; there shall surprise
The Serpent, Prince of Air, and drag in chains
Through all his realm, and there confounded leave;
Then enter into glory, and resume
His seat at God's right hand, exalted high
Above all names in Heaven; and thence shall come,
When this World's dissolution shall be ripe,
With glory and power, to judge both quick and dead—
To judge th' unfaithful dead, but to reward
His faithful, and receive them into bliss,
Whether in Heaven or Earth; for then the Earth
Shall be all Paradise, far happier place

Than this of Eden, and far happier days."
  So spake th' Archangel Michaël; then paused,
As at the World's great period; and our sire,
Replete with joy and wonder, thus replied:—
  "O Goodness infinite, Goodness immense,
That all this good of evil shall produce,
And evil turn to good—more wonderful
Than that which by creation first brought forth
Light out of darkness! Full of doubt I stand,
Whether I should repent me now of sin
By me done and occasioned, or rejoice
Much more that much more good thereof shall spring—
To God more glory, more good-will to men
From God—and over wrath grace shall abound.
But say, if our Deliverer up to Heaven
Must reascend, what will betide the few,
His faithful, left among th' unfaithful herd,
The enemies of truth? Who then shall guide
His people, who defend? Will they not deal
Worse with his followers than with him they dealt?"
  "Be sure they will," said th' Angel; "but from Heaven
He to his own a Comforter will send,
The promise of the Father, who shall dwell,
His Spirit, within them, and the law of faith,
Working through love, upon their hearts shall write,
To guide them in all truth, and also arm
With spiritual armour, able to resist
Satan's assaults, and quench his fiery darts—
What man can do against them not afraid,
Though to the death; against such cruelties
With inward consolations recompensed,
And oft supported so as shall amaze
Their proudest persecutors. For the Spirit,
Poured first on his Apostles, whom he sends
To evangelize the nations, then on all
Baptized, shall them with wondrous gifts endue

To speak all tongues, and do all miracles,
As did their Lord before them. Thus they win
Great numbers of each nation to receive
With joy the tidings brought from Heaven: at length,
Their ministry performed, and race well run,
Their doctrine and their story written left,
They die: but in their room, as they forewarn,
Wolves shall succeed for teachers, grievous wolves,
Who all the sacred mysteries of Heaven
To their own vile advantages shall turn
Of lucre and ambition, and the truth
With superstitions and traditions taint,
Left only in those written records pure,
Though not but by the Spirit understood.
Then shall they seek to avail themselves of names,
Places, and titles, and with these to join
Secular power, though feigning still to act
By spiritual; to themselves appropriating
The Spirit of God, promised alike and given
To all believers; and, from that pretence,
Spiritual laws by carnal power shall force
On every conscience—laws which none shall find
Left them enrolled, or what the Spirit within
Shall on the heart engrave. What will they then
But force the Spirit of Grace itself, and bind
His consort, Liberty? what but unbuild
His living temples, built by faith to stand—
Their own faith, not another's? for, on Earth,
Who against faith and conscience can be heard
Infallible? Yet many will presume:
Whence heavy persecution shall arise
On all who in the worship persevere
Of Spirit and Truth; the rest, far greater part,
Will deem in outward rites and specious forms
Religion satisfied; Truth shall retire
Bestuck with slanderous darts, and works of Faith

Rarely be found. So shall the world go on,
To good malignant, to bad men benign,
Under her own weight groaning, till the day
Appear of respiration to the just
And vengeance to the wicked, at return
Of Him so lately promised to thy aid,
The Woman's Seed—obscurely then foretold,
Now amplier known thy Saviour and thy Lord;
Last in the clouds from Heaven to be revealed
In glory of the Father, to dissolve
Satan with his perverted World; then raise
From the conflagrant mass, purged and refined,
New Heavens, new Earth, ages of endless date
Founded in righteousness and peace and love,
To bring forth fruits, joy and eternal bliss."
  He ended, and thus Adam last replied:—
"How soon hath thy prediction, Seer blest,
Measured this transient World, the race of Time,
Till Time stand fixed! Beyond is all abyss—
Eternity, whose end no eye can reach.
Greatly instructed I shall hence depart,
Greatly in peace of thought, and have my fill
Of knowledge, what this vessel can contain;
Beyond which was my folly to aspire.
Henceforth I learn that to obey is best,
And love with fear the only God, to walk
As in his presence, ever to observe
His providence, and on him sole depend,
Merciful over all his works, with good
Still overcoming evil, and by small
Accomplishing great things—by things deemed weak
Subverting worldly-strong, and worldly-wise
By simply meek; that suffering for Truth's sake
Is fortitude to highest victory,
And to the faithful death the gate of life—
Taught this by his example whom I now

Acknowledge my Redeemer ever blest."
  To whom thus also th' Angel last replied:—
"This having learned, thou hast attained the sum
Of wisdom; hope no higher, though all the stars
Thou knew'st by name, and all th' ethereal powers,
All secrets of the Deep, all Nature's works,
Or works of God in heaven, air, earth, or sea.
And all the riches of this world enjoy'dst,
And all the rule, one empire. Only add
Deeds to thy knowledge answerable; add faith;
Add virtue, patience, temperance; add love,
By name to come called Charity, the soul
Of all the rest: then wilt thou not be loath
To leave this Paradise, but shalt possess
A Paradise within thee, happier far.
Let us descend now, therefore, from this top
Of speculation; for the hour precise
Exacts our parting hence; and, see! the guards,
By me encamped on yonder hill, expect
Their motion, at whose front a flaming sword,
In signal of remove, waves fiercely round.
We may no longer stay. Go, waken Eve;
Her also I with gentle dreams have calmed,
Portending good, and all her spirits composed
To meek submission: thou, at season fit,
Let her with thee partake what thou hast heard—
Chiefly what may concern her faith to know,
The great deliverance by her seed to come
(For by the Woman's Seed) on all mankind—
That ye may live, which will be many days,
Both in one faith unanimous; though sad
With cause for evils past, yet much more cheered
With meditation on the happy end."
  He ended, and they both descend the hill.
Descended, Adam to the bower where Eve
Lay sleeping ran before, but found her waked;

And thus with words not sad she him received:—
"Whence thou return'st and whither went'st I know;
For God is also in sleep, and dreams advise,
Which he hath sent propitious, some great good
Presaging, since, with sorrow and heart's distress
Wearied, I fell asleep. But now lead on;
In me is no delay; with thee to go
Is to stay here; without thee here to stay
Is to go hence unwilling; thou to me
Art all things under Heaven, all places thou,
Who for my wilful crime art banished hence.
This further consolation yet secure
I carry hence: though all by me is lost,
Such favour I unworthy am vouchsafed,
By me the Promised Seed shall all restore."
So spake our mother Eve; and Adam heard
Well pleased, but answered not; for now too nigh
Th' Archangel stood, and from the other hill
To their fixed station, all in bright array,
The Cherubim descended, on the ground
Gliding meteorous, as evening mist
Risen from a river o'er the marish glides,
And gathers ground fast at the labourer's heel
Homeward returning. High in front advanced,
The brandished sword of God before them blazed,
Fierce as a comet; which with torrid heat,
And vapour as the Libyan air adust,
Began to parch that temperate clime; whereat
In either hand the hastening Angel caught
Our lingering parents, and to th' eastern gate
Led them direct, and down the cliff as fast
To the subjected plain, then disappeared.
They, looking back, all th' eastern side beheld
Of Paradise, so late their happy seat,
Waved over by that flaming brand; the gate
With dreadful faces thronged and fiery arms.

Some natural tears they dropped, but wiped them soon,
The world was all before them, where to choose
Their place of rest, and Providence their guide.
They, hand in hand, with wandering steps and slow,
Through Eden took their solitary way.

THE END OF THE TWELFTH BOOK

SELECTED
POETRY AND SONNETS

ON THE MORNING OF CHRIST'S NATIVITY

Composed 1629

I

This is the month, and this the happy morn,
Wherein the Son of Heaven's eternal King,
Of wedded maid and virgin mother born,
Our great redemption from above did bring;
For so the holy sages once did sing,
  That he our deadly forfeit should release,
And with his Father work us a perpetual peace.

II

That glorious form, that light unsufferable,
And that far-beaming blaze of majesty,
Wherewith he wont at Heaven's high council-table
To sit the midst of Trinal Unity,
He laid aside, and, here with us to be,
  Forsook the courts of everlasting day,
And chose with us a darksome house of mortal clay.

III

Say, Heavenly Muse, shall not thy sacred vein
Afford a present to the Infant God?
Hast thou no verse, no hymn, or solemn strain,
To welcome him to this his new abode,
Now while the heaven, by the Sun's team untrod,
  Hath took no print of the approaching light,
And all the spangled host keep watch in squadrons bright?

IV

See how from far upon the eastern road
The star-led wizards haste with odours sweet!
O run; prevent them with thy humble ode,

And lay it lowly at his blessèd feet;
Have thou the honour first thy Lord to greet,
And join thy voice unto the Angel choir,
From out his secret altar touched with hallowed fire.

THE HYMN

I

It was the winter wild,
While the Heaven-born Child
All meanly wrapt in the rude manger lies;
Nature, in awe to him,
Had doffed her gaudy trim,
With her great Master so to sympathize:
It was no season then for her
To wanton with the Sun, her lusty paramour.

II

Only with speeches fair
She woos the gentle air
To hide her guilty front with innocent snow,
And on her naked shame,
Pollute with sinful blame,
The saintly veil of maiden white to throw;
Confounded, that her Maker's eyes
Should look so near upon her foul deformities.

III

But he, her fears to cease,
Sent down the meek-eyed Peace:
She, crowned with olive green, came softly sliding
Down through the turning sphere,
His ready harbinger,
With turtle wing the amorous clouds dividing;
And, waving wide her myrtle wand,
She strikes a universal peace through sea and land.

IV

No war, or battle's sound,
Was heard the world around;
The idle spear and shield were high uphung;
The hookèd chariot stood,
Unstained with hostile blood;
The trumpet spake not to the armèd throng;
And kings sat still with awful eye,
As if they surely knew their sovereign Lord was by.

V

But peaceful was the night
Wherein the Prince of Light
His reign of peace upon the Earth began.
The winds, with wonder whist,
Smoothly the waters kissed,
Whispering new joys to the mild Oceàn,
Who now hath quite forgot to rave,
While birds of calm sit brooding on the charmèd wave.

VI

The stars, with deep amaze,
Stand fixed in steadfast gaze,
Bending one way their precious influence,
And will not take their flight,
For all the morning light,
Or Lucifer that often warned them thence;
But in their glimmering orbs did glow,
Until their Lord himself bespake, and bid them go.

VII

And, though the shady gloom
Had given day her room,
The Sun himself withheld his wonted speed,
And hid his head for shame,

As his inferior flame
The new-enlightened world no more should need:
He saw a greater Sun appear
Than his bright throne or burning axletree could bear.

VIII

The shepherds on the lawn,
Or ere the point of dawn,
Sat simply chatting in a rustic row;
Full little thought they then
That the mighty Pan
Was kindly come to live with them below:
Perhaps their loves, or else their sheep,
Was all that did their silly thoughts so busy keep.

IX

When such music sweet
Their hearts and ears did greet
As never was by mortal finger strook,
Divinely-warbled voice
Answering the stringèd noise,
As all their souls in blissful rapture took:
The air, such pleasure loath to lose,
With thousand echoes still prolongs each heavenly close.

X

Nature, that heard such sound
Beneath the hollow round
Of Cynthia's seat the airy region thrilling,
Now was almost won
To think her part was done,
And that her reign had here its last fulfilling:
She knew such harmony alone
Could hold all Heaven and Earth in happier union.

XI

At last surrounds their sight
A globe of circular light,
That with long beams the shamefaced Night arrayed;
The helmèd Cherubim
And sworded Seraphim
Are seen in glittering ranks with wings displayed,
Harping in loud and solemn choir,
With unexpressive notes, to Heaven's new-born Heir.

XII

Such music (as 'tis said)
Before was never made,
But when of old the Sons of Morning sung,
While the Creator great
His constellations set,
And the well balanced World on hinges hung,
And cast the dark foundations deep,
And bid the weltering waves their oozy channel keep.

XIII

Ring out, ye crystal spheres!
Once bless our human ears,
If ye have power to touch our senses so;
And let your silver chime
Move in melodious time;
And let the bass of Heaven's deep organ blow;
And with your ninefold harmony
Make up full consort to th' angelic symphony.

XIV

For, if such holy song
Enwrap our fancy long,
Time will run back and fetch the Age of Gold;
And speckled Vanity

Will sicken soon and die;
And leprous Sin will melt from earthly mould;
And Hell itself will pass away,
And leave her dolorous mansions to the peering day.

XV

Yea, Truth and Justice then
Will down return to men,
Orbed in a rainbow; and, like glories wearing,
Mercy will sit between,
Throned in celestial sheen,
With radiant feet the tissued clouds down steering;
And Heaven, as at some festival,
Will open wide the gates of her high palace-hall.

XVI

But wisest Fate says No,
This must not yet be so;
The Babe yet lies in smiling infancy
That on the bitter cross
Must redeem our loss,
So both himself and us to glorify:
Yet first, to those ychained in sleep,
The wakeful trump of doom must thunder through the deep,

XVII

With such a horrid clang
As on Mount Sinai rang,
While the red fire and smouldering clouds outbrake:
The agèd Earth, aghast
With terror of that blast,
Shall from the surface to the centre shake,
When, at the world's last session,
The dreadful Judge in middle air shall spread his throne.

XVIII

And then at last our bliss
Full and perfect is,
But now begins; for from this happy day
Th' old Dragon under ground,
In straiter limits bound,
Not half so far casts his usurpèd sway,
And, wroth to see his kingdom fail,
Swinges the scaly horror of his folded tail.

XIX

The oracles are dumb;
No voice or hideous hum
Runs through the archèd roof in words deceiving.
Apollo from his shrine
Can no more divine,
With hollow shriek the steep of Delphos leaving.
No nightly trance, or breathèd spell,
Inspires the pale-eyed priest from the prophetic cell.

XX

The lonely mountains o'er,
And the resounding shore,
A voice of weeping heard and loud lament;
From haunted spring, and dale
Edged with poplar pale,
The parting Genius is with sighing sent;
With flower-inwoven tresses torn
The Nymphs in twilight shade of tangled thickets mourn.

XXI

In consecrated earth,
And on the holy hearth,
The Lars and Lemures moan with midnight plaint;

In urns, and altars round,
A drear and dying sound
Affrights the flamens at their service quaint;
And the chill marble seems to sweat,
While each peculiar Power forgoes his wonted seat.

XXII

Peor and Baälim
Forsake their temples dim,
With that twice-battered God of Palestine;
And moonèd Ashtaroth,
Heaven's queen and mother both,
Now sits not girt with tapers' holy shine:
The Libyc Hammon shrinks his horn;
In vain the Tyrian maids their wounded Thammuz mourn.

XXIII

And sullen Moloch, fled,
Hath left in shadows dread
His burning idol all of blackest hue;
In vain with cymbals' ring
They call the grisly king,
In dismal dance about the furnace blue;
The brutish gods of Nile as fast,
Isis, and Orus, and the dog Anubis, haste.

XXIV

Nor is Osiris seen
In Memphian grove or green,
Trampling the unshowered grass with lowings loud;
Nor can he be at rest
Within his sacred chest;
Nought but profoundest Hell can be his shroud;
In vain, with timbrelled anthems dark,
The sable-stolèd sorcerers bear his worshipped ark.

XXV

He feels from Juda's land
The dreaded Infant's hand;
The rays of Bethlehem blind his dusky eyn;
Nor all the gods beside
Longer dare abide,
Not Typhon huge ending in snaky twine:
Our Babe, to show his Godhead true,
Can in his swaddling bands control the damnèd crew.

XXVI

So, when the Sun in bed,
Curtained with cloudy red,
Pillows his chin upon an orient wave,
The flocking shadows pale
Troop to th' infernal jail,
Each fettered ghost slips to his several grave,
And the yellow-skirted fays
Fly after the night-steeds, leaving their moon-loved maze.

XXVII

But see! the Virgin blest
Hath laid her Babe to rest.
Time is our tedious song should here have ending:
Heaven's youngest-teemèd star
Hath fixed her polished car,
Her sleeping Lord with handmaid lamp attending;
And all about the courtly stable
Bright-harnessed Angels sit in order serviceable.

SONG ON MAY MORNING

Now the bright morning star, day's harbinger,
Comes dancing from the east, and leads with her
The flowery May, who from her green lap throws
The yellow cowslip and the pale primrose.
  Hail, bounteous May, that dost inspire
  Mirth, and youth, and warm desire!
  Woods and groves are of thy dressing;
  Hill and dale doth boast thy blessing.
Thus we salute thee with our early song,
And welcome thee, and wish thee long.

ON SHAKESPEARE

1630

What needs my Shakespeare for his honoured bones
The labour of an age in pilèd stones?
Or that his hallowed relics should be hid
Under a star-ypointing pyramid?
Dear son of memory, great heir of fame,
What need'st thou such weak witness of thy name?
Thou in our wonder and astonishment
Hast built thyself a livelong monument.
For whilst, to th' shame of slow-endeavouring art,
Thy easy numbers flow, and that each heart
Hath from the leaves of thy unvalued book
Those Delphic lines with deep impression took,
Then thou, our fancy of itself bereaving,
Dost make us marble with too much conceiving,
And so sepúlchred in such pomp dost lie
That kings for such a tomb would wish to die.

L'ALLEGRO

Hence, loathèd Melancholy,
  Of Cerberus and blackest Midnight born
In Stygian cave forlorn
  'Mongst horrid shapes, and shrieks, and sights unholy!
Find out some uncouth cell,
  Where brooding Darkness spreads his jealous wings.
And the night-raven sings;
  There, under ebon shades and low-browed rocks,
As ragged as thy locks,
  In dark Cimmerian desert ever dwell.
But come, thou Goddess fair and free,
In Heaven yclept Euphrosyne,
And by men heart-easing Mirth;
Whom lovely Venus, at a birth,
With two sister Graces more,
To ivy-crownèd Bacchus bore:
Or whether (as some sager sing)
The frolic wind that breathes the spring,
Zephyr, with Aurora playing,
As he met her once a-Maying,
There, on beds of violets blue,
And fresh-blown roses washed in dew,
Filled her with thee, a daughter fair,
So buxom, blithe, and debonair.
Haste thee, Nymph, and bring with thee
Jest, and youthful jollity,
Quips and cranks and wanton wiles,
Nods and becks and wreathèd smiles,
Such as hang on Hebe's cheek,
And love to live in dimple sleek;
Sport that wrinkled Care derides,
And Laughter holding both his sides.
Come, and trip it as you go,
On the light fantastic toe;

And in thy right hand lead with thee
The mountain-nymph, sweet Liberty;
And, if I give thee honour due,
Mirth, admit me of thy crew,
To live with her, and live with thee,
In unreprovèd pleasures free;
To hear the lark begin his flight,
And, singing, startle the dull night,
From his watch-tower in the skies,
Till the dappled dawn doth rise;
Then to come, in spite of sorrow,
And at my window bid good-morrow,
Through the sweet-briar or the vine,
Or the twisted eglantine;
While the cock, with lively din,
Scatters the rear of darkness thin;
And to the stack, or the barn-door,
Stoutly struts his dames before:
Oft listening how the hounds and horn
Cheerly rouse the slumbering morn,
From the side of some hoar hill,
Through the high wood echoing shrill:
Sometime walking, not unseen,
By hedgerow elms, on hillocks green,
Right against the eastern gate
Where the great Sun begins his state,
Robed in flames and amber light,
The clouds in thousand liveries dight;
While the plowman, near at hand,
Whistles o'er the furrowed land,
And the milkmaid singeth blithe,
And the mower whets his scythe,
And every shepherd tells his tale
Under the hawthorn in the dale.
Straight mine eye hath caught new pleasures,
Whilst the landscape round it measures:
Russet lawns, and fallows grey,

Where the nibbling flocks do stray;
Mountains on whose barren breast
The labouring clouds do often rest;
Meadows trim, with daisies pied;
Shallow brooks, and rivers wide;
Towers and battlements it sees
Bosomed high in tufted trees,
Where perhaps some beauty lies,
The cynosure of neighbouring eyes.
Hard by a cottage chimney smokes
From betwixt two agèd oaks,
Where Corydon and Thyrsis met
Are at their savoury dinner set
Of herbs and other country messes,
Which the neat-handed Phyllis dresses;
And then in haste her bower she leaves,
With Thestylis to bind the sheaves;
Or, if the earlier season lead,
To the tanned haycock in the mead.
Sometimes, with secure delight,
The upland hamlets will invite,
When the merry bells ring round,
And the jocund rebecks sound
To many a youth and many a maid
Dancing in the chequered shade,
And young and old come forth to play
On a sunshine holiday,
Till the livelong daylight fail:
Then to the spicy nut-brown ale:
With stories told of many a feat,
How Faery Mab the junkets eat.
She was pinched and pulled, she said;
And by the Friar's lantern led,
Tells how the drudging goblin sweat
To earn his cream-bowl duly set,
When in one night, ere glimpse of morn,
His shadowy flail hath threshed the corn

That ten day-labourers could not end;
Then lies him down, the lubber fiend,
And, stretched out all the chimney's length,
Basks at the fire his hairy strength,
And crop-full out of doors he flings,
Ere the first cock his matin rings.
Thus done the tales, to bed they creep,
By whispering winds soon lulled asleep.
Towered cities please us then,
And the busy hum of men,
Where throngs of knights and barons bold,
In weeds of peace, high triumphs hold,
With store of ladies, whose bright eyes
Rain influence, and judge the prize
Of wit or arms, while both contend
To win her grace whom all commend.
There let Hymen oft appear
In saffron robe, with taper clear,
And pomp, and feast, and revelry,
With mask and antique pageantry;
Such sights as youthful poets dream
On summer eves by haunted stream.
Then to the well-trod stage anon,
If Jonson's learnèd sock be on,
Or sweetest Shakespeare, Fancy's child,
Warble his native wood-notes wild.
And ever, against eating cares,
Lap me in soft Lydian airs,
Married to immortal verse,
Such as the meeting soul may pierce,
In notes with many a winding bout
Of linkèd sweetness long drawn out
With wanton heed and giddy cunning,
The melting voice through mazes running,
Untwisting all the chains that tie
The hidden soul of harmony;
That Orpheus' self may heave his head

From golden slumber on a bed
Of heaped Elysian flowers, and hear
Such strains as would have won the ear
Of Pluto to have quite set free
His half-regained Eurydice.
These delights if thou canst give,
Mirth, with thee I mean to live.

IL PENSEROSO

Hence, vain deluding Joys,
  The brood of Folly without father bred!
How little you bested,
  Or fill the fixèd mind with all your toys!
Dwell in some idle brain,
  And fancies fond with gaudy shapes possess,
As thick and numberless
  As the gay motes that people the sun-beams,
Or likest hovering dreams,
  The fickle pensioners of Morpheus' train.
But, hail! thou Goddess sage and holy,
Hail, divinest Melancholy!
Whose saintly visage is too bright
To hit the sense of human sight,
And therefore to our weaker view
O'erlaid with black, staid Wisdom's hue;
Black, but such as in esteem
Prince Memnon's sister might beseem,
Or that starred Ethiop queen that strove
To set her beauty's praise above
The Sea-Nymphs, and their powers offended.
Yet thou art higher far descended:
Thee bright-haired Vesta long of yore
To solitary Saturn bore;
His daughter she; in Saturn's reign
Such mixture was not held a stain.
Oft in glimmering bowers and glades
He met her, and in secret shades
Of woody Ida's inmost grove,
Whilst yet there was no fear of Jove.
Come, pensive Nun, devout and pure,
Sober, steadfast, and demure,
All in a robe of darkest grain,
Flowing with majestic train,
And sable stole of cypress lawn

Over thy decent shoulders drawn.
Come; but keep thy wonted state,
With even step, and musing gait,
And looks commercing with the skies,
Thy rapt soul sitting in thine eyes:
There, held in holy passion still,
Forget thyself to marble, till
With a sad leaden downward cast
Thou fix them on the earth as fast.
And join with thee calm Peace and Quiet,
Spare Fast, that oft with gods doth diet,
And hears the Muses in a ring
Aye round about Jove's altar sing;
And add to these retired Leisure,
That in trim gardens takes his pleasure;
But, first and chiefest, with thee bring
Him that yon soars on golden wing,
Guiding the fiery-wheelèd throne,
The Cherub Contemplation;
And the mute Silence hist along,
'Less Philomel will deign a song,
In her sweetest, saddest plight,
Smoothing the rugged brow of Night,
While Cynthia checks her dragon yoke
Gently o'er th' accustomed oak.
Sweet bird, that shunn'st the noise of folly,
Most musical, most melancholy!
Thee, chauntress, oft the woods among
I woo, to hear thy even-song;
And, missing thee, I walk unseen
On the dry smooth-shaven green
To behold the wandering moon,
Riding near her highest noon,
Like one that had been led astray
Through the heaven's wide pathless way,
And oft, as if her head she bowed,
Stooping through a fleecy cloud.

Oft, on a plat of rising ground,
I hear the far-off curfew sound,
Over some wide-watered shore,
Swinging slow with sullen roar;
Or, if the air will not permit,
Some still removèd place will fit,
Where glowing embers through the room
Teach light to counterfeit a gloom,
Far from all resort of mirth,
Save the cricket on the hearth,
Or the bellman's drowsy charm
To bless the doors from nightly harm.
Or let my lamp, at midnight hour,
Be seen in some high lonely tower,
Where I may oft outwatch the Bear,
With thrice great Hermes, or unsphere
The spirit of Plato, to unfold
What worlds or what vast regions hold
The immortal mind that hath forsook
Her mansion in this fleshly nook;
And of those demons that are found
In fire, air, flood, or underground,
Whose power hath a true consent
With planet or with element.
Sometime let gorgeous Tragedy
In sceptered pall come sweeping by,
Presenting Thebes, or Pelops' line,
Or the tale of Troy divine,
Or what (though rare) of later age
Ennobled hath the buskined stage.
But, O sad Virgin! that thy power
Might raise Musaeus from his bower;
Or bid the soul of Orpheus sing
Such notes as, warbled to the string,
Drew iron tears down Pluto's cheek,
And made Hell grant what love did seek;
Or call up him that left half-told

The story of Cambuscan bold,
Of Camball, and of Algarsife,
And who had Canacè to wife,
That owned the virtuous ring and glass,
And of the wondrous horse of brass
On which the Tartar king did ride;
And if aught else great bards beside
In sage and solemn tunes have sung,
Of tourneys, and of trophies hung,
Of forests, and enchantments drear,
Where more is meant that meets the ear.
Thus, Night, oft see me in thy pale career,
Till civil-suited Morn appear,
Not tricked and frounced, as she was wont
With the Attic boy to hunt,
But kerchieft in a comely cloud,
While rocking winds are piping loud,
Or ushered with a shower still,
When the gust hath blown his fill,
Ending on the rustling leaves,
With minute-drops from off the eaves.
And, when the sun begins to fling
His flaring beams, me, Goddess, bring
To archèd walks of twilight groves,
And shadows brown, that Sylvan loves,
Of pine, or monumental oak,
Where the rude axe with heavèd stroke
Was never heard the nymphs to daunt,
Or fright them from their hallowed haunt.
There, in close covert, by some brook,
Where no profaner eye may look,
Hide me from day's garish eye,
While the bee with honeyed thigh,
That at her flowery work doth sing,
And the waters murmuring,
With such consort as they keep,
Entice the dewy-feathered Sleep.

And let some strange mysterious dream
Wave at his wings, in airy stream
Of lively portraiture displayed,
Softly on my eyelids laid;
And, as I wake, sweet music breathe
Above, about, or underneath,
Sent by some Spirit to mortals good,
Or th' unseen Genius of the wood.
But let my due feet never fail
To walk the studious cloister's pale,
And love the high embowèd roof,
With antique pillars massy-proof,
And storied windows richly dight,
Casting a dim religious light.
There let the pealing organ blow,
To the full-voiced choir below,
In service high and anthems clear,
As may with sweetness, through mine ear,
Dissolve me into ecstasies,
And bring all Heaven before mine eyes.
And may at last my weary age
Find out the peaceful hermitage,
The hairy gown and mossy cell,
Where I may sit and rightly spell
Of every star that heaven doth shew,
And every herb that sips the dew,
Till old experience do attain
To something like prophetic strain.
These pleasures, Melancholy, give;
And I with thee will choose to live.

COMUS

A MASQUE PRESENTED AT LUDLOW CASTLE

1634 etc.

THE PERSONS

The ATTENDANT SPIRIT, *afterwards in the habit of Thyrsis.*
COMUS, *with his Crew.*
THE LADY.
FIRST BROTHER.
SECOND BROTHER.
SABRINA, *the Nymph.*

The Chief Persons which presented were:

The Lord Brackley
Mr. Thomas Egerton, his Brother
The Lady Alice Egerton.

The first Scene discovers a wild wood.

The ATTENDANT SPIRIT *descends or enters.*

Before the starry threshold of Jove's court
My mansion is, where those immortal shapes
Of bright aerial spirits live insphered
In regions mild of calm and serene air,
Above the smoke and stir of this dim spot
Which men call Earth, and, with low-thoughted care,
Confined and pestered in this pinfold here,
Strive to keep up a frail and feverish being
Unmindful of the crown that Virtue gives,
After this mortal change, to her true servants
Amongst the enthroned gods on sainted seats.
Yet some there be that by due steps aspire
To lay their iust hands on that golden key

That opes the palace of eternity.
To such my errand is; and, but for such,
I would not soil these pure ambrosial weeds
With the rank vapours of this sin-worn mould.
But to my task. Neptune, besides the sway
Of every salt flood and each ebbing stream,
Took in by lot, 'twixt high and nether Jove,
Imperial rule of all the sea-girt isles
That, like to rich and various gems, inlay
The unadornèd bosom of the deep;
Which he, to grace his tributary gods,
By course commits to several government,
And gives them leave to wear their sapphire crowns
And wield their little tridents. But this Isle,
The greatest and the best of all the main,
He quarters to his blue-haired deities;
And all this tract that fronts the falling sun
A noble Peer of mickle trust and power
Has in his charge, with tempered awe to guide
An old and haughty nation, proud in arms:
Where his fair offspring, nursed in princely lore,
Are coming to attend their father's state,
And new entrusted sceptre. But their way
Lies through the perplexed paths of this drear wood,
The nodding horror of whose shady brows
Threats the forlorn and wandering passenger;
And here their tender age might suffer peril,
But that, by quick command from sovereign Jove,
I was despatched for their defence and guard:
And listen why; for I will tell you now
What never yet was heard in tale or song,
From old or modern bard, in hall or bower.
Bacchus, that first from out the purple grape
Crushed the sweet poison of misusèd wine,
After the Tuscan mariners transformed,
Coasting the Tyrrhene shore, as the winds listed,
On Circe's island fell. (Who knows not Circe,

The daughter of the Sun, whose charmèd cup
Whoever tasted lost his upright shape,
And downward fell into a grovelling swine?)
This Nymph, that gazed upon his clustering locks,
With ivy berries wreathed, and his blithe youth,
Had by him, ere he parted thence, a son
Much like his father, but his mother more,
Whom therefore she brought up, and Comus named:
Who, ripe and frolic of his full-grown age,
Roving the Celtic and Iberian fields,
At last betakes him to this ominous wood,
And, in thick shelter of black shades imbowered,
Excels his mother at her mighty art;
Offering to every weary traveller
His orient liquor in a crystal glass,
To quench the drouth of Phoebus; which as they taste
(For most do taste through fond intemperate thirst),
Soon as the potion works, their human countenance,
Th' express resemblance of the gods, is changed
Into some brutish form of wolf or bear,
Or ounce or tiger, hog, or bearded goat,
All other parts remaining as they were.
And they, so perfect is their misery,
Not once perceive their foul disfigurement,
But boast themselves more comely than before,
And all their friends and native home forget,
To roll with pleasure in a sensual sty.
Therefore, when any favoured of high Jove
Chances to pass through this adventurous glade,
Swift as the sparkle of a glancing star
I shoot from heaven, to give him safe convoy,
As now I do. But first I must put off
These my sky-robes, spun out of Iris' woof,
And take the weeds and likeness of a swain
That to the service of this house belongs,
Who, with his soft pipe and smooth-dittied song,
Well knows to still the wild winds when they roar,

And hush the waving woods; nor of less faith,
And in this office of his mountain watch
Likeliest, and nearest to the present aid
Of this occasion. But I hear the tread
Of hateful steps; I must be viewless now.

COMUS *enters, with a charming rod in one hand, his glass in the other; with him a rout of monsters, headed like sundry sorts of wild beasts, but otherwise like men and women, their apparel glistering. They come in, making a riotous and unruly noise, with torches in their hands.*

COMUS. The star that bids the shepherd fold
Now the top of heaven doth hold;
And the gilded car of day
His glowing axle doth allay
In the steep Atlantic stream;
And the slope sun his upward beam
Shoots against the dusky pole,
Pacing toward the other goal
Of his chamber in the east.
Meanwhile, welcome joy and feast.
Midnight shout and revelry,
Tipsy dance and jollity.
Braid your locks with rosy twine,
Dropping odours, dropping wine.
Rigour now is gone to bed;
And Advice with scrupulous head,
Strict Age, and sour Severity,
With their grave saws, in slumber lie.
We, that are of purer fire,
Imitate the starry choir,
Who, in their nightly watchful spheres,
Lead in swift round the months and years.
The sounds and seas, with all their finny drove,
Now to the moon in wavering morrice move;
And on the tawny sands and shelves

Trip the pert fairies and the dapper elves.
By dimpled brook and fountain-brim,
The wood-nymphs, decked with daisies trim,
Their merry wakes and pastimes keep:
What hath night to do with sleep?
Night hath better sweets to prove;
Venus now wakes, and wakens Love.
Come, let us our rites begin;
'Tis only daylight that makes sin,
Which these dun shades will ne'er report.
Hail, goddess of nocturnal sport,
Dark-veiled Cotytto, t' whom the secret flame
Of midnight torches burns! mysterious dame,
That ne'er art called but when the dragon womb
Of Stygian darkness spits her thickest gloom,
And makes one blot of all the air!
Stay thy cloudy ebon chair,
Wherein thou ridest with Hecat', and befriend
Us thy vowed priests, till utmost end
Of all thy dues be done, and none left out;
Ere the blabbing eastern scout,
The nice Morn on th' Indian steep,
From her cabined loop-hole peep,
And to the tell-tale Sun descry
Our concealed solemnity.
Come, knit hands, and beat the ground
In a light fantastic round.

THE MEASURE

Break off, break off! I feel the different pace
Of some chaste footing near about this ground.
Run to your shrouds within these brakes and trees;
Our number may affright. Some virgin sure
(For so I can distinguish by mine art)
Benighted in these woods! Now to my charms,
And to my wily trains: I shall ere long
Be well stocked with as fair a herd as grazed

About my mother Circe. Thus I hurl
My dazzling spells into the spongy air,
Of power to cheat the eye with blear illusion,
And give it false presentments, lest the place,
And my quaint habits breed astonishment,
And put the damsel to suspicious flight;
Which must not be, for that's against my course.
I, under fair pretence of friendly ends,
And well-placed words of glozing courtesy,
Baited with reasons not unplausible,
Wind me into the easy-hearted man,
And hug him into snares. When once her eye
Hath met the virtue of this magic dust,
I shall appear some harmless villager
Whom thrift keeps up about his country gear.
But here she comes; I fairly step aside,
And hearken, if I may her business hear.

THE LADY *enters.*

LADY. This way the noise was, if mine ear be true,
My best guide now. Methought it was the sound
Of riot and ill-managed merriment,
Such as the jocund flute or gamesome pipe
Stirs up among the loose unlettered hinds,
When, for their teeming flocks and granges full,
In wanton dance they praise the bounteous Pan,
And thank the gods amiss. I should be loath
To meet the rudeness and swilled insolence
Of such late wassailers; yet, oh! where else
Shall I inform my unacquainted feet
In the blind mazes of this tangled wood?
My brothers, when they saw me wearied out
With this long way, resolving here to lodge
Under the spreading favour of these pines,
Stepped, as they said, to the next thicket-side
To bring me berries, or such cooling fruit

As the kind hospitable woods provide.
They left me then when the grey-hooded Even,
Like a sad votarist in palmer's weed,
Rose from the hindmost wheels of Phoebus' wain.
But where they are, and why they came not back,
Is now the labour of my thoughts. 'Tis likeliest
They had engaged their wandering steps too far;
And envious darkness, ere they could return,
Had stole them from me. Else, O thievish Night,
Why shouldst thou, but for some felonious end,
In thy dark lantern thus close up the stars
That Nature hung in heaven, and filled their lamps
With everlasting oil to give due light
To the misled and lonely traveller?
This is the place, as well as I may guess,
Whence even now the tumult of loud mirth
Was rife, and perfect in my listening ear;
Yet nought but single darkness do I find.
What might this be? A thousand fantasies
Begin to throng into my memory,
Of calling shapes, and beckoning shadows dire,
And airy tongues that syllable men's names
On sands and shores and desert wildernesses.
These thoughts may startle well, but not astound
The virtuous mind, that ever walks attended
By a strong siding champion, Conscience.
O, welcome, pure-eyed Faith, white-handed Hope,
Thou hovering angel girt with golden wings,
And thou unblemished form of Chastity!
I see ye visibly, and now believe
That he, the Supreme Good, t' whom all things ill
Are but as slavish officers of vengeance,
Would send a glistering guardian, if need were,
To keep my life and honour unassailed.
Was I deceived, or did a sable cloud
Turn forth her silver lining on the night?
I did not err: there does a sable cloud

Turn forth her silver lining on the night,
And casts a gleam over this tufted grove.
I cannot hallo to my brothers, but
Such noise as I can make to be heard farthest
I'll venture; for my new-enlivened spirits
Prompt me, and they perhaps are not far off.

SONG

Sweet Echo, sweetest nymph, that liv'st unseen
Within thy airy shell
By slow Meander's margent green,
And in the violet-embroidered vale
Where the love-lorn nightingale
Nightly to thee her sad song mourneth well:
Canst thou not tell me of a gentle pair
That likest thy Narcissus are?
O, if thou have
Hid them in some flowery cave,
Tell me but where,
Sweet queen of parley, daughter of the sphere!
So may'st thou be translated to the skies,
And give resounding grace to all Heaven's harmonies!

COMUS. Can any mortal mixture of earth's mould
Breathe such divine enchanting ravishment?
Sure something holy lodges in that breast,
And with these raptures moves the vocal air
To testify his hidden residence.
How sweetly did they float upon the wings
Of silence, through the empty-vaulted night,
At every fall smoothing the raven down
Of darkness till it smiled! I have oft heard
My mother Circe with the Sirens three,
Amidst the flowery-kirtled Naiades,
Culling their potent herbs and baleful drugs,
Who, as they sung, would take the prisoned soul,

And lap it in Elysium: Scylla wept,
And chid her barking waves into attention,
And fell Charybdis murmured soft applause.
Yet they in pleasing slumber lulled the sense,
And in sweet madness robbed it of itself;
But such a sacred and home-felt delight,
Such sober certainty of waking bliss,
I never heard till now. I'll speak to her,
And she shall be my queen.—Hail, foreign wonder!
Whom certain these rough shades did never breed,
Unless the goddess that in rural shrine
Dwell'st here with Pan or Sylvan, by blest song,
Forbidding every bleak unkindly fog
To touch the prosperous growth of this tall wood.
LADY. Nay, gentle shepherd, ill is lost that praise
That is addressed to unattending ears.
Not any boast of skill, but extreme shift
How to regain my severed company,
Compelled me to awake the courteous Echo
To give me answer from her mossy couch.
COMUS. What chance, good Lady, hath bereft you thus?
LADY. Dim darkness and this leafy labyrinth.
COMUS. Could that divide you from near-ushering guides?
LADY. They left me weary on a grassy turf.
COMUS. By falsehood or discourtesy, or why?
LADY. To seek i' th' valley some cool friendly spring.
COMUS. And left your fair side all unguarded, Lady?
LADY. They were but twain, and purposed quick return.
COMUS. Perhaps forestalling night prevented them.
LADY. How easy my misfortune is to hit!
COMUS. Imports their loss, beside the present need?
LADY. No less than if I should my brothers lose.
COMUS. Were they of manly prime, or youthful bloom?
LADY. As smooth as Hebe's their unrazored lips.
COMUS. Two such I saw, what time the laboured ox
In his loose traces from the furrow came,
And the swinked hedger at his supper sat.

I saw them under a green mantling vine,
That crawls along the side of yon small hill,
Plucking ripe clusters from the tender shoots;
Their port was more than human, as they stood.
I took it for a faery vision
Of some gay creatures of the element,
That in the colours of the rainbow live,
And play i' th' plighted clouds. I was awe-struck
And, as I passed, I worshipped. If those you seek,
It were a journey like the path to Heaven
To help you find them.

LADY. Gentle villager,
What readiest way would bring me to that place?

COMUS. Due west it rises from this shrubby point.

LADY. To find out that, good shepherd, I suppose,
In such a scant allowance of star-light,
Would overtask the best land-pilot's art,
Without the sure guess of well-practised feet.

COMUS. I know each lane, and every alley green,
Dingle, or bushy dell, of this wild wood,
And every bosky bourn from side to side,
My daily walks and ancient neighbourhood;
And, if your stray attendance be yet lodged,
Or shroud within these limits, I shall know
Ere morrow wake, or the low-roosted lark
From her thatched pallet rouse. If otherwise,
I can conduct you, Lady, to a low
But loyal cottage, where you may be safe
Till further quest.

LADY. Shepherd, I take thy word,
And trust thy honest-offered courtesy,
Which oft is sooner found in lowly sheds,
With smoky rafters, than in tapestry halls
And courts of princes, where it first was named,
And yet is most pretended. In a place
Less warranted than this, or less secure,

I cannot be, that I should fear to change it.
Eye me, blest Providence, and square my trial
To my proportioned strength! Shepherd, lead on.

The TWO BROTHERS.

ELDER BROTHER. Umuffle, ye faint stars; and thou, fair moon,
That wont'st to love the traveller's benison,
Stoop thy pale visage through an amber cloud,
And disinherit Chaos, that reigns here
In double night of darkness and of shades;
Or, if your influence be quite dammed up
With black usurping mists, some gentle taper,
Though a rush-candle from the wicker hole
Of some clay habitation, visit us
With thy long levelled rule of streaming light,
And thou shalt be our star of Arcady,
Or Tyrian Cynosure.
SECOND BROTHER. Or, if our eyes
Be barred that happiness, might we but hear
The folded flocks, penned in their wattled cotes,
Or sound of pastoral reed with oaten stops,
Or whistle from the lodge, or village cock
Count the night-watches to his feathery dames,
'Twould be some solace yet, some little cheering,
In this close dungeon of innumerous boughs.
But, oh, that hapless virgin, our lost sister!
Where may she wander now, whither betake her
From the chill dew, amongst rude burs and thistles?
Perhaps some cold bank is her bolster now,
Or 'gainst the rugged bark of some broad elm
Leans her unpillowed head, fraught with sad fears.
What if in wild amazement and affright,
Or, while we speak, within the direful grasp
Of savage hunger, or of savage heat!
ELDER BROTHER. Peace, brother: be not over-exquisite
To cast the fashion of uncertain evils;
For, grant they be so, while they rest unknown,

What need a man forestall his date of grief,
And run to meet what he would most avoid?
Or, if they be but false alarms of fear,
How bitter is such self-delusion!
I do not think my sister so to seek,
Or so unprincipled in virtue's book,
And the sweet peace that goodness bosoms ever,
As that the single want of light and noise
(Not being in danger, as I trust she is not)
Could stir the constant mood of her calm thoughts,
And put them into misbecoming plight.
Virtue could see to do what Virtue would
By her own radiant light, though sun and moon
Were in the flat sea sunk. And Wisdom's self
Oft seeks to sweet retired solitude,
Where, with her best nurse, Contemplation,
She plumes her feathers, and lets grow her wings,
That, in the various bustle of resort,
Were all to-ruffled, and sometimes impaired.
He that has light within his own clear breast
May sit i' th' centre, and enjoy bright day:
But he that hides a dark soul and foul thoughts
Benighted walks under the mid-day sun;
Himself is his own dungeon.

SECOND BROTHER. 'Tis most true
That musing Meditation most affects
The pensive secrecy of desert cell,
Far from the cheerful haunt of men and herds,
And sits as safe as in a senate-house;
For who would rob a hermit of his weeds,
His few books, or his beads, or maple dish,
Or do his grey hairs any violence?
But Beauty, like the fair Hesperian tree
Laden with blooming gold, had need the guard
Of dragon-watch with unenchanted eye
To save her blossoms, and defend her fruit,
From the rash hand of bold Incontinence.

You may as well spread out the unsunned heaps
Of miser's treasure by an outlaw's den,
And tell me it is safe, as bid me hope
Danger will wink on Opportunity,
And let a single helpless maiden pass
Uninjured in this wild surrounding waste.
Of night or loneliness it recks me not;
I fear the dread events that dog them both,
Lest some ill-greeting touch attempt the person
Of our unownèd sister.

ELDER BROTHER. I do not, brother,
Infer as if I thought my sister's state
Secure without all doubt or controversy;
Yet, where an equal poise of hope and fear
Does arbitrate th' event, my nature is
That I incline to hope rather than fear,
And gladly banish squint suspicion.
My sister is not so defenceless left
As you imagine; she has a hidden strength,
Which you remember not.

SECOND BROTHER. What hidden strength,
Unless the strength of Heaven, if you mean that?

ELDER BROTHER. I mean that too, but yet a hidden strength,
Which, if Heaven gave it, may be termed her own.
'Tis chastity, my brother, chastity:
She that has that is clad in complete steel,
And, like a quivered nymph with arrows keen,
May trace huge forests, and unharboured heaths,
Infámous hills, and sandy perilous wilds;
Where, through the sacred rays of chastity,
No savage fierce, bandit, or mountaineer,
Will dare to soil her virgin purity.
Yea, there where very desolation dwells,
By grots and caverns shagged with horrid shades,
She may pass on with unblenched majesty,
Be it not done in pride, or in presumption.
Some say no evil thing that walks by night,

In fog or fire, by lake or moorish fen,
Blue meagre hag, or stubborn unlaid ghost,
That breaks his magic chains at curfew time,
No goblin or swart faery of the mine,
Hath hurtful power o'er true virginity.
Do ye believe me yet, or shall I call
Antiquity from the old schools of Greece
To testify the arms of chastity?
Hence had the huntress Dian her dread bow,
Fair silver-shafted queen for ever chaste,
Wherewith she tamed the brinded lioness
And spotted mountain-pard, but set at nought
The frivolous bolt of Cupid; gods and men
Feared her stern frown, and she was queen o' th' woods.
What was that snaky-headed Gorgon shield
That wise Minerva wore, unconquered virgin,
Wherewith she freezed her foes to congealed stone,
But rigid looks of chaste austerity,
And noble grace that dashed brute violence
With sudden adoration and blank awe?
So dear to Heaven is saintly chastity
That, when a soul is found sincerely so,
A thousand liveried Angels lackey her,
Driving far off each thing of sin and guilt,
And in clear dreams and solemn vision
Tell her of things that no gross ear can hear;
Till oft converse with heavenly habitants
Begin to cast a beam on th' outward shape,
The unpolluted temple of the mind,
And turns it by degrees to the soul's essence,
Till all be made immortal. But, when lust,
By unchaste looks, loose gestures, and foul talk,
But most by lewd and lavish act of sin,
Lets in defilement to the inward parts,
The soul grows clotted by contagion,
Imbodies, and imbrutes, till she quite lose
The divine property of her first being.

Such are those thick and gloomy shadows damp
Oft seen in charnel-vaults and sepulchres,
Lingering and sitting by a new-made grave,
As loath to leave the body that it loved,
And linked itself by carnal sensualty
To a degenerate and degraded state.

SECOND BROTHER. How charming is divine philosophy!
Not harsh and crabbèd, as dull fools suppose,
But musical as is Apollo's lute,
And a perpetual feast of nectared sweets,
Where no crude surfeit reigns.

ELDER BROTHER List! list! I hear
Some far-off hallo break the silent air.

SECOND BROTHER. Methought so too; what should it be?

ELDER BROTHER. For certain,
Either some one, like us, night-foundered here,
Or else some neighbour woodman, or, at worst,
Some roving robber calling to his fellows.

SECOND BROTHER. Heaven keep my sister! Again, again, and near!
Best draw, and stand upon our guard.

ELDER BROTHER. I'll hallo.
If he be friendly, he comes well: if not,
Defence is a good cause, and Heaven be for us!

The ATTENDANT SPIRIT, *habited like a shepherd.*

That hallo I should know. What are you? speak.
Come not too near; you fall on iron stakes else.

SPIRIT. What voice is that? my young Lord? speak again.

SECOND BROTHER. O brother, 'tis my father's shepherd, sure.

ELDER BROTHER. Thyrsis! whose artful strains have oft delayed
The huddling brook to hear his madrigal,
And sweetened every musk-rose of the dale.
How cam'st thou here, good swain? Hath any ram
Slipped from the fold, or young kid lost his dam,

Or straggling wether the pent flock forsook?
How couldst thou find this dark sequestered nook?
SPIRIT. O my loved master's heir, and his next joy,
I came not here on such a trivial toy
As a strayed ewe, or to pursue the stealth
Of pilfering wolf; not all the fleecy wealth
That doth enrich these downs is worth a thought
To this my errand, and the care it brought.
But, oh! my virgin Lady, where is she?
How chance she is not in your company?
ELDER BROTHER. To tell thee sadly, Shepherd, without blame
Or our neglect, we lost her as we came.
SPIRIT. Ay me unhappy! then my fears are true.
ELDER BROTHER. What fears, good Thyrsis? Prithee briefly shew.
SPIRIT. I'll tell ye. 'Tis not vain or fabulous
(Though so esteemed by shallow ignorance)
What the sage poets, taught by th' heavenly Muse.
Storied of old in high immortal verse
Of dire Chimeras and enchanted isles,
And rifted rocks whose entrance leads to Hell;
For such there be, but unbelief is blind.
Within the navel of this hideous wood,
Immured in cypress shades, a sorcerer dwells,
Of Bacchus and of Circe born, great Comus,
Deep skilled in all his mother's witcheries,
And here to every thirsty wanderer
By sly enticement gives his baneful cup,
With many murmurs mixed, whose pleasing poison
The visage quite transforms of him that drinks,
And the inglorious likeness of a beast
Fixes instead, unmoulding reason's mintage
Charactered in the face. This have I learnt
Tending my flocks hard by i' th' hilly crofts
That brow this bottom glade; whence night by night
He and his monstrous rout are heard to howl
Like stabled wolves, or tigers at their prey,

Doing abhorrèd rites to Hecate
In their obscurèd haunts of inmost bowers.
Yet have they many baits and guileful spells
To inveigle and invite th' unwary sense
Of them that pass unweeting by the way.
This evening late, by then the chewing flocks
Had ta'en their supper on the savoury herb
Of knot-grass dew-besprent, and were in fold,
I sat me down to watch upon a bank
With ivy canopied, and interwove
With flaunting honeysuckle, and began,
Wrapt in a pleasing fit of melancholy,
To meditate my rural minstrelsy,
Till fancy had her fill. But ere a close
The wonted roar was up amidst the woods,
And filled the air with barbarous dissonance;
At which I ceased, and listened them a while,
Till an unusual stop of sudden silence
Gave respite to the drowsy frighted steeds
That draw the litter of close-curtained Sleep.
At last a soft and solemn-breathing sound
Rose like a steam of rich distilled perfumes,
And stole upon the air, that even Silence
Was took ere she was ware, and wished she might
Deny her nature, and be never more,
Still to be so displaced. I was all ear,
And took in strains that might create a soul
Under the ribs of Death. But, oh! ere long
Too well I did perceive it was the voice
Of my most honoured Lady, your dear sister.
Amazed I stood, harrowed with grief and fear;
And " O poor hapless nightingale," thought I,
" How sweet thou sing'st, how near the deadly snare! "
Then down the lawns I ran with headlong haste,
Through paths and turnings often trod by day,
Till, guided by mine ear, I found the place
Where that damned wizard, hid in sly disguise

(For so by certain signs I knew), had met
Already, ere my best speed could prevent,
The aidless innocent Lady, his wished prey;
Who gently asked if he had seen such two,
Supposing him some neighbour villager.
Longer I durst not stay, but soon I guessed
Ye were the two she meant; with that I sprung
Into swift flight, till I had found you here;
But further know I not.

SECOND BROTHER. O night and shades,
How are ye joined with Hell in triple knot
Against th' unarmèd weakness of one virgin,
Alone and helpless! Is this the confidence
You gave me, brother?

ELDER BROTHER. Yes, and keep it still;
Lean on it safely; not a period
Shall be unsaid for me. Against the threats
Of malice or of sorcery, or that power
Which erring men call Chance, this I hold firm;
Virtue may be assailed, but never hurt,
Surprised by unjust force, but not enthralled:
Yea, even that which mischief meant most harm
Shall in the happy trial prove most glory.
But evil on itself shall back recoil,
And mix no more with goodness, when at last,
Gathered like scum, and settled to itself,
It shall be in eternal restless change
Self-fed and self-consumed. If this fail,
The pillared firmament is rottenness,
And earth's base built on stubble. But come, let's on!
Against th' opposing will and arm of Heaven
May never this just sword be lifted up;
But, for that damned magician, let him be girt
With all the grisly legions that troop
Under the sooty flag of Acheron,
Harpies and Hydras, or all the monstrous forms
'Twixt Africa and Ind, I'll find him out,

And force him to restore his purchase back,
Or drag him by the curls to a foul death,
Cursed as his life.
SPIRIT. Alas! good venturous youth,
I love thy courage yet, and bold emprise;
But here thy sword can do thee little stead.
Far other arms and other weapons must
Be those that quell the might of hellish charms.
He with his bare wand can unthread thy joints,
And crumble all thy sinews.
ELDER BROTHER. Why, prithee, Shepherd,
How durst thou then thyself approach so near
As to make this relation?
SPIRIT. Care and utmost shifts
How to secure the Lady from surprisal
Brought to my mind a certain shepherd lad,
Of small regard to see to, yet well skilled
In every virtuous plant and healing herb
That spreads her verdant leaf to th' morning ray.
He loved me well, and oft would beg me sing;
Which when I did, he on the tender grass
Would sit, and hearken even to ecstasy,
And in requital ope his leathern scrip,
And show me simples of a thousand names,
Telling their strange and vigorous faculties.
Amongst the rest a small unsightly root,
But of divine effect, he culled me out.
The leaf was darkish, and had prickles on it,
But in another country, as he said,
Bore a bright golden flower, but not in this soil:
Unknown, and like esteemed, and the dull swain
Treads on it daily with his clouted shoon;
And yet more med'cinal is it than that moly
That Hermes once to wise Ulysses gave.
He called it haemony, and gave it me,
And bade me keep it as of sovereign use
'Gainst all enchantments, mildew blast, or damp,

Or ghastly Furies' apparition.
I pursed it up, but little reckoning made,
Till now that this extremity compelled.
But now I find it true; for by this means
I knew the foul enchanter, though disguised,
Entered the very lime-twigs of his spells,
And yet came off. If you have this about you
(As I will give you when we go) you may
Boldly assault the necromancer's hall
Where if he be, with dauntless hardihood
And brandished blade rush on him: break his glass,
And shed the luscious liquor on the ground;
But seize his wand. Though he and his cursed crew
Fierce sign of battle make, and menace high,
Or like the sons of Vulcan, vomit smoke,
Yet will they soon retire, if he but shrink.

ELDER BROTHER. Thyrsis, lead on apace; I'll follow thee;
And some good angel bear a shield before us!

The Scene changes to a stately palace, set out with all manner of deliciousness: soft music, tables spread with all dainties. COMUS *appears with his rabble, and* THE LADY *set in an enchanted chair: to whom he offers his glass; which she puts by, and goes about to rise.*

COMUS. Nay, Lady, sit. If I but wave this wand,
Your nerves are all chained up in alabaster,
And you a statue, or as Daphne was,
Root-bound, that fled Apollo.

LADY. Fool, do not boast.
Thou canst not touch the freedom of my mind
With all thy charms, although this corporal rind
Thou hast immanacled while Heaven sees good.

COMUS. Why are you vexed, Lady? why do you frown?
Here dwell no frowns, nor anger; from these gates
Sorrow flies far. See, here be all the pleasures
That fancy can beget on youthful thoughts,
When the fresh blood grows lively, and returns

Brisk as the April buds in primrose season.
And first behold this cordial julep here,
That flames and dances in his crystal bounds,
With spirits of balm and fragrant syrups mixed.
Not that Nepenthes which the wife of Thone
In Egypt gave to Jove-born Helena
Is of such power to stir up joy as this,
To life so friendly, or so cool to thirst.
Why should you be so cruel to yourself,
And to those dainty limbs, which Nature lent
For gentle usage and soft delicacy?
But you invert the covenants of her trust,
And harshly deal, like an ill borrower,
With that which you received on other terms,
Scorning the unexempt condition
By which all mortal frailty must subsist,
Refreshment after toil, ease after pain,
That have been tired all day without repast,
And timely rest have wanted. But, fair virgin,
This will restore all soon.

LADY. 'Twill not, false traitor!
'Twill not restore the truth and honesty
That thou hast banished from thy tongue with lies.
Was this the cottage and the safe abode
Thou told'st me of? What grim aspects are these,
These ugly-headed monsters? Mercy guard me!
Hence with thy brewed enchantments, foul deceiver!
Hast thou betrayed my credulous innocence
With vizored falsehood and base forgery?
And would'st thou seek again to trap me here
With liquorish baits, fit to ensnare a brute?
Were it a draught for Juno when she banquets,
I would not taste thy treasonous offer. None
But such as are good men can give good things;
And that which is not good is not delicious
To a well-governed and wise appetite.

COMUS. O foolishness of men! that lend their ears

To those budge doctors of the Stoic fur,
And fetch their precepts from the Cynic tub,
Praising the lean and sallow Abstinence!
Wherefore did Nature pour her bounties forth
With such a full and unwithdrawing hand,
Covering the earth with odours, fruits, and flocks,
Thronging the seas with spawn innumerable,
But all to please and sate the curious taste?
And set to work millions of spinning worms,
That in their green shops weave the smooth-haired silk,
To deck her sons; and, that no corner might
Be vacant of her plenty, in her own loins
She hutched th' all-worshipped ore and precious gems,
To store her children with. If all the world
Should, in a pet of temperance, feed on pulse,
Drink the clear stream, and nothing wear but frieze,
Th' All-giver would be unthanked, would be unpraised,
Not half his riches known, and yet despised;
And we should serve him as a grudging master,
As a penurious niggard of his wealth,
And live like Nature's bastards, not her sons,
Who would be quite surcharged with her own weight,
And strangled with her waste fertility:
Th' earth cumbered, and the winged air darked with plumes,
The herds would over-multitude their lords;
The sea o'erfraught would swell, and th' unsought diamonds
Would so emblaze the forehead of the deep,
And so bestud with stars, that they below
Would grow inured to light, and come at last
To gaze upon the sun with shameless brows.
List, Lady; be not coy, and be not cozened
With that same vaunted name, Virginity.
Beauty is Nature's coin; must not be hoarded,
But must be current; and the good thereof
Consists in mutual and partaken bliss,
Unsavoury in th' enjoyment of itself.
If you let slip time, like a neglected rose

It withers on the stalk with languished head.
Beauty is Nature's brag, and must be shown
In courts, at feasts, and high solemnities,
Where most may wonder at the workmanship.
It is for homely features to keep home;
They had their name thence: coarse complexions
And cheeks of sorry grain will serve to ply
The sampler, and to tease the huswife's wool.
What need a vermeil-tinctured lip for that,
Love-darting eyes, or tresses like the morn?
There was another meaning in these gifts:
Think what, and be advised; you are but young yet.
LADY. I had not thought to have unlocked my lips
In this unhallowed air, but that this juggler
Would think to charm my judgment, as mine eyes,
Obtruding false rules pranked in reason's garb.
I hate when vice can bolt her arguments
And virtue has no tongue to check her pride.
Impostor! do not charge most innocent Nature,
As if she would her children should be riotous
With her abundance. She, good cateress,
Means her provision only to the good,
That live according to her sober laws,
And holy dictate of spare Temperance.
If every just man that now pines with want
Had but a moderate and beseeming share
Of that which lewdly-pampered Luxury
Now heaps upon some few with vast excess,
Nature's full blessings would be well dispensed
In unsuperfluous even proportion,
And she no whit encumbered with her store;
And then the Giver would be better thanked
His praise due paid: for swinish gluttony
Ne'er looks to Heaven amidst his gorgeous feast,
But with besotted base ingratitude
Crams, and blasphemes his Feeder. Shall I go on?
Or have I said enough? To him that dares

Arm his profane tongue with contemptuous words
Against the sun-clad power of chastity
Fain would I something say;—yet to what end?
Thou hast nor ear, nor soul, to apprehend
The sublime notion and high mystery
That must be uttered to unfold the sage
And serious doctrine of Virginity;
And thou art worthy that thou shouldst not know
More happiness than this thy present lot.
Enjoy your dear wit, and gay rhetoric,
That hath so well been taught her dazzling fence;
Thou art not fit to hear thyself convinced.
Yet, should I try, the uncontrollèd worth
Of this pure cause would kindle my rapt spirits
To such a flame of sacred vehemence
That dumb things would be moved to sympathize,
And the brute Earth would lend her nerves, and shake,
Till all thy magic structures, reared so high,
Were shattered into heaps o'er thy false head.
COMUS. She fables not. I feel that I do fear
Her words set off by some superior power;
And, though not mortal, yet a cold shuddering dew
Dips me all o'er, as when the wrath of Jove
Speaks thunder and the chains of Erebus
To some of Saturn's crew. I must dissemble,
And try her yet more strongly.—Come, no more!
This is mere moral babble, and direct
Against the canon laws of our foundation.
I must not suffer this; yet 'tis but the lees
And settlings of a melancholy blood.
But this will cure all straight; one sup of this
Will bathe the drooping spirits in delight
Beyond the bliss of dreams. Be wise and taste.

The BROTHERS *rush in with swords drawn, wrest his glass out of his hand, and break it against the ground: his rout make sign of resistance, but are all driven in. The* ATTENDANT SPIRIT *comes in.*

SPIRIT. What! have you let the false enchanter scape?
O ye mistook; ye should have snatched his wand,
And bound him fast. Without his rod reversed,
And backward mutters of dissevering power,
We cannot free the Lady that sits here
In stony fetters fixed and motionless.
Yet stay: be not disturbed; now I bethink me,
Some other means I have which may be used,
Which once of Meliboeus old I learnt,
The soothest shepherd that e'er piped on plains.
  There is a gentle Nymph not far from hence,
That with moist curb sways the smooth Severn stream:
Sabrina is her name: a virgin pure;
Whilom she was the daughter of Locrine,
That had the sceptre from his father Brute.
She, guiltless damsel, flying the mad pursuit
Of her enragèd stepdame, Guendolen,
Commended her fair innocence to the flood
That stayed her flight with his cross-flowing course.
The water-nymphs, that in the bottom played,
Held up their pearlèd wrists, and took her in,
Bearing her straight to agèd Nereus' hall;
Who, piteous of her woes, reared her lank head,
And gave her to his daughter to imbathe
In nectared lavers strewed with asphodel,
And through the porch and inlet of each sense
Dropt in ambrosial oils, till she revived,
And underwent a quick immortal change
Made Goddess of the river. Still she retains
Her maiden gentleness, and oft at eve
Visits the herds along the twilight meadows,
Helping all urchin blasts, and ill-luck signs
That the shrewd meddling elf delights to make,
Which she with precious vialed liquors heals:
For which the shepherds, at their festivals,
Carol her goodness loud in rustic lays,
And throw sweet garland wreaths into her stream

Of pansies, pinks, and gaudy daffodils.
And, as the old swain said, she can unlock
The clasping charm, and thaw the numbing spell,
If she be right invoked in warbled song;
For maidenhood she loves, and will be swift
To aid a virgin, such as was herself,
In hard-besetting need. This will I try,
And add the power of some adjuring verse.

SONG

Sabrina fair,
  Listen where thou art sitting
Under the glassy, cool, translucent wave,
  In twisted braids of lilies knitting
The loose train of thy amber-dropping hair;
  Listen for dear honour's sake,
  Goddess of the silver lake,
      Listen and save!

Listen, and appear to us,
In name of great Oceanus.
By the earth-shaking Neptune's mace,
And Tethys' grave majestic pace;
By hoary Nereus' wrinkled look,
And the Carpathian wizard's hook;
By scaly Triton's winding shell,
And old soothsaying Glaucus' spell;
By Leucothea's lovely hands,
And her son that rules the strands;
By Thetis' tinsel-slippered feet,
And the songs of Sirens sweet;
By dead Parthenope's dear tomb,
And fair Ligea's golden comb,
Wherewith she sits on diamond rocks
Sleeking her soft alluring locks;
By all the Nymphs that nightly dance
Upon thy streams with wily glance;

Rise, rise, and heave thy rosy head
From thy coral-paven bed,
And bridle in thy headlong wave,
Till thou our summons answered have.
Listen and save!

SABRINA *rises, attended by Water-nymphs, and sings.*

By the rushy-fringèd bank,
Where grows the willow and the osier dank,
My sliding chariot stays,
Thick set with agate, and the azurn sheen
Of turkis blue, and emerald green,
That in the channel strays;
Whilst from off the waters fleet
Thus I set my printless feet
O'er the cowslip's velvet head,
That bends not as I tread.
Gentle swain, at thy request
I am here!
SPIRIT. Goddess dear,
We implore thy powerful hand
To undo the charmèd band
Of true virgin here distressed
Through the force and through the wile
Of unblessed enchanter vile.
SABRINA. Shepherd, 'tis my office best
To help ensnarèd chastity.
Brightest Lady, look on me.
Thus I sprinkle on thy breast
Drops that from my fountain pure
I have kept of precious cure;
Thrice upon thy finger's tip,
Thrice upon thy rubied lip:
Next this marble venomed seat,
Smeared with gums of glutinous heat,
I touch with chaste palms moist and cold.

Now the spell hath lost his hold;
And I must haste ere morning hour
To wait in Amphitrite's bower.

SABRINA *descends, and* THE LADY *rises out of her seat.*

SPIRIT. Virgin, daughter of Locrine,
Sprung of old Anchises' line,
May thy brimmèd waves for this
Their full tribute never miss
From a thousand petty rills,
That tumble down the snowy hills:
Summer drouth or singèd air
Never scorch thy tresses fair,
Nor wet October's torrent flood
Thy molten crystal fill with mud;
May thy billows roll ashore
The beryl and the golden ore;
May thy lofty head be crowned
With many a tower and terrace round,
And here and there thy banks upon
With groves of myrrh and cinnamon.
Come, Lady; while Heaven lends us grace,
Let us fly this cursèd place,
Lest the sorcerer us entice
With some other new device.
Not a waste or needless sound
Till we come to holier ground.
I shall be your faithful guide
Through this gloomy covert wide;
And not many furlongs thence
Is your Father's residence,
Where this night are met in state
Many a friend to gratulate
His wished presence, and beside
All the swains that there abide
With jigs and rural dance resort.

We shall catch them at their sport,
And our sudden coming there
Will double all their mirth and cheer.
Come, let us haste; the stars grow high,
But Night sits monarch yet in the mid sky.

The Scene changes, presenting Ludlow Town, and the President's Castle: then come in Country Dancers; after them the ATTENDANT SPIRIT, *with the two* BROTHERS *and* THE LADY.

SONG

SPIRIT. Back, shepherds, back! Enough your play
Till next sun-shine holiday.
Here be, without duck or nod,
Other trippings to be trod
Of lighter toes, and such court guise
As Mercury did first devise
With the mincing Dryades
On the lawns and on the leas.

This second Song presents them to their Father and Mother.

Noble Lord and Lady bright,
I have brought ye new delight.
Here behold so goodly grown
Three fair branches of your own.
Heaven hath timely tried their youth,
Their faith, their patience, and their truth,
And sent them here through hard assays
With a crown of deathless praise,
To triumph in victorious dance
O'er sensual folly and intemperance.

The dances ended, the SPIRIT *epiloguizes.*

SPIRIT. To the ocean now I fly,
And those happy climes that lie
Where day never shuts his eye,
Up in the broad fields of the sky.

There I suck the liquid air,
All amidst the gardens fair
Of Hesperus, and his daughters three
That sing about the golden tree.
Along the crispèd shades and bowers
Revels the spruce and jocund Spring;
The Graces and the rosy-bosomed Hours
Thither all their bounties bring.
That there eternal Summer dwells,
And west winds with musky wing
About the cedarn alleys fling
Nard and cassia's balmy smells.
Iris there with humid bow
Waters the odorous banks, that blow
Flowers of more mingled hue
Than her purfled scarf can shew,
And drenches with Elysian dew
(List, mortals, if your ears be true)
Beds of hyacinth and roses,
Where young Adonis oft reposes,
Waxing well of his deep wound,
In slumber soft, and on the ground
Sadly sits th' Assyrian queen.
But far above, in spangled sheen,
Celestial Cupid, her famed son, advanced
Holds his dear Psyche, sweet entranced
After her wandering labours long,
Till free consent the gods among
Make her his eternal bride,
And from her fair unspotted side
Two blissful twins are to be born,
Youth and Joy; so Jove hath sworn.
But now my task is smoothly done:
I can fly, or I can run
Quickly to the green earth's end,
Where the bowed welkin slow doth bend,
And from thence can soar as soon

To the corners of the moon.
  Mortals, that would follow me,
Love Virtue; she alone is free.
She can teach ye how to climb
Higher than the sphery chime;
Or, if Virtue feeble were,
Heaven itself would stoop to her.

LYCIDAS

In this Monody the Author bewails a learned Friend, unfortunately drowned in his passage from Chester on the Irish Seas, 1637; and by occasion, foretells the ruin of our corrupted Clergy, then in their height.

Yet once more, O ye laurels, and once more,
Ye myrtles brown, with ivy never sere,
I come to pluck your berries harsh and crude,
And with forced fingers rude
Shatter your leaves before the mellowing year.
Bitter constraint and sad occasion dear
Compels me to disturb your season due;
For Lycidas is dead, dead ere his prime,
Young Lycidas, and hath not left his peer.
Who would not sing for Lycidas? he knew
Himself to sing, and build the lofty rhyme.
He must not float upon his watery bier
Unwept, and welter to the parching wind,
Without the meed of some melodious tear.
  Begin, then, Sisters of the sacred well
That from beneath the seat of Jove doth spring;
Begin, and somewhat loudly sweep the string.
Hence with denial vain and coy excuse:
So may some gentle Muse
With lucky words favour my destined urn,
And as he passes turn,
And bid fair peace be to my sable shroud!
  For we were nursed upon the self-same hill,
Fed the same flock, by fountain, shade, and rill;
Together both, ere the high lawns appeared
Under the opening eyelids of the Morn,
We drove a-field, and both together heard
What time the grey-fly winds her sultry horn,
Battening our flocks with the fresh dews of night,
Oft till the star that rose at evening bright
Toward heaven's descent had sloped his westering wheel.

Meanwhile the rural ditties were not mute;
Tempered to th' oaten flute,
Rough Satyrs danced, and Fauns with cloven heel
From the glad sound would not be absent long;
And old Damaetas loved to hear our song.
  But, oh! the heavy change, now thou art gone,
Now thou art gone and never must return!
Thee, Shepherd, thee the woods and desert caves,
With wild thyme and the gadding vine o'ergrown,
And all their echoes, mourn.
The willows, and the hazel copses green,
Shall now no more be seen
Fanning their joyous leaves to thy soft lays.
As killing as the canker to the rose,
Or taint-worm to the weanling herds that graze,
Or frost to flowers, that their gay wardrobe wear,
When first the white-thorn blows;
Such, Lycidas, thy loss to shepherd's ear.
  Where were ye, Nymphs, when the remorseless deep
Closed o'er the head of your loved Lycidas?
For neither were ye playing on the steep
Where your old bards, the famous Druids, lie,
Nor on the shaggy top of Mona high,
Nor yet where Deva spreads her wizard stream.
Ay me! I fondly dream
"Had ye been there,"... for what could that have done?
What could the Muse herself that Orpheus bore,
The Muse herself, for her enchanting son,
Whom universal nature did lament,
When, by the rout that made the hideous roar,
His gory visage down the stream was sent,
Down the swift Hebrus to the Lesbian shore?
  Alas! what boots it with uncessant care
To tend the homely, slighted, shepherd's trade,
And strictly meditate the thankless Muse?
Were it not better done, as others use,
To sport with Amaryllis in the shade,

Or with the tangles of Neaera's hair?
Fame is the spur that the clear spirit doth raise
(That last infirmity of noble mind)
To scorn delights and live laborious days;
But the fair guerdon when we hope to find,
And think to burst out into sudden blaze,
Comes the blind Fury with th' abhorrèd shears,
And slits the thin-spun life. "But not the praise,"
Phoebus replied, and touched my trembling ears:
"Fame is no plant that grows on mortal soil,
Nor in the glistering foil
Set off to the world, nor in broad rumour lies,
But lives and spreads aloft by those pure eyes
And perfect witness of all-judging Jove;
As he pronounces lastly on each deed,
Of so much fame in Heaven expect thy meed."
  O fountain Arethuse, and thou honoured flood,
Smooth-sliding Mincius, crowned with vocal reeds,
That strain I heard was of a higher mood.
But now my oat proceeds,
And listens to the Herald of the Sea,
That came in Neptune's plea.
He asked the waves, and asked the felon winds,
What hard mishap hath doomed this gentle swain?
And questioned every gust of rugged wings
That blows from off each beakèd promontory.
They knew not of his story;
And sage Hippotades their answer brings,
That not a blast was from his dungeon strayed:
The air was calm, and on the level brine
Sleek Panopè with all her sisters played.
It was that fatal and perfidious bark,
Built in th' eclipse, and rigged with curses dark,
That sunk so low that sacred head of thine.
  Next, Camus, reverend sire, went footing slow,
His mantle hairy, and his bonnet sedge,
Inwrought with figures dim, and on the edge

Like to that sanguine flower inscribed with woe.
"Ah! who hath reft," quoth he, "my dearest pledge?"
Last came, and last did go,
The Pilot of the Galilean Lake;
Two massy keys he bore of metals twain
(The golden opes, the iron shuts amain).
He shook his mitred locks, and stern bespake:—
"How well could I have spared for thee, young swain,
Enow of such as, for their bellies' sake,
Creep, and intrude, and climb into the fold!
Of other care they little reckoning make
Than how to scramble at the shearers' feast,
And shove away the worthy bidden guest.
Blind mouths! that scarce themselves know how to hold
A sheep-hook, or have learnt aught else the least
That to the faithful herdman's art belongs!
What recks it them? What need they? They are sped,
And, when they list, their lean and flashy songs
Grate on their scrannel pipes of wretched straw,
The hungry sheep look up, and are not fed,
But, swoln with wind and the rank mist they draw,
Rot inwardly, and foul contagion spread;
Besides what the grim wolf with privy paw
Daily devours apace, and nothing said.
But that two-handed engine at the door
Stands ready to smite once, and smite no more."
  Return, Alpheus, the dread voice is past
That shrunk thy streams; return, Sicilian Muse,
And call the vales, and bid them hither cast
Their bells and flowerets of a thousand hues.
Ye valleys low, where the mild whispers use
Of shades, and wanton winds, and gushing brooks,
On whose fresh lap the swart star sparely looks,
Throw hither all your quaint enamelled eyes,
That on the green turf suck the honeyed showers,
And purple all the ground with vernal flowers.
Bring the rathe primrose that forsaken dies,

The tufted crow-toe, and pale jessamine,
The white pink, and the pansy freaked with jet,
The glowing violet,
The musk rose, and the well-attired woodbine,
With cowslips wan that hang the pensive head,
And every flower that sad embroidery wears;
Bid amaranthus all his beauty shed,
And daffadillies fill their cups with tears,
To strew the laureate hearse where Lycid lies.
For so, to interpose a little ease,
Let our frail thoughts dally with false surmise.
Ay me! whilst thee the shores and sounding seas
Wash far away, where'er thy bones are hurled;
Whether beyond the stormy Hebrides,
Where thou perhaps under the whelming tide
Visit'st the bottom of the monstrous world;
Or whether thou, to our moist vows denied,
Sleep'st by the fable of Bellerus old,
Where the great Vision of the guarded mount
Looks toward Namancos and Bayona's hold.
Look homeward, Angel, now, and melt with ruth:
And, O ye dolphins, waft the hapless youth.
  Weep no more, woeful shepherds, weep no more,
For Lycidas, your sorrow, is not dead,
Sunk though he be beneath the watery floor.
So sinks the day-star in the ocean bed,
And yet anon repairs his drooping head,
And tricks his beams, and with new-spangled ore
Flames in the forehead of the morning sky:
So Lycidas sunk low, but mounted high,
Through the dear might of him that walked the waves,
Where, other groves and other streams along,
With nectar pure his oozy locks he laves,
And hears the unexpressive nuptial song,
In the blest kingdoms meek of joy and love.
There entertain him all the Saints above,
In solemn troops, and sweet societies,

That sing, and singing in their glory move,
And wipe the tears for ever from his eyes.
Now, Lycidas, the shepherds weep no more;
Henceforth thou art the Genius of the shore,
In thy large recompense, and shalt be good
To all that wander in that perilous flood.

Thus sang the uncouth swain to th' oaks and rills,
While the still morn went out with sandals grey:
He touched the tender stops of various quills,
With eager thought warbling his Doric lay;
And now the sun had stretched out all the hills,
And now was dropped into the western bay;
At last he rose, and twitched his mantle blue:
To-morrow to fresh woods, and pastures new.

SONNETS

I

[TO THE NIGHTINGALE]

O Nightingale that on yon bloomy spray
    Warblest at eve, when all the woods are still,
    Thou with fresh hope the lover's heart dost fill,
    While the jolly hours lead on propitious May.
Thy liquid notes that close the eye of day,
    First heard before the shallow cuckoo's bill,
    Portend success in love. O, if Jove's will
    Have linked that amorous power to thy soft lay,
Now timely sing, ere the rude bird of hate
    Foretell my hopeless doom, in some grove nigh;
    As thou from year to year hast sung too late
For my relief, yet hadst no reason why.
    Whether the Muse or Love call thee his mate,
    Both them I serve, and of their train am I.

II

[ON HIS HAVING ARRIVED AT THE AGE OF TWENTY-THREE]

How soon hath Time, the subtle thief of youth,
    Stolen on his wing my three-and-twentieth year!
    My hasting days fly on with full career,
    But my late spring no bud or blossom shew'th.
Perhaps my semblance might deceive the truth
    That I to manhood am arrived so near;
    And inward ripeness doth much less appear,
    That some more timely-happy spirits endu'th.
Yet, be it less or more, or soon or slow,
    It shall be still in strictest measure even
    To that same lot, however mean or high,
Toward which Time leads me, and the will of Heaven,
    All is, if I have grace to use it so,
    As ever in my great Task-Master's eye.

VIII

WHEN THE ASSAULT WAS INTENDED TO THE CITY

Captain or Colonel, or Knight in Arms,
Whose chance on these defenceless doors may seize,
If deed of honour did thee ever please,
Guard them, and him within protect from harms.
He can requite thee; for he knows the charms
That call fame on such gentle acts as these,
And he can spread thy name o'er lands and seas,
Whatever clime the sun's bright circle warms.
Lift not thy spear against the Muses' bower:
The great Emathian conqueror bid spare
The house of Pindarus, when temple and tower
Went to the ground; and the repeated air
Of sad Electra's poet had the power
To save th' Athenian walls from ruin bare.

X

TO THE LADY MARGARET LEY

Daughter to that good Earl, once President
Of England's Council and her Treasury,
Who lived in both unstained with gold or fee,
And left them both, more in himself content,
Till the sad breaking of that Parliament
Broke him, as that dishonest victory
At Chaeronea, fatal to liberty,
Killed with report that old man eloquent,
Though later born than to have known the days
Wherein your father flourished, yet by you,
Madam, methinks I see him living yet:
So well your words his noble virtues praise
That all both judge you to relate them true
And to possess them, honoured Margaret.

XI

ON THE DETRACTION WHICH FOLLOWED UPON MY WRITING CERTAIN TREATISES

A book was writ of late called Tetrachordon,
And woven close, both matter, form, and style;
The subject new: it walked the town a while,
Numbering good intellects; now seldom pored on.
Cries the stall-reader, "Bless us! what a word on
A title-page is this!"; and some in file
Stand spelling false, while one might walk to Mile-
End Green. Why is it harder, sirs, than Gordon,
Colkitto, or Macdonnel, or Galasp?
Those rugged names to our like mouths grow sleek,
That would have made Quintilian stare and gasp.
Thy age, like ours, O soul of Sir John Cheek,
Hated not learning worse than toad or asp,
When thou taught'st Cambridge and King Edward
Greek.

XII

ON THE SAME

I did but prompt the age to quit their clogs
By the known rules of ancient liberty,
When straight a barbarous noise environs me
Of owls and cuckoos, asses, apes, and dogs;
As when those hinds that were transformed to frogs
Railed at Latona's twin-born progeny,
Which after held the Sun and Moon in fee.
But this is got by casting pearl to hogs,
That bawl for freedom in their senseless mood,
And still revolt when truth would set them free.
Licence they mean when they cry liberty;
For who loves that must first be wise and good:
But from that mark how far they rove we see,
For all this waste of wealth and loss of blood.

XIII

TO MR. H. LAWES, ON HIS AIRS

Harry, whose tuneful and well-measured song
First taught our English music how to span
Words with just note and accent, not to scan
With Midas' ears, committing short and long,
Thy worth and skill exempts thee from the throng,
With praise enough for Envy to look wan;
To after age thou shalt be writ the man
That with smooth air couldst humour best our tongue.
Thou honour'st Verse, and Verse must lend her wing
To honour thee, the priest of Phoebus' choir,
That tun'st their happiest lines in hymn or story.
Dante shall give Fame leave to set thee higher
Than his Casella, whom he wooed to sing,
Met in the milder shades of Purgatory.

XIV

ON THE RELIGIOUS MEMORY OF MRS. CATHARINE THOMSON, MY CHRISTIAN FRIEND, DECEASED DEC. 16, 1646

When Faith and Love, which parted from thee never,
Had ripened thy just soul to dwell with God,
Meekly thou didst resign this earthy load
Of death, called life, which us from life doth sever.
Thy works, and alms, and all thy good endeavour,
Stayed not behind, nor in the grave were trod;
But, as Faith pointed with her golden rod,
Followed thee up to joy and bliss for ever.
Love led them on; and Faith, who knew them best
Thy handmaids, clad them o'er with purple beams
And azure wings, that up they flew so drest,
And spake the truth of thee on glorious themes
Before the Judge; who thenceforth bid thee rest,
And drink thy fill of pure immortal streams.

XV

ON THE LORD GENERAL FAIRFAX, AT THE SIEGE OF COLCHESTER

Fairfax, whose name in arms through Europe rings,
Filling each mouth with envy or with praise,
And all her jealous monarchs with amaze,
And rumours loud that daunt remotest kings,
Thy firm unshaken virtue ever brings
Victory home, though new rebellions raise
Their Hydra heads, and the false North displays
Her broken league to imp their serpent wings.
O yet a nobler task awaits thy hand
(For what can war but endless war still breed?)
Till truth and right from violence be freed,
And public faith cleared from the shameful brand
Of public fraud. In vain doth Valour bleed,
While Avarice and Rapine share the land.

XVI

TO THE LORD GENERAL CROMWELL, MAY 1652, ON THE PROPOSALS OF CERTAIN MINISTERS AT THE COMMITTEE FOR PROPAGATION OF THE GOSPEL

Cromwell, our chief of men, who through a cloud
Not of war only, but detractions rude,
Guided by faith and matchless fortitude,
To peace and truth thy glorious way hast ploughed,
And on the neck of crownèd Fortune proud
Hast reared God's trophies, and his work pursued,
While Darwen stream, with blood of Scots imbrued,
And Dunbar field, resounds thy praises loud,
And Worcester's laureate wreath: yet much remains
To conquer still; Peace hath her victories
No less renowned than War: new foes arise,
Threatening to bind our souls with secular chains.
Help us to save free conscience from the paw
Of hireling wolves, whose Gospel is their maw.

XVII

TO SIR HENRY VANE THE YOUNGER

Vane, young in years, but in sage counsel old,
Than whom a better senator ne'er held
The helm of Rome, when gowns, not arms, repelled
The fierce Epirot, and the African bold,
Whether to settle peace, or to unfold
The drift of hollow states, hard to be spelled;
Then to advise how war may best, upheld,
Move by her two main nerves, iron and gold,
In all her equipage; besides, to know
Both spiritual power and civil, what each means,
What severs each, thou hast learned, which few have done.
The bounds of either sword to thee we owe:
Therefore on thy firm hand Religion leans
In peace, and reckons thee her eldest son.

XVIII

ON THE LATE MASSACRE IN PIEDMONT

Avenge, O Lord, thy slaughtered saints, whose bones
Lie scattered on the Alpine mountains cold;
Even them who kept thy truth so pure of old,
When all our fathers worshipped stocks and stones,
Forget not: in thy book record their groans
Who were thy sheep, and in their ancient fold
Slain by the bloody Piemontese, that rolled
Mother with infant down the rocks. Their moans
The vales redoubled to the hills, and they
To Heaven. Their martyred blood and ashes sow
O'er all th' Italian fields, where still doth sway
The triple Tyrant; that from these may grow
A hundredfold, who, having learnt thy way,
Early may fly the Babylonian woe.

XIX

[ON HIS BLINDNESS]

When I consider how my light is spent
 Ere half my days in this dark world and wide,
 And that one talent which is death to hide
 Lodged with me useless, though my soul more bent
To serve therewith my Maker, and present
 My true account, lest he returning chide,
 "Doth God exact day-labour, light denied?"
 I fondly ask. But Patience, to prevent
That murmur, soon replies, "God doth not need
 Either man's work or his own gifts. Who best
 Bear his mild yoke, they serve him best. His state
Is kingly: thousands at his bidding speed,
 And post o'er land and ocean without rest;
 They also serve who only stand and wait."

XX

[TO MR. LAWRENCE]

Lawrence, of virtuous father virtuous son,
 Now that the fields are dank, and ways are mire,
 Where shall we sometimes meet, and by the fire
 Help waste a sullen day, what may be won
From the hard season gaining? Time will run
 On smoother, till Favonius reinspire
 The frozen earth, and clothe in fresh attire
 The lily and rose, that neither sowed nor spun.
What neat repast shall feast us, light and choice,
 Of Attic taste, with wine, whence we may rise,
 To hear the lute well touched, or artful voice
Warble immortal notes and Tuscan air?
 He who of those delights can judge, and spare
 To interpose them oft, is not unwise.

XXI

[TO CYRIACK SKINNER]

Cyriack, whose grandsire on the royal bench
 Of British Themis, with no mean applause,
 Pronounced, and in his volumes taught, our laws,
 Which others at their bar so often wrench,
Today deep thoughts resolve with me to drench
 In mirth that after no repenting draws;
 Let Euclid rest, and Archimedes pause,
 And what the Swede intend, and what the French.
To measure life learn thou betimes, and know
 Towards solid good what leads the nearest way;
 For other things mild Heaven a time ordains,
And disapproves that care, though wise in show,
 That with superfluous burden loads the day,
 And, when God sends a cheerful hour, refrains.

XXII

[TO THE SAME]

Cyriack, this three years' day these eyes, though clear,
 To outward view, of blemish or of spot,
 Bereft of light, their seeing have forgot;
 Nor to their idle orbs doth sight appear
Of sun, or moon, or star, throughout the year,
 Or man, or woman. Yet I argue not
 Against Heaven's hand or will, nor bate a jot
 Of heart or hope, but still bear up and steer
Right onward. What supports me, dost thou ask?
 The conscience, friend, to have lost them overplied
 In liberty's defence, my noble task,
Of which all Europe rings from side to side.
 This thought might lead me through the world's vain mask
 Content, though blind, had I no better guide.

XXIII

[ON HIS DECEASED WIFE]

Methought I saw my late espousèd saint
    Brought to me like Alcestis from the grave,
    Whom Jove's great son to her glad husband gave,
    Rescued from Death by force, though pale and faint.
Mine, as whom washed from spot of child-bed taint
    Purification in the Old Law did save,
    And such as yet once more I trust to have
    Full sight of her in Heaven without restraint,
Came vested all in white, pure as her mind.
    Her face was veiled; yet to my fancied sight
    Love, sweetness, goodness, in her person shined
So clear, as in no face with more delight.
    But, oh! as to embrace me she inclined,
    I waked, she fled, and day brought back my night.

SAMSON AGONISTES:

A DRAMATIC POEM

OF THAT SORT OF DRAMATIC POEM WHICH IS CALLED TRAGEDY

Tragedy, as it was anciently composed, hath been ever held the gravest, moralest, and most profitable of all other poems: therefore said by Aristotle to be of power, by raising pity and fear, or terror, to purge the mind of those and such-like passions,—that is, to temper and reduce them to just measure with a kind of delight, stirred up by reading or seeing those passions well imitated. Nor is Nature wanting in her own effects to make good his assertion; for so, in physic, things of melancholic hue and quality are used against melancholy, sour against sour, salt to remove salt humours. Hence philosophers and other gravest writers, as Cicero, Plutarch, and others, frequently cite out of tragic poets, both to adorn and illustrate their discourse. The Apostle Paul himself thought it not unworthy to insert a verse of Euripides into the text of Holy Scripture, 1 Cor. xv. 33; and Paraeus, commenting on the *Revelation*, divides the whole book, as a tragedy, into acts, distinguished each by a Chorus of heavenly harpings and song between. Heretofore men in highest dignity have laboured not a little to be thought able to compose a tragedy. Of that honour Dionysius the elder was no less ambitious than before of his attaining to the tyranny. Augustus Caesar also had begun his *Ajax*, but unable to please his own judgment with what he had begun, left it unfinished. Seneca, the philosopher, is by some thought the author of those tragedies (at least the best of them) that go under that name. Gregory Nazianzen, a Father of the Church, thought it not unbeseeming the sanctity of his person to write a tragedy, which he entitled *Christ Suffering*. This is mentioned to vindicate tragedy from the small esteem, or rather infamy, which in the account of many it undergoes at this day, with other common interludes: happening through the poet's error of intermixing comic stuff with tragic sadness and gravity, or introducing trivial and vulgar persons: which by all judicious hath been counted absurd, and brought in without discretion, corruptly to gratify the people. And, though ancient tragedy use no Prologue, yet using sometimes, in case of self-defence or explanation, that which Martial calls an Epistle, in behalf of this tragedy, coming forth after the ancient manner, much different from what among us passes for best, thus much beforehand may be *epistled*,— that Chorus is here introduced after the Greek manner, not ancient only, but modern, and still in use among the Italians. In the modelling therefore of this poem, with good reason, the Ancients and Italians are rather followed, as of much more authority and fame. The measure of verse used in the Chorus is of all sorts, called by the Greeks *Monostrophic*, or rather *Apolelymenon*, without regard had to strophe, antistrophe, or epode,—which were a kind of stanzas framed only for the music, then used with the Chorus that sung; not essential to the poem, and therefore not material: or, being divided into stanzas or pauses, they may be called *Allaeostropha*. Division into act and scene, referring chiefly to the stage (to which this work never was intended), is here omitted.

It suffices if the whole drama be found not produced beyond the fifth act. Of the style and uniformity, and that commonly called the plot, whether intricate or explicit,—which is nothing indeed but such economy, or disposition of the fable, as may stand best with verisimilitude and decorum,—they only will best judge who are not unacquainted with Aeschylus, Sophocles, and Euripides, the three tragic poets unequalled yet by any, and the best rule to all who endeavour to write tragedy. The circumscription of time wherein the whole drama begins and ends is, according to ancient rule and best example, within the space of twenty-four hours.

THE ARGUMENT

Samson, made captive, blind, and now in the prison at Gaza, there to labour as in a common workhouse, on a festival day, in the general cessation from labour, comes forth into the open air, to a place nigh, somewhat retired, there to sit a while and bemoan his condition. Where he happens at length to be visited by certain friends and equals of his tribe, which make the Chorus, who seek to comfort him what they can; then by his old father, Manoa, who endeavours the like, and withal tells him his purpose to procure his liberty by ransom; lastly, that this feast was proclaimed by the Philistines as a day of thanksgiving for their deliverance from the hands of Samson—which yet more troubles him. Manoa then departs to prosecute his endeavour with the Philistian lords for Samson's redemption; who, in the meanwhile, is visited by other persons, and, lastly, by a public officer to require his coming to the feast before the lords and people, to play or show his strength in their presence. He at first refuses, dismissing the public officer with absolute denial to come; at length persuaded inwardly that this was from God, he yields to go along with him, who came now the second time with great threatenings to fetch him. The Chorus yet remaining on the place, Manoa returns full of joyful hope to procure ere long his son's deliverance: in the midst of which discourse an Ebrew comes in haste, confusedly at first, and afterwards more distinctly, relating the catastrophe —what Samson had done to the Philistines, and by accident to himself; wherewith the tragedy ends.

THE PERSONS

SAMSON
MANOA, *the father of Samson.*
DALILA, *his wife.*
HARAPHA *of Gath.*
Public Officer.
Messenger.
Chorus of Danites.

The Scene, before the Prison in Gaza.

SAMSON. A little onward lend thy guiding hand
To these dark steps, a little further on;
For yonder bank hath choice of sun or shade.

There I am wont to sit, when any chance
Relieves me from my task of servile toil,
Daily in the common prison else enjoined me,
Where I, a prisoner chained, scarce freely draw
The air, imprisoned also, close and damp,
Unwholesome draught. But here I feel amends—
The breath of heaven fresh blowing, pure and sweet,
With day-spring born; here leave me to respire.
This day a solemn feast the people hold
To Dagon, their sea-idol, and forbid
Laborious works. Unwillingly this rest
Their superstition yields me; hence, with leave
Retiring from the popular noise, I seek
This unfrequented place, to find some ease—
Ease to the body some, none to the mind
From restless thoughts, that, like a deadly swarm
Of hornets armed, no sooner found alone
But rush upon me thronging, and present
Times past, what once I was, and what am now.
Oh, wherefore was my birth from Heaven foretold
Twice by an Angel, who at last, in sight
Of both my parents, all in flames ascended
From off the altar where an offering burned,
As in a fiery column charioting
His godlike presence, and from some great act
Or benefit revealed to Abraham's race ?
Why was my breeding ordered and prescribed
As of a person separate to God,
Designed for great exploits, if I must die
Betrayed, captívéd, and both my eyes put out,
Made of my enemies the scorn and gaze,
To grind in brazen fetters under task
With this heaven-gifted strength? O glorious strength,
Put to the labour of a beast, debased
Lower than bond-slave! Promise was that I
Should Israel from Philistian yoke deliver;
Ask for this great deliverer now, and find him

Eyeless in Gaza, at the mill with slaves,
Himself in bonds under Philistian yoke.
Yet stay; let me not rashly call in doubt
Divine prediction. What if all foretold
Had been fulfilled but through mine own default?
Whom have I to complain of but myself,
Who this high gift of strength committed to me,
In what part lodged, how easily bereft me,
Under the seal of silence could not keep,
But weakly to a woman must reveal it,
O'ercome with importunity and tears?
O impotence of mind in body strong!
But what is strength without a double share
Of wisdom? Vast, unwieldy, burdensome,
Proudly secure, yet liable to fall
By weakest subtleties; not made to rule,
But to subserve where wisdom bears command.
God, when he gave me strength, to show withal,
How slight the gift was, hung it in my hair.
But peace! I must not quarrel with the will
Of highest dispensation, which herein
Haply had ends above my reach to know.
Suffices that to me strength is my bane,
And proves the source of all my miseries—
So many, and so huge, that each apart
Would ask a life to wail. But, chief of all,
O loss of sight, of thee I must complain!
Blind among enemies! O worse than chains,
Dungeon, or beggary, or decrepit age!
Light, the prime work of God, to me is extinct,
And all her various objects of delight
Annulled, which might in part my grief have eased.
Inferior to the vilest now become
Of man or worm, the vilest here excel me:
They creep, yet see, I, dark in light, exposed
To daily fraud, contempt, abuse, and wrong,
Within doors, or without, still as a fool,

In power of others, never in my own—
Scarce half I seem to live, dead more than half.
O dark, dark, dark, amid the blaze of noon,
Irrecoverably dark, total eclipse
Without all hope of day!
O first-created beam, and thou great Word,
"Let there be light, and light was over all,"
Why am I thus bereaved thy prime decree?
The Sun to me is dark
And silent as the Moon,
When she deserts the night,
Hid in her vacant interlunar cave.
Since light so necessary is to life,
And almost life itself, if it be true
That light is in the soul,
She all in every part, why was the sight
To such a tender ball as th' eye confined,
So obvious and so easy to be quenched,
And not, as feeling, through all parts diffused,
That she might look at will through every pore?
Then had I not been thus exiled from light,
As in the land of darkness, yet in light,
To live a life half dead, a living death,
And buried; but, O yet more miserable!
Myself my sepulchre, a moving grave;
Buried, yet not exempt,
By privilege of death and burial,
From worst of other evils, pains, and wrongs;
But made hereby obnoxious more
To all the miseries of life,
Life in captivity
Among inhuman foes.
But who are these? for with joint pace I hear
The tread of many feet steering this way;
Perhaps my enemies, who come to stare
At my affliction, and perhaps to insult—
Their daily practice to afflict me more.

CHORUS. This, this is he; softly a while;
Let us not break in upon him.
O change beyond report, thought, or belief!
See how he lies at random, carelessly diffused,
With languished head unpropped,
As one past hope, abandoned,
And by himself given over,
In slavish habit, ill-fitted weeds
O'er-worn and soiled.
Or do my eyes misrepresent? Can this be he,
That heroic, that renowned,
Irresistible Samson? whom, unarmed,
No strength of man, or fiercest wild beast, could withstand:
Who tore the lion as the lion tears the kid;
Ran on embattled armies clad in iron,
And, weaponless himself,
Made arms ridiculous, useless the forgery
Of brazen shield and spear, the hammered cuirass,
Chalybean-tempered steel, and frock of mail
Adamantean proof;
But safest he who stood aloof,
When insupportably his foot advanced,
In scorn of their proud arms and warlike tools,
Spurned them to death by troops. The bold Ascalonite
Fled from his lion ramp; old warriors turned
Their plated backs under his heel,
Or grovelling soiled their crested helmets in the dust.
Then with what trivial weapon came to hand,
The jaw of a dead ass, his sword of bone,
A thousand foreskins fell, the flower of Palestine,
In Ramath-lechi, famous to this day:
Then by main force pulled up, and on his shoulders bore,
The gates of Azza, post and massy bar,
Up to the hill by Hebron, seat of giants old—
No journey of a Sabbath-day, and loaded so—
Like whom the Gentiles feign to bear up Heaven.
Which shall I first bewail,

Thy bondage or lost sight,
Prison within prison
Inseparably dark?
Thou art become (O worst imprisonment!)
The dungeon of thyself; thy soul,
(Which men enjoying sight oft without cause complain)
Imprisoned now indeed,
In real darkness of the body dwells,
Shut up from outward light
To incorporate with gloomy night;
For inward light, alas!
Puts forth no visual beam.
O mirror of our fickle state,
Since man on earth, unparalleled!
The rarer thy example stands,
By how much from the top of wondrous glory,
Strongest of mortal men,
To lowest pitch of abject fortune thou art fallen!
For him I reckon not in high estate
Whom long descent of birth,
Or the sphere of fortune, raises;
But thee, whose strength, while virtue was her mate,
Might have subdued the Earth,
Universally crowned with highest praises.
SAMSON. I hear the sound of words; their sense the air
Dissolves unjointed ere it reach my ear.
CHORUS. He speaks: let us draw nigh. Matchless in might,
The glory late of Israel, now the grief!
We come, thy friends and neighbours not unknown,
From Eshtaol and Zora's fruitful vale,
To visit or bewail thee; or, if better,
Counsel or consolation we may bring,
Salve to thy sores: apt words have power to swage
The tumours of a troubled mind,
And are as balm to festered wounds.
SAMSON. Your coming, friends, revives me; for I learn
Now of my own experience, not by talk,

How counterfeit a coin they are who " friends "
Bear in their superscription (of the most
I would be understood). In prosperous days
They swarm, but in adverse withdraw their head,
Not to be found, though sought. Ye see, O friends,
How many evils have enclosed me round;
Yet that which was the worst now least afflicts me,
Blindness; for, had I sight, confused with shame,
How could I once look up, or heave the head,
Who, like a foolish pilot, have shipwrecked
My vessel trusted to me from above,
Gloriously rigged, and for a word, a tear,
Fool! have divulged the secret gift of God
To a deceitful woman? Tell me, friends,
Am I not sung and proverbed for a fool
In every street? Do they not say, " How well
Are come upon him his deserts "? Yet why?
Immeasurable strength they might behold
In me; of wisdom nothing more than mean.
This with the other should at least have paired;
These two, proportioned ill, drove me transverse.
CHORUS Tax not divine disposal. Wisest men
Have erred, and by bad women been deceived;
And shall again, pretend they ne'er so wise.
Deject not, then, so overmuch thyself,
Who hast of sorrow thy full load besides.
Yet, truth to say, I oft have heard men wonder
Why thou should'st wed Philistian women rather
Than of thine own tribe fairer, or as fair,
At least of thy own nation, and as noble.
SAMSON. The first I saw at Timna, and she pleased
Me, not my parents, that I sought to wed
The daughter of an infidel. They knew not
That what I motioned was of God; I knew
From intimate impulse, and therefore urged
The marriage on, that, by occasion hence,
I might begin Israel's deliverance—

The work to which I was divinely called.
She proving false, the next I took to wife
(O that I never had! fond wish too late!)
Was in the vale of Sorec, Dálila,
That specious monster, my accomplished snare.
I thought it lawful from my former act,
And the same end, still watching to oppress
Israel's oppressors. Of what now I suffer
She was not the prime cause, but I myself,
Who, vanquished with a peal of words (O weakness!),
Gave up my fort of silence to a woman.
CHORUS. In seeking just occasion to provoke
The Philistine, thy country's enemy,
Thou never wast remiss, I bear thee witness;
Yet Israel still serves with all his sons.
SAMSON. That fault I take not on me, but transfer
On Israel's governors and heads of tribes,
Who, seeing those great acts which God had done
Singly by me against their conquerors,
Acknowledged not, or not at all considered,
Deliverance offered. I, on th' other side,
Used no ambition to commend my deeds;
The deeds themselves, though mute, spoke loud the doer.
But they persisted deaf, and would not seem
To count them things worth notice, till at length
Their lords, the Philistines, with gathered powers,
Entered Judea seeking me, who then
Safe to the rock of Etham was retired—
Not flying, but forecasting in what place
To set upon them, what advantaged best.
Meanwhile the men of Judah, to prevent
The harass of their land, beset me round;
I willingly on some conditions came
Into their hands, and they as gladly yield me
To the uncircumcised a welcome prey,
Bound with two cords. But cords to me were threads
Touched with the flame: on their whole host I flew

Unarmed, and with a trivial weapon felled
Their choicest youth; they only lived who fled.
Had Judah that day joined, or one whole tribe,
They had by this possessed the towers of Gath,
And lorded over them whom now they serve.
But what more oft, in nations grown corrupt,
And by their vices brought to servitude,
Than to love bondage more than liberty—
Bondage with ease than strenuous liberty—
And to despise, or envy, or suspect,
Whom God hath of his special favour raised
As their deliverer? If he aught begin,
How frequent to desert him, and at last
To heap ingratitude on worthiest deeds!
CHORUS. Thy words to my remembrance bring
How Succoth and the fort of Penuel
Their great deliverer contemned,
The matchless Gideon, in pursuit
Of Madian, and her vanquished kings;
And how ingrateful Ephraim
Had dealt with Jephtha, who by argument,
Not worse than by his shield and spear,
Defended Israel from the Ammonite,
Had not his prowess quelled their pride
In that sore battle when so many died
Without reprieve, adjudged to death
For want of well pronouncing *Shibboleth*.
SAMSON. Of such examples add me to the roll.
Me easily indeed mine may neglect,
But God's proposed deliverance not so.
CHORUS. Just are the ways of God,
And justifiable to men,
Unless there be who think not God at all.
If any be, they walk obscure;
For of such doctrine never was there school,
But the heart of the fool,
And no man therein doctor but himself.

Yet more there be who doubt his ways not just,
As to his own edicts found contradicting;
Then give the reins to wandering thought,
Regardless of his glory's diminution,
Till, by their own perplexities involved,
They ravel more, still less resolved,
But never find self-satisfying solution.
As if they would confine th' Interminable,
And tie him to his own prescript,
Who made our laws to bind us, not himself,
And hath full right to exempt
Whomso it pleases him by choice
From national obstriction, without taint
Of sin, or legal debt;
For with his own laws he can best dispense.
He would not else, who never wanted means,
Nor in respect of the enemy just cause,
To set his people free,
Have prompted this heroic Nazarite,
Against his vow of strictest purity,
To seek in marriage that fallacious bride,
Unclean, unchaste.
Down, Reason, then; at least, vain reasonings down;
Though Reason here aver
That moral verdict quits her of unclean:
Unchaste was subsequent; her stain, not his.
But see! here comes thy reverend sire,
With careful step, locks white as down,
Old Manoa: advise
Forthwith how thou ought'st to receive him.
SAMSON. Ay me! another inward grief, awaked
With mention of that name, renews th' assault.
MANOA. Brethren and men of Dan (for such ye seem,
Though in this uncouth place), if old respect,
As I suppose, towards your once gloried friend,
My son, now captive, hither hath informed
Your younger feet, while mine, cast back with age,

Came lagging after, say if he be here.
CHORUS. As signal now in low dejected state
As erst in highest, behold him where he lies.
MANOA. O miserable change! Is this the man,
That invincible Samson, far renowned,
The dread of Israel's foes, who with a strength
Equivalent to Angels' walked their streets,
None offering fight; who, single combatant,
Duelled their armies ranked in proud array,
Himself an army—now unequal match
To save himself against a coward armed
At one spear's length? O ever-failing trust
In mortal strength! and, oh, what not in man
Deceivable and vain? Nay, what thing good
Prayed for, but often proves our woe, our bane?
I prayed for children, and thought barrenness
In wedlock a reproach; I gained a son,
And such a son as all men hailed me happy:
Who would be now a father in my stead?
Oh, wherefore did God grant me my request,
And as a blessing with such pomp adorned?
Why are his gifts desirable, to tempt
Our earnest prayers, then, given with solemn hand
As graces, draw a scorpion's tail behind?
For this did the Angel twice descend? for this
Ordained thy nurture holy, as of a plant
Select and sacred? glorious for a while,
The miracle of men; then in an hour
Ensnared, assaulted, overcome, led bound,
Thy foes' derision, captive, poor and blind,
Into a dungeon thrust, to work with slaves!
Alas! methinks whom God hath chosen once
To worthiest deeds, if he through frailty err,
He should not so o'erwhelm, and as a thrall
Subject him to so foul indignities,
Be it but for honour's sake of former deeds.
SAMSON. Appoint not heavenly disposition, father.

Nothing of all these evils hath befallen me
But justly; I myself have brought them on;
Sole author I, sole cause. If aught seem vile,
As vile hath been my folly, who have profaned
The mystery of God, given me under pledge
Of vow, and have betrayed it to a woman,
A Canaanite, my faithless enemy.
This well I knew, nor was at all surprised,
But warned by oft experience. Did not she
Of Timna first betray me, and reveal
The secret wrested from me in her height
Of nuptial love professed, carrying it straight
To them who had corrupted her, my spies
And rivals? In this other was there found
More faith, who, also in her prime of love,
Spousal embraces, vitiated with gold,
Though offered only, by the scent conceived,
Her spurious first-born, treason against me?
Thrice she assayed, with flattering prayers and sighs,
And amorous reproaches, to win from me
My capital secret, in what part my strength
Lay stored, in what part summed, that she might know;
Thrice I deluded her, and turned to sport
Her importunity, each time perceiving
How openly and with what impudence
She purposed to betray me, and (which was worse
Than undissembled hate) with what contempt
She sought to make me traitor to myself.
Yet, the fourth time, when, mustering all her wiles,
With blandished parleys, feminine assaults,
Tongue-batteries, she surceased not day nor night
To storm me, over-watched and wearied out,
At times when men seek most repose and rest,
I yielded, and unlocked her all my heart,
Who, with a grain of manhood well resolved,
Might easily have shook off all her snares;
But foul effeminacy held me yoked

Her bond-slave. O indignity, O blot
To honour and religion! servile mind
Rewarded well with servile punishment!
The base degree to which I now am fallen,
These rags, this grinding, is not yet so base
As was my former servitude, ignoble,
Unmanly, ignominious, infamous,
True slavery; and that blindness worse than this,
That saw not how degenerately I served.

MANOA. I cannot praise thy marriage-choices, son—
Rather approved them not; but thou didst plead
Divine impulsion prompting how thou might'st
Find some occasion to infest our foes.
I state not that; this I am sure—our foes
Found soon occasion thereby to make thee
Their captive, and their triumph; thou the sooner
Temptation found'st, or over-potent charms,
To violate the sacred trust of silence
Deposited within thee—which to have kept
Tacit was in thy power. True; and thou bear'st
Enough, and more, the burden of that fault;
Bitterly hast thou paid, and still art paying,
That rigid score. A worse thing yet remains:—
This day the Philistines a popular feast
Here celebrate in Gaza, and proclaim
Great pomp, and sacrifice, and praises loud,
To Dagon, as their god who hath delivered
Thee, Samson, bound and blind, into their hands—
Them out of thine, who slew'st them many a slain.
So Dagon shall be magnified, and God,
Besides whom is no god, compared with idols,
Disglorified, blasphemed, and had in scorn
By th' idolatrous rout amidst their wine;
Which to have come to pass by means of thee,
Samson, of all thy sufferings think the heaviest,
Of all reproach the most with shame that ever
Could have befallen thee and thy father's house.

SAMSON Father, I do acknowledge and confess
That I this honour, I this pomp, have brought
To Dagon, and advanced his praises high
Among the heathen round—to God have brought
Dishonour, obloquy, and oped the mouths
Of idolists and atheists; have brought scandal
To Israel, diffidence of God, and doubt
In feeble hearts, propense enough before
To waver, or fall off and join with idols·
Which is my chief affliction, shame and sorrow,
The anguish of my soul, that suffers not
Mine eye to harbour sleep, or thoughts to rest.
This only hope relieves me, that the strife
With me hath end. All the contést is now
'Twixt God and Dagon. Dagon hath presumed,
Me overthrown, to enter lists with God,
His deity comparing and preferring
Before the God of Abraham. He, be sure,
Will not connive, or linger, thus provoked,
But will arise, and his great name assert.
Dagon must stoop, and shall ere long receive
Such a discomfit as shall quite despoil him
Of all these boasted trophies won on me,
And with confusion blank his worshippers.
MANOA. With cause this hope relieves thee; and these words
I as a prophecy receive; for God
(Nothing more certain) will not long defer
To vindicate the glory of his name
Against all competition, nor will long
Endure it doubtful whether God be Lord
Or Dagon. But for thee what shall be done?
Thou must not in the meanwhile, here forgot,
Lie in this miserable loathsome plight
Neglected. I already have made way
To some Philistian lords, with whom to treat
About thy ransom Well they may by this
Have satisfied their utmost of revenge,

By pains and slaveries, worse than death, inflicted
On thee, who now no more canst do them harm.
  SAMSON. Spare that proposal, father; spare the trouble
Of that solicitation. Let me here,
As I deserve, pay on my punishment,
And expiate, if possible, my crime,
Shameful garrulity. To have revealed
Secrets of men, the secrets of a friend,
How heinous had the fact been, how deserving
Contempt and scorn of all—to be excluded
All friendship, and avoided as a blab,
The mark of fool set on his front! But I
God's counsel have not kept, his holy secret
Presumptuously have published, impiously,
Weakly at least and shamefully—a sin
That Gentiles in their parables condemn
To their abyss and horrid pains confined.
  MANOA. Be penitent, and for thy fault contrite;
But act not in thy own affliction, son.
Repent the sin; but, if the punishment
Thou canst avoid, self-preservation bids;
Or th' execution leave to high disposal,
And let another hand, not thine, exact
Thy penal forfeit from thyself. Perhaps
God will relent, and quit thee all his debt;
Who ever more approves and more accepts
(Best pleased with humble and filial submission)
Him who, imploring mercy, sues for life,
Than who, self-rigorous, chooses death as due;
Which argues over-just, and self-displeased
For self-offence more than for God offended.
Reject not, then, what offered means who knows
But God hath set before us to return thee
Home to thy country and his sacred house,
Where thou may'st bring thy offerings, to avert
His further ire, with prayers and vows renewed.
  SAMSON. His pardon I implore; but, as for life,

To what end should I seek it? When in strength
All mortals I excelled, and great in hopes,
With youthful courage, and magnanimous thoughts
Of birth from Heaven foretold and high exploits,
Full of divine instinct, after some proof
Of acts indeed heroic, far beyond
The sons of Anak, famous now and blazed,
Fearless of danger, like a petty god
I walked about, admired of all, and dreaded
On hostile ground, none daring my affront—
Then, swoln with pride, into the snare I fell
Of fair fallacious looks, venereal trains,
Softened with pleasure and voluptuous life,
At length to lay my head and hallowed pledge
Of all my strength in the lascivious lap
Of a deceitful concubine, who shore me,
Like a tame wether, all my precious fleece,
Then turned me out ridiculous, despoiled,
Shaven, and disarmed among my enemies.

CHORUS. Desire of wine and all delicious drinks,
Which many a famous warrior overturns,
Thou could'st repress; nor did the dancing ruby,
Sparkling out-poured, the flavour or the smell,
Or taste, that cheers the heart of gods and men,
Allure thee from the cool crystalline stream.

SAMSON. Wherever fountain or fresh current flowed
Against the eastern ray, translucent, pure
With touch ethereal of Heaven's fiery rod,
I drank, from the clear milky juice allaying
Thirst, and refreshed; nor envied them the grape
Whose heads that turbulent liquor fills with fumes.

CHORUS. O madness! to think use of strongest wines
And strongest drinks our chief support of health,
When God with these forbidden made choice to rear
His mighty champion, strong above compare,
Whose drink was only from the liquid brook!

SAMSON. But what availed this temperance, not complete

Against another object more enticing?
What boots it at one gate to make defence,
And at another to let in the foe,
Effeminately vanquished? by which means,
Now blind, disheartened, shamed, dishonoured, quelled,
To what can I be useful? wherein serve
My nation, and the work from Heaven imposed?
But to sit idle on the household hearth,
A burdenous drone; to visitants a gaze,
Or pitied object; these redundant locks,
Robustious to no purpose, clustering down,
Vain monument of strength; till length of years
And sedentary numbness craze my limbs
To a contemptible old age obscure.
Here rather let me drudge, and earn my bread,
Till vermin, or the draff of servile food,
Consume me, and oft-invocated death
Hasten the welcome end of all my pains.

MANOA. Wilt thou then serve the Philistines with that gift
Which was expressly given thee to annoy them?
Better at home lie bed-rid, not only idle,
Inglorious, unemployed, with age outworn.
But God, who caused a fountain at thy prayer
From the dry ground to spring, thy thirst to allay
After the brunt of battle, can as easy
Cause light again within thy eyes to spring,
Wherewith to serve him better than thou hast.
And I persuade me so. Why else this strength
Miraculous yet remaining in those locks?
His might continues in thee not for naught,
Nor shall his wondrous gifts be frustrate thus.

SAMSON. All otherwise to me my thoughts portend,—
That these dark orbs no more shall treat with light,
Nor th' other light of life continue long,
But yield to double darkness nigh at hand;
So much I feel my genial spirits droop,
My hopes all flat: Nature within me seems

In all her functions weary of herself;
My race of glory run, and race of shame,
And I shall shortly be with them that rest.

MANOA. Believe not these suggestions, which proceed
From anguish of the mind, and humours black
That mingle with thy fancy. I, however,
Must not omit a father's timely care
To prosecute the means of thy deliverance
By ransom or how else: meanwhile be calm,
And healing words from these thy friends admit.

SAMSON. Oh, that torment should not be confined
To the body's wounds and sores,
With maladies innumerable
In heart, head, breast, and reins,
But must secret passage find
To th' inmost mind,
There exercise all his fierce accidents,
And on her purest spirits prey,
As on entrails, joints, and limbs,
With answerable pains, but more intense,
Though void of corporal sense!

My griefs not only pain me
As a lingering disease,
But, finding no redress, ferment and rage;
Nor less than wounds immedicable
Rankle, and fester, and gangrene,
To black mortification,
Thoughts, my tormentors, armed with daily stings,
Mangle my apprehensive tenderest parts,
Exasperate, exulcerate, and raise
Dire inflammation, which no cooling herb
Or med'cinal liquor can assuage,
Nor breath of vernal air from snowy Alp.
Sleep hath forsook and given me o'er
To death's benumbing opium as my only cure;
Thence faintings, swoonings of despair,
And sense of Heaven's desertion.

I was his nursling once and choice delight,
His destined from the womb,
Promised by heavenly message twice descending.
Under his special eye
Abstemious I grew up and thrived amain;
He led me on to mightiest deeds,
Above the nerve of mortal arm,
Against the uncircumcised, our enemies:
But now hath cast me off as never known,
And to those cruel enemies,
Whom I by his appointment had provoked,
Left me, all helpless with th' irreparable loss
Of sight, reserved alive to be repeated
The subject of their cruelty or scorn.
Nor am I in the list of them that hope;
Hopeless are all my evils, all remediless.
This one prayer yet remains, might I be heard,
No long petition—speedy death,
The close of all my miseries and the balm.
CHORUS. Many are the sayings of the wise,
In ancient and in modern books enrolled,
Extolling patience as the truest fortitude,
And to the bearing well of all calamities,
All chances incident to man's frail life,
Consolatories writ
With studied argument, and much persuasion sought,
Lenient of grief and anxious thought.
But with th' afflicted in his pangs their sound
Little prevails, or rather seems a tune
Harsh, and of dissonant mood from his complaint,
Unless he feel within
Some source of consolation from above,
Secret refreshings that repair his strength
And fainting spirits uphold.
God of our fathers! what is Man,
That thou towards him with hand so various—
Or might I say contrarious?—

Temper'st thy providence through his short course:
Not evenly, as thou rul'st
The angelic orders, and inferior creatures mute,
Irrational and brute?
Nor do I name of men the common rout,
That, wandering loose about,
Grow up and perish as the summer fly,
Heads without name, no more remembered;
But such as thou hast solemnly elected,
With gifts and graces eminently adorned,
To some great work, thy glory,
And people's safety, which in part they effect.
Yet toward these, thus dignified, thou oft,
Amidst their height of noon,
Changest thy countenance and thy hand, with no regard
Of highest favours past
From thee on them, or them to thee of service.
  Nor only dost degrade them, or remit
To life obscured, which were a fair dismission,
But throw'st them lower than thou didst exalt them high—
Unseemly falls in human eye,
Too grievous for the trespass or omission;
Oft leav'st them to the hostile sword
Of heathen and profane, their carcases
To dogs and fowls a prey, or else captívect,
Or to the unjust tribunals, under change of times,
And condemnation of the ingrateful multitude.
If these they scape, perhaps in poverty
With sickness and disease thou bow'st them down,
Painful diseases and deformed,
In crude old age;
Though not disordinate, yet causeless suffering
The punishment of dissolute days. In fine,
Just or unjust alike seem miserable,
For oft alike both come to evil end.
  So deal not with this once thy glorious champion,
The image of thy strength, and mighty minister.

What do I beg? how hast thou dealt already!
Behold him in this state calamitous, and turn
His labours, for thou canst, to peaceful end.
  But who is this? what thing of sea or land—
Female of sex it seems—
That, so bedecked, ornate, and gay,
Comes this way sailing,
Like a stately ship
Of Tarsus, bound for th' isles
Of Javan or Gadire,
With all her bravery on, and tackle trim,
Sails filled, and streamers waving,
Courted by all the winds that hold them play;
An amber scent of odorous perfume
Her harbinger, a damsel train behind?
Some rich Philistian matron she may seem;
And now, at nearer view, no other certain
Than Dalila thy wife.
  SAMSON. My wife! my traitress! let her not come near me.
  CHORUS. Yet on she moves; now stands and eyes thee fixed,
About t' have spoke; but now, with head declined,
Like a fair flower surcharged with dew, she weeps,
And words addressed seem into tears dissolved,
Wetting the borders of her silken veil.
But now again she makes address to speak.
  DALILA. With doubtful feet and wavering resolution
I came, still dreading thy displeasure, Samson;
Which to have merited, without excuse,
I cannot but acknowledge. Yet, if tears
May expiate (though the fact more evil drew
In the perverse event than I foresaw),
My penance hath not slackened, though my pardon
No way assured. But conjugal affection,
Prevailing over fear and timorous doubt,
Hath led me on, desirous to behold
Once more thy face, and know of thy estate,
If aught in my ability may serve

To lighten what thou suffer'st, and appease
Thy mind with what amends is in my power—
Though late, yet in some part to recompense
My rash but more unfortunate misdeed.
SAMSON. Out, out, hyaena! These are thy wonted arts,
And arts of every woman false like thee—
To break all faith, all vows, deceive, betray;
Then, as repentant, to submit, beseech,
And reconcilement move with feigned remorse,
Confess, and promise wonders in her change—
Not truly penitent, but chief to try
Her husband, how far urged his patience bears,
His virtue or weakness which way to assail:
Then, with more cautious and instructed skill,
Again transgresses, and again submits;
That wisest and best men, full oft beguiled,
With goodness principled not to reject
The penitent, but ever to forgive,
Are drawn to wear out miserable days,
Entangled with a poisonous bosom-snake,
If not by quick destruction soon cut off,
As I by thee, to ages an example.
DALILA. Yet hear me, Samson, not that I endeavour
To lessen or extenuate my offence,
But that, on th' other side, if it be weighed
By itself, with aggravations not surcharged,
Or else with just allowance counterpoised,
I may, if possible, thy pardon find
The easier towards me, or thy hatred less.
First granting, as I do, it was a weakness
In me, but incident to all our sex,
Curiosity, inquisitive, importune
Of secrets, then with like infirmity
To publish them—both common female faults—
Was it not weakness also to make known,
For importunity, that is for naught,
Wherein consisted all thy strength and safety?

To what I did thou show'dst me first the way.
But I to enemies revealed, and should not!
Nor should'st thou have trusted that to woman's frailty:
Ere I to thee, thou to thyself wast cruel.
Let weakness, then, with weakness come to parle,
So near related, or the same of kind;
Thine forgive mine, that men may censure thine
The gentler, if severely thou exact not
More strength from me than in thyself was found.
And what if love, which thou interpret'st hate,
The jealousy of love, powerful of sway
In human hearts, nor less in mine towards thee,
Caused what I did? I saw thee mutable
Of fancy; feared lest one day thou would'st leave me,
As her at Timna; sought by all means, therefore,
How to endear, and hold thee to me firmest:
No better way I saw than by importuning
To learn thy secrets, get into my power
Thy key of strength and safety. Thou wilt say,
"Why, then, revealed?" I was assured by those
Who tempted me that nothing was designed
Against thee but safe custody and hold.
That made for me; I knew that liberty
Would draw thee forth to perilous enterprises,
While I at home sat full of cares and fears,
Wailing thy absence in my widowed bed;
Here I should still enjoy thee, day and night,
Mine and love's prisoner, not the Philistines',
Whole to myself, unhazarded abroad,
Fearless at home of partners in my love.
These reasons in love's law have passed for good,
Though fond and reasonless to some perhaps;
And love hath oft, well meaning, wrought much woe,
Yet always pity or pardon hath obtained.
Be not unlike all others, not austere
As thou art strong, inflexible as steel.
If thou in strength all mortals dost exceed.

In uncompassionate anger do not so.
SAMSON. How cunningly the sorceress displays
Her own transgressions, to upbraid me mine!
That malice, not repentance, brought thee hither,
By this appears. I gave, thou say'st, th' example,
I led the way—bitter reproach, but true;
I to myself was false ere thou to me.
Such pardon, therefore, as I give my folly
Take to thy wicked deed; which when thou seest
Impartial, self-severe, inexorable,
Thou wilt renounce thy seeking, and much rather
Confess it feigned. Weakness is thy excuse,
And I believe it—weakness to resist
Philistian gold. If weakness may excuse,
What murderer, what traitor, parricide,
Incestuous, sacrilegious, but may plead it?
All wickedness is weakness; that plea, therefore,
With God or man will gain thee no remission.
But love constrained thee! Call it furious rage
To satisfy thy lust. Love seeks to have love;
My love how could'st thou hope, who took'st the way
To raise in me inexpiable hate,
Knowing, as needs I must, by thee betrayed?
In vain thou striv'st to cover shame with shame,
Or by evasions thy crime uncover'st more.
DALILA. Since thou determin'st weakness for no plea
In man or woman, though to thy own condemning,
Hear what assaults I had, what snares besides,
What sieges girt me round, ere I consented;
Which might have awed the best-resolved of men,
The constantest, to have yielded without blame.
It was not gold, as to my charge thou lay'st,
That wrought with me. Thou know'st the magistrates
And princes of my country came in person,
Solicited, commanded, threatened, urged,
Adjured by all the bonds of civil duty
And of religion—pressed how just it was,

How honourable, how glorious, to entrap
A common enemy, who had destroyed
Such numbers of our nation: and the priest
Was not behind, but ever at my ear,
Preaching how meritorious with the gods
It would be to ensnare an irreligious
Dishonourer of Dagon. What had I
To oppose against such powerful arguments?
Only my love of thee held long debate,
And combated in silence all these reasons
With hard contest. At length, that grounded maxim,
So rife and celebrated in the mouths
Of wisest men, that to the public good
Private respects must yield, with grave authority
Took full possession of me, and prevailed;
Virtue, as I thought, truth, duty, so enjoining.
SAMSON. I thought where all thy circling wiles would end—
In feigned religion, smooth hypocrisy!
But, had thy love, still odiously pretended,
Been, as it ought, sincere, it would have taught thee
Far other reasonings, brought forth other deeds.
I, before all the daughters of my tribe
And of my nation, chose thee from among
My enemies, loved thee, as too well thou knew'st;
Too well; unbosomed all my secrets to thee,
Not out of levity, but overpowered
By thy request, who could deny thee nothing;
Yet now am judged an enemy. Why, then,
Didst thou at first receive me for thy husband—
Then, as since then, thy country's foe professed?
Being once a wife, for me thou wast to leave
Parents and country; nor was I their subject,
Nor under their protection, but my own;
Thou mine, not theirs. If aught against my life
Thy country sought of thee, it sought unjustly,
Against the law of nature, law of nations;
No more thy country, but an impious crew

Of men conspiring to uphold their state
By worse than hostile deeds, violating the ends
For which our country is a name so dear;
Not therefore to be obeyed. But zeal moved thee;
To please thy gods thou didst it! Gods unable
To acquit themselves and prosecute their foes
But by ungodly deeds, the contradiction
Of their own deity, gods cannot be—
Less therefore to be pleased, obeyed, or feared.
These false pretexts and varnished colours failing,
Bare in thy guilt, how foul must thou appear!

DALILA. In argument with men a woman ever
Goes by the worse, whatever be her cause.

SAMSON. For want of words, no doubt, or lack of breath!
Witness when I was worried with thy peals.

DALILA. I was a fool, too rash, and quite mistaken
In what I thought would have succeeded best.
Let me obtain forgiveness of thee, Samson;
Afford me place to show what recompense
Towards thee I intend for what I have misdone,
Misguided. Only what remains past cure
Bear not too sensibly, nor still insist
To afflict thyself in vain. Though sight be lost,
Life yet hath many solaces, enjoyed
Where other senses want not their delights—
At home, in leisure and domestic ease,
Exempt from many a care and chance to which
Eyesight exposes, daily, men abroad.
I to the lords will intercede, not doubting
Their favourable ear, that I may fetch thee
From forth this loathsome prison-house, to abide
With me, where my redoubled love and care,
With nursing diligence, to me glad office,
May ever tend about thee to old age,
With all things grateful cheered, and so supplied
That what by me thou hast lost thou least shalt miss.

SAMSON. No, no; of my condition take no care;

It fits not; thou and I long since are twain;
Nor think me so unwary or accursed
To bring my feet again into the snare
Where once I have been caught. I know thy trains,
Though dearly to my cost, thy gins, and toils.
Thy fair enchanted cup, and warbling charms,
No more on me have power; their force is nulled;
So much of adder's wisdom I have learned,
To fence my ear against thy sorceries.
If in my flower of youth and strength, when all men
Loved, honoured, feared me, thou alone could hate me,
Thy husband, slight me, sell me, and forgo me,
How would'st thou use me now, blind, and thereby
Deceivable, in most things as a child
Helpless, thence easily contemned and scorned,
And last neglected! How would'st thou insult,
When I must live uxorious to thy will
In perfect thraldom! how again betray me,
Bearing my words and doings to the lords
To gloss upon, and, censuring, frown or smile!
This jail I count the house of liberty
To thine, whose doors my feet shall never enter.

DALILA. Let me approach at least, and touch thy hand.

SAMSON. Not for thy life, lest fierce remembrance wake
My sudden rage to tear thee joint by joint.
At distance I forgive thee, go with that;
Bewail thy falsehood, and the pious works
It hath brought forth to make thee memorable
Among illustrious women, faithful wives;
Cherish thy hastened widowhood with the gold
Of matrimonial treason: so farewell.

DALILA. I see thou art implacable, more deaf
To prayers than winds and seas. Yet winds to seas
Are reconciled at length, and sea to shore:
Thy anger, unappeasable, still rages,
Eternal tempest never to be calmed.
Why do I humble thus myself, and, suing

For peace, reap nothing but repulse and hate,
Bid go with evil omen, and the brand
Of infamy upon my name denounced?
To mix with thy concernments I desist
Henceforth, nor too much disapprove my own.
Fame, if not double-faced, is double-mouthed,
And with contrary blast proclaims most deeds;
On both his wings, one black, th' other white,
Bears greatest names in his wild airy flight.
My name, perhaps, among the circumcised
In Dan, in Judah, and the bordering tribes,
To all posterity may stand defamed,
With malediction mentioned, and the blot
Of falsehood most unconjugal traduced.
But in my country, where I most desire,
In Ecron, Gaza, Asdod, and in Gath,
I shall be named among the famousest
Of women, sung at solemn festivals,
Living and dead recorded, who to save
Her country from a fierce destroyer chose
Above the faith of wedlock bands; my tomb
With odours visited and annual flowers;
Not less renowned than in Mount Ephraim
Jael, who, with inhospitable guile,
Smote Sisera sleeping, through the temples nailed.
Nor shall I count it heinous to enjoy
The public marks of honour and reward
Conferred upon me for the piety
Which to my country I was judged to have shown.
At this whoever envies or repines,
I leave him to his lot, and like my own.
CHORUS. She's gone—a manifest serpent by her sting
Discovered in the end, till now concealed.
SAMSON. So let her go. God sent her to debase me,
And aggravate my folly, who committed
To such a viper his most sacred trust
Of secrecy, my safety, and my life.

CHORUS. Yet beauty, though injurious, hath strange power,
After offence returning, to regain
Love once possessed, nor can be easily
Repulsed, without much inward passion felt,
And secret sting of amorous remorse.
SAMSON. Love-quarrels oft in pleasing concord end;
Not wedlock-treachery, endangering life.
CHORUS. It is not virtue, wisdom, valour, wit,
Strength, comeliness of shape, or amplest merit.
That woman's love can win, or long inherit;
But what it is hard is to say,
Harder to hit,
Which way soever men refer it
(Much like thy riddle, Samson), in one day
Or seven though one should musing sit.
If any of these, or all, the Timnian bride
Had not so soon preferred
Thy paranymph, worthless to thee compared,
Successor in thy bed,
Nor both so loosely disallied
Their nuptials, nor this last so treacherously
Had shorn the fatal harvest of thy head.
Is it for that such outward ornament
Was lavished on their sex, that inward gifts
Were left for haste unfinished, judgment scant,
Capacity not raised to apprehend
Or value what is best
In choice, but oftest to affect the wrong?
Or was too much of self-love mixed,
Of constancy no root infixed,
That either they love nothing, or not long?
Whate'er it be, to wisest men and best,
Seeming at first all heavenly under virgin veil,
Soft, modest, meek, demure,
Once joined, the contrary she proves—a thorn
Intestine, far within defensive arms
A cleaving mischief, in his way to virtue

Adverse and turbulent; or by her charms
Draws him awry, enslaved
With dotage, and his sense depraved
To folly and shameful deeds, which ruin ends.
What pilot so expert but needs must wreck,
Embarked with such a steers-mate at the helm?
  Favoured of Heaven who finds
One virtuous, rarely found,
That in domestic good combines:
Happy that house! his way to peace is smooth:
But virtue which breaks through all opposition,
And all temptation can remove,
Most shines and most is acceptable above.
  Therefore God's universal law
Gave to the man despotic power
Over his female in due awe,
Nor from that right to part an hour,
Smile she or lour:
So shall he least confusion draw
On his whole life, not swayed
By female usurpation, nor dismayed.
  But had we best retire? I see a storm.
  SAMSON. Fair days have oft contracted wind and rain.
  CHORUS. But this another kind of tempest brings.
  SAMSON. Be less abstruse; my riddling days are past.
  CHORUS. Look now for no enchanting voice, nor fear
The bait of honeyed words; a rougher tongue
Draws hitherward; I know him by his stride,
The giant Harapha of Gath, his look
Haughty, as is his pile high-built and proud.
Comes he in peace? What wind hath blown him hither
I less conjecture than when first I saw
The sumptuous Dalila floating this way:
His habit carries peace, his brow defiance.
  SAMSON. Or peace or not, alike to me he comes.
  CHORUS. His fraught we soon shall know: he now arrives.
  HARAPHA. I come not, Samson, to condole thy chance,

As these perhaps, yet wish it had not been,
Though for no friendly intent. I am of Gath;
Men call me Harapha, of stock renowned
As Og, or Anak, and the Emims old
That Kiriathaim held. Thou know'st me now,
If thou at all art known. Much I have heard
Of thy prodigious might and feats performed,
Incredible to me, in this displeased,—
That I was never present on the place
Of those encounters, where we might have tried
Each other's force in camp or listed field;
And now am come to see of whom such noise
Hath walked about, and each limb to survey,
If thy appearance answer loud report.
SAMSON. The way to know were not to see, but taste.
HARAPHA. Dost thou already single me? I thought
Gyves and the mill had tamed thee. O that fortune
Had brought me to the field where thou art famed
To have wrought such wonders with an ass's jaw!
I should have forced thee soon with other arms,
Or left thy carcase where the ass lay thrown;
So had the glory of prowess been recovered
To Palestine, won by a Philistine
From the unforeskinned race, of whom thou bear'st
The highest name for valiant acts. That honour,
Certain to have won by mortal duel from thee,
I lose, prevented by thy eyes put out.
SAMSON. Boast not of what thou would'st have done, but do
What then thou would'st; thou seest it in thy hand.
HARAPHA. To combat with a blind man I disdain,
And thou hast need much washing to be touched.
SAMSON. Such usage as your honourable lords
Afford me, assassinated and betrayed;
Who durst not with their whole united powers
In fight withstand me single and unarmed,
Nor in the house with chamber ambushes
Close-banded durst attack me, no, not sleeping,

Till they had hired a woman with their gold,
Breaking her marriage-faith, to circumvent me.
Therefore, without feign'd shifts, let be assigned
Some narrow place enclosed, where sight may give thee,
Or rather flight, no great advantage on me;
Then put on all thy gorgeous arms, thy helmet
And brigandine of brass, thy broad habergeon,
Vant-brace and greaves and gauntlet; add thy spear,
A weaver's beam, and seven-times-folded shield:
I only with an oaken staff will meet thee,
And raise such outcries on thy clattered iron,
Which long shall not withhold me from thy head,
That in a little time, while breath remains thee,
Thou oft shalt wish thyself at Gath, to boast
Again in safety what thou would'st have done
To Samson, but shalt never see Gath more.

HARAPHA. Thou durst not thus disparage glorious arms,
Which greatest heroes have in battle worn,
Their ornament and safety, had not spells
And black enchantments, some magician's art,
Armed thee or charmed thee strong, which thou from Heaven
Feign'dst at thy birth was given thee in thy hair,
Where strength can least abide, though all thy hairs
Were bristles ranged like those that ridge the back
Of chafed wild boars or ruffled porcupines.

SAMSON. I know no spells, use no forbidden arts;
My trust is in the Living God, who gave me,
At my nativity, this strength, diffused
No less through all my sinews, joints, and bones,
Than thine, while I preserved these locks unshorn,
The pledge of my unviolated vow.
For proof hereof, if Dagon be thy god,
Go to his temple, invocate his aid
With solemnest devotion, spread before him
How highly it concerns his glory now
To frustrate and dissolve these magic spells,
Which I to be the power of Israel's God

Avow, and challenge Dagon to the test,
Offering to combat thee, his champion bold,
With th' utmost of his godhead seconded:
Then thou shalt see, or rather to thy sorrow
Soon feel, whose God is strongest, thine or mine.
HARAPHA. Presume not on thy God. Whate'er he be,
Thee he regards not, owns not, hath cut off
Quite from his people, and delivered up
Into thy enemies' hand; permitted them
To put out both thine eyes, and fettered send thee
Into the common prison, there to grind
Among the slaves and asses, thy comrádes,
As good for nothing else, no better service
With those thy boisterous locks; no worthy match
For valour to assail, nor by the sword
Of noble warrior, so to stain his honour,
But by the barber's razor best subdued.
SAMSON. All these indignities, for such they are
From thine, these evils I deserve and more,
Acknowledge them from God inflicted on me
Justly, yet despair not of his final pardon,
Whose ear is ever open, and his eye
Gracious to re-admit the suppliant;
In confidence whereof I once again
Defy thee to the trial of mortal fight,
By combat to decide whose god is God,
Thine, or whom I with Israel's sons adore.
HARAPHA. Fair honour that thou dost thy God, in trusting
He will accept thee to defend his cause,
A murderer, a revolter, and a robber!
SAMSON. Tongue-doughty giant, how dost thou prove me these?
HARAPHA. Is not thy nation subject to our lords?
Their magistrates confessed it when they took thee
As a league-breaker, and delivered bound
Into our hands; for hadst not committed
Notorious murder on those thirty men
At Ascalon, who never did thee harm,

Then, like a robber, stripp'dst them of their robes?
The Philistines, when thou hadst broke the league,
Went up with armèd powers thee only seeking,
To others did no violence nor spoil.

SAMSON. Among the daughters of the Philistines
I chose a wife, which argued me no foe,
And in your city held my nuptial feast;
But your ill-meaning politician lords,
Under pretence of bridal friends and guests,
Appointed to await me thirty spies,
Who, threatening cruel death, constrained the bride
To wring from me, and tell to them, my secret,
That solved the riddle which I had proposed.
When I perceived all set on enmity,
As on my enemies, wherever chanced,
I used hostility, and took their spoil,
To pay my underminers in their coin.
My nation was subjected to your lords!
It was the force of conquest; force with force
Is well ejected when the conquered can.
But I, a private person, whom my country
As a league-breaker gave up bound, presumed
Single rebellion, and did hostile acts!
I was no private, but a person raised,
With strength sufficient, and command from Heaven,
To free my country. If their servile minds
Me, their deliverer sent, would not receive,
But to their masters gave me up for nought,
Th' unworthier they; whence to this day they serve.
I was to do my part from Heaven assigned,
And had performed it if my known offence
Had not disabled me, not all your force.
These shifts refuted, answer thy appellant,
Though by his blindness maimed for high attempts,
Who now defies thee thrice to single fight,
As a petty enterprise of small enforce.

HARAPHA. With thee, a man condemned, a slave enrolled,

Due by the law to capital punishment!
To fight with thee no man of arms will deign.
SAMSON. Cam'st thou for this, vain boaster, to survey me,
To descant on my strength, and give thy verdict?
Come nearer; part not hence so slight informed;
But take good heed my hand survey not thee.
HARAPHA. O Baal-zebub! can my ears unused
Hear these dishonours, and not render death?
SAMSON. No man withholds thee; nothing from thy hand
Fear I incurable; bring up thy van;
My heels are fettered, but my fist is free.
HARAPHA. This insolence other kind of answer fits.
SAMSON. Go, baffled coward, lest I run upon thee,
Though in these chains, bulk without spirit vast,
And with one buffet lay thy structure low,
Or swing thee in the air, then dash thee down,
To the hazard of thy brains and shattered sides.
HARAPHA. By Astaroth, ere long thou shalt lament
These braveries, in irons loaden on thee.
CHORUS. His giantship is gone somewhat crestfallen,
Stalking with less unconscionable strides,
And lower looks, but in a sultry chafe.
SAMSON. I dread him not, nor all his giant brood,
Though fame divulge him father of five sons,
All of gigantic size, Goliah chief.
CHORUS. He will directly to the lords, I fear,
And with malicious counsel stir them up
Some way or other yet further to afflict thee.
SAMSON. He must allege some cause, and offered fight
Will not dare mention, lest a question rise
Whether he durst accept the offer or not;
And that he durst not plain enough appeared.
Much more affliction than already felt
They cannot well impose, nor I sustain,
If they intend advantage of my labours,
The work of many hands, which earns my keeping,
With no small profit daily to my owners.

But come what will; my deadliest foe will prove
My speediest friend, by death to rid me hence;
The worst that he can give to me the best.
Yet so it may fall out, because their end
Is hate, not help to me, it may with mine
Draw their own ruin who attempt the deed.

CHORUS. O, how comely it is, and how reviving
To the spirits of just men long oppressed,
When God into the hands of their deliverer
Puts invincible might,
To quell the mighty of the earth, th' oppressor,
The brute and boisterous force of violent men,
Hardy and industrious to support
Tyrannic power, but raging to pursue
The righteous, and all such as honour truth!
He all their ammunition
And feats of war defeats,
With plain heroic magnitude of mind
And celestial vigour armed;
Their armouries and magazines contemns,
Renders them useless, while
With wingèd expedition
Swift as the lightning glance he executes
His errand on the wicked, who, surprised,
Lose their defence, distracted and amazed.

But patience is more oft the exercise
Of saints, the trial of their fortitude,
Making them each his own deliverer,
And victor over all
That tyranny or fortune can inflict.
Either of these is in thy lot,
Samson, with might endued
Above the sons of men; but sight bereaved
May chance to number thee with those
Whom patience finally must crown.

This Idol's day hath been to thee no day of rest,
Labouring thy mind

More than the working day thy hands.
And yet, perhaps, more trouble is behind;
For I descry this way
Some other tending; in his hand
A sceptre or quaint staff he bears,—
Comes on amain, speed in his look.
By his habit I discern him now
A public officer, and now at hand.
His message will be short and voluble.
OFFICER. Ebrews, the prisoner Samson here I seek.
CHORUS. His manacles remark him; there he sits.
OFFICER. Samson, to thee our lords thus bid me say:
This day to Dagon is a solemn feast,
With sacrifices, triumph, pomp, and games;
Thy strength they know surpassing human rate,
And now some public proof thereof require
To honour this great feast, and great assembly.
Rise, therefore, with all speed, and come along,
Where I will see thee heartened and fresh clad,
To appear as fits before th' illustrious lords.
SAMSON. Thou know'st I am an Ebrew; therefore tell them
Our law forbids at their religious rites
My presence; for that cause I cannot come.
OFFICER. This answer, be assured, will not content them.
SAMSON. Have they not sword-players, and every sort
Of gymnic artists, wrestlers, riders, runners,
Jugglers and dancers, antics, mummers, mimics,
But they must pick me out, with shackles tired,
And over-laboured at their public mill,
To make them sport with blind activity?
Do they not seek occasion of new quarrels,
On my refusal, to distress me more,
Or make a game of my calamities?
Return the way thou cam'st; I will not come.
OFFICER. Regard thyself; this will offend them highly.
SAMSON. Myself? my conscience, and internal peace.
Can they think me so broken, so debased

With corporal servitude, that my mind ever
Will condescend to such absurd commands?
Although their drudge, to be their fool or jester,
And, in my midst of sorrow and heart-grief,
To show them feats, and play before their god—
The worst of all indignities, yet on me
Joined with supreme contempt! I will not come.
OFFICER. My message was imposed on me with speed,
Brooks no delay: is this thy resolution?
SAMSON. So take it with what speed thy message needs.
OFFICER. I am sorry what this stoutness will produce.
SAMSON. Perhaps thou shalt have cause to sorrow indeed.
CHORUS. Consider, Samson; matters now are strained
Up to the height, whether to hold or break.
He's gone, and who knows how he may report
Thy words by adding fuel to the flame?
Expect another message, more imperious,
More lordly thundering than thou well wilt bear.
SAMSON. Shall I abuse this consecrated gift
Of strength, again returning with my hair
After my great transgression—so requite
Favour renewed, and add a greater sin
By prostituting holy things to idols,
A Nazarite, in place abominable,
Vaunting my strength in honour to their Dagon?
Besides how vile, contemptible, ridiculous,
What act more execrably unclean, profane?
CHORUS. Yet with this strength thou serv'st the Philistines,
Idolatrous, uncircumcised, unclean.
SAMSON. Not in their idol-worship, but by labour
Honest and lawful to deserve my food
Of those who have me in their civil power.
CHORUS. Where the heart joins not, outward acts defile not
SAMSON. Where outward force constrains, the sentence holds:
But who constrains me to the temple of Dagon,
Not dragging? The Philistian lords command:
Commands are no constraints. If I obey them,

I do it freely, venturing to displease
God for the fear of man, and man prefer,
Set God behind; which, in his jealousy,
Shall never, unrepented, find forgiveness.
Yet that he may dispense with me, or thee,
Present in temples at idolatrous rites
For some important cause, thou need'st not doubt.
CHORUS. How thou wilt here come off surmounts my reach.
SAMSON. Be of good courage; I begin to feel
Some rousing motions in me, which dispose
To something extraordinary my thoughts.
I with this messenger will go along—
Nothing to do, be sure, that may dishonour
Our Law, or stain my vow of Nazarite.
If there be aught of presage in the mind,
This day will be remarkable in my life
By some great act, or of my days the last.
CHORUS. In time thou hast resolved: the man returns.
OFFICER. Samson, this second message from our lords
To thee I am bid say: Art thou our slave,
Our captive, at the public mill our drudge,
And dar'st thou, at our sending and command,
Dispute thy coming? Come without delay;
Or we shall find such engines to assail
And hamper thee, as thou shalt come of force,
Though thou wert firmlier fastened than a rock.
SAMSON. I could be well content to try their art,
Which to no few of them would prove pernicious;
Yet, knowing their advantages too many,
Because they shall not trail me through their streets
Like a wild beast, I am content to go.
Masters' commands come with a power resistless
To such as owe them absolute subjection;
And for a life who will not change his purpose?
(So mutable are all the ways of men!)
Yet this be sure, in nothing to comply
Scandalous or forbidden in our Law.

OFFICER. I praise thy resolution. Doff these links:
By this compliance thou wilt win the lords
To favour, and perhaps to set thee free.

SAMSON. Brethren, farewell. Your company along
I will not wish, lest it perhaps offend them
To see me girt with friends; and how the sight
Of me, as of a common enemy,
So dreaded once, may now exasperate them
I know not. Lords are lordliest in their wine;
And the well-feasted priest then soonest fired
With zeal, if aught religion seem concerned;
No less the people, on their holy-days,
Impetuous, insolent, unquenchable.
Happen what may, of me expect to hear
Nothing dishonourable, impure, unworthy
Our God, our Law, my nation, or myself;
The last of me or no I cannot warrant.

CHORUS. Go, and the Holy One
Of Israel be thy guide
To what may serve his glory best, and spread his name
Great among the heathen round;
Send thee the Angel of thy birth, to stand
Fast by thy side, who from thy father's field
Rode up in flames after his message told
Of thy conception, and be now a shield
Of fire; that Spirit that first rushed on thee
In the camp of Dan,
Be efficacious in thee now at need!
For never was from Heaven imparted
Measure of strength so great to mortal seed
As in thy wondrous actions hath been seen.
But wherefore comes old Manoa in such haste
With youthful steps? Much livelier than erewhile
He seems: supposing here to find his son,
Or of him bringing to us some glad news?

MANOA. Peace with you, brethren! My inducement hither
Was not at present here to find my son,

By order of the lords new parted hence
To come and play before them at their feast.
I heard all as I came; the city rings,
And numbers thither flock: I had no will,
Lest I should see him forced to things unseemly.
But that which moved my coming now was chiefly
To give ye part with me what hope I have
With good success to work his liberty.
  CHORUS. That hope would much rejoice us to partake
With thee. Say, reverend sire; we thirst to hear.
  MANOA. I have attempted, one by one, the lords,
Either at home, or through the high street passing,
With supplication prone and father's tears,
To accept of ransom for my son, their prisoner.
Some much averse I found, and wondrous harsh,
Contemptuous, proud, set on revenge and spite;
That part most reverenced Dagon and his priests:
Others more moderate seeming, but their aim
Private reward, for which both God and State
They easily would set to sale: a third
More generous far and civil, who confessed
They had enough revenged, having reduced
Their foe to misery beneath their fears;
The rest was magnanimity to remit,
If some convenient ransom were proposed.
What noise or shout was that? It tore the sky.
  CHORUS. Doubtless the people shouting to behold
Their once great dread, captive and blind before them,
Or at some proof of strength before them shown.
  MANOA. His ransom, if my whole inheritance
May compass it, shall willingly be paid
And numbered down. Much rather I shall choose
To live the poorest in my tribe, than richest
And he in that calamitous prison left.
No, I am fixed not to part hence without him.
For his redemption all my patrimony,
If need be, I am ready to forgo

And quit. Not wanting him, I shall want nothing.
CHORUS. Fathers are wont to lay up for their sons;
Thou for thy son art bent to lay out all:
Sons wont to nurse their parents in old age;
Thou in old age car'st how to nurse thy son,
Made older than thy age through eye-sight lost.
MANOA. It shall be my delight to tend his eyes,
And view him sitting in his house, ennobled
With all those high exploits by him achieved,
And on his shoulders waving down those locks
That of a nation armed the strength contained.
And I persuade me God hath not permitted
His strength again to grow up with his hair
Garrisoned round about him like a camp
Of faithful soldiery, were not his purpose
To use him further yet in some great service—
Not to sit idle with so great a gift
Useless, and thence ridiculous, about him.
And, since his strength with eye-sight was not lost,
God will restore him eye-sight to his strength.
CHORUS. Thy hopes are not ill founded, nor seem vain,
Of his delivery, and thy joy thereon
Conceived, agreeable to a father's love;
In both which we, as next, participate.
MANOA. I know your friendly minds, and—O, what noise!
Mercy of Heaven! what hideous noise was that?
Horribly loud, unlike the former shout.
CHORUS. Noise call you it, or universal groan,
As if the whole inhabitation perished?
Blood, death, and deathful deeds, are in that noise,
Ruin, destruction at the utmost point.
MANOA. Of ruin indeed methought I heard the noise.
Oh! it continues; they have slain my son.
CHORUS. Thy son is rather slaying them; that outcry
From slaughter of one foe could not ascend.
MANOA. Some dismal accident it needs must be.
What shall we do—stay here, or run and see?

CHORUS. Best keep together here, lest, running thither,
We unawares run into danger's mouth.
This evil on the Philistines is fallen:
From whom could else a general cry be heard?
The sufferers then will scarce molest us here;
From other hands we need not much to fear.
What if, his eye-sight (for to Israel's God
Nothing is hard) by miracle restored,
He now be dealing dole among his foes,
And over heaps of slaughtered walk his way?
MANOA. That were a joy presumptuous to be thought.
CHORUS. Yet God hath wrought things as incredible
For his people of old; what hinders now?
MANOA. He can, I know, but doubt to think he will;
Yet hope would fain subscribe, and tempts belief.
A little stay will bring some notice hither.
CHORUS. Of good or bad so great, of bad the sooner;
For evil news rides post, while good news baits.
And to our wish I see one hither speeding—
An Ebrew, as I guess, and of our tribe.
MESSENGER. O, whither shall I run, or which way fly
The sight of this so horrid spectacle,
Which erst my eyes beheld, and yet behold?
For dire imagination still pursues me.
But providence or instinct of nature seems,
Or reason, though disturbed, and scarce consulted,
To have guided me aright, I know not how,
To thee first, reverend Manoa, and to these
My countrymen, whom here I knew remaining,
As at some distance from the place of horror,
So in the sad event too much concerned.
MANOA. The accident was loud, and here before thee
With rueful cry; yet what it was we hear not.
No preface needs; thou seest we long to know.
MESSENGER. It would burst forth; but I recover breath,
And sense distract, to know well what I utter.
MANOA. Tell us the sum; the circumstance defer.

MESSENGER. Gaza yet stands; but all her sons are fallen,
All in a moment overwhelmed and fallen.
MANOA. Sad! but thou know'st to Israelites not saddest
The desolation of a hostile city.
MESSENGER. Feed on that first; there may in grief be surfeit.
MANOA. Relate by whom.
MESSENGER. By Samson.
MANOA. That still lessens
The sorrow, and coverts it nigh to joy.
MESSENGER. Ah! Manoa, I refrain too suddenly
To utter what will come at last too soon,
Lest evil tidings, with too rude irruption
Hitting thy agèd ear, should pierce too deep.
MANOA. Suspense in news is torture; speak them out.
MESSENGER. Then take the worst in brief: Samson is dead.
MANOA. The worst indeed! O, all my hopes defeated
To free him hence! but Death, who sets all free,
Hath paid his ransom now and full discharge.
What windy joy this day had I conceived,
Hopeful of his delivery, which now proves
Abortive as the first-born bloom of spring
Nipt with the lagging rear of winter's frost!
Yet, ere I give the reins to grief, say first
How died he; death to life is crown or shame.
All by him fell, thou say'st; by whom fell he?
What glorious hand gave Samson his death's wound?
MESSENGER. Unwounded of his enemies he fell.
MANOA. Wearied with slaughter, then, or how? explain.
MESSENGER. By his own hands.
MANOA. Self-violence! What cause
Brought him so soon at variance with himself
Among his foes?
MESSENGER. Inevitable cause—
At once both to destroy and be destroyed.
The edifice, where all were met to see him,
Upon their heads and on his own he pulled.
MANOA. O lastly over-strong against thyself!

A dreadful way thou took'st to thy revenge.
More than enough we know; but, while things yet
Are in confusion, give us, if thou canst,
Eye-witness of what first or last was done,
Relation more particular and distinct.
MESSENGER. Occasions drew me early to this city;
And, as the gates I entered with sun-rise,
The morning trumpets festival proclaimed
Through each high street. Little I had dispatched,
When all abroad was rumoured that this day
Samson should be brought forth, to show the people
Proof of his mighty strength in feats and games.
I sorrowed at his captive state, but minded
Not to be absent at that spectacle.
The building was a spacious theatre,
Half round on two main pillars vaulted high,
With seats where all the lords, and each degree
Of sort, might sit in order to behold;
The other side was open, where the throng
On banks and scaffolds under sky might stand:
I among these aloof obscurely stood.
The feast and noon grew high, and sacrifice
Had filled their hearts with mirth, high cheer, and wine,
When to their sports they turned. Immediately
Was Samson as a public servant brought,
In their state livery clad: before him pipes
And timbrels; on each side went armèd guards;
Both horse and foot before him and behind,
Archers and slingers, cataphracts and spears.
At sight of him the people with a shout
Rifted the air, clamouring their god with praise,
Who had made their dreadful enemy their thrall.
He patient, but undaunted, where they led him,
Came to the place; and what was set before him,
Which without help of eye might be assayed,
To heave, pull, draw, or break, he still performed
All with incredible, stupendous force,

None daring to appear antagonist.
At length, for intermission sake, they led him
Between the pillars; he his guide requested
(For so from such as nearer stood we heard),
As over-tired, to let him lean a while
With both his arms on those two massy pillars,
That to the archèd roof gave main support.
He unsuspicious led him; which when Samson
Felt in his arms, with head a while inclined,
And eyes fast fixed, he stood, as one who prayed,
Or some great matter in his mind revolved:
At last, with head erect, thus cried aloud:—
"Hitherto, Lords, what your commands imposed
I have performed, as reason was, obeying,
Not without wonder or delight beheld;
Now, of my own accord, such other trial
I mean to show you of my strength yet greater
As with amaze shall strike all who behold."
This uttered, straining all his nerves, he bowed;
As with the force of winds and waters pent
When mountains tremble, those two massy pillars
With horrible convulsion to and fro
He tugged, he shook, till down they came, and drew
The whole roof after them with burst of thunder
Upon the heads of all who sat beneath,
Lords, ladies, captains, counsellors, or priests,
Their choice nobility and flower, not only
Of this, but each Philistian city round,
Met from all parts to solemnize this feast.
Samson, with these immixed, inevitably
Pulled down the same destruction on himself;
The vulgar only scaped, who stood without.

CHORUS. O dearly bought revenge, yet glorious!
Living or dying thou hast fulfilled
The work for which thou wast foretold
To Israel, and now li'st victorious
Among thy slain self-killed;

Not willingly, but tangled in the fold
Of dire Necessity, whose law in death conjoined
Thee with thy slaughtered foes, in number more
Than all thy life had slain before.
SEMICHORUS. While their hearts were jocund and sublime,
Drunk with idolatry, drunk with wine
And fat regorged of bulls and goats,
Chaunting their idol, and preferring
Before our living Dread, who dwells
In Silo, his bright sanctuary,
Among them he a spirit of frenzy sent,
Who hurt their minds,
And urged them on with mad desire
To call in haste for their destroyer.
They, only set on sport and play,
Unweetingly importuned
Their own destruction to come speedy upon them.
So fond are mortal men,
Fallen into wrath divine,
As their own ruin on themselves to invite,
Insensate left, or to sense reprobate,
And with blindness internal struck.
SEMICHORUS. But he, though blind of sight,
Despised, and thought extinguished quite,
With inward eyes illuminated,
His fiery virtue roused
From under ashes into sudden flame,
And as an evening dragon came,
Assailant on the perchèd roosts
And nests in order ranged
Of tame villatic fowl, but as an eagle
His cloudless thunder bolted on their heads.
So Virtue, given for lost,
Depressed and overthrown, as seemed,
Like that self-begotten bird,
In the Arabian woods embossed,
That no second knows nor third,

And lay erewhile a holocaust,
From out her ashy womb now teemed,
Revives, reflourishes, then vigorous most
When most unactive deemed;
And, though her body die, her fame survives,
A secular bird, ages of lives.

MANOA. Come, come; no time for lamentation now,
Nor much more cause. Samson hath quit himself
Like Samson, and heroicly hath finished
A life heroic, on his enemies
Fully revenged—hath left them years of mourning
And lamentation to the sons of Caphtor
Through all Philistian bounds; to Israel
Honour hath left and freedom, let but them
Find courage to lay hold on this occasion;
To himself and father's house eternal fame;
And, which is best and happiest yet, all this
With God not parted from him, as was feared,
But favouring and assisting to the end.
Nothing is here for tears, nothing to wail
Or knock the breast; no weakness, no contempt,
Dispraise, or blame; nothing but well and fair,
And what may quiet us in a death so noble.
Let us go find the body where it lies
Soaked in his enemies' blood, and from the stream
With lavers pure, and cleansing herbs, wash off
The clotted gore. I, with what speed the while
(Gaza is not in plight to say us nay),
Will send for all my kindred, all my friends,
To fetch him hence, and solemnly attend,
With silent obsequy and funeral train,
Home to his father's house. There will I build him
A monument, and plant it round with shade
Of laurel ever green and branching palm,
With all his trophies hung, and acts enrolled
In copious legend, or sweet lyric song.
Thither shall all the valiant youth resort,

And from his memory inflame their breasts
To matchless valour and adventures high;
The virgins also shall, on feastful days,
Visit his tomb with flowers, only bewailing
His lot unfortunate in nuptial choice,
From whence captivity and loss of eyes.
CHORUS. All is best, though we oft doubt
What th' unsearchable dispose
Of Highest Wisdom brings about,
And ever best found in the close.
Oft he seems to hide his face,
But unexpectedly returns,
And to his faithful champion hath in place
Bore witness gloriously; whence Gaza mourns,
And all that band them to resist
His uncontrollable intent.
His servants he, with new acquist
Of true experience from this great event,
With peace and consolation hath dismissed,
And calm of mind, all passion spent.

SELECTED PROSE

THE REASON OF CHURCH GOVERNMENT *URGED AGAINST* PRELATY

(INTRODUCTION TO BOOK II)

How happy were it for this frail, and as it may be truly called mortal life of man, since all earthly things, which have the name of good and convenient in our daily use, are withal so cumbersome and full of trouble, if knowledge, yet which is the best and lightsomest possession of the mind, were, as the common saying is, no burden; and that what it wanted of being a load to any part of the body, it did not with a heavy advantage overlay upon the spirit! For not to speak of that knowledge that rests in the contemplation of natural causes and dimensions, which must needs be a lower wisdom, as the object is low, certain it is that he who hath obtained in more than the scantiest measure to know anything distinctly of God, and of his true worship; and what is infallibly good and happy in the state of man's life, what in itself evil and miserable, though vulgarly not so esteemed; he that hath obtained to know this, the only high valuable wisdom indeed, remembering also that God, even to a strictness, requires the improvement of these his entrusted gifts, cannot but sustain a sorer burden of mind, and more pressing, than any supportable toil or weight which the body can labour under; how and in what manner he shall dispose and employ those sums of knowledge and illumination, which God hath sent him into this world to trade with.

And that which aggravates the burden more is, that, having received amongst his allotted parcels certain precious truths, of such an orient lustre as no diamond can equal, which nevertheless he has in charge to put off at any cheap rate, yea, for nothing to them that will; the great merchants of this world, fearing that this course would soon discover and disgrace the false glitter of their deceitful wares, wherewith they abuse the people, like poor Indians with beads and glasses, practise by all means how they may suppress the vending of such rarities, and at such a cheapness as would undo them, and turn their trash upon their hands. Therefore, by gratifying the corrupt desires of men in fleshly doctrines, they stir them up to persecute with hatred and contempt all those that seek to bear themselves uprightly in this their spiritual factory: which they foreseeing, though they cannot but testify of truth, and the excellence of that heavenly traffic which they bring, against what opposition or danger soever, yet needs must it sit heavily upon their spirits, that being, in God's prime intention and their own, selected heralds of peace and dispensers of treasure inestimable, without price, to them that have no pence, they find in the discharge of their commission, that they are made the greatest variance and offence, a very sword and fire both in house and city over the whole earth.

This is that which the sad prophet Jeremiah laments: *Woe is me, my mother, that thou hast borne me, a man of strife and contention!* And although divine inspiration must certainly have been sweet to those ancient prophets, yet the irksomeness of that truth which they brought was so unpleasant to them, that everywhere they call it a burden. Yea, that mysterious book of Revelation, which the great Evangelist was bid to eat, as it had been some eye-brightening electuary of knowledge and foresight, though it were sweet in his mouth and in the learning, it was bitter in his belly, bitter in the denouncing. Nor was this hid from the wise poet Sophocles, who in that place of his tragedy where Tiresias is called to resolve King Oedipus in a matter which he knew would be grievous, brings him in bemoaning his lot, that he knew more than other men. For surely to every good and peaceable man, it must in nature needs be a hateful thing to be the displeaser and molester of thousands; much better would it like him doubtless to be the messenger of gladness and contentment, which is his chief intended business to all mankind, but that they resist and oppose their own true happiness.

But when God commands to take the trumpet, and blow a dolorous or a jarring blast, it lies not in man's will what he shall say, or what he shall conceal. If he shall think to be silent, as Jeremiah did, because of the reproach and derision he met with daily, *And all his familiar friends watched for his halting*, to be revenged on him for speaking the truth, he would be forced to confess as he confessed: *His word was in my heart as a burning fire shut up in my bones; I was weary with forbearing, and could not stay*. Which might teach these times not suddenly to condemn all things that are sharply spoken or vehemently written as proceeding out of stomach, virulence, and ill-nature; but to consider rather that, if the prelates have leave to say the worst that can be said, or do the worst that can be done, while they strive to keep to themselves, to their great pleasure and commodity, those things which they ought to render up, no man can be justly offended with him that shall endeavour to impart and bestow, without any gain to himself, those sharp but saving words which would be a terror and a torment in him to keep back.

For me, I have determined to lay up as the best treasure and solace of a good old age, if God vouchsafe it me, the honest liberty of free speech from my youth, where I shall think it available in so dear a concernment as the Church's good. For if I be, either by disposition or what other cause, too inquisitive, or suspicious of myself and mine own doings, who can help it? But this I foresee, that should the Church be brought under heavy oppression, and God have given me ability the while to reason against that man that should be the author of so foul a deed; or should she, by blessing from above on the industry and courage of faithful men, change this her distracted estate into better days, without the least furtherance or contribution of those few talents which God at that present had lent me; I foresee what stories I should hear within myself, all my life after, of discourage and reproach.

"Timorous and ungrateful, the Church of God is now again

at the foot of her insulting enemies, and thou bewailest. What matters it for thee, or thy bewailing? When time was, thou couldst not find a syllable of all that thou hadst read, or studied, to utter in her behalf. Yet ease and leisure was given thee for thy retired thoughts, out of the sweat of other men. Thou hadst the diligence, the parts, the language of a man, if a vain subject were to be adorned or beautified; but when the cause of God and his Church was to be pleaded, for which purpose that tongue was given thee which thou hast, God listened if he could hear thy voice among his zealous servants, but thou wert dumb as a beast: from henceforward be that which thine own brutish silence hath made thee."

Or else I should have heard on the other ear: "Slothful, and ever to be set light by, the Church hath now overcome her late distresses after the unwearied labours of many her true servants that stood up in her defence; thou also wouldst take upon thee to share amongst them of their joy: but wherefore thou? Where canst thou show any word or deed of thine which might have hastened her peace? Whatever thou dost now talk, or write, or look, is the alms of other men's active prudence and zeal. Dare not now to say or do anything better than thy former sloth and infancy; or if thou darest, thou dost impudently to make a thrifty purchase of boldness to thyself out of the painful merits of other men; what before was thy sin is now thy duty, to be abject and worthless."

These, and such like lessons as these, I know would have been my matins duly, and my evensong. But now by this little diligence, mark what a privilege I have gained with good men and saints, to claim my right of lamenting the tribulations of the Church, if she should suffer, when others, that have ventured nothing for her sake, have not the honour to be admitted mourners. But if she lift up her drooping head and prosper, among those that have something more than wished her welfare, I have my charter and freehold of rejoicing to me and my heirs. Concerning therefore this wayward subject against prelaty, the touching whereof is so distasteful and disquietous to a number of men, as by what hath been said I may deserve of charitable readers to be credited, that neither envy nor gall hath entered me upon this controversy, but the enforcement of conscience only, and a preventive fear lest the omitting of this duty should be against me, when I would store up to myself the good provision of peaceful hours: so, lest it be still imputed to me, as I have found it hath been, that some self-pleasing humour of vainglory hath incited me to contest with men of high estimation, now while green years are upon my head; from this needless surmisal I shall hope to dissuade the intelligent and equal auditor, if I can but say successfully that which in this exigent behooves me; although I would be heard only, if it might be, by the elegant and learned reader, to whom principally for a while I shall beg leave I may address myself.

To him it will be no new thing, though I tell him that if I hunted after praise, by the ostentation of wit and learning, I should not write thus out of mine own season when I have neither yet completed to my mind the full circle of my private studies, although I complain not of any insufficiency to the matter in hand; or were I ready to my wishes, it were a folly to commit anything elaborately composed to the careless and interrupted listening of these tumultuous times. Next, if I were wise only to my own ends, I would certainly take such a subject as of itself might catch applause, whereas this hath all the disadvantages on the contrary; and such a subject as the publishing whereof might be delayed at pleasure, and time enough to pencil it over with all the curious touches of art, even to the perfection of a faultless picture; whenas in this argument the not deferring is of great moment to the good speeding, that, if solidity have leisure to do her office, art cannot have much. Lastly, I should not choose this manner of writing, wherein knowing myself inferior to myself, led by the genial power of nature to another task, I have the use, as I may account it, but of my left hand.

And though I shall be foolish in saying more to this purpose, yet, since it will be such a folly as wisest men go about to commit, having only confessed and so committed, I may trust with more reason, because with more folly, to have courteous pardon.

For although a poet, soaring in the high region of his fancies, with his garland and singing robes about him, might, without apology, speak more of himself than I mean to do; yet for me sitting here below in the cool element of prose, a mortal thing among many readers of no empyreal conceit, to venture and divulge unusual things of myself, I shall petition to the gentler sort, it may not be envy to me.

I must say, therefore, that after I had for my first years, by the ceaseless diligence and care of my father (whom God recompense!), been exercised to the tongues and some sciences, as my age would suffer, by sundry masters and teachers, both at home and at the schools, it was found that whether aught was imposed me by them that had the overlooking, or betaken to of mine own choice in English, or other tongue, prosing or versing, but chiefly this latter, the style, by certain vital signs it had, was likely to live. But much latelier in the private academies of Italy, whither I was favoured to resort, perceiving that some trifles which I had in memory, composed at under twenty or thereabout (for the manner is, that everyone must give some proof of his wit and reading there), met with acceptance above what was looked for; and other things, which I had shifted in scarcity of books and conveniences to patch up amongst them, were received with written encomiums, which the Italian is not forward to bestow on men of this side the Alps; I began thus far to assent both to them and divers of my friends here at home, and not less to an inward prompting which now grew daily upon me, that by labour and intense study (which I take to be my portion in this life), joined with the strong propensity of nature, I might perhaps leave something so written to aftertimes, as they should not willingly let it die.

These thoughts at once possessed me, and these other; that if I were certain to write as men buy leases, for three lives and downward, there ought no regard be sooner had than to God's glory, by the honour and instruction of my country. For which cause, and not only for that I knew it would he hard to arrive at the second rank among the Latins, I applied myself to that resolution, which Ariosto followed against the persuasions of

Bembo, to fix all the industry and art I could unite to the adorning of my native tongue; not to make verbal curiosities the end (that were a toilsome vanity), but to be an interpreter and relater of the best and sagest things among mine own citizens throughout this island in the mother dialect. That, what the greatest and choicest wits of Athens, Rome, or modern Italy, and those Hebrews of old did for their country, I, in my proportion, with this over and above, of being a Christian, might do for mine; not caring to be once named abroad, though perhaps I could attain to that, but content with these British islands as my world; whose fortune hath hitherto been that, if the Athenians, as some say, made their small deeds great and renowned by their eloquent writers, England hath had her noble achievements made small by the unskilful handling of monks and mechanics.

Time serves not now, and perhaps I might seem too profuse, to give any certain account of what the mind at home, in the spacious circuits of her musing, hath liberty to propose to herself, though of highest hope and hardest attempting; whether that epic form whereof the two poems of Homer, and those other two of Virgil and Tasso, are a diffuse, and the book of Job a brief model: or whether the rules of Aristotle herein are strictly to be kept, or nature to be followed, which in them that know art, and use judgment, is no transgression, but an enriching of art; and lastly, what king or knight, before the conquest, might be chosen in whom to lay the pattern of a Christian hero. And as Tasso gave to a prince of Italy his choice whether he would command him to write of Godfrey's expedition against the Infidels, or Belisarius against the Goths, or Charlemain against the Lombards; if to the instinct of nature and the emboldening of art aught may be trusted, and that there be nothing adverse in our climate, or the fate of this age, it haply would be no rashness, from an equal diligence and inclination, to present the like offer in our own ancient stories; or whether those dramatic constitutions, wherein Sophocles and Euripides reign, shall be found more doctrinal and exemplary to a nation.

The scripture also affords us a divine pastoral drama in the

Song of Solomon, consisting of two persons, and a double chorus, as Origen rightly judges. And the Apocalypse of St. John is the majestic image of a high and stately tragedy, shutting up and intermingling her solemn scenes and acts with a sevenfold chorus of hallelujahs and harping symphonies: and this my opinion the grave authority of Paraeus, commenting that book, is sufficient to confirm. Or if occasion shall lead, to imitate those magnific odes and hymns, wherein Pindarus and Callimachus are in most things worthy, some others in their frame judicious, in their matter most an end faulty. But those frequent songs throughout the law and prophets beyond all these, not in their divine argument alone, but in the very critical art of composition, may be easily made appear over all the kinds of lyric poesy to be incomparable.

These abilities, wheresoever they be found, are the inspired gift of God, rarely bestowed, but yet to some (though most abuse) in every nation; and are of power, beside the office of a pulpit, to imbreed and cherish in a great people the seeds of virtue and public civility, to allay the perturbations of the mind, and set the affections in right tune; to celebrate in glorious and lofty hymns the throne and equipage of Gods' almightiness, and what he works, and what he suffers to be wrought with high providence in his Church; to sing victorious agonies of martyrs and saints, the deeds and triumphs of just and pious nations, doing valiantly through faith against the enemies of Christ; to deplore the general relapses of kingdoms and states from justice and God's true worship.

Lastly, whatsoever in religion is holy and sublime, in virtue amiable or grave, whatsoever hath passion or admiration in all the changes of that which is called fortune from without, or the wily subtleties and refluxes of man's thoughts from within; all these things with a solid and treatable smoothness to paint out and describe. Teaching over the whole book of sanctity and virtue, through all the instances of example, with such delight to those especially of soft and delicious temper, who will not so much as look upon Truth herself, unless they see her elegantly dressed; that whereas the paths of honesty and good life appear now rugged and difficult, though they be indeed easy and pleasant, they will then appear to all men both easy and pleasant, though they were rugged and difficult indeed. And what a benefit this would be to our youth and gentry, may be soon guessed by what we know of the corruption and bane which they suck in daily from the writings and interludes of libidinous and ignorant poetasters; who, having scarce ever heard of that which is the main consistence of a true poem, the choice of such persons as they ought to introduce, and what is moral and decent to each one, do for the most part lap up vicious principles in sweet pills to be swallowed down, and make the taste of virtuous documents harsh and sour.

But because the spirit of man cannot demean itself lively in this body, without some recreating intermission of labour and serious things, it were happy for the Commonwealth, if our magistrates, as in those famous governments of old, would take into their care, not only the deciding of our contentious law-cases and brawls, but the managing of our public sports and festival pastimes; that they might be, not such as were authorized a while since, the provocations of drunkenness and lust, but such as may inure and harden our bodies by martial exercises to all warlike skill and performance; and may civilize, adorn, and make discreet our minds by the learned and affable meeting of frequent Academies, and the procurement of wise and artful recitations, sweetened with eloquent and graceful enticements to the love and practice of justice, temperance, and fortitude, instructing and bettering the nation at all opportunities, that the call of wisdom and virtue may be heard everywhere, as Solomon saith: *She crieth without, she uttereth her voice in the streets, in the top of high places, in the chief concourse, and in the openings of the gates.* Whether this may not be, not only in pulpits, but after another persuasive method, at set and solemn paneguries, in theatres, porches, or what other place or way may win most upon the people to receive at once both recreation and instruction, let them in authority consult.

The thing which I had to say, and those intentions which have lived within me ever since I could conceive myself anything worth to my country, I return to crave excuse that urgent reason hath plucked from me, by an abortive and foredated discovery. And the accomplishment of them lies not but in a power above man's to promise; but that none hath by more studious ways endeavoured, and with more unwearied spirit that none shall, that I dare almost aver of myself, as far as life and free leisure will extend; and that the land had once enfranchised herself from this impertinent yoke of prelaty, under whose inquisitorious and tyrannical duncery no free and splendid wit can flourish.

Neither do I think it shame to covenant with any knowing reader, that for some few years yet I may go on trust with him toward the payment of what I am now indebted, as being a work not to be raised from the heat of youth, or the vapours of wine; like that which flows at waste from the pen of some vulgar amorist, or the trencher fury of a rhyming parasite; nor to be obtained by the invocation of Dame Memory and her siren daughters; but by devout prayer to that eternal Spirit, who can enrich with all utterance and knowledge, and sends out his Seraphim, with the hallowed fire of his altar, to touch and purify the lips of whom he pleases: to this must be added industrious and select reading, steady observation, insight into all seemly and generous arts and affairs; till which in some measure be compassed, at mine own peril and cost, I refuse not to sustain this expectation from as many as are not loath to hazard so much credulity upon the best pledges that I can give them.

Although it nothing content me to have disclosed thus much beforehand, but that I trust hereby to make it manifest with what small willingness I endure to interrupt the pursuit of no less hopes than these, and leave a calm and pleasing solitariness, fed with cheerful and confident thoughts, to embark in a troubled sea of noises and hoarse disputes, put from beholding the bright countenance of Truth in the quiet and still air of delightful studies, to come into the dim reflection of hollow antiquities sold by the seeming bulk, and there be fain to club quotations with men whose learning and belief lies in marginal stuffings; who, when they have, like good sumpters, laid ye down their horse-loads of citations and fathers at your door with a rhapsody of who and who were bishops here or there, ye may take off their pack-saddles, their day's work is done, and episcopacy, as they think, stoutly vindicated. Let any gentle apprehension, that can distinguish learned pains from unlearned drudgery, imagine what pleasure or profoundness can be in this, or what honour to deal against such adversaries.

But were it the meanest under-service, if God by his secretary Conscience enjoin it, it were sad for me if I should draw back; for me especially, now when all men offer their aid to help, ease, and lighten the difficult labours of the Church, to whose service, by the intentions of my parents and friends, I was destined of a child, and in mine own resolutions: till coming to some maturity of years, and perceiving what tyranny had invaded the Church, that he who would take orders must subscribe slave, and take an oath withal, which unless he took with a conscience that would retch, he must either straight perjure, or split his faith, I thought it better to prefer a blameless silence before the sacred office of speaking, bought and begun with servitude and forswearing. Howsoever, thus Church-outed by the prelates, hence may appear the right I have to meddle in these matters, as before the necessity and constraint appeared.

OF EDUCATION

TO MASTER SAMUEL HARTLIB

MASTER HARTLIB,

I am long since persuaded that to say and do aught worth memory and imitation, no purpose or respect should sooner move us than simply the love of God and of mankind. Nevertheless, to write now the reforming of education, though it be one of the greatest and noblest designs that can be thought on, and for the want whereof this nation perishes, I had not yet at this time been induced but by your earnest entreaties and serious conjurements; as having my mind for the present half diverted in the pursuance of some other assertions, the knowledge and the use of which cannot but be a great furtherance both to the enlargement of truth, and honest living with much more peace.

Nor should the laws of any private friendship have prevailed with me to divide thus or transpose my former thoughts; but that I see those aims, those actions which have won you with me the esteem of a person sent hither by some good providence from a far country to be the occasion and incitement of great good to this island. And (as I hear) you have obtained the same repute with men of most approved wisdom and some of the highest authority among us; not to mention the learned correspondence which you hold in foreign parts, and the extraordinary pains and diligence which you have used in this matter both here and beyond the seas, either by the definite will of God so ruling, or the peculiar sway of nature, which also is God's working.

Neither can I think that, so reputed and so valued as you are, you would, to the forfeit of your own discerning ability, impose upon me an unfit and over-ponderous argument; but that the satisfaction, which you profess to have received from those incidental discourses which we have wandered into, hath pressed and almost constrained you into a persuasion, that what you require from me in this point I neither ought nor can in conscience defer beyond this time, both of so much need at once, and so much opportunity to try what God hath determined.

I will not resist, therefore, whatever it is either of divine or human obligement that you lay upon me; but will forthwith set down in writing, as you request me, that voluntary idea, which hath long in silence presented itself to me, of a better education, in extent and comprehension far more large, and yet of time far shorter and of attainment far more certain, than hath been yet in practice. Brief I shall endeavour to be; for that which I have to say assuredly this nation hath extreme need should be done sooner than spoken. To tell you, therefore, that I have benefited herein among old renowned authors I shall spare; and to search what many modern Januas and Didactics more than ever I shall read have projected, my inclination leads me not. But if you can accept of these few observations which have flowered off, and are, as it were, the burnishing of many studious and contemplative years altogether spent in the search of religious and civil knowledge, and such as pleased you so well in the relating, I here give you them to dispose of.

The end, then, of learning is to repair the ruins of our first parents by regaining to know God aright, and out of that knowledge to love him, to imitate him, to be like him, as we may the nearest, by possessing our souls of true virtue, which, being united to the heavenly grace of faith, makes up the highest perfection. But because our understanding cannot in this body found itself but on sensible things, nor arrive so clearly to the knowledge of God and things invisible as by orderly conning over the visible and inferior creature, the same method is necessarily to be followed in all discreet teaching.

And seeing every nation affords not experience and tradition enough for all kind of learning, therefore we are chiefly taught the languages of those people who have at any time been most industrious after wisdom; so that language is but the instrument conveying to us things useful to be known. And though a linguist should pride himself to have all the tongues that Babel cleft the world into, yet if he have not studied the solid things in them as well as the words and lexicons, he were nothing so much to be esteemed a learned man as any yeoman or tradesman competently wise in his mother-dialect only.

Hence appear the many mistakes which have made learning generally so unpleasing and so unsuccessful. First, we do amiss to spend seven or eight years merely in scraping together so much miserable Latin and Greek as might be learned otherwise easily and delightfully in one year. And that which casts our proficiency therein so much behind is our time lost in too oft idle vacancies given both to schools and universities; partly in a preposterous exaction, forcing the empty wits of children to compose themes, verses, and orations, which are the acts of ripest judgment, and the final work of a head filled, by long reading and observing, with elegant maxims and copious invention.

These are not matters to be wrung from poor striplings, like blood out of the nose, or the plucking of untimely fruit; besides the ill habit which they get of wretched barbarizing against the Latin and Greek idiom with their untutored Anglicisms, odious to be read, yet not to be avoided without a well-continued and judicious conversing among pure authors, digested, which they scarce taste. Whereas, if after some preparatory grounds of speech by their certain forms got into memory they were led to the praxis thereof in some chosen short book lessoned thoroughly to them, they might then forthwith proceed to learn the substance of good things and arts in due order, which would bring the whole language quickly into their power. This I take to be the most rational and most profitable way of learning languages, and whereby we may best hope to give account to God of our youth spent herein.

And for the usual method of teaching arts, I deem it to be an old error of universities, not yet well recovered from the scholastic grossness of barbarous ages, that, instead of beginning with arts most easy (and those be such as are most obvious to the sense), they present their young unmatriculated novices at first coming with the most intellective abstractions of logic and metaphysics; so that they, having but newly left those grammatic flats and shallows where they stuck unreasonably to learn a few words with lamentable construction, and now on the sudden transported under another climate, to be tossed and turmoiled with their unballasted wits in fathomless and unquiet deeps of controversy, do, for the most part, grow into hatred and contempt of learning, mocked and deluded all this while with ragged notions and babblements, while they expected worthy and delightful knowledge; till poverty or youthful years call them importunately their several ways, and hasten them, with the sway of friends, either to an ambitious and mercenary, or ignorantly zealous divinity: some allured to the trade of law, grounding their purposes not on the prudent and heavenly contemplation of justice and equity, which was never taught them, but on the promising and pleasing thoughts of litigious terms, fat contentions, and flowing fees. Others betake them to state affairs with souls so unprincipled in virtue and true generous breeding, that flattery, and court-shifts, and tyrannous aphorisms appear to them the highest points of wisdom, instilling their barren hearts with a conscientious slavery, if, as I rather think, it be not feigned. Others, lastly, of a more delicious and airy spirit, retire themselves, knowing no better, to the enjoyments of ease and luxury, living out their days in feast and jollity; which, indeed, is the wisest and safest course of all these, unless they were with more integrity undertaken. And these are the errors, these are the fruits of mis-spending our prime youth at the schools and universities, as we do, either in learning mere words, or such things chiefly as were better unlearned.

I shall detain you no longer in the demonstration of what we should not do, but straight conduct you to a hillside, where I will point you out the right path of a virtuous and noble education; laborious indeed at the first ascent, but else so smooth, so green, so full of goodly prospect and melodious sounds on every side, that the harp of Orpheus was not more charming. I doubt not but ye shall have more ado to drive our dullest and laziest youth, our stocks and stubs, from the infinite desire of such a happy nurture, than we have now to hale and drag our choicest and hopefullest wits to that asinine feast of sow-thistles and brambles which is commonly set before them as all the food and entertainment of their tenderest and most docible age. I call, therefore, a complete and generous education, that which fits a man to perform, justly, skilfully, and magnanimously all the offices, both private and public, of peace and war. And how all this may be done between twelve and one-and-twenty, less time than is now bestowed in pure trifling at grammar and sophistry, is to be thus ordered.

First, to find out a spacious house and ground about it fit for an Academy, and big enough to lodge a hundred and fifty persons, whereof twenty or thereabout may be attendants, all under the government of one who shall be thought of desert sufficient, and ability either to do all, or wisely to direct and oversee it done. This place should be at once both school and university, not needing a remove to any other house of scholarship, except it be some peculiar college of law or physic, where they mean to be practitioners; but as for those general studies which take up all our time from Lilly to the commencing, as they term it, master of art, it should be absolute. After this pattern, as many edifices may be converted to this use as shall be needful in every city throughout this land, which would tend much to the increase of learning and civility everywhere. This number, less or more, thus collected, to the convenience of a foot-company or interchangeably two troops of cavalry, should divide their day's work into three parts as it lies orderly—their studies, their exercise, and their diet.

For their studies: first, they should begin with the chief and necessary rules of some good grammar, either that now used, or any better; and while this is doing, their speech is to be fashioned to a distinct and clear pronunciation, as near as may be to the Italian, especially in the vowels. For we Englishmen, being far northerly, do not open our mouths in the cold air wide enough to grace a southern tongue, but are observed by all other nations to speak exceeding close and inward; so that to smatter Latin with an English mouth is as ill a hearing as law French.

Next, to make them expert in the usefullest points of grammar, and withal to season them and win them early to the love of virtue and true labour, ere any flattering seducement or vain principle seize them wandering, some easy and delightful book of education would be read to them, whereof the Greeks have store, as Cebes, Plutarch, and other Socratic discourses; but in Latin we have none of classic authority extant, except the two or three first books of Quintilian and some select pieces elsewhere.

But here the main skill and groundwork will be to temper them such lectures and explanations upon every opportunity, as may lead and draw them in willing obedience, inflamed with the study of learning and the admiration of virtue, stirred up with high hopes of living to be brave men and worthy patriots, dear to God and famous to all ages: that they may despise and scorn all their childish and ill-taught qualities, to delight in manly and liberal exercises; which he who hath the art and proper eloquence to catch them with, what with mild and effectual persuasions, and what with the intimation of some fear, if need be, but chiefly by his own example, might in a short space gain them to an incredible diligence and courage, infusing into their young breasts such an ingenuous and noble ardour as would not fail to make many of them renowned and matchless men.

At the same time, some other hour of the day might be taught them the rules of arithmetic, and, soon after, the elements of geometry, even playing, as the old manner was. After evening repast till bed-time their thoughts would be best taken up in the easy grounds of religion and the story of Scripture.

The next step would be to the authors of agriculture, Cato, Varro, and Columella, for the matter is most easy; and if the language be difficult, so much the better; it is not a difficulty above their years. And here will be an occasion of inciting and enabling them hereafter to improve the tillage of their country, to recover the bad soil, and to remedy the waste that is made of good; for this was one of Hercules' praises.

Ere half these authors be read (which will soon be with plying hard and daily) they cannot choose but be masters of any ordinary prose: so that it will be then seasonable for them to learn in any modern author the use of the globes and all the maps, first with the old names and then with the new; or they might then be capable to read any compendious method of natural philosophy. And, at the same time, might be entering into the Greek tongue, after the same manner as was before prescribed in the Latin; whereby the difficulties of grammar being soon overcome, all the historical physiology of Aristotle and Theophrastus are open before them and, as I may say, under contribution. The like access will be to Vitruvius, to Seneca's *Natural Questions*, to Mela, Celsus, Pliny, or Solinus. And having thus passed the principles of arithmetic, geometry, astronomy, and geography, with a general compact of physics, they may descend in mathematics to the instrumental science of trigonometry, and from thence to fortification, architecture, enginery, or navigation. And in natural philosophy they may proceed leisurely from the history of meteors, minerals, plants, and living creatures, as far as anatomy.

Then also in course might be read to them out of some not tedious writer the institution of physic; that they may know the tempers, the humours, the seasons, and how to manage a crudity; which he who can wisely and timely do is not only a great physician to himself and to his friends, but also may at some time or other save an army by this frugal and expenseless means only, and not let the healthy and stout bodies of young men rot away under him for want of this discipline, which is a great pity, and no less a shame to the commander.

To set forward all these proceedings in nature and mathematics, what hinders but that they may procure, as oft as shall be needful, the helpful experiences of hunters, fowlers, fishermen, shepherds, gardeners, apothecaries; and in the other sciences, architects, engineers, mariners, anatomists, who, doubtless, would be ready, some for reward and some to favour such a hopeful seminary. And this would give them such a real tincture of natural knowledge as they shall never forget, but daily augment with delight. Then also those poets which are now counted most hard will be both facile and pleasant, Orpheus, Hesiod, Theocritus, Aratus, Nicander, Oppian, Dionysius; and, in Latin, Lucretius, Manilius, and the rural part of Virgil.

By this time years and good general precepts will have furnished them more distinctly with that act of reason which in ethics is called proairesis, that they may with some judgment contemplate upon moral good and evil. Then will be required a special reinforcement of constant and sound indoctrinating to set them right and firm, instructing them more amply in the knowledge of virtue and the hatred of vice, while their young and pliant affections are led through all the moral works of Plato, Xenophon, Cicero, Plutarch, Laertius, and those Locrian remnants; but still to be reduced in their nightward studies, wherewith they close the day's work, under the determinate sentence of David or Solomon, or the evangels and apostolic scriptures.

Being perfect in the knowledge of personal duty, they may then begin the study of economics. And either now or before this they may have easily learned at any odd hour the Italian tongue. And soon after, but with wariness and good antidote, it would be wholesome enough to let them taste some choice comedies, Greek, Latin, or Italian; those tragedies also that treat of household matters, as *Trachiniae*, *Alcestis*, and the like.

The next remove must be to the study of politics; to know the beginning, end, and reasons of political societies, that they may not, in a dangerous fit of the commonwealth, be such poor shaken uncertain reeds, of such a tottering conscience as many of our great councillors have lately shown themselves, but steadfast pillars of the State. After this they are to dive into the grounds of law and legal justice, delivered first and with best warrant by Moses, and, as far as human prudence can be trusted, in those extolled remains of Grecian lawgivers, Lycurgus, Solon, Zaleucus, Charondas; and thence to all the Roman edicts and tables, with their Justinian; and so down to the Saxon and common laws of England and the statutes.

Sundays also and every evening may now be understandingly spent in the highest matters of theology and church history, ancient and modern: and ere this time the Hebrew tongue at a set hour might have been gained, that the Scriptures may be now read in their own original; whereto it would be no impossibility to add the Chaldee and the Syrian dialect.

When all these employments are well conquered, then will the choice histories, heroic poems, and Attic tragedies of stateliest and most regal argument, with all the famous political orations, offer themselves; which, if they were not only read, but some of them got by memory, and solemnly pronounced with right accent and grace, as might be taught, would endue them even with the spirit and vigour of Demosthenes or Cicero, Euripides or Sophocles.

And now, lastly, will be the time to read with them those organic arts which enable men to discourse and write perspicuously, elegantly, and according to the fitted style of lofty, mean or lowly. Logic, therefore, so much as is useful, is to be referred to this due place, with all her well-couched heads and topics, until it be time to open her contracted palm into a graceful and ornate rhetoric taught out of the rule of Plato, Aristotle, Phalereus, Cicero, Hermogenes, Longinus.

To which poetry would be made subsequent, or, indeed, rather precedent, as being less subtile and fine, but more simple, sensuous, and passionate. I mean not here the prosody of a verse, which they could not but have hit on before among the rudiments of grammar, but that sublime art which in Aristotle's *Poetics*, in Horace, and the Italian commentaries of Castelvetro, Tasso, Mazzoni, and others, teaches what the laws are of a true epic poem, what of a dramatic, what of a lyric, what decorum is, which is the grand masterpiece to observe. This would make them soon perceive what despicable creatures our common rhymers and play-writers be; and show them what religious, what glorious and magnificent use might be made of poetry, both in divine and human things.

From hence, and not till now, will be the right season of forming them to be able writers and composers in every excellent matter, when they shall be thus fraught with an universal insight into things. Or whether they be to speak in Parliament or council, honour and attention would be waiting on their lips. There would then also appear in pulpits other visages, other gestures, and stuff otherwise wrought, than what we now sit under, ofttimes to as great a trial of our patience as any other that they preach to us.

These are the studies wherein our noble and our gentle youth ought to bestow their time in a disciplinary way from twelve to one-and-twenty, unless they rely more upon their ancestors dead than upon themselves living. In which methodical course it is so supposed they must proceed by the steady pace of learning onward, as at convenient times for memory's sake to retire back into the middle ward, and sometimes into the rear, of what they have been taught, until they have confirmed and solidly united the whole body of their perfected knowledge, like the last embattling of a Roman legion. Now will be worth the seeing what exercises and recreations may best agree and become these studies.

Their Exercise

The course of study hitherto briefly described is, what I can guess by reading, likest to those ancient and famous schools of Pythagoras, Plato, Isocrates, Aristotle, and such others, out of which were bred up such a number of renowned philosophers, orators, historians, poets, and princes all over Greece, Italy, and Asia, besides the flourishing studies of Cyrene and Alexandria. But herein it shall exceed them, and supply a defect as great as that which Plato noted in the commonwealth of Sparta. Whereas that city trained up their youth most for war, and these in their Academies and Lycaeum all for the gown, this institution of breeding which I here delineate shall be equally good both for peace and war. Therefore, about an hour and a half ere they eat at noon should be allowed them for exercise, and due rest afterwards; but the time for this may be enlarged at pleasure, according as their rising in the morning shall be early. The exercise which I commend first is the exact use of their weapon, to guard, and to strike safely with edge or point. This will keep them healthy, nimble, strong, and well in breath; is also the likeliest means to make them grow large and tall, and to inspire them with a gallant and fearless courage; which, being tempered with seasonable lectures and precepts to make them of true fortitude and patience, will turn into a native and heroic valour, and make them hate the cowardice of doing wrong. They must be also practised in all the locks and gripes of wrestling, wherein Englishmen are wont to excel, as need may often be in fight to tug, to grapple, and to close. And this, perhaps, will be enough wherein to prove and heat their single strength.

The interim of unsweating themselves regularly, and convenient rest before meat, may both with profit and delight be taken up in recreating and composing their travailed spirits with the solemn and divine harmonies of music heard or learned either whilst the skilful organist plies his grave and fancied descant in lofty fugues, or the whole symphony with artful and unimaginable touches adorn and grace the well-studied chords of some choice composer; sometimes the lute or soft organ-stop, waiting on elegant voices either to religious, martial, or civil ditties, which, if wise men and prophets be not extremely out, have a great power over dispositions and manners to smooth and make them gentle from rustic harshness and distempered passions. The like also would not be unexpedient after meat, to assist and cherish nature in her first concoction, and send their minds back to study in good tune and satisfaction.

Where having followed it under vigilant eyes till about two hours before supper, they are, by a sudden alarum or watchword, to be called out to their military motions, under sky or covert, according to the season, as was the Roman wont; first on foot, then, as their age permits, on horseback to all the art of cavalry; that having in sport, but with much exactness and daily muster, served out the rudiments of their soldiership in all the skill of embattling, marching, encamping, fortifying, besieging, and battering, with all the helps of ancient and modern stratagems, tactics, and warlike maxims, they may, as it were out of a long war, come forth renowned and perfect commanders in the service of their country.

They would not then, if they were trusted with fair and hopeful armies, suffer them for want of just and wise discipline to shed away from about them like sick feathers, though they be never so oft supplied; they would not suffer their empty and unrecruitable colonels of twenty men in a company to quaff out or convey into secret hoards the wages of a delusive list and a miserable remnant; yet in the meanwhile to be overmastered with a score or two of drunkards, the only soldiery left about them, or else to comply with all rapines and violences. No, certainly, if they knew aught of that knowledge which belongs to good men or good governors, they would not suffer these things.

But to return to our own institute. Besides these constant exercises at home, there is another opportunity of gaining experience to be won from pleasure itself abroad: in those vernal seasons of the year, when the air is calm and pleasant, it were an injury and sullenness against nature not to go out and see her riches and partake in her rejoicing with heaven and earth. I should not, therefore, be a persuader to them of studying much then, after two or three years that they have well laid their grounds, but to ride out in companies with prudent and staid guides to all the quarters of the land, learning and observing all places of strength, all commodities of building and of soil for towns and tillage, harbours, and ports for trade. Sometimes taking sea as far as to our navy, to learn there also what they can in the practical knowledge of sailing and of sea-fight.

These ways would try all their peculiar gifts of nature, and if there were any secret excellence among them, would fetch it out and give it fair opportunities to advance itself by, which could not but mightily redound to the good of this nation, and bring into fashion again those old admired virtues and excellencies, with far more advantage now in this purity of Christian knowledge.

Nor shall we then need the monsieurs of Paris to take our hopeful youth into their slight and prodigal custodies, and send them over back again transformed into mimics, apes, and kick-shaws. But if they desire to see other countries at three or four and twenty years of age, not to learn principles, but to enlarge experience and make wise observation, they will by that time be such as shall deserve the regard and honour of all men where they pass, and the society and friendship of those in all places who are best and most eminent. And perhaps then other nations will be glad to visit us for their breeding, or else to imitate us in their own country.

Now, lastly, for their diet there cannot be much to say, save only that it would be best in the same house; for much time else would be lost abroad, and many ill habits got; and that it should be plain, healthful, and moderate, I suppose is out of controversy.

Thus, Mr. Hartlib, you have a general view in writing, as your desire was, of that which at several times I had discoursed with you concerning the best and noblest way of education; not beginning, as some have done, from the cradle, which yet might be worth many considerations, if brevity had not been my scope. Many other circumstances also I could have mentioned; but this, to such as have the worth in them to make trial, for light and direction may be enough. Only I believe that this is not a bow for every man to shoot in that counts himself a teacher, but will require sinews almost equal to those which Homer gave Ulysses. Yet I am withal persuaded that it may prove much more easy in the assay than it now seems at distance, and much more illustrious: howbeit not more difficult than I imagine; and that imagination presents me with nothing but very happy and very possible according to best wishes, if God have so decreed, and this age have spirit and capacity enough to apprehend.

THE DOCTRINE AND DISCIPLINE OF DIVORCE

[INTRODUCTION]

TO THE PARLIAMENT OF ENGLAND WITH THE ASSEMBLY

If it were seriously asked (and it would be no untimely question), renowned Parliament, select Assembly! who of all teachers and masters, that have ever taught, hath drawn the most disciples after him, both in religion and in manners, it might be not untruly answered, Custom. Though virtue be commended for the most persuasive in her theory, and conscience in the plain demonstration of the Spirit finds most evincing; yet whether it be the secret of divine will, or the original blindness we are born in, so it happens for the most part that Custom still is silently received for the best instructor. Except it be, because her method is so glib and easy, in some manner like to that vision of Ezekiel rolling up her sudden book of implicit knowledge, for him that will to take and swallow down at pleasure; which proving but of bad nourishment in the concoction, as it was heedless in the devouring, puffs up unhealthily a certain big face of pretended learning, mistaken among credulous men for the wholesome habit of soundness and good constitution, but is indeed no other than that swollen visage of counterfeit knowledge and literature, which not only in private mars our education, but also in public is the common climber into every chair, where either religion is preached, or law reported; filling each estate of life and profession with abject and servile principles, depressing the high and heaven-born spirit of man far beneath the condition wherein either God created him, or sin hath sunk him. To pursue the allegory, Custom being but a mere face, as Echo is a mere voice, rests not in her unaccomplishment, until by secret inclination she accorporate herself with Error, who being a blind and serpentine body without a head, willingly accepts what he wants, and supplies what her incompleteness went seeking. Hence it is, that Error supports Custom, Custom countenances Error; and these two between them would persecute and chase away all truth and solid wisdom out of human life, were it not that God, rather than man, once in many ages calls together the prudent and religious counsels of men, deputed to repress the incroachments, and to work off the inveterate blots and obscurities wrought upon our minds by the subtle insinuating of Error and Custom; who, with the numerous and vulgar train of their followers, make it their chief design to envy and cry down the industry of free reasoning, under the terms of humour and innovation; as if the womb of teeming Truth were to be closed up, if she presume to bring forth aught that sorts not with their unchewed notions and suppositions. Against which notorious injury and abuse of man's free soul, to testify and oppose the utmost that study and true labour can attain, heretofore the incitement of men reputed grave hath led me among others; and now the duty and the right of an instructed Christian calls me through the chance of good or evil report, to be the sole advocate of a discountenanced truth: a high enterprise, Lord and Commons! a high enterprise and a hard, and such as every seventh son of a seventh son does not venture on. Nor have I amidst the clamour of so much envy and impertinence whither to appeal, but to the concourse of so much piety and wisdom here assembled. Bringing in my hands an ancient and most necessary, most charitable, and yet most injured statute of Moses: not repealed ever by him who only had the authority, but thrown aside with much inconsiderate neglect, under the rubbish of canonical ignorance; as once the whole Law was by some such like conveyance in Josiah's time. And he who shall endeavour the amendment of any old neglected grievance in Church or State, or in the daily course of life, if he be gifted with abilities of mind that may raise him to so high an undertaking, I grant he hath already much whereof not to repent him; yet let me aread him, not to be the foreman of any misjudged opinion, unless his resolutions be firmly seated in a square and constant mind, not conscious to itself of any deserved blame, and regardless of ungrounded suspicions. For this let him be sure, he shall be boarded presently by the ruder sort, but not by discreet and well-nurtured men, with a thousand idle descants and surmises. Who when they cannot confute the least joint or sinew of any passage in the book; yet God forbid that truth should be truth, because they have a boisterous conceit of some pretences in the writer. But were they not more busy and inquisitive than the Apostle commends, they would hear him at least, *rejoicing so the truth be preached, whether of envy or other pretence whatsoever:* for Truth is as impossible to be soiled by any outward touch, as the sunbeam; though this ill hap wait on her nativity, that she never comes into the world, but like a bastard, to the ignominy of him that brought her forth; till Time, the midwife rather than the mother of Truth, have washed and salted the infant, declared her legitimate, and churched the father of his young Minerva, from the needless causes of his purgation. Yourselves can best witness this, worthy patriots! and better will, no doubt, hereafter: for who among ye of the foremost that have travailed in her behalf to the good of Church or State, hath not been often traduced to be the agent of his own by-ends, under pretext of reformation? So much the more I shall not be unjust to hope, that however infamy or envy may work in other men to do her fretful will against this discourse, yet that the experience of your own uprightness misinterpreted will put ye in mind to give it free audience and generous construction. What though the brood of Belial, the draff of men, to whom no liberty is pleasing, but unbridled and vagabond lust without pale or partition, will laugh broad perhaps, to see so great a strength of Scripture mustering up in favour, as they suppose, of their debaucheries; they will know better when they shall hence learn, that honest liberty is the greatest foe to dishonest licence. And what though others, out of a waterish and queasy conscience, because ever crazy and never yet sound, will rail and fancy to themselves that injury and licence is the best of this book? Did not the distemper of their own stomachs affect them with a dizzy megrim, they would soon tie up their tongues and discern themselves like that Assyrian blasphemer, all this while reproaching not man, but the Almighty, the Holy One of Israel, whom they do not deny to have belawgiven his own sacred people with this very allowance, which they now call injury and licence, and dare cry shame on, and will do yet a while, till they get a little cordial sobriety to settle their qualming zeal. But this question concerns not us perhaps: indeed man's disposition, though prone to search after vain curiosities, yet when points of difficulty are to be discussed, appertaining to the removal of unreasonable wrong and burden from the perplexed life of our brother, it is incredible how cold, how dull, and far from all fellow-feeling we are, without the spur of self-concernment. Yet if the wisdom, the justice, the purity of God be to be cleared from foulest imputations, which are not yet avoided; if charity be not to be degraded and trodden down under a civil ordinance; if matrimony be not to be advanced like that exalted perdition written of to the Thessalonians, *above all that is called God*, or goodness, nay, against them both; then I dare affirm, there will be found in the contents of this book that which may concern us all. You it concerns chiefly, worthies in Parliament! on whom, as on our deliverers, all our grievances and cares, by the merit of your eminence and fortitude, are devolved. Me it concerns next, having with much labour and faithful diligence first found out, or at least with a fearless and communicative candour first published, to the manifest good of Christendom, that which, calling to witness everything mortal and immortal, I believe unfeignedly to be true. Let not other men think their conscience bound to search continually after truth, to pray for enlightening from above, to publish what they think they have so obtained, and debar me from conceiving myself tied by the same duties. Ye have now, doubtless, by the favour and appointment of God, ye have now in your hands a great and populous nation to reform; from what corruption, what blindness in religion, ye know well; in what a degenerate and fallen spirit from the apprehension of native liberty, and true manliness, I am sure ye find; with what unbounded licence rushing to whoredoms and adulteries, needs not long inquiry: insomuch that the fears, which men have of too strict a discipline, perhaps exceed the hopes that can be in others of ever introducing it with any great success. What if I should tell ye now of dispensations and indulgences, to give a little the reins, to let them play and nibble with the bait awhile; a people as hard of heart as that Egyptian colony that went to Canaan. This is the common doctrine that adulterous and injurious divorces were not connived only, but with eye open allowed of old for hardness of heart. But that opinion, I trust, by then this following argument hath been well read, will be left for one of the mysteries of an indulgent Antichrist to farm out incest by, and those his other tributary pollutions. What middle way can be taken then, may some interrupt, if we must neither turn to the right, nor to the left, and that the people hate to be reformed? Mark then, judges and lawgivers, and ye whose office it is to be our teachers, for I will utter now a doctrine, if ever any other, though neglected or not understood, yet of great and powerful importance to the governing of mankind. He who wisely would restrain the reasonable soul of man within due bounds, must first himself know perfectly, how far the territory and dominion extends of just and honest liberty. As little must he offer to bind that which God hath loosened, as to loosen that which he hath bound. The ignorance and mistake of this high point hath heaped up one huge half of all the misery that hath been since Adam. In the Gospel we shall read a supercilious crew of masters, whose holiness, or rather whose evil eye, grieving that God should be so facile to man, was to set straiter limits to obedience than God hath set, to enslave the dignity of man, to put a garrison upon his neck of empty and over-dignified precepts: and we shall read our Saviour never more grieved and troubled than to meet with such a peevish madness among men against their own freedom. How can we expect him to be less offended with us, when much of the same folly shall be found yet remaining where it least ought, to the perishing of thousands? The greatest burden in the world is superstition, not only of ceremonies in the Church, but of imaginary and scarecrow sins at home. What greater weakening, what more subtle stratagem against our Christian warfare, when besides the gross body of real transgressions to encounter, we shall be terrified by a vain and shadowy menacing of faults that are not? When things indifferent shall be set to overfront us under the banners of sin, what wonder if we be routed, and by this art of our adversary, fall into the subjection of worst and deadliest offences? The superstition of the Papist is, *Touch not, taste not*, when God bids both; and ours is, *Part not, separate not*, when God and charity both permits and commands. *Let all your things be done with charity*, saith St. Paul; and his Master saith, *She is the fulfilling of the Law*. Yet now a civil, an indifferent, a sometime dissuaded law of marriage, must be forced upon us to fulfil, not only without charity but against her. No place in heaven or earth, except hell, where charity may not enter: yet marriage, the ordinance of our solace and contentment, the remedy of our loneliness, will not admit now either of charity or mercy, to come in and mediate, or pacify the fierceness of this gentle ordinance, the unremedied loneliness of this remedy. Advise ye well, supreme Senate, if charity be thus excluded and expulsed, how ye will defend the untainted honour of your own actions and proceedings. He who marries, intends as little to conspire his own ruin, as he that swears allegiance: and as a whole people is in proportion to an ill government, so is one man to an ill marriage. If they, against any authority, covenant, or statute, may, by the sovereign edict of charity, save not only their lives but honest liberties from unworthy bondage, as well may he against any private covenant, which he never entered to his mischief, redeem himself from unsupportable disturbances to honest peace and just contentment. And much the rather, for that to resist the highest magistrate though tyrannizing, God never gave us express allowance, only he gave us reason, charity, nature, and good example to bear us out; but in this economical misfortune thus to demean ourselves, besides the warrant of those four great directors, which doth as justly belong hither, we have an express law of God, and such a law, as whereof our Saviour with a solemn threat forbade the abrogating. For no effect of tyranny can sit more heavy on the

Commonwealth, than this household unhappiness on the family. And farewell all hope of true reformation in the State, while such an evil as this lies undiscerned or unregarded in the house: on the redress whereof depends not only the spiritful and orderly life of our grown men, but the willing and careful education of our children. Let this therefore be new examined, this tenure and freehold of mankind, this native and domestic charter given us by a greater lord than that Saxon king the Confessor. Let the statutes of God be turned over, be scanned anew, and considered not altogether by the narrow intellectuals of quotationists and common placers, but (as was the ancient right of councils) by men of what liberal profession soever, of eminent spirit and breeding, joined with a diffuse and various knowledge of divine and human things; able to balance and define good and evil, right and wrong, throughout every state of life; able to show us the ways of the Lord straight and faithful as they are, not full of cranks and contradictions, and pitfalling dispenses, but with divine insight and benignity measured out to the proportion of each mind and spirit, each temper and disposition created so different each from other, and yet by the skill of wise conducting, all to become uniform in virtue. To expedite these knots were worthy a learned and memorable synod, while our enemies expect to see the expectation of the Church tired out with dependencies and independencies, how they will compound and in what calends. Doubt not, worthy senators! to vindicate the sacred honour and judgment of Moses your predecessor, from the shallow commenting of scholastics and canonists. Doubt not after him to reach out your steady hands to the misinformed and wearied life of man; to restore this his lost heritage into the household state: wherewith be sure that peace and love, the best subsistence of a Christian family, will return home from whence they are now banished; places of prostitution will be less haunted, the neighbour's bed less attempted, the yoke of prudent and manly discipline will be generally submitted to; sober and well-ordered living will soon spring up in the Commonwealth. Ye have an author great beyond exception, Moses, and one yet greater, he who hedged in from abolishing every smallest jot and tittle of precious equity contained in that law, with a more accurate and lasting Masoreth, than either the synagogue of Ezra or the Galilaean school at Tiberias hath left us. Whatever else ye can enact, will scarce concern a third part of the British name: but the benefit and good of this your magnanimous example will easily spread far beyond the banks of Tweed and the Norman isles. It would not be the first or second time, since our ancient Druids, by whom this island was the cathedral of philosophy to France, left off their pagan rights, that England hath had this honour vouchsafed from heaven, to give out reformation to the world. Who was it but our English Constantine that baptized the Roman empire? Who but the Northumbrian Willibrode, and Winifride of Devon, with their followers, were the first apostles of Germany? Who but Alcuin and Wickliff, our countrymen, opened the eyes of Europe, the one in arts, the other in religion? Let not England forget her precedence of teaching nations how to live.

Know, worthies! and exercise the privilege of your honoured country. A greater title I here bring ye than is either in the power or in the policy of Rome to give her monarchs; this glorious act will style ye the defenders of charity. Nor is this yet the highest inscription that will adorn so religious and so holy a defence as this; behold here the pure and sacred law of God, and his yet purer and more sacred name, offering themselves to you first, of all Christian reformers, to be acquitted from the long-suffered ungodly attribute of patronizing adultery. Defer not to wipe off instantly these imputative blurs and stains cast by rude fancies upon the throne and beauty itself of inviolable holiness: lest some other people more devout and wise than we bereave us this offered immortal glory, our wonted prerogative, of being the first asserters in every great vindication. For me, as far as my part leads me, I have already my greatest gain, assurance and inward satisfaction to have done in this nothing unworthy of an honest life, and studies well employed. With what event, among the wise and right understanding handful of men, I am secure. But how among the drove of custom and prejudice this will be relished by such whose capacity, since their youth run ahead into the easy creek of a system or a medulla, sails there at will under the blown physiognomy of their unlaboured rudiments; for them, what their taste will be, I have also surety sufficient, from the entire league that hath ever been between formal ignorance and grave obstinacy. Yet when I remember the little that our Saviour could prevail about this doctrine of charity against the crabbed textuists of his time, I make no wonder, but rest confident, that whoso prefers either matrimony or other ordinance before the good of man and the plain exigence of charity, let him profess Papist, or Protestant, or what he will, he is no better than a Pharisee, and understands not the Gospel: whom as a misinterpreter of Christ I openly protest against; and provoke him to the trial of this truth before all the world: and let him bethink him withal how he will solder up the shifting flaws of his ungirt permissions, his venial and unvenial dispenses, wherewith the law of God pardoning and unpardoning hath been shamefully branded for want of heed in glossing, to have eluded and baffled out all faith and chastity from the marriage-bed of that holy seed, with politic and judicial adulteries. I seek not to seduce the simple and illiterate; my errand is to find out the choicest and the learnedest, who have this high gift of wisdom to answer solidly, or to be convinced. I crave it from the piety, the learning, and the prudence which is housed in this place. It might perhaps more fitly have been written in another tongue: and I had done so, but that the esteem I have of my country's judgment, and the love I bear to my native language to serve it first with what I endeavour, make me speak it thus, ere I assay the verdict of outlandish readers. And perhaps also here I might have ended nameless, but that the address of these lines chiefly to the Parliament of England might have seemed ingrateful not to acknowledge by whose religious care, unwearied watchfulness, courageous and heroic resolutions, I enjoy the peace and studious leisure to remain.

The Honourer and Attendant of their
noble Worth and Virtues,

JOHN MILTON.

AREOPAGITICA

A SPEECH FOR THE LIBERTY OF UNLICENSED PRINTING TO THE PARLIAMENT OF ENGLAND

Τοὐλεύθερον δ᾽ ἐκεῖνο, ἔιτις θελει πόλει
Χρηστόν τι βοὐλευμ᾽ εἶς μέσον φέρειν, ἔχων.
Καὶ ταῦθ᾽, ὁ χρῄζων, λαμπρὸς ἔσθ᾽, ὁ μὴ θέλων,
Σιγᾷ, τί τούτων ἐστιν ἰσαίτερον πόλεὶ;

Euripid. Hicetid.

This is true liberty, when free-born men,
Having to advise the public, may speak free,
Which he who can, and will, deserves high praise;
Who neither can, nor will, may hold his peace:
What can be juster in a state than this?

Euripid. Hicetid.

They, who to states and governors of the Commonwealth direct their speech, High Court of Parliament, or, wanting such access in a private condition, write that which they foresee may advance the public good; I suppose them, as at the beginning of no mean endeavour, not a little altered and moved inwardly in their minds: some with doubt of what will be the success, others with fear of what will be the censure; some with hope, others with confidence of what they have to speak. And me perhaps each of these dispositions, as the subject was whereon I entered, may have at other times variously affected; and likely might in these foremost expressions now also disclose which of them swayed most, but that the very attempt of this address thus made, and the thought of whom it hath recourse to, hath got the power within me to a passion, far more welcome than incidental to a preface.

Which though I stay not to confess ere any ask, I shall be blameless, if it be no other than the joy and gratulation which it brings to all who wish and promote their country's liberty; whereof this whole discourse proposed will be a certain testimony, if not a trophy. For this is not the liberty which we can hope, that no grievance ever should arise in the Commonwealth—that let no man in this world expect; but when complaints are freely heard, deeply considered and speedily reformed, then is the utmost bound of civil liberty attained that wise men look for. To which if I now manifest by the very sound of this which I shall utter, that we are already in good part arrived, and yet from such a steep disadvantage of tyranny and superstition grounded into our principles as was beyond the manhood of a Roman recovery, it will be attributed first, as is most due, to the strong assistance of God our deliverer, next to your faithful guidance and undaunted wisdom, Lords and Commons of England. Neither is it in God's esteem the diminution of his glory, when honourable things are spoken of good men and worthy magistrates; which if I now first should begin to do, after so fair a progress of your laudable deeds, and such a long obligement upon the whole realm to your indefatigable virtues, I might be justly reckoned among the tardiest, and the unwillingest of them that praise ye.

Nevertheless there being three principal things, without which all praising is but courtship and flattery: First, when that only is praised which is solidly worth praise: next, when greatest likelihoods are brought that such things are truly and really in those persons to whom they are ascribed: the other, when he who praises, by showing that such his actual persuasion is of whom he writes, can demonstrate that he flatters not; the former two of these I have heretofore endeavoured, rescuing the employment from him who went about to impair your merits with a trivial and malignant encomium; the latter as belonging chiefly to mine own acquittal, that whom I so extolled I did not flatter, hath been reserved opportunely to this occasion.

For he who freely magnifies what hath been nobly done, and fears not to declare as freely what might be done better, gives ye the best covenant of his fidelity; and that his loyalest affection and his hope waits on your proceedings. His highest praising is not flattery, and his plainest advice is a kind of praising. For though I should affirm and hold by argument, that it would fare better with truth, with learning and the Commonwealth, if one of your published Orders, which I should name, were called in; yet at the same time it could not but much redound to the lustre of your mild and equal government, whenas private persons are hereby animated to think ye better pleased with public advice, than other statists have been delighted heretofore with public flattery. And men will then see what difference there is between the magnanimity of a triennial Parliament, and that jealous haughtiness of prelates and cabin counsellors that usurped of late, whenas they shall observe ye in the midst of your victories and successes more gently brooking written exceptions against a voted Order than other courts, which had produced nothing worth memory but the weak ostentation of wealth, would have endured the least signified dislike at any sudden proclamation.

If I should thus far presume upon the meek demeanour of your civil and gentle greatness, Lords and Commons, as what your published Order hath directly said, that to gainsay, I might defend myself with ease, if any should accuse me of being new or insolent, did they but know how much better I find ye esteem it to imitate the old and elegant humanity of Greece, than the barbaric pride of a Hunnish and Norwegian stateliness. And out of those ages, to whose polite wisdom and letters we owe that we are not yet Goths and Jutlanders, I could name him who from his private house wrote that discourse to the Parliament of Athens, that persuades them to change the form of democraty which was then established. Such honour was done in those days to men who professed the study of wisdom and eloquence, not only in their own country, but in other lands, that cities and signiories heard them gladly, and with great respect, if they had aught in public to admonish the state. Thus did Dion Prusaeus, a stranger and a private orator, counsel the Rhodians against a former edict; and I abound with other like examples, which to set here would be superfluous.

But if from the industry of a life wholly dedicated to studious labours, and those natural endowments haply not the worst for two and fifty degrees of northern latitude, so much must be derogated, as to count me not equal to any of those who had this privilege, I would obtain to be thought not so inferior, as yourselves are superior to the most of them who received their counsel: and how far you excel them, be assured, Lords and Commons, there can no greater testimony appear, than when your prudent spirit acknowledges and obeys the voice of reason from what quarter soever it be heard speaking; and renders ye as willing to repeal any Act of your own setting forth, as any set forth by your predecessors.

If ye be thus resolved, as it were injury to think ye were not, I know not what should withhold me from presenting ye with a fit instance wherein to show both that love of truth which ye eminently profess, and that uprightness of your judgment which is not wont to be partial to yourselves; by judging over again that Order which ye have ordained to regulate printing:—that no book, pamphlet, or paper shall be henceforth printed, unless the same be first approved and licensed by such, or at least one of such, as shall be thereto appointed. For that part which preserves justly every man's copy to himself, or provides for the poor, I touch not, only wish they be not made pretences to abuse and persecute honest and painful men, who offend not in either of these particulars. But that other clause of licensing books, which we thought had died with his brother quadragesimal and matrimonial when the prelates expired, I shall now attend with such a homily, as shall lay before ye, first the inventors of it to be those whom ye will be loath to own; next what is to be thought in general of reading, whatever sort the books be; and that this Order avails nothing to the suppressing of scandalous, seditious, and libellous books, which were mainly intended to be suppressed. Last, that it will be primely to the discouragement of all learning, and the stop of truth, not only by disexercising and blunting our abilities in what we know already, but by hindering and cropping the discovery that might be yet further made both in religious and civil wisdom.

I deny not, but that it is of greatest concernment in the Church and Commonwealth, to have a vigilant eye how books demean themselves as well as men; and thereafter to confine, imprison, and do sharpest justice on them as malefactors. For books are not absolutely dead things, but do contain a potency of life in them to be as active as that soul was whose progeny they are; nay, they do preserve as in a vial the purest efficacy and extraction of that living intellect that bred them. I know they are as lively, and as vigorously productive, as those fabulous dragon's teeth; and being sown up and down, may chance to spring up armed men. And yet, on the other hand, unless wariness be used, as good almost kill a man as kill a good book. Who kills a man kills a reasonable creature, God's image; but he who destroys a good book, kills reason itself, kills the image of God, as it were in the eye. Many a man lives a burden to the earth; but a good book is the precious life-blood of a master spirit, embalmed and treasured up on purpose to a life beyond life. 'Tis true, no age can restore a life, whereof perhaps there is no great loss; and revolutions of ages do not oft recover the loss of a rejected truth, for the want of which whole nations fare the worse.

We should be wary therefore what persecution we raise against the living labours of public men, how we spill that seasoned life of man, preserved and stored up in books; since we see a kind of homicide may be thus committed, sometimes a martyrdom, and if it extend to the whole impression, a kind of massacre; whereof the execution ends not in the slaying of an elemental life, but strikes at that ethereal and fifth essence, the breath of reason itself, slays an immortality rather than a life. But lest I should be condemned of introducing licence, while I oppose licensing, I refuse not the pains to be so much historical, as will serve to show what hath been done by ancient and famous commonwealths against this disorder, till the very time that this project of licensing crept out of the Inquisition, was catched up by our prelates, and hath caught some of our presbyters.

In Athens, where books and wits were ever busier than in any other part of Greece, I find but only two sorts of writings which the magistrate cared to take notice of; those either blasphemous and atheistical, or libellous. Thus the books of Protagoras were by the judges of Areopagus commanded to be burnt, and himself banished the territory for a discourse begun with his confessing not to know *whether there were gods, or whether not.* And against defaming, it was decreed that none should be traduced by name, as was the manner of Vetus Comoedia, whereby we may guess how they censured libelling. And this course was quick enough, as Cicero writes, to quell both the desperate wits of other atheists, and the open way of defaming, as the event showed. Of other sects and opinions, though tending to voluptuousness, and the denying of divine Providence, they took no heed.

Therefore we do not read that either Epicurus, or that libertine school of Cyrene, or what the Cynic impudence uttered, was ever questioned by the laws. Neither is it recorded that the writings of those old comedians were suppressed, though the acting of them were forbid; and that Plato commended the reading of Aristophanes, the loosest of them all, to his royal scholar Dionysius, is commonly known, and may be excused, if holy Chrysostom, as is reported, nightly studied so much the same author and had the art to cleanse a scurrilous vehemence into the style of a rousing sermon.

That other leading city of Greece, Lacedaemon, considering that Lycurgus their lawgiver was so addicted to elegant learning, as to have been the first that brought out of Ionia the scattered works of Homer, and sent the poet Thales from Crete to prepare and mollify the Spartan surliness with his smooth songs and odes, the better to plant among them law and civility, it is to be wondered how museless and unbookish they were, minding nought but the feats of war. There needed no licensing of books among them, for they disliked all but their own laconic apophthegms, and took a slight occasion to chase Archilochus out of their city, perhaps for composing in a higher strain than their own soldierly ballads and roundels could reach to. Or if it were for his broad verses, they were not therein so cautious but they were as dissolute in their promiscuous conversing; whence Euripides affirms in *Andromache*, that their women were all unchaste. Thus much may give us light after what sort of books were prohibited among the Greeks.

The Romans also, for many ages trained up only to a military roughness resembling most the Lacedaemonian guise, knew of learning little but what their twelve Tables, and the Pontific College with their augurs and flamens taught them in religion and law; so unacquainted with other learning, that when Carneades and Critolaus, with the Stoic Diogenes, coming ambassadors to Rome, took thereby occasion to give the city a taste of their philosophy, they were suspected for seducers by no less a man than Cato the Censor, who moved it in the Senate to dismiss them speedily, and to banish all such Attic babblers out of Italy. But Scipio and others of the noblest senators withstood him and his old Sabine austerity; honoured and admired the men; and the censor himself at last, in his old age, fell to the study of that whereof before he was so scrupulous. And yet at the same time Naevius and Plautus, the first Latin comedians, had filled the city with all the borrowed scenes of Menander and Philemon. Then began to be considered there also what was to be done to libellous books and authors; for Naevius was quickly cast into prison for his unbridled pen, and released by the tribunes upon his recantation; we read also that libels were burnt, and the makers punished by Augustus. The like severity, no doubt, was used, if aught were impiously written against their esteemed gods. Except in these two points, how the world went in books, the magistrate kept no reckoning.

And therefore Lucretius without impeachment versifies his Epicurism to Memmius, and had the honour to be set forth the second time by Cicero, so great a father of the Commonwealth; although himself disputes against that opinion in his own writings. Nor was the satirical sharpness or naked plainness of Lucilius, or Catullus, or Flaccus, by any order prohibited. And for matters of state, the story of Titus Livius, though it extolled that part which Pompey held, was not therefore suppressed by Octavius Caesar of the other faction. But that Naso was by him banished in his old age, for the wanton poems of his youth, was but a mere covert of state over some secret cause: and besides, the books were neither banished nor called in. From hence we shall meet with little else but tyranny in the Roman empire, that we may not marvel, if not so often bad as good books were silenced.

I shall therefore deem to have been large enough, in producing what among the ancients was punishable to write; save only which, all other arguments were free to treat on.

By this time the emperors were become Christians, whose discipline in this point I do not find to have been more severe than what was formerly in practice. The books of those whom they took to be grand heretics were examined, refuted, and condemned in the general Councils; and not till then were prohibited, or burnt, by authority of the emperor. As for the writings of heathen authors, unless they were plain invectives against Christianity, as those of Porphyrius and Proclus, they met with no interdict that can be cited, till about the year 400, in a Carthaginian Council, wherein bishops themselves were forbid to read the books of Gentiles, but heresies they might read: while others long before them, on the contrary, scrupled more the books of heretics than of Gentiles. And that the primitive Councils and bishops were wont only to declare what books were not commendable, passing no further, but leaving it to each one's conscience to read or to lay by, till after the year 800, is observed already by Padre Paolo, the great unmasker of the Trentine Council.

After which time the Popes of Rome, engrossing what they pleased of political rule into their own hands, extended their dominion over men's eyes, as they had before over their judgments, burning and prohibiting to be read what they fancied not; yet sparing in their censures, and the books not many which they so dealt with: till Martin V., by his bull, not only prohibited, but was the first that excommunicated the reading of heretical books; for about that time Wickliffe and Huss, growing terrible, were they who first drove the Papal Court to a stricter policy of prohibiting. Which course Leo X. and his successors followed, until the Council of Trent and the Spanish Inquisition engendering together brought forth, or perfected, those Catalogues and expurging Indexes, that rake through the entrails of many an old good author, with a violation worse than any could be offered to his tomb. Nor did they stay in matters heretical, but any subject that was not to their palate, they either condemned in a

Prohibition, or had it straight into the new purgatory of an index.

To fill up the measure of encroachment, their last invention was to ordain that no book, pamphlet, or paper should be printed (as if St. Peter had bequeathed them the keys of the press also out of Paradise) unless it were approved and licensed under the hands of two or three glutton friars. For example:

> Let the Chancellor Cini be pleased to see if in this present work be contained aught that may withstand the printing.
>
> VINCENT RABBATTA, *Vicar of Florence.*
>
> I have seen this present work, and find nothing athwart the Catholic faith and good manners: in witness whoreof I have given, etc.
>
> NICOLO CINI, *Chancellor of Florence.*
>
> Attending the precedent relation, it is allowed that this present work of Davanzati may be printed.
>
> VINCENT RABBATTA, *etc.*
>
> It may be printed, July 15.
>
> FRIAR SIMON MOMPEI D'AMELIA,
> *Chancellor of the Holy Office in Florence.*

Sure they have a conceit, if he of the bottomless pit had not long since broke prison, that this quadruple exorcism would bar him down. I fear their next design will be to get into their custody the licensing of that which they say Claudius intended, but went not through with. Vouchsafe to see another of their forms, the Roman stamp:

> Imprimatur, If it seem good to the reverend Master of the Holy Palace.
>
> BELCASTRO, *Vicegerent.*
>
> *Imprimatur, Friar Nicolo Rodolphi, Master of the Holy Palace.*

Sometimes five Imprimaturs are seen together dialogue-wise in the piazza of one title-page, complimenting and ducking each to other with their shaven reverences, whether the author, who stands by in perplexity at the foot of his epistle, shall to the press or to the sponge. These are the pretty responsories, these are the dear antiphonies, that so bewitched of late our prelates and their chaplains with the goodly echo they made; and besotted us to the gay imitation of a lordly Imprimatur, one from Lambeth House, another from the west end of Paul's; so apishly Romanizing, that the word of command still was set down in Latin; as if the learned grammatical pen that wrote it would cast no ink without Latin; or perhaps, as they thought, because no vulgar tongue was worthy to express the pure conceit of an Imprimatur, but rather, as I hope, for that our English, the language of men ever famous and foremost in the achievements of liberty, will not easily find servile letters enow to spell such a dictatory presumption English.

And thus ye have the inventors and the original of book-licensing ripped up and drawn as lineally as any pedigree. We have it not, that can be heard of, from any ancient state, or polity or church; nor by any statute left us by our ancestors elder or later; nor from the modern custom of any reformed city or church abroad, but from the most anti-christian council and the most tyrannous inquisition that ever inquired. Till then books were ever as freely admitted into the world as any other birth; the issue of the brain was no more stifled than the issue of the womb: no envious Juno sat cross-legged over the nativity of any man's intellectual offspring; but if it proved a monster, who denies, but that it was justly burnt, or sunk into the sea? But that a book, in worse condition than a peccant soul, should be to stand before a jury ere it be born to the world, and undergo yet in darkness the judgment of Radamanth and his colleagues, ere it can pass the ferry backward into light, was never heard before, till that mysterious iniquity, provoked and troubled at the first entrance of Reformation, sought out new limbos and new hells wherein they might include our books also within the number of their damned. And this was the rare morsel so officiously snatched up, and so ill-favouredly imitated by our inquisiturient bishops, and the attendant minorites their chaplains. That ye like not now these most certain authors of this licensing order, and that all sinister intention was far distant from your thoughts, when ye were importuned the passing it, all men who know the integrity of your actions, and how ye honour truth, will clear ye readily.

But some will say, what though the inventors were bad, the thing for all that may be good? It may so; yet if that thing be no such deep invention, but obvious, and easy for any man to light on, and yet best and wisest commonwealths through all ages and occasions have forborne to use it, and falsest seducers and oppressors of men were the first who took it up, and to no other purpose but to obstruct and hinder the first approach of Reformation; I am of those who believe it will be a harder alchemy than Lullius ever knew, to sublimate any good use out of such an invention. Yet this only is what I request to gain from this reason, that it may be held a dangerous and suspicious fruit, as certainly it deserves, for the tree that bore it, until I can dissect one by one the properties it has. But I have first to finish, as was propounded, what is to be thought in general of reading books, whatever sort they be, and whether be more the benefit or the harm that thence proceeds.

Not to insist upon the examples of Moses, Daniel, and Paul, who were skilful in all the learning of the Egyptians, Chaldeans, and Greeks, which could not probably be without reading their books of all sorts; in Paul especially, who thought it no defilement to insert into Holy Scripture the sentences of three Greek poets, and one of them a tragedian; the question was notwithstanding sometimes controverted among the primitive doctors, but with great odds on that side which affirmed it both lawful and profitable; as was then evidently perceived, when Julian the Apostate and subtlest enemy to our faith made a decree forbidding Christians the study of heathen learning: for, said he, they wound us with our own weapons, and with our own arts and sciences they overcome us. And indeed the Christians were put so to their shifts by this crafty means, and so much in danger to decline into all ignorance, that the two Apollinarii were fain, as a man may say, to coin all the seven liberal sciences out of the Bible, reducing it into divers forms of orations, poems, dialogues, even to the calculating of a new Christian grammar. But, saith the historian Socrates, the providence of God provided better than the industry of Apollinarius and his son, by taking away that illiterate law with the life of him who devised it. So great an injury they then held it to be deprived of Hellenic learning; and thought it a persecution more undermining, and secretly decaying the Church, than the open cruelty of Decius or Diocletian.

And perhaps it was the same politic drift that the devil whipped St. Jerome in a Lenten dream, for reading Cicero; or else it was a phantasm bred by the fever which had then seized him. For had an angel been his discipliner, unless it were for dwelling too much upon Ciceronianisms, and had chastised the reading, not the vanity, it had been plainly partial; first to correct him for grave Cicero, and not for scurril Plautus, whom he confesses to have been reading, not long before; next to correct him only, and let so many more ancient fathers wax old in those pleasant and florid studies without the lash of such a tutoring apparition; insomuch that Basil teaches how some good use may be made of *Margites*, a sportful poem, not now extant, writ by Homer; and why not then of *Morgante*, an Italian romance much to the same purpose?

But if it be agreed we shall be tried by visions, there is a vision recorded by Eusebius, far ancienter than this tale of Jerome, to the nun Eustochium, and, besides, has nothing of a fever in it. Dionysius Alexandrinus was about the year 240 a person of great name in the Church for piety and learning, who had wont to avail himself much against heretics by being conversant in their books; until a certain presbyter laid it scrupulously to his conscience, how he durst venture himself among those defiling volumes. The worthy man, loath to give offence, fell into a new debate with himself what was to be thought; when suddenly a vision sent from God (it is his own epistle that so avers it) confirmed him in these words: *Read any books whatever come to thy hands, for thou art sufficient both to judge aright.*

and to examine each matter. To this revelation he assented the sooner, as he confesses, because it was answerable to that of the Apostle to the Thessalonians, *Prove all things, hold fast that which is good*. And he might have added another remarkable saying of the same author: *To the pure, all things are pure*; not only meats and drinks, but all kind of knowledge whether of good or evil; the knowledge cannot defile, nor consequently the books, if the will and conscience be not defiled.

For books are as meats and viands are; some of good, some of evil substance; and yet God, in that unapocryphal vision, said without exception, *Rise, Peter, kill and eat*, leaving the choice to each man's discretion. Wholesome meats to a vitiated stomach differ little or nothing from unwholesome; and best books to a naughty mind are not unappliable to occasions of evil. Bad meats will scarce breed good nourishment in the healthiest concoction; but herein the difference is of bad books, that they to a discreet and judicious reader serve in many respects to discover, to confute, to forewarn, and to illustrate. Whereof what better witness can ye expect I should produce, than one of your own now sitting in Parliament, the chief of learned men reputed in this land, Mr. Selden; whose volume of natural and national laws proves, not only by great authorities brought together, but by exquisite reasons and theorems almost mathematically demonstrative, that all opinions, yea errors, known, read, and collated, are of main service and assistance toward the speedy attainment of what is truest. I conceive, therefore, that when God did enlarge the universal diet of man's body, saving ever the rules of temperance, he then also, as before, left arbitrary the dieting and repasting of our minds; as wherein every mature man might have to exercise his own leading capacity.

How great a virtue is temperance, how much of moment through the whole life of man! Yet God commits the managing so great a trust, without particular law or prescription, wholly to the demeanour of every grown man. And therefore when he himself tabled the Jews from heaven, that omer, which was every man's daily portion of manna, is computed to have been more than might have well sufficed the heartiest feeder thrice as many meals. For those actions which enter into a man, rather than issue out of him, and therefore defile not, God uses not to captivate under a perpetual childhood of prescription, but trusts him with the gift of reason to be his own chooser; there were but little work left for preaching, if law and compulsion should grow so fast upon those things which heretofore were governed only by exhortation. Solomon informs us, that much reading is a weariness to the flesh; but neither he nor other inspired author tells us that such or such reading is unlawful: yet certainly had God thought good to limit us herein, it had been much more expedient to have told us what was unlawful than what was wearisome. As for the burning of those Ephesian books by St. Paul's converts; 'tis replied the books were magic, the Syriac so renders them. It was a private act, a voluntary act, and leaves us to a voluntary imitation: the men in remorse burnt those books which were their own; the magistrate by this example is not appointed; these men practised the books, another might perhaps have read them in some sort usefully.

Good and evil we know in the field of this world grow up together almost inseparably; and the knowledge of good is so involved and interwoven with the knowledge of evil, and in so many cunning resemblances hardly to be discerned, that those confused seeds which were imposed upon Psyche as an incessant labour to cull out, and sort asunder, were not more intermixed. It was from out the rind of one apple tasted, that the knowledge of good and evil, as two twins cleaving together, leaped forth into the world. And perhaps this is that doom which Adam fell into of knowing good and evil, that is to say of knowing good by evil. As therefore the state of man now is; what wisdom can there be to choose, what continence to forbear without the knowledge of evil? He that can apprehend and consider vice with all her baits and seeming pleasures, and yet abstain, and yet distinguish, and yet prefer that which is truly better, he is the true warfaring Christian.

I cannot praise a fugitive and cloistered virtue, unexercised and unbreathed, that never sallies out and sees her adversary, but slinks out of the race, where that immortal garland is to be run for, not without dust and heat. Assuredly we bring not innocence into the world, we bring impurity much rather; that which purifies us is trial, and trial is by what is contrary. That virtue therefore which is but a youngling in the contemplation of evil, and knows not the utmost that vice promises to her followers, and rejects it, is but a blank virtue, not a pure; her whiteness is but an excremental whiteness. Which was the reason why our sage and serious poet Spenser, whom I dare be known to think a better teacher than Scotus or Aquinas, describing true temperance under the person of Guion, brings him in with his palmer through the cave of Mammon, and the bower of earthly bliss, that he might see and know, and yet abstain. Since therefore the knowledge and survey of vice is in this world so necessary to the constituting of human virtue, and the scanning of error to the confirmation of truth, how can we more safely, and with less danger, scout into the regions of sin and falsity than by reading all manner of tractates and hearing all manner of reason? And this is the benefit which may be had of books promiscuously read.

But of the harm that may result hence three kinds are usually reckoned. First, is feared the infection that may spread; but then all human learning and controversy in religious points must remove out of the world, yea the Bible itself; for that ofttimes relates blasphemy not nicely, it describes the carnal sense of wicked men not unelegantly, it brings in holiest men passionately murmuring against Providence through all the arguments of Epicurus: in other great disputes it answers dubiously and darkly to the common reader. And ask a Talmudist what ails the modesty of his marginal Keri, that Moses and all the prophets cannot persuade him to pronounce the textual Chetiv. For these causes we all know the Bible itself put by the Papist into the first rank of prohibited books. The ancientest fathers must be next removed, as Clement of Alexandria, and that Eusebian book of Evangelic preparation, transmitting our ears through a hoard of heathenish obscenities to receive the Gospel.

Who finds not that Irenaeus, Epiphanius, Jerome, and others discover more heresies than they well confute, and that oft for heresy which is the truer opinion?

Nor boots it to say for these, and all the heathen writers of greatest infection, if it must be thought so, with whom is bound up the life of human learning, that they writ in an unknown tongue, so long as we are sure those languages are known as well to the worst of men, who are both most able and most diligent to instil the poison they suck, first into the courts of princes, acquainting them with the choicest delights and criticisms of sin. As perhaps did that Petronius whom Nero called his Arbiter, the master of his revels, and the notorious ribald of Arezzo, dreaded and yet dear to the Italian courtiers. I name not him for posterity's sake, whom Henry VIII. named in merriment his vicar of hell. By which compendious way all the contagion that foreign books can infuse will find a passage to the people far easier and shorter than an Indian voyage, though it could be sailed either by the north of Cataio eastward, or of Canada westward, while our Spanish licensing gags the English press never so severely.

But on the other side that infection which is from books of controversy in religion is more doubtful and dangerous to the learned than to the ignorant; and yet those books must be permitted untouched by the licenser. It will be hard to instance where any ignorant man hath been ever seduced by papistical book in English, unless it were commended and expounded to him by some of that clergy: and indeed all such tractates, whether false or true, are as the prophecy of Isaiah was to the eunuch, not to be *understood without a guide*. But of our priests and doctors how many have been corrupted by studying the comments of Jesuits and Sorbonists, and how fast they could transfuse that corruption into the people, our experience is both late and sad. It is not forgot, since the acute and distinct Arminius was perverted merely by the perusing of a nameless discourse written at Delft, which at first he took in hand to confute.

Seeing, therefore, that those books, and those in great

abundance, which are likeliest to taint both life and doctrine, cannot be suppressed without the fall of learning and of all ability in disputation, and that these books of either sort are most and soonest catching to the learned, from whom to the common people whatever is heretical or dissolute may quickly be conveyed, and that evil manners are as perfectly learnt without books a thousand other ways which cannot be stopped, and evil doctrine not with books can propagate, except a teacher guide, which he might also do without writing, and so beyond prohibiting, I am not able to unfold, how this cautelous enterprise of licensing can be exempted from the number of vain and impossible attempts. And he who were pleasantly disposed could not well avoid to liken it to the exploit of that gallant man who thought to pound up the crows by shutting his park gate.

Besides another inconvenience, if learned men be the first receivers out of books and dispreaders both of vice and error, how shall the licensers themselves be confided in, unless we can confer upon them, or they assume to themselves above all others in the land, the grace of infallibility and uncorruptedness? And again, if it be true that a wise man, like a good refiner, can gather gold out of the drossiest volume, and that a fool will be a fool with the best book, yea or without book; there is no reason that we should deprive a wise man of any advantage to his wisdom, while we seek to restrain from a fool, that which being restrained will be no hindrance to his folly. For if there should be so much exactness always used to keep that from him which is unfit for his reading, we should in the judgment of Aristotle not only, but of Solomon and of our Saviour, not vouchsafe him good precepts, and by consequence not willingly admit him to good books; as being certain that a wise man will make better use of an idle pamphlet, than a fool will do of sacred Scripture.

'Tis next alleged we must not expose ourselves to temptations without necessity, and next to that, not employ our time in vain things. To both these objections one answer will serve, out of the grounds already laid, that to all men such books are not temptations, nor vanities, but useful drugs and materials wherewith to temper and compose effective and strong medicines, which man's life cannot want. The rest, as children and childish men, who have not the art to qualify and prepare these working minerals, well may be exhorted to forbear, but hindered forcibly they cannot be by all the licensing that Sainted Inquisition could ever yet contrive. Which is what I promised to deliver next: that this order of licensing conduces nothing to the end for which it was framed; and hath almost prevented me by being clear already while thus much hath been explaining. See the ingenuity of Truth, who, when she gets a free and willing hand, opens herself faster than the pace of method and discourse can overtake her.

It was the task which I began with, to show that no nation, or well-instituted state, if they valued books at all, did ever use this way of licensing; and it might be answered, that this is a piece of prudence lately discovered. To which I return, that as it was a thing slight and obvious to think on, so if it had been difficult to find out, there wanted not among them long since who suggested such a course; which they not following, leave us a pattern of their judgment that it was not the not knowing, but the not approving, which was the cause of their not using it.

Plato, a man of high authority, indeed, but least of all for his Commonwealth, in the book of his Laws, which no city ever yet received, fed his fancy by making many edicts to his airy burgomasters, which they who otherwise admire him wish had been rather buried and excused in the genial cups of an Academic night sitting. By which laws he seems to tolerate no kind of learning but by unalterable decree, consisting most of practical traditions, to the attainment whereof a library of smaller bulk than his own Dialogues would be abundant. And there also enacts, that no poet should so much as read to any private man what he had written, until the judges and law-keepers had seen it, and allowed it. But that Plato meant this law peculiarly to that commonwealth which he had imagined, and to no other, is evident. Why was he not else a lawgiver to himself, but a transgressor, and to be expelled by his own magistrates; both for the wanton epigrams and dialogues which he made, and his perpetual reading of Sophron Mimus and Aristophanes, books of grossest infamy, and also for commending the latter of them, though he were the malicious libeller of his chief friends, to be read by the tyrant Dionysius, who had little need of such trash to spend his time on? But that he knew this licensing of poems had reference and dependence to many other provisos there set down in his fancied republic, which in this world could have no place: and so neither he himself, nor any magistrate or city, ever imitated that course, which, taken apart from those other collateral injunctions, must needs be vain and fruitless. For if they fell upon one kind of strictness, unless their care were equal to regulate all other things of like aptness to corrupt the mind, that single endeavour they knew would be but a fond labour; to shut and fortify one gate against corruption, and be necessitated to leave others round about wide open.

If we think to regulate printing, thereby to rectify manners, we must regulate all recreations and pastimes, all that is delightful to man. No music must be heard, no song be set or sung, but what is grave and Doric. There must be licensing dancers, that no gesture, motion, or deportment be taught our youth but what by their allowance shall be thought honest; for such Plato was provided of. It will ask more than the work of twenty licensers to examine all the lutes, the violins, and the guitars in every house; they must not be suffered to prattle as they do, but must be licensed what they may say. And who shall silence all the airs and madrigals that whisper softness in chambers? The windows also, and the balconies must be thought on; there are shrewd books, with dangerous frontispieces, set to sale; who shall prohibit them, shall twenty licensers? The villages also must have their visitors to inquire what lectures the bagpipe and the rebeck reads, even to the ballatry and the gamut of every municipal fiddler, for these are the countryman's Arcadias, and his Monte Mayors.

Next, what more national corruption, for which England hears ill abroad, than household gluttony: who shall be the rectors of our daily rioting? And what shall be done to inhibit the multitudes that frequent those houses where drunkenness is sold and harboured? Our garments also should be referred to the licensing of some more sober workmasters to see them cut into a less wanton garb. Who shall regulate all the mixed conversation of our youth, male and female together, as is the fashion of this country? Who shall still appoint what shall be discoursed, what presumed, and no further? Lastly, who shall forbid and separate all idle resort, all evil company? These things will be, and must be; but how they shall be least hurtful, how least enticing, herein consists the grave and governing wisdom of a state.

To sequester out of the world into Atlantic and Utopian polities, which never can be drawn into use, will not mend our condition; but to ordain wisely as in this world of evil, in the midst whereof God hath placed us unavoidably. Nor is it Plato's licensing of books will do this, which necessarily pulls along with it so many other kinds of licensing, as will make us all both ridiculous and weary, and yet frustrate; but those unwritten, or at least unconstraining, laws of virtuous education, religious and civil nurture, which Plato there mentions as the bonds and ligaments of the commonwealth, the pillars and the sustainers of every written statute; these they be which will bear chief sway in such matters as these, when all licensing will be easily eluded. Impunity and remissness, for certain, are the bane of a commonwealth; but here the great art lies, to discern in what the law is to bid restraint and punishment, and in what things persuasion only is to work.

In every action, which is good or evil in man at ripe years, were to be under pittance and prescription and compulsion, what were virtue but a name, what praise could be then due to well-doing, what gramercy to be sober, just, or continent? Many there be that complain of divine Providence for suffering Adam to transgress; foolish tongues! When God gave him reason, he gave him freedom to choose, for reason is but choosing; he had been else a mere artificial Adam, such an Adam as he is in the motions. We ourselves esteem not of that obedience, or love, or gift, which is of force: God therefore left him free, set before him a provoking object, ever almost in his eyes; herein consisted his merit, herein the right of his reward, the praise of his abstinence. Wherefore did he create passions within us, pleasures round about us, but that these rightly tempered are the very ingredients of virtue?

They are not skilful considerers of human things, who imagine to remove sin by removing the matter of sin; for, besides that it is a huge heap increasing under the very act of diminishing, though some part of it may for a time be withdrawn from some persons, it cannot from all, in such a universal thing as books are; and when this is done, yet the sin remains entire. Though ye take from a covetous man all his treasure, he has yet one jewel left, ye cannot bereave him of his covetousness. Banish all objects of lust, shut up all youth into the severest discipline that can be exercised in any hermitage, ye cannot make them chaste, that came not thither so; such great care and wisdom is required to the right managing of this point. Suppose we could expel sin by this means; look how much we thus expel of sin, so much we expel of virtue: for the matter of them both is the same; remove that, and ye remove them both alike.

This justifies the high providence of God, who, though he command us temperance, justice, continence, yet pours out before us, even to a profuseness, all desirable things, and gives us minds that can wander beyond all limit and satiety. Why should we then affect a rigour contrary to the manner of God and of nature, by abridging or scanting those means, which books freely permitted are, both to the trial of virtue and the exercise of truth? It would be better done, to learn that the law must needs be frivolous, which goes to restrain things, uncertainly and yet equally working to good and to evil. And were I the chooser, a dram of well-doing should be preferred before many times as much the forcible hindrance of evil-doing. For God sure esteems the growth and completing of one virtuous person more than the restraint of ten vicious.

And albeit whatever thing we hear or see, sitting, walking,

travelling, or conversing, may be fitly called our book, and is of the same effect that writings are, yet grant the thing to be prohibited were only books, it appears that this Order hitherto is far insufficient to the end which it intends. Do we not see, not once or oftener, but weekly, that continued court-libel against the Parliament and City, printed, as the wet sheets can witness, and dispersed among us, for all that licensing can do? Yet this is the prime service a man would think, wherein this Order should give proof of itself. If it were executed, you'll say. But certain, if execution be remiss or blindfold now, and in this particular, what will it be hereafter and in other books? If then the Order shall not be vain and frustrate, behold a new labour, Lords and Commons, ye must repeal and proscribe all scandalous and unlicensed books already printed and divulged; after ye have drawn them up into a list, that all may know which are condemned, and which not; and ordain that no foreign books be delivered out of custody, till they have been read over. This office will require the whole time of not a few overseers, and those no vulgar men. There be also books which are partly useful and excellent, partly culpable and pernicious; this work will ask as many more officials, to make expurgations and expunctions, that the commonwealth of learning be not damnified. In fine, when the multitude of books increase upon their hands, ye must be fain to catalogue all those printers who are found frequently offending, and forbid the importation of their whole suspected typography. In a word, that this your Order may be exact and not deficient, ye must reform it perfectly according to the model of Trent and Seville, which I know ye abhor to do.

Yet though ye should condescend to this, which God forbid, the Order still would be but fruitless and defective to that end whereto ye meant it. If to prevent sects and schisms, who is so unread or so uncatechized in story, that hath not heard of many sects refusing books as a hindrance, and preserving their doctrine unmixed for many ages, only by unwritten traditions? The Christian faith, for that was once a schism, is not unknown to have spread all over Asia, ere any Gospel or Epistle was seen in writing. If the amendment of manners be aimed at, look into Italy and Spain, whether those places be one scruple the better, the honester, the wiser, the chaster, since all the inquisitional rigour that hath been executed upon books.

Another reason, whereby to make it plain that this Order will miss the end it seeks, consider by the quality which ought to be in every licenser. It cannot be denied but that he who is made judge to sit upon the birth or death of books, whether they may be wafted into this world or not, had need to be a man above the common measure, both studious, learned, and judicious; there may be else no mean mistakes in the censure of what is passable or not; which is also no mean injury. If he be of such worth as behooves him, there cannot be a more tedious and unpleasing journey-work, a greater loss of time levied upon his head, than to be made the perpetual reader of unchosen books and pamphlets, ofttimes huge volumes. There is no book that is acceptable unless at certain seasons; but to be enjoined the reading of that at all times, and in a hand scarce legible, whereof three pages would not down at any time in the fairest print, is an imposition which I cannot believe how he that values time and his own studies, or is but of a sensible nostril, should be able to endure. In this one thing I crave leave of the present licensers to be pardoned for so thinking; who doubtless took this office up, looking on it through their obedience to the Parliament, whose command perhaps made all things seem easy and unlaborious to them; but that this short trial hath wearied them out already, their own expressions and excuses to them who make so many journeys to solicit their licence are testimony enough. Seeing therefore those who now possess the employment by all evident signs wish themselves well rid of it; and that no man of worth, none that is not a plain unthrift of his own hours, is ever likely to succeed them, except he mean to put himself to the salary of a press corrector; we may easily foresee what kind of licensers we are to expect hereafter, either ignorant, imperious, and remiss, or basely pecuniary. This is what I had to show, wherein this Order cannot conduce to that end whereof it bears the intention.

I lastly proceed from the no good it can do, to the manifest hurt it causes, in being first the greatest discouragement and affront that can be offered to learning, and to learned men.

It was the complaint and lamentation of prelates, upon every least breath of a motion to remove pluralities, and distribute more equally Church revenues, that then all learning would be for ever dashed and discouraged. But as for that opinion, I never found cause to think that the tenth part of learning stood or fell with the clergy: nor could I ever but hold it for a sordid and unworthy speech of any churchman who had a competency left him. If therefore ye be loath to dishearten utterly and discontent, not the mercenary crew of false pretenders to learning, but the free and ingenuous sort of such as evidently were born to study, and love learning for itself, not for lucre or any other end but the service of God and of truth, and perhaps that lasting fame and perpetuity of praise which God and good men have consented shall be the reward of those whose published labours advance the good of mankind; then know that, so far to distrust the judgment and the honesty of one who hath but a common repute in learning, and never yet offended, as not to count him fit to print his mind without a tutor and examiner, lest he should drop a schism, or something of corruption, is the greatest displeasure and indignity to a free and knowing spirit that can be put upon him.

What advantage is it to be a man, over it is to be a boy at school, if we have only escaped the ferula to come under the fescue of an Imprimatur; if serious and elaborate writings, as if they were no more than the theme of a grammar-lad under his pedagogue, must not be uttered without the cursory eyes of a temporizing and extemporizing licenser? He who is not trusted with his own actions, his drift not being known to be evil, and standing to the hazard of law and penalty, has no great argument to think himself reputed in the Commonwealth wherein he was born for other than a fool or a foreigner. When a man writes to the world, he summons up all his reason and deliberation to assist him; he searches, meditates, is industrious, and likely consults and confers with his judicious friends; after all which done he takes himself to be informed in what he writes, as well as any that writ before him. If, in this the most consummate act of his fidelity and ripeness, no years, no industry, no former proof of his abilities can bring him to that state of maturity, as not to be still mistrusted and suspected, unless he carry all his considerate diligence, all his midnight watchings and expense of Palladian oil, to the hasty view of an unleisured licenser, perhaps much his younger, perhaps far his inferior in judgment, perhaps one who never knew the labour of book-writing, and if he be not repulsed or slighted, must appear in print like a puny with his guardian, and his censor's hand on the back of his title to be his bail and surety that he is no idiot or seducer, it cannot be but a dishonour and derogation to the author, to the book, to the privilege and dignity of learning.

And what if the author shall be one so copious of fancy, as to have many things well worth the adding come into his mind after licensing, while the book is yet under the press, which not seldom happens to the best and diligentest writers; and that perhaps a dozen times in one book? The printer dares not go beyond his licensed copy; so often then must the author trudge to his leave-giver, that those his new insertions may be viewed; and many a jaunt will be made, ere that licenser, for it must be the same man, can either be found, or found at leisure; meanwhile either the press must stand still, which is no small damage, or the author lose his accuratest thoughts, and send the book forth worse than he had made it, which to a diligent writer is the greatest melancholy and vexation that can befall.

And how can a man teach with authority, which is the life of teaching; how can he be a doctor in his book as he ought to be, or else had better be silent, whenas all he teaches, all he delivers, is but under the tuition, under the correction of his patriarchal licenser to blot or alter what precisely accords not with the hidebound humour which he calls his judgment? When every acute reader, upon the first sight of a pedantic licence, will be ready with these like words to ding the book a quoit's distance from him: I hate a pupil teacher, I endure not an instructor that comes to me under the wardship of an overseeing fist. I know nothing of the licenser, but that I have his own hand here for his arrogance; who shall warrant me his judgment? The State, sir, replies the stationer, but has a quick return: The State shall be my governors, but not my critics; they may be mistaken in the choice of a licenser, as easily as this licenser may be mistaken in an author; this is some common stuff; and he might add from Sir Francis Bacon, *That such authorized books are but the language of the times.* For though a licenser should happen to be judicious more than ordinary, which will be a great jeopardy of the next succession, yet his very office and his commission enjoins him to let pass nothing but what is vulgarly received already.

Nay, which is more lamentable, if the work of any deceased author, though never so famous in his lifetime and even to this day, come to their hands for licence to be printed, or reprinted, if there be found in his book one sentence of a venturous edge, uttered in the height of zeal (and who knows whether it might not be the dictate of a divine spirit?) yet not suiting with every low decrepit humour of their own, though it were Knox himself, the reformer of a kingdom, that spake it, they will not pardon him their dash: the sense of that great man shall to all posterity be lost, for the fearfulness or the presumptuous rashness of a perfunctory licenser. And to what an author this violence hath been lately done, and in what book of greatest consequence to be faithfully published, I could now instance, but shall forbear till a more convenient season.

Yet if these things be not resented seriously and timely by them who have the remedy in their power, but that such iron-moulds as these shall have authority to gnaw out the choicest periods of exquisitest books, and to commit such a treacherous fraud against the orphan remainders of worthiest men after death, the more sorrow will belong to that hapless race of men, whose misfortune it is to have understanding. Henceforth let no man care to learn, or care to be more than worldly-wise; for certainly in higher matters to be ignorant and slothful, to be a common steadfast dunce, will be the only pleasant life, and only in request.

And as it is a particular disesteem of every knowing person alive, and most injurious to the written labours and monuments of the dead, so to me it seems an undervaluing and vilifying of the whole nation. I cannot set so light by all the invention, the art, the wit, the grave and solid judgment which is in England, as that it can be comprehended in any twenty capacities how good soever, much less that it should not pass except their superintendence be over it, except it be sifted and strained with their strainers, that it should be uncurrent without their manual stamp. Truth and understanding are not such wares as to be monopolized and traded in by tickets and statutes and standards. We must not think to make a staple commodity of all the knowledge in the land, to mark and licence it like our broadcloth and our woolpacks. What is it but a servitude like that imposed by the Philistines, not to be allowed the sharpening of our own axes and coulters, but we must repair from all quarters to twenty licensing forges? Had anyone written and divulged erroneous things and scandalous to honest life, misusing and forfeiting the esteem had of his reason among men, if after conviction this only censure were adjudged him that he should never henceforth write but what were first examined by an appointed officer, whose hand should be annexed to pass his credit for him that now he might be safely read; it could not be apprehended less than a disgraceful punishment. Whence to include the whole nation, and those that never yet thus offended, under such a diffident and suspectful prohibition, may plainly be understood what a disparagement it is. So much the more, whenas debtors and delinquents may walk abroad without a keeper, but unoffensive books must not stir forth without a visible jailer in their title.

Nor is it to the common people less than a reproach; for if we be so jealous over them, as that we dare not trust them with an English pamphlet, what do we but censure them for a giddy, vicious, and ungrounded people; in such a sick and weak state of faith and discretion, as to be able to take nothing down but through the pipe of a licenser? That this is care or love of them, we cannot pretend, whenas, in those popish places where the laity are most hated and despised, the same strictness is used over them. Wisdom we cannot call it, because it stops but one breach of licence, nor that neither: whenas those corruptions, which it seeks to prevent, break in faster at other doors which cannot be shut.

And in conclusion it reflects to the disrepute of our ministers also, of whose labours we should hope better, and of the proficiency which their flock reaps by them, than that after all this light of the Gospel which is, and is to be, and all this continual preaching, they should still be frequented with such an unprincipled, unedified and laic rabble, as that the whiff of every new pamphlet should stagger them out of their catechism and Christian walking. This may have much reason to discourage the ministers when such a low conceit is had of all their exhortations, and the benefiting of their hearers, as that they are not thought fit to be turned loose to three sheets of paper without a licenser; that all the sermons, all the lectures preached, printed, vented in such numbers, and such volumes, as have now well nigh made all other books unsaleable, should not be armour enough against one single Enchiridion, without the castle of St. Angelo of an Imprimatur.

And lest some should persuade ye, Lords and Commons, that these arguments of learned men's discouragement at this your Order are mere flourishes, and not real, I could recount what I have seen and heard in other countries, where this kind of inquisition tyrannizes; when I have sat among their learned men, for that honour I had, and been counted happy to be born in such a place of philosophic freedom, as they supposed England was, while themselves did nothing but bemoan the servile condition into which learning amongst them was brought; that this was it which had damped the glory of Italian wits; that nothing had been there written now these many years but flattery and fustian. There it was that I found and visited the famous Galileo, grown old, a prisoner to the Inquisition, for thinking in astronomy otherwise than the Franciscan and Dominican licensers thought. And though I knew that England then was groaning loudest under the prelatical yoke, nevertheless I took it as a pledge of future happiness, that other nations were so persuaded of her liberty. Yet was it beyond my hope that those worthies were then breathing in her air, who should be her leaders to such a deliverance, as shall never be forgotten by any revolution of time that this world hath to finish. When that was once begun, it was as little in my fear that what words of complaint I heard among learned men of other parts uttered against the Inquisition, the same I should hear by as learned men at home, uttered in time of Parliament against an order of licensing; and that so generally that, when I had disclosed myself a companion of their discontent, I might say, if without envy, that he whom an honest quaestorship had endeared to the Sicilians was not more by them importuned against Verres, than the favourable opinion which I had among many who honour ye, and are known and respected by ye, loaded me with entreaties and persuasions, that I would not despair to lay together that which just reason should bring into my mind, toward the removal of an undeserved thraldom upon learning. That this is not therefore the disburdening of a particular fancy, but the common grievance of all those who had prepared their minds and studies above the vulgar pitch to advance truth in others, and from others to entertain it, thus much may satisfy.

And in their name I shall for neither friend nor foe conceal what the general murmur is; that if it come to inquisitioning again and licensing, and that we are so timorous of ourselves, and so suspicious of all men, as to fear each book and the shaking of every leaf, before we know what the contents are; if some who but of late were little better than silenced from preaching shall come now to silence us from reading, except what they please, it cannot be guessed what is intended by some but a second tyranny over learning: and will soon put it out of controversy, that bishops and presbyters are the same to us, both name and thing. That those evils of prelaty, which before from five or six and twenty sees were distributively charged upon the whole people, will now light wholly upon learning, is not obscure to us: whenas now the pastor of a small unlearned parish on the sudden shall be exalted archbishop over a large diocese of books, and yet not remove, but keep his other cure too, a mystical pluralist. He who but of late cried down the sole ordination of every novice Bachelor of Art, and denied sole jurisdiction over the simplest parishioner, shall now at home in his private chair assume both these over worthiest and excellentest books and ablest authors that write them.

This is not, ye Covenants and Protestations that we have made! this is not to put down prelaty; this is but to chop an episcopacy; this is but to translate the Palace Metropolitan from one kind of dominion into another; this is but an old canonical sleight of commuting our penance. To startle thus betimes at a mere unlicensed pamphlet will after a while be afraid of every conventicle, and a while after will make a conventicle of every Christian meeting. But I am certain that a State governed by the rules of justice and fortitude, or a Church built and founded upon the rock of faith and true knowledge, cannot be so pusillanimous. While things are yet not constituted in religion, that freedom of writing should be restrained by a discipline imitated from the prelates and learnt by them from the Inquisition, to shut us up all again into the breast of a licenser, must needs give cause of doubt and discouragement to all learned and religious men.

Who cannot but discern the fineness of this politic drift, and who are the contrivers; that while bishops were to be baited down, then all presses might be open; it was the people's birthright and privilege in time of Parliament, it was the breaking forth of light. But now, the bishops abrogated and voided out of the Church, as if our Reformation sought no more but to make room for others into their seats under another name, the episcopal arts begin to bud again, the cruse of truth must run no more oil, liberty of printing must be enthralled again under a prelatical commission of twenty, the privilege of the people nullified, and, which is worse, the freedom of learning must groan again, and to her old fetters: all this the Parliament yet sitting. Although their own late arguments and defences against the prelates might remember them, that this obstructing violence meets for the most part with an event utterly opposite to the end which it drives at: instead of suppressing sects and schisms, it raises them and invests them with a reputation. *The punishing of wits enhances their authority,* saith the Viscount St. Albans; *and a forbidden writing is thought to be a certain spark of truth that flies up in the faces of them who seek to tread it out.* This Order, therefore, may prove a nursing-mother to sects, but I shall easily show how it will be a step-dame to Truth: and first by disenabling us to the maintenance of what is known already.

Well knows he who uses to consider, that our faith and knowledge thrives by exercise, as well as our limbs and complexion. Truth is compared in Scripture to a streaming fountain; if her waters flow not in a perpetual progression, they sicken into a muddy pool of conformity and tradition. A man may be a heretic in the truth; and if he believe things only because his pastor says so, or the Assembly so determines, without knowing other reason, though his belief be true, yet the very truth he holds becomes his heresy.

There is not any burden that some would gladlier post off to another than the charge and care of their religion. There be—who knows not that there be?—of Protestants and professors who live and die in as arrant an implicit faith as any lay Papist of Loretto. A wealthy man, addicted to his pleasure and to his profits, finds religion to be a traffic so entangled, and of so many piddling accounts, that of all mysteries he cannot skill to keep a stock going upon that trade. What should he do? fain he would have the name to be religious, fain he would bear up with his neighbours in that. What does he therefore, but resolves to give over toiling, and to find himself out some factor, to whose care and credit he may commit the whole managing of his religious affairs; some divine of note and estimation that must be. To him he adheres, resigns the whole warehouse of his religion, with all the locks and keys, into his custody; and indeed makes the very person of that man his religion; esteems his associating with him a sufficient evidence and commendatory of his own piety. So that a man may say his religion is now no more within himself, but is become a dividual movable, and goes and comes near him, according as that good man frequents the house. He entertains him, gives him gifts, feasts him, lodges him; his religion comes home at night, prays, is liberally supped, and sumptuously laid to sleep; rises, is saluted, and after the malmsey, or some well-spiced brewage, and better breakfasted than he whose morning appetite would have gladly fed on green figs between Bethany and Jerusalem, his religion walks abroad at eight, and leaves his kind entertainer in the shop trading all day without his religion.

Another sort there be who, when they hear that all things shall be ordered, all things regulated and settled, nothing written but what passes through the custom-house of certain publicans that have the tonnaging and poundaging of all free-spoken truth, will straight give themselves up into your hands, make 'em and cut 'em out what religion ye please: there be delights, there be recreations and jolly pastimes that will fetch the day about from sun to sun, and rock the tedious year as in a delightful dream. What need they torture their heads with that which others have taken so strictly and so unalterably into their own purveying? These are the fruits which a dull ease and cessation of our knowledge will bring forth among the people. How goodly and how to be wished were such an obedient unanimity as this, what a fine conformity would it starch us all into! Doubtless a staunch and solid piece of framework, as any January could freeze together.

Nor much better will be the consequence even among the clergy themselves. It is no new thing never heard of before, for a parochial minister, who has his reward and is at his Hercules' pillars in a warm benefice, to be easily inclinable, if he have nothing else that may rouse up his studies, to finish his circuit in an English Concordance and a topic folio, the gatherings and savings of a sober graduateship, a Harmony and a Catena; treading the constant round of certain common doctrinal heads, attended with their uses, motives, marks, and means, out of which, as out of an alphabet, or sol-fa, by forming and transforming, joining and disjoining variously, a little bookcraft, and two hours' meditation, might furnish him unspeakably to the performance of more than a weekly charge of sermoning: not to reckon up the infinite helps of interlinearies, breviaries, synopses, and other loitering gear. But as for the multitude of sermons ready printed and piled up, on every text that is not difficult, our London trading St. Thomas in his vestry, and add to boot St. Martin and St. Hugh, have not within their hallowed limits more vendible ware of all sorts ready made: so that penury he never need fear of pulpit provision, having where so plenteously to refresh his magazine. But if his rear and flanks be not impaled, if his back door be not secured by the rigid licenser, but that a bold book may now and then issue forth and give the assault to some of his old collections in their trenches, it will concern him then to keep waking, to stand in watch, to set good guards and sentinels about his received opinions, to walk the round and counter-round with his fellow inspectors, fearing lest any of his flock be seduced, who also then would be better instructed, better exercised and disciplined. And God send that the fear of this diligence, which must then be used, do not make us affect the laziness of a licensing Church.

For if we be sure we are in the right, and do not hold the truth guiltily, which becomes not, if we ourselves condemn not our own weak and frivolous teaching, and the people for an untaught and irreligious gadding rout, what can be more fair than when a man judicious, learned, and of a conscience, for aught we know, as good as theirs that taught us what we know, shall not privily from house to house, which is more dangerous, but openly by writing publish to the world what his opinion is, what his reasons, and wherefore that which is now thought cannot be sound? Christ urged it as wherewith to justify himself, that he preached in public; yet writing is more public than preaching; and more easy to refutation, if need be, there being so many whose business and profession merely it is to be the champions of truth; which if they neglect, what can be imputed but their sloth, or unability?

Thus much we are hindered and disinured by this course of licensing, toward the true knowledge of what we seem to know. For how much it hurts and hinders the licensers themselves in the calling of their ministry, more than any secular employment, if they will discharge that office as they ought, so that of necessity they must neglect either the one duty or the other, I insist not, because it is a particular, but leave it to their own conscience, how they will decide it there.

There is yet behind of what I purposed to lay open, the incredible loss and detriment that this plot of licensing puts us to; more than if some enemy at sea should stop up all our havens and ports and creeks, it hinders and retards the importation of our richest merchandise, truth; nay, it was first established and put in practice by Antichristian malice and mystery on set purpose to extinguish, if it were possible, the light of Reformation, and to settle falsehood; little differing from that policy wherewith the Turk upholds his Alcoran, by the prohibition of printing. 'Tis not denied, but gladly confessed, we are to send our thanks and vows to Heaven louder than most of nations, for that great measure of truth which we enjoy, especially in those main points between us and the Pope, with his appurtenances the prelates: but he who thinks we are to pitch our tent here, and have attained the utmost prospect of reformation that the mortal glass wherein we contemplate can show us, till we come to beatific vision, that man by this very opinion declares that he is yet far short of truth.

Truth indeed came once into the world with her divine Master, and was a perfect shape most glorious to look on: but when he ascended, and his Apostles after him were laid asleep, then straight arose a wicked race of deceivers, who, as that story goes of the Egyptian Typhon with his conspirators, how they dealt with the good Osiris, took the virgin Truth, hewed her lovely form into a thousand pieces, and scattered them to the four winds. From that time ever since, the sad friends of Truth, such as durst appear, imitating the careful search that Isis made for the mangled body of Osiris, went up and down gathering up limb by limb, still as they could find them. We have not yet found them all, Lords and Commons, nor ever shall do, till her Master's second coming; he shall bring together every joint and member, and shall mould them into an immortal feature of loveliness and perfection. Suffer not these licensing prohibitions to stand at every place of opportunity, forbidding and disturbing them that continue seeking, that continue to do our obsequies to the torn body of our martyred saint.

We boast our light; but if we look not wisely on the sun itself, it smites us into darkness. Who can discern those planets that are oft combust, and those stars of brightest magnitude that rise and set with the sun, until the opposite motion of their orbs bring them to such a place in the firmament, where they may be seen evening or morning? The light which we have gained was given us, not to be ever staring on, but by it to discover onward things more remote from our knowledge. It is not the unfrocking of a priest, the unmitring of a bishop, and the removing him from off the presbyterian shoulders, that will make us a happy nation. No, if other things as great in the Church, and in the rule of life both economical and political, be not looked into and reformed, we have looked so long upon the blaze that Zuinglius and Calvin hath beaconed up to us, that we are stark blind. There be who perpetually complain of schisms and sects, and make it such a calamity that any man dissents from their maxims. 'Tis their own pride and ignorance which causes the disturbing, who neither will hear with meekness, nor can convince; yet all must be suppressed which is not found in their Syntagma. They are the troublers, they are the dividers of unity, who neglect and permit not others to unite those dissevered pieces which are yet wanting to the body of Truth. To be still searching what we know not by what we know, still closing up truth to truth as we find it (for all her body is homogeneal and proportional), this is the golden rule in theology as well as in arithmetic, and makes up the best harmony in a Church; not the forced and outward union of cold, and neutral, and inwardly divided minds.

Lords and Commons of England! consider what nation it is whereof ye are, and whereof ye are the governors: a nation not slow and dull, but of a quick, ingenious and piercing spirit, acute to invent, subtle and sinewy to discourse, not beneath the reach of any point the highest that human capacity can soar to. Therefore the studies of learning in her deepest sciences have been so ancient and so eminent among us, that writers of good antiquity and ablest judgment have been persuaded that even the school of Pythagoras and the Persian wisdom took beginning from the old philosophy of this island. And that wise and civil Roman, Julius Agricola, who governed once here for Caesar, preferred the natural wits of Britain before the laboured studies of the French. Nor is it for nothing that the grave and frugal Transylvanian sends out yearly from as far as the mountainous borders of Russia, and beyond the Hercynian wilderness, not their youth, but their staid men, to learn our language and our theologic arts.

Yet that which is above all this, the favour and the love of Heaven, we have great argument to think in a peculiar manner propitious and propending towards us. Why else was this nation chosen before any other, that out of her, as out of Sion, should be proclaimed and sounded forth the first tidings and trumpet of Reformation to all Europe? And had it not been the obstinate perverseness of our prelates against the divine and admirable spirit of Wickliff, to suppress him as a schismatic and innovator, perhaps neither the Bohemian Huss and Jerome, no nor the name of Luther or of Calvin, had been ever known: the glory of reforming all our neighbours had been completely ours. But now, as our obdurate clergy have with violence demeaned the matter, we are become hitherto the latest and the backwardest scholars, of whom God offered to have made us the teachers. Now once again by all concurrence of signs, and by the general instinct of holy and devout men, as they daily and solemnly express their thoughts, God is decreeing to begin some new and great period in his Church, even to the reforming of Reformation itself: what does he then but reveal himself to his servants, and as his manner is, first to his Englishmen? I say, as his manner is, first to us, though we mark not the method of his counsels, and are unworthy.

Behold now this vast city· a city of refuge, the mansion house of liberty, encompassed and surrounded with his protection; the shop of war hath not there more anvils and hammers waking, to fashion out the plates and instruments of armed justice in defence of beleaguered truth, than there be pens and heads there, sitting by their studious lamps, musing, searching, revolving new notions and ideas wherewith to present, as with their homage and their fealty, the approaching Reformation: others as fast reading, trying all things, assenting to the force of reason and convincement. What could a man require more from a nation so pliant and so prone to seek after knowledge? What wants there to such a towardly and pregnant soil, but wise and faithful labourers, to make a knowing people, a nation of prophets, of sages, and of worthies? We reckon more than five months yet to harvest; there need not be five weeks; had we but eyes to lift up, the fields are white already.

Where there is much desire to learn, there of necessity will be much arguing, much writing, many opinions; for opinion in good men is but knowledge in the making. Under these fantastic terrors of sect and schism, we wrong the earnest and zealous thirst after knowledge and understanding which God hath stirred up in this city. What some lament of, we rather should rejoice at, should rather praise this pious forwardness among men, to reassume the ill-deputed care of their religion into their own hands again. A little generous prudence, a little forbearance of one another, and some grain of charity might win all these diligences to join, and unite in one general and brotherly search after truth; could we but forgo this prelatical tradition of crowding free consciences and Christian liberties into canons and precepts of men. I doubt not, if some great and worthy stranger should come among us, wise to discern the mould and temper of a people, and how to govern it, observing the high hopes and aims, the diligent alacrity of our extended thoughts and reasonings in the pursuance of truth and freedom, but that he would cry out as Pyrrhus did, admiring the Roman docility and courage: If such were my Epirots, I would not despair the greatest design that could be attempted, to make a Church or kingdom happy.

Yet these are the men cried out against for schismatics and sectaries; as if, while the temple of the Lord was building, some cutting, some squaring the marble, others hewing the cedars, there should be a sort of irrational men who could not consider there must be many schisms and many dissections made in the quarry and in the timber, ere the house of God can be built. And when every stone is laid artfully together, it cannot be united into a continuity, it can but be contiguous in this world; neither can every piece of the building be of one form; nay rather the perfection consists in this, that, out of many moderate varieties and brotherly dissimilitudes that are not vastly disproportional, arises the goodly and the graceful symmetry that commends the whole pile and structure.

Let us therefore be more considerate builders, more wise in spiritual architecture, when great reformation is expected. For now the time seems come, wherein Moses the great prophet may sit in heaven rejoicing to see that memorable and glorious wish of his fulfilled, when not only our seventy elders, but all the Lord's people, are become prophets. No marvel then though some men, and some good men too perhaps, but young in goodness, as Joshua then was, envy them. They fret, and out of their own weakness are in agony, lest these divisions and subdivisions will undo us. The adversary again applauds, and waits the hour: when they have branched themselves out, saith he, small enough into parties and partitions, then will be our time. Fool! he sees not the firm root, out of which we all grow, though into branches: nor will beware until he see our small divided maniples cutting through at every angle of his ill-united and unwieldy brigade. And that we are to hope better of all these supposed sects and schisms, and that we shall not need that solicitude, honest perhaps, though over-timorous, of them that vex in this behalf, but shall laugh in the end at those malicious applauders of our differences, I have these reasons to persuade me.

First, when a city shall be as it were besieged and blocked about, her navigable river infested, inroads and incursions round, defiance and battle oft rumoured to be marching up even to her walls and suburb trenches, that then the people, or the greater part, more than at other times, wholly taken up with the study of highest and most important matters to be reformed, should be disputing, reasoning, reading, inventing, discoursing, even to a rarity and admiration, things not before discoursed or written of, argues first a singular goodwill, contentedness and confidence in your prudent foresight and safe government, Lords and Commons; and from thence derives itself to a gallant bravery and well-grounded contempt of their enemies, as if there were no small number of as great spirits among us, as his was, who when Rome was nigh besieged by Hannibal, being in the city, bought that piece of ground at no cheap rate, whereon Hannibal himself encamped his own regiment.

Next, it is a lively and cheerful presage of our happy success and victory. For as in a body, when the blood is fresh, the spirits pure and vigorous, not only to vital but to rational faculties, and those in the acutest and the pertest operations of wit and subtlety, it argues in what good plight and constitution the body is; so when the cheerfulness of the people is so sprightly up, as that it has not only wherewith to guard well its own freedom and safety, but to spare, and to bestow upon the solidest and sublimest points of controversy and new invention, it betokens us not degenerated, nor drooping to a fatal decay, but casting off the old and wrinkled skin of corruption to outlive these pangs and wax young again, entering the glorious ways of truth and prosperous virtue, destined to become great and honourable in these latter ages. Methinks I see in my mind a noble and puissant nation rousing herself like a strong man after sleep, and shaking her invincible locks: methinks I see her as an eagle mewing her mighty youth, and kindling her undazzled eyes at the full midday beam; purging and unscaling her long-abused sight at the fountain itself of heavenly radiance; while the whole noise of timorous and flocking birds, with those also that love the twilight, flutter about, amazed at what she means, and in their envious gabble would prognosticate a year of sects and schisms.

What would ye do then? should ye suppress all this flowery crop of knowledge and new light sprung up and yet springing daily in this city? Should ye set an oligarchy of twenty engrossers over it, to bring a famine upon our minds again, when we shall know nothing but what is measured to us by their bushel? Believe it, Lords and Commons, they who counsel ye to such a suppressing do as good as bid ye suppress yourselves; and I will soon show how. If it be desired to know the immediate cause of all this free writing and free speaking, there cannot be assigned a truer than your own mild and free and humane government. It is the liberty, Lords and Commons, which your own valorous and happy counsels have purchased us, liberty which is the nurse of all great wits; this is that which hath rarefied and enlightened our spirits like the influence of heaven; this is that which hath enfranchised, enlarged and lifted up our apprehensions, degrees above themselves.

Ye cannot make us now less capable, less knowing, less eagerly pursuing of the truth, unless ye first make yourselves, that made us so, less the lovers, less the founders of our true liberty. We can grow ignorant again, brutish, formal and slavish, as ye found us; but you then must first become that which ye cannot be, oppressive, arbitrary and tyrannous, as they were from whom ye have freed us. That our hearts are now more capacious, our thoughts more erected to the search and expectation of greatest and exactest things, is the issue of your own virtue propagated in us; ye cannot suppress that, unless ye reinforce an abrogated and merciless law, that fathers may dispatch at will their own children. And who shall then stick closest to ye, and excite others? not he who takes up arms for coat and conduct, and his four nobles of Danegelt. Although I dispraise not the defence of just immunities, yet love my peace better, if that were all. Give me the liberty to know, to utter, and to argue freely according to conscience, above all liberties.

What would be best advised, then, if it be found so hurtful and so unequal to suppress opinions for the newness or the unsuitableness to a customary acceptance, will not be my task to say. I only shall repeat what I have learned from one of your own honourable number, a right noble and pious lord, who, had he not sacrificed his life and fortunes to the Church and Commonwealth, we had not now missed and bewailed a worthy and undoubted patron of this argument. Ye know him,

I am sure; yet I for honour's sake, and may it be eternal to him, shall name him, the Lord Brook. He writing of episcopacy, and by the way treating of sects and schisms, left ye his vote, or rather now the last words of his dying charge, which I know will ever be of dear and honoured regard with ye, so full of meekness and breathing charity, that next to his last testament, who bequeathed love and peace to his disciples, I cannot call tomind where I have read or heard words more mild and peaceful. He there exhorts us to hear with patience and humility those, however they be miscalled, that desire to live purely, in such a use of God's ordinances, as the best guidance of their conscience gives them, and to tolerate them, though in some disconformity to ourselves. The book itself will tell us more at large, being published to the world, and dedicated to the Parliament by him who, both for his life and for his death, deserves that what advice he left be not laid by without perusal.

And now the time in special is, by privilege to write and speak what may help to the further discussing of matters in agitation. The temple of Janus with his two controversial faces might now not unsignificantly be set open. And though all the winds of doctrine were let loose to play upon the earth, so Truth be in the field, we do injuriously, by licensing and prohibiting, to misdoubt her strength. Let her and Falsehood grapple; who ever knew Truth put to the worse, in a free and open encounter? Her confuting is the best and surest suppressing. He who hears what praying there is for light and clearer knowledge to be sent down among us, would think of other matters to be constituted beyond the discipline of Geneva, framed and fabricked already to our hands. Yet when the new light which we beg for shines in upon us, there be who envy and oppose, if it come not first in at their casements. What a collusion is this, whenas we are exhorted by the wise man to use diligence, *to seek for wisdom as for hidden treasures* early and late, that another order shall enjoin us to know nothing but by statute? When a man hath been labouring the hardest labour in the deep mines of knowledge, hath furnished out his findings in all their equipage; drawn forth his reasons as it were a battle ranged; scattered and defeated all objections in his way; calls out his adversary into the plain, offers him the advantage of wind and sun, if he please, only that he may try the matter by dint of argument: for his opponents then to skulk, to lay ambushments, to keep a narrow bridge of licensing where the challenger should pass, though it be valour enough in soldiership, is but weakness and cowardice in the wars of Truth.

For who knows not that Truth is strong, next to the Almighty? She needs no policies, nor stratagems, nor licensings to make her victorious; those are the shifts and the defences that error uses against her power. Give her but room, and do not bind her when she sleeps, for then she speaks not true, as the old Proteus did, who spake oracles only when he was caught and bound, but then rather she turns herself into all shapes, except her own, and perhaps tunes her voice according to the time, as Micaiah did before Ahab, until she be adjured into her own likeness. Yet is it not impossible that she may have more shapes than one. What else is all that rank of things indifferent, wherein Truth may be on this side or on the other, without being unlike herself? What but a vain shadow else is the abolition of *those ordinances, that hand-writing nailed to the cross*? What great purchase is this Christian liberty which Paul so often boasts of? His doctrine is, that he who eats or eats not, regards a day or regards it not, may do either to the Lord. How many other things might be tolerated in peace, and left to conscience, had we but charity, and were it not the chief stronghold of our hypocrisy to be ever judging one another?

I fear yet this iron yoke of outward conformity hath left a slavish print upon our necks; the ghost of a linen decency yet haunts us. We stumble and are impatient at the least dividing of one visible congregation from another, though it be not in fundamentals; and through our forwardness to suppress, and our backwardness to recover any enthralled piece of truth out of the gripe of custom, we care not to keep truth separated from truth, which is the fiercest rent and disunion of all. We do not see that, while we still affect by all means a rigid external formality, we may as soon fall again into a gross conforming stupidity, a stark and dead congealment of *wood and hay and stubble*, forced and frozen together, which is more to the sudden degenerating of a Church than many subdichotomies of petty schisms.

Not that I can think well of every light separation, or that all in a Church is to be expected *gold and silver and precious stones*: it is not possible for man to sever the wheat from the tares, the good fish from the other fry; that must be the Angels' ministry at the end of mortal things. Yet if all cannot be of one mind—as who looks they should be?—this doubtless is more wholesome, more prudent, and more Christian, that many be tolerated, rather than all compelled. I mean not tolerated popery, and open superstition, which, as it extirpates all religions and civil supremacies, so itself should be extirpate, provided first that all charitable and compassionate means be used to win and regain the weak and the misled: that also which is impious or evil absolutely either against faith or manners no law can possibly permit, that intends not to unlaw itself: but those neighbouring differences, or rather indifferences, are what I speak of, whether in some point of doctrine or of discipline, which, though they may be many, yet need not interrupt *the unity of Spirit*, if we could but find among us *the bond of peace.*

In the meanwhile if any one would write, and bring his helpful hand to the slow-moving Reformation which we labour under, if Truth have spoken to him before others, or but seemed at least to speak, who hath so bejesuited us that we should trouble that man with asking licence to do so worthy a deed? and not consider this, that if it come to prohibiting, there is not aught more likely to be prohibited than truth itself; whose first appearance to our eyes, bleared and dimmed with prejudice and custom, is more unsightly and unplausible than many errors, even as the person is of many a great man slight and contemptible to see to. And what do they tell us vainly of new opinions, when this very opinion of theirs, that none must be heard but whom they like, is the worst and newest opinion of all others; and is the chief cause why sects and schisms do so much abound, and true knowledge is kept at distance from us; besides yet a greater danger which is in it.

For when God shakes a kingdom with strong and healthful commotions to a general reforming, 'tis not untrue that many sectaries and false teachers are then busiest in seducing; but yet more true it is, that God then raises to his own work men of rare abilities, and more than common industry, not only to look back and revise what hath been taught heretofore, but to gain further and go on some new enlightened steps in the discovery of truth. For such is the order of God's enlightening his Church, to dispense and deal out by degrees his beam, so as our earthly eyes may best sustain it.

Neither is God appointed and confined, where and out of what place these his chosen shall be first heard to speak; for he sees not as man sees, chooses not as man chooses, lest we should devote ourselves again to set places, and assemblies, and outward callings of men; planting our faith one while in the old Convocation house, and another while in the Chapel at Westminster; when all the faith and religion that shall be there canonized is not sufficient without plain convincement, and the charity of patient instruction to supple the least bruise of conscience, to edify the meanest Christian, who desires to walk in the Spirit, and not in the letter of human trust, for all the number of voices that can be there made; no, though Harry VII himself there, with all his liege tombs about him, should lend them voices from the dead, to swell their number.

And if the men be erroneous who appear to be the leading schismatics, what withholds us but our sloth, our self-will, and distrust in the right cause, that we do not give them gentle meetings and gentle dismissions, that we debate not and examine the matter thoroughly with liberal and frequent audience; if not for their sakes, yet for our own? seeing no man who hath tasted learning, but will confess the many ways of profiting by those who, not contented with stale receipts, are able to manage and set forth new positions to the world. And were they but as the dust and cinders of our feet, so long as in that notion they may yet serve to polish and brighten the armoury of Truth, even for that respect they were not utterly to be cast away. But if they be of those whom God hath fitted for the special use of these times with eminent and ample gifts, and those perhaps neither among the priests nor among the Pharisees, and we in the haste of a precipitant zeal shall make no distinction, but resolve to stop their mouths, because we fear they come with new and dangerous opinions, as we commonly forejudge them ere we understand them; no less than woe to us, while, thinking thus to defend the Gospel, we are found the persecutors.

There have been not a few since the beginning of this Parliament, both of the presbytery and others, who by their unlicensed books, to the contempt of an Imprimatur, first broke that triple ice clung about our hearts, and taught the people to see day: I hope that none of those were the persuaders to renew upon us this bondage which they themselves have wrought so much good by contemning. But if neither the check that Moses gave to young Joshua, nor the countermand which our Saviour gave to young John, who was so ready to prohibit those whom he thought unlicensed, be not enough to admonish our elders how unacceptable to God their testy mood of prohibiting is; if neither their own remembrance what evil hath abounded in the Church by this let of licensing, and what good they themselves have begun by transgressing it, be not enough, but that they will persuade and execute the most Dominican part of the Inquisition over us, and are already with one foot in the stirrup so active at suppressing, it would be no unequal distribution in the first place to suppress the suppressors themselves: whom the change of their condition hath puffed up, more than their late experience of harder times hath made wise.

And as for regulating the press, let no man think to have the honour of advising ye better than yourselves have done in that Order published next before this, "that no book be printed, unless the printer's and the author's name, or at least the printer's, be registered." Those which otherwise come forth, if they be found mischievous and libellous, the fire and the executioner will be the timeliest and the most effectual remedy that man's prevention can use. For this authentic Spanish policy of licensing books, if I have said aught, will prove the most unlicensed book itself within a short while; and was the immediate image of a

Star Chamber decree to that purpose made in those very times when that Court did the rest of those her pious works, for which she is now fallen from the stars with Lucifer. Whereby ye may guess what kind of state prudence, what love of the people, what care of religion or good manners there was at the contriving, although with singular hypocrisy it pretended to bind books to their good behaviour. And how it got the upper hand of your precedent Order so well constituted before, if we may believe those men whose profession gives them cause to inquire most, it may be doubted there was in it the fraud of some old patentees and monopolizers in the trade of bookselling; who under pretence of the poor in their Company not to be defrauded, and the just retaining of each man his several copy, which God forbid should be gainsaid, brought divers glossing colours to the House, which were indeed but colours, and serving to no end except it be to exercise a superiority over their neighbours; men who do not therefore labour in an honest profession to which learning is indebted, that they should be made other men's vassals. Another end is thought was aimed at by some of them in procuring by petition this Order, that, having power in their hands, malignant books might the easier scape abroad, as the event shows.

But of these sophisms and elenchs of merchandise I skill not. This I know, that errors in a good government and in a bad are equally almost incident; for what magistrate may not be misinformed, and much the sooner, if liberty of printing be reduced into the power of a few? But to redress willingly and speedily what hath been erred, and in highest authority to esteem a plain advertisement more than others have done a sumptuous bride, is a virtue (honoured Lords and Commons) answerable to your highest actions, and whereof none can participate but greatest and wisest men.

THE SECOND DEFENCE OF THE PEOPLE OF ENGLAND

AGAINST AN ANONYMOUS LIBEL

ENTITLED

'THE ROYAL BLOOD CRYING TO HEAVEN FOR VENGEANCE ON THE ENGLISH PARRICIDES'

(Translated from the Latin by Robert Fellowes)

[*SELECTED PASSAGES*]

A grateful recollection of the divine goodness is the first of human obligations; and extraordinary favours demand more solemn and devout acknowledgments: with such acknowledgments I feel it my duty to begin this work. First, because I was born at a time when the virtue of my fellow-citizens, far exceeding that of their progenitors in greatness of soul and vigour of enterprise, having invoked Heaven to witness the justice of their cause, and been clearly governed by its directions, has succeeded in delivering the commonwealth from the most grievous tyranny, and religion from the most ignominious degradation. And next, because when there suddenly arose many who, as is usual with the vulgar, basely calumniated the most illustrious achievements, and when one eminent above the rest, inflated with literary pride, and the zealous applauses of his partisans, had in a scandalous publication, which was particularly levelled against me, nefariously undertaken to plead the cause of despotism, I, who was neither deemed unequal to so renowned an adversary, nor to so great a subject, was particularly selected by the deliverers of our country, and by the general suffrage of the public, openly to vindicate the rights of the English nation, and consequently of liberty itself. Lastly, because in a matter of so much moment, and which excited such ardent expectations, I did not disappoint the hopes nor the opinions of my fellow-citizens; while men of learning and eminence abroad honoured me with unmingled approbation; while I obtained such a victory over my opponent, that notwithstanding his unparalleled assurance, he was obliged to quit the field with his courage broken and his reputation lost; and for the three years which he lived afterwards, much as he menaced and furiously as he raved, he gave me no further trouble, except that he procured the paltry aid of some despicable hirelings, and suborned some of his silly and extravagant admirers, to support him under the weight of the unexpected and recent disgrace which he had experienced. This will immediately appear Such are the signal favours which I ascribe to the divine beneficence, and which I thought it right devoutly to commemorate, not only that I might discharge a debt of gratitude, but particularly because they seem auspicious to the success of my present undertaking. For who is there, who does not identify the honour of his country with his own? And what can conduce more to the beauty or glory of one's country, than the recovery, not only of its civil but its religious liberty? And what nation or state ever obtained both, by more successful or more valorous exertion? For fortitude is seen resplendent, not only in the field of battle and amid the clash of arms, but displays its energy under every difficulty and against every assailant. Those Greeks and Romans, who are the objects of our admiration, employed hardly any other virtue in the extirpation of tyrants, than that love of liberty which made them prompt in seizing the sword, and gave them strength to use it. With facility they accomplished the undertaking, amid the general shout of praise and joy; nor did they engage in the attempt so much as an enterprise of perilous and doubtful issue, as in a contest the most glorious in which virtue could be signalized; which infallibly led to present recompence; which bound their brows with wreaths of laurel, and consigned their memories to immortal fame. For as yet, tyrants were not beheld with a superstitious reverence; as yet they were not regarded with tenderness and complacency, as the vicegerents or deputies of Christ, as they have suddenly professed to be; as yet the vulgar, stupefied by the subtle casuistry of the priest, had not degenerated into a state of barbarism, more gross than that which disgraces the most senseless natives of Hindostan. For these make mischievous demons, whose malice they cannot resist, the objects of their religious adoration: while those elevate impotent tyrants, in order to shield them from destruction, into the rank of gods; and, to their own cost, consecrate the pests of the human race. But against this dark array of long-received opinions, superstitions, obloquy, and fears, which some dread even more than the enemy himself, the English had to contend; and all this, under the light of better information, and favoured by an impulse from above, they overcame with such singular enthusiasm and bravery, that, great as were the numbers engaged in the contest, the grandeur of conception, and loftiness of spirit which were universally displayed, merited for each individual more than a mediocrity of fame; and Britain, which was formerly styled the hot-bed of tyranny, will hereafter deserve to be celebrated for endless ages, as a soil most genial to the growth of liberty. During the mighty struggle, no anarchy, no licentiousness was seen; no illusions of glory, no extravagant emulation of the ancients inflamed them with a thirst for ideal liberty; but the rectitude of their lives, and the sobriety of their habits, taught them the only true and safe road to real liberty; and they took up arms only to defend the sanctity of the laws and the rights of conscience. Relying on the divine assistance, they used every honourable exertion to break the yoke of slavery; of the praise of which, though I claim no share to myself, yet I can easily repel any charge which may be adduced against me, either of want of courage, or want of zeal. For though I did not participate in the toils or dangers of the war, yet I was at the same time engaged in a service not less hazardous to myself and more beneficial to my fellow-citizens; nor, in the adverse turns of our affairs, did I ever betray any symptoms of pusillanimity and dejection; or shew myself more afraid than became me of malice or of death: For since from my youth I was devoted to the pursuits of literature, and my mind had always been stronger than my body, I did not court the labours of a camp, in which any common person would have been of more service than myself, but resorted to that employment in which my exertions were likely to be of most avail. Thus, with the better part of my frame I contributed as much as possible to the good of my country, and to the success of the glorious cause in which we were engaged; and I thought that if God willed the success of such glorious achievements, it was equally agreeable to his will that there should be others by whom those achievements should be recorded with dignity and elegance; and that the truth, which had been defended by arms, should also be defended by reason; which is the best and only legitimate means of defending it. Hence, while I applaud those who were victorious in the field, I will not complain of the province which was assigned me; but rather congratulate myself upon it, and thank the Author of all good for having placed me in a station, which may be an object of envy to others rather than of regret to myself. I am far from wishing to make any vain or arrogant comparisons, or to speak ostentatiously of myself; but, in a cause so great and glorious, and particularly on an occasion when I am called by the general suffrage to defend the very defenders of that cause, I can hardly refrain from assuming a more lofty and swelling tone than the simplicity of an exordium may seem to justify: and much as I may be surpassed in the powers of eloquence and copiousness of diction, by the illustrious orators of antiquity; yet the subject of which I treat was never surpassed in any age, in dignity, or in interest. It has excited such general and such ardent expectation, that I imagine myself not in the forum or on the rostra, surrounded only by the people of Athens or of Rome, but about to address in this, as I did in my former Defence, the whole collective body of people, cities, states, and councils of the wise and eminent, through the wide expanse of anxious and listening Europe. I seem to survey, as from a towering height, the far extended tracts of sea and land, and innumerable crowds of spectators, betraying in their looks the liveliest interest, and sensations the most congenial with my own. Here I behold the stout and manly prowess of the Germans disdaining servitude; there the generous and lively impetuosity of the French; on this side, the calm and stately valour of the Spaniard; on that, the composed and wary magnanimity of the Italian. Of all the lovers of liberty and virtue, the magnanimous and the wise, in whatever quarter they may be found, some secretly favour, others openly approve; some greet me with congratulations and applause; others, who had long been proof against conviction, at last yield themselves captive to the force of truth. Surrounded by congregated multitudes, I now imagine that, from the columns of Hercules to the Indian Ocean, I behold the nations of the earth recovering that liberty which they so long had lost; and that the people of this island are transporting to other countries a plant of more beneficial qualities, and more noble growth, than that which Triptolemus is reported to have carried from region to region; that they are disseminating the blessings of civilization and freedom among cities, kingdoms, and nations.

* * * * *

You see under what a cloud of disgrace Salmasius laboured to depress me. But ought he to have relinquished a post of honourable exertion to mingle in foreign controversies, or to have deserted the service of the church for political and external discussions, in which he had no knowledge and no concern? Ought he to have made a truce with the pope? and, what was most base of all, after the utmost bitterness of hostility, to have sought a reconciliation with the bishops? Let us now come to the charges which were brought against myself. Is there anything reprehensible in my manners or my conduct? Surely nothing. What no one, not totally divested of all generous sensibility, would have done, he reproaches me with want of beauty and loss of sight.

"A monster huge and hideous, void of sight."

I certainly never supposed that I should have been obliged to enter into a competition for beauty with the Cyclops; but he immediately corrects himself, and says, "though not indeed huge, for there cannot be a more spare, shrivelled, and bloodless form." It is of no moment to say anything of personal appearance, yet lest (as the Spanish vulgar, implicitly confiding in the relations of their priests, believe of heretics) any one, from the representations of my enemies, should be led to imagine that I have either the head of a dog, or the horn of a rhinoceros, I will say something on the subject, that I may have an opportunity of paying my grateful acknowledgments to the Deity, and of refuting the most shameless lies. I do not believe that I was ever once noted for deformity, by any one who ever saw me; but the praise of beauty I am not anxious to obtain. My stature certainly is not tall; but it rather approaches the middle than the diminutive. Yet what if it were diminutive when so many men, illustrious both in peace and war, have been the same? And how can that be called diminutive, which is great enough for every virtuous achievement? Nor, though very thin, was I ever deficient in courage or in strength; and I was wont constantly to exercise myself in the use of the broadsword, as long as it comported with my habit and my years. Armed with this weapon, as I usually was, I should have thought myself quite a match for any one, though much stronger than myself, and I felt perfectly secure against the assault of any open enemy. At this moment I have the same courage, the same strength, though not the same eyes; yet so little do they betray any external appearance of injury, that they are as unclouded and bright as the eyes of those who most distinctly see. In this instance alone I am a dissembler against my will. My face, which is said to indicate a total privation of blood, is of a complexion entirely opposite to the pale and the cadaverous; so that, though I am more than forty years old, there is scarcely any one to whom I do not appear ten years younger than I am; and the smoothness of my skin is not, in the least, affected by the wrinkles of age. If there be one particle of falsehood in this relation, I should deservedly incur the ridicule of many thousands of my countrymen, and even many foreigners to whom I am personally known. But if he, in a matter so foreign to his purpose, shall be found to have asserted so many shameless and gratuitous falsehoods, you may the more readily estimate the quantity of his veracity on other topics. Thus much necessity compelled me to assert concerning my personal appearance. Respecting yours, though I have been informed that it is most insignificant and contemptible, a perfect mirror of the worthlessness of your character and the malevolence of your heart, I say nothing, and no one will be anxious that anything should be said. I wish that I could with equal facility refute what this barbarous opponent has said of my blindness; but I cannot do it; and I must submit to the affliction. It is not so wretched to be blind, as it is not to be capable of enduring blindness. But why should I not endure a misfortune, which it behoves every one to be prepared to endure if it should happen; which may, in the common course of things, happen to any man; and which has been known to happen to the most distinguished and virtuous persons in history. Shall I mention those wise and ancient bards, whose misfortunes the gods are said to have compensated by superior endowments, and whom men so much revered, that they chose rather to impute their want of sight to the injustice of heaven than to their own want of innocence or virtue? What is reported of the Augur Tiresias is well known, of whom Apollonius sung thus in his Argonauts:

'To men he dar'd the will divine disclose,
Nor fear'd what Jove might in his wrath impose.
The gods assigned him age; without decay;
But snatched the blessing of his sight away.'

But God himself is truth; in propagating which, as men display a greater integrity and zeal, they approach nearer to the similitude of God, and possess a greater portion of his love. We cannot suppose the deity envious of truth, or unwilling that it should be freely communicated to mankind. The loss of sight, therefore, which this inspired sage, who was so eager in promoting knowledge among men, sustained, cannot be considered as a judicial punishment. Or shall I mention those worthies who were as distinguished for wisdom in the cabinet, as for valour in the field? And first, Timoleon of Corinth, who delivered his city and all Sicily from the yoke of slavery; than whom there never lived in any age, a more virtuous man, or a more incorrupt statesman: Next Appius Claudius, whose discreet counsels in the senate, though they could not restore sight to his own eyes, saved Italy from the formidable inroads of Pyrrhus: then Caecilius Metellus the high-priest, who lost his sight, while he saved, not only the city, but the palladium, the protection of the city, and the most sacred relics, from the destruction of the flames. On other occasions Providence has indeed given conspicuous proofs of its regard for such singular exertions of patriotism and virtue; what, therefore, happened to so great and so good a man, I can hardly place in the catalogue of misfortunes. Why should I mention others of later times, as Dandolo of Venice, the incomparable Doge; or Boemar Zisca, the bravest of generals, and the champion of the cross; or Jerome Zanchius, and some other theologians of the highest reputation? For it is evident that the patriarch Isaac, than whom no man ever enjoyed more of the divine regard, lived blind for many years; and perhaps also his son Jacob, who was equally an object of the divine benevolence. And in short, did not our Saviour himself clearly declare that that poor man whom he restored to sight had not been born blind, either on account of his own sins or those of his progenitors? And with respect to myself, though I have accurately examined my conduct, and scrutinized my soul, I call thee, O God, the searcher of hearts, to witness, that I am not conscious, either in the more early or in the later periods of my life, of having committed any enormity, which might deservedly have marked me out as a fit object for such a calamitous visitation. But since my enemies boast that this affliction is only a retribution for the transgressions of my pen, I again invoke the Almighty to witness, that I never, at any time, wrote anything which I did not think agreeable to truth, to justice, and to piety. This was my persuasion then, and I feel the same persuasion now. Nor was I ever prompted to such exertions by the influence of ambition, by the lust of lucre or of praise; it was only by the conviction of duty and the feeling of patriotism, a disinterested passion for the extension of civil and religious liberty. Thus, therefore, when I was publicly solicited to write a reply to the Defence of the royal cause, when I had to contend with the pressure of sickness, and with the apprehension of soon losing the sight of my remaining eye, and when my medical attendants clearly announced, that if I did engage in the work, it would be irreparably lost, their premonitions caused no hesitation and inspired no dismay. I would not have listened to the voice even of Esculapius himself from the shrine of Epidauris, in preference to the suggestions of the heavenly monitor within my breast; my resolution was unshaken, though the alternative was either the loss of my sight, or the desertion of my duty: and I called to mind those two destinies, which the oracle of Delphi announced to the son of Thetis:

> "*Two fates may lead me to the realms of night;*
> *If staying here, around Troy's wall I fight,*
> *To my dear home no more must I return;*
> *But lasting glory will adorn my urn.*
> *But, if I withdraw from the martial strife,*
> *Short is my fame, but long will be my life.*" *Il.* ix.

I considered that many had purchased a less good by a greater evil, the meed of glory by the loss of life; but that I might procure great good by little suffering; that though I am blind, I might still discharge the most honourable duties, the performance of which, as it is something more durable than glory, ought to be an object of superior admiration and esteem; I resolved, therefore, to make the short interval of sight, which was left me to enjoy, as beneficial as possible to the public interest. Thus it is clear by what motives I was governed in the measures which I took, and the losses which I sustained. Let then the calumniators of the divine goodness cease to revile, or to make me the object of their superstitious imaginations. Let them consider, that my situation, such as it is, is neither an object of my shame or my regret, that my resolutions are too firm to be shaken, that I am not depressed by any sense of the divine displeasure; that, on the other hand, in the most momentous periods, I have had full experience of the divine favour and protection; and that, in the solace and the strength which have been infused into me from above, I have been enabled to do the will of God; that I may oftener think on what he has bestowed, than on what he has withheld; that, in short, I am unwilling to exchange my consciousness of rectitude with that of any other person; and that I feel the recollection a treasured store of tranquillity and delight. But, if the choice were necessary, I would, sir, prefer my blindness to yours; yours is a cloud spread over the mind, which darkens both the light of reason and of conscience; mine keeps from my view only the coloured surfaces of things, while it leaves me at liberty to contemplate the beauty and stability of virtue and of truth. How many things are there besides which I would not willingly see; how many which I must see against my will; and how few which I feel any anxiety to see! There is, as the apostle has remarked, a way to strength through weakness. Let me then be the most feeble creature alive, as long as that feebleness serves to invigorate the energies of my rational and immortal spirit; as long as in that obscurity, in which I am enveloped, the light of the divine presence more clearly shines, then, in proportion as I am weak, I shall be invincibly strong; and in proportion as I am blind, I shall more clearly see. O! that I may thus be perfected by feebleness, and irradiated by obscurity! And, indeed, in my blindness, I enjoy in no inconsiderable degree the favour of the Deity, who regards me with more tenderness and compassion in proportion as I am able to behold nothing but himself. Alas! for him who insults me, who maligns and merits public execration! For the divine law not only shields me from injury, but almost renders me too sacred to attack; not indeed so much from the privation of my sight, as from the overshadowing of those heavenly wings which seemed to have occasioned this obscurity; and which, when occasioned, he is wont to illuminate with an interior light, more precious and more pure.

* * * * *

I will now mention who and whence I am. I was born at London, of an honest family; my father was distinguished by the undeviating integrity of his life; my mother, by the esteem in which she was held, and the alms which she bestowed. My father destined me from a child to the pursuits of literature; and my appetite for knowledge was so voracious, that, from twelve years of age, I hardly ever left my studies, or went to bed before midnight. This primarily led to my loss of sight. My eyes were naturally weak, and I was subject to frequent head-aches; which, however, could not chill the ardour of my curiosity, or retard the progress of my improvement. My father had me daily instructed in the grammar-school, and by other masters at home. He then, after I had acquired a proficiency in various languages, and had made a considerable progress in philosophy, sent me to the University of Cambridge. Here I passed seven years in the usual course of instruction and study, with the approbation of the good, and without any stain upon my character, till I took the degree of Master of Arts. After this I did not, as this miscreant feigns, run away into Italy, but of my own accord retired to my father's house, whither I was accompanied by the regrets of most of the fellows of the college, who shewed me no common marks of friendship and esteem. On my father's estate, where he had determined to pass the remainder of his days, I enjoyed an interval of uninterrupted leisure, which I entirely devoted to the perusal of the Greek and Latin classics; though I occasionally visited the metropolis, either for the sake of purchasing books, or of learning something new in mathematics or in music, in which I, at that time, found a source of pleasure and amusement. In this manner I spent five years till my mother's death. I then became anxious to visit foreign parts, and particularly Italy. My father gave me his permission, and I left home with one servant. On my departure, the celebrated Henry Wotton, who had long been king James's ambassador at Venice, gave me a signal proof of his regard, in an elegant letter which he wrote, breathing not only the warmest friendship, but containing some maxims of conduct which I found very useful in my travels. The noble Thomas Scudamore, king Charles's ambassador, to whom I carried letters of recommendation, received me most courteously at Paris. His lordship gave me a card of introduction to the learned Hugo Grotius, at that time ambassador from the queen of Sweden to the French court; whose acquaintance I anxiously desired, and to whose house I was accompanied by some of his lordship's friends. A few days after, when I set out for Italy, he gave me letters to the English merchants on my route, that they might shew me any civilities in their power. Taking ship at Nice, I arrived at Genoa, and afterwards visited Leghorn, Pisa, and Florence. In the latter city, which I have always more particularly esteemed for the elegance of its dialect, its genius, and its taste, I stopped about two months; when I contracted an intimacy with many persons of rank and learning; and was a constant attendant at their literary parties; a practice which prevails there, and tends so much to the diffusion of knowledge, and the preservation of friendship No time will ever abolish the agreeable recollections which I cherish of Jacob Gaddi, Carolo Dati, Frescobaldo, Cultellero, Bonomatthai, Clementillo, Francisco, and many others. From Florence I went to Siena, thence to Rome, where, after I had spent about two months in viewing the antiquities of that renowned city, where I experienced the most friendly attentions from Lucas Holstein, and other learned and ingenious men, I continued my route to Naples. There I was introduced by a certain recluse, with whom I had travelled from Rome, to John Baptista Manso, marquis of Villa, a nobleman of distinguished rank and authority, to whom Torquato Tasso, the illustrious poet, inscribed his book on friendship. During my stay, he gave me singular proofs of his regard. he himself conducted me round the city, and to the palace of the viceroy; and more than once paid me a visit at my lodgings. On my departure he gravely apologized for not having shewn me more civility, which he said he had been restrained from doing, because I had spoken with so little reserve on matters of religion. When I was preparing to pass over into Sicily and Greece, the melancholy intelligence which I received of the civil commotions in England made me alter my purpose; for I thought it base to be travelling for amusement abroad, while my fellow-citizens were fighting for liberty at home. While I was on my way back to Rome, some merchants informed me that the English Jesuits had formed a plot against me if I returned to Rome, because I had spoken too freely on religion; for it was a rule which I laid down to myself in those places, never to be the first to begin any conversation on religion; but if any questions were put to me concerning my faith, to declare it without any reserve or fear. I, nevertheless, returned to Rome. I took no steps to conceal either my person or my character; and for about the space of two months I again openly defended, as I had done before, the reformed religion in the very metropolis of popery. By the favour of God, I got safe back to Florence, where I was received with as much affection as if I had returned to my native country. There I stopped as many months as I had done before, except that I made an excursion for a few days to Lucca; and, crossing the Apennines, passed through Bologna and Ferrara to Venice. After I had spent a month in surveying the curiosities of this city, and had put on board a ship the books which I had collected in Italy, I proceeded through Verona and Milan, and along the Leman lake to Geneva. The mention of this city brings to my recollection the slandering More, and makes me again call the Deity to witness, that in all those places in which vice meets with so little discouragement, and is practised with so little shame, I never once deviated from the paths of integrity and virtue, and perpetually reflected that, though my conduct might escape the notice of men, it could not elude the inspection of God. At Geneva I held daily conferences with John Deodati, the learned professor of Theology. Then pursuing my former route through France, I returned to my native country, after an absence of one year and about three months; at the time when Charles, having broken the peace, was renewing what is called the episcopal war with the Scots, in which the royalists being routed in the first encounter, and the English being universally and justly disaffected, the necessity of his affairs at last obliged him to convene a parliament. As soon as I was able, I hired a spacious house in the city for myself and my books; where I again with rapture renewed my literary pursuits, and where I calmly awaited the issue of the contest, which I trusted to the wise conduct of Providence, and to the courage of the people. The vigour of the parliament had begun to humble the pride of the bishops. As long as the liberty of speech was no longer subject to control, all mouths began to be opened against the bishops: some complained of the vices of the individuals, others of those of the order. They said that it was unjust that they alone should differ from the model of other reformed churches; that the government of the church should be according to the pattern of other churches, and particularly the word of God. This awakened all my attention and my zeal. I saw that a way was opening for the establishment of real liberty; that the foundation was laying for the deliverance of man from the yoke of slavery and superstition; that the principles of religion, which were the first objects of our care, would exert a salutary influence on the manners and constitution of the republic; and as I had from my youth studied the distinctions between religious and civil rights, I perceived that if I ever wished to be of use, I ought at least not to be wanting to my country, to the church, and to so many of my fellow-Christians, in a crisis of so much danger, I therefore determined to relinquish the other pursuits in which I was engaged, and to transfer the whole force of my talents and my industry to this one important object. I accordingly wrote two books to a friend concerning the reformation of the Church of England. Afterwards, when two bishops of superior distinction vindicated their privileges against some principal ministers, I thought that on those topics, to the consideration of which I was led solely by my love of truth, and my reverence for Christianity, I should not probably write worse than those who were contending only for their own emoluments and usurpations. I therefore answered the one in two books, of which the first is inscribed, Concerning Prelatical Episcopacy, and the other Concerning the Mode of Ecclesiastical Government; and I replied to the other in some Animadversions, and soon after in an Apology. On this occasion it was supposed that I brought a timely succour to the ministers, who were hardly a match for the eloquence of their opponents; and from that time I was actively employed in refuting any answers that appeared. When the bishops could no longer resist the multitude of their assailants, I had leisure to turn my thoughts to other subjects; to the promotion of real and substantial liberty; which is rather to be sought from within than from without;

and whose existence depends, not so much on the terror of the sword, as on sobriety of conduct and integrity of life. When, therefore, I perceived that there were three species of liberty which are essential to the happiness of social life—religious, domestic, and civil; and as I had already written concerning the first, and the magistrates were strenuously active in obtaining the third, I determined to turn my attention to the second, or the domestic species. As this seemed to involve three material questions, the conditions of the conjugal tie, the education of the children, and the free publication of the thoughts, I made them objects of distinct consideration. I explained my sentiments, not only concerning the solemnization of the marriage, but the dissolution, if circumstances rendered it necessary; and I drew my arguments from the divine law, which Christ did not abolish, or publish another more grievous than that of Moses. I stated my own opinions, and those of others, concerning the exclusive exception of fornication, which our illustrious Selden has since, in his Hebrew Wife, more copiously discussed; for he in vain makes a vaunt of liberty in the senate or in the forum, who languishes under the vilest servitude, to an inferior at home. On this subject, therefore, I published some books which were more particularly necessary at that time, when man and wife were often the most inveterate foes, when the man often stayed to take care of his children at home, while the mother of the family was seen in the camp of the enemy, threatening death and destruction to her husband. I then discussed the principles of education in a summary manner, but sufficiently copious for those who attend seriously to the subject; than which nothing can be more necessary to principle the minds of men in virtue, the only genuine source of political and individual liberty, the only true safeguard of states, the bulwark of their prosperity and renown. Lastly, I wrote my Areopagitica, in order to deliver the press from the restraints with which it was encumbered; that the power of determining what was true and what was false, what ought to be published and what to be suppressed, might no longer be entrusted to a few illiterate and illiberal individuals who refused their sanction to any work which contained views or sentiments at all above the level of the vulgar superstition. On the last species of civil liberty, I said nothing, because I saw that sufficient attention was paid to it by the magistrates; nor did I write anything on the prerogative of the crown, till the king, voted an enemy by the parliament, and vanquished in the field, was summoned before the tribunal which condemned him to lose his head. But when, at length, some presbyterian ministers, who had formerly been the most bitter enemies to Charles, became jealous of the growth of the independents, and of their ascendancy in the parliament, most tumultuously clamoured against the sentence, and did all in their power to prevent the execution, though they were not angry, so much on account of the act itself, as because it was not the act of their party; and when they dared to affirm, that the doctrine of the protestants, and of all the reformed churches, was abhorrent to such an atrocious proceeding against kings; I thought that it became me to oppose such a glaring falsehood; and accordingly, without any immediate or personal application to Charles, I shewed, in an abstract consideration of the question, what might lawfully be done against tyrants; and in support of what I advanced, produced the opinions of the most celebrated divines; while I vehemently inveighed against the egregious ignorance or effrontery of men, who professed better things, and from whom better things might have been expected. That book did not make its appearance till after the death of Charles, and was written rather to reconcile the minds of the people to the event, than to discuss the legitimacy of that particular sentence which concerned the magistrates, and which was already executed. Such were the fruits of my private studies, which I gratuitously presented to the church and to the state; and for which I was recompensed by nothing but impunity; though the actions themselves procured me peace of conscience, and the approbation of the good; while I exercised that freedom of discussion which I loved. Others, without labour or desert, got possession of honours and emoluments; but no one ever knew me either soliciting anything myself or through the medium of my friends, ever beheld me in a supplicating posture at the doors of the senate, or the levees of the great. I usually kept myself secluded at home, where my own property, part of which had been withheld during the civil commotions, and part of which had been absorbed in the oppressive contributions which I had to sustain, afforded me a scanty subsistence. When I was released from these engagements, and thought that I was about to enjoy an interval of uninterrupted ease, I turned my thoughts to a continued history of my country, from the earliest times to the present period. I had already finished four books, when, after the subversion of the monarchy, and the establishment of a republic, I was surprised by an invitation from the council of state, who desired my services in the office for foreign affairs. A book appeared soon after, which was ascribed to the king, and contained the most invidious charges against the parliament. I was ordered to answer it; and opposed the Iconoclast to his Icon. I did not insult over fallen majesty, as is pretended; I only preferred queen Truth to king Charles. The charge of insult, which I saw that the malevolent would urge, I was at some pains to remove in the beginning of the work; and as often as possible in other places. Salmasius then appeared, to whom they were not, as More says, long in looking about for an opponent, but immediately appointed me, who happened at the time to be present in the council. I have thus, sir, given some account of myself, in order to stop your mouth, and to remove any prejudices which your falsehoods and misrepresentations might cause even good men to entertain against me.

* * * * *

Oliver Cromwell was sprung from a line of illustrious ancestors, who were distinguished for the civil functions which they sustained under the monarchy, and still more for the part which they took in restoring and establishing true religion in this country. In the vigour and maturity of his life, which he passed in retirement, he was conspicuous for nothing more than for the strictness of his religious habits, and the innocence of his life; and he had tacitly cherished in his breast that flame of piety which was afterwards to stand him in so much stead on the greatest occasions, and in the most critical exigencies. In the last parliament which was called by the king, he was elected to represent his native town, when he soon became distinguished by the justness of his opinions, and the vigour and decision of his counsels. When the sword was drawn, he offered his services, and was appointed to a troop of horse, whose numbers were soon increased by the pious and the good, who flocked from all quarters to his standard; and in a short time he almost surpassed the greatest generals in the magnitude and the rapidity of his achievements. Nor is this surprising; for he was a soldier disciplined to perfection in the knowledge of himself. He had either extinguished, or by habit had learned to subdue, the whole host of vain hopes, fears, and passions, which infest the soul. He first acquired the government of himself, and over himself acquired the most signal victories; so that on the first day he took the field against the external enemy, he was a veteran in arms, consummately practised in the toils and exigencies of war. It is not possible for me in the narrow limits in which I circumscribe myself on this occasion, to enumerate the many towns which he has taken, the many battles which he has won. The whole surface of the British empire has been the scene of his exploits, and the theatre of his triumphs; which alone would furnish ample materials for a history, and want a copiousness of narration not inferior to the magnitude and diversity of the transactions. This alone seems to be a sufficient proof of his extraordinary and almost supernatural virtue, that by the vigour of his genius, or the excellence of his discipline, adapted, not more to the necessities of war than to the precepts of Christianity, the good and the brave were from all quarters attracted to his camp, not only as to the best school of military talents, but of piety and virtue; and that during the whole war, and the occasional intervals of peace, amid so many vicissitudes of faction and of events, he retained and still retains the obedience of his troops, not by largesses or indulgence, but by his sole authority and the regularity of his pay. In this instance his fame may rival that of Cyrus, of Epaminondas, or any of the great generals of antiquity. Hence he collected an army as numerous and as well equipped as any one ever did in so short a time; which was uniformly obedient to his orders, and dear to the affections of the citizens; which was formidable to the enemy in the field, but never cruel to those who laid down their arms; which committed no lawless ravages on the persons or the property of the inhabitants; who, when they compared their conduct with the turbulence, the intemperance, the impiety, and the debauchery of the royalists, were wont to salute them as friends, and to consider them as guests. They were a stay to the good, a terror to the evil, and the warmest advocates for every exertion of piety and virtue. Nor would it be right to pass over the name of Fairfax, who united the utmost fortitude with the utmost courage; and the spotless innocence of whose life seemed to point him out as the peculiar favourite of Heaven. Justly, indeed, may you be excited to receive this wreath of praise; though you have retired as much as possible from the world, and seek those shades of privacy which were the delight of Scipio. Nor was it only the enemy whom you subdued, but you have triumphed over that flame of ambition and that lust of glory which are wont to make the best and the greatest of men their slaves. The purity of your virtues and the splendour of your actions consecrate those sweets of ease which you enjoy, and which constitute the wished-for haven of the toils of man. Such was the ease which, when the heroes of antiquity possessed, after a life of exertion and glory not greater than yours, the poets, in despair of finding ideas or expressions better suited to the subject, feigned that they were received into heaven, and invited to recline at the tables of the gods. But whether it were your health, which I principally believe, or any other motive which caused you to retire, of this I am convinced, that nothing could have induced you to relinquish the service of your country, if you had not known that in your successor liberty would meet with a protector, and England with a stay to its safety, and a pillar to its glory. For, while you, O Cromwell, are left among us, he hardly shews a proper confidence in the Supreme, who distrusts the security of England; when he sees that you are in so special a manner the favoured object of the divine regard. But there was another department of the war, which was destined for your exclusive exertions.

Without entering into any length of detail, I will, if possible, describe some of the most memorable actions, with as much brevity as you performed them with celerity. After the loss o' all Ireland, with the exception of one city, you in one battle immediately discomfited the forces of the rebels: and were busily employed in settling the country, when you were suddenly recalled to the war in Scotland. Hence you proceeded with unwearied diligence against the Scots, who were on the point of making an irruption into England with the king in their train: and in about the space of one year you entirely subdued, and added to the English dominion, that kingdom which all our monarchs, during a period of 800 years, had in vain struggled to subject. In one battle you almost annihilated the remainder of their forces, who, in a fit of desperation, had made a sudden incursion into England, then almost destitute of garrisons, and got as far as Worcester; where you came up with them by forced marches, and captured almost the whole of their nobility. A profound peace ensued; when we found, though indeed not then for the first time, that you were as wise in the cabinet as valiant in the field. It was your constant endeavour in the senate either to induce them to adhere to those treaties which they had entered into with the enemy, or speedily to adjust others which promised to be beneficial to the country. But when you saw that the business was artfully procrastinated, that every one was more intent on his own selfish interest than on the public good, that the people complained of the disappointments which they had experienced, and the fallacious promises by which they had been gulled, that they were the dupes of a few overbearing individuals, you put an end to their domination. A new parliament is summoned; and the right of election given to those to whom it was expedient. They meet; but do nothing; and, after having wearied themselves by their mutual dissensions, and fully exposed their incapacity to the observation of the country, they consent to a voluntary dissolution. In this state of desolation, to which we were reduced, you, O Cromwell! alone remained to conduct the government, and to save the country. We all willingly yield the palm of sovereignty to your unrivalled ability and virtue, except the few among us, who, either ambitions of honours which they have not the capacity to sustain, or who envy those which are conferred on one more worthy than themselves, or else who do not know that nothing in the world is more pleasing to God, more agreeable to reason, more politically just, or more generally useful, than that the supreme power should be vested in the best and the wisest of men. Such, O Cromwell, all acknowledge you to be; such are the services which you have rendered, as the leader of our councils, the general of our armies, and the father of your country. For this is the tender appellation by which all the good among us salute you from the very soul. Other names you neither have nor could endure; and you deservedly reject that pomp of title which attracts the gaze and admiration of the multitude. For what is a title but a certain definite mode of dignity; but actions such as yours surpass, not only the bounds of our admiration, but our titles; and, like the points of pyramids, which are lost in the clouds, they soar above the possibilities of titular commendation. But since, though it be not fit, it may be expedient, that the highest pitch of virtue should be circumscribed within the bounds of some human appellation, you endured to receive, for the public good, a title most like to that of the father of your country; not to exalt, but rather to bring you nearer to the level of ordinary men; the title of king was unworthy the transcendent majesty of your character. For if you had been captivated by a name over which, as a private man, you had so completely triumphed and crumbled into dust, you would have been doing the same thing as if, after having subdued some idolatrous nation by the help of the true God, you should afterwards fall down and worship the gods which you had vanquished. Do you then, sir, continue your course with the same unrivalled magnanimity; it sits well upon you; —to you our country owes its liberties: nor can you sustain a character at once more momentous and more august than that of the author, the guardian, and the preserver of our liberties;

and hence you have not only eclipsed the achievements of all our kings, but even those which have been fabled of our heroes. Often reflect what a dear pledge the beloved land of your nativity has entrusted to your care; and that liberty which she once expected only from the chosen flower of her talents and her virtues, she now expects from you only, and by you only hopes to obtain. Revere the fond expectations which we cherish, the solicitudes of your anxious country; revere the looks and the wounds of your brave companions in arms, who, under your banners, have so strenuously fought for liberty; revere the shades of those who perished in the contest; revere also the opinions and the hopes which foreign states entertain concerning us, who promise to themselves so many advantages from that liberty which we have so bravely acquired, from the establishment of that new government which has begun to shed its splendour on the world, which, if it be suffered to vanish like a dream, would involve us in the deepest abyss of shame; and lastly, revere yourself; and, after having endured so many sufferings and encountered so many perils for the sake of liberty, do not suffer it, now it is obtained, either to be violated by yourself, or in any one instance impaired by others. You cannot be truly free unless we are free too; for such is the nature of things, that he who entrenches on the liberty of others, is the first to lose his own and become a slave. But if you, who have hitherto been the patron and tutelary genius of liberty, if you, who are exceeded by no one in justice, in piety, and goodness, should hereafter invade that liberty which you have defended, your conduct must be fatally operative, not only against the cause of liberty, but the general interests of piety and virtue. Your integrity and virtue will appear to have evaporated, your faith in religion to have been small; your character with posterity will dwindle into insignificance, by which a most destructive blow will be levelled against the happiness of mankind. The work which you have undertaken is of incalculable moment, which will thoroughly sift and expose every principle and sensation of your heart, which will fully display the vigour and genius of your character, which will evince whether you really possess those great qualities of piety, fidelity, justice, and self-denial, which made us believe that you were elevated by the special direction of the Deity to the highest pinnacle of power. At once wisely and discreetly to hold the sceptre over three powerful nations, to persuade people to relinquish inveterate and corrupt for new and more beneficial maxims and institutions, to penetrate into the remotest parts of the country, to have the mind present and operative in every quarter, to watch against surprise, to provide against danger, to reject the blandishments of pleasure and pomp of power;—these are exertions compared with which the labour of war is mere pastime, which will require every energy and employ every faculty that you possess; which demand a man supported from above, and almost instructed by immediate inspiration. These and more than these are, no doubt, the objects which occupy your attention and engross your soul; as well as the means by which you may accomplish these important ends, and render our liberty at once more ample and more secure. And this you can, in my opinion, in no other way so readily effect, as by associating in your councils the companions of your dangers and your toils, men of exemplary modesty, integrity, and courage; whose hearts have not been hardened in cruelty and rendered insensible to pity by the sight of so much ravage and so much death, but whom it has rather inspired with the love of justice, with a respect for religion, and with the feeling of compassion, and who are more zealously interested in the preservation of liberty, in proportion as they have encountered more perils in its defence. They are not strangers or foreigners, a hireling rout scraped together from the dregs of the people, but, for the most part, men of the better conditions in life, of families not disgraced if not ennobled, of fortunes either ample or moderate; and what if some among them are recommended by their poverty? for it was not the lust of ravage which brought them into the field; it was the calamitous aspect of the times, which, in the most critical circumstances, and often amid the most disastrous turn of fortune, roused them to attempt the deliverance of their country from the fangs of despotism. They were men prepared, not only to debate, but to fight; not only to argue in the senate, but to engage the enemy in the field. But unless we will continually cherish indefinite and illusory expectations, I see not in whom we can place any confidence, if not in these men and such as these. We have the surest and most indubitable pledge of their fidelity in this, that they have already exposed themselves to death in the service of their country; of their piety in this, that they have been always wont to ascribe the whole glory of their successes to the favour of the Deity, whose help they have so suppliantly implored, and so conspicuously obtained; of their justice in this, that they even brought the king to trial, and when his guilt was proved, refused to save his life; of their moderation in our own uniform experience of its effects, and because, if by any outrage, they should disturb the peace which they have procured, they themselves will be the first to feel the miseries which it will occasion, the first to meet the havoc of the sword, and the first again to risk their lives for all those comforts and distinctions which they have so happily acquired; and lastly, of their fortitude in this, that there is no instance of any people who ever recovered their liberty with so much courage and success; and therefore let us not suppose, that there can be any persons who will be more zealous in preserving it. I now feel myself irresistibly compelled to commemorate the names of some of those who have most conspicuously signalized themselves in these times: and first thine, O Fleetwood! whom I have known from a boy to the present blooming maturity of your military fame, to have been inferior to none in humanity, in gentleness, in benignity of disposition, whose intrepidity in the combat, and whose clemency in victory, have been acknowledged even by the enemy. next thine, O Lambert! who, with a mere handful of men, checked the progress, and sustained the attack, of the Duke of Hamilton, who was attended by the whole flower and vigour of the Scottish youth: next thine, O Desborough! and thine, O Hawley! who wast always conspicuous in the heat of the combat, and the thickest of the fight; thine, O Overton! who hast been most endeared to me now for so many years by the similitude of our studies, the suavity of your manners, and the more than fraternal sympathy of our hearts; you, who, in the memorable battle of Marston Moor, when our left wing was put to the rout, were beheld with admiration, making head against the enemy with your infantry and repelling his attack, amid the thickest of the carnage; and lastly you, who, in the Scotch war, when under the auspices of Cromwell, occupied the coast of Fife, opened a passage beyond Stirling, and made the Scotch of the west, and of the north, and even the remotest Orkneys, confess your humanity, and submit to your power. Besides these, I will mention some as celebrated for their political wisdom and their civil virtues, whom you, sir, have admitted into your councils, and who are known to me by friendship or by fame. Whitlocke, Pickering, Strickland, Sydenham, Sydney. (a name indissolubly attached to the interests of liberty,) Montacute, Laurence, both of highly cultivated minds and polished taste; besides many other citizens of singular merit, some of whom were distinguished by their exertions in the senate, and others in the field. To these men, whose talents are so splendid, and whose worth has been so thoroughly tried, you would without doubt do right to trust the protection of our liberties; nor would it be easy to say to whom they might more safely be entrusted. Then, if you leave the church to its own government, and relieve yourself and the other public functionaries from a charge so onerous, and so incompatible with your functions; and will no longer suffer two powers, so different as the civil and the ecclesiastical, to commit fornication together, by their mutual and delusive aids in appearance to strengthen, but in reality to weaken and finally to subvert, each other, if you shall remove all power of persecution out of the church, (but persecution will never cease, so long as men are bribed to preach the gospel by a mercenary salary, which is forcibly extorted, rather than gratuitously bestowed, which serves only to poison religion and to strangle truth,) you will then effectually have cast those money-changers out of the temple, who do not merely truckle with doves but with the Dove itself, with the Spirit of the Most High. Then, since there are often in a republic men who have the same itch for making a multiplicity of laws, as some poetasters have for making many verses, and since laws are usually worse in proportion as they are more numerous, if you shall not enact so many new laws as you abolish old, which do not operate so much as warnings against evil, as impediments in the way of good, and if you shall retain only those which are necessary, which do not confound the distinctions of good and evil, which while they prevent the frauds of the wicked, do not prohibit the innocent freedoms of the good, which punish crimes, without interdicting those things which are lawful only on account of the abuses to which they may occasionally be exposed. For the intention of laws is to check the commission of vice; but liberty is the best school of virtue, and affords the strongest encouragements to the practice. Then, if you make a better provision for the education of our youth than has hitherto been made, if you prevent the promiscuous instruction of the docile and the indocile, of the idle and the diligent, at the public cost, but reserve the rewards of learning for the learned, and of merit for the meritorious. If you permit the free discussion of truth without any hazard to the author, or any subjection to the caprice of an individual, which is the best way to make truth flourish and knowledge abound, the censure of the half-learned, the envy, the pusillanimity, or the prejudice which measures the discoveries of others, and in short every degree of wisdom, by the measure of its own capacity, will be prevented from doling out information to us according to their own arbitrary choice. Lastly, if you shall not dread to hear any truth, or any falsehood, whatever it may be, but if you shall least of all listen to those who think that they can never be free till the liberties of others depend on their caprice, and who attempt nothing with so much zeal and vehemence as to fetter, not only the bodies but the minds of men, who labour to introduce into the state the worst of all tyrannies, the tyranny of their own depraved habits and pernicious opinions, you will always be dear to those who think not merely that their own sect or faction, but that all citizens of all descriptions, should enjoy equal rights and equal laws. If there be any one who think that this is not liberty enough, he appears to me to be rather inflamed with the lust of ambition or of anarchy, than with the love of a genuine and well-regulated liberty; and particularly since the circumstances of the country, which has been so convulsed by the storms of faction, which are yet hardly still, do not permit us to adopt a more perfect or desirable form of government.

For it is of no little consequence, O citizens, by what principles you are governed, either in acquiring liberty, or in retaining it when acquired. And unless that liberty which is of such a kind as arms can neither procure nor take away, which alone is the fruit of piety, of justice, of temperance, and unadulterated virtue, shall have taken deep root in your minds and hearts, there will not long be wanting one who will snatch from you by treachery what you have acquired by arms. War has made many great whom peace makes small. If after being released from the toils of war, you neglect the arts of peace, if your peace and your liberty be a state of warfare, if war be your only virtue, the summit of your praise, you will, believe me, soon find peace the most adverse to your interests. Your peace will be only a more distressing war, and that which you imagined liberty will prove the worst of slavery. Unless by the means of piety, not frothy and loquacious, but operative, unadulterated, and sincere, you clear the horizon of the mind from those mists of superstition which arise from the ignorance of true religion, you will aways have those who will bend your necks to the yoke as if you were brutes, who, notwithstanding all your triumphs, will put you up to the highest bidder, as if you were mere booty made in war; and will find an exuberant source of wealth in your ignorance and superstition. Unless you will subjugate the propensity to avarice, to ambition, and sensuality, and expel all luxury from yourselves and from your families, you will find that you have cherished a more stubborn and intractable despot at home, than you ever encountered in the field; and even your very bowels will be continually teeming with an intolerable progeny of tyrants. Let these be the first enemies whom you subdue; this constitutes the campaign of peace; these are triumphs, difficult indeed, but bloodless; and far more honourable than those trophies which are purchased only by slaughter and by rapine.

Unless you are victors in this service, it is in vain that you have been victorious over the despotic enemy in the field. For if you think that it is a more grand, a more beneficial, or a more wise policy, to invent subtle expedients for increasing the revenue, to multiply our naval and military force, to rival in craft the ambassadors of foreign states, to form skilful treaties and alliances, than to administer unpolluted justice to the people, to redress the injured, and to succour the distressed, and speedily to restore to every one his own, you are involved in a cloud of error; and too late will you perceive, when the illusion of those mighty benefits has vanished, that in neglecting these, which you now think inferior considerations, you have only been precipitating your own ruin and despair. The fidelity of enemies and allies is frail and perishing, unless it be cemented by the principles of justice; that wealth and those honours, which most covet, readily change masters; they forsake the idle, and repair where virtue, where industry, where patience flourish most. Thus nation precipitates the downfall of nation; thus the more sound part of one people subverts the more corrupt; thus you obtained the ascendant over the royalists. If you plunge into the same depravity, if you imitate their excesses, and hanker after the same vanities, you will become royalists as well as they, and liable to be subdued by the same enemies, or by others in your turn; who, placing their reliance on the same religious principles, the same patience, the same integrity and discretion which made you strong, will deservedly triumph over you who are immersed in debauchery, in the luxury and the sloth of kings. Then, as if God was weary of protecting you, you will be seen to have passed through the fire, that you might perish in the smoke; the contempt which you will then experience will be great as the admiration which you now enjoy; and, what may in future profit others, but cannot benefit yourselves, you will leave a salutary proof what great things the solid reality of virtue and of piety might have effected, when the mere counterfeit and varnished resemblance could attempt such mighty achievements, and make such considerable advances towards the execution. For, if either through your want of knowledge, your want of constancy, or your want of virtue, attempts so noble, and actions so glorious, have had an issue so unfortunate, it does not therefore follow, that better men should be either less daring in their projects or less sanguine in their hopes. But from such an abyss of corruption into which you so readily fall, no one, not even Cromwell himself, nor a whole nation of Brutuses, if they were alive, could deliver you if they would, or would deliver you if they could. For who would vindicate your right of unrestrained suffrage, or of choosing what representatives you liked best, merely that you might elect the creatures of your own faction, whoever they might be, or him, however small might be his worth, who would give you the most lavish feasts, and enable you to drink to the greatest excess? Thus not wisdom and authority, but turbulence and gluttony, would soon exalt the vilest miscreants from our taverns and our brothels, from our towns and villages, to the rank and dignity of senators. For, should the management of the republic be entrusted to persons to whom no one would willingly entrust the management of his private concerns; and the treasury of the state be left to the care of those who had lavished their own fortunes in an infamous prodigality? Should they have the charge of the public purse, which they would soon convert into a private, by their unprincipled peculations? Are they fit to be the legislators of a whole people who themselves know not what law, what reason, what right and wrong, what crooked and straight, what licit and illicit means? who think that all power consists in outrage, all dignity in the parade of insolence? who neglect every other consideration for the corrupt gratification of their friendships, or the prosecution of their resentments? who disperse their own relations and creatures through the provinces, for the sake of levying taxes and confiscating goods; men, for the greater part, the most profligate and vile, who buy up for themselves what they pretend to expose to sale, who thence collect an exorbitant mass of wealth, which they fraudulently divert from the public service; who thus spread their pillage through the country, and in a moment emerge from penury and rags to a state of splendour and of wealth? Who could endure such thievish servants, such vicegerents of their lords? Who could believe that the masters and the patrons of a banditti could be the proper guardians of liberty? or who would suppose that he should ever be made one hair more free by such a set of public functionaries, (though they might amount to five hundred elected in this manner from the counties and boroughs,) when among them who are the very guardians of liberty, and to whose custody it is committed, there must be so many, who know not either how to use or to enjoy liberty, who neither understand the principles nor merit the possession? But, what is worthy of remark, those who are the most unworthy of liberty are wont to behave most ungratefully towards their deliverers. Among such persons, who would be willing either to fight for liberty, or to encounter the least peril in its defence? It is not agreeable to the nature of things that such persons ever should be free. However much they may brawl about liberty, they are slaves, both at home and abroad, but without perceiving it, and when they do perceive it, like unruly horses that are impatient of the bit, they will endeavour to throw off the yoke, not from the love of genuine liberty, (which a good man only loves and knows how to obtain), but from the impulses of pride and little passions. But though they often attempt it by arms, they will make no advances to the execution; they may change their masters, but will never be able to get rid of their servitude. This often happened to the ancient Romans, wasted by excess, and enervated by luxury: and it has still more so been the fate of the moderns; when, after a long interval of years, they aspired, under the auspices of Crescentius, Nomentanus, and afterwards of Nicolas Rentius, who had assumed the title of Tribune of the People, to restore the splendour and re-establish the government of ancient Rome. For, instead of fretting with vexation, or thinking that you can lay the blame on any one but yourselves, know that to be free is the same thing as to be pious, to be wise, to be temperate and just, to be frugal and abstinent, and lastly, to be magnanimous and brave; so to be the opposite of all these is the same as to be a slave; and it usually happens, by the appointment, and as it were retributive justice, of the Deity, that that people which cannot govern themselves, and moderate their passions, but crouch under the slavery of their lusts, should be delivered up to the sway of those whom they abhor, and made to submit to an involuntary servitude. It is also sanctioned by the dictates of justice and by the constitution of nature, that he who from the imbecility or derangement of his intellect, is incapable of governing himself, should, like a minor, be committed to the government of another; and least of all should he be appointed to superintend the affairs of others or the interest of the state. You, therefore, who wish to remain free, either instantly be wise, or, as soon as possible, cease to be fools, if you think slavery an intolerable evil, learn obedience to reason and the government of yourselves; and finally bid adieu to your dissensions, your jealousies, your superstitions, your outrages, your rapine, and your lusts. Unless you will spare no pains to effect this, you must be judged unfit, both by God and mankind, to be entrusted with the possession of liberty and the administration of the government; but will rather, like a nation in a state of pupilage, want some active and courageous guardian to undertake the management of your affairs. With respect to myself, whatever turn things may take, I thought that my exertions on the present occasion would be serviceable to my country, and as they have been cheerfully bestowed, I hope that they have not been bestowed in vain. And I have not circumscribed my defence of liberty within any petty circle around me, but have made it so general and comprehensive, that the justice and the reasonableness of such uncommon occurrences, explained and defended, both among my countrymen and among foreigners, and which all good men cannot but approve, may serve to exalt the glory of my country, and to excite the imitation of posterity. If the conclusion do not answer to the beginning, that is their concern, I have delivered my testimony, I would almost say, have erected a monument, that will not readily be destroyed, to the reality of those singular and mighty achievements which were above all praise. As the epic poet, who adheres at all to the rules of that species of composition, does not profess to describe the whole life of the hero whom he celebrates, but only some particular action of his life, as the resentment of

Achilles at Troy, the return of Ulysses, or the coming of Aeneas into Italy; so it will be sufficient, either for my justification or apology, that I have heroically celebrated at least one exploit of my countrymen; I pass by the rest, for who could recite the achievements of a whole people? If after such a display of courage and of vigour, you basely relinquish the path of virtue, if you do anything unworthy of yourselves, posterity will sit in judgment on your conduct. They will see that the foundations were well laid; that the beginning (nay, it was more than a beginning) was glorious; but with deep emotions of concern will they regret, that those were wanting who might have completed the structure. They will lament that perseverance was not conjoined with such exertions and such virtues. They will see that there was a rich harvest of glory, and an opportunity afforded for the greatest achievements, but that men only were wanting for the execution; while they were not wanting who could rightly counsel, exhort, inspire, and bind an unfading wreath of praise round the brows of the illustrious actors in so glorious a scene.

NOTES

The careful reader of Milton is advised (and here assumed) to have the Bible and Ovid's *Metamorphoses* within easy reach. To save space, glosses of words are not repeated and no attempt is made to note all the echoes of Gen. 1-3 in *Paradise Lost* or of Judg. 13-16 in *Samson Agonistes*.

For the prose, page and line numbers are cited; for poetry, line numbers only.

PARADISE LOST

The second edition of *Paradise Lost* arranged the ten books of the first edition into twelve (separating Book vii and Book viii, and the present Book xi and Book xii), added the prose arguments to the beginnings of the books, and included two commendatory poems, one in Latin by Samuel Barrows and one in English by Andrew Marvell.

Verse. Italian and Spanish poets: it is not clear what poets Milton had in mind, though Tasso wrote a blank verse poem on the Creation.

Book I

Arg. midst of things: the *in medias res* opening, like the invocation to the Muse, the catalogue in 376*f.*, and the simile of the bees in 768*f.*, follows the epic conventions of Homer and Virgil.

not in the centre: perhaps referring to Dante, who placed hell in the center of the earth. The influence of Dante on *Paradise Lost* is very slight.

Pandemonium: a word invented by Milton, modeled perhaps on "pantheon."

4. *greater Man:* Christ, whose defeat of Satan is the theme of *Paradise Regained*.

6. *Muse:* Urania. See note on vii, 1.

8. *Shepherd:* Moses, assumed the author of the Book of Genesis which is Milton's source, who received the law from Mount Sinai according to Exod. 19:20, and from Mount Horeb according to Deut. 4:10.

11. *Siloa's brook:* See Isa. 8:6. It is called a "pool" in John 9:7. The "oracle of God" is the temple of Jerusalem (Ps. 28:2).

15. *Aonian mount:* Helicon, sacred to the Muses. "Above" means that Christian themes surpass the range of classical ones.

17. Milton appeals to the Holy Spirit, traditionally represented as a dove (Luke 3:22), as the inspirer of the Christian poet and prophet. Line 21 refers to Gen. 1:2 (in the 1611 version read "brooded" for "moved": cf. vii, 235). Milton did not accept the orthodox view of the Holy Spirit as the third person of the Trinity.

37. The chief Scriptural sources for the fall of Satan are Isa. 14:12; Luke 10:18; II Pet. 2:4; Jude 6; and Rev. 12:9*f* See also Hesiod, *Theogony,* 722, for the "nine" of 50.

57. *witnessed:* showed forth.

59. We should perhaps read "Angels' ken," taking ken as a noun.

68. *still urges:* continually afflicts.

74. It is three times as far from heaven to hell as it is from the center of the earth to the pole of the *primum mobile* (for which see the note to ii, 1052).

81. For Beelzebub ("Lord of flies") see Matt. 12:24.

82. *thence:* Satan means "adversary." His name before his fall is rendered "Lucifer" in the 1611 version of Isa. 14:12. Cf. v, 760; vii, 131; and x, 425.

84. An echo both of *Aeneid,* ii. 274, and of Isa. 14:12.

116. *by fate:* By denying that God is uniquely God, Satan automatically becomes a fatalist. God's will is the real fate (vii, 173).

127. *Powers:* Tradition said that there was a hierarchy of nine orders of angels: Seraphim, Cherubim, Thrones, Dominions, Virtues, Powers, Principalities, Archangels and Angels. Milton uses these names, but seems to have no definite hierarchical scheme in mind. For "Seraphim" see Isa. 6:2; for "Cherubim" see Exod. 25:19. The "im" is the Hebrew plural ending. Most of the other names come from Eph. 1:21 and Col. 1:16, by way of a famous work attributed to Dionysius the Areopagite (see Acts 17:34) called *On the Divine Hierarchy.*

176. *his:* The older form of "its," the retention of which enables

Milton to preserve an ambiguity between the natural object and the personified force. Cf. "her" in 592.

186. *afflicted:* struck down.

198*f.* The mother of the Titans who rebelled against Zeus or Jove was Earth (Ge). See Hesiod's *Theogony*. Briareus (*Aeneid,* x. 565*f.*) was a Titan with a hundred arms, compared by Don Quixote with his windmill; Typhon (a Giant rather than a Titan, though the two were often confused) was the father of Cerberus; Tarsus is in Asia Minor. For the leviathan, often mentioned in the Bible, see especially Job 41 and Isa. 27:1. The story of the whale mistaken for an island, which is in the Arabian Nights, was sometimes interpreted as an allegory of sin and temptation.

224. *horrid:* bristling.

226. *incumbent:* leaning on.

230. Earthquakes were formerly explained as caused by the escaping of air imprisoned under the earth. Pelorus is in Sicily near Etna.

288. *Tuscan artist:* Galileo, who lived at Florence in the valley of the Arno, near which is the town of Fiesole.

294. *ammiral:* leading flagship in a fleet.

301. For "legion" as associated with Satan see Luke 8:30.

303*f.* Vallombrosa is near Florence in Tuscany, the modern name of Etruria. Orion is associated with storms as a winter constellation. For the overthrow of the army of Pharaoh ("Memphian" because Memphis was the chief city of ancient Egypt) when pursuing the Israelites ("sojourners of Goshen") see Exod. 14. Busiris was an Egyptian king who persecuted foreigners. The identification with the Pharaoh of the Exodus appears to be Milton's own.

320. *virtue:* valor.

339. *Amram's son:* Moses. See Exod. 10:12*f.*

341. *warping:* writhing forward. A nautical term.

353. "Rhine or the Danube." At the fall of Rome, the Vandals crossed Spain and invaded North Africa.

387. See Ps. 80:1, and Exod. 25:19.

392*f.* Moloch (Heb. *melek,* king) was a sun-god whose rites included the burning of living children. For the destruction of his cult by Josiah (418) see II Kings 23. Verse 10 explains Tophet and Hinnom, the latter a valley near Jerusalem of which "Gehenna" is the Greek name, names later used as synonyms ("types") of hell. The Ammonites lived east of the Jordan, and the names in 397-399 are Ammonite place-names. Directly south, and east of the Dead Sea ("Asphaltic pool"), was Moab, whose god Chemosh also demanded human sacrifice (II Kings 3:27). The place-names in 407-411 are all Moabite. For "the opprobrious hill" (the Mount of Olives) see I Kings 6:7, and II Kings, 23:13. For Peor, or Baal-Peor, see Num. 25.

422. "Baals and Astartes"; "im" is a masculine and "oth" a feminine plural ending. These were gods of the Phoenicians, whose chief cities were Sidon (441) and Tyre. Baal was a general name for a god; Astarte (Ashtoreth or Ishtar) was a moon-goddess, also identified with Venus.

444. *king:* Solomon. See I Kings 11:1-5.

446. *Thammuz:* Adonis, the dying god of vegetation, whose annual death in the autumn was ceremonially lamented by women. A Syrian river with a red sediment bore his name for the reason given in 451. For his cult in Jerusalem see Ezek. 8:14.

457*f*. Dagon belonged to the Philistines, whose five chief cities are listed in 464-466. See I Sam. 5:1-5.

460. *grunsel:* threshold.

469. For Abbana and Pharphar see II Kings 5:12. The leper Rimmon lost was Naaman, in the same chapter. For Ahaz see II Kings 16.

478*f*. Osiris was the dying god of Egypt; Isis was his sister and wife; Horus their son. They were associated respectively with the bull, the cow and the hawk. The story of the golden calf is in Exod. 32 (for "borrowed" see Exod. 12:35); for the "rebel king" (Jeroboam) see I Kings 12:20*f*.

487. See Exod. 12:29.

490. For Belial ("worthlessness") see especially II Cor. 6:15. It was not the name of a god (492).

495. See I Sam. 2:12*f*. The following lines have a contemporary reference.

503. See Gen. 19:4*f*. and Judg. 19:22*f*. Belial is mentioned in the latter story.

508. Javan (Gen. 10:2) is the Hebrew form of Ion, eponymous ancestor of the Ionians or Greeks of Asia Minor.

510*f*. The story of the overthrow of Titan or Uranus by Chronos or Saturn (cf. x, 583), who with his consort Rhea was then overthrown by Zeus or Jupiter (Jove), is told in Hesiod's *Theogony*, 168*f*. and 468*f*. Saturn's followers fled across the Adriatic to Italy, thence to France and the British Isles (520-521). In Greece (the "Doric land") there were shrines of Zeus at Mount Ida in Crete, reputed his birthplace, and at Dodona in Epirus. The "Delphian cliff" is Parnassus.

517. The pagans had no heaven higher than the middle of the three regions into which the sphere of air was formerly divided, the region of clouds. Cf. Eph. 2:2, often alluded to by Milton.

534. *Azazel:* The demon of the wilderness mentioned in Lev. 16:8. The 1611 version renders his name "scapegoat" in a curious mistranslation which has established itself in the language.

536. *advanced:* lifted up.

550. For the Dorian as the martial mode see Plato, *Republic,* iii.

575. The battles of the cranes and the pygmies are referred to in the *Iliad,* iii. 3*f.*

576. *Phlegra:* The battlefield of the Giants and the gods (Ovid, *Metamorphoses,* x. 151).

578. The "seven against Thebes" is the subject of a tragedy by Aeschylus; Ilium is Troy.

580. *Uther's son:* Arthur. Tristram was his most famous Armoric (Breton) knight.

583*f.* Places recalling the wars of Christians and Saracens in history and romance. Aspramont and Montalban are in southern France; Fontarabbia is for Roncesvalles, where Roland (not Charlemagne) was killed.

597. *disastrous:* Originally a technical term in astrology (*astrum,* star).

624. *event:* outcome.

674. Until the publication of Boyle's *Sceptical Chymist* (1661), it was generally believed that all minerals were made of sulphur and mercury (and, according to some, salt).

676. *pioneers:* sappers.

678. *Mammon:* "wealth" (like Belial an abstract word and not a name). See Matt. 6:24. Cf. Spenser, *The Faerie Queene,* II, vii.

694*f.* A general comparison to the buildings of Babylon and Egypt ("Alcairo," 718, is Memphis, near Cairo) is intended, though a more specific reference to the tower of Babel and the pyramids may be included.

703. *founded:* melted.

704. *bullion dross:* the scum rising from the molten metal.

716. *bossy:* in relief.

720. Bel (Baal) had a temple at Babylon (Herodotus, i), and Serapis (a late development of Osiris) one at Memphis, besides the "Serapeum" at Alexandria where the famous library was.

739. *Ausonian:* Italian.

740. *Mulciber:* Hephaestus or Vulcan, builder of the palaces on Olympus. For his fall to Lemnos see *Iliad* i. 591*f.* Milton believed that many classical myths were later (xi, 11) and distorted versions of Biblical ones.

750. *engines:* devices.

774. *expatiate:* walk about.

781. The chief authority for locating the pygmies in India is Pliny.

797. *frequent:* crowded.

Book II

Arg. Chaos: Note how the personification of abstractions, Chaos, Night, Sin, and Death, increases the feeling of mysterious amorphousness.

2. *Ormus:* Hormuz, a city on the Persian gulf, a market for precious stones.

4. This line combines Virgil's "barbaric gold" (*Aeneid,* ii. 504) with a reference to the custom in Eastern coronations of sprinkling a dust of gold and pearl on the king. See *Antony and Cleopatra,* II, v, 45.

75. *proper:* natural. When it was believed that everything was made of earth, water, air, fire and quintessence, the principle that each element seeks its own sphere accounted for many phenomena: solids or liquids in the air fall to earth or water; springs of water rise in earth; bubbles of air rise in water; fires rise in air. Hence spirits, made of the heavenly element of quintessence, naturally rise to the heavens. Belial insinuates that if the motion is natural, it need not require an effort of will.

79. *insulting:* leaping upon.

89. *exercise:* torment.

124. *fact:* deed.

127. *scope:* target.

165. *amain:* in haste.

182. *racking:* scudding.

330. *determined:* made an end of.

337. *reluctance:* resistance.

352. Cf. *Iliad,* i. 530; *Aeneid,* ix. 106; and Isa. 45:23.

375. *original:* i.e., Adam.

387. *States:* estates, representatives.

406. Cf. Exod. 10:21. The phrase is echoed in xii, 188.

407. *uncouth:* unknown.

409. *abrupt:* gap.

412. *stations:* guards.

432. Cf. *Aeneid,* vi. 126*f.* A passage several times echoed.

457. *intend:* consider.

517. *alchemy:* metallic alloy, i.e., brass.

518. *explained:* proclaimed.

531. *shun the goal:* cf. Horace, *Odes,* I. i. 4.

539. Typhoeus, a hundred-headed Giant buried under Mount Etna, was the father of Typhon (i, 199).

541. *Alcides:* Hercules, who after conquering the king of Oechalia in Thessaly was sent a poisoned shirt, in his anguish flung his companion Lichas into the sea between Euboea and Attica, and then burned himself on a funeral pyre on Mount Oeta in Thessaly. See Ovid, *Metamorphoses,* ix. 134*f.*, and Sophocles' *Trachiniae.*

564. *apathy:* withdrawal from passion, of the kind counseled by the Stoics.

575*f.* Milton shows that the roots of Styx, Acheron, Cocytus and Phlegethon mean respectively hatred, sorrow, wailing and burning. Lethe (forgetfulness, referred to by Moloch in 74) is usually separated from the others: Dante puts it at the top of Purgatory.

592. The lake, or marsh, of Serbonis is in northern Egypt, and Mount Casius is near it. Damiata (Damietta) is at the mouth of the Nile. The story is from Diodorus Siculus, i.

600. *starve:* freeze to death.

611-4. For Medusa and Tantalus see Ovid, *Metamorphoses,* iv. 458*f.* and 655*f.*

639. Ternate and Tidore are islands in the Moluccas.

641. "Through the Indian Ocean to the Cape of Good Hope."

642. *stemming:* pressing forward.

647. *impaled:* encircled.

660*f.* Satan passing Sin and Death recalls Ulysses (1019-1020) passing between the cliff Scylla and the whirlpool Charybdis in the straits of Messina between Calabria in Italy and Sicily (Trinacria). For the transformation of Scylla by herbs thrown by Circe into the water she bathed in, see Ovid, *Metamorphoses,* xiv. 18*f.*

662. *night-hag:* Hecate. Cf. *Macbeth,* III, v.

665. Lapland was the traditional home of witches.

692. *third part:* so in Rev. 12:4. Cf. v, 710.

709. *Ophiuchus:* "serpent-bearer"; a northern ("arctic") constellation in which a famous comet appeared in 1618.

752*f*. A kind of parody of the legend that Minerva, the goddess of wisdom, was born from the forehead of Jupiter. The Biblical source is Jas. 1:15.

772. *pitch:* height.

842. *buxom:* yielding.

883. *Erebus:* a Classical name for (upper) hell.

898. These are the four principles of chaos, whose four possible combinations produce the humors in the organic world and the elements in the inorganic one (fire and choler are hot and dry; air and blood hot and moist; water and phlegm cold and moist; earth and melancholy [cf. x, 294, and xi, 544] cold and dry).

900. *embryon atoms* suggests the *semina rerum* of Lucretius (cf. Ovid, *Metamorphoses,* i. 9), who thought of atoms as varied in shape and capable of growth.

904. Barca and Cyrene are respectively a desert and a city in Libya.

905-906. *levied . . . :* raised to fight in the wars of the winds, and to give weight to the otherwise too light wings of those winds. The elliptical style, like the vague elusive imagery, is deliberate.

907. *He:* one of the "champions" of 898.

913. *pregnant causes:* elements capable of growth.

920. *pealed:* deafened.

935*f*. God's will permits Satan's journey, and on the level of chaos that will appears in the form of chance.

939. *Syrtis:* quicksand in north Africa.

943. The Arimaspians were a one-eyed tribe of Scythians in north Russia continually trying to steal treasures of gold guarded by griffins (Herodotus, iii).

964-965. Orcus and Ades (Hades) are names of Pluto, god of hell. Demogorgon is not classical, but is often mentioned by Renaissance poets. See Spenser, *The Faerie Queene,* I, i, 37, and IV, ii, 47.

1004. Heaven as the sky should be distinguished from the empyrean heaven of 1006.

1017. *Argo:* the ship of the Argonauts. For the clashing rocks see Ovid, *Metamorphoses,* xv. 338.

1029. *utmost orb:* outermost sphere (*primum mobile;* see below).

1048. Heaven is apparently square (x, 381), but its shape cannot be seen at Satan's distance.

1051. The chain comes from the *Iliad,* viii. 18*f.* It has had a long history as a symbol in poetry and philosophy, one development of which is the "scale of nature" in this poem (v, 509-512).

1052. *world:* the created universe, conceived by Milton according to the older "Ptolemaic" view of it as a series of concentric spheres, with the earth at the center. This center consisted of four layers or sub-spheres, the earth proper, then the water, the air (divided into three regions), and a sphere of fire (ignored by Milton, and no longer much believed in when he wrote). Cf. v, 180*f.* Above this "sublunary" world were the planets in the following order: Moon, Mercury, Venus, Sun, Mars, Jupiter, Saturn. Then came the sphere of fixed stars, thought of as all in one plane and as not moving with respect to each other. Outside this was a "crystalline" sphere, and outside that was a vast shell called the *primum mobile.* Cf. iii, 481*f.* These last two spheres, though made of quintessence, were thought of as liquid and solid respectively. All moved circularly from west to east except the *primum mobile,* which had a diurnal rotation from east to west (cf. viii, 134).

Above this universe Milton puts the empyrean heaven, with a wall of battlements separating it from chaos, which extends beneath it and around the cosmos. The cosmos is linked to heaven by a flight of stairs extending through a small crack in the *primum mobile,* through which Satan enters. Below chaos is hell, separated from chaos by a gate guarded by Sin and Death.

Book III

7. *hear'st thou rather:* dost thou prefer to be called.

16. *utter:* outer. "Through hell and through chaos."

17. A reference to the *Hymn to Night,* a Greek poem attributed to Orpheus.

25-26. *drop serene* (*gutta serena*) and *suffusion* are technical terms for total and partial blindness.

35-36. All these are blind poets or prophets. Thamyris is mentioned by Homer (*Iliad,* ii. 595); Maeonides is Homer himself, traditionally blind; Tiresias is the blind prophet of *Oedipus Rex* (Ovid, *Metamorphoses,* iii. 323*f.*) and Phineus, the victim of the Harpies, was a Thracian king (*Aeneid,* iii. 210-244).

72. *sublime:* aloft.

73. *stoop:* pounce.

75-76. *firmament:* sky. The *primum mobile* is a solid in the midst of a chaos which is never definitely water or air.

80. The source book for Milton's theological views is his Latin treatise *The Christian Doctrine,* which was not published until 1825. The issues raised in God the Father's ambrosial harangue are dealt with more fully in Part One of that work, as follows: foreknowledge, Chap. iii; predestination, Chap. iv; election, Chap. viii; atonement, Chap. xiv; imputation (291), Chap. xxii.

140. *substantially:* Milton regards the Son as of like substance with the Father (Arian view), not as of the same substance (Athanasian or orthodox view).

208. *sacred and devote:* doomed to destruction.

217. Notice the careful paralleling of the council in heaven with the council in hell, each leading up to a unique volunteer.

227. *passed:* pledged.

247. See Ps. 16:10. There are many other Scriptural echoes in this speech.

255. *maugre:* in spite of.

287. See I Cor. 15:22.

317. *anointed:* the literal meaning of "Messiah."

341. See I Cor. 15:28.

432. Imaus is in the Himalayas, where the Ganges and the Hydaspes (Jhelum) rise. Sericana was vaguely located near Tibet; the wagons driven with sails come from a contemporary geographical work, Peter Heylin's *Cosmography.*

444*f*. The goal of Satan's enterprise, an attack on heaven which falls just short of heaven, is the same as that of unacceptable human efforts to reach heaven, whether by violence (suicide) or by guile (hypocritical disguise).

456. *unkindly:* unnaturally.

459. *some:* i.e., Ariosto, whose *Orlando Furioso,* canto 34, is the source of Milton's conception of a Fools' Paradise.

461. The translated saints are Enoch and Elijah, glanced at again in 521-522 below. Milton does not follow up his suggestion of "middle spirits."

463. See Gen. 6:1-4.

468. *Sennaar:* Shinar, the plain of Babel (see Gen. 11:2). Milton regularly avoids "sh" and "ch" whenever he can, though the pro-

nunciations indicated by such spellings as "voutsafe," "adventrous," and "vultur" have to be obliterated in a modernized text.

469*f*. These fables are traditional. The real Empedocles was the philosopher whose principle of "like attracts like" underlies vii, 240.

475. Carmelites, Dominicans, and Franciscans.

483. *trepidation:* The retrograde movement of the sphere of fixed stars which produces the precession of the equinoxes, to account for which the crystalline sphere was invented (Ptolemaic view); or a slow wobble of the earth in its rotation on its axis (Copernican view). *talked:* discussed, i.e., by the rival theories.

484*f*. Satire on the Roman Catholic interpretation of Matt. 16:19. Note too the ironic use of the Catholic term "limbo," generally associated with "embryos and idiots" (474).

510. See Gen. 28:11-17.

516. *mysteriously was meant:* had an allegorical meaning. Cf. Dante, *Purgatorio,* ix.

518. Milton identifies the crystalline sphere with the "sea of jasper" of Rev. 4:6.

535-537. From the north to the south of the Holy Land. Paneas is the later Greek name of Dan (Judg. 18:29).

558. *fleecy star:* Aries, directly opposite Libra in the Zodiac, and just below the constellation Andromeda in the western sky.

568. For the Hesperides, here and in iv, 250 below, see note to *Comus,* 393.

575. *by centre or eccentric:* toward or from the center (of the earth).

576. *longitude:* latitude (cf. "breadth," 560).

588. Sunspots were noted by Galileo in 1609.

597. See Exod. 28:17*f*., and Rev. 21:19*f*.

598. *stone:* The philosopher's stone or elixir (607) sought by the alchemists, which would turn metals to gold and, in the form of potable gold (608) preserve health. The alchemic process was an attempt to isolate the true ("native," 605) form of the "first matter" for which Proteus was a frequent symbol (e.g., Bacon, *Wisdom of the Ancients*), by means of distilling and heating operations in vessels called alembics ("limbec," 605). At a certain stage the "fixing of mercury" ("Hermes," 603, see note on i, 674) was essential. Proteus (see *Odyssey,* iv. 454*f*.) was a sea-god who could take many shapes, but would foretell the future if caught and held.

610. See note on iv, 669, below. The sun is the planet that causes

the "growth" of gold and precious stones, hence the sun does what the alchemist tries to do.

623. Rev. 19:17.

648. The name Uriel ("fire of God") comes from II Esdras. For the "seven eyes" see Zech. 4:10, and Rev. 4:5.

730. *triform:* crescent, full and waning. The classical moon-goddess had three forms, Luna, Diana and Hecate, and was called *diva triformis* by Horace.

742. *Niphates:* a mountain in Armenia near Assyria (iv, 126).

Book IV

1*f*. See Rev. 12:12.

10. *accuser:* the literal meaning of *diabolos,* from which the word "devil" comes.

32*f*. These lines are said by Milton's nephew to have been written as early as 1642 as the opening speech of a tragedy on the paradise lost theme.

132. Paradise is the eastern (Gen. 2:8) part of Eden: see 209-210 below. For Paradise as a mountain (so also in Dante and Ariosto) see Ezek. 28:14.

134. *champaign head:* flat summit.

162. Saba or Sheba was part of the territory called Arabia Felix.

168. See Tob. 8. Asmodeus was a devil in love with a girl betrothed to Tobit's son Tobias, and had killed her seven previous suitors. On the advice of the angel Raphael, Tobit drove him away (and into Egypt) with the smell of burning fish. On the approach of Satan, Milton changes his imagery of spicy odors to a pungent stink.

172. *savage:* woody.

176. *perplexed:* complicated.

180. Cf. John 10:1*f*.

211. Auran was on the Euphrates; Seleucia, on the Tigris, near Bagdad, was founded by Seleucus, one of the "Grecian king" Alexander's generals. For Telassar see Isa. 37:12.

233. The four streams are traditionally the Nile, Euphrates, Tigris, and Indus, but Milton does not seem to follow this. However, the river in line 223 is the Tigris. See ix, 71.

239. *error:* meandering.

242. *knots:* flower-beds; *boon:* bountiful.

255. *irriguous:* well-watered.

256. That is, the thorns on the rose came after the fall of Adam. Cf. Gen. 3:18.

266. The name of the pastoral god Pan means "all," hence "universal." For the Graces see Hesiod, *Theogony,* 64; for the Hours see *Iliad,* v. 749. The "perpetual spring" (and summer and autumn) was a traditional attribute of Paradise.

269*f*. *Enna:* in Sicily. For Proserpine see Ovid, *Metamorphoses,* v. 385*f*. Daphne, a Syrian town on the Orontes river, had a fountain sacred to Apollo; the Castalian spring, on Parnassus near Delphi, was "inspired" by the oracle there. Diodorus Siculus, iii, explains that Bacchus got his Greek name Dionysus from his sojourn as an infant on the island of Nysa in the Triton river in Libya, where he had been hidden with his mother Amalthea by his father Ammon, whose legitimate consort was Rhea. Ammon was an Egyptian god identified with Jupiter in classical times and, by Milton and others, with Noah's son Ham (Cham), ancestor of the Africans.

280*f*. The legend (from Heylin's *Cosmography*) that Abyssinian princes were educated in a place of seclusion in Mount Amara was used later by Samuel Johnson in *Rasselas*. The passage here is an important influence also on Coleridge's *Kubla Khan*. The legend that the Nile rises in Paradise is also suggested by Heylin, but is of very ancient origin.

299. Cf. I Cor. 11:7*f*. See 14-15 for the lines immediately following.

313. *dishonest:* unchaste.

337. *purpose:* conversation.

352. *ruminating:* cud-chewing.

397. Satan's assumption of these animal shapes anticipates their later or "fallen" forms; they are not yet beasts of prey. Cf. Isa. 11:6.

460. Compare the story of Narcissus in Ovid, *Metamorphoses,* iii. 407*f*., often interpreted as an allegory of self-will.

486. *individual:* inseparable.

499. Jupiter and Juno here mean the sun and the air.

541. *with right aspect:* directly opposite.

557. *thwarts:* crosses.

592. *prime orb:* the sun. As usual, Milton puts the Copernican and Ptolemaic explanations beside one another without committing himself.

628. *manuring:* cultivating by hand.

652. *charm:* song.

669. *influence:* the doctrine of astrology that the stars affected the

growth of living things including metals, a belief which has left the words saturnine, jovial, martial, mercurial and lunatic in our language. The word mercury for quicksilver recalls the belief that each planet fostered a metal. See note to iii, 598.

688. *divide the night:* i.e., into watches.

703. *emblem:* inlaid work.

707-708. Classical woodland deities.

711. *hymenaean:* marriage song.

712. *genial:* nuptial.

714. Pandora ("all-gifted," 715) opened through curiosity a box containing all the world's evils. See Hesiod, *Works and Days,* 81*f.* Her husband was Epimetheus, the stupid ("unwiser," cf. Hesiod, *Theogony,* 511) brother of Prometheus, referred to in 719. They were sons of Iapetos, identified by Milton with Noah's son Japhet.

744*f.* See I Tim. 4:1-3.

751. *propriety:* property.

776*f.* It was nine o'clock.

785. Half turning left and half right.

788. Ithuriel and Zephon both mean "discovery" or "search."

971. *limitary:* set to guard boundaries.

985. *alarmed:* on guard.

987. Mountains in the Canary Isles and northwest Africa.

997. *yet seen:* i.e., as the Zodiacal sign of Libra. The scales are from *Iliad,* viii. 69-72, and Isa. 40:12.

998. *Astraea:* Virgo.

Book V

5. *vapors:* see note to 484 below.

23. *balmy reed:* balsam.

106. *frames:* frames into.

117. *God:* angel. Cf. xii, 201 below with Exod. 13:21.

150. *numerous:* metrical. The hymn which follows is based on Ps. 148.

166. *fairest of stars:* Venus; its two names as morning and evening star respectively, Lucifer and Hesperus, are often used by Milton.

177. The word "planet" means etymologically "wanderer."

178. *not without song:* the music of the spheres could be heard by Adam before his fall.

181. *quaternion:* fourfold combination.

189. *uncoloured:* of one color.

214. *pampered:* luxuriant. For the vine as the "spouse" of the elm see Virgil, *Georgics,* ii. 367.

221. See note to iv, 168.

249. *ardors:* Seraphim, traditionally spirits of fire and love as the Cherubim were of light and contemplation. Medieval painters colored them red and blue respectively.

264-265. Islands in the Aegean Sea.

266. *prone:* downward.

272. For the phoenix see Ovid, *Metamorphoses,* xv. 391*f;* Milton has altered the place of its pyre from Heliopolis (Gr. "city of the sun") to Thebes, both Egyptian cities.

277. *six:* cf. Isa. 6:2.

285. *grain:* dye. Maia's son was Mercury or Hermes, the messenger (Gr. *angelos*) of the gods.

297. *enormous:* unruly.

336. *kindliest:* most natural.

340*f*. The Black Sea and Carthaginian coasts produced fruit, notably cherries and figs. Alcinous was a king visited by Ulysses (*Odyssey,* vii. 125*f*.), whose gardens had the Paradisal attribute of perpetual spring and harvest.

345. *must:* unfermented liquor; similarly *meaths.*

349. *unfumed:* unburnt (in contrast to incense).

378. *Pomona:* the Roman goddess of fruits.

382. The judgment of Paris took place on Mount Ida in Asia Minor.

412. *concoct:* begin to digest.

419. The spots on the moon were formerly explained as exhalations rising from the earth below.

430. *pearly grain:* manna. See Exod. 16:14.

435-436. Cf. Tob. 12:19.

440. *empiric:* concerned with the practical side of alchemy, which was also a speculative philosophy.

447. See Gen. 6:2.

484*f*. Creation forms a scale of consciousness extending through angels, men, animals, plants, minerals and chaos. As all creation is from God (see note to vii, 170), there is in it a tendency to reascend to its Creator. The crucial stage is where the physical part of man passes into the intelligent part. According to contemporary physiology, the link consisted of three sets of "spirits," natural, vital or cordial and animal, which were formed by the humors and acted on the body, the emotions, and the intellect respectively. We still use the phrase "animal spirits," though in the sense of "cordial spirits" (viii, 466: cf. iv, 805).

583. *great year:* the interval of time in which the precession of equinoxes is completed, generally estimated at 26,000 years. The year that began at this point presumably ends at the point described in iii, 336-341. Milton held the Arian view that the Son was created, but "this day" (603) refers, not to the actual begetting of Christ (cf. iii, 383, and v, 835*f.*), but to his first manifestation or epiphany.

603. Ps. 2:6-7; Hebrews 1:3.

689. *north:* see Isa. 14:13, which also explains line 766.

750. *triple degrees:* i.e., nine orders (see note to i, 127).

799. *this:* the fact that angels need no law.

890. *devoted:* doomed.

906. *retorted:* flung back (without words).

Book VI

4. *cave:* cf. Hesiod, *Theogony,* 748, and Ovid, *Metamorphoses,* ii. 112-114.

10. *obsequious:* obediently following.

19. *procinct:* readiness.

29. *servant of God:* the literal meaning of "Abdiel."

58. *reluctant:* struggling.

69. *obvious:* lying in the way.

84. *argument:* device, inscription.

93. *hosting:* mustering.

99*f.* Cf. II Thess. 2:4.

115. *realty:* loyalty, or perhaps a misprint for "fealty."

161. *success:* fortune.

239. *moment:* momentum, the weight that turns the scale.

329. *griding:* cutting through.

365. For Adrammalech see II Kings 17:31. Asmadai is the Asmodeus of iv, 168.

371-372. The origin of these names is uncertain.

387. *deformed:* ugly.

399. *cubic:* perhaps literally (cf. "globe," ii, 512). The angels can fight in three dimensions.

404. *unobnoxious:* not subject to pain.

411. *prevalent:* victorious.

447. For Nisroch see II Kings 19:37.

467-468. Paraphrase: Such an inventor in my opinion deserves no less gratitude than we owe for our deliverance to Satan.

479. Airy and fiery particles.

493. *effect:* performance.

512. *foam:* pumice.

514. *adusted:* dried.

519. *missive ruin:* sent-forth destruction. *incentive reed:* torch lighting the fuse.

520. *pernicious:* swift (as well as destructive).

541. *sad:* settled.

555. *interview:* confrontation.

560. *composure:* armistice, with pun on the meaning mixture.

581. *amused:* wondering.

587. *embowelled:* filled.

605. *tire:* rank.

644. Cf. Ovid, *Metamorphoses,* i. 151*f.*

674. *advised:* with his mind settled.

679. *assessor:* sharer of the seat.

699. Notice the anticipation of the three-day interval of Christ's later sufferings and triumph.

709. *unction:* see note on iii, 317.

739. Cf. Rev. 20:1.

750*f.* The description of the chariot is based on Ezek. 1. The "four shapes" reappear in Rev. 4:6-8, and were later identified with the four evangelists.

761. *Urim:* "lights" on the high-priest's breastplate. See Exod. 28:30.

766. *bickering:* flashing.

771. Cf. II Sam. 22:11.

777. *reduced:* led back.

778. *circumfused:* spread around.

779. The archetype of the Church: see Rom. 12:5. Christ's present action anticipates his later one of cleansing the temple.

788. Cf. *Aeneid,* i. 11 (also in ix, 729).

838. *plagues:* blows.

868. *ruining:* falling.

Book VII

1*f.* *Urania,* one of the nine Muses haunting Mount Olympus, associated with hymns of praise to the gods and with astronomy.

Milton makes her a specifically Christian inspiring power, an aspect ("sister") of the Wisdom mentioned, and also personified as female, in Prov. 8. For Wisdom as a part of God's creating power, the subject of this book, see Wisd. of Sol., especially Chap. 7.

4*f*. Pegasus, the winged horse of the Muses and the symbol of poetic inspiration, was also ridden by Bellerophon (18), the slayer of the Chimera (*Iliad,* vi. 200*f*.), who attempted to fly to heaven with him, and for his presumption was flung down on a plain in Asia Minor. The allegory relates both to Milton himself and to the inadequacy of a pagan approach to a Christian theme. Nevertheless Milton's account of creation, though a close paraphrase of Gen. 1, makes some use of Ovid, Lucretius and Plato's *Timaeus* (cf. "great idea," 557).

9. *converse:* live with.

23. *rapt above the pole:* caught up above the *primum mobile*. The scene of the second half of the poem is confined to the earth.

32*f*. Orpheus, the Thracian poet who was the son of Calliope, the Muse of epic poetry, was torn to pieces by a mob of infuriated Bacchantes, female worshippers of Bacchus, who had a shrine in the mountain range of Rhodope in Thrace. Cf. Ovid, *Metamorphoses,* xi. 1*f*.

59. *repealed:* called back.

92. *so late:* the conception of time relates only to the manifestation, to men or to angels (cf. v, 580), of what God does, and not to God's eternal existence or his creative acts, which latter thus do not strictly "precede" the creation. Hence the six days of creation are to God the same as an instant (154). Cf. 176-179 below, and the note on v, 583.

94. *absolved:* finished.

103. *unapparent:* (a) invisible to Adam; (b) not taking definite form.

152. *fondly:* foolishly.

162. *inhabit lax:* spread into the vacated places.

170*f*. Chaos is not strictly a creation, nor can it be co-eternal with God. It must, then, be that into which God's purpose chooses not to extend itself. The creation is therefore simply from God, not by God out of something else, whether matter, forms or nothing (*ex nihilo*). On the other hand, created things are independent of God, and conscious creatures have the free will to turn against him. Thus Milton tries to steer a course between the view that something is eternally not God (Manichean) and the view that everything is God (pantheistic).

200-201. The Scriptural echoes are from Jer. 50:25, and Zech. 6:1.

216. An anticipation of Mark 4:39. Note the rhythm of the line.

225-60. Apart from the paraphrase of Gen. 1, the following Scriptural echoes are important: Prov. 8:27; Job 26:7; Ps. 19:4; and Job 38:7.

238. *tartareous:* tending to the bottom of creation or hell (Tartarus).

261. The "firmament" is heaven in the sense of the sky, stretching from the air to the fixed stars. Its lower boundary is the sea, its upper one the watery or crystalline sphere. Thus Milton interprets the phrase "in the midst of the waters," in Gen. 1:6.

282. *genial:* fertilizing.

299. *torrent rapture:* headlong speed.

323. *implicit:* tangled.

325. *gemmed:* budded.

327. *tufts:* groves.

366. *horns:* an allusion to Galileo's discovery of the phases of Venus.

367. *tincture:* absorption of sun's light by the planets, which have little light of their own (368).

375. Cf. Job 38:31.

388. *reptile:* includes fish.

403. *bank:* make a bank in.

406. *dropped:* spotted.

409. *smooth:* the smooth sea.

421. *summed their pens:* became "full-fledged."

423. *in prospect:* viewed from a distance.

425. *loosely:* separately; *region,* upper air.

451. *soul:* perhaps "fowl."

457. *wons:* dwells.

471. *behemoth:* see Job 40:15*f.*

490. The worker bees were often regarded as female.

502. *consummate:* completed.

511. *correspond:* communicate.

565. Cf. Ps. 24:7.

619. *hyaline:* glass. See note to iv, 518.

620. *immense:* unmeasurable.

Book VIII

23. *punctual:* small as a point.

36. *sumless:* immeasurable.

61. *pomp:* procession.

65. *facile:* gracious.

83*f*. Among the Ptolemaic conceptions developed to "save appearances" were the eccentric sphere, a planetary rotation which, though around the earth, was not centered on the earth, and the epicycle, a subsidiary circular movement of the revolving planet.

99. *officious:* serviceable.

124. *attractive virtue:* magnetic attraction. The discovery that the earth and other heavenly bodies (cf. iii, 583) were magnetic immediately preceded Newton's conception of gravitation.

130. *three:* rotation on its axis, revolution around the sun, and the rotation of the pole around the ecliptic (cf. note to iii, 483).

132. *thwart obliquities:* irregular movements. See note to 83 above.

134. The daily rotation of the *primum mobile* (see note to ii, 1052), which does not exist on the hypothesis of a moving earth.

142. *terrestrial moon:* the moon assumed to be habitable like the earth. Cf. v, 263.

150. *male and female:* direct and reflected.

153-158. Paraphrase: It may well be wondered whether the only function of the stars is to shine for man, considering how many there are and how little light each one gives.

164. *inoffensive:* free of interference (so in x, 305).

167*f*. Raphael's point is not that Adam's descendants should not study astronomy, but that (a) his own message is concerned with revelation, with the sort of knowledge later given in the Bible, and not with science; (b) whatever may be true of the universe as a whole, the center of Adam's world is clearly Adam; (c) in preparing for his ordeal Adam should concentrate on the will of God within him rather than on the works of God outside him. It is for this last reason that Raphael particularly warns Adam against the idolizing of Eve which in fact turned out to be the cause of his fall. Cf. xii, 575-576 below.

268. *went:* walked.

316. *submiss:* prostrate.

330. *die:* become mortal (see the next line).

384. *sort:* be appropriate.

387. *intense:* aspiring. *remiss,* recessive.

421. *through all numbers absolute:* perfect in all details.

573. *that skill:* i.e., self-esteem.

631. The Cape Verde ("green") islands.

632. *Hesperian:* western.

Book IX

5. *venial:* innocent.

15*f*. The references are to *Iliad,* xxii; *Aeneid,* xii; *Odyssey,* i; and *Aeneid,* i. Achilles' foe was Hector; Turnus was the rival of Aeneas; "the Greek" is Ulysses; and Aeneas was the son of Cytherea or Venus. Milton refers to each epic in its aspect as a song of wrath.

26. *long choosing:* Milton's ambition to write a poem like *Paradise Lost* is recorded in his Cambridge valedictory, *At a Vacation Exercise,* 1629.

33. *furniture:* equipment.

35. *impreses:* devices on shields.

36. *bases:* embroidered silk coverings.

38. *sewers:* butlers. *seneschals,* stewards.

44. *age:* i.e., of the world. The question whether nature was losing its energy was much debated in Milton's time. Milton discussed it in an early Latin poem, *Natura non Pati Senium.*

63*f*. Satan flies for three days around the equator on the side of the earth opposite the sun, then for two days around each colure (one of two meridians of longitude at right angles to each other).

78. *pool Maeotis:* the sea of Azov.

80. *Orontes:* a river in Syria. The ocean barred at Darien in Panama is of course the Atlantic. The encircling movements of Satan are in keeping with the serpentine nature he is about to assume.

88. *of thoughts revolved:* i.e., because of the hesitation of his thoughts. *sentence,* decision.

95. *doubt:* suspicion.

112. *gradual:* going up the "scale of nature" to the human.

121. *siege of contraries:* dwelling of conflicting emotions.

170. *obnoxious:* exposed.

191. *close:* hidden.

270. *virgin:* innocent, unfallen.

292. *entire:* unimpaired.

330. *front:* forehead.

353. *still erect:* continually on guard.

358. *mind:* remind.

367. *approve:* prove.

371. *securer:* more confident.

387. *Oread or Dryad:* nymph of mountain or tree. *Delia:* Diana, born on the island of Delos (x, 296).

393*f*. *Pales:* Roman pastoral goddess. For the story of Pomona and Vertumnus see Ovid, *Metamorphoses,* xiv. 623*f*. Ceres "in her prime" was the first to teach men agriculture. See Ovid, *Metamorphoses,* v. 341.

436. *voluble:* rolling.

440. For the gardens of Adonis, the dying and "revived" god, see especially Spenser, *The Faerie Queene,* III, vi. Laertes' son is Ulysses. See note to iv, 341. The "sapient king" is Solomon. See I Kings 3, and the Song of Songs 7:2. Being in the Bible, Solomon is historical ("not mystic").

446. *annoy:* pollute.

500. Cf. Ezek. 28:13.

502. *spires:* coils.

505*f*. The story of Cadmus, the founder of Thebes, who with his wife Harmonia or Hermione was changed to a serpent, is told in Ovid, *Metamorphoses,* iv. 563*f*. "Changed" means "were the changed forms of:" The "god" of 506 is Esculapius, who was worshipped in the form of a serpent (Ovid, *Metamorphoses,* xv. 626*f*.) and had a temple at Epidaurus in Argolis. According to Plutarch's life of Alexander, Alexander's mother Olympias told him that his father was Jupiter Ammon (see note to iv, 269), who came to her in the form of a serpent. Jupiter in Rome ("Capitoline;" 508) was reputed the father of Scipio Africanus, whose mother's name, if it matters, was Sempronia.

522. *herd:* the men transformed to animals by Circe. See *Odyssey,* x.

525. *turret:* towering.

529-530. Satan may have spoken either by means of the serpent's tongue or independently of it.

558. *demur:* doubt.

563. *of mute:* from a dumb condition.

581. Serpents were popularly believed to be fond of fennel and to suckle sheep and goats.

613. *spirited:* inspired.

623. *their provision:* i.e., until there are enough men to eat them.

624. *bearth:* birth, the things she bears.

653. *daughter of his voice:* a Hebraism. *the rest:* for the rest.

745*f*. Beginning with her dream (iv, 800), Eve has been listening to Satan more unconsciously than consciously, and she now repeats his arguments as though they were her own.

771. *author unsuspect:* authority not to be suspected.

793. *boon:* exuberant.

800. *not without song:* an ironic echo of v, 178.

805. *others:* i.e., other gods.

953. *certain:* resolved.

980. *oblige:* involve in guilt.

998. See I Timothy 2:14.

1017*f*. The word "savor," taste, comes from *sapere,* to know. As in the case of the fallen angels (vi, 558*f*.), Milton associates punning with a sinful nature.

1034. *toy:* caress.

1059. Judg. 16:19-20.

1079. *last:* worst. The difference between the sexual relations of Adam and Eve here and those in iv, 741*f*. is that these are generalized, based not on the love of Adam for Eve but on the desire of a man for a woman.

1101. *figtree:* the banyan tree of Southern India, often described by travelers. The incorrect statement that its leaves are broad is due to Pliny.

1111. *Amazonian targe:* shield of an Amazon.

1133. *intermitted:* broken.

1164. *expressed immutable:* shown to be steadfast.

Book X

29. Construe: "to make appear accountable," i.e., to justify.

57. Cf. John 5:22.

77. *derived:* transferred.

89. *coast:* region.

106. *obvious:* attending, meeting.

135. *devolved:* concentrated.

156. *person:* role.

163*f*. The cursing of the serpent in Gen. 3:14-15 is consistent with the Genesis account of the Fall, which makes no mention of Satan, but hardly with the New Testament doctrine that the serpent was a disguise for the devil. Milton is somewhat perplexed by the compulsion to have it both ways.

165. *unable:* i.e., the serpent was unable.

184*f*. See Luke 10:18; Eph. 2:2; Ps. 68:18; Col. 2:15; Rom. 17:20.

215. See John 13:5; Phil. 2:7.

217. *or:* whether. The animals who provided the coats must have been either killed or given new coats.

219. *thought not much:* did not mind. *enemies:* sinners.

222. See Isa. 5:10.

246. *sympathy:* see notes to ii, 75, and viii, 124.

288. *shoaling:* making compact.

290. *Cronian Sea:* Arctic Ocean.

291. *imagined way:* the North-East passage, often attempted by English explorers, along the north shore of Siberia where the Pechora river debouches. For "Cathaian" see notes to xi, 388, 390.

296. *Delos:* One of the Cyclades group in the Aegean Sea, said to have been originally a floating island created by Poseidon with his trident (cf. Death's mace), and anchored to its present place by Zeus.

297. *Gorgonian:* petrifying. See note on ii, 611.

302. *wall:* the *primum mobile.*

307*f*. According to Herodotus, vii, Xerxes in his invasion of Greece ordered the sea to be scourged for the trouble it gave him to build a pontoon bridge over the Hellespont. Xerxes is the Ahasuerus of Esther, and his capital Susa is the Biblical "Shushan," traditionally associated with Memnon, for whom see Ovid, *Metamorphoses,* xiii. 579*f*.

313. *pontifical:* pertaining to bridge-building.

321. The passage between earth and heaven (iii, 510) is joined by the new bridge to hell.

328. Scorpio, near which is the constellation of the Centaur, is well away from Aries, where the sun (and Uriel) are.

337. *covertures:* the fig-leaves.

364. *consequence:* mutual connection.

413. *planet-struck:* the planets themselves were affected as they were later to affect humans (cf. "moonstruck," as in xi, 485).

415. *causey:* the original form of the word "causeway."

426. *paragoned:* compared.

430. *observed:* obeyed.

432. *Astracan:* a Russian outpost on the Volga near Tartary.

433. *Bactrian Sophy:* Shah of Persia.

435. *Aladule:* Armenia. Casbeen and Tauris (Tabriz) are cities in Persia.

445. *state:* canopy.

449. *fulgent:* glowing.

457. *divan:* council.

513. *supplanted:* tripped up. Satan's metamorphosis is based on Ovid, *Metamorphoses,* iv. 576*f.*

524*f.* Most of these serpents are fabulous. The amphisbaena had a head at both ends; the cerastes was a horned serpent; the hydrus was a water-snake, the ellops a swordfish, and the dipsas produced a raging thirst by its bite. African serpents were supposed to have sprung from the blood-drops of Medusa's head when Perseus flew over Libya with it. See Ovid, *Metamorphoses,* iv. 617-620. Ophiusa, traditionally full of snakes, is near Majorca; Python was a huge serpent killed by Apollo at the site of his oracle; in honor of his victory the Pythian games (ii, 530) were instituted. See Ovid, *Metamorphoses,* i. 438*f.*

535. *just:* regular.

546. *exploding:* driving off the stage.

560. *Megaera:* one of the three Furies, generally represented, like Medusa, with snakes in their hair.

562. *bituminous lake:* the Dead Sea. For the destruction of Sodom see Gen. 19. The legendary "apples of Sodom" were beautiful outside but full of ashes inside.

568. *drugged:* sickened.

576. Perhaps derived from the story of Manto in Ariosto, *Orlando Furioso,* canto 43.

580*f.* Ophion, whose name means "serpent," was a Titan who originally ruled Olympus. The name of his consort Eurynome means "wide-ruling." Milton seems to identify her with Eve in Eve's aspect of "our general mother"; but the meaning of "encroaching" here is obscure. Ops or Rhea was Saturn's consort; her son Zeus or Jove had a shrine at Mount Dicte in Crete, near his birthplace Ida. Cf. i, 510*f.*, and note.

590. *pale horse:* see Rev. 6:8.

601. *unhide-bound:* loose-skinned.

643. See Rev. 15:3.

645. *extenuate:* make slight.

659. The influence of the planets (which for the first time can be malignant) is most powerful when a conjunction ("synod") of them is a sixth, a quarter, a third or half the distance of the Zodiac apart (i.e., separated by two, three, four, or six signs).

668*f*. Winter was created either by tilting the earth 23½° on its axis (Copernican view) or by pushing the sun to a corresponding degree ("like distant breadth," 673) out of the orbit of the celestial equator into the ecliptic (Ptolemaic view). The following lines trace the sun's apparent movement between the Tropics of Cancer and Capricorn.

674. Pleiades and Gemini: for the reasons for Milton's epithets see Ovid, *Metamorphoses,* xiii. 293, and viii. 301.

680-687. If Adam had not fallen, the unfallen equivalents of the Eskimos and penguins would have had the sun continually circling the horizon, never rising nor setting, along with a temperate climate.

686. *Estotiland:* Labrador.

688. Thyestes' brother Atreus served him the flesh of his own sons at a banquet. See Ovid, *Metamorphoses,* xv. 462.

693. *sideral blast:* malignant starry (sidereal) influence. The word "consider" is of astrological origin.

696. *Norumbega:* New England. *Samoed:* Siberian.

698. *flaw:* gust.

699*f*. The first four winds mentioned come from the north; the next two (702) from the south; Eurus (705) is the east ("Levant") and Zephyr the west ("Ponent") wind; the winds in 706 are from the south-east and south-west respectively. The last two are Italian names; the others are classical.

739. *redound:* flow back.

741. Adam's sins weigh heavily on him, in spite of being at their natural center, where, according to the physics of Milton's time, they should weigh nothing at all.

807. Things act according to their own natures and not according to the nature of whatever acts on them. If man is finite, his punishment should be finite too, regardless of the infinity of God.

872. *pretended:* held out.

978. *as in our evils:* in such evils as ours.

996. *object:* Eve herself.

1071. *foment:* heat (by focussing the sun's rays).

1073. *attrite:* kindled by friction.

1075. *tine:* kindle.

Book XI

2. *mercy-seat:* see Exod. 25:18, and 12:253 below.

3. *prevenient grace:* grace that comes before repentance.

4. *stony* (adjective as noun): see Ezek. 11:19.

5. See Rom. 8:26.

12. In Ovid's version of the flood story (*Metamorphoses,* i. 312*f.*) the survivors, Deucalion and Pyrrha, prayed before the shrine of Themis, and then repeopled the earth by throwing stones on the ground which turned into human beings. Milton's allusion to them thus carries on the metaphor of line 4.

15. Cf. iii, 487.

18. Cf. Rev. 8:3.

74. See Exod. 19:16 (cf. note to i, 8 above); Matt. 24:31.

86. *defended:* prohibited.

95-96. See Gen. 3:22-23. Milton has explained the reason for God's fear of Adam's touching the tree of life more coherently in lines 57-62 above.

105. *remorse:* pity.

114. Cf. Dan. 10:13-14.

129*f.* Janus, the god of gates and of the new year, was represented with two faces. The four faces of the Cherubim, and the phrase "spangled with eyes," are based on Ezek. 1. For the story of Argus, slain by Hermes, who put him to sleep with the pastoral pipe and his magic caduceus, see Ovid, *Metamorphoses,* i. 668*f.*

135. *Leucothea:* goddess of the dawn: cf. note to *Comus,* 868.

159. The word Eve means mother (Gen. 3:20), and, in the form Eva, is an anagram of *Ave,* hail (Luke 1:28. Cf. also Raphael's greeting, v, 385, and xii, 379 below).

182. *subscribed:* consented.

183. *eclipsed:* darkened by pollution. Cf. x, 413.

185*f.* The eagle and the lion become hunters—an anticipation of the similar change in human society that begins with Nimrod (xii, 24*f.*).

213. See Gen 32:1-2, and II Kings 6:17.

242. *Meliboea:* a town in Thessaly, a center of the trade in Tyrian purple; Sarra is Tyre itself.

247. *zodiac:* belt.

338. *virtual:* filled with energy.

383. *second Adam:* Christ (I Cor. 15:45*f.*). See Luke 4:5.

388. *seat of Cathaian Khan:* capital of the Chinese, or rather Mongolian, khan.

389. *Temir:* Tamburlaine, the Mongol conqueror.

390. *Paquin:* Peiping. *Sinaean:* Chinese. Milton (incorrectly) distinguishes Paquin from Cambalu, and China from Cathay.

392. *Chersonese:* south-east Asia.

393*f*. Of the names not still familiar, Ecbatan and Hispahan are Persian cities; Bizance is Constantinople or Byzantium, held by the Turks (396); Negus is the title of the king of Abyssinia; Ercoco is on the Red Sea; the three towns of 399 are on the East African coast; Sofala is in Mozambique, famous for its traffic in gold, and so, like many other places, conjecturally identified with Solomon's Ophir (I Kings 9:28); the names in 403-404 all belong to northwest Africa.

409. *Atabalipa:* the Inca king conquered and killed by Pizarro. *yet unspoiled:* i.e., not yet discovered.

410. *Geryon's sons:* the Spaniards.

414. Euphrasy and rue were plants supposed to be good for the eyes.

416. *well of life:* see Ps. 36:9, and Rev. 22:1.

429*f*. The story of Cain and Abel, Gen. 4:1*f*.

433. *sord:* turf.

487. *marasmus:* consumption.

496-497. Note the verbal echoes from *Macbeth*.

518. *image:* Appetite personified as a false god, as in Philipp. 3:19.

544. See note to ii, 898. Hopefulness was the normal effect of the blood or "sanguine" humor.

556*f*. The story of Cain's descendants, who invented music and metallurgy. See Gen. 4:16*f*.

562. *instinct:* practiced.

573. *fusil:* cast.

574*f*. The story of Seth's descendants, identified by Milton with the "sons of God" of Gen. 6:1-4.

620. *troll:* wag.

638*f*. The story of the earlier antediluvians. The scene is partly based on the description of Achilles' shield in the *Iliad*, xviii. 478*f*.

642. *giants:* see Gen. 6:4, and line 688 below.

651. *makes:* in the first edition "tacks," i.e., equalizes.

665. *one:* Enoch. See Gen. 5:24, and Jude 14.

712*f*. The story of the later antediluvians and the flood. Some details come from Ovid, *Metamorphoses*, i.

735. *sevens and pairs:* reconciling by brute strength Gen. 6:19 with 7:2, which come from different sources.

736-737. Cf. I Pet. 3:20.

766. *dispensed:* distributed.

831. *hornèd:* branching.

835. *orcs:* sea-monsters.

840*f*. The story of the end of the flood, Gen. 8. *hull:* drift.

866. *listed:* striped.

Book XII

1. *bates:* stops to eat.

24. *one:* Nimrod, traditionally the founder of the world's first monarchy at Babylon (Babel). His name may mean rebel (36).

34. That is, the phrase "before the Lord" (Gen. 10:9) means "against the Lord."

41. *gurge:* spring. Milton probably means the Dead Sea area. Cf. x, 562.

53. *various spirit:* spirit of faction, in contrast to the gift of tongues at Pentecost.

62. *confusion:* the Hebrew interpretation of the word Babel (Gen. 11:9).

101. *irreverent son:* Ham. See Gen. 9:22*f*. From here on it is unnecessary to itemize Milton's summary of the Old Testament narrative.

130*f*. Ur, Abraham's home, is west of the Euphrates and Haran (Gen. 11:31) east of it; for Shechem and Moreh see Gen. 12:6. Michael then outlines the boundaries of Canaan according to Num. 24: north, Hamath in Syria; east, Mount Hermon or Senir (146) and the Jordan; south, the desert, and west, the Mediterranean, on the shore of which was Mount Carmel.

191. *river-dragon:* see Ezek. 29:3.

207. *defends between:* stops by coming in between.

225. *senate:* the council of seventy elders chosen by Moses (Exod. 24:9).

232. *types:* the ceremonial code of the Jews is not literally binding on Christians, but is to be taken as an allegory of the spiritual truths revealed by the Gospel.

241. *in figure:* as a prototype. See Acts 3:22.

255. *seven lamps:* see Exod. 25:37. Milton follows Josephus in seeing a reference to the planets in the number.

265. Josh. 10:12*f*.

267. *Israel:* the name both of Jacob and of his descendants.

288. *natural pravity:* depraved nature.

291. *shadowy:* cf. Heb. 10:1, and note to line 232 above.

295. *imputed:* transferred.

298-299. The paradox of the law is that man must be morally perfect to satisfy the law, and no man can be.

310. Joshua and Jesus are the same word, meaning "Saviour." The story of the Exodus is a "type" of the fact that not the law (Moses) but only the Saviour can enter and conquer man's promised land (cf. *P.R.*, i, 7).

348. *kings:* of Persia.

356. Referring to the struggle for the high-priesthood described in II Macc. 3, which disrupted the royal succession of the line of David, so that Jesus, David's direct descendant, was born in obscurity.

358. *stranger:* the word includes the Syrian and Roman conquerors of Palestine as well as Herod.

364. *solemn:* heralding.

380-381. A denial of the Immaculate Conception is implied.

386*f*. The dense mass of Biblical echoes in the next hundred lines cannot all be annotated here.

401. *appaid:* satisfied.

403-404. See Rom. 13:10.

442. *profluent:* running.

486. *Comforter:* see John 14:16, 26.

508. *wolves:* see Acts 20:29, a favorite text of Milton's.

526. See II Cor. 3:17, and cf. I Cor. 6:19.

540. *respiration:* revival.

591. *expect their motion:* await the order to advance.

640. *subjected:* lying beneath.

NATIVITY ODE

5. *holy sages:* Hebrew prophets.

6. *deadly forfeit:* the penalty of death which Adam incurred by his fall. *release:* remit.

11. The traditional position of Christ in the Trinity, "on the

right hand of the Father," Heb. 1:3. Milton's view of the Trinity is at this time orthodox (cf. notes to *P.L.*, i, 17, and iii, 140).

24. *prevent:* anticipate.

28. See Isa. 6:6.

39. *guilty:* nature is thought of as having fallen along with, and in consequence of, the fall of Adam, man apart from divine grace being the "natural man."

49. *ready:* making ready.

53*f*. Christ was born during an interval of peace in the Roman Empire; the hanging up of arms (55) symbolized this. Cf. Isa. 2:4.

56. *hookèd:* with scythes on the wheels.

64. *whist:* hushed.

68. *birds of calm:* the halcyon birds or kingfishers, supposed to have their nesting time at the winter solstice during a period of calm while their nests floated on the water. For the story of Alcyone see Ovid, *Metamorphoses,* xi. 384*f*. For the larger implications of "brooding" see note to *P.L.*, i, 17, and cf. line 50 above.

71. *influence:* see note to *P.L.*, iv, 669.

74. *Lucifer:* Venus as the morning star.

75. *orbs:* spheres (see note to *P.L.* ii, 1052). The glimmering is presumably produced by the rising sun.

83. Cf. Mal. 4:2.

89. *Pan:* the Greek pastoral god, identified with Christ in the latter's role of the good shepherd. See E. K.'s note to line 54 of "May," in Spenser's *Shepheards Calender.*

92. *silly:* innocent.

98. *took:* enchanted.

103. The sound is heard piercing ("thrilling") the region or upper air (see *P.L.*, vii, 425, and note to *Comus,* 3), immediately below the sphere of the moon (Cynthia).

119. See Job 38:7.

122. Cf. *P.L.*, vii, 242. The "hinges" may derive from the figure of the boxes which Plato uses to describe the spheres in *Republic,* x.

124. Cf. Job 38:11, and Ps. 89:9. See also note to *P.L.*, vii, 216, and line 67 above.

125. The doctrine that the revolution of the spheres produces a music (or single concord) inaudible to man since his fall derives chiefly from Plato (*Republic,* x). Here the harmony of the order of nature with the song of the angels is a portent of the Last Judgement which creates a new heaven and a new earth (Rev. 21:1).

135. The golden age was traditionally a period of happiness, simplicity and equality, followed by silver, brazen and iron ages of worsening virtue. See Ovid, *Metamorphoses,* i. 89*f*.: another favorite source of the idea was Boethius' *Consolation of Philosophy*. In Christianity it becomes a symbol of the unfallen world.

141. Based partly on Ps. 75:10-11, and partly on the Classical myth that Astraea, goddess of justice, forsook the world after the golden age. See Ovid, *Metamorphoses,* i. 150.

146. *tissued:* shot through with gold and silver.

158. Cf. Exod. 19:6 and *P.L.,* xi, 74-76.

173*f*. Milton's chief source here is Plutarch's essay *On the Cessation of Oracles,* a famous story from which is quoted by E. K. (see note to 89).

191. Roman deities. Lars were household gods (190) and Lemurs ghosts (189).

194. *flamens:* Roman priests. *quaint:* mystical.

195. A frequent omen of disaster. Cf. Virgil, *Georgics,* i. 480.

197*f*. For Peor, Baalim, Dagon (199), Ashtaroth, Thammuz and Moloch, see notes to *P.L.,* i, 392-457.

199. Palestine derived its name from the Philistines.

203. For Hammon, represented as a horned ram, see note to *P.L.,* iv, 269.

212. These gods were represented in the forms of a cow, a hawk and a jackal respectively. Cf. note to *P.L.,* i, 478.

213. Osiris was represented as a bull and had a shrine at Memphis in Egypt. The grass is "unshowered" (215) because it never rains in Egypt. The reference to his ark comes from Herodotus, ii.

226. For Typhon, a giant half man and half serpent, see note to *P.L.,* i, 198; Typhon was also the name of the evil being of Egyptian mythology.

228. The reference is to the story of the infant Hercules strangling serpents in his cradle. Ovid, *Metamorphoses,* ix. 67.

232. Cf. Shakespeare, *Hamlet,* I, i, 161; *A Midsummer-Night's Dream,* III, ii, 379-382.

236. *maze:* pattern of dancing, such as "fairy rings" are supposed to represent.

240. *youngest-teemèd:* latest born.

ON SHAKESPEARE

This poem appeared in the Second Shakespeare Folio of 1632.

8. *monument:* the reference seems to be to Shakespeare's monument in the church at Stratford, which Milton evidently expected to be reproduced as a frontispiece.

10. *heart:* another reading is "part."

11. *unvalued:* invaluable.

12. *Delphic:* inspired by Apollo as god of poetry.

L'ALLEGRO

This poem and *Il Penseroso* may have been written while Milton was still at Cambridge. One of his academic exercises at Cambridge was on the theme "Whether Day is better than Night." See E. M. W. Tillyard, *English Association Pamphlet* No. 82, July, 1932. They are usually, however, assigned to the Horton period. L'Allegro is Italian for "the cheerful man."

10. The Cimmerians lived in a realm of perpetual darkness (Ovid, *Metamorphoses,* xi. 592).

12. Euphrosyne ("mirth," as in the next line) was one of the three Graces, born of Bacchus (whose emblem was the ivy) and Venus. The other two were called Aglaia and Thalia.

17. *some sager:* the myth that the Graces were born of the west wind and the dawn appears to be Milton's own.

24. *buxom:* agreeable; similarly *debonair.*

27. *cranks:* jokes, puns.

29. *Hebe:* the handmaiden of the gods.

36. Mountain nymphs were called Oreads. The traditional association of liberty with the mountains recurs in Wordsworth's *The Two Voices.*

45. *spite:* contempt. The one who comes may be either the poet or the lark; the latter seems more probable.

55. *hoar:* pale grey (its color at dawn, cf. 71, and *Lycidas,* 187).

57. *not unseen:* in contrast to the mood of *Il Penseroso,* 65.

60. *state:* procession.

67. *tells his tale:* counts his tally of sheep (or perhaps "tells his story," i.e., of his love).

80. *cynosure:* ("dog's tail," i.e., the pole star, which forms the tip of the tail of the constellation called the Little Bear), object of attention (because so closely watched by sailors).

83. Conventional pastoral names, like Phyllis (86) and Thestylis (88).

87. *bower:* cottage.

91. *secure:* carefree.

94. *rebecks:* three-stringed fiddles.

102*f*. The process of changing "fairies" from malignant demons into household pets was largely due to Shakespeare, who introduces Queen Mab into *Romeo and Juliet,* I, iv, and whose Puck (*A Midsummer-Night's Dream,* II, i) is identified both with the "Friar's lantern" (104) or will-o'-the-wisp, and with Robin Goodfellow, the best known of the farmhouse brownies who were supposed to pinch lazy or slovenly maids (103) and to dispose of bits of food left out for them.

122. *influence:* the ladies are seated in the galleries above the tournament field and their eyes are compared to stars.

125. *Hymen:* god of marriage. His yellow robe and candle were traditional in masques.

132. *sock:* the shoe worn by actors in classical comedy.

134. This line is intended of course to refer only to the lighter and more fanciful comedies of Shakespeare, such as *As You Like It* or *A Midsummer-Night's Dream.*

136. *Lydian airs:* said by Plato, *Republic,* iii, to be sensual and erotic.

138. *meeting soul:* the soul attracted to the harmony of music because it is itself "harmonious." Cf. *The Merchant of Venice,* V, i, 83*f*.

139. *bout:* turn.

140*f*. These lines refer to contrapuntal love-songs like the madrigal.

144. There is a reference to what we now call the tonic chord.

145. Orpheus by the power of his music prevailed on Pluto to restore his dead wife Eurydice, with the condition, which he was unable to keep, that he should not look at her on the way back. See Ovid, *Metamorphoses,* x.

IL PENSEROSO

This poem presents an intricate series of parallels and contrasts to its predecessor, especially in its opening invocation and its final couplet. The title is Italian for "the thoughtful man."

3. *bested:* profit.

10 *Morpheus:* god of sleep: cf. Ovid, *Metamorphoses,* xi. 592-596, and *L'Allegro,* 10.

16. Cf. Spenser, *The Faerie Queene,* I, i, 4, and Song of Songs 1:5. Black is also the color of melancholy (*Samson Agonistes,* 600).

18. Memnon, son of Tithonus and Aurora (cf. note to *P.L.,* x, 307), was a prince of Ethiopia described as the handsomest of men by Homer (*Odyssey,* xi. 522); he had a sister named Hemera or Himera.

19. The boast of Cassiopeia was not about her own beauty but about that of her daughter Andromeda. See Ovid, *Metamorphoses,* iv. 670*f.*

23. This myth is Milton's own: Vesta is the goddess of the hearth and of chastity (cf. the "vestal virgins") and the name Saturn combines the ideas of melancholy, thought to be due to "saturnine" influence, the golden age which was the period of "Saturn's reign," and contemplation, with which Saturn was associated (cf. Dante, *Paradiso,* xxi). The metal produced by Saturn's influence was lead. Cf. 43 below.

30. Jove, born on Mount Ida in Crete, revolted against his father Saturn and overthrew him.

35. "A black robe of fine crape."

54. Cf. Ezek. 1 and 10, and see note to *P.L.,* v, 249.

55. *hist:* beckon.

59. The chariot of the moon was drawn by dragons Cf. Shakespeare, *A Midsummer-Night's Dream,* III, ii, 379. The meaning of "accustomed" in the next line is not clear.

83. *bellman:* night-watchman who announced the hours, often adding a blessing.

87. *outwatch the Bear:* stay up all night, as it never sets.

88. Hermes Trismegistus ("thrice-great"), an Alexandrian deity who owed his name to the Greek Hermes and his attributes to the Egyptian god of wisdom Thoth, was the patron of occult studies, especially alchemy, and was believed to be the actual author of

some of the Alexandrian "hermetic" literature. *unsphere:* draw down from his present sphere (cf. note to *Comus,* 3).

89*f.* The question of the habitation of departed souls is touched on in Plato, *Republic,* x; but speculations about spirits or demons of the elements belong rather to the occult and Neoplatonic traditions which were revived in the sixteenth century and still enjoyed some vogue in Milton's time. Cf. notes to *L'Allegro,* 102, and *Comus,* 3.

98. *pall:* robe or mantle.

99. Most Greek tragedies were based on the stories of the kings of Thebes, including Oedipus; the stories of the kings of Argos (Pelops being first of the line and grandfather of Agamemnon) and the stories of the Trojan war.

102. Tragic actors wore the high boot or buskin (cf. *L'Allegro,* 132).

104. Musaeus, like Orpheus, was a pre-Homeric and largely legendary poet. For Orpheus see note to *L'Allegro,* 145.

109. *him:* Chaucer, who left the *Squire's Tale* unfinished. The outline of the story and its main characters as far as Chaucer told it is given in 110-115. Cf. Spenser, *The Faerie Queene,* IV, iii, 32*f.*

116*f.* Referring to the romances of Boiardo, Ariosto, Tasso and Spenser, which abound in tournaments, magicians, forest scenes, and allegory (120).

123. *tricked and frounced:* dressed up with her hair curled.

124. *Attic boy:* Cephalus, beloved by Aurora, goddess of the dawn (122), whose love for his wife Procris met a tragic end in consequence. See Ovid, *Metamorphoses,* vii. 675*f.*

130. *minute-drops:* drops falling at intervals.

134. Sylvanus was a god of forests.

148. *wave at:* i.e., come floating along with.

156. *pale:* precinct.

158. *massy-proof:* apparently "sturdy enough to hold up the roof."

170. *spell:* consider.

COMUS

Comus was written by Milton in honor of the installation of Sir John Egerton, Earl of Bridgewater, at Ludlow Castle as Lord President of Wales. He wrote it at the instigation of the composer Henry Lawes, at the time employed in the Egerton household. It was the second masque Milton wrote for the family, the first being *Arcades*. Lawes composed the music for the songs, directed the performance, edited Milton's text for it, and took the part of the Attendant Spirit (Thyrsis). It is unlikely that Milton saw the performance. The three "persons who presented" were the Earl's children.

Comus was published separately in 1637 and later in the collected edition of 1645 (1673): Milton's manuscript (Cambridge MS) and an acting text (Bridgewater MS) also survive. The title dates from the eighteenth century, and the eighteenth-century music of Arne and Handel, especially Arne's fine setting of lines 119-126, is better known today than the original Lawes music.

The masque was a form of Renaissance drama that had grown up in connection with court festivities. It differed from the ordinary play in its greater emphasis on music and on elaborate scenery and costumes (less true of *Comus,* where Milton had an unusually free hand). Its characters usually represented gods or moral qualities; its action led up to a compliment to the member of the audience in whose honor it had been composed; its actors normally belonged to the same social group as the audience, and it often ended in a dance in which the audience joined the actors. One striking feature of the masque was a middle section known as the antimasque, in which a different group of characters, often in animal disguise, rushed in and changed the action abruptly to the ribald and farcical.

3. *insphered:* all the characters of *Comus* except the Lady and her brothers are elemental spirits (see note to *Il Penseroso,* 89). The Attendant Spirit lives in a lower Paradise located in the "region" or upper air above the clouds (cf. *P.L.,* vii, 425, and *Nativity Ode,* 103 and notes), and Echo also is in the sphere ("shell," 231) of air, on a lower plane; Sabrina (824*f.*) is a water-spirit. Comus and his rout claim to be fire-spirits like the will-o'-the-wisp (cf. 433), and hence of "purer" (111) material than human beings. Gnomes or earth-spirits are referred to in 436 and 734. Such beings are quite distinct from ghosts (469*f.*).

7. *pestered:* hobbled. *pinfold:* animal pound.

16. *ambrosial:* heavenly. Ambrosia was the food of the gods, and nectar (479) their drink.

18*f.* After the overthrow of Saturn (cf. *Il Penseroso,* 30 and note), Jupiter divided the empire of the universe with his brothers Neptune and Pluto, taking heaven and earth for himself and giving the sea to Neptune and hell to Pluto ("nether Jove").

25. *by course:* in turn. *several:* separate.

27. *this isle:* Britain. Albion was traditionally a son of Neptune (Spenser, *The Faerie Queene,* IV, xi, 16).

29. *quarters:* divides into four, the western (30) part, Wales (33), being under the presidency of the Earl of Bridgewater (31).

34. *offspring:* notice how "the persons who presented" are identified with their dramatic roles. Cf. 966*f.* below.

46*f.* The story that Bacchus as an infant was kidnapped by Italian ("Tuscan") pirates, and thereupon transformed the ship into an arbor, its ropes into vines and the pirates into dolphins, comes from Ovid, *Metamorphoses,* iii. 607*f.* The Tyrrhenian sea is on the west of Italy. The affair between Bacchus and Circe is Milton's invention.

49. *listed:* shifted.

50. For Circe see *Odyssey,* x, and Ovid, *Metamorphoses,* xiv. 247*f.* The allegorical implications of the story made it a favorite of Renaissance poets; the Alcina of Ariosto's *Orlando Furioso,* vi, and the Acrasia of *The Faerie Queene,* II, xii, have also influenced Milton.

58. Comus means "revelry" (Gr. *komos,* from which the word "comedy" is probably derived). It had previously been employed as a masque name by Ben Jonson.

60. *Celtic and Iberian:* French and Spanish.

65. *orient:* glowing red like the dawn.

69. A classical variant of Gen. 1:27.

84. *swain:* an allusion to Henry Lawes, whose musical powers are compared with those of Orpheus (87).

90. *likeliest:* most suitable.

Stage Dir. The entry of the antimasque (see above); for the glistering apparel cf. *The Tempest,* IV, i, 225*f.*

97. *stream:* the ocean was conceived by Homer as a great river surrounding the earth. The sun is thought of as passing under the earth back to the east (for "chamber," 101, cf. Ps. 19:5).

116. *morrice:* the traditional dance of English folk festivals.

129. *Cotytto:* Thracian witch-goddess worshiped with obscene nocturnal rites.

131. *dragon:* see note to *Il Penseroso,* 59.

135. For Hecate as patroness of witches cf. *Macbeth,* III, v, 10, and Ovid, *Metamorphoses,* vii. 94.

139. *nice:* prudish.

142. *solemnity:* festival.

Stage Dir. *The Measure:* a dance occurs at this point.

154. *spongy:* the air absorbs the "dust" (165) thrown by Comus into the air.

168. *fairly:* quietly.

189. *votarist:* man under a vow, especially a vow to journey to the Holy Land. *palmer:* a pilgrim who had been there and carried a palm-leaf in token.

203. *perfect:* distinct.

204. *single:* total.

215. *Chastity:* the reader expects "charity" (I Cor. 13:13): for Milton the two virtues are, on the Lady's level, much the same, except that "charity" would require a more explicitly Christian setting.

230. Echo was a nymph in love with Narcissus, who after his death pined away until only her voice was left. See Ovid, *Metamorphoses,* iii. 351*f*. The Meander river is in Asia Minor. The "echo song" was a favorite of Renaissance poets and musicians.

251. *fall:* cadence, like "close" in 548.

253. For Scylla and Charybdis see note to *P.L.,* ii, 660. The haunt of the Sirens was nearby; cf. *Odyssey,* xii, and Ovid, *Metamorphoses,* xiv. 88. The association of Circe with nymphs is from Ovid, *Metamorphoses,* xiv. 264*f*.

277*f*. The technical name for this kind of dialogue, much used in Greek drama, is stichomythia.

293. *swinked:* tired out.

299. *element:* the air. Comus's flattery of the brothers is also the poet's.

301. *plighted:* folded.

313. *bosky bourn:* brook shadowed by bushes.

318. *thatched pallet:* straw nest.

341-342. For "cynosure" see note to *L'Allegro,* 80. The Phoenicians from Tyre were the greatest sailors of the ancient world. According to Ovid, *Metamorphoses,* ii. 505-507, the Little Bear is the stellified form of Arcas, son of Jupiter and Callisto, an Arcadian princess who herself became the Great Bear.

344. *wattled cotes:* sheepfolds surrounded with palisades of stakes

366. *to seek:* unprepared; similarly *unprincipled* (367).

393. The tree in the garden of the Hesperides (daughters of the Titan Atlas living in an island in the Atlantic) bore golden fruit and was guarded by a dragon. To gather the fruit and kill the dragon was one of the labors of Hercules. See Ovid, *Metamorphoses,*

iv. 637, and ix. 190. The word "unenchanted" (i.e., unable to be enchanted) glances at the story of Argus: see note to *P.L.*, xi, 129.

407. *unownèd:* unprotected.

434. *hag:* female evil spirit. For "blue" cf. the blue eyes of Sycorax in *The Tempest,* I, ii, 269.

441*f*. The beasts hunted by Diana and the head of Medusa (presented to Minerva by Perseus and placed by her on her shield [Ovid, *Metamorphoses,* iv, 802-803]) are interpreted as allegories of lust tamed by chastity. The theme of the invulnerability of Chastity is treated at length by Spenser in Book III of *The Faerie Queene* (the legend of Britomart).

461. Cf. I Cor. 6:19, and *P.L.*, v, 497.

470*f*. These lines are derived from Plato's *Phaedo.*

494*f*. Another compliment to Lawes, who acted the part.

515*f*. The story of the Chimera is in the *Iliad;* episodes dealing with enchanted isles and a descent to hell are in the *Odyssey.*

547. "To play on my rustic pipe."

553. *frighted:* the Cambridge MS has "flighted," which may well be right.

554. *litter:* reclining chariot.

568. *lawns:* open spaces in forests, hence paths.

607. *purchase:* prey.

619. The reference is apparently to Milton himself, in which case the plant bearing a golden flower in another land (633, cf. *Lycidas,* 78-82) given to Thyrsis (Lawes) in exchange for his music must represent poetry.

621. *virtuous:* possessing healing properties. Such plants were called "simples" (627).

636. In the *Odyssey* Ulysses is able to resist Circe through the virtues of an herb called moly. The equivalent plant here, haemony, seems to have got its name from Haemonia, Thessaly, a land famous for magic and healing. But a more natural association would be with Orpheus (see notes to 84 and 619), whose name is linked with Mt. Haemus in neighboring Thrace (Ovid, *Metamorphoses,* ii. 219; x, 77).

652. Cf. Spenser, *The Faerie Queene,* II, xii, 57.

660. *nerves:* tendons, muscles.

661. Daphne was a nymph changed to a laurel tree when pursued by Apollo. See Ovid, *Metamorphoses,* i. 547*f*.

675. *Nepenthes,* drug inducing forgetfulness of sorrow, given to

Helen of Troy, a daughter of Zeus, by Polydamna, the wife of an Egyptian named Thone. See *Odyssey,* iv. 220*f*.

700. *liquorish* (perhaps better "lickerish"): delicious (pejorative).

701. Cf. *Iliad,* i. 584.

707. *budge:* fur used on doctoral hoods.

708. A tub was the reputed habitat of Diogenes, leader of the ascetic school of philosophy called cynicism.

733. *deep:* of the earth. Cf. "centre" in 382.

760. *bolt:* refine.

801. *set off:* supported by.

804. *Erebus:* hell, in which some of the Titans who fought with Saturn against Jupiter were imprisoned after being defeated by Jupiter's thunderbolts.

813. Cf. *P.L.,* ix, 1017 and note.

816. Cf. Ovid, *Metamorphoses,* xiv. 300.

822. *Meliboeus:* a pastoral name referring to Spenser (see *The Faerie Queene,* II, x, 19). Sabrina is the Roman name for the Severn river, near Ludlow Castle. According to the (mostly fabulous) history of Geoffrey of Monmouth, Britain was settled by the Trojan Brutus (828), grandson of Aeneas (son of Anchises, 923), whose son Locrine became enamored of Estrild. Locrine's jealous queen Gwendolen (830) had Estrild and her daughter Sabrina flung into the Severn, which took its name from Sabrina.

835. *Nereus:* a sea-god, usually spoken of as very old (871), whose fifty daughters were the ocean nymphs or Nereids. Cf. Ovid, *Metamorphoses,* ii. 268*f*. and Spenser, *The Faerie Queene,* III, iv, 40*f*.

838. *asphodel:* lily growing in Elysium (*Odyssey,* xi. 538). Nectar and ambrosia (840, see 16 and note) conferred immortality (841).

845. *urchin blasts:* blights caused by mischievous fairies.

868*f*. Oceanus is the original god of the sea in Homer and Hesiod; Tethys was his consort; Neptune, whose consort was Amphitrite (921), is called "earth-shaker" by Homer; for Nereus see note to 835; the Carpathian wizard is Proteus, who carried a sheep-hook (see note to *P.L.,* iii, 598); Triton, a merman, was Neptune's herald (cf. *Lycidas,* 89), represented as blowing a conch or "wreathed horn" (Wordsworth); Glaucus was a fisherman changed to a sea-god with the power of prophecy (*Aeneid,* v. 823; Spenser, *The Faerie Queene,* IV, xi, 13); Leucothea ("white goddess") was Ino, the wife of the mad Athamas, who to escape him plunged into the sea with her son Melicertes, both being rescued by dolphins and deified (Ovid, *Metamorphoses,* iv. 539*f*.); Thetis was a Nereid and the mother of Achilles, called "silver-footed" by Homer; for the Sirens see 253 and note; Parthenope and Ligea were names of Sirens, the former's tomb being shown near Naples.

929. *tresses:* (a) the nymph's hair; (b) the bushes along the river bank.

958. The dance of the shepherds (actors in the masque) gives way to the general dance in which the audience joins.

963. Mercury was traditionally the leader of a chorus of dancing nymphs; Dryades are tree-nymphs.

970. *timely:* early.

980*f*. The lower Paradise in the sphere of air inhabited by the Attendant Spirit (cf. note to 3) is identified with (a) the Atlantic islands of the blest, including Elysium (996, cf. *Odyssey,* iv. 561-564) and the garden of the Hesperides (393 and note); (b) the Earthly Paradise (see note to *P.L.,* iv, 266); (c) the gardens of Adonis described by Spenser in *The Faerie Queene,* III, vi, where we also find the "Assyrian queen" (Venus, first worshiped in Assyria) as well as Cupid and Psyche, whose story is told in Apuleius' *Metamorphoses.*

995. *purfled:* embroidered.

LYCIDAS

Lycidas was Milton's contribution to a memorial volume of verses on the death by drowning of Edward King prepared by some of King's associates at Cambridge, of whom Milton was one, though not a close friend. King was preparing to enter the Church, and had (unlike Milton) just gained a fellowship. His merits as a poet are considerably enhanced by Milton.

The pastoral convention of describing poets and lovers as shepherds began with Theocritus of Sicily (133), whose *Idyls* are written in the Doric (189) dialect of Greek spoken there. Theocritus also established the main types of the convention, of which the elegy was one. Virgil's *Eclogues* transmitted the pastoral tradition to the Renaissance, when it mingled with the pastoral symbolism of the Bible (Abel, Ps. 23, the conception of Christ as the good shepherd, and the religious meanings of "pastor" and "flock"), an important connecting link being Virgil's fourth or "Messianic" eclogue. The treatment of religion in the pastoral often took the form of satire on clerical abuses (e.g., "May," "July," and "September" in Spenser's *Shepheards Calender*), and the treatment of poetry, and of love or friendship, often involved a discussion of fame (e.g., "October" and "December").

1-2. The laurel, myrtle and ivy were traditional garlands of the poet. Notice how the theme of the unripeness of the poet modulates into the theme of premature death.

6. *dear:* deeply concerning.

13. *welter:* roll about, suggesting an image picked up in 126.

15. *sacred well:* either Aganippe, the well at the foot of Helicon, where the Muses danced about the altar of Jove (*Il Penseroso,* 47-48), or the Pierian spring at the foot of Olympus, where they were born.

19. *Muse:* poet.

36. *Damaetas:* pastoral name for an older scholar at Cambridge, not certainly identified.

50. Cf. Theocritus, *Idyl,* i. 66*f*., and Virgil, *Eclogue,* x. 9*f*.

53*f*. The Druids of Britain, a priesthood which included a caste of bards, had one of their main centers in Mona (Anglesey). The Dee (Roman Deva) is nearby; its frequent changes of course were supposed to be auguries of the welfare of the country, hence "wizard" (55). The "steep" (52) is a mountain in North Wales where there was said to be a Druid cemetery. All these places are near the scene of King's death.

58. *Orpheus:* see note to *P.L.,* vii, 32. His head floated down the river Hebrus ("swift," according to *Aeneid,* i. 317) and was carried to the island of Lesbos. See Ovid, *Metamorphoses,* xi. 1*f*.

68-69. Pastoral names, the latter occurring in two Renaissance Latin poets, Joannes Secundus and George Buchanan.

70. *clear:* noble.

75. *Fury:* Atropos, strictly a Fate, whose function it was to cut the threads of human lives spun and woven by her two sisters.

85. Arethusa is in Sicily, the home of Theocritus; the Mincius, a tributary of the Po, is near Virgil's birthplace Mantua.

89. *herald:* Triton. See note on *Comus,* 868.

96. *Hippotades*: Aeolus, god of winds. For his "dungeon" cf. *Aeneid,* i. 52*f*.

99. *Panope:* a Nereid. See *Aeneid,* v. 240.

103. *Camus:* the river-god of the Cam, here the symbol of Cambridge. The river-weeds and grass growing along the river are de-

scribed as the (academic) dress of the god (104). Cf. *Comus,* 929 and note.

106. *flower:* the hyacinth, which has red markings on its petals resembling the Greek word *ai* (alas). The legend is that they were produced by the blood of a Spartan youth Hyacinthus, and were inscribed on it by Apollo, who had been responsible for his death. See Ovid, *Metamorphoses,* x. 214*f*. The basis of the story is a "dying god" myth like that of Adonis, hence its appropriateness.

107. *pledge:* child.

109. *Pilot:* Peter (see Luke 5:2-4); to whom were given the keys (traditionally two) of heaven (Matt. 16:19), and who became the first bishop of the Church ("mitred," 112). For the gold and iron cf. *P.L.,* ii, 327-328.

115*f*. Cf. John 10:1 (with *P.L.,* iv, 193), Matt. 22:8 (for 118) and Ezek. 34. See also Ruskin's *Sesame and Lilies.*

122. *sped:* prosperous.

123. *flashy:* insipid.

124. *scrannel:* squeaking.

128. *wolf:* the symbol of the degradation of the Church, associated here with anti-Protestant tendencies, whether Anglican or Catholic.

130. *two-handed:* an allegory variously explained as the two houses of Parliament, the spiritual and temporal power, or the Law and Gospel of the Bible (cf. Rev. 1:16). *engine:* instrument of human or divine justice, explained as a sword (cf. *P.L.,* vi, 251), axe (cf. Matt. 3:10), flail (cf. Spenser, *The Faerie Queene,* V, ii, 24), and sickle (cf. Rev. 14:16), none of which accounts for both "door" and "smite once." It is far more important to notice the link in imagery with 75

132. *Alpheus:* a river in Arcadia. Its god loved the nymph Arethusa, and when she fled to Sicily to escape him, plunged under the sea and rose again in Sicily. Cf. Ovid, *Metamorphoses,* v. 574*f*. The reference to him marks the end of the second episode, as the reference to Arethusa (85) marked the end of the first, and anticipates the final theme of resurrection from the sea.

136. *use:* live in.

138. *swart star:* Sirius the dog-star, which rises in July.

142. *rathe:* early.

153. *false:* the body of Lycidas is not present.

160. *Bellerus:* a personified form of Bellerium (Land's End in Cornwall).

161. St. Michael's Mount, near Land's End, has a seat-shaped forma-

tion in which St. Michael was said to sit. As it faces south, he would be looking across the Bay of Biscay toward Galicia in north-west Spain, where Namancos and Bayona are located.

164. The allusion is to the story of Arion, whose skill in music caused dolphins to bear him to the shore. Arion symbolizes the salvation of the poet, as Orpheus (63) symbolizes his death. The Christian form of the same symbol is in 173 (cf. Matt. 14:24-31).

174. Cf. Rev. 22:2; 19:9 (176); and 7:17 (181).

183. *Genius:* in classical terms a local divinity (*Nativity Ode,* 186); in Christian terms a guardian angel like St. Michael (181) or the Attendant Spirit in *Comus.*

184. *large recompense:* contrast with line 122 above.

186. *uncouth swain:* unknown poet (Milton).

188. *quills:* hollow reeds of pastoral pipes.

192. *blue:* the conventional color of the shepherd's cloak.

SONNETS

I. 14. *serve:* the language is that of the Courtly Love convention, rarely used by Milton.

II. This sonnet formed part of a letter sent to a friend who had reproached Milton with spending too much time in study and retirement.

VIII. *Assault:* the Royalist campaign of 1642 consisted of a drive on London which was turned back without a battle.

1. *Colonel:* pronounce as spelt.

10. *Emathian:* Macedonian. *conqueror:* Alexander the Great, who was said to have spared Pindar's house when he destroyed Thebes.

13. Plutarch, in his life of Lysander, says that the destruction of Athens, after its defeat by Sparta, was averted when an officer repeated the opening chorus of Euripides' *Electra.*

X. 1. *Earl:* Sir James Ley, Earl of Marlborough, who under Charles I was Lord High Treasurer and President of the Council, but died in 1629 when the king seized power (see Table). Lady Margaret, his oldest daughter, married a Parliamentary captain.

6. *dishonest:* shameful. The battle of Chaeronea resulted in the conquest of Greece by Philip of Macedon; the shock of its news killed the aged Athenian orator Isocrates.

XI. *certain treatises:* the divorce pamphlets, of which the third was *Tetrachordon* (Gr. "four strings," because based on four Scriptural texts). Milton's views on divorce had been denounced by a Puritan clergyman in a sermon to Parliament.

7. *spelling:* interpreting. *Mile-End Green:* in the far east of London; the doggerel rhyme is deliberate.

9. These three names seem all to have been possessed by one person, a lieutenant in the army of the Royalist leader Montrose.

11. Quintilian advised writers not to use cacophonous foreign names (*Oratory,* viii).

12. *Cheek* (Cheke): tutor to Edward VI and professor of Greek at Cambridge. He lived when Greek was still the object of some prejudice.

XII. 5. Latona, mother by Zeus of Apollo the sun-god and Artemis the moon-goddess (7), was prevented by some peasants, who were changed to frogs in consequence, from drinking at a lake. See Ovid, *Metamorphoses,* vi. 317*f.*

XIII. For Lawes see the introductory note to *Comus.* This sonnet first appeared in Lawes' publication *Choice Psalms.*

4. Midas, king of Phrygia, was given ass's ears by Apollo because he preferred the music of Pan. Ovid, *Metamorphoses,* xi. 153*f.* *committing:* placing against one another.

9. *honour'st Verse:* Lawes composed in the Baroque monodic style of accompanied aria which, in contrast to elaborate contrapuntal forms like the madrigal, preserved the integrity of the words, and was far more popular with poets.

11. *story:* glossed in *Choice Psalms* as "the story of Ariadne set by him in music." The author of the "story" was William Cartwright.

13. See Dante, *Purgatorio,* ii, 76*f.*

XIV. Mrs. Thomason's husband, a close friend of Milton's, was a London publisher who made an important collection of Civil War pamphlets.

XV. The capture of Colchester in Essex by the Parliamentary general Fairfax was one of the decisive events of the second Civil War.

7. *north:* Scotland, an ally of Parliament in the first Civil War, swung over to the Royalists in the second.

8. *imp:* graft feathers into an injured (falcon's) wing.

XVI. The occasion of this sonnet was a brief submitted by a

group of clergymen to a Parliamentary committee appointed by Cromwell to examine the state of the Church. The general drift of the brief was in favor of intolerance and clerical censorship.

7. The battle of Preston, 1648.

14. *maw:* a kind of pun based on "law." Cf. Matt. 7:15, and Philipp. 3:19.

XVII. 4. The allusion is to the role of the Roman Senate in the invasions of Italy by Pyrrhus (of Epirus) and Hannibal.

6. *hollow:* pun on Holland. Vane was conducting negotiations with the Dutch after hostilities had broken out. Cf. *P.L.*, vi, 578.

11. Vane was one of the most consistent supporters of religious toleration.

XVIII. A massacre of Waldensians, with incidents like those described in line 8, took place in Piedmont on Easter Day, 1655. Cromwell's protest against it was handled by Milton as Latin Secretary.

1. Cf. Rev. 6:10.

4. The Waldensians had been in existence since the twelfth century, and became Protestants at the Reformation.

10. *sow:* i.e., "the blood of the martyrs is the seed of the Church."

12. *triple:* the Papal tiara has three crowns.

14. The Papal court is described in a sonnet of Petrarch as a "wicked Babylon" and a "fountain of woe."

XIX. 3. Matt. 25:14-30.

XX. 1. *father:* Henry Lawrence, father of Milton's friend Edward, was President of the Council under Cromwell.

6. *Favonius:* the west wind.

8. Matt. 6:28.

13. *spare:* "spare time" seems a more natural meaning than "forbear," which is also possible.

XXI. 1. Cyriack Skinner, evidently an amateur mathematician (7), had been a pupil of Milton's; his grandfather was the legal writer Sir Edward Coke, Chief Justice under James I.

2. *Themis:* goddess of justice.

8. An attack on Poland by Charles X of Sweden and the policies of Cardinal Mazarin in France were prominent in the news of the time.

XXII. 12. *rings:* the flatter reading "talks" has more authority.

XXIII. 2. Alcestis, after dying for her husband Admetus, was delivered from Death by Hercules, Jove's son, and restored to Admetus, who did not recognize her because she was veiled. Milton never saw his second wife.

5*f*. A contrast is intended between the Law (Lev. 12) and the Gospel (Rev. 7:13-14).

SAMSON AGONISTES

The word "agonistes" means a wrestler or athlete, Samson's role at the moment of his death, and also, in a more general sense, a struggler or fighter.

Intro. Aristotle: The passage is a paraphrase of Aristotle's doctrine of tragic catharsis (*Poetics,* vi), but the analogy of homeopathic medicine shows Renaissance influence.

Paraeus: a sixteenth-century German Protestant theologian.

Dionysius, tyrant of Sicily and friend of Plato, won a prize for tragedy.

Ajax: The story is told in Suetonius' life of Augustus. Milton's phrase echoes his comment on his own unfinished poem, *The Passion.*

Gregory Nazianzen, a famous Father of the Church, was apparently not the author of *Christus Patiens.*

Italians: Tasso had written a tragedy on the Greek model.

Monostrophic: Not divided, like the choruses of Greek tragedies and like the Pindaric ode, into the three lyrical stanzas mentioned below. The two long words mean "free" and "irregular."

It suffices . . . : It is enough to give the impression of dramatic completeness (without numbering the acts).

Arg. relating the catastrophe: which takes place offstage, as regularly in Greek tragedy and in the Book of Job. *by accident:* incidentally.

13. Dagon (see note to *P.L.*, i, 457) was a fertility god, but the Hebrews derived his name from a root meaning "fish."

55. *secure:* rash.

118. *diffused:* relaxed; similarly *languished* (119).

133. *Chalybean:* made by the Chalybes, a tribe of smiths living on the Black Sea.

136. *insupportably:* irresistibly.

138. Ascalon was one of the five chief Philistine cities (see *P.L.*, i, 464-466). The other four are mentioned in 981.

145. This scene was one originally considered by Milton as the subject for his Samson tragedy. Ramath-Lechi means "the wielding of the jaw-bone."

148. Hebron is about forty miles from Gaza ("Azza," 147); for its giants see Num. 13:22, 33.

150. For Atlas see Ovid, *Metamorphoses,* ii. 296*f.* Cf. *P.L.*, ii, 306.

167*f.* The wheel of fortune, which comes mainly from Boethius, became in the Middle Ages the central image of tragedy. Cf. the opening of Chaucer's *Troilus.*

181. Cf. Judg. 13:2, with Josh. 15:33.

247. *ambition:* attempt to get support.

278*f.* For Gideon and Jephthah, predecessors of Samson in the office of "judge," see Judg. 8, 11, and 12.

295. Ps. 14:1.

312. *national obstriction:* the law given to Israel, according to which Dalila, being a Philistine, was unclean (321) as well as unchaste.

318. For the Nazarites see Num. 6, and Judg. 13:4-5.

332. *Dan:* the Israelite tribe to which Samson and his chorus belonged, and who in the division of Canaan had been allotted the portion then held by the Philistines. Their later migration is recorded in Judg. 18.

373. *appoint:* limit.

500. Referring mainly to Tantalus and Prometheus; Aeschylus' tragedy of *Prometheus Bound* is a major influence on *Samson Agonistes.*

528. *sons of Anak:* giants. See note to 148.

533. *venereal trains:* sexual wiles.

548. The purest springs were thought to be those rising toward the east.

549. *rod:* the ray of the sun, associated with the rod of Moses (Num. 20:8).

581. Judg. 15:18-19, carrying on the image of 549.

600. *black:* melancholy (Gr. "black bile").

612. *accidents:* symptoms. The imagery suggests an allegorical reading of the torments of Prometheus.

662. *mood:* mode (in music).

694. Cf. *Iliad,* i. 5.

701. *disordinate:* intemperate. Milton himself suffered greatly from gout, often regarded as caused by intemperance.

715-716. Tarsus is evidently identified with Tarshish (Isa. 23:1); for Javan see note to *P.L.*, i, 508; Gadire is the modern Cadiz in Spain.

720. *amber:* ambergris.

727. *declined:* the literal meaning of "Dalila."

748. The hyena, according to legend, could assume speech to decoy human victims.

934. *cup:* cf. *Comus,* 51, and Jer. 51:7. *charms:* enchanting songs.

936. Cf. Ps. 58:4-5.

971. For the personification of Fame see *Aeneid,* iv. 173, and Ovid, *Metamorphoses,* xii. 43*f*.

989. *Jael:* see Judges 4 and 5.

993. *piety:* patriotism. The Dalila episode certainly is closely connected with the argument of the divorce pamphlets. Whether Milton himself is still brooding about his first marriage, thirty years and two wives later, is another matter.

1020. *paranymph:* best man.

1030. *affect:* prefer.

1048. "That co-operates (with her husband) for the good of the home."

1068. Harapha (Heb. "the giant," probably derived by Milton from the Hebrew text of II Sam. 21:22) belongs to the dramatic type of the *miles gloriosus* or cowardly braggart, frequent in comedy but rare in tragedy.

1075. *fraught:* cargo, hence business. Harapha is compared to towers like Babel ("pile," 1069) and tall ships like those in the Armada.

1080-1081. Giants of old Canaan. See Deut. 2:10-11, 3:11; Num. 13, and Gen. 14:5.

1092 *single:* challenge (to single combat).

1096. *with:* perhaps "wish."

1109. *assassinated:* ambushed.

1120. Brigandine is plate armor, habergeon a coat of mail, vantbrace armor for the arms. The contrast between simple and elaborate weapons recurs in the story of David's fight with Goliath (Harapha's son).

1122. Cf. I Sam. 17:7, and *Iliad,* vii. 220.

1220. *appellant:* challenger.

1228. *descant on:* slander.

1237. *baffled:* disgraced as a knight.

1248. The brothers of Goliath were begotten by the editorializings on II Sam. 21:19 which began with I Chron. 20:5.

1307. *voluble:* concise.

1342. *joined:* enjoined.

1367. Note that Samson's position in Philistine society is based on a clear separation of spiritual and temporal authority. Cf. Sonnet XVII (to Vane), 11.

1619. *cataphracts:* armed cavalry.

1647-1648. See note to *P.L.*, i, 230.

1669. *sublime:* uplifted.

1674. *Silo:* Shiloh: cf. Josh. 18:1, and *P.L.*, i, 11.

1675. The god-inspired frenzy, like the "Necessity" of 1666 and the hybris or proud mind of 1669, belongs to the Greek conception of tragedy. Line 1686 marks the final transfer of the tragic catastrophe from Samson to the Philistines.

1692. *dragon:* serpent.

1695. *villatic:* barnyard. The eagle and thunderbolt are associated as being both emblems of Zeus.

1699. For the phoenix see Ovid, *Metamorphoses,* xv. 391*f*. There was only one phoenix at a time (1701); it lived in Arabia for five centuries (*saecula* in Latin, hence "secular," 1707), and then it burned itself completely ("holocaust," 1702) and rose as a new phoenix from its ashes. Here it is compared to virtue, but in Christian poetry it is usually an allegory of the death and resurrection of Christ.

1713. *Caphtor:* Crete, from which the Hebrews believed the Philistines to have come (Amos 9:7).

1751. *in place:* on this spot.

REASON OF CHURCH GOVERNMENT URGED AGAINST PRELATY

Prelaty: rule of bishops. "Reason" in Milton is a revolutionary word connected with the struggle for liberty (*P.L.*, xii, 82-85).

428. 10. *factory:* trading post.

20. See Jer. 15:10.

26. See Rev. 10:9: the phrase "mysterious book of Revelation" is an oxymoron.

27. *electuary:* medicine.

30. See Sophocles, *Oedipus Rex,* 316*f*., and cf. note to *P.L.*, iii, 35.

429. 7. Jer. 20:9-10.

13. *stomach:* arrogance.

430. 22. *infancy:* inarticulateness.

431. 9. *equal:* fair.

432. 37. Ariosto's remark to Cardinal Bembo that he would rather be a major Italian than a minor Latin poet was one of the turning points in the humanist controversy over whether poetry in the major forms (epic and tragedy) should be written in the modern languages or not.

433. 15. *mechanics:* pedants.

25. *before the conquest:* Alfred the Great is compared to Ulysses in Milton's notebook.

27. *prince:* the Duke of Ferrara, patron of Tasso, who eventually chose the subject of Godfrey of Boulogne and the First Crusade for his *Jerusalem Delivered.*

32. Cf. *P.L.*, ix, 44-45.

434. 2. Origen, the great Alexandrian scholar, is quoted by Paraeus in his commentary on Revelation referred to here and in the Introduction to *Samson Agonistes.*

8. *Callimachus:* an Alexandrian poet of the third century B.C.

10. *frequent songs:* e.g., David's lament over Jonathan, II Sam. 1; Deborah's war-song, Judg. 5; Moses' song, Exod. 15.

435. 29. Prov. 8:2-3; "she" is Wisdom.

32. *paneguries:* religious festivals.

33. *porches:* church-porches, where sermons dealing with moral matters were preached to crowds in the street.

436. 17. *Dame Memory:* the Muses were daughters of Jupiter and Mnemosyne (Memory).

18. *Spirit:* see Isa. 6, *P.L.*, i, 17 and note, and *Nativity Ode,* 28.

37. *sumpters:* packasses.

OF EDUCATION

Samuel Hartlib, a Prussian exile living in England, was a disciple of the Czech educational reformer Comenius, who advocated a system of education moving from the concrete to the abstract, beginning with natural and scientific knowledge and ending with abstract principles. This was in harmony with the empiric program of knowledge laid down by Bacon, but directly opposite to the medieval and Renaissance system still in force in Milton's day, which was based on the "seven liberal arts." This was a deductive approach to knowledge which began with the "trivium" of grammar, rhetoric, and logic, learned through the writing of "themes" or "disputations" arguing on one side or other of a general question, and then moved on to the "quadrivium" (arithmetic, geometry, astronomy, and music), in which the sciences were included. Milton adopts the general inductive plan of Hartlib, and agrees with his policy of a less grammar-bound approach to languages, but his educational values are still humanistic. Milton also has in mind two major precepts of Plato: that education is for both body and mind and for both peace and war.

439. 6. *voluntary idea:* spontaneously evolved form.

14. *Januas and Didactics:* a reference to two works on education by Comenius. Janua means "door" (i.e., to Latin).

440. 11. *preposterous:* inverted in position or order. For the significance of the term see introductory note.

21. *conversing among:* getting acquainted with.

24. *praxis:* application.

35. *unmatriculated:* inexperienced.

442. 19. William Lilly or Lily was the author of the standard beginners' book in Latin grammar.

20. *absolute:* self-contained.

36. *smatter:* mispronounce.

37. *law French:* the debased jargon of French origin used in English law courts.

443. 6. Cebes, a disciple of Socrates who appears in the *Phaedo,* was assumed to be the author of the *Pinax,* a moral allegory of human life.

27. *playing:* a number game played with the hands was sometimes used in schools to teach arithmetic.

36. *Hercules' praises:* one of Hercules' labors was the cleansing of the filthy Augean stables, allegorically interpreted as the manuring of the soil.

444. 9*f.* Theophrastus was the chief classical authority on botany, Vitruvius on architecture, Pomponius Mela on geography, and Celsus and Pliny on medicine and natural history. Solinus was the author of a general compendium of geographical knowledge.

10. *under contribution:* to be used for reference.

23. *crudity:* attack of indigestion. The basis of medical study was the relation of the four humors (see note to *P.L.*, ii, 898) to one another ("tempers") and to their environment ("seasons").

445. 1*f*. A list of didactic and pastoral poets. A poem on the virtues of gems was attributed to Orpheus; Aratus wrote on astronomy and meteorology; Nicander on poisons; Oppian on fishing and hunting, and Dionysius of Alexandria on geography. Manilius' poem in five books on astronomy was still standard for that subject. The *Georgics* and *Eclogues* constitute "the rural part of Virgil."

6. *proairesis:* free choice by the will of its end. A technical term in Aristotle's *Ethics.*

12. Diogenes Laertius' *Lives of the Philosophers* and a treatise called *On the Soul of the World,* falsely attributed to the Timaeus (who came from Locris) of Plato's dialogue, are referred to.

14. *determinate sentence:* inspired or canonical maxim.

18. *economics:* household management.

23. For *Alcestis* (by Euripides) see note to Sonnet XXIII; Sophocles' *Trachiniae* also deals with a self-sacrificing wife.

33. Zaleucus and Charondas were, like Solon and Lycurgus, authors, or reputed authors, of Greek codes of law.

34. The definitive codification of Roman law by Justinian included the edicts or special statements of procedure laid down by praetors and followed as precedents, and the original statutory law of Rome known as the "Twelve Tables."

446. 4. *Chaldee:* Aramaic, in which a few passages of the Old Testament are written. Some of the oldest New Testament MSS are in Syriac.

14. *organic:* creative.

20. Phalereus and Hermogenes were rhetoricians (many of the obscurer names in Milton's lists are not intended to be anything but names).

23. *sensuous:* derived from sense experience (without the moral implications of "sensual"). The word seems to be Milton's invention.

26. Castelvetro commented on Aristotle's *Poetics;* Tasso is referred to because of his critical treatises on epic; Mazzoni defended Dante against Renaissance humanist criticism.

28. *decorum:* propriety, especially the choice of style suitable

to the speaker or theme (for the three classes of style see lines 15-16). It was the central conception of contemporary rhetoric.

447. 24. *Cyrene:* Libya, where there was a medical school in ancient times.

28. The words "Academy" and "Lyceum" describe the schools of Plato and Aristotle respectively.

449. 3. This paragraph reflects the dissatisfaction of Parliamentary supporters with the management of their armies, which, under the command of Essex, encountered an almost unbroken series of defeats in the first year or two of the war.

7. *unrecruitable:* no good at getting or keeping recruits.

450. 1. *kickshaws:* fops. The word is derived from *quelque chose.*

25. See *Odyssey,* xxi.

THE DOCTRINE AND DISCIPLINE OF DIVORCE

Doctrine and Discipline: theory and practice.

451. 12. See Ezek. 3:1-3.

452. 1. The image is that of a monster with a serpentine body and a female face. See Spenser, *The Faerie Queene,* I, i, 14.

28. *Moses:* see Deut. 24:1-2. Deuteronomy is generally identified with the book of the law rediscovered in the reign of Josiah (line 31, cf. II Kings 22).

453. 10. Philipp. 1:18.

17. *churched the father:* an ironic reference to the Anglican rite of "churching" or purifying ("needless . . . purgation") of women after childbirth. See notes to *P.L.,* ii, 752, and Sonnet XXIII, 5.

454. 1. *Assyrian blasphemer:* Rabshakeh. See II Kings 19.

18. II Thess. 2:3-4 was the chief source for the doctrine of the Antichrist ("exalted perdition").

455. 6. *Egyptian colony:* the Israelites. Cf. Mark 10:5.

31. Cf. Matt. 23.

456. 9. See I Cor. 16:14, and Rom. 13:10.

33. *economical:* pertaining to the family.

36. See Matt. 5:19-20.

457. 8. Some of the statutes of Edward the Confessor still formed part of English law.

10. *intellectuals:* brains.

23. *expectation:* the general sense is that the enemies of the Church are waiting to see its patience exhausted in attempting to compromise at various times ("calends") with conflicts of opinion.

458. 2. *Masoreth:* commentary on the law. Rabbinical Judaism began with Ezra and had one of its main centers at Tiberias in Galilee.

6. *Norman isles:* the Channel Islands.

8. *Druids:* see note to *Areopagitica,* 495, line 3.

11. The Emperor Constantine's career began in Britain.

12-13. Missionaries living about A.D. 700. Winifride is St. Boniface.

14. *Alcuin:* a British scholar and monk invited by Charlemagne to his court to reform education in France.

459. 1. *medulla:* abstract.

AREOPAGITICA

The immediate occasion of *Areopagitica* was an order for the supervision of printing passed by Parliament in 1643, some clauses of which are quoted by Milton. From the Parliamentary point of view this order legalized censorship, which under Charles had depended only on a Star Chamber directive. The Parliamentary order retained the general form and the machinery for enforcement (inspection by the Company of Stationers) adopted by its predecessor. The title is derived from the Areopagus or high court of Athens, implicitly compared by Milton with Parliament, and, in particular, from an oration addressed to it by Isocrates called *Logos Areopagiticos.*

460. 5. *altered:* disturbed.

7. *censure:* opinion.

461. 11. *Roman recovery:* Rome under the later Emperors was no longer, as Gibbon said, "capable of a rational freedom."

29. *him:* Bishop Hall, whose defense of episcopacy, also addressed to Parliament, had started the "Smectymnuus" controversy (see Table).

462. 7. *statists:* statesmen.

9. *triennial:* Parliament had so constituted itself in 1641.

10. *cabin:* cabinet.

23. *stateliness:* arrogance.

26. *him:* Isocrates. See introductory note.

31. *signiories:* tyrannies.

33. Dion Chrysostom, a Greek orator, tried to persuade the Rhodians not to allow their rulers to put their names on ancient monuments.

463. 20. *copy:* copyright.

24. *quadragesimal and matrimonial:* the enforcing of canon laws governing Lenten fasts and sacramental marriage. The power of bishops had "expired" when they were excluded from the House of Lords in 1641.

464. 8. *dragon's teeth:* see Ovid, *Metamorphoses,* vii. 121*f.*

25. *fifth essence:* see *P.L.,* iii. 716, and note to ii, 75.

36. *Protagoras:* the story is told in Cicero's *Nature of the Gods,* referred to in the next sentence but one.

465. 4. *Vetus Comoedia:* the Old Comedy of Aristophanes, which made (licensed) personal attacks on public figures.

11. Aristippus of Cyrene taught an extreme form of Epicureanism.

17. Chrysostom ("golden-mouthed") was bishop of Constantinople in the fourth century.

22. These stories are told in Plutarch's life of Lycurgus.

29. *laconic:* the word is derived from Laconia, Sparta.

30. *Archilochus:* a lyric poet of the seventh century B.C., who wrote an epigram on his own cowardice in war.

466. 2. *Pontific College:* a group of priests who administered Roman religion, including the duties of the flamens or priests of individual gods.

4. This story comes from Plutarch's life of Cato: Carneades, as a rhetorical exercise, had first defended and then attacked justice. Cato, who lived on a Sabine farm (line 11), learned Greek in his old age.

14. The comedies of Naevius (which are lost) also included personal caricatures. Roman comedy was largely paraphrased from Greek originals (Menander and Philemon).

24. Lucretius dedicated his *On the Nature of Things* to the praetor Memmius. Cicero, according to a doubtful tradition, was its editor ("set forth"), though, as a Stoic, he attacked its Epicureanism.

29. *Flaccus:* Horace.

30. *the story of Titus Livius:* the history of Livy.

32. *Naso:* Ovid, banished to the Black Sea by Augustus.

467. 11. The attacks of the Neoplatonic philosophers Porphyry and Proclus against Christianity have, naturally, been lost.

20. *Padre Paolo:* Pietro Sarpi, a monk who was a leader of the Venetians in their struggle with the Papacy. His *History of the Council of Trent,* translated into English in 1620, is Milton's chief source here.

468. 1. *purgatory:* pun on Index Expurgatorius, a list of passages to be expunged from permitted books. "Prohibition" refers to the index of books prohibited in their entirety.

25. *Claudius:* part of a sentence from Suetonius' life of Claudius, which may be translated "whether he should allow the privilege of breaking wind silently or noisily at a banquet," is quoted by Milton at this point in a note. The note is usually suppressed in teaching editions—an odd sidelight on the history of censorship.

469. 5. Responsories and antiphonies are parts of the Roman mass.

9. The residences of the Archbishop of Canterbury and the Bishop of London.

27. *sat cross-legged:* thus preventing by sympathetic magic the birth of Hercules. See Ovid, *Metamorphoses,* ix. 281*f.*

32. *Radamanth:* judge of hell. See *Aeneid,* vi. 562*f.*

34. *mysterious iniquity:* the power of Antichrist (II Thess. 2:7).

470. 2. *minorites:* Franciscan friars.

16. *Lullius:* Raymond Lully, a thirteenth-century mystic and logician. *sublimate:* extract (cf. *P.L.,* i, 235).

24. Cf. Acts 7:22, and 22:3; Dan. 1:17.

28. *tragedian:* Euripides. Cf. I Cor. 15:33 and Introduction to *Samson Agonistes.* The sentence is perhaps from a comedian, Menander.

29. *primitive doctors:* teachers of the apostolic Church.

471. 1. This story is told in the *Ecclesiastical History* of Socrates Scholasticus (line 5).

10. *Decius or Diocletian:* persecuting emperors.

11. *devil:* Jerome's own account of his experience (in a letter to the nun Eustochium, line 27) locates it in heaven.

21. Basil was bishop of Caesarea in the fourth century.

22. *Margites,* of which only a line or two remains, was attributed to Homer by Plato and Aristotle.

23. *Morgante Maggiore* (1488), a romance about a good-natured giant by Luigi Pulci, started a literary vogue carried on by Ariosto. The first book was translated by Byron.

26. Eusebius was the chief authority on the early history of the Church.

472. 3. I Thess. 5:21. Cf. Titus 1:15.

10. See Acts 10:9-16.

14. *naughty:* worthless.

21. Selden's legal masterpiece *De Jure Naturali et Gentium* was much studied by Milton, especially for his divorce tracts. Milton's translation of its title is echoed in *Samson Agonistes,* 890.

36. *omer:* see Exod. 16:16*f.*

473. 3. *defile not:* see Matt. 15:17-20.

8. *Solomon:* Ecclesiastes 12:12.

14. *magic:* see Acts 19:19.

18. *appointed:* bound.

25. The story of Psyche is told in Apuleius' *Metamorphoses,* iv-vi.

36. *warfaring:* perhaps "wayfaring."

474. 9. *excremental:* see Matt. 23:27.

10. See Spenser, *The Faerie Queene,* II, vii and xii. The Palmer is not with Guyon in the Mammon episode.

31. *Keri:* "to be read." A marginal note providing a euphemism for the written word (Chetiv) in the text. Such glosses arose in the Rabbinical or Talmudic period of Judaism.

35*f.* Clement of Alexandria and the others are apologists of the early Christian Church who all described at some length the pagan and heretical doctrines they attacked.

475. 10. *criticisms:* subtleties.

12. *ribald of Arezzo:* more commonly known as Aretino.

15. *vicar of hell:* Milton probably intended the reference to be to Skelton, though a cousin of Anne Boleyn named Sir Francis Brian had the nickname.

29. See Acts 8:28-35.

31. *Sorbonists:* Dominican scholars at the Sorbonne in Paris.

33. *Arminius:* a Dutch theologian who attacked Calvinism, giving a higher place to free will. He was in bad odor with Milton's party because of the agreement of his views with those of the Anglicans, whom the Puritans often called Arminians, but Milton's own theology is far closer to Arminius than to Calvin.

476. 10. *cautelous:* deceitful.

28. Aristotle, *Ethics,* I, iii; Solomon, Prov. 23:9; Christ, Matt. 7:6.

477. 3. *want:* be without.

4. *qualify:* compound (drugs).

478. 1. *epigrams:* some of these, whether genuine or not, are quoted by Diogenes Laertius (see note to p. 445, line 12), Plato's dialogue form was developed partly from the *Mimes* of Sophron. Aristophanes is one of the speakers in the *Symposium.* For Dionysius see the Introduction to *Samson Agonistes.*

21. The Doric was the martial mode: see *Republic,* iii, and *P.L.,* i, 550.

23. *honest:* chaste.

32. *visitors:* an ironic reference to the "visitations" ordered by the Established Church, which were particularly severe on "lectures" or Puritanic sermons. Similar irony is in the word "officials," p. 481, line 21.

35. Sidney's *Arcadia* and Montemayor's *Diana* were sixteenth-century pastoral prose romances.

479. 13. *Atlantic:* the story of Atlantis comes from Plato's *Timaeus* and *Critias.*

32. *gramercy:* thanks.

37. *motions:* puppet-shows.

481. 5. *court-libel:* a Royalist weekly called *Mercurius Aulicus* (Court News), published at Oxford and still circulating.

23. *damnified:* injured.

483. 5. *pluralities:* the practice of giving several Church offices to one incumbent.

27. *fescue:* pointer.

484. 7. *Palladian oil:* Pallas Athene taught men the use of oil and was the goddess of wisdom.

11. *puny:* minor.

32. *patriarchal:* with a glance at its meaning "archiepiscopal."

485. 7. From Bacon's *Advertisement touching the Controversies of the Church of England.*

19. Knox's *History of the Reformation in Scotland* had just appeared in an expurgated edition. He may be the author referred to in the next sentence.

29. *moulds:* rusts.

486. 11. *tickets:* credit slips.

14. See I Sam. 13:19-22.

35. *pipe:* feeding tube.

487. 19. *Enchiridion:* handbook.

20. *castle of St. Angelo:* the papal prison in Rome.

488. 11. *he:* Cicero, at one time a quaestor (treasurer) in Sicily, who wrote seven orations attacking the grafter Verres.

32. *name:* "presbyter" and "priest" come from the same Greek word (*presbyteros,* elder).

489. 2. *sole ordination:* ordination by bishops only.

7. The Solemn League and Covenant between Scotland and (Parliamentary) England was signed in 1643; the Protestation was a document drawn up by Parliament in 1641 against the king.

8. *chop:* exchange.

9. *Palace Metropolitan:* the Archbishop of Canterbury's palace at Lambeth.

11. *commuting:* exchanging one penance for another, as allowed by canon law.

32. *twenty:* the Star Chamber order (see introductory note) had stipulated that only twenty printers should be allowed in London and that their company should have the right of search against unauthorized printers. The Parliamentary order, as Milton repeatedly hints, had confirmed this monopoly.

490. 3. *St. Albans:* Bacon (see note to p. 485, line 7).

20. *professors:* Puritans.

24. *mysteries:* trades (with pun).

491. 5. *he:* cf. Matt. 21:18-19.

12. Tonnage and poundage were excise taxes, the control of which was disputed by King and Parliament.

28. *at his Hercules' pillars:* as far as he wants to go.

31. *topic folio:* commonplace book.

32. *Harmony:* of the Gospels. *Catena:* collection of quotations.

492. 4. St. Thomas and St. Martin's are in Cheapside; St. Hugh's is unidentified. "Vestry" presumably means "near neighborhood." The sense is that nothing is easier to buy than sermons.

9. *impaled:* fenced in.

38. *Christ:* see John 28:19-21.

493. 3. *particular:* personal matter.

13. Printing was prohibited in Turkey at that time.

20. *glass:* see I Cor. 13:12.

27. The story of how the body of Osiris was torn into fourteen pieces by his enemy Typhon, which were then sought for and gathered up by Isis, is told by Plutarch in his essay *On Isis and Osiris.*

494. 6. *combust:* a planet was supposed to lose its "influence" when it got too near the sun. This applied particularly to Venus and Mercury.

23. *Syntagma:* handbook.

28. *golden rule:* rule of three.

35. *discourse:* reason.

495. 3. The notion that the Magi of Persia were taught by the Druids of Britain was derived from Pliny, *Natural History,* xxx. For Pythagoras cf. the "Abaris" story in Herodotus iv. See also the opening sentences of Diogenes Laertius.

6. This statement comes from Tacitus' *Life of Agricola.*

8. Transylvania was at that time a Protestant country. The "Hercynian wilderness" means the forests of the Harz mountains in Germany.

20. Jerome of Prague was burned in 1416.

23. *demeaned:* handled.

496. 31. *Pyrrhus:* see note to Sonnet XVII, 4.

32. *docility:* discipline.

36. See I Kings 6:7.

497. 13. See Num. 11:24-29.

25. *maniples:* guerrillas.

32*f*. Cf. note to Sonnet VIII.

498. 7. The story is told by Livy, xxvi.

27. *mewing:* perhaps "newing."

28. The eagle was thought to be able to look directly on the sun. For "unscaling" cf. Acts 9:18.

36. *engrossers:* monopolizers. See note to p. 489, line 32.

499. 25. *coat and conduct:* uniform and transportation (paid for out of public taxes).

26. *nobles:* silver coins. *Danegelt:* ship-money, a tax originally levied to pay off the Danes. The next sentence means that unjust taxation alone is not worth going to war about.

500. 2. Robert Greville, Lord Brooke, was a Parliamentary general, recently killed in battle. His book attacked episcopacy and admitted the principle of toleration.

19. Janus, the god of the new year, was represented with two

faces: the gates of his temple were opened in wartime. Milton does not mean the Civil War but the war of Eph. 6:12.

28. *discipline of Geneva:* Presbyterian system of Church government.

32. Cf. Prov. 16:16.

501. 5. *bridge:* cf. Spenser, *The Faerie Queene,* V, ii, 4.

12. *Proteus:* see note to *P.L.*, iii, 598.

15. *Micaiah:* see I Kings 22.

20. See Eph. 2:15-16; Col. 2:13-14; and, for the next sentences, Gal. 5:1, and Rom. 14:5-8.

29. *linen:* referring to High Church vestments.

502. 1. I Cor. 3:12.

5. Rev. 18:12; Matt. 13:24-30.

20. Eph. 4:3.

503. 16. The Convocation was the Anglican, and the Assembly (p. 490, line 15) the Puritan name for the Church council. The Assembly, after 1643, met in the Henry VII Chapel in Westminster Abbey.

18. *canonized:* made canon law.

504. 11. *triple:* see note to Sonnet XVIII, 12.

15. Num. 11:24-29; Luke 9:49-50.

505. 22. *elenchs:* quibbles.

SECOND DEFENCE

In writing this pamphlet Milton had two antagonists chiefly in mind. One was the author of the pamphlet mentioned on the title page, erroneously supposed by Milton to be Alexander More, who had ridiculed Milton's blindness, courage, and physical appearance. The other was Claude Salmasius, the chief Continental spokesman for the Royalists, against whom Milton had written the *First Defence.*

510. 16. *Triptolemus:* son of Ceres and king of Eleusis in Attica, who taught men agriculture (Ovid, *Metamorphoses,* v. 646).

34. *Cyclops:* Polyphemus, the giant blinded by Ulysses. The line quoted is from *Aeneid,* iii. 658.

512. 21. *Tiresias:* see note to *P.L.*, iii, 35.

513. 1*f*. The lives of Timoleon and Appius Claudius are in Plutarch. The palladium rescued by Metellus was traditionally the one brought by Aeneas. Dandolo of Venice led an expedition against

Constantinople in the twelfth century; Zisca was a Bohemian general who befriended Huss; Zanchius was an Italian Protestant scholar of the sixteenth century. See also Gen. 27:1 and 48:10; and John 9:2-3.

514. 7. See note to *P.L.*, ix, 505.

13. *son of Thetis:* Achilles.

515. 15. *apostle:* see Heb. 11:34.

516. 28. Wotton's life was written by Izaak Walton. The original edition of *Comus* printed a letter of his to Milton praising the poem.

36. Grotius influenced Milton through his writings on law, his commentaries on Scripture (which supported Milton's views of divorce) and his poem on the loss of Paradise, *Adamus Exul.*

37. *queen of Sweden:* Christina, whose admiration for Milton caused great humiliation to Salmasius, who was at her court. A panegyric of her is included in the *Second Defence.*

517. 21. One of Milton's Latin poems is an epistle to Manso; references to most of his other Continental friends mentioned here may be found in his letters.

518. 23. John Diodati was the uncle of Milton's close friend Charles Diodati, in whose memory he wrote *Epitaphium Damonis.*

519. 21. *two bishops:* Hall and Ussher.

520. 17. For Selden see note to p. 472, line 21. The book referred to here appeared later than Milton's divorce tracts.

523. 36. Epaminondas was the Theban general who broke the power of Sparta.

529. 25*f*. *Fleetwood . . . :* perhaps Milton's own notes on these Cromwellian leaders will be annotation enough for the general reader.

530. 35. See Matt. 21:12, and note to *P.L.*, i, 17.

535. 28. *Rentius:* Rienzi, whose attempt to restore the Roman Republic in the Middle Ages failed, as did that of a predecessor, Crescentius of Nomentum.

Rinehart Editions